10-01

OUR LITERARY HERITAGE
SECOND EDITION

DESMOND PACEY

Revision by Michael Pacey

McGraw-Hill Ryerson Limited
Toronto   Montreal

ISBN 0-07-548493-5

   4567890   D   098

Printed and bound in Canada

Canadian Cataloguing in Publication Data

Main entry under title:
Our literary heritage

Includes index.
ISBN 0-07-548493-5

1. English literature. 2. Canadian literature (English).*
3. American literature. I. Pacey, Desmond, 1917-1975.
II. Pacey, Michael, date

PN6014.087 1982   820'.8   C82-094989-2

ACKNOWLEDGMENTS

Grateful acknowledgment is made to publishers and owners of copyrighted material for permission to reprint the selections listed:

JOHN G. AYLEN. The works of Duncan Campbell Scott are reproduced with the permission of John G. Aylen of Ottawa, Canada.

CLARKE, IRWIN & CO. LTD. "Ypres," from *The Mysterious Naked Man* by Alden Nowlan © 1969 by Clarke, Irwin & Company Limited. Used by permission.

FABER AND FABER LTD. "Musée des Beaux Arts" and "Lay your Sleeping Head, My Love" from *Collected Poems* by W. H. Auden. "The Love Song of J. Alfred Prufrock" and "The Hollow Men" from *Collected Poems 1909-1962* by T. S. Eliot. Reprinted by permission of Faber and Faber Ltd.

JOHN FARQUHARSON, LTD., LONDON. "Prologue to *The Canterbury Tales*," and "The Pardoner's Tale," from *The Canterbury Tales* by Geoffrey Chaucer, translated by Nevill Coghill. (The Folio Society, 1956). Reprinted by permission of John Farquharson Ltd.

A. LEONARD GROVE. "Snow" by F. P. Grove, by permission of A. Leonard Grove, Toronto.

HARCOURT BRACE JOVANOVICH. "The Secret Life of Walter Mitty," copyright © 1942 James Thurber. Copyright © 1970 Helen Thurber. From *My World—And Welcome To It,* published by Harcourt Brace Jovanovich. "Chicago" from *Chicago Poems* by Carl Sandburg, copyright 1916 by Holt, Rinehart and Winston, Inc; copyright 1944 by Carl Sandburg. "Caboose Thoughts," "Prayers of Steel," and "Cool Tombs" from *Cornhuskers* by Carl Sandburg, copyright 1918 by Holt, Rinehart and Winston Inc; copyright 1946 by Carl Sandburg. Reprinted by permission of Harcourt Brace Jovanovich, Inc.

DAVID HIGHAM ASSOC. LTD. "Do Not Go Gentle into That Good Night," "The Force that . . . Drives the Flower," "And Death Shall Have No Dominion," "Poem in October," "A Refusal to Mourn . . .," "Fern Hill" and "Memories of Christmas" from *Collected Poems* and *Quite Early One Morning* by Dylan Thomas. Reprinted by permission of David Higham Associates Ltd.

HOGARTH PRESS LTD. Excerpt from Chapter 3 of *A Room of One's Own* by Virginia Woolf. By permission of the Author's Literary Estate and The Hogarth Press Ltd.

HOLT, RINEHART AND WINSTON INC. "The Pasture," "Mending Wall," "Fire and Ice," "Birches," "Stopping by Woods . . ." and "Out, Out" from *The Poetry of Robert Frost,* edited by Edward Connery Lathem. Copyright 1916, 1923, 1930, 1939 © 1967, 1969 by Holt, Rinehart and Winston, Copyright 1944, 1951 © 1958 by Robert Frost. Copyright © 1967 by Lesley Frost Ballantine, Reprinted by permission of Holt, Rinehart and Winston, Publishers.

HOUSE OF ANANSI PRESS. "This is a Photograph of Me" from *The Circle Game* by Margaret Atwood © 1966. Reprinted by permission of House of Anansi Press, Toronto.

MACLENNAN. "Scotchman's Return" by Hugh MacLennan is reprinted by permission of the author.

MACMILLAN OF CANADA. "The Blue Kimono" from *Morley Callaghan's Stories* by Morley Callaghan. Copyright, Canada, 1959, by Morley Callaghan. Reprinted by permission of Macmillan of Canada, A Division of Gage Publishing Ltd.

MACMILLAN OF LONDON. "When You Are Old," "Red Hanrahan's Song," "The Song of Wandering Aengus," "September 1913," "Wild Swans," "Sailing to Byzantium" and "Among School Children" from *Collected Poems* by W. B. Yeats and Anne Yeats. Reprinted by permission of Macmillan London Ltd.

MCCLELLAND AND STEWART LTD. "David," "Slug in Woods," "Canada: Case History," "Vancouver Lights" and "Anglosaxon Street" from *Collected Poems* by Earle Birney. "The Sparrows," "For E.J.P." and "Suzanne" from *Selected Poems* by Leonard Cohen. "To Set Our House in Order" from *A Bird in the House* by Margaret Laurence. "Song for Naomi," "Anglo-Canadian," "The Bull Calf" and "Keine Lazarovitch" from *Collected Poems* by Irving Layton. "My Financial Career" from *Literary Lapses* by Stephen Leacock. "Mortimer Griffin, Shalinsky . . ." from *Cocksure* by Mordecai Richler. "The Young Ravens . . ." from *Earths Enigmas* by Charles G. D. Roberts. "The Lamp at Noon" from *The Lamp at Noon and other Stories* by Sinclair Ross. "The Canadian Authors Meet," "Saturday Sundae," "Flux,"

"Conflict" and "Tourist Time" from *Selected Poems* by F. R. Scott. "Sea Cliff," "The Lonely Land," "News of the Phoenix" and "The Archer" from *Collected Poems* by A. J. M. Smith. Reprinted by permission of the Canadian publishers, McClelland and Stewart, Toronto.

MCGRAW-HILL INC. Glossary entries from *Concise Dictionary of Literary Terms* by Harry Shaw © by McGraw-Hill Inc. Reprinted by permission of McGraw-Hill Inc.

MCGRAW-HILL RYERSON LTD. "Autobiographical," "For the Sisters . . .," "Rocking Chair," and "Lookout: Mount Royal" from *The Collected Poems of A. M. Klein.* "Dance of the Happy Shades" from *Dance of the Happy Shades* by Alice Munro. Reprinted by permission of McGraw-Hill Ryerson Ltd.

NEWLOVE. "Good Company, Fine Houses" and "Lady, Lady." Copyright 1965, 1968, 1977 by John Newlove.

NOWLAN. "The Bull Moose" by Alden Nowlan is reprinted by permission of the author.

OBERON PRESS. "Flight of the Roller Coaster" and "Downtown Corner News Stand" are reprinted from *Collected Poems of Raymond Souster,* Volume III, by Raymond Souster, by permission of Oberon Press.

ONDAATJE. "A House Divided," "Bear Hug" and "The Gate in His Head" from *There's a Trick With a Knife I'm Learning to Do* by Michael Ondaatje. Reprinted by permission of the author.

OXFORD UNIVERSITY PRESS. "Dream 2: Brian the Still-Hunter" from *The Journals of Susanna Moodie* by Margaret Atwood © Oxford University Press 1970. "the animals in that country" from *The Animals in That Country* by Margaret Atwood © Margaret Atwood, by permission of the publisher.

PRATT. "The Shark," "From Stone to Steel," "The Truant" and "Come Away, Death" from *Collected Poems* by E. J. Pratt. Reprinted by permission of Viola and Claire Pratt.

RANDOM HOUSE INC. "Their Lonely Betters," copyright 1951 by W. H. Auden. Reprinted from *W. H. Auden: Collected Poems.* "Remarks Upon Receiving the Nobel Prize" from *Essays, Speeches & Public Letters,* by William Faulkner. By permission of Random House Inc.

ROBERTS. "Tantramar Revisited," "The Sower," "The Potato Harvest" and "Ice" from *Selected Poems* by Charles G. D. Roberts. Reprinted by permission of Joan Roberts.

CHARLES SCRIBNER'S SONS. "In Another Country" from *Men Without Women* by Ernest Hemingway. Copyright 1972 by Charles Scribner's Sons; copyright renewed 1955 by Ernest Hemingway (New York: Charles Scribner's Sons, 1927). Reprinted with permission of Charles Scribner's Sons.

SOCIETY OF AUTHORS. "Lovliest of Trees," "Is My Team Ploughing," "When Smoke Stood Up . . .," "When I Was One-and-Twenty," "To An Athlete . . ." and "The Chestnut . . ." by A. E. Housman. Reprinted by permission of The Society of Authors as the literary representative of the Estate of A. E. Housman, and Jonathan Cape Ltd., publishers of A. E. Housman's *Collected Poems.*

VIKING PENGUIN INC. "Araby" from *Dubliners* by James Joyce. Originally published by B. W. Huebsch in 1916. Definitive text copyright © 1967 by the Estate of James Joyce. Reprinted by permission of Viking Penguin Inc.

WILSON. "The Window," by Ethel Wilson, is reprinted by permission of the Estate of Ethel Davis Wilson, and Bull, Housser and Tupper.

Every reasonable care has been taken to trace ownership of copyrighted material. Information will be welcomed which will enable the publishers to rectify any reference or credit.

PREFACE

This anthology of literature in English is designed especially for Canadian students; its special feature is the inclusion in one volume of representative selections from English, American, and Canadian literature. The Canadian's literary heritage is a three-fold one: his English speech and institutions, and in many cases his English ancestry, make him part of the English tradition; his proximity to and close relations with the United States allow him to feel almost equally at home in the American tradition; and of course he must be aware of the young literature of his own country, preferably both in French and in English. This necessity to know the literature of at least three countries—for, indeed, a case could be made for his knowing also the literatures of France, the other countries of the Commonwealth, and many of the literatures of Europe—may at times seem burdensome; but it is really a challenge and an opportunity, a means of personal enrichment.

Personal enrichment is the prime aim of this anthology. It is an attempt to bring together the "best of the best," the finest work of the finest authors who have written in the three countries concerned. The pieces selected are those that the editor himself has found, over the years, to be most memorable, to be capable of arousing over and over again that profound sense of delight which is literature's chief function. If this book is not taught and studied as a source of delight, it is being improperly approached.

But personal enrichment involves more than delight. This book should allow the student to feel that he has been in contact with the great minds and great spirits of the English-speaking tradition. New ideas, new sensations, new awareness—a sense of a world which is infinitely complex and endlessly interesting—these should be the by-products of reading these selections. The student should be able to see the way in which certain ideas, certain attitudes to experience, have been born and have developed. He should see also something of the development of English, American, and Canadian society, and of the way in which social institutions and social changes are reflected in, and sometimes affected by, the literature of the period.

To this end, the anthology has been arranged historically. In order to avoid some of the pitfalls of the merely superficial "survey," however, the number of authors represented has been kept relatively low, and the aim has been to give sufficiently large samples of the authors' work to allow the student to get a real sense of their individual styles and thoughts. The selections may seem to favour poetry rather than prose. This is partly because the editor believes that poetry is the real glory of the English literary tradition, and partly because prose, being less condensed and intense than poetry, takes up more space and is therefore more difficult to represent in small samples. The novel and the play, for example, are almost impossible to represent other than as wholes, and for this reason these forms have been omitted. The shorter prose forms—the essay, the meditation, the diary, the brief biography, the short story—will, it is hoped, be found to be adequately represented.

A constant attempt has been made throughout the book to maintain a sensible balance between the literatures of the various periods and between the literatures of the three countries. As far as possible, whole works rather than excerpts have been used, in order that the student may see the total structure of the selection. In many cases, however, this has been impossible; long poems such as *The Canterbury Tales*, for example, could not have been included even in a book several times this length. In such instances, an effort has been made to select a passage which is in itself a unit; the whole of "The Pardoner's Tale" in *The Canterbury Tales* has been included. Where an excerpt from a prose work has had to be selected, every effort has been made to choose a passage or passages representative and self-explanatory.

Each of the major periods is prefaced by an historical introduction, which attempts to explain the background out of which the literature of that period sprang and to sketch the main outlines of the literary development of this era. A biographical and critical introduction has been provided for each author, also, and these introductions frequently relate one author to another or suggest his role in the literary history of his time and place. Brief explanatory footnotes have been provided where necessary to illuminate obscure references in the selections. Finally, the dates of the selections have been indicated; dates appearing at the left are the dates of composition; dates at the right are the dates of publication. All these aids to the teacher and student, however, have been provided merely as rough guides, and it is hoped that users of the book will supplement them with material drawn from histories of English, American, and Canadian literature, and from other reference books. Certainly the introductions should not be "learned," in the sense of seeking to memorize a whole series of titles and dates. The focus should be kept on the literature as literature, and the background regarded simply as background.

It remains to thank those who have helped in the planning and preparation of this book. My chief thanks must go to Professor A. M. Kinloch of the University of New Brunswick, who is responsible for the Anglo-Saxon portion of the book and who, in collaboration with Professor Fred Cogswell, translated *Beowulf* into modern English. I am also grateful to Professors D. R. Galloway, J. K. Johnstone, and A. R. Donaldson, who read various portions of the text in manuscript, and to the many New Brunswick high school teachers, and notably Sister Brendan, Mr. R. E. Hawkes, and Miss Jennie Wilson, who gave me valuable advice. I have enjoyed the co-operation of the English Curriculum Sub-Committee of the New Brunswick Department of Education, and of the officers of The Ryerson Press and The Macmillan Company of Canada. Finally, I should like to thank those teachers who, in Caledonia High School in Ontario in the nineteen-thirties, enhanced my own enjoyment of literature: Mrs. Kay Dobson Riddell, Miss Vera M. Cox, and Miss Lily P. Hunter.

DESMOND PACEY

In the fifteen years since my father wrote the preface reprinted above, *Our Literary Heritage* has enjoyed continued popularity with students and teachers alike. The result of this popularity is the revised and expanded text before you, a product of both students' and teachers' experience with the book.

Revisions in the new edition of *Our Literary Heritage* are of two basic types: replacing or deleting selections because of a change in critical evaluation over the past fifteen years, or for the sake of contemporary relevance; and greatly expanding the modern Canadian section. A full thirteen writers whose reputations have been established or enhanced in the past two decades have been added. Space would simply not permit us to correspondingly increase the modern British and American sections, and since this is a Canadian textbook, we deemed this expansion to the Canadian section essential. So much has happened in the world of Canadian literature in the past fifteen years, I know my father would be the first to enthusiastically suggest this change.

Thanks and acknowledgements are due to Hugh Duplisea of the Department of Education, the English teachers who suggested the revisions—Blaine Hatt, Betty Harvey, Ken Lamey, John Farthing and Nada Sparks—my brother Peter who, like myself, is a poet and veteran of high-school English instruction in New Brunswick, and my mother, Mrs. W. C. D. (Mary) Pacey, whose advice helped me maintain the spirit in which my father created this collection—"the best of the best, the finest work of the finest authors."

MICHAEL PACEY

CONTENTS

Italics for titles indicate poetry selections.

THE SEVENTEENTH CENTURY (1603-1660)

THE ROMANTIC PERIOD (1785-1836)

THE VICTORIAN PERIOD (1837-1901)

ENGLISH LITERATURE

AMERICAN LITERATURE

THE TWENTIETH CENTURY

CANADIAN LITERATURE

400   **500**   **600**   **700**

• Romans evacuate Britain

• Christian missionaries arrive in Britain

• Anglo-Saxon invasion of Britain begins

THE
ANGLO-SAXON
PERIOD
(to 1066)

800	900	1000	1100

• *Beowulf* manuscript

• Battle of Brunanburh

usion of Bede's *Ecclesiastical History*

By A.D. 500, Angles and Saxons were crossing to Britain in large numbers from what is now North Germany, Denmark, Holland, and the Frisian Islands; and by 600, the Romano-British province of Britannia had virtually ceased to exist. In its place was "Engla-lond"—England.

At first, the Anglo-Saxons kept their continental social organization. Each king had his company of warriors, chosen partly for noble birth and partly for prowess in battle. In peace they advised him, and in war they were at once his bodyguard and the hard core of his army. They were paid for their service by the ruler's generous gifts of jewellery and armour, and by his protection; but the most powerful bond of union was the love and loyalty between warrior and lord. The exchange of gifts was the symbol, not the origin, of this love.

Although they fought among themselves, the Anglo-Saxons had a powerful feeling that they were a part of one common Germanic culture, pagan in spirit and northern in origin. "The Wanderer" and "The Seafarer" are Anglo-Saxon poems which bewail the hard fate of a man who has lost his lord and praise the pagan virtues of stoicism and courage. "The Complaint of Deor" and other poems show a knowledge of Weland the Smith, and of other continental and Scandinavian heroes. A background of common emotional values which survived in "The Battle of Brunanburh" and "The Battle of Maldon," both tenth century poems, lies behind most Anglo-Saxon poetry; and, in general, Northern Europe has probably never felt or expressed such a close cultural unity since, and this same cultural inheritance appears in *Beowulf*, the finest surviving Anglo-Saxon product.

The conversion of the Anglo-Saxons to Christianity affected the pagan literature and also produced much poetry which was entirely Christian in origin and treatment. Stories from the Bible and from Christian legend replaced the stories from Scandinavia. One of these new poems is a nine-line Hymn by Caedmon, the first English poet whose name is known. Soon, longer works were written, and the Anglo-Saxon poems "Genesis," "Exodus," "Daniel," and "Judith" all tell stories from the Vulgate Bible. Even in these, however, the pagan spirit still lives on, but in the work of Cynewulf, a new and more sophisticated Christianity appears. The figures in the five poems attributed to him, "Andreas," "Elene," "Juliana," "Christ," and "The Fates of the Apostles," are much less stern than the figures in other Anglo-Saxon poetry, and the poet shows a much wider knowledge of the human mind and emotions. In his work, the hero is no longer the bravest, but the most deeply Christian figure. Of all the religious poems, however, the best is probably "The Dream of the Rood"; in this poem, the poet's imaginative sympathy with his subject, the subtlety of mood, the intimacy of tone and the magnificent and symbolic language combine to produce poetry of a very high order.

In general, Anglo-Saxon poetry uses a special vocabulary, many of the words found in poetry not occurring in prose. The poets used many compound words; e.g., "sad-minded," "middle-earth." Some are metaphors which are thought to have lost their metaphorical quality; they are known as "kennings." Rhyme and stanzaic form are hardly ever used; instead, each single verse is unified by alliteration which spans a central caesura; e.g.,

Wuldres wealdend   / /   woroldare forgeaf

Versification of this type is illustrated in the translation of *Beowulf* in this volume; it is found in other Germanic countries, and remained common in England till the time of Chaucer.

A.M.K.

FROM Beowulf

(translated into modern English verse
by A. M. Kinloch and Fred Cogswell)

The Anglo-Saxon poem *Beowulf* has survived from the Dark Ages in one manuscript only, the manuscript Cotton Vitellius A xv, which is now in the British Museum in London. The history of this manuscript has been almost as stormy as the age it deals with. It seems to have been written about the year A.D. 1000, but no one knows what was happening to it for about 500 years after that. In 1700 it was presented to the English nation but even then it was not safe, for, in 1731, while it was lodged in Ashburnham House in London, a fire broke out which scorched the manuscript at the edges. It was then allowed to crumble at the edges for almost a century and a half until finally, between 1860 and 1870, proper steps were taken to prevent further deterioration. During this period of neglect, however, two transcripts had been made, and these fortunately preserve some words which have since disappeared from the edges of the pages of the original manuscript.

The manuscript was written about the year 1000, but the poem seems to have been composed long before this. Although the exact date of its composition is not known, most scholars think it was composed during the eighth century A.D., when the material and mental civilization of England would agree more or less with that pictured in the poem. This would make *Beowulf* almost one thousand years older than England's next great epic, *Paradise Lost*.

An epic *Beowulf* certainly is. Its hero, Beowulf, is a man upon whom the destiny of a nation depends, for the Danes find no help against the monster Grendel until Beowulf arrives to kill him. Its setting is ample, for, while the main action takes place in Southern Scandinavia, episodes and digressions range from the Geat raid on Frisia to the Gothic empire of the Black Sea. Deeds and actions are on a heroic scale, for Beowulf knows that each battle must bring absolute victory or certain death. The movement of the poem, circulating among palace, field of combat, and the sea, is deliberate and ceremonious.

The material of the poem includes some things which are historical, like Hygelac's Frisian expedition, and much that is supernatural and legendary, like Grendel, the monster-enemy of the Danes. The hero, Beowulf, probably contains elements of both kinds; he may have had a historical existence, but he can hardly have had the enormous strength the poem gives him. The poem contains much that is pagan, but over it all is a Christian colouring which is most noticeable in the speeches of Hrothgar. In this amalgam of the historical, the legendary, the pagan, and the Christian, the poem stands at the beginning of a long tradition culminating in Spenser's *Faerie Queene*. In *Beowulf* all these divers strains are unified by the manly tone and epic style of the poem.

The theme of the poem is the nobility of its hero, Beowulf. In his youth he was a mighty fighter, and in his old age he is a wise and peaceable ruler who dies fighting to protect his land and his people from a ravaging dragon. The theme is developed against a background of generous kings and loyal and brave warriors. Throughout the poem there are telling contrasts of emotion. Social life produces pleasure which gives way to the tense anticipation of battle; battle produces a fierce delight which in turn gives way to the joy of victory or the sadness of defeat and death.

In the manuscript the poem is divided into forty-three sections. Each section is numbered, although the numbering is not entirely consistent. The sections vary in length from 43 verse-lines to 142 verse-lines. The manuscript does not indicate the end of one verse-line and the beginning of the next, being written continuously across the page as if its contents were prose. Sometimes words are run together; at other times one word is split. The contraction 7 is regularly used for *ond*.

Here are lines 260-266 as they appear in the original manuscript (lines 236-240 on page 11) but transliterated into the characters used by most modern editors:

. . . wesynt gumcynnes
geata leode 7higelaces heorðgeneatas
wæs min fæder folcum gecyþed æþele
ordfruma ecgþeow haten gebad wintra
worn ærhe onweg hwurfe. gamol ofgear
dum hine gear we geman witena wel
hwylc wide geond eorþan . . .

Most editors would print this passage as:

We synt gumcynnes   Geata leode
ond Higelaces   heorðgeneatas.
Wæs min fæder   folcum gecyþed,
æþele ordfruma,   Ecgþeow haten.
Gebad wintra worn,   ær he on weg hwurfe,
gamol of geardum   hine gearwe geman
witena welhwylc   wide geond eorþan.

This helps to show the basis of Anglo-Saxon prosody. Verse lines are unrhymed, and each verse-line is divided by a caesura into two half-lines which are in turn linked to each other by alliteration.

The valour of Vikings[1]   vigorous heroes
Deeds of the Spear-Danes[2]   doughty in days gone by,
Ring high in the hall!   hark to the harp of the *scald*![3]

Often did Scyld[4] Scefing   scorner of chieftains,
Mar with his men   merriment and feasting,
Taking by terror,   the tribute of tribes.
Wan in the world's way   once that man was
But he flourished far   under the frame of sky,
Growing in greatness   and guarding his gains
Till the proud tribes   past the whale's path[5]   10
Gave gifts to him.   That was a good king!

To this Scyld Scefing   God sent a son
Out of pure pity   for plight of the people,
Living their lives   in a lordless land,
Their dire distress   too long endured.
But Beow[6] the brave   blessed as a boy
Found favour with God,   for fame of the Scyld's son
Waxed like Dane warriors   over the world's land.

[1]Scandinavian sea-rovers and warriors who made widespread raids on the coastline of the rest of Europe and at one time ruled an extensive kingdom in Britain. They may even have reached North America as early as the tenth century.
[2]At the imagined time of Beowulf, the Danes lived in S. Sweden.
[3]The professional poet of the Scandinavian tribe.
[4]The Danes are often called Scylds, Scyldings, etc.   [5]*the whale's path*. The sea.
[6]The manuscript here reads *Beowulf*, but this is probably a scribe's error.

Like him a young lord   should love to bestow   20
War-gear and weapons   worthy of warriors
Free with his father's   fast-guarded possessions,
So when in his dotage   the enemy is dealing
Hot war to his homeland   all of his henchmen
Smite with their strong swords   to succour him
And poor folk follow   where his footsteps lead.
As every nation knows   no man has grown
Here on earth to honour   or in heaven save by deeds.

Still hearty and hale   was Scyld when his hour came
To pay with his power   the price[7] God asks of men.
Carried by the kin   he cared for and cherished   30
Scyld's corpse to the shore came   where a strong ship[8] rode
As he on his bed bade   when the death-breath was in him.

Long in the land then   had ruled the loved lord
Blessed by his liege men bestower of rings[9]
But now high in the harbour   hung the curved prow,
Ice-rigged and ready,   the craft of a ruler;
There gently the bearers bore the great prince,
Laid him in the hull's hold   hard by the mast.
Great was the gear   gathered and given,
The war-freight and fortune   of far-away lands,   40
Helmets and hauberks[10] as none ever heard of
Bronze swords and chain-mail   heaped on Scyld's bosom,
All treasure to take   into the sea's talons;
For full was the freight with fruit of their giving
When sad in their spirit they sent the ship seaward
And gilded his going   with a banner of gold.
But hushed then were heroes   and hinds[11] too were still,
Who has taken that treasure   no tongue can tell.

Then God after Scyld's going   gave to his people
Beow, the bountiful,   blessed among men   50
High among heroes   till Healfdene his son,
War-lord of warriors,   wrought in his stead.

Healfdene the Hale   headed the Scyldings,
Knowing not death   till full of deeds and days,
Leaving four children   worthy of chieftains,
Heorogar and Hrothgar   and Halga the good

---

[7]Death.   [8]When a king in Anglo-Saxon times died, his body might be placed in a ship and the ship pushed out to sea, as is done here.   [9]Here, as elsewhere throughout *Beowulf*, the Anglo-Saxon word "beag" translated as "ring" may include arm-bracelets, neck-chains, head-circlets, etc.   [10]Coats of mail.   [11]Servants.

And she who was the only   queen and bride of Onela
The Heathesclyfing[12],   Yrse[13], I heard.

Good hap and great honour   had Hrothgar in battle;
Waxing with warriors   won by his prowess   60
The blades of his war-band   bristled and grew.
He for his high deeds   thankful to heaven
Gathered builders and wrights   to lift with great labour
A hall higher than any   that man heard of ever.
And there on a dais   Hrothgar intended
To share with the Scylds   all his cherished treasure,
Meting God's store   to great men and common,
Save for the public land   and the lives of men.

Where in the wide world   artisans wandered
Hrothgar haled them   home to his hall.   70
Many hands made its raising   a matter of months.
Finished and fitted   and fit for his heroes,
Mightiest of mead-halls,   meeter than any
For bestowing of rings   and treasures at banquets,
Square on a high hill   stood Heorot[14]
Named thus by a namester   who knew all the words,
High and wide-gabled   and waiting for its wyrd[15].
Although that time of torment   lay far in the future:
The smiting of strange swords,   red sorrows to come,
War-flames and feuding   between fathers and sons[16].   80

Then a dread demon   lurked in the darkness,
Hearing the harp   each day in the hall
Mingle its sound   with the song of the scop[17].
Sweetly the man sang   of the glad strokes of God,
Firming the earth's face   and filling the sea.
High in the heaven   hung He the moon and sun,
Lighting the living clay   He breathed upon.
Great in His glory   God, too, garlanded
With grass and growth   all his great earth,
Making with mercy   all manner of life.   90

So well lived the warriors   in weal and luxury
Till Hell loosed its hold   of a hideous fiend

[12]This and other words ending in *scylfing* refer to the Swedes.
[13]Her name is not given in the manuscript but has been discovered by scholars.
[14]The name given to the hall Hrothgar had caused to be built. See the next line.   [15]Fate.
[16]*fathers and sons*. As the later lines tell,Heorot was destroyed when a group from
     another tribe, the Heathobards, led by Hrothgar's son-in-law Ingeld, made an
     otherwise unsuccessful attack on the land of the Danes.
[17]Another word for the "scald"; see footnote 3.

Grendel the grim   infamous and gray
As a marsh mist   marking the fenland.
Long had he lived   in the land of monsters
Condemned by the Creator   with the race of Cain.
Mad in his malice   that man murdered,
But he no gear nor glory   gained from Abel slain,
Harried hence from men   for heinous crime.
Thence[18] sprang all spectres   unholy in spirit,   100
Fouler in form,   Hell-fiends and demons,
Ogres and giants   who gird at God.
Hard by His hap   they have their reward.

Foul in the night-fall   Grendel the fiend
Waited for the Ring-Danes[19]   weary of wassail
To drain their mead-cups   and drop themselves down.
He crept to the high hall   and here he saw heroes
Full from the feast   as they slept on the floor
Senseless to sorrow   of sons of the earth.
Then did the fierce fiend   fume in damned fury.   110
Gore-greedy and grim   he snatched in his jaws
There of the shield-thanes   to the number of thirty
And flew to the fen   full of his prize.

Dim in the dawn   the Ring-Danes awaking
Saw the tell-tale blood   the track of the monster.
As once they had given   great joy to the wassail,
So now they lamented   the loss of their comrades,
And Hrothgar the hero   heart-smitten with sorrow
Mourned for his men   murdered unmanfully
And gazed in his grief   on the tracks of grim Grendel.   120
Too hateful that struggle,   strenuous and too long

But the dire Grendel   determined on slaughter
Fared forth in the evening   each night for the feast.
Once men knew malice   lurked near to the mead-hall
Wisdom it was   for those who were weary
To seek for their shelter   in a safer house
And lie in a bed   less exposed to the mere
Now that they noted   how near Grendel was.
He fled far off   who escaped the fiend.

---

[18]The medieval world held that monsters, demons, etc., were the descendants of Cain.
[19]Most Germanic tribes had a number of names, each calling attention to a different aspect
    of the tribe's existence; here, for example, the Danes' wealth is alluded to. See
    "Spear-Danes" 1. 2.

Alone against all others did Grendel prevail,   130
Vaunting to victory invincible evil
Until Hrothgar's hall was emptied of heroes.
Twelve years of torment the lord of the Scyldings
Hopeless of succour suffered deep grief
Sad did the news spread over the swan's bath[20]
How Hrothgar the hardy was harried by Grendel,
Year after year, with no yielding in view,
For the price of Grendel's peace no Dane would pay.
No wisemen dree the doom darker than death
From the cold killer who keeps black ambush   140
On misty moors against old men and young
When dark mists draw the day and devils glide
Hither from Hell but where they hie
In their world wandering no one can tell.

Horrible humility on Hrothgar's people
Inflicted this fiend fierce from the fen,
Harrying with hatred the hall of Heorot,
In the night noises knowing his hour.
One place[21] at his peril was pure from his touch,
The chief throne of honour where the Scyld chieftain   150
Gave gifts to his men as God gives of His grace.
No evil can ever over giving prevail.
Often the chief of the Scyld-Danes shrouded in sorrow
Summoned in secret his sages to council.
Oft did they dispute the best way to deal with
The horrible stealth of the sudden attacks.
Sometimes they sacrificed[22], saying long prayers,
Asking the demons to aid them the devil to doom,
Turning their hearts to Hell, the hope of the heathen,
For little they'd learned of the one true Lord,   160
Maker of men and judge of man's deeds,
And none of them knew of the Omnipotent
God in His glory grateful for praise.
Woe-full is the wyrd of the wicked
Who thrust forever flaming into Hell
Sin-sick and hopeless their immortal souls.
But good is the goal of the God-seeking man.
He finds eternal bliss in his Father's bosom.

---

[20]*the swan's bath.* The sea. [21]Some critics hold that the throne was protected by God.
[22]At the time when Grendel's attacks were imagined to have occurred, the Danes were not yet Christian.

This king Hrothgar,   kinsman[23] of Healfdene,
Worried his wits   with the woe of his times   170
But wise though he was   still his grief remained.
No country could conquer   nor council assail
The power that preyed   on his people,
Horrible and hideous   out of the night's hell.
Too hateful that struggle,   strenuous and too long.

News of these deeds   done by grim Grendel
Came back to Beowulf[24]   brave thane of the Geats[25].
Hale in the mead-hall   and high in his breeding,
Stalwart he stood   the strongest of men.
He fitted a stout ship   for the sea's buffeting,   180
Well-oared and thick-decked,   to his kin declaring
That he would ride the swan-road   to rescue Hrothgar,
Renowned among Spear-Danes,   in his need for men.
All of his liege-men   loyal in their love
Talked not of terrors   to turn him aside
But inspecting the omens   for weal and for woe
They bade Beowulf   blithe on his voyage
Fare with his fourteen   fine men of his choosing,
Picked for their fierceness   from the fiery Geats.
Skilled as a sea-man   he set out for his ship,   190
Steering by safe ways   his men down to the shore.

Caught under the cliff   close in the bay's cleft
Upright the ship rode   where currents swirled
Languid and light   along the shore.
Into its broad bows   bounded the swordsmen.
High in its hull   they heaped the bright armour,
Strong swords and spears   sharp for fierce thrusting.
Lashed they the lot   tight against losing,
And pointed with pride   the prow of the vessel
Seaward at last   on the longed-for voyage.   200
Running before the wind   and riding the waves
Blithe did the brave ship   with its bird-shaped prow
Forge through the foam   till fair in the sun
Of the next day's dawn   gleamed the dear land
Clipped with sea-cliffs   steep hills and wide capes.
The Geats stepped ashore   swift from their vessel,

[23]In an age when news travelled slowly, to mention a man's relationship to a warrior of
  wide renown was a good way of enabling an audience to "place" him.
[24]This is the first mention of the hero of the poem.
[25]A Scandinavian tribe living probably in what is now S. Sweden.

Making their mail ring   as they moored it,
Paying God thanks   that the passage was easy.

Came he whose care it was   to keep safe the coast-line,
The Scylding soldier,   and saw from the cliff   210
The war-shields and swords,   the spears of the Geats,
Handled by hale warriors �= high over the gang-plank.
Then Hrothgar's thane   thundered his horse
Sharp to the shore,   shaking his spear
With thrusts of his hands,   and formally demanded:
"What manner of men   armoured in mail
Are you, sailing your tall ship   safe o'er the sea-ways?
Tell me, the sentinel   whose trust is
The watch and the ward   of the wave's edge
Lest the foe's fleet   light on the Dane's land.   220
No mailed man ever   as openly as you
From a tall ship   leaped down to this land
Without the will   of our warriors,
Nor ever on earth   saw I a war-man
Sturdier in stature   than your stout leader.
If his form and face   speak him fair
That man mighty of arms   is no mere house-carl[26].
Now, certes, you must say   what siring[27] have you;
Hard would be your hap   to hie into Dane-land
Farther than the fore shore ⏑ foreign to our knowing.   230
Listen then to leal council,   outland voyagers,
Often the best news   you can announce
As wise warriors   is whence you have come."

Then did bold Beowulf,   the war-band's leader,
Answer the sentry   out of his store of words:
"We here are Geats,   hearthmen of Hygelac[28].
My father was famous   far among nations:
To the ends of the earth   was the noble Ecgtheow
By wise-men remembered   when he went from the world,
His fork beard white   with the weight of winters.   240
Here have we hied   to Healfdene's son,
Hrothgar the prince,   who protects his people,
Kindly as friends we come,   asking good counsel.
We have deeds to do   for your Danish lord
Great as his glory.   We come for that goal.
If there be truth   in tales told

[26]A servant, and hence below a warrior in rank and prowess.   [27]See footnote 23.
[28]King of the Geats; for Beowulf's mention of him at this point, see footnote 23.

Some mysterious malice   lurking in mists,
Dread demon of darkness   terrible and dire,
Heaps humiliation   on Hrothgar's hall,
Murdering his men   by midnight sallies.   250

"I would of my wisdom   show Hrothgar the wise
How to deal death   to the death-dealing fiend
That even this evil   mayhap may end
And his sorrow-surge   cease to flame.
It may be through me   mercy may come,
Or perhaps he will suffer   this sickness and sorrow
To rankle and gnaw   at the ribs of his realm
As long as this great hall   stands high by the mere."

Calm in his saddle   the sentry heard him
And resolute still   the Scyld replied: 260
"Clever and close-reasoning   comrades of arms
Must weigh in their minds   the merits of deeds
As well as the weight   of what words may pass.
You claim that your company   calls Hrothgar friend.
Snatch up your swords,   your spears and your armour,
And go without guile   where I shall guide you,
And I shall make my young men   mount guard with fierce weapons
Over your new-tarred vessel,   vowing to keep it
Free from all foemen   till fairly at last
The wood of its curved prow   clearing the whale's way[29]   270
Will carry your leader   safe o'er the sea-lane
Home to the land   where the brave Geats live,
God willing he die not   gripped by dread Grendel."

Onward the Geats moved   at the warder's words.
Their stately ship   with its wide hull
Rode at the anchor-rope   on the rising tide.
Fine-tempered by fire,   reflecting the sun,
Upon the men's helms,   the boar-images[30]
Gleamed over the gold   on the cheek-guards:
So gave the coast-guard   care and safe conduct   280
To the fierce fighters   footing as one
Till they could see   clear in the distance
Mighty Heorot,   highest of all halls,
Girded with timbers   and gilded with gold.
Most-famed among men   in many lands
Shone that great hall   where Hrothgar was king.

[29]*the whale's way.* The sea.
[30]The figure of a boar was a common device in the decoration of Scandinavian helmets. It
    might be embossed on the helmet's plating or affixed above it as a kind of crest.

The war-tried warder   pointed the way
To the great building   built for brave men
That they might march   there without delay.
Then did the Scyld thane   speak to them thus: 290
"May God, the Father,   guide you on your going
And keep you safe   with the staff of His mercy.
But I keep the care   of the sea-cliff,
Watching the waves   to ward off foe-men;
Now back I go   to keep my guard."

The street was studded   with bright stones
And the shining path   showed the way.
Hand-forged and hard,   the hauberk shone
And its rings sang   of the armour's iron.
Barely had Beowulf   and his brave thanes   300
Halted at Heorot,   home of the Spear-Danes,
When tired from travel   over land-trail and sea,
They stood their broad shields   the strongest men know,
Against the hall's side   and sat down on the bench.
Then rang the ring-mail,   the war-armour,
Ash-tipped and together   the tall spears stood,
The war-gear of the Geats   wealthy in weapons.
Then a proud thane   challenged their lineage:
"From where in the world   have you wandered,
Bringing these shields,   garnished with gold,   310
These grey-hued hauberks   and helms with their visors,
And this high heap of spears   for the harvest of blood?
I am Hrothgar's herald   and his attendant,
And outlanders more gallant   have not met my gaze.
I think that you come   to visit Hrothgar
Not as outcasts   exiled by kinsmen
But great in the pride   of your mind and heart."

Straight then in his strength   stood Beowulf,
Proud resolute   under his helm,
And duly with dignity   answered the Dane: 320
"Hygelac's hall   and his table we share.
To Healfdene's heir   and to him only,
That well-loved king   worthy of warriors,
My mouth would declare   the thoughts of my mind
Provided that prince   would let us approach
So mighty a man.   Beowulf is my name."

Then Wulfgar the wise,   the war-thane

From the race of the Vandals[31]   rose to reply:
"Since you pray permission   for your project
I shall hie hence   to the home of the Dane-lord,   330
So free with his gear,   great giver of rings,
And bring back to you   whatever word
That wise man   may wish to give."

Swiftly he sped   thence to the steading
Where gray-haired and wrinkled   Hrothgar was
Seated in state   surrounded by war-thanes.
Then the valiant Vandal   versed in the court's way
Went straight to the seat   where Hrothgar sat.
Full in the face   of the Danes' lord
Frankly he looked   and manfully spoke: 340
"Over the ocean   a long way
To this land have come   thanes of the Geats.
The lord who leads them   is called Beowulf.
They would like, my lord,   to talk with you.
Do not, gracious Hrothgar,   deny what they ask.
Like earls they are   armed for attack.
A masterly man   indeed must be
The thane who brought   these warriors hither."

Then spoke prince Hrothgar,   protector of Scyldings:
"Well did I know him   when he was a child.   350
Ecgtheow his father was,   he whom Hrethel
King of the Geats,   Ecgtheow's kinsmen,
Wedded to his one   well-dowered daughter.
Now has Ecgtheow's son   come to a true friend
Seeking to save   the land of the Spear-Danes.
Moreover sailors   who sailed over sea,
Bearing treasure for thanks   to the land of the Geats
Have recounted his courage   and strength of his clasp
That in one hand-hold   can quell thirty men.
Surely God has given   this good man   360
To the beleaguered   and desperate Danes
As a stout staff   against Grendel.
So for the spirit   he has shown us
I shall reward him   with rings and riches.
Call this company   of his kinsmen
And bid them altogether   hither to me here,
And tell them too   when you answer them
That they are welcome   in the land of the Danes."

[31]Another Scandinavian nation originally from S. Sweden. F. Klaeber, *Beowulf*, 3rd. ed., Boston, 1950, p. 141 suggests that Wulfgar may have been a refugee from a blood-feud, or a mercenary.

[32] . . . spoke words from inside:

"I convey to you   what the Dane-king commands;
Knows all your lineage   my victorious lord,   370
He welcomes you here   and your heroes as well
Who sailed with you safe   over the swan's bath.
Wearing your helms and armour   you are now welcome
To see and have speech   with Hrothgar the king,
But leave your long spears   where you have piled them,
Your war-shields as well,   there to await
Whatever may fare   from the conference."

Then girded with thanes   a fine company,
Big-thewed and brawny   Beowulf rose.
Some where they were   waited to guard   380
All the war-weapons   as their war-lord commanded,
But the rest of the warriors   rushed as one man
While Wulfgar directed   under Heorot's roof-tree.

[33] . . . hard under his helm   till he stood by the hearth.
While his corselet,   pride of the smith's craft,
Burned in the light,   Beowulf spoke:
"I bring greetings   to you, great Hrothgar.
I come, a young thane   of Hygelac's kin.
Brave works have I done,   deeds worthy of Danes,
In the years of my youth   far in the Geat's land.   390
Heard I at home   Heorot's affliction,
Grim Grendel's curse   bearing grisly death.
Often by sailors   is the tale told
How this great hall   high Heorot
Ever is useless   and empty of warriors
After the sunset glow   goes under the sky's dome.
Hark now, King Hrothgar,   how the best of my men—
Wisest they were   among war-thanes—
Gave me advice   to visit you,
Seeing my strength   when spattered and stained   400
With gore of my foeman   I return from the wars.
In one battle I bound   of the brood of giants
Five enormous champions   and destroyed them all.
Many I massacred   of monsters that swim.
Dire was the distress   I endured from them
In that fierce fray   far on the sea,
Avenging in darkness   destruction of Geats.

[32]A few words are missing from the manuscript here; presumably Wulfgar is speaking from
    the doorway of the hall to the Geats waiting outside.
[33]Again a few words are missing from the manuscript.

Truly those demons   brought doom on themselves.
Now Grendel the monster   alone I would meet.
Therefore I pray you,   protector of Danes   410
And shield of the Scyldings,   to grant me one boon.
Do not refuse me   who have fared so far.
Let me do my duty   and drive that demon
From Heorot's hall   far and forever
Helped only by those   stern thanes of my troop.
I have heard also   how the grim monster
Out of war-wantonness   cares nothing for weapons.
So that Hygelac,   my liege lord
May boast the better   of my bravery
I shall scorn the sword   and the shelter of shield.   420
With both my bare hands   I shall grip Grendel
And fight the death-fight,   one foe against another.
The blow that death deals   let the loser take,
Accepting in silence   the judgment of God.
I think that the monster   if he can manage
Will make a meal   of the mighty Geats
Who wait in the hall   where the battle will be
As this fearless fiend   has often done.
You will never need   in a death-napkin
To cover[34] the head   of my heavy clay,   430
For if dire death   deign to take me
He will carry my corpse   intent to devour them
As he takes all slain men,   intending sepulchre.
But the outcast killer   cruel Grendel
Recklessly rends them,   staining his retreat
With bleak bones and blood   over the moors.
If I die then,   of my broken body
You need not care   much how to dispose.
If red war ravage me,   return to Hygelac
His excellent breastplate   of burnished mail   440
Wrought by Weland[35],   wizard of war-smiths,
For Hrethel the Geat   whose relic it was.
No will man wields   can alter wyrd."

Then the Scyld's protector,   Hrothgar, replied:
"Because of deeds done   and aid delivered
You come to us,   Beowulf, my friend.
Your father's fighting   started a blood feud.
He with his bare hands   killed Heatholaf

[34]Covering the head of a corpse at the time of burial was a Scandinavian custom.
[35]The mighty smith of Scandinavian and Germanic legend.

The while he abode among the Wylfings[36].
When the Geats fearful of war refused him asylum   450
Over the rolling seas he found a refuge
Safe with the South-Danes, the Ar-Scyldings[37].
Lord of all Dane-land a little time only,
I was young then, holding a wide kingdom
And ruling a city rich in warriors.
I stood in the stead of a stouter than I,
Heorogar he was, Healfdene's son,
My bravest brother, by death betrayed.
I settled with silver your sire's homicide,
Sending a store of ancient treasure   460
Over the waves to the wronged Wylfing.
Then Ecgtheow swore that he would keep peace.
It shames me now to tell any man
The humbling here in Heorot's hall
That Grendel has given with his grim sallies.
Day after day my hall-guard dwindles
Thrown by their wyrd into Grendel's power.
Yet God of His goodness may make us with ease
Free from the fury of that perilous fiend.
Often at evening over their ale-cups   470
My challenging thanes, pride of the Scyldings,
Vowed there to watch in the mead-hall wary,
Tossing terrible swords till Grendel should come.
But always next morning when the day's light dawned
That banquet hall and its benches were red with blood
Spilled from stout warriors spoiled in the fight
Then had I fewer thanes. Death had taken them.
Take seats at our banquet and tell us the details
Of wars won by valour as your mind wills."

Bare in the mead-hall a bench was cleared   480
That the Geat-thanes might sit together.
Resolute still and renowned for their strength
All the stout warriors at once took their seats.
Then a thane carrying a carved ale-keg
Served them with sweet and sparkling drink.
From time to time in the glad throng
The song of the scop rang clear in the hall
Where mingled in merriment the mighty men,
Stalwart and strong both the Dane and the Geat.

[36]Probably a N. Germanic tribe located on the south shore of the Baltic.
[37]Anglo-Saxon *ar* here probably meant "honour."

Unferth[38] the thane,   son of Ecglaf,   490
Sat at the feet   of the king of the Scyldings.
This voyage of Beowulf,   valiant sea-farer,
Jarred all the joy   from his jealous heart,
Greedy of greatness   by any man garnered
Save for his own deeds   under the sky's dome.
And now he rose openly,   showing resentment:
"Are you that Beowulf   who boasted with Breca[39],
So foolish to vaunt   the skill of your swimming
That vain of your valour   both of you bade
Good-bye to all caution,   cleaving the current   500
Over the dread deeps   of death-dealing ocean?
Neither friend nor foe   could prevent that faring,
The anxious trip   you two took in the water.
Both of you embraced   the billows in your arms,
Out there threshing with hands   and gliding through the waves;
The sea rolled its wave-swell   whipped by winter winds
And there you two   toiled for seven nights
Weary and perilous   in the power of the water.
Then did Breca the brawny   beat you at swimming.
Clear in the morning   the current carried   510
The stronger man   out of the sea's swell
Hence to the home   of the Heathoreames[40].
From there he made his way   to his own land
Where he held in the love   of his loyal people
A city, a throne,   and a treasure as well.
Thus the brag of Breca,   the son of Beanstan,
In all that he said   there was made good.
Though fierce you have fared   in the grim fight,
And sturdy and scatheless   have ever survived,
A worse wyrd, I think,   is waiting for you   520
If you spend a whole night   watching for Grendel."

Thus did Ecgtheow's son   answer the thane:
"Too much you have drunk   and talked about Breca,
And all on his side,   O Unferth, my friend.
But I shall talk now,   tell truth of the matter.
I in the sea   stronger was than Breca.
More of its malice   than any one man
My body bore   from the wave's buffets.
Boys were we both   all inexperienced
When brash in our boasting,   we bargained together   530

[38]His name means "un-peace."
[39]A Prince of the Brondings, a tribe from S. Scandinavia.   [40]A tribe of S. Norway.

To pit our two lives   against the sea's peril.
But we never went back   on the words of our brag.
We held in our hands   the hilts of bare swords
To ward off the whales   that lurk in the waves.
Unable was Breca,   breasting the swell
Though he divided the water   with all his strength
To distance me,   nor would I abandon him.
Then did we two   for the space of five nights
Stay in the sea,   swimming together
Till the cross-currents   crested with foam   540
Drove us unwilling   in different directions.
And the cruel north wind   as night closed in
Over the furious waves   fought us like a foe,
Buffeting fiercely   in the bitter cold.
Then raged around me   the aroused sea-whales
And I would have perished   in their perilous path
Had I not my hauberk,   hard garment of war
With its hand-woven links   well plated with gold.
It lay on my breast,   light and snug fitting
And protected me   against my enemies.   550
Fast-fisted was I   for one fell moment
Gripped in the grasp   of a grisly fiend
Who drew me down   to the deep sea-floor.
Hardly by good hap   did my sword-hand turn,
Letting me drive   deep with deadly sword
Hilting it home   in the monster's maw.
Thus did the dire fray   destroy the sea-beast.
And thus did these loathly creatures   thrust close to me,
But like a brave man   I beat them away.
When I swung my good sword   surely these monsters   560
Mindful to make   a meal of me
Had no reason then   to relish their feast.
They had gathered for banquet   near the sea-bottom
Who shoreward were washed   on the morning tide.
So spoiled were their sides   from thrusts of my sword
They never have hindered   seafarers again.
Grandly the good light   —God's bright sun—
Stood in the east-sky   and the waves sank
Showing the sea-capes   swept by the wind.
If his courage lasts   sometimes Fate saves   570
The determined warrior   not destined to die,
Such was my case   as it turned out.
Nine of the sea-beasts   I slew with my sword.
I have never heard   of a harder fight

Under the arched sky   or in the sea's stream
Waged ever by any   more wretched man;
Weary I won free   from that web of foes.
Finally the foam-race   through the sea carried me
Till I escaped with my life   in the land of the Finns[41].
Never, O Unferth,   have I heard   580
Of your doing such deeds   by dint of your sword.
Neither you nor Breca   in any vigorous battle
Wrought such a work   with your red weapons.
(But I must not mention   my exploits too much);
You killed your own brother,   closest of kinsmen,
And Hell-damned are you now,   however clever you are.
And now, Unferth,   son of Ecglaf,
I tell you the truth,   this terrible monster
Had not had heart   for his horrible deeds
To humble your king   in Heorot hall   590
Were you as a warrior   what you claim for yourself
In the merit and skill   of spirit and mind.
But Grendel has learned   he need not fear
Any desperate deeds   done in hostility
From the sharpened and deadly   swords of the Danes,
The victorious clan   to which you belong.
The oppressor takes   his terrible toll,
Showing no mercy   on the Danish people.
He does whatever evil   that his will pleases—
He kills and despatches,   knowing no man   600
Will rise up against him   from the ranks of the Spear-Danes.
But him shall I teach   in our terrible trial
The valour and strength   of the thanes of the Geats.
Gaily the brave man   . bears to the banquet
After the clear dawn   of another day
When the bright sun   in the south-sky
Scatters his splendour   over all men."

     The spirits of Hrothgar   were roused by this speech.
The king of the Bright-Danes   old and renowned
As prince of his people   believed in this aid,
Perceiving in Beowulf   resolute intent.   610

     Then did merriment   and mirthful speech
Through the hall resound   with a cheerful noise.
Wealhtheow[42], the queen,   wearing gold rings,

[41]Modern Finland lies east of Sweden; however, the poet may have meant the Lapps of
  Finmarken in N. Norway.
[42]Hrothgar's queen. Her name means "foreign slave or captive" and she belongs to the nation
  of the Helmings (see 1. 621); however, little is known of this nation.

Rose royally   to receive Beowulf;
Forward she came,   courteous in the hall.
First a full cup   she filled for her husband,
Urging the Dane-guard   to give himself joy
For the loyal love   of his people.
Hrothgar the hero   accepted the cup
And eager as ever   took part in the banquet.   620
Then the Helming woman   went to each member,
Giving both old and young   a rich goblet for drinking.
At last the ringed queen,   that excellent woman
To Beowulf bore   a cup of bright mead[43].
Greeting the Geat-thane,   gladly she gave
High honour to God   for help from these crimes.
Boldly did Beowulf,   fierce slayer in battle,
Take Wealhtheow's welcome   and with it the cup.
Then Ecgtheow's son,   that resolute war-thane,
Strong and war-ready   rendered this speech: 630
"When I sat in my ship   and put out to sea
Amid my men,   one meaning I had:
To win completely   goodwill of your people
Or failing that feat   to find my death
In the grimmest of combats   gripped by the fiend.
Either a man's deed   shall I do here
Or meet my death   in this banqueting hall."

These words of the Geat-thane   brave in their forecast
Delighted the noble   queen of the people
And she went in the glow   of her gold ornaments   640
To sit by the side   of her Scylding lord.
Again in the great hall   brave words were spoken
As the Spear-Danes   shouted their victories
Until the time came   when Healfdene's son[44]
Wished to retire   to rest for the night.
He knew that there   in the high hall
Men had decided   to way-lay the monster
From when the sun's light   was seen first by man
Until the time   when night's black tide
With its shadow shapes   gliding like ghosts   650
Crept over the world   dark under the skies.
All his warriors rose   at Hrothgar's sign.
Then Hrothgar,   the son of Healfdene,
Bade Beowulf   the best of luck

[43]A fermented drink resembling wine or very strong beer.
[44]Hrothgar. The oblique reference here is probably to remind the audience of Hrothgar's
    greatness; see note to 1. 169.

And willed him his mead hall   with these words:
"Since I could lift   either hand or shield
I have not entrusted   this mighty house
To any man   other than you.
Take guard and charge now   of this noblest of houses.
Consider the thoughts   men think of you   660
And be warlike in valour   to ward off our foes.
All that you wish   will be always yours
If you leave with your life   this brave enterprise."

      Then Hrothgar, head of the Danes,   left the hall
And with him went   his warlike company.
That leader longed   to join Wealhtheow,
His excellent queen   in her royal bed,
For the good God,   glory of kings,
Had given a warder   to watch against Grendel.
This special service   did Beowulf do   670
Keeping with care   for the king of the Danes
Guard against Grendel,   the monster of evil.
The great hero   trusted completely
In God's grace   and his spirited strength.
Then Beowulf put off   his iron coat,
Unhelmed his head,   and to his thrall
Consigned his carved sword   wrought of choice iron,
Bidding him guard   his gear with care.
Then Beowulf the Geat   in brave forecast
Spoke before settling   his frame to sleep: 680
"I deem not myself   meaner than Grendel
Where strength is required   in warfare and fighting.
No sword shall I use   to take his life
Though I at my ease   might kill him so.
Nothing he knows   of the skills of a thane
Like striking against me   and cutting my shield
Even if he has won fame   for his fierce fighting.
But without swords   shall we strive tonight
If he weaponless   wills to attack.
And may the holy Lord,   almighty God,   690
Grant glory   in the game of blood
To whichever hand   seems just to Him."
Then on the pillow   nobly this warrior
Rested his head   while all around him
Many a stout seaman   stretched in the hall.
No man of them there   thought that he ever
Would return again   after that time
To the people   or the loved land

Or the royal city   where he was raised,
For they knew that death   had already destroyed   700
Too many of the Danes   in that dire hall.
But God with His help   wove a victory web
That through one man's skill   the Geats might triumph
Over their enemy   and manifest ever
That Almighty God   is Ruler of men.
Then moved the monster   in the mid-night
Stalking in silence   dark in the shadows.
Placed as protectors   in the high hall
All of the warriors   were sleeping save one.
Men thought that this demon   unless the Lord willed   710
Could not drag them down   to the deep shadows.
But Beowulf,   biding the outcome,
Hostile and wary   watched for the foe.
Then from the moors   and the misty hills
Grendel came baleful,   bearing God's wrath.
That dire demon,   mankind's destroyer,
Was seeking by stealth   to snatch in his jaws
One of the thanes   there in the high hall.
Carefully he crept   forward under the sky
Right to the point where   he might most readily   720
Spy on the gilded hall   with its gables of gold.
This was not the first time   he attacked Hrothgar's house.
Not in his whole life   before that or after
Did he find such thanes   or fare so evilly.
Joyless this creature   came to the hall doors.
When with his fist   he first touched them,
All the oak doors   opened at once,
Though fastened with bands   forged in the fire.
Starving for slaughter   he swept into the hall.
Fiercely the fiend   strode over the floor,   730
And the flame of his eyes   flared on the pavement.
There he saw sleeping   in the hall of the Scyldings
War-thanes and kinsmen,   a good company.
The wretch rejoiced,   for before day came
He intended to tear   with his ravening teeth
Firm flesh and life-blood   from the body of each
Should it be given him   to gorge in gore
As his foul joy   fully expected.
But it was not then fated   that any more men
The monster might snatch   after that night.   740
For the brave Beowulf,   blood-kin of Hygelac,
Watched what the ravager   would grip in his grasp.

He unhesitating   with his first attack
Went to a warrior[45]   where he was sleeping
And tore at his flesh   then with his teeth,
Rended his joints   with ravaging jaws,
And drank the bright blood   that boiled from his veins,
Gulping down gobbets   of evil gore.
In a flash   the fiend had devoured
Hands and feet   and all of the dead thane.   750
Then that cursed of God   came still closer
To have in the grip   of his grasping hands
The determined war-thane   where watching he lay.
Beowulf welcomed   him with hostility
And on one arm   raised himself up.

      Then the fiend found   a worthy foeman.
Never had he   harder hand-grip
Met in a match   from any man
In any corner   of the Dane's land.
Fear filled his mind   and daunted his spirit.   760
Then longed he to leave,   to lose himself
In the dread darkness,   the home of devils,
But he could not break   the grip of Beowulf.
This was not what   he was wont to find.
Then the bold Beowulf,   blood-kin of Hygelac,
Remembering his speech   made in the evening,
Raised himself upright   and steady returned
Great Grendel's grip   till his fingers cracked.
He tried to evade   but the brave earl
Avid for victory   stepped farther in.   770
Fain was the fiend   to flee if he could
Thence to his lair   in the fen-land,
For he felt the force   of Beowulf's fingers,
The terrible throat-grip   of the furious thane.
O grievous to him   was the grim journey
That malicious monster   made to Heorot!

      Long the hall rang   loud with the noise
And a deep draught   of panic was poured
For every bold Dane   who dwelt in that city.
Both fighters were furious   to combat with frenzy.   780
A wonder it was   in their warring
A hall could stand   such savage onslaught
And the lofty lodge   did not collapse
From the strength   of strenuous attackers.

[45]His name was Hondscioh although we do not learn this till much later in the poem.

But it was bound   inside and out
And firm-fitted   with forged iron bands
Cunningly crafted   by excellent smiths.
Many main benches   inlaid with gold
Were sprung from the floor   while these two fought.
The Danish elders   never expected   790
Any man to damage   that antler-hung hall
By dint of any force   but devouring flame.
A new noise   swelled up loudly
And terrible terror   troubled the Danes
To hear through the wall   the howling of Grendel,
That Hell-bound fiend,   foe of the Lord,
As he cried in his fear   a shriek of despair
And screamed at the shock   of his wounds.
But Beowulf   the brawniest man
That in the world was   held him fast in his clutch.   800

      Then the proud prince,   protector of earls,
Made up his mind   more than all else
Never to let   this lethal assailant
Out of his grasp   while still he had breath
For he deemed that its life   was useless to men.
Many of Beowulf's earls   now brandished their blades.
Determined to protect   their illustrious prince.
But these wise-thanes   resolute in war
And bent on battle   to beat the demon
Were not aware   that no man-made sword   810
Though forged of pure iron   could harm that foe
Who blunted all blades   by dint of a spell.
Dire was to be the day   of its despatching,
Far from the world   into the power of fiends.
Oft had God's grim foe   greatly afflicted
By menace and stealth   the spirits of men,
But he found now   that no longer
His flesh would avail   for Hygelac's kinsman
Held him fast   in his hand.
Each hated the other   with a lethal hate.   820
Now had the Hell-fiend   a bodily hurt,
Grisly a great wound   gaped in his shoulder,
Sinews were parted   and joints torn asunder.
Fate then to Beowulf   gave glory in battle,
For Grendel was forced   to flee to the fen,
Destined for death   from his dire wound.
There did he seek   his wretched lair,
Knowing more plainly   the days of his life

Were now numbered   and at an end.
After the siege   of his murderous slaughters   830
The dearest desire   of every Dane
From hind to Hrothgar   had been realized.
Wise and resolute   the thane of the Geats
Had come hither   from a distant land
Resolved to cleanse   the hall of Hrothgar,
Delivering it whole   from the fiend's malice,
And glad was that man,   mindful of merit
That that night's deed   would bring among men.
He from the Geat's home   in the land of the Danes
Bravely had boasted   and made the boast good.   840
He too had remedied   all the sad distress
The Danes had endured,   that dire affliction
Granted by God   for them to undergo.
The token was clear,   his task was completed
When Beowulf then   after brave battle
Laid Grendel's whole arm   hand, shoulder and all,
Under the hall-roof   of high Heorot.

    Next morning there crowded   many war-thanes
Round the great hall   as I have heard,
And princes and earls,   peers of the people,   850
Went far and near   over wide stretching ways,
Viewing with wonder   the width of the tracks[46].
Not great was their grief   for Grendel slain
Who examined the spoor   that monster made
When worsted in war   and well-nigh dead
He fled to the lake   where the Hell-fiends live,
Leaving behind him   a trail of black blood.
There the water welled   in hideous waves
Mingled with gore   hot from the slaughter.
The horrible monster,   hidden from the hour   860
He gave up his life   and his Godless ghost,
Lay dead in his refuge   far out in the fen;
Hell in its fury   held hold of him there.
Then the old warriors   and young ones as well
Mounted on horse-back   merry in spirit
And rode their proud steeds   back from the lake,
Telling the tale   of Beowulf's deed.
Many were the men   who often declared
That in all the world   between the two seas
Washed by the tide   under the ringed sky   870

[46]i.e. Grendel's footprints.

There never was   a better shield-thane
More worthy than Beowulf   to wear a king's crown.
Nor did they indeed   ere talking was done
In any way   impute blame to their lord,
The gracious Hrothgar;   he was a good king.
Then did these brave   experienced war-thanes
Let their bay horses   gallop and race
Wherever the land's face   was known to be fair.
One of Hrothgar's thanes   was a powerful poet
Who held in his head   many heroic songs.   880
He knew as no man   all the old traditions
And could put new words   in their proper order.
From time to time   he would recite
With the skill of Aesop   Beowulf's story,
All its action in order   and words interlocked.
He also retold   all tales he had heard
Concerning the deeds   of prince Sigmund[47].
Much that was marvellous   sang he of Sigmund,
His woeful wars   and his wide journeys.
Evils and wickedness   few were aware of   890
Save for his fast friend,   his nephew Fitela;
With him did his uncle   these matters discuss,
For shoulder to shoulder   in the shield-play
Fierce had they fought   in every battle,
And their sharp swords   together had slain
A myriad monsters   in deadly combat.
Far-flung and mighty   was Sigmund's fame,
Nor did it diminish   after his death-day
When the fierce warrior   hardened in battle
Slew the great dragon   guarding its hoard.   900
All alone there   under a grey stone
Did the brave prince   that daring deed,
Not even Fitela   was with him then.
He thrust his fine sword   through the stout beast,
And its iron point   pierced to the wall;
But the dragon died   a bloody death.
So by his strength   Sigmund succeeded
And had at his will   a wealth[48] of gold rings.
Then did stern Sigmund,   the son of Waels,
Heap the bright hoard   high in his ship's hull   910

[47]A legendary Germanic hero descended through his father, King Volsung, from Woden the
    god of war. The story of his fighting a dragon, told in 11. 898-906 is peculiar to *Beowulf*.
    Beowulf's own third and last battle is also against a dragon.
[48]In Germanic legend, dragons are often guardians of treasure which passes into the hands
    of whoever kills the dragon, as happens in the end of *Beowulf*.

And fare with it seaward,   while flesh of the dragon
Weltered and melted   in its own heat.
For actions of valour   performed in all lands
Men hailed him   as Sigmund the hero,
Famous protector: thus he had prospered.
Sigmund flourished   after the courage
And powerful strength   of Heremod[49]
In his exile   had lessened.
Heremod was betrayed   in the Jutes'[50] land
And done to death   by dire enemies.   920
Too long over him   his heart's unhappiness
Swept in full waves   of deepest woe
Filling with sorrow   all his people's lives
And those of his war-thanes   without exception.
Many wise men   looking to him
For the realm's remedy   deemed that this ruler
Filling his father's rank   would prosper
And hold the good land   home of all Danes
With its people and stronghold   and riches as well,
Therefore his actions   by his friends were deplored.   930
Now in Denmark,   Hygelac's kin,
The bold Beowulf,   became most popular,
Loved by his friends   and by all mankind:
But wickedness won   in Heremod's heart.

　　　At times the thanes raced,   running their horses
Along the paved way,   the yellow street;
By this time the morning   was wearing on.
Many brave men   marched to the hall
To look at the marvel,   the wonderful thing.
Even the great guard   of the realm's riches,   940
Hrothgar the king,   sure of his excellence,
Came from the queen's rooms   along with this retinue,
Wealhtheow the queen   and her few attendants.
They took together   the path to the hall.
Then Hrothgar went   up to the hall
And stood on the stones   hard by the steps.
He looked up   at the high roof
That glittered gold   with its bright gilding
And gazed at Grendel's   grim hand and arm:
"Praise be to God   for what I see now.   950
Much hostility   and humbling had I

[49]A legendary king of the Danes.   [50]Hereditary enemies of the Danes. A Danish
king driven into exile by his countrymen might understandably flee to their enemies.

Hard to endure   from this Grendel;
But the good Lord,   God of all glory,
May with His Mercy   still work miracles.
I thought not long ago   I should never live
To see any succour   for the worst of my woes
When this high Heorot,   best of all halls,
Was stained red with blood   shed in warfare
And deep dejection   dimmed the spirits
Of my wily counsellors   who in their wisdom   960
Deemed it impossible   to hold the Dane's keep
Free from the fierce sallies   of that furious devil.
Now one man alone   through the Lord's might
Has done that deed   we could not do
Through all our skill   banded together.
Yes, whatever woman   brought from her womb
Such a son as he   into the world,
Well may she boast   if she be living
That the good Lord gave   her a great gift;
He helped her well   at her childbirth.   970
Now bold Beowulf,   best of all men,
Here to my heart   I hold you close
As a strong son.   Be such to me
And guard from now on   our new kinship.
Whatever you wish   in all the world
Shall be my gift   if I have power to give.
For a smaller service   to a poorer swordsman
I have often bestowed   from our treasure
A royal reward   and a rare honour.
You yourself have ensured   by your deeds done   980
Fame that shall live   for ever and ever.
May the Almighty   as He has done already
Reward you richly   for what you deserve."

        Then Beowulf,   the son of Ecgtheow,
Rose to reply   to Hrothgar the king:
"It was with the greatest   of good will
That we did   that deed of daring,
Fought that fight,   braving the foe
In all his uncanny   malice and might.
I would have wished   with all my heart   990
You could have seen   your enemy
Lying as he was   in battle, but dead.
Had not his body   slipped from my hands,
That fell fiend   I would have forced

Down on his bed   of dire death.
Then he would have lain   struggling for life,
Held in the grip   of my dread grasp.
But the divine Lord   did not desire
My hand should hold   the hostile foe
Tight to prevent   his prudent escape.   1000
Too strong was the foe   in his fleeing.
Behind him he left   hand, arm, and shoulder,
Sad sacrifice   to save his life.
But even so,   the evil creature
Cheated not death   from this deed.
It will not leave   any longer life
To this terrible   tyrant of evil,
For the hurt he had   from my dread hands
Has bound him fast   in the bonds of death.
There will this wretch   stained with his guilt[51]   1010
Wait till the dawn   of his doom's day
When God in His glory   shall judge him."

     Unferth, son of Ecglaf,   was silent now
About any boasting   of brave deeds
As the noble Danes   up at the high roof
Gazed on the hand   and fingers of Grendel
Where the ability   of Beowulf
Had hung there   that terrible trophy.
Each place in front   for a fingernail,
And each finger-tip   was just like steel.   1020
So hideous the claw   of this heathen fighter
All the crowd declared   in a chorus
That no forged sword   held in brave hands
Had edge to touch   this terrible fiend
In such a way   as to wound in battle
The blood-stained grip   of Grendel.
Then duly was   the order given
That many hands   of men and women
Might decorate   the banquet hall.
Rich hangings were there   and tapestries   1030
Woven with gold   shone from its walls,
Showing the Scyldings   wonderful sights.
The bright building   was badly damaged;
In spite of   its iron bands.
The strong door hinges   were all sprung
And the inside benches   battered and smashed.

[51] i.e. The guilt of killing many Danes.

Only the roof   survived intact
When that monster,   guilty of crimes,
Full of despair   fled for his life.
Let him who will   fly from death;   1040
That fell fate   he cannot avoid
For each living soul   on this sad earth
Will come at last   to a place prepared,
A narrow room   where his body sleeps
Fast in the grave   after this life's feast.

    Then it was time   and fitting as well
That Healfdene's son   should go to his hall,
For fain was the king   to join the feast.
I have never heard   of any nation
Where a greater band   of brave warriors   1050
Bore themselves better   around a lord
More liberal   with rings and land.
Men in their prime   stepped to the benches
And glad were they all   for the abundant fare.
Courteously then   the close kinsmen,
Hrothgar the king   and Hrothulf,
His sister's son,   accepted together
Many full cups   in the high hall.
Heorot within   was thronged with friends,
For at that time   the Danish nation   1060
Never had done   a treacherous deed.
Then Hrothgar,   son of Healfdene,
Gave rich presents   to brave Beowulf,
A fighting standard   as fee for conquest,
Heavy with glint   of gold embroidery.
And while the thanes watched,   Scylding and Geat,
A helmet, a hauberk,   and a huge sword
Famed for its forging,   of fabulous price,
Were brought and bestowed   on Beowulf too.
Strong in the hall   the hero stood   1070
And drained a draught   from a drinking cup.
Nor should he be shamed   before shield-thanes
To receive royally   these rich gifts.
I have not heard   of many men
Who gave four gifts   of golden worth
In a friendlier way   to some one else
At any banquet   anywhere.
A wire-bound rim   around the helm
Protected the head   so that filed swords
Hardened in battle   could not harm   1080

The brave war-thane   who carried his shield
Into the fray   against his foes.
Then the proud prince,   protector of earls,
Ordered eight horses   with decorated bridles
To be brought   there before him
Inside the high walls   of Heorot's hall.
On one sat a saddle   skilfully inlaid
That glittered and glowed   with jewels and gold.
It was the war-seat   of the high king
Whenever that warrior,   Healfdene's son,   1090
Rode at his foemen   to fight with the sword.
Never in battle   bloody with carnage
Did this king's force   falter or fail.
Then the great lord,   protector of Danes,
Gave to Beowulf   both horses and weapons,
And he told him   to use them well.
Thus this great prince,   illustrious lord,
Who guarded with his blood   his warriors' wealth,
Rewarded Beowulf   for his stormy battle
Most nobly   with horses   1100
And gave to him   gear of great worth.
No man finds fault   with these gifts
If he relates   the real truth.
Then to each one   of the brave thanes
On the banquet benches   those who had sailed
Over the sea   in Beowulf's ship
The king gave   a rich heirloom
And ordered gold   as a blood-gift
For that poor thane   whom Grendel
Had wickedly   worsted and slain[52].   1110
More men than he   that monster had murdered,
But Beowulf then   and all-knowing God
Delivered the Danes   from this doom.
As He does still,   upon that day
The Great Judge   ruled the lives of men.
Deep understanding   and mind's forethought
Are everywhere   best in the world;
Who grows old   on this vexed earth
Shall meet much   to love and hate.
Then there was music   mingled with singing   1120
Glad in the presence   of Healfdene's son.
The wooden-framed harp[53]   rang in the hall

---

[52]As the poet has told in ll. 743-750.   [53]The Anglo-Saxon harp was small and, as the
poet says, wooden-framed.

And many tales   were told with skill.
Then Hrothgar's scop   turned to the guests
On the oak benches   and began to tell
The fable of Finn[54]   and his fated men
Suddenly stricken   with disaster
And of how Hnaef,   the Dane-thane,
In the fierce fighting   in Frisia
Was doomed to die   a warrior's death.   1130
No rag of reason   had Queen Hildeburh
To praise the good faith   of Finn's people,
For in the fighting,   from spear-wounds,
Adored and innocent   of evil intention,
Both her brave son   and brother were slain.
O she was then   a woeful woman!
But not without cause   the daughter of Hoc[55]
Wept for the fate   befalling her kin,
For when day dawned   she saw by its light
There foully slaughtered   her fallen kinsmen   1140
Whom she had held   as her greatest joy.
Save for a few   all of Finn's thanes
Were swept away   in the war-fury.
He could not stand   against Hengest
Nor force from the fields   his[56] few followers
Who had come unscathed   from the combat.
Then did they offer   these terms to Finn,
For the Dane's use   the Frisians should free
Another hall[57]   with floor and high seat
And each of two bands,   Frisians and Danes,   1150
Should rule over   one half the hall,
And daily there Finn,   the son of Folcwalda[58],
Should honour the thanes   of Hengest's troop,
The Dane warriors,   with costly gifts,
With presents of rings,   and rare treasures

[54]*Finn*. A probably legendary king of the Frisians.
    As this episode is handled rather elliptically in *Beowulf*, an account of it follows:
        Finn, king of the Frisians, has a Danish queen, Hildeburh (1. 1132). A roving band of
Danes, led by Hildeburh's brother Hnaef, attack Finn for reasons the poet does not state.
In the fighting Hnaef is killed and both sides lose heavily in a drawn battle (11. 1143-1147).
After Hnaef's death, leadership of the Danes falls to Hengest (1. 1145), and Hengest and
Finn make a truce on terms given in 11. 1148-1175.
        The Danes and some of the Frisians spend the winter together in Finnsburh in Frisia.
In the spring a Danish warrior, Hunlafing, urges Hengest to break the truce (1. 1225-1228).
Guthlaf and Oslaf, two Danish warriors, provide the occasion for Hengest to do this
(11. 1232-1236), and fighting breaks out again between Danes and Frisians. This time
the Danes are victorious and Finn is killed (1. 1238). Queen Hildeburh is carried back to
the land of the Danes along with the treasure of the Frisians (11. 1239-1255).
[55]Father of Hildeburh and Hnaef.   [56]i.e., Hengest's.   [57]This hall was to be built to
    replace the one presumably wrecked in the first fight between Frisians and Danes.
[58]The father of Finn; his name probably means "ruler of the people."

Of great value   carved out of gold;
As much wealth   to the warlike Danes
Should Finn give   as he first gave
To his fast friends,   the Frisians
Who followed him   in their banqueting hall.   1160
Both sides concurred   in this compact of peace.
Then the son of Folcwalda   solemnly swore
To brave Hengest   an unbreakable oath
Kindly to treat   all the survivors,
Using the Danes   as his elders deemed;
And that none of his men   would mar this truce
Either by word   or evil deed,
Nor mention with malice   the facts of the case,
How the Danes having lost   their liberal lord
Were loyally serving   his killer[59]   1170
Forced by their fate   to do so.
Finally Finn swore   that if the Frisians
Were rash to remind   of this murderous feud
The edge of the sword   should settle the matter.
A funeral pyre[60]   was piled high,
Heaped with gold   got from the hoard,
And here the cold corpse   of Hnaef,
Bravest in battle   of war-Danes,
Was placed with his gear   firm on the pyre.
His blood-stained hauberk   and iron-hard helm   1180
Gilt with the image   of a golden boar
Could be seen plain   on the pyre's peak,
And many earls   earth-fallen in battle
Or carried off   by grievous wounds.
Then at Hnaef's pyre   Hildeburh commanded
Her own son be sent   to the singeing flames
And his body burned   on the blazing pyre
Hard by the shoulder   of his uncle.
She lamented their dying   with dirges,
And the war-thane was placed   on the funeral pyre.   1190
The great flames leaped   up to the clouds,
Roaring in front   of the burial mound.
Men's heads dissolved   like melted wax
And the gashed wounds   which weapons had made
Burst open and gushed   great gobbets of blood.
What war had seized   fire-thirst devoured,
Greedy to drink   both Frisian and Dane:

[59]*serving his killer.* To do this was to incur grave reproach in Germanic thought.
[60]Burning the dead was another Germanic burial custom.

Life and full vigour   had fled from them.
Reft of their friends   the warriors
Departed   leaving Danes lingering,   1200
Home to houses and towns   throughout Frisia.
Hengest, however,   having no choice,
Stayed fast with Finn   that blood-stained winter.
That lord longed   for his own land
Though he could not sail   across the sea
The curving prow   of his proud ship
For the ocean boiled   with a storm
And wrestled   with the north wind
While winter locked   the active waves
In fast fetters   of rigid ice   1210
Until at last   as still happens
At the right time   the turning year
Brought bright weather   gloriously constant.
Winter was fled   and everywhere
The earth's breast   showed fair and bright,
And this alien lord   in his exile
Dearly desired   home to depart,
But his bitter thoughts   burned more for revenge
On the grievous harms   he had suffered
Than for voyages   over the sea.   1220
He pondered the problem   how to provoke
A grim battle   where he might bear
The fate of the Frisians   fell in his mind.
When Hunlafing[61]   placed in his hands
An excellent sword   gleaming in battle
Whose edges were known   to the Frisian warriors,
He did not deny   the ways of the world.
Thus a dire death,   a cruel doom,
In his own home   overtook Finn
Slain by the sword   of the daring Hengest   1230
After the good thanes,   Guslaf and Oslaf[62],
Fierce from their journey   over the sea,
Referred to the fury   of that forced battle
And boldly blamed Finn   for all their sorrows:
Their great grief   would not let them rest.
Then the hall was decked   with dead Frisians.
Among his warriors   was King Finn slain
And Hildeburh his queen   haled as a prisoner.
After this battle   the victorious Danes

[61]A Danish warrior; see note to 1. 1127.   [62]Danish warriors; see note to 1. 1127. They have evidently been on a voyage, although the poet gives no details of the voyage.

Heaped in the holds of their long ships   1240
Brooches and jewels cunningly carved,
All gear they could get out of the king's house.
On their voyage the noble queen
They carried off, their arms' captive,
To their own people in Denmark.

  This song was sung as the scop's tale;
Then was the revel a general thing,
And the guests gave a glad noise
As among them mingled the servants
Pouring out wine from the wonderful casks.   1250
Then walked Wealhtheow, wearing her circlet
Wrought of pure gold, forth to the place where
Firm in their faith and fully at peace
Sat those good men, uncle and nephew[63].
There Unferth the orator sat at the Dane-king's feet.
Him each man admired for magnanimous spirit
Though in the melee he had shown no mercy
Nor granted kindness to his nearest kin.
Then Wealhtheow the queen spoke in this wise:
"Take this gold goblet, my bountiful lord.   1260
Be glad as a man should, O gracious king,
And speak to this Geat[64] with generous words.
Be liberal to all the Geats,
Mindful of benefits from near and far.
Oft have men said that you wish to have
A worthy warrior for your son's weal.
And now that Heorot, that bright hall,
Wherein you gave your gifts of rings,
Is purified of that fell demon,
Give many gifts while yet you may   1270
And when the day comes of your destined doom
Leave your loyal kin a land and a folk
Fit for the gift of a great king.
I know that Hrothulf is a generous thane.
If you, great Hrothgar, king of the Danes,
Should depart from this world before his leaving,
He will mind with mercy all his young men.
As well, I am sure, he will use our children
If he remembers the many favours
And all the honour we allowed him   1280
When he was a child under this roof."

[63]Hrothgar and Hrothulf. [64]Beowulf.

Then did she move   to the bench where her sons,
Hrethric and Hrothmund   and the other young men,
Sons of Scyld-warriors   were sitting together.
Beside the two brothers   sat Beowulf,
That excellent man,   stout thane of the Geats.
A drinking cup   was carried to him
And he was given   a most gracious greeting;
On him were pressed   presents of spun-gold,
And a corselet,   two arm-bracelets,   1290
And the greatest chain   of graven gold
I have ever heard of   for a hero's neck.
No man has told   of a nobler jewel
Given by any human   underneath the skies
Since Hama[65] haled   to his beautiful city
That priceless jewel   with its precious setting,
The bright necklace   of the Brosings[66].
That man by malice   met his death
When he fled the hate   of cunning Eormanric[67].
Hygelac the Geat,   grandson of Swerting,   1300
Held the necklace   on that last occasion
When as a warrior   under his standard
He gathered treasure   and guarded it with death.
But he too heard   the voice of his pride
Sealing his fate   in a war against Frisia[68].
That powerful prince   took the necklace
With its precious stones   along with him
Over the bowl   of the waters[69];
And he died in combat   under his shield.
Then Hygelac's corpse   and his corselet   1310
And the necklace   that belonged to the Brosings
Passed into the power   of the valiant Franks[70].
The foreign foemen   foraged in plunder
Among the bodies   of the Geatish dead
Where calm they lay   cut down in the combat.
Thus the Franks kept the field   after the fray.

[65]In the medieval stories of Dietrich von Bern, Hama is sometimes a follower of Dietrich and sometimes a follower of Dietrich's enemy Eormanric.
[66]A Scandinavian tribe, possibly the same as the Brisings of Norse legend. The necklace had magical power.   [67]Historically, king of the Ostrogothic empire which stretched from the Baltic to the Black Sea in the middle of the fourth century A.D. In legend he became, as here, a prototype of cunning and ferocity.
[68]*war against Frisia.* Hygelac's disastrous Frisian expedition is historical. It took place about 521 A.D. and is recorded by Gregory of Tours in his *Historia Francorum.* He mentions Hygelac as "Chlochilaichus."   [69]*the bowl of the waters.* The sea.
[70]The Germanic tribe who occupied the north of what is now W. Germany and eastern France. At this time they were ruled by the Merovingian Kings. The poet makes no distinction between Franks and Frisians.

Heorot rang　　with the warriors' applause
And, standing in front　　of the king's guard,
Hrothgar's queen　　spoke once again:
"Wear round your neck　　this royal chain.　　　　　　　　　1320
May it bring you,　　my dear Beowulf,
Good favour of fortune　　while you are young.
Wear too this corselet　　come from the king's house,
The hoarding place　　of the nation's treasure,
And may you flourish　　firm as its iron.
Make yourself known　　for strength in the striving
And be kind in counsel　　to these children[71];
Nor shall you fail from me　　to find reward.
Wherever in the world　　the wind blows
Or the salt sea rolls　　or cities stand　　　　　　　　　　1330
Men will always praise　　what you have done.
As long as you live,　　noble Beowulf,
May you thrive　　as you deserve.
I wish you wealth　　worthy your greatness.
Be kind to my son[72]　　in your time of happiness.
Each of my two sons[73]　　is true to the other,
Loyal to his lord　　and gentle in spirit.
Our earls are united,　　our people well disposed,
And these warriors　　now at their wassail
In all their duties　　do as I command."　　　　　　　　　1340
Then Wealhtheow went　　back to her seat.
At this best of banquets　　the bold warriors
Drained to the dregs　　their draughts of wine,
Nor were they aware　　of the grim wyrd[74]
Ordained for them　　from the first of days;
But that fate　　soon overtook
Many nobles　　after night came
When mighty Hrothgar　　weary of feasting
Had gone to his rest　　in his own quarters.

[71]Hrethric and Hrothmund. Wealhtheow seems to fear some danger to them possibly from
　　Hrothulf their cousin. See ll. 1274-1281 and the notes thereto.
[72]Wealhtheow seems to commend one son, possibly Hrethric the elder, specially to
　　Beowulf's care.　　[73]See footnote 72.　　[74]*grim wyrd*. Renewed attacks, now to be made
　　by Grendel's mother in revenge for the death of her son.

Free from the terror of Grendel, the Danish thanes may now sleep in the hall once again. This they do, to find next morning that Grendel's mother, in revenge for the death of her offspring, has broken into the hall and killed and carried away the warrior Aeschere. Stricken anew with grief, Hrothgar sends for Beowulf who at once agrees to deal with this fresh menace. The trail left by Grendel's mother is followed to a lonely and forbidding lake, thick with water-monsters. Nothing daunted, Beowulf dives into the lake and fights and kills Grendel's mother, in a battle in a cave below the lake. Then, loaded with gifts from Hrothgar, he returns home. After Beowulf has ruled the Geats for fifty years, a firebreathing dragon's hoard is robbed by a fugitive slave. In revenge the monster devastates the land of the Geats. Beowulf, although sensing that his days are ending, fights the dragon and kills it, but is mortally wounded himself. War and disaster after his death are foretold, and Beowulf's people bury him royally and mourn him deeply. The poem ends with the lines:

"Thus the Geatish people, the sharers of Beowulf's hearth, mourned the death of their lord. Of all men who were kings in this world, they judged him the mildest and most gentle, the most loved by his people, and the most deserving of praise."

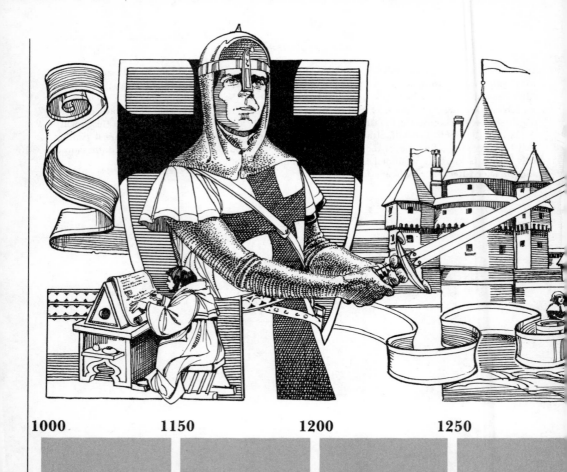

1000   1150   1200   1250

● Norman Conquest

● Magna Carta

● Founding of Oxford University

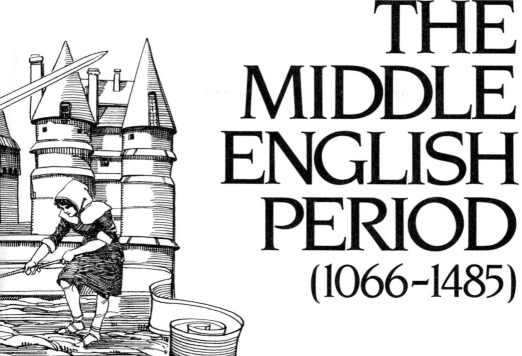

THE MIDDLE ENGLISH PERIOD (1066-1485)

1350	1400	1450	1500

• *Sir Gawain and the Green Knight*

• Beginning of Hundred Years' War

• Black Death   Reign of Henry VII – end of feudalism •

• Peasants' Revolt   Malory: *Morte d'Arthur* •

• Chaucer: *Canterbury Tales*

The Norman Conquest of 1066 might have been expected to put an end to literature in English: French became the language of the aristocracy, Latin remained the language of the scholars, and English was left to the speech of the lower classes. There was, indeed, a temporary halt, but the net effect of the Conquest was to enrich rather than to impoverish English language and literature. Shortly after the end of the twelfth century, wise and witty English poems such as "The Owl and the Nightingale" and long verse-chronicles such as Layamon's *Brut* were beginning to appear; by the thirteenth century English was beginning to establish itself again as the official language of government; and by the fourteenth century English literature had entered one of its great creative periods. In the meantime, many new words, literary forms, and social attitudes had entered England from France, and the whole character of English language and literature had been altered. To read *Beowulf* is to read a poem with a spirit and a language alien to us; to read *The Canterbury Tales* is to read a poem which in language and thought is recognizably our own.

This change in temper as a result of Norman influence had indeed begun before the Conquest, but was greatly accelerated by it. Old English literature is essentially a northern, Scandinavian literature, vigorous, virile, and stirring, but rather stark, humourless, and forbidding; Middle English literature is a southern, Gallic literature, stressing love and tenderness as much as strength and courage, and possessing a gaiety and delicacy seldom found in Old English. The change can perhaps be expressed most clearly and simply by saying that the hero of the old epic, the Warrior, is replaced by the hero of the new romance, the Knight.

English society underwent many upheavals between 1066 and 1485. There was the struggle of the Norman King and his barons to impose their will on the Anglo-Saxons; the struggle of the barons to assert their rights against those of the King, culminating in the signing of the Magna Carta in 1215; the struggle of serfs to win their freedom from the King and barons, symbolized most vividly by the Peasants' Revolt of 1381; the struggle of the Scots to assert their freedom from the English, climaxed by the battle of Bannockburn in 1314; the struggle of the English to resist the claims of the French Kings, leading to the Hundred Years' War which broke out in 1337 and saw the great English victories of Crécy (1346), Poitiers (1356), and Agincourt (1455); the devastating Black Death, or plague, which swept over England several times in the fourteenth century and wiped out over a third of its population; revolts of such powerful nobles as the Percies (1403); the struggle between the houses of York and Lancaster for the English throne, precipitating the Wars of the Roses which left England in a disturbed state throughout the rest of the fifteenth century; and finally the attempts of successive Popes to claim and maintain both spiritual and temporal authority over England, and the stirrings (such as those of Wycliffe) against the worldliness and materialism of parts of the late medieval church.

In spite of these struggles, however, the English nation gradually consolidated itself during these four centuries. Agriculture continued to be the basis of the economy, but trade and industry developed and brought with them the rise of a new middle class. The universities of Oxford and Cambridge were founded, and many new schools were established. Gradually a strong national consciousness was forged in the furnace of foreign and civil war.

Medieval society in England, as in the other parts of Western Europe, was dominated by two great institutions—feudalism and the church. Around these two institutions the literature of the period may conveniently be grouped.

Out of feudalism, with its ideal of fealty to the baron, grew chivalry, the elaborate code of conduct by which the medieval knight must live. And out of chivalry grew the medieval romance, the mirror of its ideals. The romance flourished in France in the thirteenth century, and soon spread to England. Unlike the old epics, which they nevertheless resembled in being long narrative poems, the romances were frankly fictional, more concerned with feeling than with action, and dealt in the strange, the fanciful, and the wonderful. They laid much stress on love and respect for women, and were full of colour and elaborate description. Many of them dealt with the legendary exploits of King Arthur and his Knights of the Round Table, others with the French hero Charlemagne, and still others with heroes of ancient, especially Roman, history. Early examples of the English romance, such as *Havelok the Dane* and *Arthur and Merlin*, appeared at the end of the thirteenth century, but the greatest of them is *Sir Gawain and the Green Knight*, which probably belongs to the late fourteenth century. Chaucer wove romances into the fabric of his *Canterbury Tales*, and Sir Thomas Malory, in the late fifteenth century, gathered together his prose version of the Arthurian cycle.

Many of the romances stress moral aspiration, or by means of allegory (as in the stories dealing with the quest for the Holy Grail) seek religious significance; so even this secular form could be said to owe nearly as much to the church as to feudalism. On other literary forms of the period the influence of the church was more direct and unmistakable. Stories of the lives of the saints, often embellished with legendary material reminiscent of the romances (see, for example, the legend of Saint George and the dragon), were a popular literary form, as were the "exempla," short tales told to teach a moral lesson, and the fables, in which animals were manipulated to point a human moral. The church also inspired many lyrics, songs which glorified the Virgin, a saint, or Jesus Christ himself. Drama, too, was heavily under religious influence: plays began as parts of the service of worship, and gradually evolved into the miracle and morality plays which employed biblical and allegorical characters to enforce the truths of Christian belief and conduct.

Not all the literature of the period, however, was chivalric or Christian in inspiration. Secular lyrics, such as the famous "Cuckoo Song," were written in praise of natural scenery or earthly love; the common people relished scandalous or racy stories known as fabliaux which related comic episodes of mistaken identity, intentional or unintentional adultery, and various farcical pranks; and the popular ballads, relating violent or pathetic events of everyday experience in a simple, memorable, repetitive style, flourished in the fifteenth century.

One conspicuous feature of medieval literature was its anonymity. Apart from Layamon, of whom our knowledge is very scanty, we know virtually nothing of individual authors until the time of Chaucer. But in the latter half of the fourteenth century four writers appeared of whom we have considerable knowledge. Geoffrey Chaucer was by far the greatest of these, but his contemporaries John Gower, William Langland, and John Wycliffe were also important figures. Gower wrote three long poems, one in French, one in Latin, and one in English, but it is the latter, *Confessio Amantis*, a collection of love stories written in octosyllabic couplets, which is his most famous work. Gower is a more explicit preacher than Chaucer, and lacks his humour and force, but he writes easily and gracefully. William Langland, in *The Vision of Piers Plowman*, challenged the conscience of his time by his trenchant attack on the abuses of laity and clergy alike. *Piers Plowman* is interesting both for its allegorical satire and for its verse form, for it is one of the last works to be written in the Old English alliterative style. The third writer, Wycliffe, was rather a preacher and reformer than an artist. He is best known as a forerunner of the Reformation in England, and for founding an order of poor priests known as Lollards as a protest against the worldliness of the medieval church; but he wrote many sermons and played a major role in the first English translation of the Bible.

Another important writer of this late fourteenth century is known simply as the "Pearl Poet." The sole surviving manuscript of his work includes four poems: "The Pearl," "Patience," "Purity," and "Sir Gawain and the Green Knight." The first of these is a religious allegory in elegiac form; the next two are biblical narratives of a didactic sort; the last is the finest metrical romance in English, the vigorous and colourful story of Sir Gawain's double ordeal, test of both his courage and his chastity. All four are interesting from the standpoint of style, in that they combine the Anglo-Saxon alliterative line with the device of rhyme imported from France.

The promise, indeed the achievement, of the late fourteenth century was not carried on into the fifteenth. The most probable reasons for this dearth of literature in the fifteenth century are the disrupting effect of the Wars of the Roses and the rapid changes in the language, which made rhyme and syllabification very uncertain. Chaucer's chief English disciples, Lydgate and Occleve, were uninspired imitators; only in Scotland, where King James I, Henryson, and Dunbar carried on the tradition, was Chaucer's example immediately fruitful. The rough and ready rhymes of John Skelton were almost all that England could show of verse in the fifteenth century—for the fifteenth was the great century of the popular ballad, with its brisk rhythms, its dramatic scenes, and its powerful emotional effects.

When Henry Tudor defeated Richard III at Bosworth Field in 1485 and began his reign as Henry VII, feudal England had virtually reached conclusion. It is fitting that in that same year the first English printer, William Caxton, should have published Sir Thomas Malory's *Morte d'Arthur*, the repository of the chivalric conventions which were no longer much more than a heroic memory. The England of the Tudors was indisputably modern England, and its literature the first great phase of modern English literature.

MIDDLE ENGLISH LYRICS

A lyric is a brief, personal poem with strong melodic and emotional qualities; in England, it reached its peaks of development in the Elizabethan and Romantic periods; but the lyric has been written in every age. In the Old English period, there are lyrical passages in *Beowulf* and religious poems such as Caedmon's hymn. The introduction of Latin hymns and, after the Norman Conquest, the songs of the French troubadours, provided the English lyric with a new style and a new subject-matter. The new style consisted of the substitution of rhyme and accent for the native prosody of stress and alliteration; the new subject-matter was courtly love and nature description, although religion continued to be the chief subject. Most of the Middle English lyrics which have survived come from the thirteenth, fourteenth, and fifteenth centuries. In the selections which follow, "The Cuckoo Song" exemplifies the nature lyric, "Alysoun" the love lyric, "Ubi Sunt Qui Ante Nos Fuerunt?" the lyric common to all ages which laments the transitoriness of human life, and "I Syng of a Myden" the religious lyric.

The language of these lyrics may at first glance appear unintelligible, but if the student will follow the sound rather than the spelling he will find that most of the words are familiar.

The Cuckoo Song

Sumer is icumen in,
Lhude[1] sing cuccu!
Groweth sed and bloweth med[2]
And springth the wode nu[3].
Sing cuccu!

Awe[4] bleteth after lomb,
Lhouth[5] after calve cu,
Bulluc sterteth[6], bucke verteth[7].
Murie sing cuccu!
Cuccu, cuccu,
Wel singes thu, cuccu.
Ne swik[8] thu naver nu!

Sing cuccu nu, Sing cuccu!
Sing cuccu, Sing cuccu nu!

Ms. c. 1240

[1]Loudly.   [2]Blooms (the) meadow.
[3]Now.   [4]Ewe.   [5]Lows.   [6]Leaps.
[7]Breaks wind.   [8]Cease.

Alysoun

Bytuene Mersh and Averil
When spray biginneth to springe,
The lutel foul hath hire wyl
On hyre lud[1] to synge.

[1]Song, sound.

Ich libbe[2] in lovelonginge
For semlokest[3] of alle thynge;
He[4] may me blisse bringe,
Icham[5] in hire baundoun[6].
    An hendy hap[7] ichabbe[8] yhent,[9]
    Ichot[10] from hevene it is me sent— 10
    From alle wymmen mi love is lent[11],
    And lyht on Alysoun.

On heu hire her is fayr ynoh,
Hire browe broune, hire eye blake,
With lossum chere[12] he on me loh[13];
With middel smal and wel ymake[14].
Bote he me wolle[15] to hire take
Forte buen[16] hire owen make[17],
Longe to lyven ichulle[18] forsake
And feye[19] fallen adoun.
    An hendy hap &c.

Nihtes when y wende[20] and wake—
For-thi[21] myn wonges[22] waxeth won[23]—
Leuedi[24], al for thine sake,
Longinge is ylent[25] me on.

[2]Live.   [3]Fairest.   [4]She. (Also in ll. 15 and 17.)
[5]I am.   [6]Power.
[7]*Hendy hap.* Pleasant fortune.   [8]I have.
[9]Received.   [10]I know.   [11]Gone.
[12]*lossum chere.* Lovely complexion.
[13]Laughed.   [14]Made.   [15]Will.   [16]Be.
[17]Mate.   [18]I will.   [19]Fated to die.
[20]Turn.   [21]Therefore.   [22]Cheeks.
[23]Pallid.   [24]Lady.   [25]Arrived.

In world nis[26] non so wyter[27] mon
That al hire bounte[28] telle con;
Hire swyre[29] is whittore than the swon,
And feyrest may in toune.
    An hendy hap &c.   30

Icham for wowyng al forwake[30],
Wery so water in wore[31];
Lest eny reve me[32] my make
Ychabbe y-yyrned yore[33].
Betere is tholien whyle sore[34]
Then mournen evermore;
Geynest under gore[35],
Herkne to my roun[36].
    An hendy hap &c.

        Ms. c. 1310

[26]Is not.   [27]Wise.   [28]Goodness.
[29]Neck.   [30]Wearied with waking.
[31]Sea beach.   [32]*reve me*. Take from me.
[33]*Ychabbe y-yyrned yore.* I have yearned for a long time.
[34]*tholien whyle sore.* Suffer sorrow for a time.
[35]*Geynest under gore.* Handsomest under (any) garment.
[36]Song.

Ubi Sunt Qui Ante Nos Fuerunt?

Were[1] beth they that biforen us weren,
Houndes ladden[2] and havekes[3] beren,[4]
    And hadden feld and wode?

[1]Where.   [2]Led.   [3]Hawks.   [4]Bore.

The riche levedies[5] in hoere[6] bour,
That wereden gold in hoere tressour[7],
    With hoere brightte rode[8];
Eten and drounken, and maden hem glad;
Hoere lif was al with gamen i-lad[9],
    Men kneleden hem biforen;
They beren hem wel swithe heye[10];   10
And in a twincling of an eye
    Hoere soules weren forloren.

Were is that lawhing[11] and that song,
That trayling and that proude gong[12],
    Tho havekes and tho houndes?
Al that joye is went[13] away,
That wele is comen to weylaway,
    To manye harde stoundes[14].

Hoere paradis they nomen[15] here,
And nou they lyen in helle i-fere[16];   20
    The fuir hit brennes[17] hevere:
Long is ay, and long is o,
Long is wy, and long is wo;
    Thennes ne cometh they nevere.

        Ms. c. 1275

[5]Ladies.   [6]Their.   [7]Tresses.
[8]Redness (i.e. complexion).
[9]*with gamen i-lad.* Led in sport.
[10]*beren . . . heye.* Bore themselves very high (proudly).
[11]Laughing.   [12]*proude gong.* Stately gait.
[13]Gone.   [14]Moments.   [15]Took.
[16]In company.   [17]Burns.

I Syng of a Myden

I syng of a myden   that is makeles[1],
Kyng of alle kynges   to here sone che ches[2].

He cam also stylle[3]   ther his moder was
As dew in Aprille,   that fallyt[4] on the gras.

[1]Matchless, peerless.   [2]Chose.   [3]*also stylle.* As quietly.   [4]Falleth.

He cam also stylle   to his moderes bowr
As dew in Aprille,   that fallyt on the flour.

He cam also stylle   ther his moder lay
As dew in Aprille,   that fallyt on the spray.

Moder and mayden   was never non but che—
Wel may swych[5] a lady   Godes moder be.

Ms. c. 1450

[5]Such.

GEOFFREY CHAUCER (1344?-1400)

The exact date of Chaucer's birth, usually given as 1340, is uncertain, but recent scholarship tends to place it as late as 1343 or 1344. The son of a prosperous London wine merchant, he led an active life in the public service. He fought in the Hundred Years' War against France, was sent abroad several times on diplomatic missions, and in 1374 was appointed Controller of Customs in the Port of London. During the twelve years that he held this important post he wrote his great verse romance, *Troilus and Criseyde*. In 1389 he was made Clerk of the King's Works, and thus was in charge of the construction and repair of the royal and public buildings, bridges, walls, wharves, and other port facilities.

Chaucer was, then, a busy man of affairs; he was also a scholar. He acquired a broad knowledge of the medieval sciences, of ancient and contemporary literature, and of philosophy and theology. He was especially influenced by modern French and Italian writers such as Froissart, Deschamps, Dante, Petrarch, and Boccaccio, but he always so adapted others' work to his own purposes as to make it virtually new and original.

His greatest work, *The Canterbury Tales*, is a case in point. Such collections of tales were very popular in the Middle Ages, but Chaucer's collection at least equals and in some respects excels its models. The same is true of the individual tales, most of which are borrowed from other authors such as Boccaccio or Dante or from folk-lore, but which always emerge as greater stories from Chaucer's transforming imagination.

The Canterbury Tales are, like all great works of art, both of their own time and of all time. They constitute by far the most comprehensive record we possess of English life in the fourteenth century, and yet they are more than a mere picture of contemporary manners. In these tales, as Dryden put it, "We have our forefathers and great-grand-dames all before us, as they were in Chaucer's days. Their general characters are still remaining in mankind, and even in England, though they are called by other names than those of Monks, and Friars, and Canons, and Lady Abbesses, and Nuns; for mankind is ever the same."

The debt which English literature owes to Chaucer is immense. His humour, which ranges all the way from broad farce to subtle wit, his power of characterization, his narrative artistry, and his metrical skill all had a great influence on succeeding writers. In particular, he imported the iambic pentameter line from France, and it became the great line of English verse.

By the time of Chaucer, the English language had been greatly enriched by French words and phrases, and had lost most of its inflections except the final "e." Usually the final "e" should be pronounced as a separate syllable in Chaucerian verse, and its pronunciation has been indicated in the text below by a dot above it thus: "ė." If the verse is read in this way, it will be found quite regular. In reading it, too, the student should sound the words either aloud or in his mind, and he will then find that most of the words are familiar to him, however strange their spelling may appear.

The Canterbury Tales: The Prologue

Here bygynneth the Book of the tales of Caunterbury

Whan that Aprille with his shoures soote[1]
The droghte of March hath perced to the roote,
And bathed every veyne in swich licour[2]
Of which vertu engendred is the flour;
Whan Zephirus eek with his swete breeth
Inspired hath in every holt[3] and heeth
The tendre croppes, and the yonge sonne
Hath in the Ram his halfe cours y-ronne[4],
And smale foweles maken melodye,
That slepen al the nyght with open ye,   10
So priketh hem Nature in hir corages[5],
Thanne longen folk to goon on pilgrimages,
And palmeres for to seken straunge strondes,
To ferne halwes, kowthe in sondry londes[6];
And specially, from every shires ende
Of Engelond, to Caunterbury they wende,
The hooly blisful martir[7] for to seke,
That hem hath holpen whan that they were seeke[8].

[1]Sweet.   [2]*swich licour.* Such moisture.   [3]Wood.   [4]*Hath in . . . y-ronne.* Has run through
    his half-course in the sign of Aries.   [5]*So priketh . . . corages.* Nature so stirs their hearts.
[6]*To ferne . . . londes.* To distant shrines, known in many lands.   [7]St. Thomas à Becket.
[8]Sick.

(translated by NEVILL COGHILL)

When In April the sweet showers fall
And pierce the drought of March to the root, and all
The veins are bathed in liquor of such power
As will bring on the engendering of the flower,
When also Zephyrus[1] with his sweet breath
Exhales an air in every grove and heath
Upon the tender shoots, and the young sun
His half-course in the sight of the Ram has run,[2]
And the small fowl are making melody,
That sleep away the night with open eye   10
(So nature pricks them and their heart engages),
Then people long to go on pilgrimages,
And palmers[3] long to seek the stranger strands

[1]The warm west wind.
[2]*young sun . . . run.* The Ram is one of the signs of the Zodiac; the sun has passed half through this
    period after March 21.
[3]Pilgrims.

Of far-off saints, hallowed in sundry lands,
And specially, from every shire's end
In England, down to Canterbury[4] they wend
To seek the holy blissful martyr,[5] quick
In giving help to them when they were sick.
   It happened in that season that one day
In Southwark,[6] at the Tabard,[7] as I lay   20
Ready to go on pilgrimage and start
For Canterbury, most devout at heart,
At night there came into that hostelry
Some nine and twenty in a company
Of sundry folk happening then to fall
In fellowship, and they were pilgrims all
That towards Canterbury meant to ride.
The rooms and stables of the inn were wide;
They made us easy, all was of the best.
And shortly, when the sun had gone to rest,   30
By speaking to them all upon the trip
I soon was one of them in fellowship,
And promised to rise early and take the way
To Canterbury, as you heard me say.
   But none the less, while I have time and space,
Before my story takes a further pace,
It seems a reasonable thing to say
What their condition was, the full array
Of each of them, as it appeared to me,
According to profession and degree,   40
And what apparel they were riding in;
And at a Knight I therefore will begin.
There was a KNIGHT, a most distinguished man,
Who from the day on which he first began
To ride abroad had followed chivalry,
Truth, honor, generousness and courtesy.
He had done nobly in his sovereign's war
And ridden into battle, no man more,
As well in Christian as in heathen places,
And ever honored for his noble graces. . . .[8]   50
And though so much distinguished, he was wise

---

[4]A town about fifty-five miles southeast of London, the site of Canterbury Cathedral.
[5]*holy blissful martyr.* Saint Thomas aBecket, the archbishop who in 1170 was murdered in Canterbury
    Cathedral by ambitious agents of the king.
[6]A town outside London, where the Canterbury road began.
[7]A short, sleeveless coat; here, the "sign" and the name of the inn.
[8]*He had . . . graces.* The knight has also fought in three major Crusades, which Chaucer goes on to
    specify in detail in the lines omitted here.

And in his bearing modest as a maid.
He never yet a boorish thing had said
In all his life to any, come what might;
He was a true, a perfect gentle-knight.
   Speaking of his equipment, he possessed
Fine horses, but he was not gaily dressed.
He wore a fustian tunic stained and dark
With smudges where his armor had left mark;
Just home from service, he had joined our ranks   60
To do his pilgrimage and render thanks.

   He had his son with him, a fine young SQUIRE,
A lover and cadet,[9] a lad of fire
With locks as curly as if they had been pressed.
He was some twenty years of age, I guessed.
In stature he was of a moderate length,
With wonderful agility and strength.
He'd seen some service with the cavalry
In Flanders and Artois and Picardy[10]
And had done valiantly in little space   70
Of time, in hope to win his lady's grace.
He was embroidered like a meadow bright
And full of freshest flowers, red and white.
Singing he was, or fluting all the day;
He was as fresh as is the month of May.
Short was his gown, the sleeves were long and wide;
He knew the way to sit a horse and ride.
He could make songs and poems and recite,
Knew how to joust and dance, to draw and write.
He loved so hotly that till dawn grew pale   80
He slept as little as a nightingale.
Courteous he was, lowly and serviceable,
And carved to serve his father at the table.[11]

   There was a YEOMAN[12] with him at his side,
No other servant; so he chose to ride.
This Yeoman wore a coat and hood of green,
And peacock-feathered arrows, bright and keen
And neatly sheathed, hung at his belt the while

[9]*A lover and cadet.* The Squire, following the code of courtly love and chivalry, is not yet a knight, but is already in the service of a lady.
[10]*In Flanders ... Picardy.* Like Chaucer himself, he has fought in battles of the Hundred Years' War.
[11]*And carved ... table.* One of the duties of the personal squire or attendant.
[12]An attendant not so high in rank as a squire, but a little higher than a page.

—For he could dress his gear in yeoman style,
His arrows never dropped their feathers low—   90
And in his hand he bore a mighty bow.
His head was like a nut, his face was brown.
He knew the whole of woodcraft up and down.
A saucy brace was on his arm to ward
It from the bowstring, and a shield and sword
Hung at one side, and at the other slipped
A jaunty dirk, spear-sharp and well-equipped.
A medal of Saint Christopher[13] he wore
Of shining silver on his breast, and bore
A hunting horn, well slung and burnished clean,   100
That dangled from a baldrick[14] of bright green.
He was a proper forester I guess.

    There also was a NUN, a Prioress,[15]
Her way of smiling very simple and coy;
Her greatest oath was only "By Saint Loy!"[16]
And she was known as Madam Eglantyne.
And well she sang a service, with a fine
Intoning through her nose, as was most seemly,
And she spoke daintily in French, extremely,
After the school of Stratford-atte-Bowe;[17]   110
French in the Paris style she did not know.
At meat her manners were well taught withal;
No morsel from her lips did she let fall,
Nor dipped her fingers in the sauce too deep;
But she could carry a morsel up and keep
The smallest drop from falling on her breast.
For courtliness she had a special zest.
And she would wipe her upper lip so clean
That not a trace of grease was to be seen
Upon the cup where she had drunk; to eat,   120
She reached a hand sedately for the meat.
She certainly was very entertaining,
Pleasant and friendly in her ways, and straining
To counterfeit a courtly kind of grace,
A stately bearing fitting to her place,

---

[13]*Saint Christopher*. Patron of foresters and travellers.
[14]Carrying-belt.
[15]Superior officer of a religious order.
[16]*Saint Loy*. Saint Eligious, who was remembered for his courtesy and craftsmanship—he had been a bishop and a goldsmith. The "oath" is a mild one.
[17]*Stratford-atte-Bow*. There was a Benedictine nunnery of Saint Leonard in this village near London, and if the Prioress did not come from there, she had been educated there. The French taught in the schools of England was by this time much less polished than that of Paris.

And to seem dignified in all her dealings,
As for her sympathies and tender feelings,
She was so charitably solicitous
She used to weep if she but saw a mouse
Caught in a trap, if it were dead or bleeding.   130
And she had little dogs she would be feeding
With roasted flesh, or milk, or fine white bread.
Sorely she wept if one of them were dead
Or someone took a stick and made it smart;
She was all sentiment and tender heart.
Her veil was gathered in a seemly way,
Her nose was elegant, her eyes glass-gray;
Her mouth was very small, but soft and red,
Her forehead, certainly, was fair of spread,
Almost a span across the brows, I own;   140
She was indeed by no means undergrown.
Her cloak, I noticed, had a graceful charm.
She wore a coral trinket on her arm,
A set of beads, the gaudies tricked in green,
Whence hung a golden brooch of brightest sheen
On which there first was graven a crowned *A*,
And lower, *Amor vincit omnia*.[18]

    Another NUN, the chaplain at her cell,
Was riding with her, and three PRIESTS as well.
    A MONK[19] there was, one of the finest sort   150
Who rode the country; hunting was his sport.
A manly man, to be an Abbot able;
Many a dainty horse he had in stable.
His bridle, when he rode, a man might hear
Jingling in a whistling wind as clear,
Aye, and as loud as does the chapel bell
Where my lord Monk was Prior of the cell.
The Rule of good Saint Benet or Maur[20]
As old and strict he tended to ignore;
He let go by the things of yesterday   160
And took the modern world's more spacious way.
He did not rate that text at a plucked hen
Which says that hunters are not holy men
And that a monk uncloistered is a mere

[18]*Amor . . . omnia.* Latin for "love conquers all."
[19]The monk belongs to the "regular" clergy, those bound to a monastic life by *regulae*, or strict rules
    of discipline.
[20]*Saint Benet or Saint Maur.* Saint Benedict or his disciple, Saint Maur. Saint Benedict was the founder
    of monasticism in western Europe.

Fish out of water, flapping on the pier,
That is to say a monk out of his cloister.
That was a text he held not worth an oyster;
And I agreed and said his views were sound;
Was he to study till his head went round
Poring over books in cloisters? Must he toil   170
As Austin[21] bade and till the very soil?
Was he to leave the world upon the shelf?
Let Austin have his labor to himself.
    This Monk was therefore a good man to horse;
Greyhounds he had, as swift as birds, to course.
Hunting a hare or riding at a fence
Was all his fun, he spared for no expense.
I saw his sleeves were garnished at the hand
With fine gray fur, the finest in the land,
And on his hood, to fasten it at his chin   180
He had a wrought-gold cunningly fashioned pin;
Into a lover's knot it seemed to pass.
His head was bald and shone like looking glass;
So did his face, as if it had been greased.
He was a fat and personable priest;
His prominent eyeballs never seemed to settle
And glittered like the flame beneath a kettle;
Supple his boots, his horse in fine condition.
He was a prelate[22] fit for exhibition,
He was not pale like a tormented soul.   190
He liked a fat swan best, and roasted whole.
His palfrey was as brown as is a berry. . . .

    There was a MERCHANT with a forking beard
And motley[23] dress; high on his horse he sat,
Upon his head a flemish beaver hat
And on his feet daintily buckled boots.
In solemn tones he spoke of his pursuits,
Harping upon his gains—he never lost.
The sea should be kept free at any cost
(He thought) upon the Harwich-Holland range.[24]   200
He was expert at currency-exchange.
This estimable Merchant so had set
His wits to work, none knew he was in debt,

[21]Saint Augustine, one of the greatest of the Church Fathers, wrote much upon the subject of self-discipline.
[22]One who ranks high in the Church.
[23]Cloth of mixed colors.
[24]*The sea . . . range.* The merchant wants the sea between England and Holland kept free of pirates.

He was so stately in negotiation,
Loan, bargain and commercial obligation.
He was an excellent fellow all the same;
To tell the truth I do not know his name.

    An OXFORD CLERIC,[25] still a student though,
One who had taken logic long ago,
Was there; his horse was thinner than a rake,   210
And he was not too fat, I undertake,
But had a hollow look, a sober stare;
The thread upon his overcoat was bare.
He had found no preferment[26] in the church
And he was too unworldly to make search
For secular employment. By his bed
He preferred having twenty books in red
And black, of Aristole's philosophy,
To having fine clothes, fiddle or psaltery.
Though a philosopher, as I have told,   220
He had not found the stone for making gold.[27]
What ever money from his friends he took
He spent on learning or another book
And prayed for them most earnestly, returning
Thanks to them thus for paying for his learning.
His only care was study, and indeed
He never spoke a word more than was need,
Formal at that, respectful in the extreme,
Short, to the point, and lofty in his theme.
The thought of moral virtue filled his speech   230
And he would gladly learn, and gladly teach. . . .

    There was a FRANKLIN[28] with him, it appeared;
White as a daisy-petal was his beard.
A sanguine man, high-colored and benign,
He loved a morning sop of cake in wine.
He lived for pleasure and had always done,
For he was Epicurus'[29] very son,
In whose opinion sensual delight
Was the one true felicity in sight.

[25]The Cleric (clerk, or student) is perhaps a Master of Arts, but he is still training for entrance into the priesthood or holy orders.
[26]"Living," or appointment to a parish.
[27]*stone . . . gold.* "Philosopher's stone," an imaginary stone believed to have the power of transmuting base metals into gold.
[28]A landed proprietor or gentleman farmer.
[29]A Greek philosopher.

As noted as Saint Julian[30] was for bounty   240
He made his household free to all the County.
His bread, his ale were finest of the fine
And no one had a better stock of wine.
His house was never short of bake-meat pies,
Of fish and flesh, and these in such supplies
It positively snowed with meat and drink
And all the dainties that a man could think.
According to the seasons of the year
Changes of dish were ordered to appear.
He kept fat partridges in coops, beyond,   250
Many a bream and pike were in his pond.
Woe to the cook whose sauces had no sting
Or who was unprepared in anything!
And in his hall a table stood arrayed
And ready all day long, with places laid.
As Justice at the Sessions none stood higher;[31]
He often had been Member for the Shire.[32]
A dagger and a little purse of silk
Hung at his girdle, white as morning milk.
As Sheriff he checked audit,[33] every entry.   260
He was a model among landed gentry. . . .

There was a SKIPPER hailing from far west;
He came from Dartmouth,[34] so I understood.
He rode a farmer's horse as best he could,
And wore a woolen gown that reached his knee.
A dagger on a lanyard falling free
Hung from his neck under his arm and down.
The summer heat had tanned his color brown,
And certainly he was an excellent fellow.
Many a draught of vintage, red and yellow,   270
He'd drawn at Bordeaux, while the trader snored;
The nicer rules of conscience he ignored.
If, when he fought, the enemy vessel sank,
He sent his prisoners home; they walked the plank.
As for his skill in reckoning his tides,
Currents and many another risk besides,
Moons, harbors, pilots, he had such dispatch

---

[30]*Saint Julian.* Patron saint of hospitality.
[31]*As Justice . . . higher.* He presided at sessions of the local court.
[32]*Member . . . Shire.* Member of Parliament.
[33]*As Sheriff . . . audit.* He was a sheriff and an auditor.
[34]An old port in southwest England, not far from Plymouth.

That none from Hull[35] to Carthage[36] was his match. . . .

    A worthy WOMAN from beside BATH city
Was with us, somewhat deaf, which was a pity.   280
In making cloth she showed so great a bent
She bettered those of Ypres and of Ghent.[37]
In all the parish not a dame dared stir
Towards the altar steps in front of her,
And if indeed they did, so wrath was she
As to be quite put out of charity.[38]
Her kerchiefs were of finely woven ground;
I dared have sworn they weighed a good ten pound,
The one she wore on Sunday, on her head.
Her hose were of the finest scarlet red   290
And gartered tight; her shoes were soft and new.
Bold was her face, handsome, and red in hue.
A worthy woman all her life, what's more
She'd had five husbands, all at the church door,[39]
Apart from other company in youth;
No need just now to speak of that, forsooth.
And she had thrice been to Jerusalem,
Seen many strange rivers and passed over them;
She'd been to Rome and also to Boulogne,
St. James of Compostella and Cologne,[40]   300
And she was skilled in wandering by the way.
She had gap-teeth, set widely, truth to say.
Easily on an ambling horse she sat
Well wimpled up, and on her head a hat
As broad as is a buckler or a shield;
She had a flowing mantle that cocealed
Large hips, her heels spurred sharply under that.
In company she like to laugh and chat
And knew the remedies for love's mischances,   310
An art in which she knew the oldest dances.

    A holy-minded man of good renown

[35]An English port.
[36]Perhaps the North African port called Carthage, or the Spanish port Cartagena. (The word Chaucer used was *Cartage*.)
[37]*Ypres . . . Ghent.* Cities in Flanders famous for their woolen goods.
[38]*In all . . . charity.* One's position in the procession to the offering at church was a sign of one's rank. If any other "wife" tried to take precedence over her, she became so angry that no one gave anything.
[39]*at the church door.* Marriage ceremonies in the Middle Ages took place at the church door.
[40]*And she . . . Cologne.* She had made pilgrimages to most of the important European religious shrines.

There was, and poor, the PARSON[41] to a town,
Yet he was rich in holy thought and work.
He also was a learned man, a clerk,
Who truly knew Christ's gospel and would preach it
Devoutly to parishioners, and teach it.
Benign and wonderfully diligent,
And patient when adversity was sent
(For so he proved in great adversity)   320
He much disliked extorting tithe[42] or fee,
Nay rather he preferred beyond a doubt
Giving to poor parishioners round about
From his own goods and Easter offerings.
He found sufficiency in little things.
Wide was his parish, with houses far asunder,
Yet he neglected not in rain or thunder,
In sickness, or in trouble, to pay call
On the remotest whether great or small
Upon his feet, and in his hand a stave.   330
A noble example to his sheep he gave,
A doer of the word before he taught it,
And it was from the gospel he had caught it.
This little proverb he would add thereto
That if gold rust, what then will iron do?
For if a priest be foul in whom we trust
No wonder that a common man should rust;
And shame it is to see—let priests take stock—
A dunged-up shepherd and a snowy flock.
The true example that a priest should give
Is one of cleanness, how the sheep should live.   340
He did not set his benefice to hire[43]
And leave his sheep encumbered in the mire
Or run to London to earn easy bread
By singing masses for the wealthy dead,
Or find some Brotherhood and get enrolled.[44]
He stayed at home and watched over his fold
So that no wolf should make the sheep miscarry.
He was a shepherd and no mercenary.
Holy and virtuous he was, but then
Never contemptuous of sinful men,   350

---

[41]The Parson belongs to the "secular" clergy, or those who are out in the world and not bound by monastic rules.
[42]Portion of one's income (literally, one-tenth) contributed by members to the support of a church.
[43]*He did . . . hire.* He did not hire someone to perform his duties.
[44]*Or run . . . enrolled.* The offerings would be rich in London; the private chaplain to a guild or association of tradesmen would live well.

Never disdainful, never too proud or fine,
But was discreet in teaching and benign.
His business was to show a fair behavior
And draw men thus to Heaven and their Saviour,
Unless indeed a man were obstinate;
And such, whether of high or low estate,
He put to sharp rebuke to say the least.
I think there never was a better priest.
He sought no pomp or glory in his dealings,
No scrupulosity had spiced his feelings.   360
Christ and His Twelve Apostles and their lore
He taught, but followed it himself before.

    There was a PLOWMAN with him there, his brother.
Many a load of dung one time or other
He must have carted through the morning dew.
He was an honest worker, good and true,
Living in peace and perfect charity.
And, as the gospel bade him, so did he;
God he loved best, with all his heart and mind,
And then his neighbor as himself, repined   370
At no misfortune, slacked for no content,
For steadily about his work he went
To thrash his corn, to dig or to manure
Or make a ditch; and he would help the poor
For love of Christ and never take a penny
If he could help it, and, as prompt as any,
He paid his tithes in full when they were due,
On what he owned, and on his earnings too.
He wore a tabard smock and rode a mare. . . .

    The MILLER was a chap of sixteen stone,[45]   380
A great stout fellow big in brawn and bone.
He did well out of them, for he could go
And win the ram at any wrestling show.[46]
Broad, knotty and short-shouldered, he would boast
He could heave any door off hinge and post,
Or take a run and break it with his head.
His beard, like any sow or fox, was red
And broad as well, as though it were a spade;
And, at its very tip, his nose displayed
A wart on which there stood a tuft of hair   390

---

[45]A unit of mass, now 6.3 kg.
[46]*And win . . . show.* Livestock were often the prizes for winning wrestling matches at country fairs.

Red as the bristles in an old sow's ear.
His nostrils were as black as they were wide,
He had a sword and buckler at his side,
His mighty mouth was like a furnace door.
A wrangler and buffoon, he had a store
Of tavern stories, filthy in the main.
His was a master-hand at stealing grain.
He felt it with his thumb and thus he knew
Its quality and took three times his due—
A thumb of gold,[47] by God, to gauge an oat!   400
He wore a hood of blue and a white coat.
He liked to play his bagpipes up and down
And that was how he took us out of town. . . .

    The REEVE[48] was old and choleric and thin;
His beard was shaven closely to the skin,
His shorn hair came abruptly to a stop
Above his ears, and he was docked on top
Just like a priest; his legs were long and lean,
They were like sticks, no calf was to be seen.
He kept his bins and garners[49] very trim;   410
No auditor could gain a point on him.[50]
And he could judge by watching drought and rain
The yield he might expect from seed and grain.
His master's sheep, his animals and hens,
Pigs, horses, dairies, stores and cattle pens
Were wholly trusted to his government.
And he was under contract to present
The accounts, right from his master's earliest years.
No one had ever caught him in arrears.
No bailiff,[51] serf or herdsman dared to kick,   420
He knew their dodges, knew their every trick;
Feared like the plague he was, by those beneath.
He had a charming house upon a heath,
Shadowed in green by trees above the sward.[52]
A better hand at bargains than his lord,
He had grown rich and had a store of treasure
Well tucked away, yet out it came to pleasure
His lord with subtle loans or gifts of goods

---

[47]*thumb of gold.* A proverbial expression: "An honest miller has a golden thumb."
[48]An estate manager.
[49]Granaries.
[50]*2o auditor . . . him.* He knew how to balance (or juggle) his accounts.
[51]Estate officer.
[52]Grassy land.

To earn his thanks, and even coats and hoods.
When young he'd learnt a useful trade and still   430
He was a carpenter of first-rate skill.
The stallion-cob[53] he rode at a slow trot
Was dapple-gray and bore the name of Scot.
He wore an overcoat of bluish shade
And rather long; he had a rusty blade
Slung at his side. He came, as I heard tell,
From Norfolk, near a place called Baldeswell.
His coat was tucked under his belt and splayed.
He rode the hindmost of our cavalcade. . . .

He[54] and a gentle PARDONER[55] rode together,   440
A bird from Charing Cross of the same feather,
Just back from visiting the Court of Rome.
He loudly sang, "Come hither, love, come home!"
The Summoner sang deep seconds to this song,
No trumpet ever sounded half so strong.
This Pardoner had hair as yellow as wax
Hanging down smoothly like a hank of flax.
In driblets fell these locks behind his head
Down to his shoulders which they overspread;
Thinly they fell, like rattails, one by one.   450
He wore no hood upon his head, for fun;
The hood inside his wallet[56] had been stowed,
He aimed at riding in the latest mode;
But for a little cap his head was bare
And he had bulging eyeballs, like a hare.
He'd sewed a holy relic on his cap;
His wallet lay before him on his lap,
Brimful of pardons come from Rome all hot.
He had the same small voice a goat has got.
His chin no beard had harbored, nor would harbor,   460
Smoother than ever chin was left by barber. . . .
There was no pardoner of equal grace,
For in his trunk he had a pillowcase

---

[53]Good, solid stallion.
[54]The Summoner, whose description is here omitted. The Summoner was one who summoned people to an ecclesiastical court to answer for certain crimes that were not tried in civil court.
[55]One (often lower than the priest in the orders of the Church) who had been licensed to grant, in return for offerings to the Church, indulgences—documents that granted remission of punishment in Purgatory for sins already confessed. The office of pardoner was grossly abused in the Middle Ages and was finally abolished by the Church. This Pardoner comes from the Hospital of the Blessed Mary of Rouncivalle, a religious institution near Charing Cross in Chaucer's London.
[56]Travelling bag.

Which he asserted was Our Lady's veil.
He said he had a gobbet of the sail
Saint Peter had the time when he made bold
To walk the waves, till Jesu Christ took hold.[57]
He had a cross of metal set with stones
And, in a glass, a rubble of pigs' bones.
And with these relics, any time he found   470
Some poor up-country parson to astound,
On one short day, in money down, he drew
More than the parson in a month or two,
And by his flatteries and prevarication
Made monkeys of the priest and congregation.
But still to do him justice first and last
In church he was a noble ecclesiast.
How well he read a lesson or told a story!
But best of all he sang an Offertory,[58]
For well he knew that when that song was sung   480
He'd have to preach and tune his honey-tongue
And (well he could) win silver from the crowd.
That's why he sang so merrily and loud.

Now I have told you shortly, in a clause,
The rank, the array, the number and the cause
Of our assembly in this company
In Southwark, at that high-class hostelry
Known as the Tabard, close beside the Bell.[59]

                                                      1386-1400

[57]*the sail . . . took hold.* See Matthew 14:24-31.
[58]An anthem sung in the Mass, following the Creed, while the offerings of the congregation are
    made.
[59]Another inn.

The Pardoner's Tale

It's of three rioters I have to tell
Who long before the morning service bell
Were sitting in a tavern for a drink.
And as they sat, they heard the hand-bell clink
Before a coffin going to the grave;
One of them called the little tavern-knave
And said "Go and find out at once—look spry!—
Whose corpse is in that coffin passing by;
And see you get the name correctly too."
"Sir," said the boy, "no need, I promise you;   10
Two hours before you came here I was told.

He was a friend of yours in days of old,
And suddenly, last night, the man was slain,
Upon his bench, face up, dead drunk again.
There came a privy thief, they call him Death,
Who kills us all round here, and in a breath
He speared him through the heart, he never stirred.
And then Death went his way without a word.
He's killed a thousand in the present plague,
And, sir, it doesn't do to be too vague   20
If you should meet him; you had best be wary.
Be on your guard with such an adversary,
Be primed to meet him everywhere you go,
That's what my mother said. It's all I know."
   The publican joined in with, "By St. Mary.
What the child says is right; you'd best be wary,
This very year he killed, in a large village
A mile away, man, woman, serf at tillage,
Page in the household, children—all there were.
Yes, I imagine that he lives round there.   30
It's well to be prepared in these alarms,
He might do you dishonour!" "Huh, God's arms!"
The rioter said, "Is he so fierce to meet?
I'll search for him, by Jesus, street by street.
God's blessed bones! I'll register a vow!
Here, chaps! The three of us together now,
Hold up your hands, like me, and we'll be brothers
In this affair, and each defend the others,
And we will kill this traitor Death, I say!
Away with him as he has made away   40
With all our friends. God's dignity! To-night!"
   They made their bargain, swore with appetite,
These three, to live and die for one another
As brother-born might swear to his born brother.
And up they started in their drunken rage
And made towards this village which the page
And publican had spoken of before.
Many and grisly were the oaths they swore,
Tearing Christ's blessed body to a shred;
"If we can only catch him, Death is dead!"   50
   When they had gone not fully half a mile,
Just as they were about to cross a stile,
They came upon a very poor old man
Who humbly greeted them and thus began,
"God look to you, my lords, and give you quiet!"
To which the proudest of these men of riot

Gave back the answer, "What, old fool? Give place!
Why are you all wrapped up except your face?
Why live so long? Isn't it time to die?"
   The old, old fellow looked him in the eye   60
And said, "Because I never yet have found,
Though I have walked to India, searching round
Village and city on my pilgrimage,
One who would change his youth to have my age.
And so my age is mine and must be still
Upon me, for such time as God may will.
   "Not even Death, alas, will take my life;
So, like a wretched prisoner at strife
Within himself, I walk alone and wait
About the earth, which is my mother's gate,[1]   70
Knock-knocking with my staff from night to noon
And crying, 'Mother, open to me soon!
Look at me, mother, won't you let me in?
See how I wither, flesh and blood and skin!
Alas! When will these bones be laid to rest?
Mother, I would exchange—for that were best—
The wardrobe in my chamber, standing there
So long, for yours! Aye, for a shirt of hair
To wrap me in!' She has refused her grace,
Whence comes the pallor of my withered face.   80
   "But it dishonoured you when you began
To speak so roughly, sir, to an old man,
Unless he had injured you in word or deed.
It says in holy writ, as you may read,
'Thou shalt rise up before the hoary head
And honour it.' And therefore be it said
'Do no more harm to an old man than you,
Being now young, would have another do
When you are old'—if you should live till then.
And so may God be with you, gentlemen,   90
For I must go whither I have to go."
   "By God," the gambler said, "you shan't do so,
You don't get off so easy, by St. John!
I heard you mention, just a moment gone,
A certain traitor Death who singles out
And kills the fine young fellows hereabout.
And you're his spy, by God! You wait a bit.
Say where he is or you shall pay for it,
By God and by the Holy Sacrament!

[1]*mother's gate.* The grave, entrance to "mother earth."

I say you've joined together by consent 100
To kill us younger folk, you thieving swine!"
   "Well, sirs," he said, "if it be your design
To find out Death, turn up this crooked way
Towards that grove. I left him there to-day
Under a tree, and there you'll find him waiting.
He isn't one to hide for all your prating.
You see that oak? He won't be far to find.
And God protect you that redeemed mankind,
Aye, and amend you!" Thus that ancient man.

   At once the three young rioters began 110
To run, and reached the tree, and there they found
A pile of golden florins[2] on the ground,
New-coined, eight bushels of them as they thought.
No longer was it Death those fellows sought,
For they were all so thrilled to see the sight,
The florins were so beautiful and bright,
That down they sat beside the precious pile.
The wickedest spoke first after a while.
"Brothers," he said, "you listen to what I say.
I'm pretty sharp although I joke away. 120
It's clear that Fortune has bestowed this treasure
To let us live in jollity and pleasure.
Light come, light go! We'll spend it as we ought.
God's precious dignity! Who would have thought
This morning was to be our lucky day?
   "If one could only get the gold away,
Back to my house, or else to yours, perhaps—
For as you know, the gold is ours, chaps—
We'd all be at the top of fortune, hey?
But certainly it can't be done by day. 130
People would call us robbers—a strong gang,
So our own property would make us hang.
No, we must bring this treasure back by night
Some prudent way, and keep it out of sight.
And so as a solution I propose
We draw for lots and see the way it goes.
The one who draws the longest, lucky man,
Shall run to town as quickly as he can
To fetch us bread and wine—but keep things dark—
While two remain in hiding here to mark 140
Our heap of treasure. If there's no delay,

[2]Coins worth a third of a pound sterling, or seventy-five cents.

When night comes down we'll carry it away,
All three of us, wherever we have planned."
    He gathered lots and hid them in his hand
Bidding them draw for where the luck should fall.
It fell upon the youngest of them all,
And off he ran at once towards the town.
    As soon as he had gone the first sat down
And thus began a parley with the other:
"You know that you can trust me as a brother;   150
Now let me tell you where your profit lies;
You know our friend has gone to get supplies
And here's a lot of gold that is to be
Divided equally amongst us three.
Nevertheless, if I could shape things thus
So that we shared it out—the two of us—
Wouldn't you take it as a friendly turn?"
    "But how?" the other said with some concern,
"Because he knows the gold's with me and you;
What can we tell him? What are we to do?"   160
    "Is it a bargain," said the first, "or no?
For I can tell you in a word or so
What's to be done to bring the thing about."
"Trust me," the other said, "you needn't doubt
My word, I won't betray you, I'll be true."
    "Well," said his friend, "you see that we are two,
And two are twice as powerful as one.
Now look; when he comes back, get up in fun
To have a wrestle; then, as you attack,
I'll up and put my dagger through his back   170
While you and he are struggling, as in game;
Then draw your dagger too and do the same.
Then all this money will be ours to spend,
Divided equally of course, dear friend.
Then we can gratify our lusts and fill
The day with dicing at our own sweet will."
Thus these two miscreants agreed to slay
The third and youngest, as you heard me say.
    The youngest, as he ran towards the town,
Kept turning over, rolling up and down   180
Within his heart the beauty of those bright
New florins, saying, "Lord, to think I might
Have all that treasure to myself alone!
Could there be anyone beneath the throne
Of God so happy as I then should be?"

And so the Fiend, our common enemy,
Was given power to put it in his thought
That there was always poison to be bought,
And that with poison he could kill his friends.
To men in such a state the Devil sends   190
Thoughts of this kind, and has a full permission
To lure them on to sorrow and perdition;
For this young man was utterly content
To kill them both and never to repent.
    And on he ran, he had no thought to tarry,
Came to the town, found an apothecary
And said, "Sell me some poison if you will,
I have a lot of rats I want to kill
And there's a polecat too about my yard
That takes my chickens and it hits me hard;   200
But I'll get even, as is only right,
With vermin that destroy a man by night."
    The chemist answered, "I've a preparation
Which you shall have, and by my soul's salvation
If any living creature eat or drink
A mouthful, ere he has the time to think,
Though he took less than makes a grain of wheat,
You'll see him fall down dying at your feet;
Yes, die he must, and in so short a while
You'd hardly have the time to walk a mile,   210
The poison is so strong, you understand."
    This cursed fellow grabbed into his hand
The box of poison and away he ran
Into a neighbouring street, and found a man
Who lent him three large bottles. He withdrew
And deftly poured the poison into two.
He kept the third one clean, as well he might,
For his own drink, meaning to work all night
Stacking the gold and carrying it away.
And when this rioter, this devil's clay,   220
Had filled his bottles up with wine, all three,
Back to rejoin his comrades sauntered he.
    Why make a sermon of it? Why waste breath?
Exactly in the way they'd planned his death
They fell on him and slew him, two to one.
Then said the first of them when this was done,
"Now for a drink. Sit down and let's be merry,
For later on there'll be the corpse to bury."
    And, as it happened, reaching for a sup,

He took a bottle full of poison up   230
And drank; and his companion, nothing loth,
Drank from it also, and they perished both.

   There is, in Avicenna's long relation[3]
Concerning poison and its operation,
Trust me, no ghastlier section to transcend
What these two wretches suffered at their end.
Thus these two murderers received their due,
So did the treacherous young poisoner too.

   O cursed sin! O blackguardly excess!
O treacherous homicide! O wickedness!   240
O gluttony that lusted on and diced!
O blasphemy that took the name of Christ
With habit-hardened oaths that pride began!
Alas, how comes it that a mortal man,
That thou, to thy Creator, Him that wrought thee,
That paid His precious blood for thee and bought thee,
Art so unnatural and false within?
   Dearly beloved, God forgive your sin
And keep you from the vice of avarice!
My holy pardon frees you all of this,   250
Provided that you make the right approaches,
That is with sterling, rings, or silver brooches.
Bow down your heads under this holy bull!
Come on, you women, offer up your wool!
I'll write your name into my ledger; so!
Into the bliss of Heaven you shall go.
For I'll absolve you by my holy power,
You that make offering, clean as at the hour
When you were born. . . . That, sirs, is how I preach
And Jesu Christ, soul's healer, aye, the leech   260
Of every soul, grant pardon and relieve you
Of sin, for that is best, I won't deceive you.

                                 1386-1400

---

[3]*Avicenna's long relation.* A work on medicine by an Arabian physician (A.D. 980-1037).

THE POPULAR BALLAD

The ballad was originally a song intended as the accompaniment to a dance, but gradually the narrative element became more important and the ballad became what it has remained: a song that tells a story. There are two main types of ballads: the popular or traditional ballad, of which the authorship is anonymous, and the literary or art-ballad, which is written in imitation of the popular ballad by a known individual. The popular ballads almost all belong to the late Middle Ages; the literary ballads began to be written in the late eighteenth century as the result of the romantic revival of interest in the Middle Ages.

The popular ballads may have been originally written by one man or a group of men, but in either case they were passed on from generation to generation by word of mouth. As a result, their original forms underwent mutation, and most of the ballads can be found in various versions. Unlike most lyrics, they are objective poems, and the attention is on the characters and events of the story rather than on the personal views or feelings of the narrator. They deal for the most part with upper-class individuals and families, and are hence aristocratic rather than democratic in tone. They are composed in simple stanzas of two main sorts: couplets made up of two rhyming four-stress lines, or the so-called "ballad stanza." In this ballad stanza, there are four lines of which the second and fourth almost always rhyme, and the first and third sometimes rhyme; the first and third lines are iambic tetrameter, the second and fourth iambic trimeter. There are, however, many variations of this pattern.

The versification of the popular ballad is usually rather uneven, and the style simple and direct. Frequent use is made of a refrain and of "incremental repetition" whereby a line or phrase is repeated with slight changes. Bright colours, and magic numbers such as three and seven, often occur. There is a minimum of background information, word-painting, or psychological subtlety: the effect aimed for is sparse, clear, and definite. The ballads are of various lengths, depending upon whether they relate a single episode or a series; most of them are short enough to be readily committed to memory. For the same reason, their rhythms tend to be strong and emphatic.

The popular ballads have considerable variety of subject-matter, but most of them involve either love or battle. The motives of jealousy and revenge are common, and almost always the feelings and events portrayed are violent. The material is drawn from history or from folk-lore.

The dates given at the end of each of the following four ballads refer, of course, to their first appearance in print. Notice that two of them are dated 1765, indicating that they first appeared in print in the famous collection of ballads made by Thomas Percy, *Reliques of Ancient English Poetry*. In manuscript or oral form, however, all four of the ballads below belong to the late Middle Ages.

Edward

'Why dois[1] your brand sae drap wi
    bluid[2],
            Edward, Edward,
Why dois your brand sae drap wi bluid,
  And why sae sad gang[3] yee O?"
"O I hae killed my hauke sae guid[4],
            Mither, mither,

I hae killed my hauke sae guid,
  And I had nae mair bot[5] hee O."

"Your haukis bluid was nevir sae reid,
            Edward, Edward, 10
Your haukis bluid was nevir sae reid,
  My deir son I tell thee O."

[1]Does.
[2]*sae drap wi bluid*. So drop with blood.
[3]Walk.   [4]Good.

[5]*nae mair bot*. No more but.

"O I hae killed my reid-roan steid,
        Mither, mither,
O I hae killed my reid-roan steid,
    That erst was sae fair and frie O."

"Your steid was auld, and ye hae gat
        mair,
            Edward, Edward,
Your steid was auld, and ye hae gat
        mair,
    Sum other dule ye drie[6] O."   20
"O I hae killed my fadir deir,
        Mither, mither,
O I hae killed my fadir deir,
    Alas, and wae is mee O!"

"And whatten penance wul ye drie for
        that,
            Edward, Edward?
And whatten penance will ye drie for
        that?
    My deir son, now tell me O."
"Ile set my feit in yonder boat,
        Mither, mither,
Ile set my feit in yonder boat,   31
    And Ile fáre ovir the sea O."

"And what wul ye doe wi your towirs
        and your ha,[7]
            Edward, Edward?
And what wul ye doe wi your towirs
        and your ha,

That were sae fair to see O?"
"Ile let thame stand tul they doun fa,
        Mither, mither,
Ile let thame stand tul they doun fa,
    For here nevir mair maun I bee O."

"And what wul ye leive to your bairns
        and your wife,   41
            Edward, Edward?
And what wul ye leive to your bairns
        and your wife,
    Whan ye gang ovir the sea O?"

"The warldis[8] room, late them beg
        thrae life,
            Mither, mither,
The warldis room, late them beg thrae
        life,
    For thame nevir mair wul I see O."

"And what wul ye leive to your ain
        mither deir,
            Edward, Edward?
And what wul ye leive to your ain
        mither deir?   51
    My deir son, now tell me O."
"The curse of hell frae me sall ye beir,
        Mither, mither,
The curse of hell frae me sall ye beir,
    Sic counseils ye gave to me O."

                                1765

---

[6]*Sum other dule ye drie.* Some other grief you are
    enduring.
[7]Hall.   [8]World's.

The Three Ravens

There were three ravens sat on a tree,
    Downe a downe, hay down, hay
        downe
There were three ravens sat on a tree,
    With a downe
There were three ravens sat on a tree,
They were as blacke as they might be.
    With a downe derrie, derrie, derrie,
        downe, downe.

The one of them said to his mate,
"Downe in yonder greene field,   10
There lies a knight slain under his
        shield.

"His hounds they lie downe at his
        feete,
So well they can their master keepe.

"His haukes they flie so eagerly,
There's no fowle dare him come nie."

Downe there comes a fallow doe[1],
As great with yong as she might goe.

She lift up his bloudy hed,
And kist his wounds that were so red.

She got him up upon her backe,   20
And carried him to earthen lake[2].

She buried him before the prime[3],
She was dead herselfe ere even-song
        time.

God send every gentleman,
Such haukes, such hounds, and such a
        leman[4].
                                1611

[1]fallow doe. I.e. the knight's lady.
[2]Pit.   [3]First hour of the day.
[4]Sweetheart.

The Twa Corbies

As I was walking all alane,
I heard twa corbies[1] making a mane;
The tane unto the t'other say,
"Where sall we gang and dine to-day?"

"In behint yon auld fail dyke[3],
I wot there lies a new slain knight;
And naebody kens that he lies there,
But his hawk, his hound, and lady fair.

"His hound is to the hunting gane,
His hawk to fetch the wild-fowl hame,   10

His lady's ta'en another mate,
So we may mak our dinner sweet.

"Ye'll sit on his white hause-bane[4],
And I'll pike out his bonny blue een;
Wi ae lock o his gowden hair
We'll theek[5] our nest when it grows bare.

"Mony a one for him makes mane,
But nane sall ken where he is gane;
Oer his white banes, when they are bare,
The wind sall blaw for evermair."   20
                                1803

[1]Ravens.   [2]Moan.   [3]Turf wall.   [4]Neck-bone.   [5]Thatch.

Sir Patrick Spens

The king sits in Dumferling toune,
  Drinking the blude-reid wine:
"O whar will I get guid sailor,
  To sail this schip of mine?"

Up and spak an eldern knicht,
  Sat at the kings richt kne:
"Sir Patrick Spens is the best sailor
  That sails upon the se."

The king has written a braid[1] letter,
  And signd it wi his hand,   10
And sent it to Sir Patrick Spens,
  Was walking on the sand.

The first line that Sir Patrick red,
  A loud lauch lauched he;
The next line that Sir Patrick red,
  The teir blinded his ee.

"O wha is this has don this deid,
  This ill deid don to me,

To send me out this time o' the yeir,
  To sail upon the se!   20

"Mak hast, mak haste, my mirry men
    all,
  Our guid schip sails the morne:"
"O say na sae, my master deir,
  For I feir a deadlie storme.

"Late late yestreen I saw the new
    moone,
  Wi the auld moone in hir arme,
And I feir, I feir, my deir master,
  That we will cum to harme."

O our Scots nobles wer richt laith
  To weet their cork-heild schoone[2]; 30
Bot lang owre a' the play wer playd,
  Thair hats they swam aboone[3].

---

[1]Long.

[2]*laith . . . schoone.* Loath to wet their cork-heeled
  shoes.
[3]*Thair hats . . . aboone.* I.e. They were in over
  their heads.

1400　　　　　　　　**1450**　　　　　　　　**1500**

● Columbus to the West I▮

Skeleton: *Magnificence* ●

● More:

THE SIXTEENTH CENTURY (1485-1603)

1550	1600	1650

● Founding of the Royal Exchange

● Spenser: *Prothalamion*

● Reign of Elizabeth I –Tudor Period

● Bacon: *Essays*

● Sidney: *Astrophel and Stella*

● Hakluyt: *Voyages*

● Shakespeare: Sonnets

The Tudor period, and especially the Elizabethan period (1558-1603), was one of tremendous progress in English literature. At its beginning, England was lagging far behind France and Italy; by its end, thanks to the work of Spenser, Shakespeare, and a host of lesser writers and artists, England was in the lead.

The literary progress was accompanied by, and in part the result of, great political, religious, economic, and cultural changes. Politically, the period saw Henry VII (1485-1509) deprive the feudal barons of their power, unify the nation, and initiate a new aristocracy of wealth; Henry VIII (1509-1547) successfully challenge the authority of the Pope and enormously increase England's wealth and standard of education; and, after the troubled interludes of Edward VI (1547-1553) and Mary I (1553-1558), Elizabeth I break the rival power of Spain, sponsor the voyages of such seamen as Drake and Frobisher, and found the East India Company to expand English power in the East. In religion, the period felt the full impact of the Reformation in England for the first time: Henry VIII established the independent Church of England with himself as head, and in his reign Erasmus, More, and Tyndale made their attacks upon the corruption of the Church of Rome, while in Europe, Luther and Calvin led the Protestant revolt; during the brief reign of Edward VI, England became a strongly Protestant country; Mary I tried to turn the tide back to Catholicism by a series of bloody martyrdoms; under Elizabeth, the English compromise was worked out, by which the Church of England retained some Catholic doctrine and ritual but remained separate and independent. This compromise did not suit some of the more extreme Protestants, and as Elizabeth's reign went on they came to agitate more and more strongly for the purification of the Church of England from surviving traces of Catholicism, and thus earned for themselves the name of Puritans.

In economics, the growth of trade and industry which had begun in the late Middle Ages continued and accelerated. Diaz's voyage around the Cape in 1486, Columbus' discovery of America in 1492, the voyages of Cabot, da Gama, Cortes, Drake, and others—these explorations and discoveries multiplied the size of the known world and made possible a tremendous expansion of commerce. English seamen laid the foundation of the world-wide system of trade that made England a great world power. The foundation of the Royal Exchange in 1566 is symptomatic of this growing commercial activity. Gradually, but perceptibly, the power in the state was beginning to shift from the landed aristocracy to the commercial middle class.

Culturally, the period saw the Renaissance, which had begun in Italy in the fourteenth century, spread to England and alter the whole temper of civilization. The Renaissance is a complex and controversial phenomenon, but it may be summarized as a gradual change in the character of European culture which put an end to medieval habits of thought and ushered in the modern age. It was the result partly of natural development, partly of the effects of the Eastern influences brought by trade, and partly of the new wealth which for the first time since the fall of Rome made it possible for European men to enjoy leisure and learning. The other-worldliness of the medieval world gave way to a critical and optimistic interest in the affairs, beauties, attractions, and possibilities of *this* world. Medieval civilization was God-centered; Renaissance civilization was man-centered. Medieval man submitted to the authority of the Pope, the Emperor, the Church Fathers; Renaissance man affirmed his individuality, subjected all things to scrutiny, experiment, and analysis. This stress on man and his immediate earthly environment changed the quality of art and literature and led to the development of modern science. Instead of pale and spiritual Virgins, the painters now portrayed lovely women even if they still purported to be pictures of the Virgin; poets turned to earthly love and beauty for their subjects; the lives of saints were replaced by the lives of outstanding men and women; drama ceased, as in the medieval mystery and morality plays, to deal exclusively with religious subjects, and concerned itself instead with the problems of men of action, with questions of statecraft, military ambition, sexual jealousy, and the like.

All of these developments had their effect upon the literature of the period. The rise of a strong nation-state under the Tudors stimulated English nationalism and devotion to a stable monarchy: hence the adulation accorded to Queen Elizabeth in Spenser's *Faerie Queene*, for example, and the stress on a stable throne which is the theme of Shakespeare's historical plays. The religious upheavals are reflected in the puritan moral tone of parts of Spenser's writings, in Marlowe's religious cynicism, in the questionings of divine justice that occur in so many of Shakespeare's tragedies. The economic expansion and the discovery of new lands are reflected directly in Hakluyt's accounts of the voyages of the Elizabethan seamen, and indirectly in the many images of geography, cartography, and navigation which dot the poetry and prose of the period. The most obvious effect was that of the Renaissance, which led to the passionate love lyrics of Wyatt, Surrey, and Sidney, the sense of almost infinite human potentiality which pervades the plays of Marlowe and Shakespeare, the scientific interests of Francis Bacon, and the spirit of exuberance and optimism which marks so much of the literature of this age.

It was in poetry that the Tudor literary revival first became evident. The reign of Henry VII saw little except the work of two holdovers from the fifteenth century, the languorous Stephen Hawes and the rough and ready John Skelton. But in the reign of Henry VIII the new movement got underway with the melodious lyrics of Sir Thomas Wyatt and the Earl of Surrey, who frankly modelled their work on Italian poetry and sought to give England a poetry of comparable beauty. In the early years of Elizabeth's reign Thomas Sackville (1536-1608) and George Gascoigne (1525-1577) kept poetry alive; the great outburst came in the last decades of the century with the splendid work of Spenser, Sidney, Raleigh, Marlowe, Shakespeare, Campion, Daniel, Drayton, and a host of others too numerous to mention. England was called a nest of singing birds; every courtier felt it part of his duty to write poetry; sonnet sequences by the hundreds appeared; and English poetry was the admiration of all Europe.

Elizabethan drama developed more slowly, but if anything reached even greater heights. The mystery and morality plays of the late Middle Ages continued into the sixteenth century, though the former rapidly lost ground as they were not liked by the Protestants. The morality plays maintained a vigorous life, but they assimilated influences both from the Reformation and the Renaissance. In Skelton's morality play, *Magnificence*, written about 1516, the virtues are not the usual Christian ones but humanistic virtues such as Good Hope, Circumspection, and Perseverance. In others knowledge tends to replace piety, and ignorance the Devil, thus clearly showing the influence of the Renaissance. Another group shows the influence of the Reformation, pillorying the alleged corruption of the Catholic priests. In the second half of the sixteenth century changes came quickly. Plays were performed in universities and schools, at the Inns of Court, and by touring groups of professional actors. The nature of the plays was changed by the influence of classical drama, especially that of Seneca, and of the Italian *commedia erudita*. Outstanding comedies of the early Elizabethan period were *Ralph Roister Doister*, written by Nicholas Udall and performed at Westminster or Eton about 1549, and *Gammer Gurton's Needle*, written by W.S. (William Stevenson?) and performed at Christ's College in 1554. The chief early tragedy was Sackville's *Gorboduc* (1561-2), in which the influence of Seneca is apparent in the unrelieved seriousness, the abundance of declamation, and the plethora of bloody crimes. Gradually, however, a more independent and national drama was emerging, the main early example being *Cambyses* (1569), probably the work of Thomas Preston, a Cambridge don. In the 1580's the tide of development became a flood: John Lyly wrote graceful and fanciful English comedies which in some ways anticipated Shakespeare's *Love's Labour's Lost*, *A Midsummer Night's Dream*, and others; Thomas Kyd did in tragedy what Lyly did in comedy, that is, brought classical models into conformity with national tastes; Christopher Marlowe, beginning with *Tamburlaine* in 1588, did more than any other single individual to prepare the way for Shakespeare by laying the chief stress on character and by skilfully using blank verse; and Robert Greene wrote romantic comedies which prefigure such Shakespearean plays as *As You Like It*. Finally, of course, Shakespeare combined in one person the tender romantic fancy of Greene, the wit and grace of Lyly, the tragic violence of Kyd, the power and eloquence of Marlowe.

Sixteenth century prose lagged behind poetry and drama, but nevertheless showed a striking development. Renaissance influences were reflected in the many books concerned with the improvement of the individual and his society, the expression of the humanist ideal. The first of these was Sir Thomas More's *Utopia* (1516), which although written in Latin is regarded as the masterpiece of English humanism. He was followed by Sir Thomas Elyot, whose *The Governour* (1531) is a treatise on ethics and education, Sir John Cheke, whose *Heart of Sedition* (1549) is an essay on politics, Sir Thomas Wilson, whose *Art of Rhetorique* (1553) recommends purity and simplicity of language, and Sir Roger Ascham, the most popular and pungent of the group, whose *Toxophilus* (1545) and *The Scholemaster* (1570) are both thoroughly English in their ideals and subject-matter, the former being a treatise on the long bow and the importance of physical exercise, and the latter a practical essay on education and the importance of the English language.

The religious controversies of the time were also reflected in the prose of the sixteenth century. There were the various translations of the Bible—by Tyndale, Coverdale, and Latimer—which were to culminate early in the next century in the Authorized or King James Version. There were the various tracts and pamphlets involved in the Marprelate controversy between the Puritans and Anglicans. There was John Foxe's *Actes and Monuments* (1563), better known as "Foxe's Book of Martyrs," which bitterly attacked the Catholic purge of the Protestants in the reign of Bloody Mary. Above all, there was Richard Hooker's grave and eloquent defence of the Anglican *via media*, *Of The Laws of Ecclesiastical Polity* (1594).

The new spirit of nationalism found expression in the many chronicles which sought to glorify the English past: Edward Hall's *Chronicle* (1542), Raphael Holin-shed's *Chronicles of England, Scotland, and Ireland* (1577), John Stow's *Chronicles of England* (1580), and William Camden's *Britannia* (1586). A work of a similar sort, but concerned with England's glorious present rather than her past, was Richard Hakluyt's proud record of English sea-discoverers: *The Principal Navigations, Voyages, and Discoveries of the English Nation* (1589).

The sixteenth century also saw the beginnings of English literary criticism, in Gascoigne's *Certayne Notes of Instruction* (1575), Stephen Gosson's *School of Abuse* (1579), William Webbe's *Discourse of English Poetrie* (1586), George Puttenham's *The Arte of English Poesie* (1589), Sidney's *Defence of Poesie* (1595), Thomas Campion's *Observations in the Art of English Poesie* (1602), and Samuel Daniel's *A Defence of Ryme* (1603). This interest in literary history and criticism reflected both the new national pride and the new interest in art which the Renaissance had brought.

English prose fiction did not really develop as an important literary form until the early eighteenth century, but it had its tentative beginnings in the sixteenth. John Lyly's *Euphues* (1578-80) is a romance with a very thin plot and a most involved style; Sir Philip Sidney's *Arcadia* (1590) is an expression of pastoral idealism, and Robert Greene, Thomas Lodge, and Nicholas Breton wrote similar prose romances. In the last decade of the century, prose fiction became more realistic; Greene himself made the change, and was followed by Thomas Nashe (*The Unfortunate Traveller*, 1594) and Thomas Deloney (*Jack of Newbury*, 1598). But none of these books can compete in interest with Elizabethan poetry or drama.

The other prose form which came to birth in the sixteenth century was the essay, which in the hands of Francis Bacon was brought to near perfection at its first appearance.

The sixteenth century, then, saw the development of English poetry and drama to unexampled heights, and the foundations laid for most of the prose forms. It was an age of both great achievement and great promise.

SIR THOMAS WYATT (1503-1542)

Sir Thomas Wyatt was a graduate of Cambridge, a member of the court of Henry VIII, and a diplomat who made several missions to France and Italy. He was knighted for his services to the king, but fell out of favour and was twice imprisoned in the Tower of London. His last few years were spent as an English diplomat in Spain. He died of a fever caught while conducting the Spanish Ambassador to London.

Wyatt was the pioneer of the modern English lyric. Impressed by the melodic grace of Italian lyrics, and especially by the sonnets of Petrarch, he sought to give English poetry the harmony it had lost in the fifteenth century. He did not fully succeed—his lines are sometimes rough and uncertain in accent, and he often allows his rhymes to fall on unaccented syllables—but he did much to prepare the way for the great Elizabethan lyricists.

Wyatt is also important historically for importing the sonnet to England. His sonnets are greatly influenced by those of Petrarch, but they often have his own note of manly vigour. He also, unlike Petrarch, often ended his sonnets with a couplet, thus taking a step in the direction of the Shakespearean or English sonnet form.

The Lover Compareth His State to a Ship in Perilous Storm Tossed on the Sea

My galley, chargèd with forgetfulness,
Thorough sharp seas, in winter nights, doth pass
'Tween rock and rock; and eke mine enemy, alas,
That is my lord, steereth with cruelness;
And every oar, a thought in readiness,
As though that death were light in such a case.
An endless wind doth tear the sail apace
Of forcèd sighs and trusty fearfulness;
A rain of tears, a cloud of dark disdain,
Hath done the wearied cords great hinderance;
Wreathèd with error and eke with ignorance.
The stars be hid that led me to this pain;
   Drownèd is Reason, that should me comfort;
   And I remain, despairing of the port.

1557

The Lover for Shamefastness Hideth His Desire Within His Faithful Heart

The long love that in my thought doth harbour,
And in mine heart doth keep his residence,
Into my face presseth with bold pretence,
And therein campeth, spreading his banner.
She that me learneth to love and suffer,
And wills that my trust and lustès negligence
Be reigned by reason, shame, and reverence,
With his hardiness taketh displeasure.

Wherewith all unto the heart's forest he fleeth,
Leaving his enterprise with pain and cry,
And there him hideth, and not appeareth.
What may I do when my master feareth,
   But in the field with him to live and die?
   For good is the life, ending faithfully.

1557

The Lover Beseecheth His Mistress
Not to Forget His Steadfast Faith and True Intent

Forget not yet the tried intent
Of such a truth as I have meant,
My great travail so gladly spent,
   Forget not yet.

Forget not yet when first began
The weary life ye know, since whan
The suit, the service, none tell can;
   Forget not yet.

Forget not yet the great assays,
The cruel wrong, the scornful ways,   10

The painful patience in denays,
   Forget not yet.

Forget not yet, forget not this,
How long ago hath been, and is
The mind that never meant amiss,
   Forget not yet.

Forget not then thine own approved,
The which so long hath thee so loved,
Whose steadfast faith yet never moved;
   Forget not this.   20

1815

The Lover Complaineth the Unkindness of His Love

My lute, awake! perform the last
Labour that thou and I shall waste,
And end that I have now begun;
For when this song is sung and past,
My lute, be still, for I have done.

As to be heard where ear is none,
As lead to grave in marble stone,
My song may pierce her heart as soon;
Should we then sigh, or sing, or moan?
No, no, my lute, for I have done.   10

The rocks do not so cruelly
Repulse the waves continually,
As she my suit and affection;
So that I am past remedy,
Whereby my lute and I have done.

Proud of the spoil that thou hast got
Of simple hearts thorough Love's shot,
By whom, unkind, thou hast them won,
Think not he hath his bow forgot,
Although my lute and I have done.   20

Vengeance shall fall on thy disdain
That makest but game on earnest pain.
Think not alone under the sun
Unquit to cause thy lovers plain,
Although my lute and I have done.

Perchance thee lie withered and old
The winter nights that are so cold,
Plaining in vain unto the moon;
Thy wishes then dare not be told;
Care then who list, for I have done.   30

And then may chance thee to repent
The time that thou hast lost and spent
To cause thy lovers sigh and swoon;
Then shalt thou know beauty but lent,
And wish and want, as I have done.

Now cease, my lute, this is the last
Labour that thou and I shall waste,
And ended is that we begun;
Now is this song both sung and past,
My lute, be still, for I have done.   40

1557

THE EARL OF SURREY (1517?-1547)

Henry Howard, Earl of Surrey, was born fourteen years after Wyatt, and was his disciple. Their names are always linked together in literary history, partly because they supplemented one another in introducing Italian lyricism into English poetry, and partly because their work appeared together in *Tottel's Miscellany*, a book of lyrics published in 1557 and much in demand throughout the Elizabethan period.

Surrey was the son of Lord Thomas Howard, third Duke of Norfolk, and as a youth was the close companion of Henry VIII's son, the Duke of Richmond. He became a courtier and served with the English Army in Flanders, but his haughtiness and pugnacity eventually proved his undoing. He was accused of treason, imprisoned in the Tower, and executed on January 19, 1547.

Surrey's poetry has not the strength of Wyatt's, but it has more grace and sweetness. In his sonnets he moved from Petrarch's form of an octave and sestet to the English form of three quatrains and a final couplet. His chief distinction, however, is his introduction of blank verse into English in his translation of parts of Virgil's *Aeneid*.

Description of Spring,
Wherein Each Thing Renews, Save Only the Lover

The soote season that bud and bloom forth brings,
With green hath clad the hill and eke the vale;
The nightingale with feathers new she sings,
The turtle to her make hath told her tale.
Summer is come, for every spray now springs,
The hart hath hung his old head on the pale,
The buck in brake his winter coat he flings,
The fishes flete with new repaired scale,
The adder all her slough away she slings,
The swift swallow pursueth the flyës smale,
The busy bee her honey now she mings,—
Winter is worn, that was the flowers' bale:
   And thus I see, among these pleasant things
   Each care decays, and yet my sorrow springs.

1557

The Frailty and Hurtfulness of Beauty

Brittle beauty, that nature made so frail,
Whereof the gift is small, and short the season;
Flow'ring today, tomorrow apt to fail,
Tickle treasure, abhorrèd of reason;
Dangerous to deal with, vain, of none avail,
Costly in keeping, past not worth two peason;
Slipper in sliding, as is an eelës tail,
Hard to obtain, once gotten, not geason;
Jewel of jeopardy that peril doth assail,
False and untrue, enticèd oft to treason,
Enemy to youth; that most may I bewail.
Ah, bitter sweet, infecting as the poison,
　　Thou farest as fruit that with the frost is taken,
　　Today ready ripe, tomorrow all to-shaken.

　　　　　　　　　　　　　　　　　　　　　　1557

Of the Death of Sir T. W. the Elder

　Wyatt resteth here, that quick could never rest;
Whose heavenly gifts increased by disdain,
And virtue sank the deeper in his breast;
Such profit he by envy could obtain.

　A head where wisdom mysteries did frame,
Whose hammers beat still in that lively brain
As on a stithy where that some work of fame
Was daily wrought, to turn to Britain's gain.

　A visage stern and mild, where both did grow,
Vice to contemn, in virtue to rejoice;　　　　　　　　　　10
Amid great storms, whom grace assured so
To live upright and smile at fortune's choice.

　A hand that taught what might be said in rhyme;
That reft Chaucer the glory of his wit:
A mark, the which (unparfited, for time)
Some may approach, but never none shall hit.

　A tongue that served in foreign realms his king;
Whose courteous talk to virtue did enflame
Each noble heart; a worthy guide to bring
Our English youth by travail unto fame.　　　　　　　　　20

　An eye whose judgment none affect could blind,
Friends to allure, and foes to reconcile;
Whose piercing look did represent a mind
With virtue fraught, reposèd, void of guile.

A heart where dread was never so impress'd,
To hide the thought that might the truth advance;
In neither fortune loft, nor yet repress'd,
To swell in wealth, or yield unto mischance.
A valiant corps, where force and beauty met;
Happy, alas, too happy, but for foes!   30
Lived, and ran the race, that Nature set:
Of manhood's shape, where she the mould did lose.
But to the heavens that simple soul is fled,
Which left with such as covet Christ to know
Witness of faith that never shall be dead,
Sent for our health, but not received so.
Thus, for our guilt, this jewel have we lost;
The earth his bones, the heavens possess his ghost.

1542?   1557

EDMUND SPENSER (1552-1599)

The task of restoring grace and harmony to English poetry, begun by Wyatt and Surrey, was completed by Edmund Spenser, the first great craftsman of modern English poetry. His melodic and technical skill was such that Charles Lamb called him a "poet's poet." He was also a serious moralist and the author of the first modern English epic.

Spenser was born in London of middle-class parents and was educated at Merchant Taylor's School and Pembroke College, Cambridge. At Cambridge he became involved in the Puritan controversy, and was himself influenced by Puritan ideas. In 1580 Spenser became secretary to Lord Grey, and accompanied him to Ireland where, in 1586, he became the owner of the confiscated castle of Kilcolman and was visited by Sir Walter Raleigh. In 1594 he married Elizabeth Boyle, and in 1598 he fled Ireland shortly before his castle was burned during the Tyrone rebellion. He died in London in 1599.

The main characteristics of Spenser's style are his gift for melody, his elaborate word-painting, his lavish but harmonious use of metaphors and similes, his leisurely, majestic rhythms, and his conscious concern for structure. In thought he seeks to combine the best features of the Renaissance—its belief in man's potentialities, in human love, in earthly beauty, and in the value of art—with the moral idealism and religious devotion of the Reformation. This sometimes leads him into shallow compromises, but at its best it produces an effect of sensuous beauty and moral seriousness.

Of the poems below, it should be said that the sonnets are from the sonnet sequence *Amoretti*, published in 1595, in which Spenser paid court to the lady who became his wife; *Prothalamion* is a marriage song written by Spenser in 1596 for the double marriage of Lady Elizabeth and Lady Katherine Somerset, daughters of the Earl of Worcester; we see here the poet interested in deepening the theme of love through an intricately allusive and symbolic style. The poem moves from the "empty shadowes" of court to a pastoral scene where a delicate tension can be maintained between the idealized existence described and hoped for, and the shifting fortunes of actual life—". . . here fits not well/Old woes, but joys, to tell . . ." (l. 141-2).

from *Amoretti*

I

Happy ye leaves! when as those lilly hands,
Which hold my life in their dead doing[1] might,
Shall handle you, and hold in loves soft bands,
Lyke captives trembling at the victors sight;
And happy lines! on which, with starry light,
Those lamping[2] eyes will deigne sometimes to look,
And reade the sorrowes of my dying spright[3],
Written with teares in harts close bleeding book;
And happy rymes! bath'd in the sacred brooke
Of Helicon[4], whence she derived is,
When ye behold that angels blessed looke,
My soules long lacked foode, my heavens blis.
Leaves, lines, and rymes, seeke her to please alone,
Whom if ye please, I care for other none.

XXXIV

Lyke as a ship that through the ocean wyde,
By conduct of some star doth make her way,
Whenas a storme hath dimd her trusty guyde,
Out of her course doth wander far astray,
So I, whose star, that wont with her bright ray,
Me to direct, with cloudes is overcast,
Doe wander now in darknesse and dismay,
Through hidden perils round about me plast[5].
Yet hope I well that when this storme is past
My *Helice*[6], the lodestar of my lyfe,
Will shine again, and looke on me at last,
With lovely light to cleare my cloudy grief.
Till then I wander carefull[7] comfortlesse,
In secret sorrow and sad pensivenesse.

XLVII

Like as a huntsman after weary chase,
Seeing the game from him escap'd away,
Sits down to rest him in some shady place,
With panting hounds beguilèd of their prey:
So after long pursuit and vain assay,

---

[1]*dead doing*. Doing to death.   [2]Light-shedding.   [3]Spirit.
[4]A mountain in Greece, sacred to the Muses.
[5]Placed.   [6]Helice, daughter of the king of Arcadia. Zeus fell in love with her, and his wife
Hera, jealous, changed her into a she-bear. Zeus made her the Pole Star.   [7]Full of care.

When I all weary had the chase forsook,
The gentle deer return'd the self-same way,
Thinking to quench her thirst at the next brook.
There she beholding me with milder look,
Sought not to fly, but fearless still did bide:
Till I in hand her yet half trembling took,
And with her own goodwill her firmly tied.
Strange thing, me seem'd, to see a beast so wild,
So goodly won, with her own will beguil'd.

LXXV

One day I wrote her name upon the strand,
But came the waves and washèd it away:
Agayne I wrote it with a second hand,
But came the tyde, and made my paynes his pray.
Vayne man, sayd she, that doest in vaine assay
A mortall thing so to immortalize!
For I my selve shall lyke to this decay,
And eek my name bee wypèd out lykewize.
Not so (quod I), let baser things devize
To dy in dust, but you shall live by fame:
My verse your vertues rare shall eternize,
And in the hevens wryte your glorious name;
Where, whenas death shall all the world subdew,
Our love shall live, and later life renew.

                                                    1595

Prothalamion[1]

CALM was the day, and through the trembling air
Sweet-breathing Zephyrus did softly play
A gentle spirit, that lightly did delay
Hot Titan's beams, which then did glister fair;
When I (whom sullen care,
Through discontent of my long fruitless stay
In prince's court, and expectation vain
Of idle hopes, which still do fly away
Like empty shadows, did afflict my brain),
Walk'd forth to ease my pain   10
Along the shore of silver-streaming Thames;

---

[1] A marriage song written for the double wedding of Lady Katherine and Lady Elizabeth
   Somerset, November 8, 1596.

Whose rutty bank, the which his river hems,
Was painted all with variable flowers,
And all the meads adorn'd with dainty gems
Fit to deck maidens' bowers,
And crown their paramours,
Against the bridal day, which is not long:
   Sweet Thames run softly, till I end my song.

There, in a meadow, by the river's side,
A flock of nymphs I chancèd to espy,   20
All lovely daughters of the flood thereby,
With goodly greenish locks, all loose untied,
As each had been a bride;
And each one had a little wicker basket,
Made of fine twigs, entrailèd² curiously,
In which they gathered flowers to fill their flasket³,
And with fine fingers cropt full feateously⁴
The tender stalks on high.
Of every sort, which in that meadow grew,
They gathered some; the violet, pallid blue,   30
The little daisy, that at evening closes,
The virgin lily, and the primrose true,
With store of vermeil roses,
To deck their bridegrooms' posies
Against the bridal day, which was not long:
   Sweet Thames run softly, till I end my song.

With that I saw two swans of goodly hue
Come softly swimming down along the Lee;
Two fairer birds I yet did never see;
The snow which doth the top of Pindus strew,   40
Did never whiter shew,
Nor Jove himself, when he a swan would be,
For love of Leda, whiter did appear;
Yet Leda was (they say) as white as he,
Yet not so white as these, nor nothing near;
So purely white they were,
That even the gentle stream, the which them bare,
Seem'd foul to them, and bad his billows spare
To wet their silken feathers, lest they might
Soil their fair plumes with water not so fair,   50
And mar their beauties bright,

²Twisted.   ³Long shallow basket.   ⁴Deftly.

That shone as heaven's light,
Against their bridal day, which was not long:
   Sweet Thames run softly, till I end my song.

Eftsoons the nymphs, which now had flowers their fill,
Ran all in haste to see that silver brood,
As they came floating on the crystal flood;
Whom when they saw, they stood amazèd still,
Their wond'ring eyes to fill;
Them seem'd they never saw a sight so fair,   60
Of fowls so lovely, that they sure did deem
Them heavenly born, or to be that same pair
Which through the sky draw Venus' silver team;
For sure they did not seem
To be begot of any earthly seed,
But rather angels, or of angels' breed;
Yet were they bred of Somers-heat, they say,
In sweetest season, when each flower and weed
The earth did fresh array;
So fresh they seem'd as day,   70
Even as their bridal day, which was not long:
   Sweet Thames run softly, till I end my song.

Then forth they all out of their baskets drew
Great store of flowers, the honour of the field,
That to the sense did fragrant odours yield,
All which upon those goodly birds they threw
And all the waves did strew,
That like old Peneus' waters they did seem,
When down along by pleasant Tempe's shore,
Scatt'red with flowers, through Thessaly they stream,   80
That they appear through lilies' plenteous store,
Like a bride's chamber floor.
Two of those nymphs, meanwhile, two garlands bound
Of freshest flowers which in that mead they found,
The which presenting all in trim array,
Their snowy foreheads therewithal they crown'd,
Whilst one did sing this lay,
Prepar'd against that day,
Against their bridal day, which was not long:
   Sweet Thames run softly, till I end my song.   90

"Ye gentle birds, the world's fair ornament,
And heaven's glory, whom this happy hour
Doth lead unto your lovers' blissful bower,

Joy may you have, and gentle heart's content
Of your love's complement;
And let fair Venus, that is Queen of Love,
With her heart-quelling son upon you smile,
Whose smile, they say, hath virtue to remove
All love's dislike, and friendship's faulty guile
For ever to assoil.   100
Let endless Peace your steadfast hearts accord,
And blessed Plenty wait upon your board:
And let your bed with pleasures chaste abound,
That fruitful issue may to you afford,
Which may your foes confound,
And make your joys redound
Upon your bridal day, which is not long:
   Sweet Thames run softly, till I end my song."

So ended she; and all the rest around
To her redoubled that her undersong,   110
Which said their bridal day should not be long;
And gentle Echo from the neighbour ground
Their accents did resound.
So forth those joyous birds did pass along,
Adown the Lee, that to them murmur'd low,
As he would speak, but that he lack'd a tongue,
Yet did by signs his glad affection show,
Making his stream run slow.
And all the fowl which in his flood did dwell
Gan flock about these twain, that did excel   120
The rest, so far as Cynthia doth shend[5]
The lesser stars.   So they, enranged well,
Did on those two attend,
And their best service lend
Against their wedding day, which was not long:
   Sweet Thames run softly, till I end my song.

At length they all to merry London came,
To merry London, my most kindly nurse,
That to me gave this life's first native source,
Though from another place I take my name[6],   130
An house of ancient fame.
There when they came, whereas those bricky towers[7]

[5]Put to shame.
[6]*Though from another . . . name.* Spenser claimed relationship with the Spensers of Althorp.
[7]*those bricky towers.* The Temple, originally the abode of the Knights Templar, but since 1346
  occupied by a society of lawyers.

The which on Thames' broad aged back do ride,
Where now the studious lawyers have their bowers,
Their whilom wont the Templar Knights to bide,
Till they decay'd through pride:
Next whereunto there stands a stately place,
Where oft I gainèd gifts and goodly grace
Of that great lord, which therein wont to dwell[3],
Whose want too well now feels my friendless case: 140
But ah! here fits not well
Old woes, but joys, to tell
Against the bridal day, which is not long:
    Sweet Thames run softly, till I end my song.

Yet therein now doth lodge a noble peer,
Great England's glory, and the world's wide wonder,
Whose dreadful name late through all Spain did thunder,
And Hercules' two pillars standing near
Did make to quake and fear:
Fair branch of honour, flower of chivalry,   150
That fillest England with thy triumph's fame,
Joy have thou of thy noble victory,
And endless happiness of thine own name
That promiseth the same;
That through thy prowess, and victorious arms,
Thy country may be freed from foreign harms;
And great Eliza's glorious name may ring
Through all the world, fill'd with thy wide alarms,
Which some brave Muse may sing
To ages following,   160
Upon the bridal day, which is not long:
    Sweet Thames run softly, till I end my song.
From those high towers this noble lord issuing,
Like radiant Hesper, when his golden hair
In th' ocean billows he hath bathèd fair,
Descended to the river's open viewing,
With a great train ensuing.
Above the rest were goodly to be seen
Two gentle knights of lovely face and feature,
Beseeming well the bower of any queen,   170
With gifts of wit, and ornaments of nature,
Fit for so goodly stature,

[3]*Next whereunto . . . case.* In November, 1596, Spenser was staying with the Earl of Essex, at Essex House, where he had lived in earlier years when it belonged to his erstwhile patron the Earl of Leicester.

That like the twins of Jove they seem'd in sight,
Which deck the baldric of the heavens bright;
They two, forth pacing to the river's side,
Received those two fair brides, their love's delight;
Which, at th' appointed tide,
Each one did make his bride
Against their bridal day, which is not long:
    Sweet Thames run softly, till I end my song.

1596

SIR PHILIP SIDNEY (1554-1586)

Spenser gave English verse fluidity and ease; Sidney and Raleigh gave it resonance and strength. And Sidney himself was the closest English approximation to the Renaissance ideal of the all-round man, "skilled in all the virtues, public and private."

Sir Philip Sidney, the son of Sir Henry Sidney, was born at the beautiful family estate of Penshurst, and was educated at Shrewsbury School and Oxford University. In 1572, he went on the continental tour then customary for young gentlemen, and was hiding in the British Embassy in Paris on August 24 when French Protestants were martyred in the Massacre of St. Bartholomew. After continuing his travels in Germany and Italy, he returned to England to become a brilliant courtier and diplomat. He was killed at Zutphen in the Low Countries in 1586, and in his dying moments is reputed to have refused a drink of water with the chivalrous words, "Thy need is greater than mine."

Sidney's writings consist of the pastoral romance, *Arcadia*, the sonnet sequence *Astrophel and Stella* (written as the result of his unsuccessful courtship of the beautiful Penelope Devereux), and his critical work, *Apologie for Poetrie*, afterwards called *Defence of Poesie*.

FROM Astrophel and Stella[1]

I

Loving in truth, and fain in verse my love to show,
That she, dear she, might take some pleasure of my pain,—
Pleasure might cause her read, reading might make her know,
Knowledge might pity win, and pity grace obtain,—
I sought fit words to paint the blackest face of woe;
Studying inventions fine, her wits to entertain,
Oft turning others' leaves, to see if thence would flow
Some fresh and fruitful showers upon my sunburn'd brain.
But words came halting forth, wanting Invention's stay;
Invention, Nature's child, fled step-dame Study's blows;
And others' feet still seem'd but strangers in my way.
Thus, great with child to speak, and helpless in my throes,
Biting my truant pen, beating myself for spite;
"Fool," said my Muse to me, "look in thy heart, and write."

---

[1]*Astrophel and Stella.* I.e., star-lover and star; or the poet and Penelope Devereux, with whom Sidney was once in love but who married Lord Rich in 1581. In September, 1583, Sidney himself married Frances Walsingham.

VII

When Nature made her chief work, Stella's eyes,
In colour black why wrapt she beams so bright?
Would she in beamy black, like painter wise,
Frame daintiest lustre, mix'd of shades and light?
Or did she else that sober hue devise,
In object best to knit and strength our sight;
Lest, if no veil these brave gleams did disguise,
They, sunlike, should more dazzle than delight?
Or would she her miraculous power show,
That, whereas black seems beauty's contrary,
She even in black doth make all beauties flow?
Both so, and thus,—she, minding Love should be
Plac'd ever there, gave him this mourning weed
To honour all their deaths who for her bleed.

XXXI

With how sad steps, O Moon, thou climb'st the skies!
How silently, and with how wan a face!
What, may it be that even in heav'nly place
That busy archer his sharp arrows tries!
Sure, if that long-with-love-acquainted eyes
Can judge of love, thou feel'st a lover's case,
I read it in thy looks; thy languished grace,
To me, that feel the like, thy state descries.
Then, ev'n of fellowship, O Moon, tell me,
Is constant love deem'd there but want of wit?
Are beauties there as proud as here they be?
Do they above love to be lov'd, and yet
Those lovers scorn whom that love doth possess?
Do they call virtue there ungratefulness?

XLI

Having this day[2] my horse, my hand, my lance
Guided so well that I obtain'd the prize,
Both by the judgment of the English eyes
And of some sent from that sweet enemy France;
Horsemen my skill in horsemanship advance,
Town folks my strength; a daintier judge applies
His praise to sleight which from good use doth rise;
Some lucky wits impute it but to chance;

---

[2] In April, 1581, Sidney took part in a tournament at Whitehall in honour of the emissaries of the Duke of Anjou.

Others, because of both sides I do take
My blood from them who did excell in this,
Think Nature me a man-at-arms did make.
How far they shot awry! The true cause is,
Stella look'd on, and from her heav'nly face
Sent forth the beams which made so fair my race.

CX

Leave me, O Love, which reachest but to dust;
And thou, my mind, aspire to higher things;
Grow rich in that which never taketh rust;
Whatever fades, but fading pleasure brings.
Draw in thy beams, and humble all thy might
To that sweet yoke where lasting freedoms be;
Which breaks the clouds, and opens forth the light,
That both doth shine, and give us sight to see.
O take fast hold; let that light be thy guide
In this small course which birth draws out to death,
And think how evil becometh him to slide,
Who seeketh heav'n, and comes of heav'nly breath.
Then farewell, world; thy uttermost I see:
Eternal Love, maintain thy life in me.

c. 1580-82   1598

FROM *Arcadia*

My true-love hath my heart, and I have his,
By just exchange one for the other given:
I hold his dear, and mine he cannot miss;
There never was a bargain better driven.
His heart in me keeps me and him in one;
My heart in him his thoughts and senses guides:
He loves my heart for once it was his own;
I cherish his because in me it bides.
His heart his wound received from my sight;
My heart was wounded with his wounded heart;
For as from me on him his hurt did light,
So still, methought, in me his hurt did smart:
Both equal hurt, in this change sought our bliss,
My true-love hath my heart, and I have his.

1580?   1593

SIR WALTER RALEIGH (1552?-1618)

Like Sidney, Raleigh was a man of many parts: explorer, statesman, admiral, historian, soldier, and poet. The son of a Devonshire knight, he went to Oriel College, Oxford, fought for the Protestant cause in the Low Countries, accompanied Sir Humphrey Gilbert on his first voyage to North America, became one of the luminaries of Queen Elizabeth's court, discovered and occupied the colony of Virginia for his queen, was an admiral in the English expeditions to Cadiz and the Azores, and played a prominent part in the defeat of the Spanish Armada in 1588. In spite of such brilliant accomplishments, and the chivalric manners which are reflected in the legend of his throwing down his cloak for Elizabeth to walk upon, Raleigh was not always in favour at court even during her reign. After the queen's death and the accession of James I, Raleigh was almost constantly in trouble. For a long time he was imprisoned in the Tower, and he was finally beheaded there on October 29, 1618. During his imprisonment he wrote his *History of the World*, one of the finest specimens of Elizabethan prose.

The selections which follow include Raleigh's witty and realistic reply to Marlowe's "The Passionate Shepherd to his Love," and the uniquely sensuous spiritual poem, "The Passionate Man's Pilgrimage."

The Nymph's Reply[1]

If all the world and love were young,
And truth in every shepherd's tongue,
These pretty pleasures might me move
To live with thee and be thy love.

Time drives the flocks from field to
  fold,
When rivers rage and rocks grow cold,
And Philomel[2] becometh dumb;
The rest complains of cares to come.

The flowers do fade, and wanton fields
To wayward winter reckoning yields; 10
A honey tongue, a heart of gall,
Is fancy's spring, but sorrow's fall.

Thy gowns, thy shoes, thy beds of roses,
Thy cap, thy kirtle, and thy posies
Soon break, soon wither, soon
   forgotten,—
In folly ripe, in reason rotten.

[1]Reply to Marlowe's "The Passionate Shepherd
 to His Love." See page 115.
[2]The nightingale.

Thy belt of straw and ivy buds,
The coral clasps and amber studs,
All these in me no means can move
To come to thee and be thy love.   20

But could youth last and love still breed,
Had joys no date nor age no need,
Then these delights my mind might move
To live with thee and be thy love.

1600

The Passionate Man's Pilgrimage

Supposed to be written by one at the point of death

Give me my scallop-shell[1] of quiet,
My staff of faith to walk upon,
My scrip[2] of joy, immortal diet,
My bottle of salvation,
My gown of glory, hope's true gage,
And thus I'll take my pilgrimage.

Blood must be my body's balmer,
No other balm will there be given,
Whilst my soul, like a white palmer,
Travels to the land of heaven;   10
Over the silver mountains,
Where spring the nectar fountains;
And there I'll kiss
The bowl of bliss,
And drink my eternal fill
On every milken hill.

My soul will be a-dry before,
But after it will ne'er thirst more;
And by the happy blissful way
More peaceful pilgrims I shall see,   20
That have shook off their gowns of clay,
And go apparelled fresh like me.
I'll bring them first
To slake their thirst,

And then to taste those nectar suckets[3],
At the clear wells
Where sweetness dwells,
Drawn up by saints in crystal buckets.

And when our bottles and all we
Are fill'd with immortality,   30
Then the holy paths we'll travel,
Strew'd with rubies thick as gravel,
Ceilings of diamonds, sapphire floors,
High walls of coral, and pearl bowers.

From thence to heaven's bribeless hall
Where no corrupted voices brawl,
No conscience molten into gold,
Nor forg'd accusers bought and sold,
No cause deferr'd, nor vain-spent
          journey,
For there Christ is the king's attorney,   40
Who pleads for all without degrees,
And he hath angels[4], but no fees.
When the grand twelve million jury
Of our sins and sinful fury,
'Gainst our souls black verdicts give,

[3]Sweetmeats.
[1]The badge of the returning pilgrim.   [2]Wallet.   [4]An old English gold coin.

Christ pleads his death, and then we
    live.
Be thou my speaker, taintless pleader,
Unblotted lawyer, true proceeder,
Thou movest salvation even for alms,
Not with a bribed lawyer's palms.   50
And this is my eternal plea
To him that made heaven, earth, and
    sea,

Seeing my flesh must die so soon,
And want a head to dine next noon,
Just at the stroke when my veins start
    and spread,
Set on my soul an everlasting head.
Then am I ready, like a palmer fit,
To tread those blest paths which
    before I writ.

                         1604

RICHARD HAKLUYT (1553?-1616)

Richard Hakluyt was born in London about 1553, and educated at Westminster School and Oxford. He took Holy Orders, and was successively chaplain of the English embassy in Paris, rector of Witheringsett, Suffolk, archdeacon of Westminster, and rector of Godney, Lincolnshire. His chief interest, however, and real claim to fame, lay in collecting records of the voyages of English seamen. The interest began when, as a schoolboy, he saw a map of the world in the room of his cousin and (in his own words) "resolved . . . I would by God's assistance prosecute that knowledge and kind of literature." With great diligence he proceeded to collect every available account of English navigation, publishing them in their final three volume form in 1599 as *The Principal Navigations, Voyages . . . and Discoveries of the English Nation made by Sea or over Land to the Remote and Farthest Distant Quarters of the Earth . . . within the Compass*

of these 1500 Years. His book reflects not only the Elizabethan interest in the New World and in the science of navigation, but also the patriotic spirit of the age: Hakluyt wished to prove England the great sea-power of the world.

The excerpt below, in which the spelling and punctuation have been somewhat modernized, is taken from a report of the voyage of Sir Humphrey Gilbert to what is now Canada. The report was written, Hakluyt tells us, "by M. Edward Haie gentlemen, and principall actour in the same voyage, who alone continued unto the end, and by Gods speciall assistance returned home with his retinue safe and entire." It is interesting to note that Sir Walter Raleigh, Gilbert's half-brother, set out on this voyage but that his ship was forced to turn back to Plymouth by the outbreak of contagious disease among the crew.

                         111

FROM The Voyage of Sir Humphrey Gilbert to Newfoundland, 1583

. . . Now having made ready our shipping, that is to say, the *Delight*, the *Golden Hind*, and the *Squirrel*, and put aboard our provision, which was wines, bread or rusk, fish wet and dry, sweet oils, besides many other, as marmalades, figs, lemons barrelled, and such like; also we had other necessary provisions for trimming our ships, nets and lines to fish withal,

boats or pinnaces fit for discovery. In brief, we were supplied of our wants commodiously, as if we had been in a country or some city populous and plentiful of all things.

We departed from this harbour of St. John's upon Tuesday the twentieth of August, which we found by exact observation to be in 47 degrees 40 minutes.

And the next day by night we were at Cape Race, 25 leagues from the same harbour.

This Cape lies South Southwest from St. John's: it is a low land, being off from the Cape about half a league: within the sea rises up a rock against the point of the Cape, which thereby is easily known. It is in latitude 46 degrees 25 minutes.

Under this Cape we were becalmed a small time, during which we laid out hooks and lines to take cod, and drew in less than two hours fish so large and in such abundance that many days after we fed upon no other provision.

From hence we shaped our course to Sable Island, if conveniently it would so fall out, also directly to Cape Breton.

Sable lies to the seaward of Cape Breton about 25 leagues, whither we were determined to go upon intelligence we had of a Portuguese (during our abode in St. John's) who was himself present when the Portuguese (above thirty years past) did put into the same island both neat and swine to breed, which were since exceedingly multiplied. This seemed unto us very happy tidings, to have in an island lying so near the main, which we intended to plant upon, such store of cattle, whereby we might at all times conveniently be relieved of victual, and served of store for breed.

In this course we trended along the coast, which from Cape Race stretches into the Northwest, making a bay which some called Trepassa. Then it goes out again toward the west, and makes a point, which with Cape Race lies in manner east and west. But this point inclines to the north; to the west of which goes in the bay of Placentia. We sent men on land to take view of the soil along this coast, whereof they made good report, and some of them had will to be planted there. They saw pease growing in great abundance everywhere.

The distance between Cape Race and Cape Breton is 87 leagues, in which navigation we spent 8 days, having many times the wind indifferent good: yet could we never attain sight of any land all that time, seeing we were hindered by the current. At last we fell into such flats and dangers, that hardly any of us escaped: where nevertheless we lost our Admiral with all the men and provision, not knowing certainly the place . . .

THE MANNER OUR ADMIRAL
WAS LOST

Upon Tuesday the 27th of August, toward the evening, our General[1] caused them in his frigate[2] to sound, who found white sand at 35 fathom, being then in latitude about 44 degrees.

Wednesday toward night the wind came South, and we bare with the land all that night, west northwest, contrary to the mind of master Cox: nevertheless we followed the Admiral[3], deprived of power to prevent a mischief, which by no contradiction could be brought to hold other course, alleging they could not make the ship to work better, nor to lie otherwise.

The evening was fair and pleasant, yet not without token of storm to ensue, and most part of this Wednesday night, like the swan that sings before her death,

[1]Sir Humphrey Gilbert.
[2]*The Squirrel.*   [3]In the *Delight.*

they in the Admiral, or *Delight*, continued in sounding of trumpets, with drums and fifes: also winding the cornets, hautboys: and in the end of their jollity, left with the battle and ringing of doleful knells.

Towards the evening also we caught in the *Golden Hind* a very mighty porpoise, with a harping iron, having first striken divers of them, and brought away part of their flesh, sticking upon the iron, but could recover only that one. These also passing through the ocean, in herds, did portend storm. I omit to recite frivolous reports by them in the frigate of strange voices, the same night, which scared some from the helm.

Thursday the 29 of August, the wind rose, and blew vehemently at South and by east, bringing withal rain, and thick mist, so that we could not see a cable length before us. And betimes in the morning we were altogether run and folded in amongst flats and sands, amongst which we found shoal and deep in every three or four ships' length, after we began to sound: but first we were upon them unawares, until master Cox, looking out, discerned (in his judgment) white cliffs, crying land withal, though we could not afterward descry any land, it being very likely the breaking of the sea white, which seemed to be white cliffs, through the haze and thick weather.

Immediately tokens were given unto the *Delight*, to cast about to seaward, which, being the greater ship, and of burden 120 tons, was yet foremost upon the breach, keeping so ill watch, that they knew not the danger before they felt the same, too late to recover it: for presently the Admiral struck aground, and had soon after her stern and hinder parts beaten in pieces: whereupon the rest (that is to say the frigate in which was the General, and the *Golden Hind*) cast about east southeast, bearing to the south, even for our lives into the wind's eye, because that way carried us to the seaward. Making out from this danger, we sounded one while seven fathom, then four fathom and less, again deeper, immediately four fathom, then but three fathom, the sea going mightily and high. At last we recovered (God be thanked), in some despair, to sea room enough.

In this distress, we had vigilant eye unto the Admiral, whom we saw cast away, without power to give the men succour, neither could we espy any of the men that leaped overboard to save themselves, either in the same pinnace, or upon rafters, and such like means presenting themselves to men in those extremities: for we desired to save the men by every possible means. But all in vain, since God had determined their ruin: yet all that day, and part of the next, we beat up and down as near to the wreck as was possible for us, looking out if by good hap we might espy any of them.

This was a heavy and grievous event, to lose at one blow our chief ship freighted with great provision, gathered together with much travail, care, long time, and difficulty. But more was the loss of our men, which perished to the number almost of a hundred souls. . . .

After this heavy chance, we continued in beating the sea up and down, expecting when the weather would clear up that we might yet bear in with the land, which we judged not far off, either the continent or some island. . . .

Our people lost courage daily after this ill success, the weather continuing thick and blustering, with increase of cold, winter drawing on, which took from them all hope of amendment, settling an assurance of worse weather to grow upon us every day. The leeside of us lay full of flats and dangers inevitable, if the wind blew hard at south. Some again doubted we were engulfed in the Bay of St. Lawrence, the coast full of dangers, and unto us unknown. But above all, provision waxed scant, and hope of supply was gone with the loss of our Admiral.

Those in the frigate were already pinched with spare allowance, and want of clothes chiefly, whereupon they besought the General to return for England, before they all perished. And to them of the *Golden Hind*, they made signs of their distress, pointing to their mouths, and to their clothes thin and ragged; then immediately they also of the *Golden Hind* grew to be of the same opinion and desire to return home.

The former reasons having also moved the General to have compassion of his poor men, in whom he saw no want of good will, but of means fit to perform the action they came for, resolved upon retirement; and calling the Captain and Master of the *Hind*, he yielded them many reasons inforcing this unexpected return, withal protesting himself greatly satisfied with that he had seen, and knew already.

Reiterating these words, "Be content, we have seen enough, and take no care of expense past: I will set you forth royally next spring, if God send us safe home. Therefore I pray you let us no longer strive here, where we fight against the elements."

Omitting circumstance, how unwillingly the Captain and Master of the *Hind* condescended to this motion, his own company can testify: yet comforted with the General's promise of a speedy return at spring, and induced by other apparent reasons, proving it an impossibility to accomplish the action at that time, it was concluded on all hands to retire.

So upon Saturday in the afternoon of the 31st. of August, we changed our course, and returned back for England. . .

1599

CHRISTOPHER MARLOWE (1564-1593)

Marlowe is best known as a dramatist, but his non-dramatic poetry has much of the richness, colour, and verve that make his plays so exciting.

He was born at Canterbury about two months before Shakespeare's birth at Stratford, attended the King's School at Canterbury from 1579 to 1581, and then entered Corpus Christi College, Cambridge, receiving his B.A. in 1584 and his M.A. in 1587. He made his sensational debut as a playwright with *Tamburlaine the Great*, and followed its success with *Dr. Faustus*, *The Jew of Malta*, and *Edward II*. A controversial man of extreme opinions and quick temper, Marlowe was killed in a tavern brawl in Deptford at the age of twenty-nine.

As a dramatist, Marlowe's chief gifts were his strong grasp of character and his skilful use of blank verse, which Ben Jonson called "Marlowe's mighty line." As a non-dramatic poet, he is remarkable for his sensuousness and his melodic effects. There is about his poetry as about his plays a spirit of exuberance which marks him clearly as a man of the Renaissance. "The Passionate Shepherd to His Love" was perhaps the most famous of all Elizabethan lyrics and provoked many replies and parodies of which Sir Walter Raleigh's "Nymph's Reply" is one example.

The Passionate Shepherd to His Love

Come live with me and be my love,
And we will all the pleasures prove,
That valleys, groves, hills, and fields,
Woods, or steepy mountain yields.

And we will sit upon the rocks,
Seeing the shepherds feed their flocks,
By shallow rivers, to whose falls
Melodious birds sing madrigals.

And I will make thee beds of roses,
And a thousand fragrant posies,   10
A cap of flowers and a kirtle
Embroider'd all with leaves of myrtle:

A gown made of the finest wool,
Which from our pretty lambs we pull;
Fair lined slippers for the cold,
With buckles of the purest gold:

A belt of straw and ivy buds,
With coral clasps and amber studs;
And if these pleasures may thee move,
Come live with me and be my love.   20

The shepherd swains shall dance and sing
For thy delight each May morning;
If these delights thy mind may move,
Then live with me and be my love.

1599

WILLIAM SHAKESPEARE (1564-1616)

Shakespeare was born in Stratford-on-Avon, Warwickshire, on or about April 23, 1564, the eldest son and third child of Mary Arden and John Shakespeare, a glove-maker and alderman. He probably attended the Stratford Grammar School, where he would have received a sound classical training. At the age of eighteen he married the twenty-six year old Ann Hathaway, by whom he had three children, Susanna, Hamnet, and Judith. About 1587 he left Stratford for London, where he early identified himself with the theatre. By 1592 he was making a reputation for himself as an actor and playwright, and in 1593 and 1594 he published, respectively, the narrative poems *Venus and Adonis* and *The Rape of Lucrece*. By 1597 he was sufficiently successful financially to buy New Place, a large house in Stratford, and he had written twelve plays by 1598. About 1611 he seems gradually to have retired from London to Stratford, where he died on April 23, 1616. His plays were first published together in 1623 in a large format known as the First Folio.

Shakespeare's fame rests chiefly on his almost forty plays written over a twenty-year period, from roughly 1590 to 1610. But he was also a fine lyric poet, as the songs in his plays and his sonnets abundantly prove. His one hundred and fifty-four sonnets were probably written between 1593 and 1596, at the height of the sonnet's vogue, but they were not published until 1609. They have provoked much speculation, especially concerning the identity of the "W.H." to whom the sonnets are dedicated, and of the dark lady and the rival poet mentioned in the poems. It is quite possible, however, that the sonnets have little if any biographical basis, and that Shakespeare was simply following the sonnet conventions in treating the usual themes of the beauty of his lady, the intensity of his love for her, the assurance of her immortality through his verse, the sufferings of the frustrated lover, and so on. The most valid approach is to appreciate the sonnets for their poetic qualities, for the mastery they display of the difficult sonnet form.

Sonnets

XVIII

Shall I compare thee to a summer's day?
Thou art more lovely and more temperate:
Rough winds do shake the darling buds of May,
And summer's lease hath all too short a date:
Sometime too hot the eye of heaven shines,
And often is his gold complexion dimm'd;

And every fair from fair sometime declines,
By chance or nature's changing course untrimm'd;
But thy eternal summer shall not fade
Nor lose possession of that fair thou ow'st;
Nor shall Death brag thou wander'st in his shade,
When in eternal lines to time thou grow'st:
   So long as men can breathe or eyes can see,
   So long lives this and this gives life to thee.

XXIX

When, in disgrace with fortune and men's eyes,
I all alone beweep my outcast state
And trouble deaf heaven with my bootless cries
And look upon myself and curse my fate,
Wishing me like to one more rich in hope,
Featur'd like him, like him with friends possess'd,
Desiring this man's art and that man's scope,
With what I most enjoy contented least;
Yet in these thoughts myself almost despising,
Haply I think on thee, and then my state,
Like to the lark at break of day arising
From sullen earth, sings hymns at heaven's gate;
   For thy sweet love remember'd such wealth brings
   That then I scorn to change my state with kings.

XXX

When to the sessions of sweet silent thought
I summon up remembrance of things past,
I sigh the lack of many a thing I sought,
And with old woes new wail my dear time's waste:
Then can I drown an eye, unus'd to flow,
For precious friends hid in death's dateless night,
And weep afresh love's long since cancell'd woe,
And moan the expense of many a vanish'd sight;
Then can I grieve at grievances foregone,
And heavily from woe to woe tell o'er
The sad account of fore-bemoanèd moan,
Which I new pay as if not paid before.
   But if the while I think on thee, dear friend,
   All losses are restor'd, and sorrows end.

CVI

When in the chronicle of wasted time
I see descriptions of the fairest wights,
And beauty making beautiful old rhyme
In praise of ladies dead and lovely knights,

Then, in the blazon of sweet beauty's best,
Of hand, of foot, of lip, of eye, of brow,
I see their antique pen would have express'd
Even such a beauty as you master now.
So all their praises are but prophecies
Of this our time, all you prefiguring;
And, for they look'd but with divining eyes,
They had not skill enough your worth to sing:
    For we, which now behold these present days,
    Have eyes to wonder, but lack tongues to praise.

CXVI

Let me not to the marriage of true minds
Admit impediments.   Love is not love
Which alters when it alteration finds,
Or bends with the remover to remove:
O no! it is an ever-fixèd mark
That looks on tempests and is never shaken;
It is the star to every wandering bark,
Whose worth's unknown, although his height be taken.
Love's not Time's fool, though rosy lips and cheeks
Within his bending sickle's compass come;
Love alters not with his brief hours and weeks,
But bears it out even to the edge of doom.
    If this be error and upon me proved,
    I never writ, nor no man ever loved.

CXXX

My mistress' eyes are nothing like the sun;
Coral is far more red than her lips' red:
If snow be white, why then her breasts are dun;
If hairs be wires, black wires grow on her head.
I have seen roses damask'd, red and white,
But no such roses see I in her cheeks;
And in some perfumes is there more delight
Than in the breath that from my mistress reeks.
I love to hear her speak, yet well I know
That music hath a far more pleasing sound:
I grant I never saw a goddess go,
My mistress, when she walks, treads on the ground:
    And yet, by heaven, I think my love as rare
    As any she beli'd with false compare.

c. 1594-1604?   1609

Songs from the Plays

FROM TWO GENTLEMEN
OF VERONA

Who is Silvia? what is she,
  That all our swains commend her?
Holy, fair, and wise is she;
  The heaven such grace did lend her,
That she might admired be.

Is she kind as she is fair?
  For beauty lives with kindness.
Love doth to her eyes repair
  To help him of his blindness,
And, being helped, inhabits there.

Then to Silvia let us sing,
  That Silvia is excelling;
She excels each mortal thing
  Upon the dull earth dwelling:
To her let us garlands bring.
c. 1592   1598

FROM CYMBELINE

Fear no more the heat o' the sun,
  Nor the furious winter's rages;
Thou thy worldly task hast done,
  Home art gone, and ta'en thy wages.
Golden lads and girls all must,
As chimney-sweepers, come to dust.

Fear no more the frown o' the great;
  Thou art past the tyrant's stroke;
Care no more to clothe and eat;
  To thee the reed is as the oak.   10
The scepter, learning, physic, must
All follow this, and come to dust.

Fear no more the lightning-flash,
  Nor the all-dreaded thunder-stone,
Fear not slander, censure rash;
  Thou hast finished joy and moan.
All lovers young, all lovers must
Consign to thee, and come to dust.

No exorciser harm thee!
  Nor no witchcraft charm thee!   20
Ghost unlaid forbear thee!
  Nothing ill come near thee!
Quiet consummation have,
  And renownèd be thy grave!
1610   1623

FROM MUCH ADO
ABOUT NOTHING

Sigh no more, ladies, sigh no more!
  Men were deceivers ever.
One foot in sea and one on shore,
  To one thing constant never:
Then sigh not so, but let them go,
  And be you blithe and bonny,
Converting all your sounds of woe
  Into Hey nonny, nonny!

Sing no more ditties, sing no moe
  Of dumps so dull and heavy!
The fraud of men were ever so,
  Since summer first was leafy:
Then sigh not so, but let them go,
  And be you blithe and bonny,
Converting all your sounds of woe
  Into Hey nonny, nonny!
1598   1600

FROM THE TEMPEST

  Where the bee sucks, there suck I;
  In a cowslip's bell I lie;
  There I couch when owls do cry.
  On the bat's back I do fly
  After summer merrily.
Merrily, merrily, shall I live now
Under the blossom that hangs on the
  bough.
1611   1623

FRANCIS BACON (1561-1626)

No man in English literary history is more puzzling than Bacon. Pope put it most neatly when he called him "the wisest, brightest, meanest of mankind"—for here was a man who first gave systematic expression to the philosophy of modern science, whose legal knowledge was such that he became Lord Chancellor of England, whose essays were the first and in some ways most penetrating ever written in English, and yet a man who bitterly prosecuted his own patron and who was found guilty of taking bribes while occupying the highest judicial position in his country. "Knowledge is power," he asserted: and in those words is the clue to his character. He was ambitious, power-hungry; but in his defence it can be said that he wanted power in order to bring benefit to mankind rather than to himself alone.

Bacon was born on January 22, 1561, the youngest son of Sir Nicholas Bacon, Lord Keeper of the Great Seal. From 1573 to 1576 he attended Trinity College, Cambridge, and from 1576 to 1579 served at the English Embassy in Paris. The sudden death of his father compelled him to choose a profession, and he completed legal studies at Gray's Inn and was called to the bar in 1582. He was elected to Parliament in 1584, and remained a member for over twenty years. In 1593 he was unsuccessful in seeking the offices of Solicitor-General and Attorney-General, in spite of the efforts made on his behalf by the Queen's favourite, and his friend and patron, the Earl of Essex. When Essex fell from favour and was tried for insurrection in 1601, Bacon took a prominent part in his fatal prosecution. The accession of James I in 1603 soon advanced Bacon's fortunes: he was knighted in 1603, became Solicitor-General in 1607, Attorney-General in 1613, Lord Keeper of the Great Seal in 1614, and Lord Chancellor and Baron Verulam in 1618. Three years later a parliamentary committee found him guilty of corruption; he was briefly imprisoned in the Tower, and spent the rest of his life in retirement and study. He died on April 9, 1626, of a chill caught while testing the preservative powers of snow.

Bacon's philosophical works, such as *The Advancement of Learning* (1605) and *Novum Organum* (1620), were devoted to the exposition of the inductive method of reasoning, or the forming of hypotheses on the basis of detailed observation of particular facts, which is the basis of modern science. His best purely literary works are his *Essays*, which appeared in several editions between 1597 and 1625. The essay had originated in France in 1580 with the work of Montaigne, but Bacon was the first to practise the form in English. As the examples below will indicate, he brought to the form his keen legal brain, his broad learning, and his wide practical experience of men and affairs.

Of Truth

What is truth? said jesting Pilate; and would not stay for an answer. Certainly there be that delight in giddiness, and count it as bondage to fix a belief; affecting free-will in thinking, as well as in acting. And though the sects of philosophers of that kind be gone, yet there remain certain discoursing wits which are of the same veins, though there be not so much blood in them as was in those of the ancients. But it is not only the difficulty and labour which men take in finding out of truth; nor again that when it is found it imposeth upon men's thoughts, that doth bring lies in favor; but a natural though corrupt love of the lie itself. One of the later schools of the Grecians examineth the matter and is at a stand to think what should be in it, that men should love lies, where neither they make for pleasure, as with poets, nor for advantage, as with the merchant; but for the lie's sake. But I cannot tell; this same truth is a naked and open day-light, that doth not show the masks and mummeries and triumphs of the world, half so stately and daintily as candle-lights. Truth may perhaps come to the price of a pearl, that showeth best by day; but it will not rise to the price of a diamond or carbuncle, that showeth best in varied lights. A mixture of a lie doth ever add pleasure. Doth any man doubt, that if there were taken out of men's minds, vain opinions, flattering hopes, false valuations, imaginations as one would, and the like, but it would leave the minds of a number of men poor shrunken things, full of melancholy and indisposition, and unpleasing to themselves? One of the Fathers[1], in great severity, called poesy *vinum daemonum*, because it filleth the imagination; and yet it is but with the shadow of a lie. But it is not the lie that passeth through the mind, but the lie that sinketh in and settleth in it, that doth the hurt; such as we spake of before. But howsoever these things are thus in men's depraved judgments and affections, yet truth, which only doth judge itself, teacheth that the inquiry of truth, which is the love-making or wooing of it, the knowledge of truth, which is the presence of it, and the belief of truth, which is the enjoying of it, is the sovereign good of human nature. The first creature of God, in the works of the days, was the light of the sense; the last was the light of reason; and his sabbath work ever since is the illumination of His Spirit. First He breathed light upon the face of the matter or chaos; then He breathed light into the face of man; and still He breatheth and inspireth light into the face of His chosen. The poet[2] that beautified the sect that was otherwise inferior to the rest, saith yet excellently well: "It is a pleasure to stand upon the shore and to see ships tossed upon the sea; a pleasure to stand in the window of a castle and to see a battle and the adventures thereof below; but no pleasure is comparable to the standing upon the vantage ground of truth (a hill not to be commanded, and where the air is always clear and serene), and to see the errors and wanderings and mists and tempests in the vale below"; so always that this prospect be with pity, and not with swelling or pride. Certainly, it is heaven upon earth, to have a man's mind move in charity, rest in providence, and turn upon the poles of truth.

To pass from theological and philosophical truth to the truth of civil business; it will be acknowledged even by those that practise it not, that clear and round dealing is the honour of man's nature; and that mixture of falsehood is like alloy in coin of gold and silver, which may make the metal work the better, but it embaseth it. For these winding and crooked courses are the goings of the serpent; which goeth basely upon the belly, and not upon the feet. There is no vice that doth so cover a man with shame as to be found false and perfidious. And therefore Montaigne saith prettily, when he inquired the reason why the word of the lie should be such a disgrace and such an odious charge. Saith he, "If it be well weighed, to say that a man lieth, is as much to say, as that he is brave towards God and a coward towards men." For a lie faces God, and shrinks from man. Surely the wickedness of falsehood and breach of faith cannot possibly be so highly expressed, as in that it shall be the last peal to call the judgments of God upon the generations of men; it being foretold that when Christ cometh, "He shall not find faith upon earth."

[1]St. Augustine.
[2]Lucretius, Roman poet of the Epicurean school.

Of Studies

Studies serve for delight, for ornament, and for ability. Their chief use for delight is in privateness and retiring; for ornament, is in discourse; and for ability, is in the judgment and disposition of business. For expert men can execute, and perhaps judge of particulars, one by one; but the general counsels, and the plots and marshalling of affairs, come best from those that are learned. To spend too much time in studies is sloth; to use them too much for ornament, is affectation; to make judgment wholly by their rules, is the humour of a scholar. They perfect nature, and are perfected by experience: for natural abilities are like natural plants, that need pruning, by study; and studies themselves do give forth directions too much at large, except they be bounded in by experience. Crafty men contemn studies, simple men admire them, and wise men use them; for they teach not their own use; but that is a wisdom without them, and above them, won by observation. Read not to contradict and confute; nor to believe and take for granted; nor to find talk and discourse; but to weigh and consider. Some books are to be tasted, others to be swallowed, and some few to be chewed and digested; that is, some books are to be read only in parts; others to be read, but not curiously; and some few to be read wholly, and with diligence and attention. Some books also may be read by deputy, and extracts made of them by others; but that would be only in the less important arguments, and the meaner sort of books; else distilled books are like common distilled waters, flashy things. Reading maketh a full man; conference a ready man; and writing an exact man. And therefore, if a man write little, he had need have a great memory; and if he read little, he had need have much cunning, to seem to know that he doth not. Histories make men wise; poets witty; the mathematics subtile; natural philosophy deep; moral grave; logic and rhetoric able to contend. "Abeunt studia in mores[1]." Nay, there is no stond or impediment in the wit but may be wrought out by fit studies; like as diseases of the body may have appropriate exercises. Bowling is good for the stone and reins; shooting for the lungs and breast; gentle walking for the stomach; riding for the head; and the like. So if a man's wit be wandering, let him study the mathematics; for in demonstrations, if his wit be called away never so little, he must begin again. If his wit be not apt to distinguish or find differences, let him study the Schoolmen; for they are *cumini sectores*[2]. If he be not apt to beat over matters, and to call up one thing to prove and illustrate another, let him study the lawyers' cases. So every defect of the mind may have a special receipt.

1597

[1]"Studies pass into manners." (Ovid)
[2]Splitters of hairs.

1600　　　　　　　　**1610**　　　　　　　　**1620**

● Jonson: *Epigrammes*

● Authorized Version of the Bible

● Death of Shakespeare

● Marlowe: *Tamburlaine the Great*

THE SEVENTEENTH CENTURY
(1603-1660)

1640	1650	1660

• Execution of Charles I

• Herbert: *The Temple*

Milton: *Paradise Lost* •

• Browne: *Religio Medici*

• Herrick: *Noble Numbers*

ath of Donne, father of Metaphysical Poetry

Marvell: *The Garden* •

In literary terms, the seventeenth century comprises the period from the accession of James I in 1603 to the Restoration of the Stuart monarchy in 1660. After the Restoration, literature changed direction and followed paths which led into the eighteenth century.

Unlike the Elizabethan period, in which internal conflict had been kept to a minimum by the political tact and skill of the queen and her advisors, the seventeenth century was a period of great stress and strain. James I (1603-1625) antagonized many of the people by his high-handed measures and his extravagant claims of royal prerogative; Charles I (1625-1649) made matters even worse, and by his refusal to allow Parliament to control his expenditures precipitated the Civil War in 1642 and his own execution in 1649; from 1653 to 1658 Oliver Cromwell ruled England with an iron hand as Lord Protector; after an interval of confusion Charles II was restored to the throne in 1660. The political struggle was thus a violent one, involving the conflict of parliamentary privilege against royal prerogative, of democratic liberty against monarchical absolutism, and of all shades of opinion between these two extremes.

Of at least equal importance was the religious conflict. The extreme Protestants under Elizabeth had been growing increasingly uneasy, and when James I came to the throne and made his famous pronouncement, "No bishop, no king!" their mood became rebellious. Many of them left the country for Holland and America; those who remained were ripe for civil war. When the Parliamentary forces triumphed in the War, the Puritans, who made up the majority of the Parliamentary party, were in no mood to be charitable to their old enemies, and were as severe in their attacks on the Church of England as Archbishop Laud had been in his attacks upon them.

Closely associated with the political and religious conflicts were social and economic struggles. The Renaissance and the Reformation had a good deal in common: both stressed the rights of the individual, the value of free discussion, the inevitability of change. But they carried within themselves also the seeds of dissension: the Renaissance, with its stress on the values of earthly love and beauty, tended in its extreme manifestations to permit moral laxity, a devil-may-care attitude of "Eat, drink, and be merry, for tomorrow you die"; the Reformation, on the other hand, rebelled against the medieval Church not for its strictness but for its laxity; instead of encouraging moral license and religious scepticism, it stood for an even closer walk with God, a greater purity of belief and conduct. The Royalist supporters, the Cavaliers as they were called, tended to follow the Renaissance ideals of gaiety, sensuous pleasure, and easy scepticism; the Puritan wing of the Parliamentary party (the Roundheads) stood for austerity, moral seriousness, and strict piety.

In economic terms, the struggle was a development of the rift which had been growing slowly since the time of Chaucer between the landed aristocracy and the commercial middle class. Most of the landed aristocracy, and their rural dependents and servants, supported the Royal cause; most of the city merchants, and especially the merchants of London, supported the privileges of Parliament.

The Civil War, then, was not a simple struggle of Parliament against King, but in some sense also a struggle of Puritan against Anglican, Reformation against Renaissance, city merchant against rural land owner.

An even more basic conflict than the Civil War was the developing intellectual conflict between the remnants of the medieval, scholastic outlook and the modern, rational temper. The medieval mind had relied upon faith and authority; the modern mind relied rather upon reason and experiment. All the leading philosophers of seventeenth century England—Bacon, Hobbes, Locke, and Newton—belonged to the rationalist school. More and more of the old accepted ideas were subjected to critical scrutiny, and many of them were discarded as mere superstition. The way was being prepared for the conflicts of religion and science which were to develop in later centuries, and the effect of all the questioning of hitherto-received opinions was to make men of the seventeenth century anxious and apprehensive.

This disintegration in society was matched by a similar break-up in literature. The writers of the Elizabethan period, whatever their superficial differences, all belonged to the same general school. It is often difficult to say whether a given sonnet was written by Sidney, Spenser, Shakespeare, Raleigh, or Drayton. But this unity gave way to diversity in the seventeenth century. Instead of one school of poets there were three: Donne and his metaphysical followers, whose work stressed wit and passion and who revolted against the sweetness and conventionality of the Elizabethan lyrical tradition; Jonson and his disciples, "the sons of Ben," who prided themselves on the classical polish of their verse, its neatness and economy as against the elaborate eloquence of Spenser; and finally the Spenserians such as the Fletchers, Wither, and Browne, who sought to perpetuate the majestic, magnificent, sensuous verse of Edmund Spenser. To this last school, in a sense, belonged the greatest poet of the period, John Milton, though he eventually surpassed his master in depth and range.

Similar diversity and conflict is evident in the dramatic history of the period. Shakespeare continued to write until his death in 1616, but he had a rival in Ben Jonson, who disliked fantastic comedy, chronicle plays, and tragedy on the grand scale, and preferred to write realistic comedies to "shew an Image of the times,/And sport with human follies, not with crimes," or classical tragedies which obeyed the Aristotelian rules of unity of time, place, and action and were scholarly and accurate in their historical detail. Lesser dramatists such as John Fletcher, Francis Beaumont, Philip Massinger, Thomas Middleton, Cyril Tourneur, John Webster, and John Ford attempted to carry on the Elizabethan dramatic tradition, but their work became increasingly sophisticated, artificial, and abnormal. More and more attacks were made upon the theatre by the Puritans, who associated it with the court and with moral depravity. When the Puritans triumphed in the Civil War, the theatres were abruptly closed; and when English drama re-emerged after the Restoration it was a very different product.

It is in the prose of the seventeenth century that we see the greatest diversity of all. By the Restoration, the foundations had been laid of all forms of English prose except the novel and the short story. The Authorized Version of the Bible, published under the auspices of James I in 1611, had an immense influence on all subsequent English prose. Historical writing, already initiated in earlier periods, was made much more scholarly and systematic. Biography also made rapid advances in the seventeenth century. Izaak Walton, more popularly known as the author of that whimsical treatise on fishing, *The Compleat Angler* (1653), wrote biographies of Donne, Hooker, and George Herbert; and Thomas Fuller included many biographical sketches in his historical works such as *The Church History of Britain* (1655).

As we should expect in an age of such intense religious controversy, many works on religion were published. There were the eloquent sermons of Lancelot Andrewes, John Donne, and Jeremy Taylor; the devotional writings of Donne, Taylor, Herbert, and Traherne; the books setting forth the author's personal religious beliefs, such as Sir Thomas Browne's *Religio Medici* (1642) and Milton's *De Doctrina Christiana* (1659); and the multitude of controversial religious pamphlets, of which Milton's are almost the only ones which have survived.

The growth of scientific thought and philosophical speculation produced many books. Following such pioneer works as Francis Bacon's *Novum Organum* (1620) came Robert Burton's *Anatomy of Melancholy* (1621), a serious and yet intermittently humorous treatise on psychological disorders, Thomas Hobbes' *Elements of Law, Natural and Politic* (1650), *Leviathan* (1651), and *Questions concerning Liberty, Necessity and Chance* (1656), and James Harrington's *Oceania* (1656), to mention but a few of the more prominent.

The short essay, as Bacon had introduced it, had no direct descendants in the seventeenth century, but it had close relatives in the commonplace books such as Ben Jonson's *Timber* and the "characters" of Sir Thomas Overbury and John Earle. In the latter, the writer took an occupation such as that of the milkmaid or scholar and sought to delineate its distinguishing characteristics. It was a quaint and often charming form which in many ways resembles the modern familiar essay.

The seventeenth century is a curious mixture of the old and the new, the mythical and the scientific. Even in such scientifically minded writers as Bacon, Burton, and Browne there is much that is merely quaint and superstitious. It was an era in which old values were crumbling, in which competing ways of life and thought struggled for the mastery. The greatest literary figure of the age, John Milton, derives his greatness in part from the fact that in an age of disintegration he made the most heroic effort at reintegration. In him all the issues of the age come to a burning focus.

BEN JONSON (1572-1637)

Dramatist, lyric poet, and literary critic, Ben Jonson was perhaps the most influential writer of his day. As dramatist he rivalled Shakespeare; as poet he rivalled Donne; and as critic he was pre-eminent.

Jonson was the posthumous son of a clergyman of Scottish descent, and was brought up by his stepfather, a London bricklayer. He attended Westminster School where he derived a great love of the classics from his master William

Camden, the famous antiquarian. For a few years he followed his stepfather's trade, served briefly in the army, and in 1597 began to work for Henslowe's company as an actor and playwright. In the following year he killed a fellow actor in a duel, was imprisoned, but escaped death by pleading benefit of clergy. In 1598, also, appeared the first of his brilliant series of satirical and realistic comedies, *Every Man in His Humour*, with Shakespeare as a member of the cast. The first of his classical tragedies, *Sejanus*, appeared in 1603, and the first of his masques (a form combining music, dance, and dialogue somewhat like the modern opera) in 1605. In 1616 he was given a pension by James I, and became in effect the first poet laureate. After the death of his patron, James I, in 1625, his fortunes began to decline: he lost his library in a fire, he suffered a paralytic stroke in 1628, and he quarrelled with Inigo Jones, his collaborator in the masques, in 1630. On his death in 1637, he was buried in Westminster Abbey.

Besides his many plays and masques, Jonson wrote three volumes of poetry—*Epigrammes*, *The Forrest*, and *Underwoods*—and a prose work entitled *Timber, or Discoveries Made upon Men and Matter*. His poems marked a departure from the Spenserian tradition in their classical restraint, brevity, and wit, and they inspired a group of disciples known as the "tribe of Ben." The best of the tribe is Robert Herrick. In *Timber*, Jonson expounded his classical standards of taste and judgment, frequently quoting from or paraphrasing the Greek and Latin authors whom he so admired.

Songs from Cynthia's Revels[1]

Queen and huntress, chaste and fair,
Now the sun is laid to sleep,
Seated in thy silver chair
State in wonted manner keep:
   Hesperus entreats thy light,
   Goddess excellently bright.

Earth, let not thy envious shade
Dare itself to interpose;
Cynthia's shining orb was made

Heaven to clear when day did close
   Bless us then with wishèd sight,
   Goddess excellently bright.

Lay thy bow of pearl apart
And thy crystal-shining quiver;
Give unto the flying hart
Space to breathe, how short soever:
   Thou that mak'st a day of night,
   Goddess excellently bright.

Slow, slow, fresh fount, keep time with my salt tears,
   Yet slower yet, oh faintly, gentle springs;
List to the heavy part the music bears,
   Woe weeps out her division when she sings.
      Droop herbs and flowers;
      Fall grief in showers;
      Our beauties are not ours;
      Oh, I could still,
(Like melting snow, upon some craggy hill)
      Drop, drop, drop, drop,
Since Nature's pride is now a wither'd daffodil.

1601

[1]A comedy by Jonson, satirizing some hangers-on at court. These songs are sung by Hesperus, god of the evening star, to Cynthia, goddess of the moon.

FROM *Epicoene*[1]*, or the Silent Woman*

Still to be neat, still to be drest,
As you were going to a feast;
Still to be powder'd, still perfum'd:
Lady, it is to be presum'd,
Though art's hid causes are not found,
All is not sweet, all is not sound.

Give me a look, give me a face,
That makes simplicity a grace;
Robes loosely flowing, hair as free:
Such sweet neglect more taketh me
Than all th' adulteries of art;
They strike mine eyes, but not my heart.

1609   1616

[1]Another comedy by Jonson, first acted in 1609,
and one of the most popular of his works.

To Celia

Drink to me only with thine eyes,
And I will pledge with mine;
Or leave a kiss but in the cup,
And I'll not look for wine.
The thirst that from the soul doth rise
Doth ask a drink divine;
But might I of Jove's nectar sup,
I would not change for thine.

I sent thee late a rosy wreath,
Not so much honouring thee
As giving it a hope, that there
It could not withered be.
But thou thereon didst only breathe,
And sent'st it back to me;
Since when it grows, and smells, I swear,
Not of itself, but thee.

1616

The Triumph of Charis

See the chariot at hand here of Love,
Wherein my lady rideth!
Each that draws is a swan or a dove,
And well the car Love guideth.
As she goes, all hearts do duty
Unto her beauty;
And enamour'd, do wish, so they might
But enjoy such a sight,
That they still were to run by her side,
Through swords, through seas, whither
she would ride.

Do but look on her eyes, they do light
All that Love's world compriseth!
Do but look on her hair, it is bright
As Love's star when it riseth!
Do but mark, her forehead's smoother
Than words that soothe her;

And from her arched brows, such a grace
Sheds itself through the face
As alone there triumphs to the life
All the gain, all the good, of the elements'
strife.

Have you seen but a bright lily grow,
Before rude hands have touch'd it?
Ha' you mark'd but the fall o' the snow
Before the soil hath smutch'd it?
Ha' you felt the wool of beaver?
Or swan's down ever?
Or have smelt o' the bud o' the briar?
Or the nard in the fire?
Or have tasted the bag of the bee?
Oh so white! Oh so soft! Oh so sweet is
she!

1640

To the Memory of My Beloved the Author, Mr. William Shakespeare, and What He Hath Left Us[1]

To draw no envy, Shakespeare, on thy name,
Am I thus ample to thy book and fame;
While I confess thy writings to be such
As neither man nor muse can praise too much;
'Tis true, and all men's suffrage. But these ways
Were not the paths I meant unto thy praise;
For seeliest[2] ignorance on these may light,
Which, when it sounds at best, but echoes right;
Or blind affection, which doth ne'er advance
The truth, but gropes, and urgeth all by chance;   10
Or crafty malice might pretend this praise,
And think to ruin, where it seem'd to raise.
These are, as some infamous bawd or whore
Should praise a matron; what could hurt her more?
But thou art proof against them, and indeed,
Above th' ill fortune of them, or the need.
I therefore will begin. Soul of the age!
The applause, delight, the wonder of our stage!
My Shakespeare, rise! I will not lodge thee by
Chaucer, or Spenser, or bid Beaumont lie   20
A little further, to make thee a room:
Thou art a monument without a tomb,
And art alive still while thy book doth live
And we have wits to read and praise to give.
That I not mix thee so, my brain excuses,
I mean with great, but disproportion'd Muses,
For if I thought my judgment were of years,
I should commit thee surely with thy peers,
And tell how far thou didst our Lyly outshine,
Or sporting Kyd, or Marlowe's mighty line.   30
And though thou hadst small Latin and less Greek,
From thence to honour thee, I would not seek
For names; but call forth thund'ring Æschylus,
Euripides, and Sophocles to us;
Pacuvius[3], Accius, him of Cordova dead,
To life again, to hear thy buskin tread,
And shake a stage; or, when thy socks[4] were on,

---

[1]This poem was prefaced to the first folio edition of Shakespeare's works, 1623.   [2]Simplest, most artless.
[3]Pacuvius (220-129 B.C.), Accius (b. 170 B.C.), Seneca (d. A.D. 65), Roman writers of tragedy.
[4]The low shoe of comedy, in contrast with the buskin or high shoe of tragedy.

Leave thee alone for the comparison
Of all that insolent Greece or haughty Rome
Sent forth, or since did from their ashes come.   40
Triumph, my Britain, thou hast one to show
To whom all scenes of Europe homage owe.
He was not of an age, but for all time!
And all the Muses still were in their prime,
When, like Apollo, he came forth to warm
Our ears, or like a Mercury to charm!
Nature herself was proud of his designs
And joy'd to wear the dressing of his lines,
Which were so richly spun, and woven so fit,
As, since, she will vouchsafe no other wit.   50
The merry Greek, tart Aristophanes,
Neat Terence, witty Plautus, now not please,
But antiquated and deserted lie,
As they were not of Nature's family.
Yet must I not give Nature all; thy art,
My gentle Shakespeare, must enjoy a part.
For though the poet's matter nature be,
His art doth give the fashion; and, that he
Who casts to write a living line, must sweat,
(Such as thine are) and strike the second heat   60
Upon the Muses' anvil; turn the same
(And himself with it) that he thinks to frame,
Or, for the laurel, he may gain a scorn;
For a good poet's made, as well as born;
And such wert thou. Look how the father's face
Lives in his issue, even so the race
Of Shakespeare's mind and manners brightly shines
In his well-turned, and true-filed lines;
In each of which he seems to shake a lance,
As brandish'd at the eyes of ignorance.   70
Sweet Swan of Avon! what a sight it were
To see thee in our waters yet appear,
And make those flights upon the banks of Thames[5],
That so did take Eliza, and our James!
But stay, I see thee in the hemisphere
Advanc'd, and made a constellation there!
Shine forth, thou star of poets, and with rage
Or influence, chide or cheer the drooping stage;
Which, since thy flight from hence, hath mourn'd like night,
And despairs day, but for thy volume's light.   80

                                          1623

[5]The Globe theatre was situated on the south bank of the Thames.

FROM

Timber: Or Discoveries Made upon Men and Matter

DE SHAKESPEARE NOSTRATI

I remember the players have often mentioned it as an honour to Shakespeare, that in his writing (whatsoever he penned) he never blotted out a line. My answer hath been, "Would he had blotted a thousand!" which they thought a malevolent speech. I had not told posterity this but for their ignorance who chose that circumstance to commend their friend by wherein he most faulted; and to justify mine own candour, for I loved the man, and do honour his memory on this side idolatry as much as any. He was, indeed, honest, and of an open and free nature; had an excellent phantasy, brave notions, and gentle expressions, wherein he flowed with that facility that sometimes it was necessary he should be stopped. "Sufflaminandas erat" (he ought to have been clogged) as Augustus said of Haterius. His wit was in his own power; would the rule of it had been so, too! Many times he fell into those things could not escape laughter, as when he said in the person of Caesar, one speaking to him, "Caesar, thou dost me wrong." He replied, "Caesar did never wrong but with just cause"; and such like, which were ridiculous. But he redeemed his vices with his virtues. There was ever more in him to be praised than to be pardoned.

DE STILO, ET OPTIMO SCRIBENDI GENERE[1]

For a man to write well, there are required three necessaries—to read the best authors, observe the best speakers, and much exercise of his own style. In style, to consider what ought to be written, and after what manner, he must first think

[1] "Of style, and the best form of writing."

and excogitate his matter, then choose his words, and examine the weight of either. Then take care, in placing and ranking both matter and words, that the composition be comely; and to do this with diligence and often. No matter how slow the style be at first, so it be laboured and accurate; seek the best, and be not glad of the forward conceits, or first words, that offer themselves to us; but judge of what we invent, and order what we approve. Repeat often what we have formerly written; which beside that it help the consequence, and makes the juncture better, it quickens the heat of imagination, that often cools in the time of setting down, and gives it new strength, as if it grew lustier by the going back. As we see in the contention of leaping, they jump farthest that fetch their race largest; or, as in throwing a dart or javelin, we force back our arms to make our loose the stronger. Yet, if we have a fair gale of wind, I forbid not the steering out of our sail, so the favour of the gale deceive us not. For all that we invent doth please us in the conception or birth, else we would never set it down. But the safest is to return to our judgment, and handle over again those things the easiness of which might make them justly suspected. So did the best writers in their beginnings; they imposed upon themselves care and industry; they did nothing rashly; they obtained first to write well, and then custom made it easy and a habit. By little and little their matter showed itself to them more plentifully; their words answered, their composition followed; and all, as in a well-ordered family, presented itself in the place. So that the sum of all is, ready writing makes not good writing, but good writing brings on ready writing. Yet, when we think we have got the faculty, it is even then good to resist it, as to give a horse a check sometimes with a bit, which doth not so much stop his course as stir his mettle. Again, whither a man's genius is best able to reach, thither it should more and more contend, lift and dilate itself; as men of low stature raise themselves on their toes, and so oftimes get even, if not eminent. Besides, as it is fit for grown and able writers to stand of themselves, and work with their own strength, to trust and endeavour by their own faculties, so it is fit for the beginner and learner to study others and the best. For the mind and memory are more sharply exercised in comprehending another man's things than our own; and such as accustom themselves and are familiar with the best authors shall ever and anon find somewhat of them in themselves, and in the expression of their minds, even when they feel it not, be able to utter something like theirs, which hath an authority above their own. Nay, sometimes it is the reward of a man's study, the praise of quoting another man fitly; and though a man be more prone and able for one kind of writing than another, yet he must exercise all. For as in an instrument, so in style, there must be a harmony and consent of parts.

1640

JOHN DONNE (1571?-1631)

John Donne, along with Ben Jonson, was one of the two most influential poets of the seventeenth century; he was also one of its greatest preachers.

Donne was the son of a well-to-do London ironmonger, and was educated at both Oxford and Cambridge. He did not take a degree at either university, however, because his family was Roman Catholic. He briefly studied law at Lincoln's Inn in London, and in 1596 and 1597 sailed in the expeditions of the Earl of Essex to Cadiz and the Azores. From 1598 to 1602 he was secretary to Sir Thomas Egerton, Lord Keeper of the Great Seal, but lost this post through a clandestine marriage with Anne More, niece of his employer's wife. He was in poor circumstances for several years, but found a valuable patron in Sir Robert Drury, with whom he went to the Continent in 1611. Meanwhile Donne had been deeply considering the rival claims of the Anglican and Roman Catholic churches, and at some indeterminate point in his career decided to transfer to the former. He was ordained in the Church of England in 1615, soon won fame for his eloquent sermons, and in 1621 was made Dean of St. Paul's. There his sermons attracted great crowds, of whom James I and Charles I were frequently members. Donne's wife died in 1623, and from then until his own death in 1631 Donne was much ob-sessed with death and with preparing himself to meet it without fear.

Donne was a man of many conflicts. He was torn between the piety of his family and the gaiety of the universities and the court, between Catholicism and Anglicanism, between physical and spiritual love, between faith and doubt, between the fear of God and the love of God, between secular ambition and sacred devotion. His poetry and prose clearly reflect these conflicts. His early love poems were sensual and cynical; the love poems he wrote to Anne More had a much more idealistic cast; the religious poems of his later years recorded his passionate search for an assured faith. His sermons so impressed their hearers because they came from the mind and heart of a man who had himself known sin and the agonies of guilt and doubt.

Donne was the founder of what Dryden called the "metaphysical" school of poetry, which included George Herbert, Henry Vaughan, Richard Crashaw, Thomas Traherne, and Andrew Marvell. Donne and his followers reacted against the smoothness and sensuousness of Elizabethan poetry to write in a manner that is abrupt, fantastic, paradoxical, and at once passionate and intellectual. Instead of the conventional metaphors and similies comparing a woman's teeth to pearls, her lips to cherries and so on—comparisons based on physical resemblances—the metaphysical poets used surprising comparisons (or 'conceits') based on similarities of idea and function, such as Donne's famous comparison of himself and his wife to a pair of compasses. Whether writing of religion or love—their favourite subjects—the metaphysical poets united passion and thought, and wrote with great excitement and intensity. Sometimes they became overly fantastic, even absurd—but at their best they were distinctive and original.

Donne, then, was a great innovator. He founded a new school by reacting against all the main features of Spenserian poetry. He had no use for the artificialities of the pastoral with its make-believe shepherds and shepherdesses, for the frequent mythological references to Diana, Apollo, and the like, for allegory, for the neo-Platonic idealization of woman and love, for long-drawn-out descriptions of persons and places, for smooth, regular, soporific metres, for the subordination of meaning to melody. His poems are nearer to excited speech than to song, and they are distinguished by their explosive force, their wit, passion, and extraordinary honesty.

In prose, Donne was the author of the religious tract *Pseudo-Martyr* (1610), of over one hundred and fifty sermons, and of *Devotions Upon Emergent Occasions* (1624). This latter book was written from notes made by Donne during a six-week illness in 1623, when he was in daily fear of death and could hear the passing-bell tolling out for others who had died.

The Bait

Come live with me, and be my love,
And we will some new pleasures prove
Of golden sands, and crystal brooks,
With silken lines, and silver hooks.

There will the river whispering run
Warm'd by thy eyes, more than the sun;
And there the'enamour'd fish will stay,
Begging themselves they may betray.

When thou wilt swim in that live bath,
Each fish, which every channel hath,   10
Will amorously to thee swim,
Gladder to catch thee, than thou him.

If thou, to be so seen, be'st loth,
By sun or moon, thou dark'nest both,

And if myself have leave to see,
I need not their light, having thee.

Let others freeze with angling reeds,
And cut their legs with shells and weeds,
Or treacherously poor fish beset,   19
With strangling snare, or windowy net.

Let coarse bold hands from slimy nest
The bedded fish in banks out-wrest;
Or curious traitors, sleeve-silk flies,
Bewitch poor fishes' wand'ring eyes.

For thee, thou need'st no such deceit,
For thou thyself art thine own bait:
That fish, that is not catch'd thereby,
Alas! is wiser far than I.

c. 1590-1601?   1633

Song

Sweetest love, I do not go,
  For weariness of thee,
Nor in hope the world can show
  A fitter love for me;

But since that I
Must die at last, 'tis best,
Thus to use myself in jest
  Thus by feign'd deaths to die.

Yesternight the sun went hence,
And yet is here to-day; 10
He hath no desire nor sense,
Nor half so short a way:
Then fear not me,
But believe that I shall make
Speedier journeys, since I take
More wings and spurs than he.

O how feeble is man's power,
That if good fortune fall,
Cannot add another hour,
Nor a lost hour recall! 20
But come bad chance,
And we join to'it our strength,
And we teach it art and length,
Itself o'er us to'advance.

When thou sigh'st, thou sigh'st not wind,
But sigh'st my soul away;
When thou weep'st, unkindly kind,
My life's blood doth decay.
It cannot be
That thou lov'st me, as thou say'st, 30
If in thine my life thou waste,
That art the best of me.

Let not thy divining heart
Forethink me any ill;
Destiny may take thy part,
And may thy fears fulfil;
But think that we
Are but turn'd aside to sleep;
They who one another keep
Alive, ne'er parted be. 40

1612? 1633

A Valediction: Forbidding Mourning

As virtuous men pass mildly away,
And whisper to their souls, to go,
Whilst some of their sad friends do say,
"The breath goes now," and some say,
"No."

So let us melt, and make no noise,
No tear-floods, nor sigh-tempests move;
'Twere profanation of our joys
To tell the laity our love.

Moving of th' earth brings harms and
fears;
Men reckon what it did, and meant; 10
But trepidation of the spheres,
Though greater far, is innocent.

Dull sublunary lovers' love
(Whose soul is sense) cannot admit
Absence, because it doth remove
Those things which elemented it.

But we by a love so much refin'd,
That ourselves know not what it is,

Inter-assurèd of the mind,
Care less, eyes, lips, and hands to miss.

Our two souls therefore, which are one,
Though I must go, endure not yet 22
A breach, but an expansion,
Like gold to airy thinness beat.

If they be two, they are two so
As stiff twin compasses are two;
Thy soul, the fix'd foot, makes no show
To move, but doth, if the' other do.

And though it in the centre sit,
Yet when the other far doth roam, 30
It leans, and hearkens after it,
And grows erect, as that comes home.

Such wilt thou be to me, who must
Like th' other foot, obliquely run;
Thy firmness makes my circle just,
And makes me end where I begun.

1612? 1633

Epigrams

A BURNT SHIP

Out of a fired ship, which by no way
But drowning could be rescued from the flame,
Some men leap'd forth, and ever as they came
Near the foes' ships, did by their shot decay;
So all were lost, which in the ship were found,
   They in the sea being burnt, they in the burnt ship drown'd.

A LAME BEGGAR

I am unable, yonder beggar cries,
To stand, or move; if he say true, he lies.

1633

Holy Sonnets

VII

At the round earth's imagin'd corners blow
Your trumpets, angels, and arise, arise
From death, you numberless infinities
Of souls, and to your scatter'd bodies go;
All whom the flood did, and fire shall o'erthrow,
All whom war, death, age, agues, tyrannies,
Despair, law, chance hath slain, and you, whose eyes
Shall behold God, and never taste death's woe.
But let them sleep, Lord, and me mourn a space;
For, if above all these my sins abound,
'Tis late to ask abundance of Thy grace,
When we are there.   Here on this lowly ground,
Teach me how to repent, for that's as good
As if Thou hadst seal'd my pardon with Thy blood.

X

Death, be not proud, though some have called thee
Mighty and dreadful, for thou art not so;
For those, whom thou think'st thou dost overthrow,
Die not, poor Death, nor yet canst thou kill me.
From rest and sleep, which but thy pictures be,
Much pleasure, then from thee much more must flow,
And soonest our best men with thee do go,
Rest of their bones, and soul's delivery.

Thou art slave to Fate, Chance, kings, and desperate men,
And dost with poison, war, and sickness dwell,
And poppy, or charms can make us sleep as well,
And better than thy stroke; why swell'st thou then?
One short sleep past, we wake eternally,
And Death shall be no more; Death, thou shalt die.

c. 1617?   1633

A Hymn to God the Father

Wilt Thou forgive that sin where I begun,
  Which was my sin, though it were done before?
Wilt Thou forgive that sin, through which I run,
  And do run still, though still I do deplore?
    When Thou hast done, Thou hast not done,
      For I have more.

Wilt Thou forgive that sin which I have won
  Others to sin, and made my sin their door?
Wilt Thou forgive that sin which I did shun
  A year or two, but wallowed in, a score?
    When Thou hast done, Thou hast not done,
      For I have more.

I have a sin of fear, that when I have spun
  My last thread, I shall perish on the shore;
But swear by Thyself, that at my death Thy Son
  Shall shine as he shines now, and heretofore;
    And, having done that, Thou hast done;
      I fear no more.

1623?   1633

FROM Devotions upon Emergent Occasions

XVI. MEDITATION

We have a convenient author who writ a discourse of bells when he was prisoner in Turkey. How would he have enlarged himself if he had been my fellow prisoner in this sick-bed so near to that steeple which never ceases no more than the harmony of the spheres, but is more heard! When the Turks took Constantinople, they melted the bells into ordnance; I have heard both bells and ordnance but never been so much affected with those as with these bells. I have lain near a steeple in which there are said to be more than thirty bells and near another where there is one so big as that the clapper is said to weigh more than six hundred pounds, yet never so affected as here. Here the bells can scarce solemnize the funeral of any person but that I knew him or knew that he was my neighbour. We dwelt in houses near to one another before, but now he is gone into that house into which I must follow him. There is a way of correcting the children of great persons, that other children are corrected in their behalf and in their names, and this works upon them who had indeed more deserved it. And when these bells tell me that now one and now another is buried, must not I acknowledge that they have the correction due to me and paid the debt I owe? There is a story of a bell in a monastery which, when any of the house was sick to death, rung always voluntarily, and they knew the inevitableness of the danger by that. It rung once when no man was sick, but the next day one of the house fell from the steeple and died, and the bell held the reputation of a prophet still. If these bells that warn to a funeral now were appropriated to none, may not I by the hour of the funeral supply? How many men that stand at an execution, if they would ask, for what dies that man, should hear their own faults condemned and see themselves executed by attorney! We scarce hear of any man preferred but we think of ourselves that we might very well have been that man; why might not I have been that man that is carried to his grave now? Could I fit myself to stand or sit in any man's place, and not to lie in any man's grave? I may lack much of the good parts of the meanest, but I lack nothing of the mortality of the weakest; they may have acquired better abilities than I, but I was born to as many infirmities as they. To be an incumbent by lying down in a grave, to be a doctor by teaching mortification by example, by dying, though I may have seniors, others may be older than I, yet I have pro-

ceeded apace in a good university and gone a great way in a little time by the furtherance of a vehement fever; and whomsoever these bells bring to the ground today, if he and I had been compared yesterday, perchance I should have been thought likelier to come to this preferment than he. God hath kept the power of death in his own hands lest any man should bribe death. If man knew the gain of death, the ease of death, he would solicit, he would provoke death to assist him by any hand which he might use. But as when men see many of their own professions preferred, it ministers a hope that that may light upon them; so when these hourly bells tell me of so many funerals of men like me, it presents, if not a desire that it may, yet a comfort whensoever mine shall come.

XVII. MEDITATION

Perchance he for whom this bell tolls may be so ill as that he knows not it tolls for him; and perchance I may think myself so much better than I am as that they who are about me and see my state may have caused it to toll for me, and I know not that. The church is catholic, universal, so are all her actions; all that she does belongs to all. When she baptizes a child, that action concerns me; for that child is thereby connected to that body which is my head too and ingrafted into that body whereof I am a member. And when she buries a man, that action concerns me. All mankind is of one author, and is one volume; when one man dies, one chapter is not torn out of the book, but translated into a better language; and every chapter must be so translated. God employs several translators; some pieces are translated by age, some by sickness, some by war, some by justice; but God's hand is in every translation, and his hand shall bind up all our scattered leaves again for that library where every book shall lie open to one another. As therefore the bell that rings to a sermon calls not upon the preacher only but upon the congregation to come, so this bell calls us all; but how much more me who am brought so near the door by this sickness! There was a contention as far as a suit—in which piety and dignity, religion and estimation, were mingled—which of the religious orders should ring to prayers first in the morning; and it was determined that they should ring first who rose earliest. If we understand aright the dignity of this bell that tolls for our evening prayer, we would be glad to make it ours by rising early, in that application, that it might be ours as well as his, whose indeed it is. The bell doth toll for him that thinks it doth; and though it intermit again, yet from that minute that that occasion wrought upon him he is united to God. Who casts not up his eye to the sun when it rises? but who takes off his eye from a comet when that breaks out? Who bends not his ear to any bell which upon any occasion rings? but who can remove it from that bell which is passing a piece of himself out of this world? No man is an island entire of itself; every man is a piece of the continent, a part of the main. If a clod be washed away by the sea, Europe is the less, as well as if a promontory were, as well as if a manor of thy friend's or of thy own were. Any man's death diminishes me, because I am involved in mankind, and therefore never send to know for whom the bell tolls; it tolls for thee. Neither can we call this a begging of misery or a borrowing of misery, as though we were not miserable enough of ourselves but must fetch in more from the next house, in taking upon us the misery of our neighbours. Truly it were an excusable covetousness if we did, for affliction is a treasure, and scarce any man hath enough of it. No man hath affliction enough that is not matured and ripened by it and made fit for God by that affliction. If a man carry treasure in bullion or in a wedge of gold and have none coined into current money, his treasure will not defray him as he travels. Tribulation is treasure in the nature of it, but it is not current money in the use of it, except we get nearer and nearer our home, heaven, by it. Another man may be sick too, and sick to death, and this affliction may lie in his bowels as gold in a mine and be of no use to him; but this bell that tells me of his affliction digs out and applies that gold to me, if by this consideration of another's danger I take mine own into contemplation and so secure myself by making my recourse to my God, who is our only security.

1624

SIR THOMAS OVERBURY (1581-1613)

Sir Thomas Overbury was the author of the most popular "character book" of the seventeenth century. In these character books, brief portraits were given of representative citizens such as the schoolmaster or of representative family figures such as the father or the eldest son. The form was largely based on the similar portraits of the Greek writer Theophrastus, and it was extremely popular throughout the seventeenth century. This popularity reflected the new interest in man and his social relations which was part of the spirit of the Renaissance.

Overbury was born in Warwickshire, received his B.A. from Oxford in 1598, and studied law in London. He became a member of the court of James I, and was knighted in 1608. He involved himself in court intrigues, and as a result of his indiscretions was imprisoned in the Tower of London. He died in the Tower, the victim of mysterious poisoning, in September, 1613.

Overbury's book, *A Wife, Now a Widow*, was first published in 1614; in its first edition it con-sisted only of a long poem, but in subsequent editions more and more prose characters, "written by himself and other learned gentlemen his friends," were added, until by 1622 there were no less than eighty-two characters. Prob-ably few of the characters were the work of Overbury himself: he was the compiler, and many of the sketches were written by such men as John Webster, the dramatist.

FROM His Wife . . . and Divers More Characters

A GOOD WIFE

Is a man's best movable, a scion incor-porate with the stock, bringing forth sweet fruit; one that to her husband is more than a friend, less than a trouble; an equal with him in the yoke. Calamities and troubles she shares alike, nothing pleases her that doth not him. She is relative in all; and he without her, but half himself. She is his absent hands, eyes, ears, and mouth; his present and absent all. She frames her nature unto his how-soever: the hyacinth follows not the sun more willingly. Stubbornness and obsti-nacy are herbs that grow not in her garden. She leaves tattling to the gossips of the town, and is more seen than heard. Her household is her charge; her care to that makes her seldom non-resident. Her pride is but to be cleanly, and her thrift not to be prodigal. By her discretion she hath children, not wantons; a husband without her is a misery in man's apparel; none but she hath an aged husband, to whom she is both a staff and a chair. To conclude, she is both wise and religious, which makes her all this.

A FAIR AND HAPPY MILKMAID

Is a country wench, that is so far from making herself beautiful by art that one look of hers is able to put all face-physic out of countenance. She knows a fair look is but a dumb orator to commend virtue, therefore minds it not. All her excellencies stand in her so silently as if they had stolen upon her without her knowledge. The lining of her apparel (which is herself) is far better than the outside of tissue[1]: for though she be not arrayed in the spoil of the silkworm, she is decked in innocency, a far better wearing. She doth not, with lying long abed, spoil both her complexion and conditions; nature hath taught her too immoderate sleep is rust to the soul: she rises therefore with chanti-cleer, her dame's cock, and at night makes the lamb her curfew. In milking a cow, and straining the teats through her fingers, it seems that so sweet a milk-press makes the milk the whiter or sweeter; for never came almond glove or aromatic ointment on her palm to taint it. The golden ears of corn fall and kiss her feet when she reaps them, as if they wished to be bound and led prisoners by the same hand that felled them. Her breath is her own, which scents all the year long of June, like a new made hay-cock. She makes her hands hard with labour, and her heart soft with pity; and when winter evenings fall early (sitting at her merry

[1] Rich cloth.

wheel), she sings a defiance to the giddy wheel of fortune. She doth all things with so sweet a grace it seems ignorance will not suffer her to do ill, being her mind is to do well. She bestows her year's wages at next fair; and in choosing her garments, counts no bravery[2] in the world like decency. The garden and bee-hive are all her physic and chirurgery, and she lives the longer for it. She dares go alone, and unfold sheep in the night, and fears no manner of ill, because she means none; yet to say truth, she is never alone, for she is still accompanied with old songs, honest thoughts, and prayers, but short ones; yet they have their efficacy, in that they are not palled with ensuing idle cogitations. Lastly, her dreams are so chaste that she dare tell them; only a Friday's dream is all her superstition; that she conceals for fear of anger. Thus lives she, and all her care is that she may die in the springtime, to have store of flowers stuck upon her winding-sheet.

A FRANKLIN

His outside is an ancient yeoman of England, though his inside may give arms (with the best gentlemen) and n'er see the herald. There is no truer servant in the house than himself. Though he be master, he says not to his servants, Go to field, but, Let us go; and with his own eye doth both fatten his flock and set forward all manner of husbandry. He is taught by nature to be contented with a little; his own fold yields him both food and raiment; he is pleased with any nourishment God sends, whilst curious gluttony ransacks, as it were, Noah's ark for food, only to feed the riot of one meal. He is ne'er

known to go to law; understanding to be law-bound among men is like to be hidebound among beasts; they thrive not under it; in that such men sleep as unquietly as if their pillows were stuffed with lawyer's pen knives. When he builds, no poor tenant's cottage hinders his prospect; they are indeed his alms-houses, though there be painted on them no such superscription; he never sits up late but when he hunts the badger, the vowed foe of his lambs; nor uses he any cruelty but when he hunts the hare, nor subtlety, but when he sets snares for the snite, or pitfalls for the blackbird; nor oppression, but when in the month of July, he goes to the next river, and shears his sheep. He allows of honest pastime, and thinks not the bones of the dead anything bruised, or the worse for it, though the lasses dance in the churchyard after evensong. Rock Monday[3], and the wake in summer, shrovings[4], the watchful catches on Christmas Eve, hoky, or seed cake, these he yearly keeps, yet holds them no relics of popery. He is not so inquisitive after news derived from the privy closet, when the finding an eyrie of hawks in his own ground, or the foaling of a colt come of a good strain, are tidings more pleasant, more profitable. He is lord paramount within himself, though he hold by never so mean a tenure; and dies the more contentedly (though he leave his heir young) in regard he leaves him not liable to a covetous guardian. Lastly, to end him, he cares not when his end comes, he needs not fear his audit, for his *quietus* is in heaven.

1616

[2]Fine dress.

[3]The Monday following Twelfth-night, when spinning was resumed after the Christmas holidays.
[4]The festivities attendant on Shrove Tuesday.

ROBERT HERRICK (1591-1674)

Robert Herrick was the leading disciple of Ben Jonson and one of the most delightful lyricists of the seventeenth century. He was born in London, the son of a wealthy goldsmith, and was himself a goldsmith's apprentice from 1607 to 1613. In that latter year he entered Cambridge University, receiving his B.A. in 1617 and his M.A. in 1620. He took holy orders, and in 1629 became vicar of Dean Prior in Devonshire. He remained in Dean Prior until he was ejected by the Puritans in 1647; lived in London until the Restoration; returned to his vicarage in 1662 and died there, in the same year as Milton, 1674.

Herrick's *Noble Numbers* was published in 1647, his *Hesperides* in 1648. The qualities and subject-matter of his verse are well summed up in the prefatory poem or "Argument" of *Hesperides;* he is a poet of the pleasant aspects of nature, of the pleasant months of the year, of the happy festivals of rural life, of the joys of innocent love, of the delights of fantasy and fairyland, and of the more comforting elements of religion. He lacks Jonson's intellectual range and social realism, but has his master's neatness and polish. And he has a dawn-like freshness all his own.

The Argument of His Book

I sing of brooks, of blossoms, birds, and bowers,
Of April, May, of June and July flowers.
I sing of May-poles, hock-carts, wassails, wakes,
Of bridegrooms, brides, and of their bridal-cakes.
I write of youth, of love, and have access
By these to sing of cleanly wantonness.
I sing of dews, of rains, and piece by piece
Of balm, of oil, of spice, and ambergris.
I sing of times trans-shifting; and I write
How roses first came red, and lilies white.
I write of groves, of twilights, and I sing
The court of Mab, and of the fairy king.
I write of Hell; I sing (and ever shall)
Of Heaven, and hope to have it after all.

1648

Delight in Disorder

A sweet disorder in the dress
Kindles in clothes a wantonness;
A lawn about the shoulders thrown
Into a fine distraction;
An erring lace, which here and there
Enthrals the crimson stomacher;
A cuff neglectful, and thereby
Ribands to flow confusedly;
A winning wave, deserving note,
In the tempestuous petticoat;
A careless shoe-string, in whose tie
I see a wild civility;—
Do more bewitch me, than when art
Is too precise in every part.

1648

Corinna's Going A-Maying

Get up, get up for shame, the blooming morn
Upon her wings presents the god unshorn.
  See how Aurora throws her fair
  Fresh-quilted colours through the air:
  Get up, sweet slug-a-bed, and see
  The dew bespangling herb and tree.
Each flower has wept and bow'd toward the east
Above an hour since: yet you not drest,
  Nay! not so much as out of bed?
  When all the birds have matins said   10
  And sung their thankful hymns, 'tis sin,
  Nay, profanation, to keep in,
Whenas a thousand virgins on this day
Spring, sooner than the lark, to fetch in May.

Rise and put on your foliage, and be seen
To come forth, like the spring-time, fresh and green,
  And sweet as Flora.   Take no care
  For jewels for your gown or hair:
  Fear not; the leaves will strew
  Gems in abundance upon you: 20
Besides, the childhood of the day has kept,
Against you come, some orient pearls unwept;
  Come and receive them while the light
  Hangs on the dew-locks of the night:
  And Titan on the eastern hill
  Retires himself, or else stands still
Till you come forth.   Wash, dress, be brief in praying:
Few beads are best when once we go a-Maying.

Come, my Corinna, come; and, coming, mark
How each field turns a street, each street a park   30
  Made green and trimm'd with trees; see how
  Devotion gives each house a bough
  Or branch; each porch, each door ere this
  An ark, a tabernacle is,
Made up of white-thorn, neatly interwove;
As if here were those cooler shades of love.
  Can such delights be in the street
  And open fields and we not see't?
  Come, we'll abroad; and let's obey
  The proclamation made for May: 40

And sin no more, as we have done, by staying;
But, my Corinna, come, let's go a-Maying.

There's not a budding boy or girl this day
But is got up, and gone to bring in May.
   A deal of youth, ere this, is come
   Back, and with white-thorn laden, home.
   Some have despatch'd their cakes and cream
   Before that we have left to dream:
And some have wept, and woo'd, and plighted troth,
And chose their priest, ere we can cast off sloth: 50
   Many a green-gown has been given;
   Many a kiss, both odd and even:
   Many a glance too has been sent
   From out the eye, love's firmament;
Many a jest told of the keys betraying
This night, and locks pick'd, yet we're not a-Maying.

Come, let us go while we are in our prime;
And take the harmless folly of the time.
   We shall grow old apace, and die
   Before we know our liberty.   60
   Our life is short, and our days run
   As fast away as does the sun;
And as a vapour, or a drop of rain,
Once lost, can ne'er be found again,
   So when or you or I are made
   A fable, song, or fleeting shade,
   All love, all liking, all delight
   Lies drown'd with us in endless night.
Then while time serves, and we are but decaying,
Come, my Corinna, come, let's go a-Maying.   70

                        1648

To the Virgins, to Make Much of Time

Gather ye rosebuds while ye may,
   Old Time is still a-flying;
And this same flower that smiles today,
   Tomorrow will be dying.

The glorious lamp of heaven, the Sun,
   The higher he's a-getting,
The sooner will his race be run,
   And nearer he's to setting.

That age is best which is the first,
   When youth and blood are warmer;
But being spent, the worse and worst
   Times still succeed the former.

Then be not coy, but use your time,
   And while ye may, go marry;
For having lost but once your prime,
   You may forever tarry.

                        1648

Another Grace for a Child

What God gives, and what we take,
'Tis a gift for Christ his sake:
Be the meal of beans and peas,
God be thank'd for those, and these:
Have we flesh, or have we fish,

All are fragments from His dish.
He His church save, and the king,
And our peace here, like a spring,
Make it ever flourishing.

1648

GEORGE HERBERT (1593-1633)

As Herrick was the chief of Jonson's disciples, Herbert was the chief of Donne's. And just as Herrick lacked his master's intellectual power but had a greater sweetness and freshness, so did Herbert lack Donne's tortured intensity and mental gymnastics but possess a clear, pure, devotional humility of his own.

Herbert was born at Montgomery on the Welsh border, April 3, 1593, of a distinguished land-owning family. His father died when the boy was four years old, and he was brought up by his mother, a woman famous for her intelligence, wit, and piety. Herbert was educated at Westminster School and Trinity College, Cambridge. He received his B.A. in 1613, was elected a fellow of his college in 1614, and was appointed University Orator in 1620. This latter post brought him into contact with the great, and he began to spend a lot of time at the court of James I. After the death of his patron, James,

in 1625, he retired to the country, decided to enter the Church, and after some years of hesitation was inducted as rector of Bemerton in April, 1630. During the last three years of his life he devoted himself to the labours of a country parson with exemplary zeal and fidelity. He died on March 1, 1633.

Herbert's chief works were a book of verse, *The Temple*, published just after his death, and a book of prose, *A Priest to the Temple*, which is a manual for the country parson. His poems reflect his struggle to choose between academic preferment, court favour, and God's service, but the struggle is less agonizing than Donne's. His work is quieter, more relaxed, and more straightforward than his master's, but it has the same combination of strong feeling and logical thought, similarly surprising metaphors and similes, and a similarly experimental attitude towards metre.

The Collar

I struck the board, and cried, "No more!
    I will abroad.
What! shall I ever sigh and pine?
My lines and life are free; free as the road,
    Loose as the wind, as large as store.
        Shall I be still in suit?
Have I no harvest but a thorn
To let me blood, and not restore
What I have lost with cordial fruit?
        Sure there was wine
Before my sighs did dry it; there was corn
    Before my tears did drown it.
    Is the year only lost to me?
        Have I no bays to crown it,

10

No flowers, no garlands gay? all blasted?
    All wasted?
Not so, my heart; but there is fruit,
    And thou hast hands.
Recover all thy sigh-blown age
On double pleasures; leave thy cold dispute   20
Of what is fit and not; forsake thy cage,
    Thy rope of sands
Which petty thoughts have made; and made to thee
    Good cable, to enforce and draw,
      And be thy law,
While thou didst wink and wouldst not see.
    Away! take heed;
    I will abroad.
Call in thy death's-head there, tie up thy fears:
    He that forbears   30
    To suit and serve his need
    Deserves his load."
But as I rav'd, and grew more fierce and wild
    At every word,
Me thoughts I heard one calling, "Child";
    And I replied, "My Lord."

        1633

The Pulley

    When God at first made man,
Having a glass of blessings standing by,
    "Let us," said He, "pour on him all we can;
Let the world's riches, which dispersed lie,
    Contract into a span."

    So strength first made a way;
Then beauty flow'd, then wisdom, honour, pleasure.
    When almost all was out, God made a stay,
Perceiving that, alone of all His treasure,
    Rest in the bottom lay.   10

    "For if I should," said He,
"Bestow this jewel also on My creature,
    He would adore My gifts instead of Me,
And rest in Nature, not the God of Nature:
    So both should losers be.

"Yet let him keep the rest,
But keep them with repining restlessness:
Let him be rich and weary, that at least,
If goodness lead him not, yet weariness
May toss him to My breast."   20

1633

The Elixir

Teach me, my God and King,
In all things thee to see,
And what I do in anything
To do it as for thee.

Not rudely, as a beast,
To run into an action;
But still to make thee prepossest,
And give it his perfection.

A man that looks on glass,
On it may stay his eye;   10
Or if he pleaseth, through it pass,
And then the heav'n espy.

All may of thee partake:
Nothing can be so mean,
Which with his tincture—"for thy
sake"—
Will not grow bright and clean.

A servant with this clause
Makes drudgery divine:
Who sweeps a room as for thy laws,
Makes that and th' action fine.   20

This is the famous stone
That turneth all to gold;
For that which God doth touch and own
Cannot for less be told.

1633

IZAAK WALTON (1593-1683)

Izaak Walton was born in Stafford of yeoman stock, was apprenticed to an ironmonger in London, and became a freeman of that company in 1618. His literary interests were probably aroused by his friendships with Ben Jonson, Michael Drayton, and John Donne, the latter of whom was for some years vicar of St. Dunstan's Church, near Walton's home. An Anglican and a Royalist, he was too old to fight for the King in the Civil War, but he was entrusted with some of the crown jewels after Charles' defeat at the battle of Worcester in 1651. He lived quietly in London for the remainder of his long life, taking little part in the violent upheavals of the Commonwealth and Restoration regimes.

Walton's most famous work is *The Compleat Angler, or the Contemplative Man's Recreation* (1653), the most delightful of all books on the art of fishing. His first literary work, however, was the *Life of Dr. John Donne*, which first appeared as an introduction to an edition of Donne's sermons published in 1640. He also wrote biographies of Sir Henry Wotton (1651), Richard Hooker (1665), George Herbert (1670), and Robert Sanderson (1678).

Walton's biographies are the most readable today of all those produced in the seventeenth century. They are more formal than his *Compleat Angler*, but they are enlivened with anecdotes and with touches of humour. He is not always accurate, but he is always honest. The chief defect of his biographies is that his own dislike of controversy led him to play down the controversial and less pleasant aspects of his subjects' characters. The Donne of his portrait is a less tempestuous and agonized figure than other sources of information, including Donne's own writings, lead us to envisage. The stress is on Donne the scholar and preacher; Donne the rebel and cynic is scarcely in evidence.

FROM The Life of Dr. John Donne

Master John Donne was born in London in the year 1573[1], of good and virtuous parents; and though his own learning and other multiplied merits may justly appear sufficient to dignify both himself and his posterity, yet the reader may be pleased to know that his father was masculinely and lineally descended from a very ancient family in Wales, where many of his name now live that deserve and have great reputation in that country.

By his mother he was descended of the family of the famous and learned Sir Thomas More, sometime Lord Chancellor of England, as also from that worthy and laborious Judge Rastall, who left posterity the vast statutes of the law of this nation most exactly abridged.

He had his first breeding in his father's house, where a private tutor had the care of him until the tenth year of his age; and in his eleventh year was sent to the University of Oxford, having at that time a good command both of the French and Latin tongue. This and some other of his remarkable abilities made one then give this censure of him: "That this age had brought forth another Picus Mirandola," of whom story says, "That he was rather born, than made wise by study."

There he remained for some years in Hart Hall, having for the advancement of his studies tutors of several sciences to attend and instruct him, till time made him capable and his learning expressed in public exercises declared him worthy to receive his first degree in the schools; which he forebore by advice from his friends, who being for their religion of the Romish persuasion were conscionably

averse to some parts of the oath that is always tendered at those times and not to be refused by those that expect the titulary honour of their studies.

About the fourteenth year of his age he was transplanted from Oxford to Cambridge; where, that he might receive nourishment from both soils, he stayed till his seventeenth year; all which time he was a most laborious student, often changing his studies but endeavouring to take no degree for the reasons formerly mentioned.

About the seventeenth year of his age he was removed to London and then admitted into Lincoln's Inn with an intent to study the law; where he gave great testimonies of his wit, his learning, and of his improvement in that profession which never served him for other use than an ornament and self-satisfaction.

His father died before his admission into this society and being a merchant left him his portion in money (it was £3000). His mother and those to whose care he was committed were watchful to improve his knowledge and to that end appointed him tutors both in the mathematics and in all the other liberal sciences to attend him. But with these arts they were advised to instil into him particular principles of the Romish Church; of which those tutors professed (though secretly) themselves to be members.

They had almost obliged him to their faith, having for their advantage, besides many opportunities, the example of his dear and pious parents, which was a most powerful persuasion and did work much upon him, as he professeth in his preface to his Pseudo-Martyr . . .

[1]Modern scholars put the date back to 1571.

He was now entered into the eighteenth year of his age; and at that time had betrothed himself to no religion that might give him any other denomination than a Christian. And reason and piety had both persuaded him that there could be no such sin as schism if an adherence to some visible church were not necessary.

About the nineteenth year of his age he, being then unresolved what religion to adhere to and considering how much it concerned his soul to choose the most orthodox, did therefore, though his youth and health promised him a long life, to rectify all scruples that might concern that, presently lay aside all study of the law and of all other sciences that might give him a denomination; and begun seriously to survey, and consider the body of divinity as it was then controverted betwixt the Reformed and the Roman Church. And as "God's blessed Spirit did then awaken him to the search and in that industry did never forsake him" — they be his own words — "so he calls the same Holy Spirit to witness this protestation; that in that disquisition and search he proceeded with humility and diffidence in himself, and by that which he took to be the safest way, namely, frequent prayers and an indifferent affection to both parties"; and indeed, truth had too much light about her to be hid from so sharp an enquirer; and he had too much ingenuity not to acknowledge he had found her.

Being to undertake this search, he believed the Cardinal Bellarmine to be the best defender of the Roman cause and therefore betook himself to the examination of his reasons. The cause was weighty, and wilful delays had been inexcusable both towards God and his own conscience; he therefore proceeded in this search with all moderate haste, and about the twentieth year of his age did show the then Dean of Gloucester, whose name my memory hath now lost, all the cardinal's works marked with many weighty observations under his own hand; which words were bequeathed by him at his death as a legacy to a most dear friend.

About a year following he resolved to travel; and the Earl of Essex going first the Cadiz and after the Island voyages, the first *anno* 1596, the second 1597, he took the advantage of those opportunities, waited upon his lordship, and was an eye-witness of those happy and unhappy employments.

But he returned not back into England till he had stayed some years first in Italy and then in Spain, where he made many useful observations of those countries, their laws and manner of government, and returned perfect in their languages.

The time that he spent in Spain was at his first going into Italy designed for travelling to the Holy Land and for viewing Jerusalem and the sepulchre of our Saviour. But at his being in the furthest parts of Italy, the disappointment of company or of a safe convoy or the uncertainty of returns of money into those remote parts denied him that happiness; which he did often occasionally mention with a deploration.

Not long after his return into England, that exemplary pattern of gravity and wisdom, the Lord Ellesmere[2], then Keeper of the Great Seal and Lord Chancellor of England, taking notice of his learning, languages, and other abilities and much affecting his person and behaviour, took him to be his chief secretary, supposing

[2]Sir Thomas Egerton became Lord Ellesmere in 1603 after Donne had left his service.

and intending it to be an introduction to some more weighty employment in the state; for which, his lordship did often protest, he thought him very fit.

Nor did his lordship in this time of Master Donne's attendance upon him account him to be so much his servant as to forget he was his friend; and to testify it did always use him with much courtesy, appointing him a place at his own table, to which he esteemed his company and discourse to be a great ornament.

He continued that employment for the space of five years, being daily useful and not mercenary to his friends. During which time he—I dare not say unhappily —fell into such a liking as, with her approbation, increased into a love with a young gentlewoman that lived in that family who was niece to the Lady Ellesmere, and daughter to Sir George More, then Chancellor of the Garter and Lieutenant of the Tower.

Sir George had some intimation of it and, knowing prevention to be a great part of wisdom, did therefore remove her with much haste from that to his own house at Lothesley, in the County of Surrey; but too late, by reason of some faithful promises which were so interchangeably passed as never to be violated by either party.

These promises were only known to themselves, and the friends of both parties used much diligence and many arguments to kill or cool their affections to each other. But in vain; for love is a flattering mischief that hath denied aged and wise men a foresight of those evils that too often prove to be the children of that blind father, a passion, that carries us to commit errors with as much ease as whirlwinds remove feathers and begets in us an unwearied industry to the attain-

ment of what we desire. And such an industry did, notwithstanding much watchfulness against it, bring them secretly together—I forbear to tell the manner how—and at last to a marriage too without the allowance of those friends whose approbation always was and ever will be necessary to make even a virtuous love become lawful.

And that the knowledge of their marriage might not fall like an unexpected tempest on those that were unwilling to have it so and that pre-apprehensions might make it the less enormous when it was known, it was purposely whispered into the ears of many that it was so, yet by none that could affirm it. But to put a period to the jealousies of Sir George— doubt often begetting more restless thoughts than the certain knowledge of what we fear—the news was in favour to Mr. Donne and with his allowance made known to Sir George by his honourable friend and neighbour Henry, Earl of Northumberland. But it was to Sir George so immeasurably unwelcome and so transported him that as though his passion of anger and inconsideration might exceed theirs of love and error he presently engaged his sister, the Lady Ellesmere, to join with him to procure her lord to discharge Mr. Donne of the place he held under his lordship. This request was followed with violence; and though Sir George were remembered that errors might be overpunished and desired therefore to forbear till second considerations might clear some scruples, yet he became restless until his suit was granted and the punishment executed. And though the Lord Chancellor did not at Mr. Donne's dismission give him such a commendation as the great Emperor Charles the Fifth did of his secretary

Eraso, when he presented him to his son and successor, Philip the Second, saying, "That in his Eraso he gave to him a greater gift than all his estate and all the kingdoms which he then resigned to him"; yet the Lord Chancellor said, "He parted with a friend and such a secretary as was fitter to serve a king than a subject."

Immediately after his dismission from his service, he sent a sad letter to his wife to acquaint her with it; and after the subscription of his name writ

"John Donne, Anne Donne, Undone," and God knows it proved too true.

For this bitter physic of Mr. Donne's dismission was not strong enough to purge out all Sir George's choler; for he was not satisfied till Mr. Donne and his sometime compupil in Cambridge that married him, Samuel Brooke, who was after Doctor of Divinity, and Master of Trinity College, and his brother Mr. Christopher Brooke, sometime Mr. Donne's chamber-fellow in Lincoln's Inn, who gave Mr. Donne his wife and witnessed the marriage, were all committed to three several prisons.

Mr. Donne was first enlarged[3], who neither gave rest to his body or brain nor to any friend in whom he might hope to have an interest until he had procured an enlargement for his two imprisoned friends.

He was now at liberty; but his days were still cloudy, and being past these troubles, others did still multiply upon him; for his wife was, to her extreme sorrow, detained from him; and though with Jacob he endured not an hard service for her, yet he lost a good one and was forced to make good his title and to

get possession of her by a long and restless suit in law; which proved troublesome and sadly chargeable to him whose youth and travel and needless bounty had brought his estate into a narrow compass.

It is observed, and most truly, that silence and submission are charming qualities and work most upon passionate men; and it proved so with Sir George; for these and a general report of Mr. Donne's merits, together with his winning behaviour, which when it would entice had a strange kind of elegant irresistible art, these and time had so dispassionated Sir George that as the world had approved his daugher's choice so he also could not but see a more than ordinary merit in his new son. And this at last melted him into so much remorse—for love and anger are so like agues as to have hot and cold fits, and love in parents, though it may be quenched, yet is easily rekindled and expires not till death denies mankind a natural heat—that he laboured his son's restoration to his place, using to that end both his own and his sister's power to her lord; but with no success; for his answer was, "That though he was unfeignedly sorry for what he had done, yet it was inconsistent with his place and credit to discharge and readmit servants at the request of passionate petitioners."

Sir George's endeavour for Mr. Donne's readmission was by all means to be kept secret, for men do more naturally reluct for errors than submit to put on those blemishes that attend their visible acknowledgment. But however it was not long before Sir George appeared to be so far reconciled as to wish their happiness and not to deny them his parental blessing, but yet refused to contribute any

[3] I.e., given his release from prison.

means that might conduce to their livelihood.

Mr. Donne's estate was the greatest part spent in many and chargeable travels, books, and dear-bought experience; he out of all employment that might yield a support for himself and his wife, who had been curiously and plentifully educated; both their natures generous and accustomed to confer and not to receive courtesies; these and other considerations, but chiefly that his wife was to bear a part in his sufferings, surrounded him with many sad thoughts and some apparent apprehensions of want.

But his sorrows were lessened and his wants prevented by the seasonable courtesy of their noble kinsman, Sir Francis Wolley, of Pirford in Surrey, who entreated them to a cohabitation with him; where they remained with much freedom to themselves and equal content to him for some years; and as their charge increased—she had yearly a child —so did his love and bounty. . . .

1640

JOHN MILTON (1608-1674)

John Milton was the greatest poet of the mid-seventeenth century and, along with Chaucer and Shakespeare, one of the three greatest English writers of all time.

He was born in Bread Street, Cheapside, London, the son of a successful scrivener, and was educated at St. Paul's School and Christ's College, Cambridge (B.A., 1629, M.A., 1632). After leaving Cambridge he retired to his father's country estate at Horton in Buckinghamshire to prepare himself by study and meditation for his vocation as a poet. From 1637 to 1639 he travelled abroad, chiefly in Italy, and on his return began to keep a private school. In 1641 he began to publish a series of tracts against episcopacy, and in 1642 he married Mary Powell, daughter of Royalist parents; she left him shortly after the wedding and did not return for three years. He continued to teach and write Puritan pamphlets during the Civil War, and after the execution of Charles I in 1649 he was appointed Latin Secretary to the new Council of State. In a few years he became blind, and had to have assistance in his official duties, one of his assistants being the poet Andrew Marvell. His first wife died in 1652, leaving three daughters, and in 1656 he married Catharine Woodcock, who died two years later. He remained Latin Secretary until the Restoration, when as a leading Puritan he was arrested and heavily fined. On his release he set to work on the three great poems of his maturity:

Paradise Lost (1667), *Paradise Regained* (1671) and *Samson Agonistes* (1671). He had married his third wife, Elizabeth Minshull, in 1662, and with her and his daughters he lived quietly in London until his death in 1674. He was buried beside his father in St. Giles', Cripplegate.

Milton's literary career may be subdivided into three fairly distinct periods: the University and Horton period, from 1623 to 1637, in which he wrote such relatively brief poems as the "Ode on Christ's Nativity," "L'Allegro" and "Il Penseroso," "Comus" and "Lycidas"; the Civil War and Commonwealth years, from 1639 to 1660, in which he wrote mainly prose pamphlets and a few sonnets; and his final period, 1660 to 1674, in which he wrote his three long poems and some miscellaneous prose.

Milton was a product of both the Reformation and the Renaissance, and tried to combine the best features of those two great movements in his view of life and in his writing. To the Reformation tradition he owed his deep knowledge of the Bible, of theology, and of Church history, his moral seriousness, and his concern for liberty of conscience; to the Renaissance tradition he owed his intimate knowledge of the Greek and Latin classics, his interest in contemporary science, his delight in natural beauty, his devotion to the arts, and his belief in the potentialities of the individual human being. He was far from being the sour, dour fellow that we are inclined to picture as the conventional

Puritan: he was a lover of life, learning, and liberty. His great positive conviction was the supreme importance of individual liberty, of the right of every individual to search freely for the truth.

Milton was both a profound thinker and a skilled craftsman. His early poems were written mainly in rhyme, and show influences of Spenser, Jonson, and even, to a slight degree, of Donne; he gradually mastered a style all his own, a style marked by majesty and controlled splendour; in the three great poems of his maturity he used blank verse with increasing freedom and flexibility. His prose has a similar amplitude and power.

Milton's influence has been enduring. In the eighteenth century poets such as James Thomson and William Blake were deeply in his debt; in the early nineteenth century his influence was apparent on Wordsworth, Shelley, and Keats; in the Victorian period he influenced Tennyson and Arnold. He has always been regarded as the classic exponent of the English tradition of liberty, and his *Areopagitica* as the classic defence of the principle of freedom of the press.

On Shakespeare

What needs my Shakespeare for his honored bones
The labor of an age in pilèd stones?[1]
Or that his hallowed relics should be hid
Under a star-ypointing pyramid?
Dear son of memory,[2] great heir of fame,
What need'st thou such weak witness of thy name?
Thou in our wonder and astonishment
Hast built thyself a livelong monument.
For whilst, to the shame of slow-endeavoring art,
Thy easy numbers flow, and that each heart   10
Hath from the leaves of thy unvalued[3] book
Those Delphic[4] lines with deep impression took,
Then thou, our fancy of itself bereaving,
Dost make us marble with too much conceiving,[5]
And so sepulchred[6] in such pomp dost lie
That kings for such a tomb would wish to die.

1632

[1]During Milton's time, many people complained that Shakespeare's bones were buried in lowly Stratford, without an impressive monument. Milton first answers this complaint, then describes Shakespeare's true eternal monuments.
[2]In Greek mythology, Memory (the goddess Mnemosyne) is the mother of the Muses, inspirer of poets, and, as Milton suggests, by association the mother of poets as well.
[3]Beyond a fixed value.
[4]Inspired, prophetic; relating to the ancient oracle at Delphi, in Greek mythology.
[5]We all become the monuments of Shakespeare's tomb as, enchanted and motionless, we read his book.
[6]Put in a tomb.

Lycidas

In This Monody the Author Bewails a Learned Friend, Edward King, Unfortunately Drowned in His Passage from Chester on the Irish Seas, 1637; and, by Occasion, Foretells the Ruin of Our Corrupted Clergy, Then in Their Height.

Yet once more[1], O ye laurels, and once more,
Ye myrtles brown, with ivy[2] never sere,
I come to pluck your berries harsh and crude,
And with forced fingers rude
Shatter your leaves before the mellowing year.
Bitter constraint, and sad occasion dear
Compels me to disturb your season due;
For Lycidas[3] is dead, dead ere his prime,
Young Lycidas, and hath not left his peer.
Who would not sing for Lycidas? he well knew   10
Himself to sing, and build the lofty rhyme.
He must not float upon his watery bier
Unwept, and welter[4] to the parching wind,
Without the meed[5] of some melodious tear[6].
Begin, then, Sisters[7] of the sacred well
That from beneath the seat of Jove doth spring;
Begin, and somewhat loudly sweep the string.
Hence with denial vain and coy excuse.
So may some gentle Muse
With lucky words favour my destined urn,   20
And as he passes turn,
And bid fair peace be to my sable shroud!
For we were nursed upon the self-same hill,
Fed the same flock, by fountain, shade, and rill.
Together both, ere the high lawns appeared
Under the opening eyelids of the Morn,
We drove a-field, and both together heard
What time the gray-fly winds her sultry horn,
Battening our flocks with the fresh dews of night,
Oft till the star that rose, at evening, bright   30
Towards heaven's descent had sloped his westering wheel.
Meanwhile the rural ditties were not mute;
Tempered to the oaten flute,

[1]An interval of four years separates "Lycidas" from "Comus," Milton's most ambitious poem before "Lycidas."
[2]*laurels . . . myrtles . . . ivy.* Evergreens with which poets were traditionally crowned.
[3]A typical shepherd's name in the pastoral elegies.
[4]Toss about. King's body was never recovered.   [5]Tribute.
[6]*melodious tear.* A conventional figure for elegiac verse.
[7]The Muses, to whom certain springs (wells) were sacred.

Rough Satyrs danced, and Fauns with cloven heel
From the glad sound would not be absent long;
And old Damoetas[8] loved to hear our song.
    But, oh! the heavy change, now thou art gone,
Now thou art gone and never must return!
Thee, Shepherd, thee the woods and desert caves,
With wild thyme and the gadding[9] vine o'ergrown,   40
And all their echoes, mourn.
The willows, and the hazel copses green,
Shall now no more be seen
Fanning their joyous leaves to thy soft lays.
As killing as the canker[10] to the rose,
Or taint-worm to the weanling herds that graze,
Or frost to flowers, that their gay wardrobe wear,
When first the white-thorn blows;
Such, Lycidas, thy loss to shepherd's ear.
    Where were ye, Nymphs, when the remorseless deep   50
Closed o'er the head of your loved Lycidas?
For neither were ye playing on the steep
Where your old bards, the famous Druids[11], lie,
Nor on the shaggy top of Mona[12] high,
Nor yet where Deva[13] spreads her wizard stream.
Ay me! I fondly[14] dream
"Had ye been there," . . . for what could that have done?
What could the Muse[15] herself that Orpheus bore,
The Muse herself, for her enchanting son,
Whom universal nature did lament,   60
When, by the rout[16] that made the hideous roar,
His gory visage down the stream was sent,
Down the swift Hebrus to the Lesbian shore?
    Alas! what boots it with uncessant care
To tend the homely, slighted, shepherd's trade,
And strictly meditate the thankless Muse?
Were it not better done, as others use,
To sport with Amaryllis[17] in the shade,
Or with the tangles of Neaera's hair?
Fame is the spur that the clear spirit doth raise   70
(That last infirmity of noble mind)

[8]Another type name from pastoral poetry. Possibly the reference is to some tutor at the university.
[9]Straggling.   [10]The canker worm.
[11]The minstrel-priests of the ancient Celts of Britain.
[12]The Roman name for the isle of Anglesey, off the Welsh coast.
[13]The river Dee, which flows between England and Wales into the Irish Sea and has magical
   associations.   [14]Foolishly.   [15]Calliope, the Muse of epic poetry.
[16]The group of frenzied women of Thrace who tore Orpheus in pieces. See Ovid: *Metamorphoses*,
   Book XI, ll. 1-60.   [17]*Amaryllis . . . Neaera.* Typical names of maidens in pastoral poetry.

To scorn delights, and live laborious days;
But the fair guerdon when we hope to find,
And think to burst out into sudden blaze,
Comes the blind Fury[18] with the abhorrèd shears,
And slits the thin-spun life. "But not the praise,"
Phoebus[19] replied, and touched my trembling ears[20]:
"Fame is no plant that grows on mortal soil,
Nor in the glistering foil[21]
Set off to the world, nor in broad rumour lies,   80
But lives and spreads aloft by those pure eyes,
And perfect witness of all-judging Jove;
As he pronounces lastly on each deed,
Of so much fame in heaven expect thy meed."

 O fountain Arethuse[22], and thou honoured flood,
Smooth-sliding Mincius, crowned with vocal reeds,
That strain I heard was of a higher mood.
But now my oat[23] proceeds,
And listens to the Herald of the Sea[24]
That came in Neptune's plea.   90
He asked the waves, and asked the felon winds,
What hard mishap hath doomed this gentle swain?
And questioned every gust of rugged wings
That blows from off each beakèd promontory.
They knew not of his story;
And sage Hippotades[25] their answer brings;
That not a blast was from his dungeon strayed,
The air was calm, and on the level brine
Sleek Panope[26] with all her sisters played.
It was that fatal and perfidious bark,   100
Built in the eclipse[27], and rigged with curses dark,
That sunk so low that sacred head of thine.

 Next, Camus[28], reverend sire, went footing slow,
His mantle hairy, and his bonnet sedge,
Inwrought with figures dim, and on the edge

---

[18]*blind Fury.* It is Atropos, one of the three Fates in classical mythology, who cuts the thread of life
 Milton presumably changed "Fate" to "Fury" to intensify the effect of the line.
[19]Apollo, god of poetic inspiration.
[20]*touched my trembling ears.* A Virgilian figure meaning to recall something to one's mind.
[21]Glittering gold or silver leaf, placed under gems to make them shine more brilliantly.
[22]*fountain Arethuse . . . Mincius.* Arethusa, a spring in Sicily, the country of Theocritus, represents the
 Greek tradition of pastoral poetry, as Mincius, the river near which Virgil was born, does the
 Latin. [23]The shepherd's pipe of oat straw.
[24]*Herald of the Sea.* Triton, Neptune's agent who comes to plead his master's innocence.
[25]Aeolus (son of Hippotes), god of the winds. [26]One of the fifty Nereids, or sea nymphs.
[27]The proverbial omen of ill fortune.
[28]A personification of the river Cam, which flows through Cambridge.

Like to that sanguine[29] flower inscribed with woe.
"Ah! who hath reft[30]," quoth he, "my dearest pledge[31]?"
Last came, and last did go,
The Pilot[32] of the Galilean Lake;
Two massy keys he bore of metals twain   110
(The golden opes, the iron shuts amain[33]).
He shook his mitred locks, and stern bespake:—
"How well could I have spared for thee, young swain,
Enow of such as, for their bellies' sake,
Creep, and intrude, and climb into the fold!
Of other care they little reckoning make
Than how to scramble at the shearers' feast,
And shove away the worthy bidden guest.
Blind mouths! that scarce themselves know how to hold
A sheep-hook, or have learnt aught else the least   120
That to the faithful herdman's art belongs!
What recks it them? What need they? They are sped;
And, when they list, their lean and flashy songs
Grate on their scrannel[34] pipes of wretched straw;
The hungry sheep look up, and are not fed,
But, swoln with wind and the rank mist they draw,
Rot inwardly, and foul contagion spread;
Besides what the grim wolf[35] with privy paw[36]
Daily devours apace, and nothing said.
But that two-handed engine[37] at the door   130
Stands ready to smite once, and smite no more."
     Return, Alpheus[38]; the dread voice is past
That shrunk thy streams; return, Sicilian Muse,
And call the vales, and bid them hither cast
Their bells and flowerets of a thousand hues.
Ye valleys low, where the mild whispers use
Of shades, and wanton winds, and gushing brooks,
On whose fresh lap the swart star[39] sparely looks,

---

[29]Literally, "bloody." The flower referred to is the purple hyacinth, named for the youth Hyacinthus, slain by Apollo. The hyacinth was reputed to be marked *ai, ai* (woe! woe!).
[30]Snatched away.   [31]Child.
[32]St. Peter, the legendary keeper of the keys of heaven. See Matthew 16:19.
[33]With force.   [34]Thin, harsh.   [35]The Roman Catholic Church?
[36]*privy paw.* Secret proselytizing.
[37]*that two-handed engine.* The exact meaning of this phrase has been widely debated. Milton obviously believes that some agency or group will soon bring about reform, but whether he meant to suggest that the two Houses of Parliament would do the smiting, or that the smiting would be done by a heavy axe or sword, is not clear.
[38]A river whose god was the lover of Arethusa, referred to in 1. 85. The invocation to Alpheus and the Sicilian Muse signifies Milton's return to the pastoral strain after the digression on the corruption of the Church.
[39]The Dog Star, Sirius, whose baleful influence blasts or makes "swart" the summer's flowers.

Throw hither all your quaint enamelled eyes,
That on the green turf suck the honeyed showers,   140
And purple all the ground with vernal flowers.
Bring the rathe primrose that forsaken dies,
The tufted crow-toe, and pale jessamine,
The white pink, and the pansy freaked with jet,
The glowing violet,
The musk rose, and the well-attired woodbine,
With cowslips wan that hang the pensive head,
And every flower that sad embroidery wears;
Bid amaranthus all his beauty shed,
And daffadillies fill their cups with tears,   150
To strew the laureate hearse where Lycid lies.
For so, to interpose a little ease,
Let our frail thoughts dally with false surmise.
Ay me! whilst thee the shores and sounding seas
Wash far away, where'er thy bones are hurled;
Whether beyond the stormy Hebrides,
Where thou perhaps under the whelming tide
Visit'st the bottom of the monstrous world;
Or whether thou, to our moist vows denied,
Sleep'st by the fable of Bellerus[40] old,   160
Where the great Vision of the guarded mount[41]
Looks toward Namancos and Bayona's hold[42].
Look homeward[43], Angel, now, and melt with ruth:
And, O ye dolphins, waft the hapless youth.
　　Weep no more, woeful shepherds, weep no more,
For Lycidas, your sorrow, is not dead,
Sunk though he be beneath the watery floor.
So sinks the day-star[44] in the ocean bed,
And yet anon repairs his drooping head,
And tricks his beams, and with new-spangled ore   170
Flames in the forehead of the morning sky:
So Lycidas sunk low, but mounted high,
Through the dear might of Him that walked the waves,
Where, other groves and other streams along,
With nectar pure his oozy locks he laves,
And hears the unexpressive nuptial song,
In the blest kingdoms meek of joy and love.
There entertain him all the Saints above,

[40]The abode of the fabulous Bellerus—Land's End, the southwestern extremity of England.
[41]St. Michael's Mount in Cornwall, under the protection of the sword of St. Michael the Archangel.
[42]*Namancos and Bayona's hold.* Stronghold in Spain.
[43]*Look homeward.* Be on guard against internal enemies and dangers.
[44]The sun.

In solemn troops, and sweet societies,
That sing, and singing in their glory move,   180
And wipe the tears for ever from his eyes.
Now, Lycidas, the shepherds weep no more;
Henceforth thou art the Genius[45] of the shore,
In thy large recompense, and shalt be good
To all that wander in that perilous flood.

Thus sang the uncouth swain to the oaks and rills,
While the still morn went out with sandals gray:
He touched the tender stops of various quills,
With eager thought warbling his Doric lay:
And now the sun had stretched out all the hills,   190
And now was dropt into the western bay;
At last he rose, and twitched his mantle blue:
To-morrow to fresh woods, and pastures new.

[45]Guardian spirit.
                                                        1638

On His Having Arrived at the Age of Twenty-three [1]

How soon hath Time, the subtle thief of youth,
Stolen on his wing my three and twentieth year!
My hasting days fly on with full career,[2]
But my late spring no bud or blossom show'th.
Perhaps my semblance might deceive the truth,
That I to manhood am arrived so near,
And inward ripeness doth much less appear,
That some more timely-happy spirits[3] endu'th.[4]
Yet be it less or more, or soon or slow,
It shall be still[5] in strictest measure even[6]   10
To that same lot, however mean or high,
Toward which Time leads me, and the will of Heaven;
All is, if I have grace to use it so,
As ever in my great Taskmaster's eye.[7]
1629-1632   1645

[1]This sonnet was contained in a letter of December 1632, in which Milton complained to a friend of
    his own lack of accomplishment.
[2]Speed.
[3]Those who have matured as one would normally expect.
[4]Invest.
[5]Always.
[6]Level, equivalent.
[7]God, the great Taskmaster, foresees all things; I must learn to use my talents (have "inward ripe-
    ness") in the way that he wishes.

On the Late Massacre in Piemont[1]

Avenge, O Lord, thy slaughter'd saints, whose bones
   Lie scatter'd on the Alpine mountains cold,
   Ev'n them who kept thy truth so pure of old,
   When all our fathers worshipp'd stocks and stones,
Forget not: in thy book record their groans
   Who were thy sheep and in their ancient fold
   Slain by the bloody Piemontese that roll'd
   Mother with infant down the rocks.   Their moans
The vales redoubl'd to the hills, and they
   To heav'n.   Their martyr'd blood and ashes sow
O'er all th' Italian fields where still doth sway
The triple tyrant; that from these may grow
   A hundred-fold, who having learnt thy way
   Early may fly the Babylonian woe.
1655   1673

[1]The Waldenses, a Protestant sect in northern Italy, were massacred in April, 1655.

On His Blindness[1]

When I consider how my light is spent,
   Ere half my days, in this dark world and wide,
   And that one talent which is death to hide,
   Lodg'd with me useless, though my soul more bent
To serve therewith my Maker, and present
   My true account, lest he returning chide,
   "Doth God exact day-labour, light denied?"
   I fondly ask.   But Patience, to prevent
That murmur, soon replies, "God doth not need
   Either man's work or his own gifts; who best
   Bear his mild yoke, they serve him best; his state
Is kingly; thousands at his bidding speed
   And post o'er land and ocean without rest:
   They also serve who only stand and wait."
1655?   1673

[1]Milton became totally blind in 1651.

To Mr. Lawrence[1]

Lawrence, of virtuous father virtuous son,
   Now that the fields are dank, and ways are mire,

[1]Edward Lawrence (1633-1679), son of the president of Cromwell's Council of State.

Where shall we sometimes meet, and by the fire
Help waste a sullen day; what may be won
From the hard season gaining?   Time will run
On smoother, till Favonius re-inspire
The frozen earth, and clothe in fresh attire
The lily and rose, that neither sow'd nor spun.
What neat repast shall feast us, light and choice,   90
Of Attic taste, with wine, whence we may rise
To hear the lute well touch'd, or artful voice
Warble immortal notes and Tuscan air?
He who of those delights can judge, and spare
To interpose them oft, is not unwise.

1655   1673

FROM Areopagitica[1]

. . . I deny not but that it is of greatest concernment in the church and commonwealth to have a vigilant eye how books demean themselves, as well as men, and thereafter to confine, imprison, and do sharpest justice on them as malefactors. For books are not absolutely dead things, but do contain a potency of life in them to be as active as that soul was whose progeny they are; nay, they do preserve as in a vial the purest efficacy and extraction of that living intellect that bred them. I know they are as lively, and as vigorously productive, as those fabulous dragon's teeth; and being sown up and down, may chance to spring up armed men. And yet, on the other hand, unless wariness be used, as good almost kill a man as kill a good book: who kills a man kills a reasonable creature, God's image; but he who destroys a good book, kills reason itself, kills the image of God, as it were, in the eye. Many a man lives a burden to the earth; but a good book is the precious life-blood of a master spirit embalmed and treasured up on purpose to a life beyond life. 'Tis true, no age can restore a life, whereof, perhaps, there is no great loss; and revolutions of ages do not oft recover the loss of a rejected truth, for the want of which whole nations fare the worse. We should be wary, therefore, what persecution we raise against the living labours of public men, how we spill that seasoned life of man preserved and stored up in books; since we see a kind of homicide may be thus committed, sometimes a martyrdom; and if it extend to the whole impression, a kind of massacre, whereof the execution ends not in the slaying of an elemental life, but strikes at that ethereal and fifth essence, the breath of reason itself, slays an immortality rather than a life. . . .

Good and evil we know in the field of this world grow up together almost inseparably; and the knowledge of good is so involved and interwoven with the knowledge of evil, and in so many cunning resemblances hardly to be discerned, that those confused seeds which

[1] The title is taken from an oration delivered by Isocrates to the Areopagus, a selected group of wise men who acted as a court in ancient Athens.

were imposed on Psyche as an incessant labour to cull out and sort asunder, were not more intermixed. It was from out the rind of one apple tasted that the knowledge of good and evil, as two twins cleaving together, leaped forth into the world. And perhaps this is that doom which Adam fell into of knowing good and evil, that is to say, of knowing good by evil. As therefore the state of man now is, what wisdom can there be to choose, what continence to forbear, without the knowledge of evil? He that can apprehend and consider vice with all her baits and seeming pleasures, and yet abstain, and yet distinguish, and yet prefer that which is truly better, he is the true warfaring Christian. I cannot praise a fugitive and cloistered virtue, unexercised and unbreathed, that never sallies out and sees her adversary, but slinks out of the race where that immortal garland is to be run for, not without dust and heat. Assuredly we bring not innocence into the world, we bring impurity much rather; that which purifies us is trial, and trial is by what is contrary. That virtue therefore which is but a youngling in the conemtplation of evil, and knows not the utmost that vice promises to her followers, and rejects it, is but a blank virtue, not a pure; her whiteness is but an excremental whiteness, which was the reason why our sage and serious poet Spenser, whom I dare be known to think a better teacher than Scotus or Aquinas, describing true temperance under the person of Guyon, brings him in with his palmer through the cave of Mammon and the bower of earthly bliss, that he might see and know, and yet abstain. Since therefore the knowledge and survey of vice is in this world so necessary to the constituting of human virtue, and the scanning of error to the confirmation of truth, how can we more safely, and with less danger, scout into the regions of sin and falsity than by reading all manner of tractates and hearing all manner of reason? And this is the benefit which may be had of books promiscuously read. . . .

1644

ANDREW MARVELL (1621-1678)

Andrew Marvell's poetry is a unique combination of metaphysical wit and sensuous delight in nature and in love. His "To His Coy Mistress" is considered by many critics to be the most passionate and convincing love lyric in English, and his "The Garden" combines detailed observation with a sort of mystical ecstasy.

Marvell was born at Winestead near Hull, in north-eastern England, and educated at Hull Grammar School (of which his father was headmaster) and at Trinity College, Cambridge (B.A., 1639). After a prolonged Continental tour, Marvell in 1650 became tutor to the daughter of Lord Fairfax at the latter's beautiful country estate at Nun Appleton, Yorkshire. It was at this estate that he wrote many of his poems about gardens and country life. In 1653 he became tutor to Oliver Cromwell's ward, William Dutton, and in 1657 he was appointed assistant to John Milton in the Latin Secretaryship. In 1659 Marvell was elected Member of Parliament for Hull, and held the seat until his death in 1678.

An opponent of the Restoration, and a severe critic of Charles II and his ministers, Marvell wrote a number of political satires in his later life, but he is chiefly remembered for his poems on love and nature. His poems did not appear in book form until after his death.

The Garden

How vainly men themselves amaze
To win the palm, the oak, or bays,
And their incessant labours see
Crowned from some single herb, or tree,
Whose short and narrow-vergèd shade
Does prudently their toils upbraid;
While all flowers and all trees do close
To weave the garlands of repose!

Fair Quiet, have I found thee here,
And Innocence, thy sister dear?   10
Mistaken long, I sought you then
In busy companies of men.
Your sacred plants, if here below,
Only among the plants will grow;
Society is all but rude
To this delicious solitude.

No white nor red was ever seen
So amorous as this lovely green.
Fond lovers, cruel as their flame,
Cut in these trees their mistress' name:
Little, alas, they know or heed   21
How far these beauties hers exceed!
Fair trees, wheresoe'er your barks I
          wound,
No name shall but your own be found.

When we have run our passion's heat,
Love hither makes his best retreat.
The gods, that mortal beauty chase,
Still in a tree did end their race:
Apollo hunted Daphne so,
Only that she might laurel grow;   30
And Pan did after Syrinx speed,
Not as a nymph, but for a reed.

What wondrous life is this I lead!
Ripe apples drop about my head;
The luscious clusters of the vine
Upon my mouth do crush their wine;

The nectarine and curious peach
Into my hands themselves do reach;
Stumbling on melons, as I pass,
Insnared with flowers, I fall on grass. 40

Meanwhile the mind, from pleasure less
Withdraws into its happiness;
The mind, that ocean where each kind
Does straight its own resemblance find;
Yet it creates, transcending these,
Far other worlds and other seas,
Annihilating all that's made
To a green thought in a green shade.

Here at the fountain's sliding foot,
Or at some fruit-tree's mossy root,   50
Casting the body's vest aside,
My soul into the boughs does glide:
There, like a bird, it sits and sings,
Then whets and combs its silver wings,
And, till prepared for longer flight,
Waves in its plumes the various light.

Such was that happy garden-state,
While man there walked without a mate:
After a place so pure and sweet,
What other help could yet be meet!   60
But 'twas beyond a mortal's share
To wander solitary there:
Two paradises 'twere in one
To live in paradise alone.

How well the skilful gardener drew,
Of flowers and herbs, this dial new;
Where, from above, the milder sun
Does through a fragrant zodiac run;
And, as it works, the industrious bee
Computes its time as well as we!   70
How could such sweet and wholesome
          hours
Be reckoned but with herbs and flowers?

1681

The Definition of Love

My love is of a birth as rare
As 'tis, for object, strange and high;
It was begotten by Despair
Upon Impossibility.

Magnanimous Despair alone
Could show me so divine a thing,
Where feeble Hope could ne'er have
    flown
But vainly flapped its tinsel wing.

And yet I quickly might arrive
Where my extended soul is fixed;   10
But Fate does iron wedges drive,
And always crowds itself betwixt.

For Fate with jealous eyes does see
Two perfect loves, nor lets them close;
Their union would her ruin be,
And her tyrannic power depose.

And therefore her decrees of steel
Us as the distant poles have placed,
(Though Love's whole world on us
    doth wheel),
Not by themselves to be embraced;   20

Unless the giddy heaven fall,
And earth some new convulsion tear,
And, us to join, the world should all
Be cramped into a planisphere.

As lines, so loves, oblique may well
Themselves in every angle greet;
But ours, so truly parallel,
Though infinite, can never meet.

Therefore the love which us doth bind,
But Fate so enviously debars,
Is the conjunction of the mind,
And opposition of the stars.

1681

To His Coy Mistress

  Had we but world enough, and time,
This coyness, lady, were no crime.
We would sit down, and think which way
To walk, and pass our long love's day.
Thou by the Indian Ganges' side
Shouldst rubies find; I by the tide
Of Humber would complain. I would
Love you ten years before the flood,
And you should, if you please, refuse
Till the conversion of the Jews.   10
My vegetable love should grow
Vaster than empires and more slow;
An hundred years should go to praise
Thine eyes, and on thy forehead gaze;
Two hundred to adore each breast,
But thirty thousand to the rest;
An age at least to every part,
And the last age should show your heart.

For, lady, you deserve this state,
Nor would I love at lower rate.   20
  But at my back I always hear
Time's wingèd chariot hurrying near;
And yonder all before us lie
Deserts of vast eternity.
Thy beauty shall no more be found,
Nor, in thy marble vault, shall sound
My echoing song; then worms shall try
That long-preserved virginity,
And your quaint honour turn to dust,
And into ashes all my lust: 30
The grave's a fine and private place,
But none, I think, do there embrace.
  Now therefore, while the youthful hue
Sits on thy skin like morning lew,
And while thy willing soul transpires
At every pore with instant fires,

Now let us sport us while we may,
And now, like amorous birds of prey,
Rather at once our time devour
Than languish in his slow-chapped power.
Let us roll all our strength and all   41

Our sweetness up into one ball,
And tear our pleasures with rough strife
Thorough the iron gates of life;
Thus, though we cannot make our sun
Stand still, yet we will make him run.

1681

HENRY VAUGHAN (1622-1695)

Henry Vaughan is another member of the metaphysical school of poets, and his verse is distinguished by its radiant sense of the presence of God. Vaughan was born in Wales and educated at Jesus College, Oxford. During the Civil War he was imprisoned for a period as a Royalist. Released, he returned to his Welsh birthplace and spent the remainder of his long life as a country doctor. His first book, *Poems*, was published in 1646 and his second, *Olor Iscanus* (The Swan of Usk) in 1651, but it was his third book, *Silex Scintillans* (Sparks from the Flint), published in 1655, which contained most of his memorable poetry and established his reputation. His earlier books were light, witty, and secular, but a serious illness in the early 1650's turned his mind to God and he determined to "exchange vain and vicious subjects for divine themes and celestial praise."

Vaughan is a mystic who seeks full communion with God, and he sees God as a great light which shines amidst the darkness of the world. He feels that the child is in contact with God, but that the adult person is corrupted by the world of time and must seek to recover the innocent happiness of childhood. This recovery can often be effected by renewing contact with nature, which is the language of God. In style, Vaughan's poems are simple and casual, fluid and flexible, but they achieve great intensity by the brilliance and clarity of his images.

The Retreat

Happy those early days, when I
Shined in my angel infancy;
Before I understood this place
Appointed for my second race,
Or taught my soul to fancy aught
But a white, celestial thought;
When yet I had not walked above
A mile or two from my first Love,
And looking back, at that short space,
Could see a glimpse of His bright face; 10
When on some gilded cloud or flower
My gazing soul would dwell an hour,
And in those weaker glories spy
Some shadows of eternity;
Before I taught my tongue to wound
My conscience with a sinful sound,

Or had the black art to dispense
A several sin to every sense,
But felt through all this fleshly dress
Bright shoots of everlastingness.   20
  Oh, how I long to travel back,
And tread again that ancient track!
That I might once more reach that plain
Where first I left my glorious train;
From whence the enlightened spirit sees
That shady city of palm trees.
But, ah! my soul with too much stay
Is drunk, and staggers in the way.
Some men a forward motion love;
But I by backward steps would move, 30
And when this dust falls to the urn,
In that state I came, return.

1655

Peace

My soul, there is a country
  Far beyond the stars,
Where stands a wingèd sentry
  All skilful in the wars.
There, above noise and danger,
  Sweet Peace sits crowned with smiles,
And One born in a manger
  Commands the beauteous files.
He is thy gracious friend,
  And—O my soul, awake!—   10

Did in pure love descend
  To die here for thy sake.
If thou canst get but thither,
  There grows the flower of peace,
The rose that cannot wither,
  Thy fortress and thy ease.
Leave, then, thy foolish ranges;
  For none can thee secure
But One who never changes,
  Thy God, thy life, thy cure.   20

1655

The World

I saw eternity the other night
Like a great ring of pure and endless light,
  All calm as it was bright;
And round beneath it, time, in hours, days, years,
  Driven by the spheres,
Like a vast shadow moved, in which the world
  And all her train were hurled.

The doting lover in his quaintest strain
  Did there complain;
Near him, his lute, his fancy, and his flights,   10
  Wit's sour delights,
With gloves and knots, the silly snares of pleasure,
  Yet his dear treasure,
All scattered lay, while he his eyes did pour
  Upon a flower.

The darksome statesman, hung with weights and woe,
Like a thick midnight fog, moved there so slow
  He did not stay nor go;
Condemning thoughts, like mad eclipses, scowl
  Upon his soul,   20
And crowds of crying witnesses without
  Pursued him with one shout.

Yet digged the mole, and lest his ways be found,
  Worked under ground,
Where he did clutch his prey.   But one did see
  That policy:
Churches and altars fed him; perjuries
  Were gnats and flies;
It rained about him blood and tears; but he
  Drank them as free.   30

The fearful miser on a heap of rust
Sat pining all his life there, did scarce trust
  His own hands with the dust;
Yet would not place one piece[1] above, but lives
  In fear of thieves.
Thousands there were as frantic as himself,
  And hugged each one his pelf:
The downright epicure placed heaven in sense,
  And scorned pretense;
While others, slipped into a wide excess,   40
  Said little less;
The weaker sort, slight trivial wares enslave,
  Who think them brave;
And poor, despised Truth sat counting by
  Their victory.

Yet some, who all this while did weep and sing,
And sing and weep, soared up into the ring;
  But most would use no wing.
"O fools!" said I, "thus to prefer dark night
  Before true light!   50
To live in grots and caves, and hate the day
  Because it shows the way,
The way which from this dead and dark abode
  Leads up to God;
A way where you might tread the sun and be
  More bright than he!"
But, as I did their madness so discuss,
  One whispered thus:
"This ring the Bridegroom did for none provide,
  But for His bride."   60

                                              1655

<hr>

[1]I.e., invest one coin. See St. Matthew 6:20.

They Are All Gone into the World of Light

They are all gone into the world of light,
 And I alone sit lingering here!
Their very memory is fair and bright,
 And my sad thoughts doth clear.

It glows and glitters in my cloudy breast,
 Like stars upon some gloomy grove,
Or those faint beams in which this hill is dressed
 After the sun's remove.

I see them walking in an air of glory,
 Whose light doth trample on my days;   10
My days, which are at best but dull and hoary,
 Mere glimmerings and decays.

O holy hope, and high humility,
 High as the heavens above!
These are your walks, and you have showed them me
 To kindle my cold love.

Dear, beauteous death! the jewel of the just,
 Shining nowhere but in the dark;
What mysteries do lie beyond thy dust,
 Could man outlook that mark!   20

He that hath found some fledged bird's nest may know
 At first sight if the bird be flown;
But what fair well or grove he sings in now,
 That is to him unknown.

And yet, as angels in some brighter dreams
 Call to the soul when man doth sleep,
So some strange thoughts transcend our wonted themes,
 And into glory peep.

If a star were confined into a tomb,
 Her captive flames must needs burn there;   30
But when the hand that locked her up gives room,
 She'll shine through all the sphere.

O Father of eternal life, and all
    Created glories under Thee!
Resume Thy spirit from this world of thrall
    Into true liberty!

Either disperse these mists, which blot and fill
    My perspective still as they pass;
Or else remove me hence unto that hill
    Where I shall need no glass.   40

1655

1660   **1680**   **1700**

• Royal Society founded

• Bloodless Revolution

Defoe: *Robinson Crusoe*, first English r

• Dryden: *Absalom and Achitophel*

THE RESTORATION AND EIGHTEENTH CENTURY (1660–1784)

1740	1760	1780

Boswell: *The Life of Samuel Johnson, LL.D.* •

• Swift: *Gulliver's Travels*   Goldsmith: *She Stoops to Conquer* •

• Johnson's *Dictionary*

Dryden: *An Essay of Dramatic Poesy* •

• Pope: *An Essay on Man*   • Sterne: *Tristram Shandy*

• Fielding: *Tom Jones*   Isaac Newton discovers gravity •

Blake: *Songs of Innocence* •

After the turmoil of the first two thirds of the seventeenth century, the task of the next period was to restore order and stability. Fortunately the new rationalism and scientific spirit, the steady rise of which was signalized by the foundation of the Royal Society for the Advancement of Learning in 1662, provided a means whereby order might be sought. To moderate the passions aroused by the political and religious conflicts of the previous age, writers and thinkers appealed to "nature" and "reason." It is necessary to put these words in quotation marks, for they had meanings somewhat different from the meanings of the words today. By "nature" they meant not woods, rivers, and trees, nor a primitive state of things, but the orderly, logical, reasonable plan of the universe. Thanks to the new discoveries of scientists, such as Boyle and Newton, the men of this period saw the universe as a wonderfully ordered whole, a cosmos in which only man's affairs were in chaos. If man were to take his proper place in this universe, he should order his own personal life and the system of his society, and thus become a harmonious part of the greater harmony. By "reason" they meant not so much intellectualism, speculative thinking, but common sense, an orderly, calm, balanced consideration of every question.

This tendency to seek order and balance was strengthened, in the realms of literature and the other arts, by the strong prestige in this period of the classical literature of Greece and Rome. The Renaissance had revived interest in this classical literature, and we have seen that Ben Jonson was strongly influenced by it in his writings in the early seventeenth century. In the Restoration and eighteenth century, this interest became more widespread, and attempts were made to achieve in English literature the clarity, balance, and harmony which were the chief virtues of the ancients. For this reason, this age is often labelled the neo-classical period in English literature.

But, of course, order and stability, whether in politics, religion, or literature, were not achieved immediately. The first three decades of the Restoration period were almost as chaotic as the three which preceded them. The restored Charles II was a brilliant, witty, pleasure-loving man who made of his Court a palace of pleasure; his immorality and ostentation offended the Puritans, many of whom, such as the old blind Puritan poet John Milton, had to go into hiding or, worse, were imprisoned or beheaded. Moreover, Charles was suspected of having Roman Catholic leanings, and his brother James, the legal heir, was known to be a Catholic. When James succeeded to the throne in 1685, an attempt was made to oust him in favour of the Duke of Monmouth, Charles' illegitimate son and a Protestant. Although the Monmouth Rebellion was eventually crushed, James did not last long. He had none of Charles' wit, tact, or personal charm; as a Catholic he seemed to favour his co-religionists, and in 1688, he was compelled to abdicate in the Bloodless Revolution. This revolution marked the end of absolute monarchy in England; William and James' daughter Mary were brought over from Holland as joint constitutional sovereigns in 1689.

During the next hundred years the system of cabinet and parliamentary government that we know today gradually but steadily evolved. As early as the reign of William and Mary, two parties emerged: the Whigs, made up mainly of the commercial middle classes and of the Puritans, and the Tories, representing the landed gentry, the country squires, and most of the Anglican clergy. The real power came to reside not with the monarch, whose function was largely symbolic and ceremonial, but with the elected Prime Minister, his cabinet, and the majority party in the House of Commons. The fierce struggle between royal prerogative and parliamentary privilege had been decided in favour of the latter.

The religious struggle between the Puritans and the Anglicans was also largely resolved in the last decades of the seventeenth and early decades of the eighteenth century. Neither group gave up its convictions, but by the Toleration Act of 1689 they did agree to live side by side in peace: freedom of worship was accorded to all except Catholics (they were not to get their freedom until early in the nineteenth century), although the Church of England remained the official or established religion of the country. Generally, the intense religious feeling which had marked the earlier seventeenth century subsided; most men settled into a complacent, lip-serving Christianity which Jonathan Swift was to satirize. A new wave of religious excitement began in the middle of the eighteenth century with the work of John Wesley, but for a long time it affected only a minority of the lower classes: such passionate enthusiasm as Wesley aroused seemed faintly ridiculous to most of the educated, rational men of the time.

It was in science and philosophy, rather than in religious thought, that the greatest intellectual advances of the Restoration and eighteenth century were made. In 1661 Robert Boyle promulgated his famous law regarding the behaviour of gases; in 1662, as we have seen, the Royal Society was founded and began a systematic attempt to increase scientific learning; in 1666 Isaac Newton conceived the law of gravitation from the falling apple, and proceeded to portray the universe as an intricate system of mechanical laws; in 1675 the Greenwich Observatory was established; in 1690 John Locke published his *Essay Concerning the Human Understanding*, in which he argued that all knowledge is derived from sensory observation; in 1709 appeared Bishop Berkeley's *Essay towards a New Theory of Vision*, a brilliant piece of psychological analysis, and in 1710 his even more penetrating *Treatise concerning the Principles of Human Understanding*; in 1739 came David Hume's *Treatise on Human Nature*, a lucid discussion of the way the human mind works in acquiring knowledge of the external world; in 1749 appeared David Hartley's *Observations on Man*, a book which by its expression of the theory of the association of ideas was to have a great effect on William Wordsworth; in 1757 there came Richard Price's *Review of the*

Principal Questions in Morals, in which he argued that right and wrong are simple ideas perceived immediately and intuitively by the reason; in 1771 Joseph Priestley discovered oxygen; in 1776 Edward Gibbon published his monumental, rational, and sceptical *Decline and Fall of the Roman Empire,* and in the same year Adam Smith published his *Inquiry into the Nature and Causes of the Wealth of Nations,* a book which virtually founded the subject of political economy and sought for the first time to subject economics to rational scrutiny.

Such a long list of books may mean little to those who have not read them; but their titles alone reveal to us much of the spirit of the age. Notice how frequently these titles involve the words "man" or "human," and how frequently they imply rational investigation. When Pope wrote "the proper study of mankind is man," he was echoing the dominant belief of his age. It was a human-centred age, an age which believed that man and man's social relations were capable of being understood and ordered. It was a sceptical, analytical, critical age, believing in reason and prepared to discard every belief that could not be reasonably demonstrated.

The literature of the period strongly reflects this attitude. Poets such as Dryden, Pope, Swift, Johnson, Gay, Prior do not write of their own love affairs, or directly of their own joys and sorrows, but subject social and philosophical questions to rational analysis. They are objective, critical, probing poets, and their style is plain, neat, sharp, balanced, and incisive. We remember their lines not for their decorative beauty, as we remember Spenser's or Keats', nor for their passionate intensity, as we remember Donne's or Hopkins', but for their wit, their brevity, their cleverness. Instead of landscape or love, their interests are politics, morals, social behaviour. Frequently they write satires, mocking in the name of common sense all follies and irrational forms of conduct and belief.

This critical, sceptical spirit informs the prose of the period too. Pepys in his *Diary* studies himself and his society, and records his observations with almost the detailed care of a modern sociological investigator determined to omit no detail however seemingly insignificant; Dryden is the first great literary critic in English because he subjects literary questions to the same sort of scrutiny that Locke applied to the human mind or Newton to the universe; Swift in his great prose satires such as *Gulliver's Travels* brings into question all accepted ideas about the nature of man, the basis of his society, the reality of his beliefs; Addison and Steele, in their essays, probe less deeply but still sensibly and perceptively into contemporary social relationships; Dr. Johnson in his *Lives of the Poets* seeks to give a reasoned estimate of each of the leading English poets, subjecting their work to sustained scrutiny and seeking to argue his conclusions from logical premises; and James Boswell, in his *Life of Samuel Johnson,* observes Johnson's every act and word as closely as if Johnson were a laboratory specimen.

There was one literary form, scarcely born at the time of the Restoration, which was nourished by this new self-critical spirit—the English novel. The novel is essentially a realistic study of man in his environment, and it is therefore not surprising that the eighteenth century was the first great period of the English novel. John Bunyan's allegorical *Pilgrim's Progress*, and Addison and Steele's portraits of Sir Roger de Coverley and his friends in the *Spectator*, both helped to prepare the way for the novel. But Daniel Defoe, in his *Robinson Crusoe* (1719) and *Moll Flanders* (1722), Samuel Richardson in his *Pamela* (1740) and *Clarissa* (1747), Henry Fielding in *Joseph Andrews* (1742) and *Tom Jones* (1749), Tobias Smollet in his *Roderick Random* (1748) and *Humphry Clinker* (1771) and Laurence Sterne in his *Tristram Shandy* (1760-1767) and *Sentimental Journey* (1768) established the novel as one of the greatest of all literary forms. By the nineteenth century critics were complaining about the "tyranny of the novel"; in the seventeenth century the novel could hardly have been said to exist.

The drama of the Restoration and eighteenth century shared the critical, witty, scrutinizing spirit and the balanced, orderly form of poetry and the novel. It was an age above all of comedy, principally the comedy of manners which holds up contemporary fads and fashions to ridicule. The comedy of the Restoration, as written by such playwrights as William Wycherley, George Etherege, and William Congreve, was dry, brilliant, epigrammatic, and often indecent; the comedy of the mid-eighteenth century, as produced by Oliver Goldsmith (*She Stoops to Conquer*, 1773) and Richard Brinsley Sheridan (*The Rivals*, 1775 and *The School for Scandal*, 1777), was a little less caustic, a little more superficial and artificial, but still elegant, graceful, and witty. Tragedy fared much worse; perhaps the rational view of life excludes great tragedy. Such attempts as were made—Dryden's *All for Love* (1678) for example, or Addison's *Cato* (1713)—failed in their aim to write English tragedy in accordance with the rules of the ancients. In drama as in fiction, the ambition of the writers of the period was to laugh folly out of court, to ridicule disorder and bad taste, and to establish stability, order, and harmony in the individual and society.

Such were the dominant characteristics of the literature from the Restoration of Charles II in 1660 to the death of Dr. Johnson in 1784. But well before Johnson's death, in spite of the dogmatic assurance with which he expounded his common-sense opinions and his neo-classical literary values, signs of change were evident. Man is not only a rational being; he has feelings, passions, irrational drives and compulsions: and the truth of this was being realized even when rationalism was at its height. As early as 1726, in his *Winter*, James Thomson had returned elaborate nature description to poetry; in the seventeen-forties, Blair's *Grave* and Young's *Night Thoughts* reintroduced mystery, melancholy, and wonder; Gray and Collins, in the 'forties and 'fifties, stood half-way between neo-classical restraint and romantic enthusiasm; and in the last decades of the century Cowper, Burns, and Blake wrote poetry which in its strength of feeling and imaginative vision was much closer to the romantic than to the neo-classical school. A similar development was underway in the novel. Horace Walpole's *Castle of Otranto*, in 1764, started the vogue for mystery, magic, and the exotic in place or time which culminated in the Gothic romances of the late eighteenth and early nineteenth centuries, while Oliver Goldsmith, in *The Vicar of*

Wakefield (1766) and Henry Mackenzie, in *The Man of Feeling* (1771) initiated the novel of sentiment. By 1784, in other words, the neo-classical movement was being steadily undermined by the forces that were to erupt in romanticism.

JOHN DRYDEN (1631-1700)

Dryden was the dominant literary figure of the Restoration era, and as the first of the English neo-classical school of poetry he remained influential until the late eighteenth century. His heroic couplets, balanced lines, and witty turns of phrase created a vogue that endured for a century. His reputation declined somewhat in the nineteenth century, because of the dominance of romantic canons of taste, but in the present century, owing to the homage paid to him by T. S. Eliot and others, he has again been recognized as one of the great English poets and critics.

Dryden was born on August 9, 1631, in Aldwinckle, Northamptonshire, of a family that supported the Parliamentary cause. He was educated at Westminster School and Trinity College, Cambridge, receiving his B.A. in 1654. He made his bow as a poet in 1658, with his *Heroic Stanzas* on the death of Cromwell. Like most Englishmen, however, he welcomed the Restoration of Charles II, and became a staunch Anglican and Royalist. On December 1, 1663, Dryden married Lady Elizabeth Howard, with whose brother, Sir Robert, he collaborated on his first heroic play, *The Indian Queen* (1664). During the next twenty years Dryden wrote nearly thirty plays, most popular being his "heroic" plays, spectacular productions in which exotic characters presented stirring if incredible scenes of love and valour. He also wrote many comedies for the stage, and poems such as *Annus Mirabilis* (1666) dealing with the fire of London and the Dutch War, *Absalom and Achitophel* (1681) attacking those who were promoting the claims of the Duke of Monmouth to the throne, *Mac Flecknoe* (1682) ridiculing his rival poets and especially Thomas Shadwell, and *Religio Laici* (1683) expounding his Anglican beliefs. In 1670 Dryden was appointed Poet Laureate and Historiographer Royal by Charles II, and these appointments were confirmed later by James II. Shortly after the accession of the Catholic James II, Dryden himself was converted to Catholicism—but probably from

genuine conviction rather than from a desire to please the king. With the Revolution of 1688, Dryden fell upon less fortunate times. As a Catholic, he refused to take the oath of allegiance to William and Mary, and thus lost all his public offices. He had to depend solely on his pen for a living. He turned again to the stage, translated various Latin poets into English, published poems such as "Alexander's Feast" and "Ode for St. Cecilia's Day," and compiled an anthology of stories from Chaucer, Boccaccio, and others under the title of *Fables Ancient and Modern*. He died on May 1, 1700, and was buried in Westminster Abbey.

Dryden's poetry is remarkably objective: it deals not with his personal feelings but with the world about him. Most of his poems were occasioned by some external event. To the events and personalities of his time he applied the test of reason, and frequently adopted the form of satire to laugh men out of their follies. Living in the aftermath of revolution, he believed that the sensible thing was to seek stability, and he therefore attacked all those who would disturb the existing order. His own changes in politics and religion were not really inconsistent, for they were all in the direction of a more and more conservative view of life. His conservatism, like Swift's and Pope's in the next generation, arose not from a blind admiration of things as they were, but from a fear that by inexpert tampering they might easily be made worse. But he was no dogmatist; his conclusions were always tentative. His constant search for truth can be seen in his literary criticism, whether it is the early *Essay on Dramatic Poetry* (1668) or the late introduction to *Fables* (1700): he carefully weighed both sides of the case in an attempt to reach a sensible conclusion. In both his poetry and his prose his chief virtues were clarity, neatness, energy, and balance. He had a sharp, quick mind, and a great capacity for turning a memorable phrase. He helped to refine the language, to turn it away from rhetorical extravagance to the stuff of plain speech.

FROM *Mac Flecknoe*[1]

All human things are subject to decay,
And when fate summons, monarchs must obey.
This Flecknoe found, who, like Augustus, young
Was called to empire, and had governed long;
In prose and verse was owned, without dispute,
Through all the realms of Nonsense absolute.
This aged prince, now flourishing in peace,
And blessed with issue of a large increase;
Worn out with business, did at length debate
To settle the succession of the State;   10
And, pondering which of all his sons was fit
To reign, and wage immortal war with wit,
Cried; " 'Tis resolved; for nature pleads, that he
Should only rule, who most resembles me.
Sh—— alone my perfect image bears,
Mature in dullness from his tender years:
Sh—— alone, of all my sons, is he
Who stands confirmed in full stupidity.
The rest to some faint meaning make pretense,
But Sh—— never deviates into sense.   20
Some beams of wit on other souls may fall,
Strike through, and make a lucid interval;
But Sh——'s genuine night admits no ray,
His rising fogs prevail upon the day.
Besides, his goodly fabric fills the eye,
And seems designed for thoughtless majesty;
Thoughtless as monarch oaks that shade the plain,
And, spread in solemn state, supinely reign.
Heywood and Shirley[2] were but types of thee,
Thou last great prophet of tautology.   30
Even I, a dunce of more renown than they,
Was sent before but to prepare thy way;
And, coarsely clad in Norwich drugget, came
To teach the nations in thy greater name.
My warbling lute, the lute I whilom strung,
When to King John[3] of Portugal I sung,
Was but the prelude to that glorious day,
When thou on silver Thames didst cut thy way,

---

[1]This poem arose out of a literary quarrel between Dryden and Thomas Shadwell, a poet
   and playwright on the Whig side. Shadwell is portrayed as the son of Richard
   Flecknoe, a mediocre versifier who died in 1678.
[2]Heywood and Shirley were late Elizabethan dramatists.
[3]John IV of Portugal, whose patronage Flecknoe had enjoyed.

With well-timed oars before the royal barge,
Swelled with the pride of thy celestial charge; 40
And big with hymn, commander of a host,
The like was ne'er in Epsom blankets tossed.
Methinks I see the new Arion[4] sail,
The lute still trembling underneath thy nail.
At thy well-sharpened thumb from shore to shore
The treble squeaks for fear, the basses roar;
Echoes from Pissing Alley Sh—— call,
And Sh—— they resound from Aston Hall.
About thy boat the little fishes throng,
As at the morning toast that floats along. 50
Sometimes, as prince of thy harmonious band,
Thou wield'st thy papers in thy threshing hand.
St. André's[5] feet ne'er kept more equal time,
Not e'en the feet of thy own *Psyche's*[6] rime;
Though they in number as in sense excel:
So just, so like tautology, they fell,
That, pale with envy, Singleton[7] forswore
The lute and sword, which he in triumph bore,
And vowed he ne'er would act Villerius more."
Here stopped the good old sire, and wept for joy 60
In silent raptures of the hopeful boy.
All arguments, but most his plays, persuade,
That for anointed dullness he was made.

1682

[4]A Greek musician, saved from drowning by a dolphin.   [5]A French dancing-master.
[6]An opera by Shadwell.   [7]An opera singer who took the role of Villenus in Davenant's
    Siege of Rhodes.

FROM *Absalom and Achitophel*[1]

... Of these the false Achitophel[2] was first;
A name to all succeeding ages curst:
For close designs and crooked counsels fit,
Sagacious, bold, and turbulent of wit,
Restless, unfix'd in principles and place,
In pow'r unpleas'd, impatient of disgrace;
A fiery soul, which, working out its way,
Fretted the pigmy body to decay:

[1]In the form of a scriptural parable, this poem tells of the efforts to exclude James II from succession
    to the throne. The English are referred to as the Jews, Cromwell as Saul, Charles II as David,
    London as Jerusalem, etc.
[2]*false Achitophel*. The Earl of Shaftesbury, prominent Whig who was believed to be promoting the
    cause of the Duke of Monmouth.

And o'er-inform'd the tenement of clay.
A daring pilot in extremity;   10
Pleas'd with the danger, when the waves went high
He sought the storms; but, for a calm unfit,
Would steer too nigh the sands, to boast his wit.
Great wits are sure to madness near allied,
And thin partitions do their bounds divide;
Else why should he, with wealth and honour blest,
Refuse his age the needful hours of rest?
Punish a body which he could not please,
Bankrupt of life, yet prodigal of ease?
And all to leave what with his toil he won,   20
To that unfeather'd two-legg'd thing, a son:
Got, while his soul did huddled notions try;
And born a shapeless lump, like anarchy.
In friendship false, implacable in hate,
Resolv'd to ruin or to rule the state;
To compass this the triple bond³ he broke;
The pillars of the public safety shook,
And fitted Israel for a foreign yoke:
Then, seiz'd with fear, yet still affecting fame,
Usurp'd a patriot's all-atoning name.   30
So easy still it proves in factious times
With public zeal to cancel private crimes.
How safe is treason, and how sacred ill,
Where none can sin against the people's will!
Where crowds can wink, and no offense be known,
Since in another's guilt they find their own!
Yet, fame deserv'd, no enemy can grudge;
The statesman we abhor, but praise the judge.
In Israel's courts ne'er sat an Abbethdin⁴
With more discerning eyes or hands more clean,   40
Unbrib'd, unsought, the wretched to redress;
Swift of dispatch, and easy of access.
O, had he been content to serve the crown,
With virtues only proper to the gown,
Or had the rankness of the soil been freed
From cockle, that oppress'd the noble seed,
David for him his tuneful harp had strung,
And Heav'n had wanted one immortal song.
But wild Ambition loves to slide, not stand,
And Fortune's ice prefers to Virtue's land.   50

³The Triple Alliance between England, Holland, and Sweden.
⁴President of the Jewish judicature, hence a reference to Shaftesbury's Lord Chancellor-
   ship, 1672-1673.

Achitophel, grown weary to possess
A lawful fame, and lazy happiness,
Disdain'd the golden fruit to gather free
And lent the crowd his arm to shake the tree.
Now, manifest of crimes, contriv'd long since,
He stood at bold defiance with his prince:
Held up the buckler of the people's cause
Against the crown; and skulk'd behind the laws.
The wish'd occasion of the plot he takes;
Some circumstances finds, but more he makes.   60
By buzzing emissaries, fills the ears
Of list'ning crowds with jealousies and fears
Of arbitrary counsels brought to light,
And proves the king himself a Jebusite.
Weak arguments! which yet he knew full well
Were strong with people easy to rebel.
For, govern'd by the moon, the giddy Jews
Tread the same track when she the prime renews:
And once in twenty years, their scribes record,
By natural instinct they change their lord.   70

1681

FROM An Essay of Dramatic Poesy[1]

. . . "But to return whence I have digressed: I dare boldly affirm these two things of the English drama: First, that we have many plays of ours as regular as any of theirs [the French], and which, besides, have more variety of plot and characters; and secondly, that in most of the irregular plays of Shakespeare or Fletcher (for Ben Jonson's are for the most part regular), there is a more masculine fancy and greater spirit in the writing than there is in any of the French. I could produce, even in Shakespeare's and Fletcher's works, some plays which are almost exactly formed; as *The Merry Wives of Windsor*, and *The Scornful Lady*:

but because (generally speaking) Shakespeare, who writ first, did not perfectly observe the laws of comedy, and Fletcher, who came nearer to perfection, yet through carelessness made many faults, I will take the pattern of a perfect play from Ben Jonson, who was a careful and learned observer of the dramatic laws, and from all his comedies I shall select *The Silent Woman*, of which I will make a short examen, according to those rules which the French observe."

As Neander was beginning to examine *The Silent Woman*, Eugenius, earnestly regarding him: "I beseech you, Neander," said he, "gratify the company, and me in particular, so far, as before you speak of the play, to give us a character of the author; and tell us frankly your opinion, whether you do not think all

[1]An essay in the form of a dialogue among four men: Eugenius (Charles Sackville, a poet), Crites (Sir Robert Howard, a dramatist), Lisideus (Sir Charles Sedley, another playwright), and Neander (Dryden himself).

writers, both French and English, ought to give place to him."

"I fear," replied Neander, "that in obeying your commands I shall draw some envy on myself. Besides, in performing them, it will be first necessary to speak somewhat of Shakespeare and Fletcher, his rivals in poesy; and one of them, in my opinion, at least his equal, and perhaps his superior.

"To begin, then, with Shakespeare. He was the man who of all modern, and perhaps ancient poets, had the largest and most comprehensive soul. All the images of nature were still present to him, and he drew them, not laboriously, but luckily; when he describes anything, you more than see it, you feel it too. Those who accuse him to have wanted learning, give him the greater commendation: he was naturally learned; he needed not the spectacles of books to read nature; he looked inwards, and found her there. I cannot say he is everywhere alike; were he so, I should do him injury to compare him with the greatest of mankind. He is many times flat, insipid, his comic wit degenerating into clenches[2], his serious swelling into bombast. But he is always great, when some great occasion is presented to him; no man can say he ever had a fit subject for his wit, and did not then raise himself as high above the rest of poets,

Quantum lenta solent inter viburna cupressi.[3]

The consideration of this made Mr. Hales of Eton say that there was no subject of which any poet ever writ, but he would produce it much better done in Shakespeare; and however others are now generally preferred before him, yet the age wherein he lived, which had contemporaries with him Fletcher and Jonson, never equaled them to him in their esteem: and in the last king's court, when Ben's reputation was at highest, Sir John Suckling, and with him the greater part of the courtiers, set our Shakespeare far above him.

. . . "As for Jonson, to whose character I am now arrived, if we look upon him while he was himself (for his last plays were but his dotages), I think him the most learned and judicious writer which any theater ever had. He was a most severe judge of himself, as well as others. One cannot say he wanted wit, but rather that he was frugal of it. In his works you find little to retrench or alter. Wit, and language, and humour also in some measure, we had before him; but something of art was wanting to the drama, till he came. He managed his strength to more advantage than any who preceded him. You seldom find him making love in any of his scenes, or endeavouring to move the passions; his genius was too sullen and saturnine to do it gracefully, especially when he knew he came after those who had performed both to such an height. Humor was his proper sphere; and in that he delighted most to represent mechanic people. He was deeply conversant in the Ancients, both Greek and Latin, and he borrowed boldly from them; there is scarce a poet or historian among the Roman authors of those times, whom he has not translated in *Sejanus* and *Catiline*[4]. But he has done his robberies so openly, that one may see he fears not to be taxed by any law. He invades authors like a monarch; and what would be theft in other poets,

---

[2]Puns.

[3]"As much as cypresses stand out amid shrubs."
    (Virgil).

[4]*Sejanus* and *Catiline.* Jonson's two tragedies on classical subjects.

is only victory in him. With the spoils of these writers he so represents old Rome to us, in its rites, ceremonies, and customs, that if one of their poets had written either of his tragedies, we had seen less of it than in him. If there was any fault in his language, it was, that he weaved it too closely and laboriously, in his comedies especially; perhaps, too, he did a little too much Romanize our tongue, leaving the words which he translated almost as much Latin as he found them: wherein, though he learnedly followed their language, he did not enough comply with the idiom of ours.

If I would compare him with Shakespeare, I must acknowledge him the more correct poet, but Shakespeare the greater wit. Shakespeare was the Homer, or father of our dramatic poets; Jonson was the Virgil, the pattern of elaborate writing; I admire him, but I love Shakespeare. To conclude of him; as he has given us the most correct plays, so in the precepts which he has laid down in his *Discoveries*[5], we have as many and profitable rules for perfecting the stage, as any wherewith the French can furnish us . . ."

1668

[5] *Timber*, or *Discoveries*, see p. 132.

from Fables, Ancient and Modern

. . . He [Chaucer] must have been a man of a most wonderful comprehensive nature, because, as it has been truly observed of him, he has taken into the compass of his *Canterbury Tales* the various manners and humours (as we now call them) of the whole English nation, in his age. Not a single character has escaped him. All his pilgrims are severally distinguished from each other; and not only in their inclinations, but in their very physiognomies and persons. Baptista Porta[1] could not have described their natures better than by the marks which the poet gives them. The matter and manner of their tales, and of their telling, are so suited to their different educations, humours, and callings, that each of them would be improper in any other mouth. Even the grave and serious characters are distinguished by their several sorts of gravity: their discourses are such as belong to their age, their calling, and their

[1] Italian doctor, author of *De Humana Physiognomie* (1586).

breeding; such as are becoming of them, and of them only. Some of his persons are vicious, and some virtuous; some are unlearned, or (as Chaucer calls them) lewd, and some are learned. Even the ribaldry of the low characters is different: the Reeve, the Miller, and the Cook, are several men, and distinguished from each other as much as the mincing Lady-Prioress and the broad-speaking, gap-toothed Wife of Bath. But enough of this; there is such a variety of game springing up before me that I am distracted in my choice, and know not which to follow. 'Tis sufficient to say, according to the proverb, that here is God's plenty. We have our forefathers and great-grand-dames all before us, as they were in Chaucer's days: their general characters are still remaining in mankind, and even in England, though they are called by other names than those of Monks, and Friars, and Canons, and Lady Abbesses, and Nuns; for mankind is ever the same, and nothing lost out of Nature, though everything is altered. May I have leave to do myself the justice (since my enemies will do me none, and are so far from granting me to be a good poet that they will not allow me so much as to be a Christian, or a moral man), may I have leave, I say, to inform my reader, that I have confined my choice to such tales of Chaucer as savour nothing of immodesty. If I had desired more to please than to instruct, the *Reeve*, the *Miller*, the *Shipman*, the *Merchant*, the *Sumner*, and, above all, the *Wife of Bath*, in the Prologue to her *Tale*, would have procured me as many friends and readers, as there are *beaux* and ladies of pleasure in the town. But I will no more offend against good manners: I am sensible, as I ought to be, of the scandal I have given by my loose writings; and make what reparation I am able by this public acknowledgement. If anything of this nature, or of profaneness, be crept into these poems, I am so far from defending it, that I disown it. *Totum hoc indictum volo*[2].

1700

[2]"All this I wish unsaid."

SAMUEL PEPYS (1633-1703)

Samuel Pepys, the greatest diarist in English, was born and lived most of his life in London. He was the son of a tailor, educated at St. Paul's School and at Trinity Hall and Magdalene College, Cambridge. In 1656 he entered the employ of Sir Edward Montague (afterwards Earl of Sandwich), his father's first cousin, and through his patronage was appointed Clerk of the Acts after the Restoration. In 1665 he became surveyor-general of the victualling office, and in 1672 secretary of the Admiralty. In these two posts he did much to reform abuses in the Navy, and to bring the service up to a high standard of efficiency. His career received a check in 1679, when he was imprisoned for alleged complicity in the Popish Plot and lost his secretaryship. He was subsequently reappointed to the post, but lost it finally in 1688 in the revolution that compelled James II to abdicate. Thereafter Pepys lived in retirement at Clapham until his death in 1703.

His famous diary opens on January 1, 1660, when Pepys was still a poor and obscure young man; it closes on May 31, 1669, by which time, as he proudly records, he was rich, famous, and an intimate of the great. The diary was written in code, and remained undeciphered in the library of Magdalene College until 1825. Its unique interest derives from the frankness, fullness, and gusto with which Pepys records his personal life, and from the detailed vividness with which he depicts the stirring public events of his period—the Restoration, the Plague, the Great Fire of London, the Dutch War. It is one of the strangest coincidences of literary history that the second most interesting diary in English was written by a friend and contemporary of Pepys—John Evelyn, whom Pepys mentions in the excerpt which follows.

FROM The Diary of Samuel Pepys[1]

1665

(MAY) 5TH. After dinner to Mr. Evelyn's; he being abroad, we walked in his garden, and a lovely, noble ground he hath indeed. And, among other rarities, a hive of bees, so as, being hived in glass, you may see the bees making their honey and combs mighty pleasantly. This day, after I had suffered my own hair to grow long in order to wearing it, I find the convenience of periwigs is so great that I have cut off all short again and will keep to periwigs.

[1]It has been considered unnecessary to identify all the persons and places mentioned by Pepys. The student is advised to concentrate on the over-all effect.

(AUGUST) 31ST. The plague having a great increase this week, beyond all expectation, of almost 2,000, making the general bill 7,000, odd 100; and the plague above 6,000. Thus this month ends with great sadness upon the public through the greatness of the plague everywhere through the kingdom almost. Every day sadder and sadder news of its increase. In the city died this week 7,496, and of them 6,102 of the plague. But it is feared that the true number of the dead this week is near 10,000; partly from the poor that cannot be taken notice of, through the greatness of the number, and partly from the Quakers and others that will not have any bell ring for them.

1666

(JANUARY) 28TH. The King come to me of himself and told me, "Mr. Pepys," says he, "I do give you thanks for your good service all this year, and I assure you I am very sensible of it." And the Duke of York[2] did tell me with pleasure that he had read over my discourse about pursers and would have it ordered in my way, and so fell from one discourse to another.

(MARCH) 10TH. I find at home Mrs. Pierce and Knipp come to dine with me. We were mighty merry; and, after dinner, I carried them and my wife out by coach to the New Exchange, and there I did give my Valentine, Mrs. Pierce, a dozen pair of gloves and a pair of silk stockings, and Knipp for company, though my wife had, with my consent, laid out 20s. on her the other day, six pairs of gloves. The truth is, I do indulge myself a little the more in pleasure, knowing that this is the proper age of my life to do it and out of

my observation that most men that do thrive in the world do forget to take pleasure during the time that they are getting their estate, but reserve that till they have got one, and then it is too late for them to enjoy it.

(AUGUST) 19TH. Comes by agreement Mr. Reeves, bringing me a lanthorn, with pictures in glass, to make strange things appear on a wall, very pretty. We did also at night see Jupiter and his girdle and satellites, very fine, with my twelve foot glass, but could not Saturn, he being very dark. Spong and I had also several fine discourses upon the globes this afternoon, particularly why the fixed stars do not rise and set at the same hour all the year long, which he could not demonstrate nor I neither.

(SEPTEMBER) 2ND. Some of our maids sitting up late last night to get things against our feast today, Jane called us up about three in the morning to tell us of a great fire they saw in the city. So I rose and slipped on my nightgown and went to her window; and thought it to be on the back side of Mark Lane at the farthest; but, being unused to such fires as followed, I thought it far enough off; and so went to bed again and to sleep. About seven rose again to dress myself, and there looked out at the window and saw the fire not so much as it was, and further off. So to my closet to set things to rights, after yesterday's cleaning. By and by Jane comes and tells me that she hears that above 300 houses have been burned down tonight by the fire we saw and that it is now burning down all Fish Street by London Bridge. So I made myself ready presently, and walked to the Tower[3]; and there got upon one of the

[2] The Duke of York was Charles II's younger brother and was to succeed to the throne as James II.

[3] The Tower of London.

high places, Sir J. Robinson's little son going up with me; and there I did see the houses at that end of the bridge all on fire and infinite great fire on this and the other side the end of the bridge. So down, with my heart full of trouble, to the lieutenant of the Tower, who tells me that it begun this morning in the King's baker's house in Pudding Lane and that it had burned down St. Magnus' Church and most part of Fish Street already. So I down to the water-side, and there got a boat, and through bridge, and there saw a lamentable fire. Poor Mitchell's house, as far as the Old Swan, already burned that way, and the fire running further, that in a very little time it got as far as the Steel-yard, while I was there. Everybody endeavouring to remove their goods, and flinging them into the river or bringing them unto lighters that lay off; poor people staying in their houses as long as till the very fire touched them, and then running into boats or clambering from one pair of stairs, by the water-side, to another. And among other things, the poor pigeons, I perceive, were loth to leave their houses, but hovered about the windows and balconies, till they burned their wings and fell down. Having stayed and in an hour's time seen the fire rage every way, and nobody, to my sight, endeavouring to quench it, but to remove their goods and leave all to the fire, and having seen it get as far as the Steel-yard, and the wind mighty high and driving it into the city; and everything, after so long a drought, proving combustible, even the very stones of churches;...I to Whitehall, with a gentleman with me, who desired to go off from the Tower, to see the fire, in my boat; and there up to the King's closet in the chapel, where people came about me, and I did give them an account

dismayed them all, and word was carried in to the King. So I was called for, and did tell the King and Duke of York what I saw; and that, unless His Majesty did command houses to be pulled down, nothing could stop the fire. They seemed much troubled, and the King commanded me to go to my Lord Mayor from him and command him to spare no houses, but to pull down before the fire every way. The Duke of York bid me tell him that if he would have any more soldiers, he shall; and so did Lord Arlington afterwards, as a great secret. Here meeting with Captain Cocke, I in his coach, which he lent me, and Creed with me to Paul's[4]; and there walked along Watling Street, as well as I could, every creature coming away laden with goods to save, and, here and there, sick people carried away in beds, extraordinary good goods carried in carts and on backs. At last met my Lord Mayor in Canning Street, like a man spent, with handerchief about his neck. To the King's message he cried, like a fainting woman, "Lord! What can I do? I am spent! People will not obey me. I have been pulling down houses but the fire overtakes us faster than we can do it." That he needed no more soldiers and that, for himself, he must go and refresh himself, having been up all night. So he left me, and I him, and walked home; seeing people all almost distracted, and no manner of means used to quench the fire. The houses, too, so very thick thereabouts, and full of matter for burning, as pitch and tar, in Thames Street; and warehouses of oil and wines and brandy and other things. . . . Met with the King and Duke of York in their barge, and with them to Queenhithe, and there called Sir Richard Browne

[4]St. Paul's Cathedral.

to them. Their order was only to pull down houses apace, and so below bridge at water-side; but this little was or could be done, the fire coming upon them so fast. Good hopes there was of stopping it at the Three Cranes above and at Buttolph's Wharf below bridge, if care be used; but the wind carries it into the city so as we know not, by the water-side, what it do there. River full of lighters and boats taking the goods, and good goods swimming in the water; and only I observed that hardly one lighter or boat in three that had the goods of a house in but there was a pair of virginals in it. Having seen as much as I could now, I away to Whitehall by appointment, and there walked to St. James's Park; and there met my wife and Creed and Wood, and his wife, and walked to my boat; and there upon the water again, and to the fire up and down, it still increasing and the wind great. So near the fire as could for smoke; and all over the Thames, with one's face in the wind you were almost burned with a shower of fire-drops. This is very true, so as houses were burned by these drops and flakes of fire three or four, nay, five or six houses one from another. When we could endure no more upon the water, we to a little ale-house on the Bankside over against the Three Cranes, and there stayed till it was dark almost, and saw the fire grow; and, as it grew darker, appeared more and more; and in corners and upon steeples and between churches and houses, as far as we could see up the hill of the city, in a most horrid, malicious, bloody flame, not like the fine flame of an ordinary fire. Barbary and her husband away before us. We stayed till, it being darkish, we saw the fire as only one entire arch of fire from this to the other side of the bridge and in a bow up the hill for an arch of above a mile long. It made me weep to see it. The churches, houses, and all on fire and flaming at once; and a horrid noise the flames made, and the cracking of houses at their ruin. So home with a sad heart; and there find everybody discoursing and lamenting the fire; and poor Tom Hater come with some few of his goods saved out of his house, which was burned upon Fish Street Hill. I invited him to lie at my house, and did receive his goods; but was deceived in his lying there, the news coming every moment of the growth of the fire; so as we were forced to begin to pack up our own goods and prepare for their removal; and did by moonshine, it being brave, dry, and moonshine and warm weather, carry much of my goods into the garden; and Mr. Hater and I did remove my money and iron chests into my cellar, as thinking that the safest place. And got my bags of gold into my office, ready to carry away, and my chief papers of accounts also there, and my tallies into a box by themselves.

(SEPTEMBER) 5TH. I lay down in the office again upon W. Hewer's quilt, being mighty weary and sore in my feet with going till I was hardly able to stand. About two in the morning my wife calls me up and tells me of new cries of fire, it being come to Barking Church, which is the bottom of our lane. I up; and finding it so, resolved presently to take her away, and did, and took my gold, which was about £2,350, W. Hewer and Jane down by Proundy's boat to Woolwich. But Lord! what a sad sight it was by moonlight to see the whole city almost on fire that you might see it as plain at Woolwich as if you were by it. There, when I come, I find the gates shut, but no guard kept at all, which troubled me, because of discourses now begun that there is a plot in it and that the French had done it. I got the gates open, and to Mr. Shelden's, where I locked up my gold and charged my wife and W. Hewer never to leave the room without one of them in it night and day. So back again, by the way seeing my goods well in the lighters at Deptford and watched well by people. Home, and whereas I expected to have seen our house on fire, it being now about seven o'clock, it was not. But to the fire, and there find greater hopes than I expected; for my confidence of finding our office on fire was such that I durst not ask anybody how it was with us till I come and saw it was not burned. But going to the fire, I find, by the blowing up of houses and the great help given by the workmen out of the King's yards, sent up by Sir W. Penn, there is a good stop given to it, as well at Mark Lane end as ours; it having only burned the dial of Barking Church and part of the porch, and was there quenched. I up to the top of Barking steeple, and there saw the saddest sight of desolation that I ever saw; everywhere great fires, oil-cellars and brim-stone and other things burning. I became afraid to stay there long and therefore down again as fast as I could, the fire being spread as far as I could see it; and to Sir W. Penn's, and there eat a piece of cold meat, having eaten nothing since Sunday, but the remains of Sunday's dinner. Here I met with Mr. Young and Whistler; and, having removed all my things and received good hopes that the fire at our end is stopped, they and I walked into the town, and find Fenchurch Street, Gracious Street, and Lombard Street all in dust. The Exchange a sad sight, noth-ing standing there of all the statues or pillars but Sir Thomas Gresham's picture in the corner. Into Moorfields, our feet ready to burn walking through the town among hot coals, and find that full of people and poor wretches carrying their goods there and everybody keeping his goods together by themselves; and a great blessing it is to them that it is fair weather for them to keep abroad night and day; drunk there, and paid twopence for a plain penny loaf. Thence homeward, having passed through Cheapside and Newgate Market, all burned; and seen Anthony Joyce's house in fire; and took up, which I keep by me, a piece of glass of the Mercers' Chapel in the street, where much more was, so melted and buckled with the heat of the fire like parchment. I also did see a poor cat taken out of a hole in a chimney, joining to the wall of the Exchange, with the hair all burnt off the body, and yet alive. So home at night, and find there good hopes of saving our office; but great endeavours watching all night and having men ready; and so we lodged them in the office, and had drink and bread and cheese for them. And I lay down and slept a good night about midnight, though, when I rose, I heard that there had been a great alarm of French and Dutch being risen, which proved nothing.

(DECEMBER) 25TH. Lay pretty long in bed, and then rose, leaving my wife desirous to sleep, having sat up till four this morning seeing her maids make mince-pies. I go to church, where our parson Mills made a good sermon. Then home, and dined well on some good ribs of beef roasted and mince-pies; only my wife, brother, and Barker, and plenty of good wine of my own, and my heart full of true joy; and thanks to God Almighty for the goodness of my condition at this day!

(DECEMBER) 31ST. Blessed be God! and I pray God make me thankful for it, I do

1665

find myself worth in money, all good, above £6,200; which is above £1,800 more than I was the last year. Thus ends this year of public wonder and mischief to this nation and therefore generally wished by all people to have an end. . . .

1825

JONATHAN SWIFT (1667-1745)

Jonathan Swift is the greatest English prose satirist, and an interesting minor neo-classical poet. Because his insight into human nature was so pitiless and penetrating, many readers find his work disturbing. They picture him as a bull in a china-shop, blindly destroying all their cherished illusions. In fact he was a very clear, systematic thinker, a rather too sensitive idealist, and a devout Christian who sought to ridicule man out of his false pride, out of his subordination of his reason to his passions, out of his stupidity, cruelty, intolerance, and greed.

Swift was the posthumous son of an Englishman who had settled in Ireland, and thanks to the kindness of an uncle was educated at Kilkenny Grammar School and Trinity College, Dublin. In 1689 he became secretary to Sir William Temple of Moor Park, Surrey, and, except for a brief period in 1694-5 when he returned to Ireland and was ordained in the Church of England, remained in that post until Temple's death in 1699. His service with Temple had brought him into contact with King William and the Whig party, but his hopes of political preferment were blasted in 1702 by William's death. He returned to his small Irish parish to wait for preferment in the Church, but it too was slow in coming. Meanwhile Swift had turned to writing, and his first books, *The Battle of the Books* and *A Tale of a Tub*, were published in 1704. The second of these especially, a satirical attack on religious extremism and the corruptions of modern learning, was a literary sensation, and established Swift as the genius of the age. He became the intimate of all the leading writers of the period, including Addison, Steele, Pope, Gay, and Prior. In 1710 Swift switched his allegiance from the Whig to the Tory party, chiefly because he believed that the

latter was more likely to preserve the rights of the Church of England. He now became the chief Tory propagandist, and editor of their paper, *The Examiner*. The death of Queen Anne in 1714 put the Tory party in eclipse for many years, and Swift's political hopes were again blasted. He returned to Ireland, where he spent the rest of his life (apart from brief visits to London) as Dean of St. Patrick's Cathedral in Dublin. He felt something of an exile in Ireland, but made himself popular with the Irish by defending their interests against the English government. In 1742, the fits of deafness and dizziness from which he had long suffered culminated in insanity, and three years later he died, leaving his estate to found a hospital for the insane. Probably because of his poor health, Swift never married, but had close friendships with two women: Esther Johnson ("Stella") and Esther Vanhomrigh ("Vanessa"). To the former he wrote his famous *Journal to Stella*, and about his relations with the latter the poem "Cadenus and Vanessa."

Swift's satires are subtle and ironical in argument, but rest on a set of simple convictions. His basic conviction is that man is a *rational* creature, and should always act like one. He is convinced also that the natural world is rational, and that man should attempt to conform to its laws rather than indulge in eccentricity. He is therefore against "enthusiasm," by which he means pretensions on the part of individuals to special and direct insight, whether in religion, philosophy, politics, or morality. His fear of ill-considered changes led him, like Dryden, to Toryism in politics. In religion, he felt that the time-tested and moderate Church of England was much superior to any of the new dissenting sects that were springing up.

These convictions are given classic expression in Swift's greatest single satire, *Gulliver's Travels* (1726). The imaginary voyages which he there relates provided many opportunities for satirical reflections on the follies and vices of his countrymen, whom he alternately compares and contrasts with the inhabitants of the imaginary lands Gulliver visits. In "A Modest Proposal" (1729), Swift attempted to shock the people of England into a new policy towards the Irish by ironically suggesting that they should carry their harsh policies to their logical conclusion.

A Modest Proposal[1]

It is a melancholy object to those who walk through this great town[2], or travel in the country, when they see the streets, roads, and cabin doors crowded with beggars of the female sex, followed by three, four, or six children, all in rags and importuning every passenger for an alms. These mothers, instead of being able to work for their honest livelihood, are forced to employ all their time in strolling to beg sustenance for their helpless infants; who as they grow up either turn thieves, for want of work, or leave their dear native country to fight for the pretender in Spain, or sell themselves to the Barbados.

I think it is agreed by all parties that this prodigious number of children in the arms, or on the backs, or at the heels of their fathers, is, in the present deplorable state of the kingdom, a very great additional grievance; and therefore whoever could find out a fair, cheap, and easy method of making these children sound, useful members of the commonwealth would deserve so well of the public as to have his statue set up for a preserver of the nation.

But my intention is very far from being confined to provide only for the children of professed beggars: it is of a much greater extent and shall take in the whole number of infants at a certain age, who are born of parents in effect as little able to support them as those who demand our charity in the streets.

As to my own part, having turned my thoughts for many years upon this important subject and maturely weighed the several schemes of our projectors, I have always found them grossly mistaken in their computation. It is true, a child just dropped from its dam may be supported by her milk for a solar year, with little other nourishment: at most not above the value of two shillings which the mother may certainly get, or the value in scraps, by her lawful occupation of begging; and it is exactly at one year old that I propose to provide for them in such a manner, as, instead of being a charge upon their parents or the parish, or wanting food and raiment for the rest of their lives, they shall, on the contrary, contribute to the feeding and partly to the clothing of many thousands.

There is likewise another great advantage in my scheme, that it will prevent those voluntary abortions and that horrid practice of women murdering their bastard children, alas! too frequent among us, sacrificing the poor innocent babes, I doubt more to avoid the expense than the shame which would move tears

[1] In reading this sketch, the student should keep reminding himself that Swift has his tongue in his cheek. The whole essay is a model of subtle and mocking irony, occasionally at the expense of the Irish, but usually at the expense of the English, and especially the absentee English landlords.

[2] Dublin.

and pity in the most savage and inhuman breast.

The number of souls in this kingdom being usually reckoned one million and a half, of these I calculate there may be about two hundred thousand couple, whose wives are breeders; from which number I subtract thirty thousand couple, who are able to maintain their own children (although I apprehend there cannot be so many, under the present distresses of the kingdom), but this being granted, there will remain an hundred and seventy thousand breeders. I again subtract fifty thousand for those women who miscarry, or whose children die by accident or disease within the year. There only remains one hundred and twenty thousand children of poor parents annually born. The question therefore is, How this number shall be reared and provided for? which, as I have already said, under the present situation of affairs, is utterly impossible by all the methods hitherto proposed. For we can neither employ them in handicraft or agriculture; we neither build houses (I mean in the country) nor cultivate land: they can very seldom pick up a livelihood by stealing till they arrive at six years old, except where they are of towardly parts; although I confess they learn the rudiments much earlier, during which time they can, however, be properly looked upon only as probationers; as I have been informed by a principal gentleman in the county of Cavan, who protested to me that he never knew above one or two instances under the age of six, even in a part of the kingdom so renowned for the quickest proficiency in that art.

I am assured by our merchants that a boy or a girl before twelve years old is no salable commodity; and even when they come to this age they will not yield above three pounds, or three pounds and half a crown at most, on the exchange; which cannot turn to account either to the parents or kingdom, the charge of nutriment and rags having been at least four times that value.

I shall now therefore humbly propose my own thoughts, which I hope will not be liable to the least objection.

I have been assured by a very knowing American of my acquaintance in London that a young healthy child well nursed is at a year old a most delicious, nourishing, and wholesome food, whether stewed, roasted, baked, or boiled; and I make no doubt that it will equally serve in a fricassee or a ragout.

I do therefore humbly offer it to public consideration that of the hundred and twenty thousand children already computed, twenty thousand may be reserved for breed, whereof only one-fourth part to be males; which is more than we allow to sheep, black cattle, or swine; and my reason is that these children are seldom the fruits of marriage, a circumstance not much regarded by our savages; therefore one male will be sufficient to serve four females. That the remaining hundred thousand may, at a year old, be offered in sale to the persons of quality and fortune through the kingdom; always advising the mother to let them suck plentifully in the last month, so as to render them plump and fat for a good table. A child will make two dishes at an entertainment for friends; and when the family dines alone, the fore or hind quarter will make a reasonable dish, and seasoned with a little pepper or salt will be very good boiled on the fourth day, especially in winter.

I have reckoned upon a medium that a child just born will weigh twelve pounds, and in a solar year, if tolerably nursed, will increase to twenty-eight pounds.

I grant this food will be somewhat dear, and therefore very proper for landlords, who, as they have already devoured most of the parents, seem to have the best title to the children.

Infant's flesh will be in season throughout the year, but more plentifully in March, and a little before and after: for we are told by a grave author, an eminent French physician, that fish being a prolific diet, there are more children born in Roman Catholic countries about nine months after Lent than at any other season; therefore, reckoning a year after Lent the markets will be more glutted than usual, because the number of popish infants is at least three to one in this kingdom: and therefore it will have one other collateral advantage, by lessening the number of papists among us.

I have already computed the charge of nursing a beggar's child (in which list I reckon all cottagers, labourers, and four-fifths of the farmers) to be about two shillings per annum, rags included; and I believe no gentlemen would repine to give ten shillings for the carcass of a good fat child, which, as I have said, will make four dishes of excellent nutritive meat, when he has only some particular friend or his own family to dine with him. Thus the squire will learn to be a good landlord and grow popular among his tenants; the mother will have eight shillings net profit and be fit for work till she produces another child.

Those who are more thrifty (as I must confess the times require) may flay the carcass; the skin of which artificially dressed will make admirable gloves for ladies and summer boots for fine gentlemen.

As to our city of Dublin, shambles[3] may be appointed for this purpose in the most convenient parts of it, and butchers we may be assured will not be wanting; although I rather recommend buying the children alive and dressing them hot from the knife as we do roasting pigs.

A very worthy person, a true lover of his country, and whose virtues I highly esteem, was lately pleased, in discoursing on this matter, to offer a refinement upon my scheme. He said that many gentlemen of this kingdom, having of late destroyed their deer, he conceived that the want of venison might be well supplied by the bodies of young lads and maidens, not exceeding fourteen years of age nor under twelve; so great a number of both sexes in every country being now ready to starve for want of work and service; and these to be disposed of by their parents, if alive, or otherwise by their nearest relations. But with due deference to so excellent a friend and so deserving a patriot, I cannot be altogether in his sentiments; for as to the males, my American acquaintance assured me from frequent experience that their flesh was generally tough and lean, like that of our schoolboys, by continual exercise, and their taste disagreeable; and to fatten them would not answer the charge. Then as to the females, it would, I think with humble submission be a loss to the public, because they soon would become breeders themselves: and besides, it is not improbable that some scrupulous people might be apt to censure such a practice (although indeed very unjustly), as a little bordering upon cruelty; which, I confess, has always

[3]Slaughterhouses.

been with me the strongest objection against any project, however so well intended.

But in order to justify my friend, he confessed that this expedient was put into his head by the famous Psalmanazar[4], a native of the island Formosa, who came from thence to London above twenty years ago: and in conversation told my friend that in his country when any young person happened to be put to death, the executioner sold the carcass to persons of quality as a prime dainty; and that in his time the body of a plump girl of fifteen, who was crucified for an attempt to poison the emperor, was sold to his imperial majesty's prime minister of state, and other great mandarins of the court, in joints from the gibbet, at four hundred crowns. Neither indeed can I deny that if the same use were made of several plump young girls in this town, who, without one single groat to their fortunes, cannot stir abroad without a chair, and appear at a playhouse and assemblies in foreign fineries which they never will pay for, the kingdom would not be the worse.

Some persons of a desponding spirit are in great concern about that vast number of poor people, who are aged, diseased, or maimed; and I have been desired to employ my thoughts, what course may be taken to ease the nation of so grievous an incumbrance. But I am not in the least pain upon that matter, because it is very well known that they are every day dying and rotting, by cold and famine and filth and vermin, as fast as can be reasonably expected. And as to the young labourers, they are now in al-

most as hopeful a condition: they cannot get work, and consequently pine away for want of nourishment to a degree that if at any time they are accidentally hired to common labour, they have not strength to perform it; and thus the country and themselves are happily delivered from the evils to come.

I have too long digressed and therefore shall return to my subject. I think the advantages, by the proposal which I have made, are obvious and many, as well as of the highest importance.

For first, as I have already observed, it would greatly lessen the number of papists, with whom we are yearly overrun, being the principal breeders of the nation, as well as our most dangerous enemies, and who stay at home on purpose to deliver the kingdom to the pretender, hoping to take their advantage by the absence of so many good protestants, who have chosen rather to leave their country than stay at home and pay tithes against their conscience to an Episcopal curate.

Secondly, the poorer tenants will have something valuable of their own, which by law may be made liable to distress, and help to pay their landlords' rent; their corn and cattle being already seized, and money a thing unknown.

Thirdly, whereas the maintenance of a hundred thousand children, from two years old and upward cannot be computed at less than ten shillings a piece per annum, the nation's stock will be thereby increased fifty thousand pounds per annum, besides the profit of a new dish introduced to the tables of all gentlemen of fortune in the kingdom, who have any refinement in taste. And the money will circulate among ourselves, the goods being entirely of our own growth and manufacture.

[4]An impostor who passed himself off in London as a native of Formosa and who wrote a book about the island.

Fourthly, the constant breeders, beside the gain of eight shillings sterling per annum by the sale of their children, will be rid of the charge of maintaining them after the first year.

Fifthly, this food would likewise bring great custom to taverns: where the vintners will certainly be so prudent as to procure the best receipts for dressing it to perfection, and consequently have their houses frequented by all the fine gentlemen, who justly value themselves upon their knowledge in good eating: and a skilful cook, who understands how to oblige his guests, will contrive to make it as expensive as they please.

Sixthly, this would be a great inducement to marriage, which all wise nations have either encouraged by rewards or enforced by laws and penalties. It would increase the care and tenderness of mothers toward their children, when they were sure of a settlement for life to the poor babes, provided in some sort by the public, to their annual profit instead of expense. We should see an honest emulation among the married women, which of them could bring the fattest child to market. Men would become as fond of their wives during the time of their pregnancy as they are now of their mares in foal, their cows in calf, or sows when they are ready to farrow; nor offer to beat or kick them (as is too frequent a practice) for fear of a miscarriage.

Many other advantages might be enumerated. For instance, the addition of some thousand carcasses in our exportation of barreled beef, the propagation of swine's flesh, and improvement in the art of making good bacon, so much wanted among us by the great destruction of pigs, too frequent at our tables; which are no way comparable in taste or magnificence to a well-grown, fat, yearling child, which roasted whole will make a considerable figure at a lord mayor's feast, or any other public entertainment. But this and many others I omit, being studious of brevity.

Supposing that one thousand families in this city would be constant customers for infants' flesh, besides others who might have it at merry-meetings, particularly weddings and christenings, I compute that Dublin would take off annually about twenty thousand carcasses; and the rest of the kingdom (where probably they will be sold somewhat cheaper) the remaining eighty thousand.

I can think of no one objection that will possibly be raised against this proposal, unless it should be urged that the number of people will be thereby much lessened in the kingdom. This I freely own, and it was indeed one principal design in offering it to the world. I desire the reader will observe that I calculate my remedy for this one individual kingdom of Ireland, and for no other that ever was, is, or, I think, ever can be upon earth. Therefore let no man talk to me of other expedients[5]; of taxing our absentees at five shillings a pound: of using neither clothes nor household furniture, except what is of our own growth and manufacture: of utterly rejecting the materials and instruments that promote foreign luxury: of curing the expensiveness of pride, vanity, idleness, and gaming in our women: of introducing a vein of parsimony, prudence, and temperance: of learning to love our country, in the want of which we differ even from Laplanders and the

[5]Here, as elsewhere, of course, Swift is being ironical. These "expedients" are really the remedies he would recommend.

inhabitants of Topinamboo: of quitting our animosities and factions, nor acting any longer like the Jews, who were murdering one another at the very moment their city was taken: of being a little cautious not to sell our country and conscience for nothing: of teaching landlords to have at least one degree of mercy toward their tenants: lastly, of putting a spirit of honesty, industry, and skill into into our shopkeepers; who, if a resolution could now be taken to buy only our native goods, would immediately unite to cheat and exact upon us in the price, the measure, and the goodness, nor could ever yet be brought to make one fair proposal of just dealing, though often and earnestly invited to it.

Therefore, I repeat, let no man talk to me of these and the like expedients, till he has at least some glimpse of hope that there will be ever some hearty and sincere attempt to put them in practice.

But as to myself, having been wearied out for many years with offering vain, idle, visionary thoughts, and at length utterly despairing of success, I fortunately fell upon this proposal; which, as it is wholly new, so it has something solid and real, of no expense and little trouble, full in our own power, and whereby we can incur no danger in disobliging England. For this kind of commodity will not bear exportation, the flesh being of too tender a consistence to admit a long continuance in salt, although perhaps I could name a country which would be glad to eat up our whole nation without it.

After all, I am not so violently bent upon my own opinion as to reject any offer proposed by wise men, which shall be found equally innocent, cheap, easy, and effectual. But before something of that kind shall be advanced in contradiction to my scheme, and offering a better, I desire the author or authors will be pleased maturely to consider two points. First, as things now stand, how they will be able to find food and raiment for an hundred thousand useless mouths and backs. And secondly, there being a round million of creatures in human figure throughout this kingdom, whose whole subsistence put into a common stock would leave them in debt two millions of pounds sterling, adding those who are beggars by profession to the bulk of farmers, cottagers, and labourers, with their wives and children, who are beggars in effect; I desire those politicians, who dislike my overture, and may perhaps be so bold as to attempt an answer, that they will first ask the parents of these mortals, whether they would not at this day think it a great happiness to have been sold for food at a year old in the manner I prescribe, and thereby have avoided such a perpetual scene of misfortunes as they have since gone through by the oppression of landlords, the impossibility of paying rent without money or trade, the want of common sustenance, with neither house nor clothes to cover them from the inclemencies of the weather, and the most inevitable prospect of entailing the like or greater miseries upon their breed for ever.

I profess, in the sincerity of my heart, that I have not the least personal interest in endeavouring to promote this necessary work, having no other motive than the public good of my country, by advancing our trade, providing for infants, relieving the poor, and giving some pleasure to the rich. I have no children by which I can propose to get a single penny; the youngest being nine years old, and my wife past child-bearing. 1729

JOSEPH ADDISON (1672-1719) and
RICHARD STEELE (1672-1729)

Although Addison and Steele wrote many things separately, it is chiefly for their collaboration on the periodicals *The Tatler* (1709-1711) and *The Spectator* (1711-1713) that they are remembered. They were born in the same year (Addison in Wiltshire and Steele in Dublin), met first at Charterhouse School, consolidated their friendship at Oxford, and remained friends almost until Addison's death. After university, Addison entered the government service and became, successively, Commissioner of Appeals, Under-Secretary of State, Chief Secretary for Ireland, and Secretary of State; Steele, for his part, served in the army, and became gentleman waiter to Prince George of Denmark, gazetteer, commissioner of stamps, Member of Parliament for Stockbridge, and supervisor of Drury Lane Theatre. Both then, were active men of affairs, although their personalities were quite distinct: Addison was prudent, studious, and restrained; Steele reckless, pleasure-loving, and impulsive. Expressive of this difference is the fact that Addison's best known work, apart from his periodical essays, was the stiff classical tragedy *Cato*, whereas Steele wrote sentimental comedies such as *The Tender Husband* and *The Conscious Lovers*.

It was Steele who founded *The Tatler*, virtually the first literary periodical in English, but Addison almost immediately became his collaborator. Two months after *The Tatler* ceased publication, the first issue of *The Spectator* appeared, and throughout the latter's two-year existence the two friends contributed to it equally. The periodicals found their audience chiefly in the well-to-do men of the middle class who in Queen Anne's reign patronized the coffee-houses of London. The aim of the editors was to entertain and instruct the members of this class, then rapidly rising in importance.

The essays appearing in *The Tatler* and *The Spectator* were rather different from those of Bacon. They were more informal, more personal, more whimsical. They were also more various, including character sketches, familiar letters, table talk, discussions of current events and fashions, literary criticism, and sketches that somewhat resembled the modern short story, as well as the more formal and didactic discussions of general topics such as Bacon wrote. What Addison and Steele did, in effect, was to invent the familiar essay. The form had many subsequent practitioners; Oliver Goldsmith in the mid-eighteenth century, and Charles Lamb and Washington Irving in the early nineteenth, were the best-known. Addison and Steele also, by their series of essays dealing with Sir Roger de Coverley and his friends, did something to prepare the way for the English novel. In addition, they helped to consolidate a direct, correct, and colloquial English prose style.

Mr. Spectator

NO. 1. THURSDAY, MARCH 1, 1711

*Non fumum ex fulgore, sed ex fumo dare lucem
Cogitat, ut speciosa dehinc miracula promat.*[1]

Hor. Ars. Poet. 143.

*One with a flash begins, and ends in smoke;
Another out of smoke brings glorious light,
And, without raising expectation high,
Surprises us with dazzling miracles.*

Roscommon

[1] "He thinks not how to give you smoke from light, but light from smoke, that he may draw his bright wonders forth after." (Horace, *Art of Poetry*).

I have observed that a reader seldom peruses a book with pleasure, till he knows whether the writer of it be a black or a fair man, of a mild or choleric disposition, married or a bachelor, with other particulars of the like nature, that conduce very much to the right understanding of an author. To gratify this curiosity, which is so natural to a reader, I design this paper, and my next, as prefatory discourses to my following writings, and shall give some account in them of the several persons that are engaged in this work. As the chief trouble of compiling, digesting, and correcting will fall to my share, I must do myself the justice to open the work with my own history.

I was born to a small hereditary estate, which, according to the tradition of the village where it lies, was bounded by the same hedges and ditches in William the Conqueror's time that it is at present, and has been delivered down from father to son whole and entire, without the loss or acquisition of a single field or meadow, during the space of six hundred years. There runs a story in the family that when my mother was gone with child of me about three months, she dreamt that she was brought to bed of a judge. Whether this might proceed from a lawsuit which was then depending in the family, or my father's being a justice of the peace, I cannot determine; for I am not so vain as to think it presaged any dignity that I should arrive at in my future life, though that was the interpretation which the neighbourhood put upon it. The gravity of my behaviour at my very first appearance in the world seemed to favour my mother's dreams; for, as she often told me, I threw away my rattle before I was two months old, and would not make use of my coral until they had taken away the bells from it.

As for the rest of my infancy, there being nothing in it remarkable, I shall pass it over in silence. I find that during my nonage I had the reputation of a very sullen youth, but was always a favourite of my schoolmaster, who used to say, that my parts were solid, and would wear well. I had not been long at the university, before I distinguished myself by a most profound silence; for, during the space of eight years, excepting in the public exercises of the college, I scarce uttered the quantity of a hundred words; and indeed do not remember that I ever spoke three sentences together in my whole life. Whilst I was in this learned body, I applied myself with so much diligence to my studies, that there are very few celebrated books, either in the learned or the modern tongues, which I am not acquainted with.

Upon the death of my father, I was resolved to travel into foreign countries, and therefore left the university, with the character of an odd unaccountable fellow, that had a great deal of learning, if I would not show it. An insatiable thirst after knowledge carried me into all the countries of Europe, in which there was anything new or strange to be seen; nay, to such a degree was my curiosity raised, that having read the controversies of some great men concerning the antiquities of Egypt, I made a voyage to Grand Cairo, on purpose to take the measure of a pyramid; and as soon as I had set myself right in that particular, returned to my native country with great satisfaction.

I have passed my latter years in this city, where I am frequently seen in most public places, though there are not above half a dozen of my select friends that know me; of whom my next paper shall give a more particular account. There is no place of general resort, wherein I do not often make my appearance; sometimes I am seen thrusting my head into a round of politicians at Will's, and listening with great attention to the narratives that are made in these little circular audiences. Sometimes I smoke a pipe at Child's, and whilst I seem attentive to nothing but the Postman, overhear the conversation of every table in the room. I appear on Sunday nights at St. James's coffee-house, and sometimes join the little committees of politics in the inner room, as one who comes there to hear and improve. My face is likewise very well known at the Grecian, the Cocoa-tree, and in the theatres both of Drury-Lane and the Hay-market. I have been taken for a merchant upon the Exchange for above these ten years, and sometimes pass for a Jew in the assembly of stock-jobbers at Jonathon's. In short, wherever I see a cluster of people, I always mix with them, though I never open my lips but in my own club.

Thus I live in the world rather as a Spectator of mankind, than as one of the species, by which means I have made myself a speculative statesman, soldier, merchant, and artisan, without ever meddling with any practical part in life. I am very well versed in the theory of a husband or a father, and can discern the errors in the economy, business, and diversion of others, better than those who are engaged in them; as standers-by discover blots which are apt to escape those who are in the game. I never espoused any party with violence, and am resolved to observe an exact neutrality between the Whigs and Tories, unless I shall be forced to declare myself by the hostilities of either side. In short, I have acted in all the parts of my life as a looker-on, which is the character I intend to preserve in this paper.

I have given the reader just so much of my history and character as to let him see I am not altogether unqualified for the business I have undertaken. As for other particulars in my life and adventures, I shall insert them in following papers, as I shall see occasion. In the meantime, when I consider how much I have seen, read, and heard, I begin to blame my own taciturnity; and since I have neither time nor inclination, to communicate the fulness of my heart in speech, I am resolved to do it in writing, and to print myself out, if possible, before I die. I have been often told by my friends, that it is a pity so many useful discoveries which I have made should be in the possession of a silent man. For this reason, therefore, I shall publish a sheet-full of thoughts every morning, for the benefit of my contemporaries; and if I can any way contribute to the diversion or improvement of the country in which I live, I shall leave it when I am summoned out of it, with the secret satisfaction of thinking that I have not lived in vain.

There are three very material points which I have not spoken to in this paper; and which, for several important reasons, I must keep to myself, at least for some time: I mean, an account of my name, my age, and my lodgings. I must confess, I would gratify my reader in anything that is reasonable; but as for these three particulars, though I am sensible they might tend very much to the embellishment of my paper, I cannot yet come to a resolution of communicating them to the public. They would indeed draw me out of that obscurity which I have enjoyed for many years, and expose me in public places to several salutes and civilities, which have been always very disagreeable to me; for the greatest pain I can suffer, is the being talked to, and being stared at. It is for this reason likewise, that I keep my complexion and dress as very great secrets; though it is not impossible but I may make discoveries of both in the progress of the work I have undertaken.

After having been thus particular upon myself, I shall, in tomorrow's paper, give an account of these gentlemen who are concerned with me in this work; for, as I have before intimated, a plan of it is laid and concerted, as all other matters of importance are, in a club. However, as my friends have engaged me to stand in the front, those who have a mind to correspond with me may direct their letters to the Spectator, at Mr. Buckley's, in Little Britain. For I must further acquaint the reader, that, though our club meets only on Tuesdays and Thursdays, we have appointed a committee to sit every night, for the inspection of all such papers as may contribute to the advancement of the public weal.

—Addison, 1711

The Club

NO. 2. FRIDAY, MARCH 2, 1711

—Ast alii sex
Et plures uno conclamant ore[1].

Juv. Sat. vii. 167.

The first of our society is a gentleman of Worcestershire, of ancient descent, a baronet, his name Sir Roger de Coverley. His great grandfather was inventor of that famous country-dance which is called after him. All who know that shire are very well acquainted with the parts and merits of Sir Roger. He is a gentleman that is very singular in his behaviour, but his singularities proceed from his good sense, and are contradictions to the manners of the world, only as he thinks the world is in the wrong. However, this humour creates him no enemies, for he does nothing with sourness or obstinacy; and his being unconfined to modes and forms, makes him but the readier and more capable to please and oblige all who know him. When he is in town, he lives in Soho Square. It is said, he keeps himself a bachelor, by reason he was crossed in love by a perverse beautiful widow of the next county to him. Before this disappointment, Sir Roger was what you call a fine gentleman, had often supped with my Lord Rochester[2] and Sir George Etherege[3], fought a duel upon his first coming to town, and kicked Bully Dawson[4] in a public coffee house for calling him youngster. But being ill used by the above mentioned widow, he was very serious for

[1] "Six more at least join their consenting voice." (Juvenal)

[2] A poet and wit (1647-1680).
[3] A dramatist (1635-1691).
[4] A London swindler of the time.

a year and a half, and though, his temper being naturally jovial, he at last got over it, he grew careless of himself, and never dressed afterwards. He continues to wear a coat and doublet of the same cut that were in fashion at the time of his repulse, which, in his merry humours, he tells us, has been in and out twelve times since he first wore it. It is said Sir Roger grew humble in his desires after he had forgot his cruel beauty, inasmuch that it is reported he has frequently offended in point of chastity with beggars and gypsies; but this is looked upon, by his friends, rather as matter of raillery than truth. He is now in his fifty-sixth year, cheerful, gay, and hearty; keeps a good house both in town and country; a great lover of mankind; but there is such a mirthful cast in his behaviour, that he is rather beloved than esteemed.

His tenants grow rich, his servants look satisfied, all the young women profess love to him, and the young men are glad of his company. When he comes into a house, he calls the servants by their names, and talks all the way up stairs to a visit. I must not omit, that Sir Roger is a justice of the quorum; that he fills the chair at a quarter-session with great abilities, and three months ago, gained universal applause, by explaining a passage in the game-act.

The gentleman next in esteem and authority among us, is another bachelor, who is a member of the Inner Temple; a man of great probity, wit, and understanding; but he has chosen his place of residence rather to obey the direction of an old humoursome father, than in pursuit of his own inclinations. He was placed there to study the laws of the land, and is the most learned of any of the house in those of the stage. Aristotle and Longinus are much better understood by him than Littleton or Coke[5]. The father sends up every post questions relating to marriage articles, leases, and tenures, in the neighbourhood; all which questions he agrees with an attorney to answer and take care of in the lump. He is studying the passions themselves, when he should be inquiring into the debates among men which arise from them. He knows the argument of each of the orations of Demosthenes and Tully; but not one case in the reports of our own courts. No one ever took him for a fool, but none, except his intimate friends, know he has a great deal of wit. This turn makes him at once both disinterested and agreeable. As few of his thoughts are drawn from business, they are most of them fit for conversation. His taste of books is a little too just for the age he lives in; he has read all, but approves of very few. His familiarity with the customs, manners, actions, and writings of the ancients, makes him a very delicate observer of what occurs to him in the present world. He is an excellent critic, and the time of the play is his hour of business; exactly at five he passes through New Inn, crosses through Russell court, and takes a turn at Will's, till the play begins; he has his shoes rubbed, and his periwig powdered, at the barber's as you go into the Rose. It is for the good of the audience when he is at a play; for the actors have an ambition to please him.

The person of next consideration is Sir Andrew Freeport, a merchant of great eminence in the city of London, a person of indefatigable industry, strong reason,

---

[5]I.e., he knew more of literary criticism than of the law.

and great experience. His notions of trade are noble and generous, and, as every rich man has usually some sly way of jesting, which would make no great figure were he not a rich man, he calls the sea the British Common. He is acquainted with commerce in all its parts, and will tell you that it is a stupid and barbarous way to extend dominion by arms; for true power is to be got by arts and industry. He will often argue that if this part of our trade were well cultivated, we should gain from one nation;—and if another, from another. I have heard him prove, that diligence makes more lasting acquisitions than valor, and that sloth has ruined more nations than the sword. He abounds in several frugal maxims, amongst which the greatest favourite is, "A penny saved is a penny got." A general trader of good sense is pleasanter company than a general scholar; and Sir Andrew having a natural unaffected eloquence, the perspicuity of his discourse gives the same pleasure that wit would in another man. He has made his fortunes himself; and says that England may be richer than other kingdoms, by as plain methods as he himself is richer than other men; though at the same time I can say this of him, that there is not a point in the compass but blows home a ship in which he is an owner.

Next to Sir Andrew in the club-room sits Captain Sentry, a gentleman of great courage, good understanding, but invincible modesty. He is one of those that deserve very well, but are very awkward at putting their talents within the observation of such as should take notice of them. He was some years a captain, and behaved himself with great gallantry in several engagements and at several sieges; but having a small estate of his own, and being next heir to Sir Roger, he has quitted a way of life, in which no man can rise suitably to his merit, who is not something of a courtier as well as a soldier. I have heard him often lament, that in a profession where merit is placed in so conspicuous a view, impudence should get the better of modesty. When he has talked to this purpose, I never heard him make a sour expression, but frankly confess that he left the world, because he was not fit for it. A strict honesty and an even regular behaviour are in themselves obstacles to him that must press through crowds who endeavour at the same end with himself, the favour of a commander. He will, however, in his way of talk, excuse generals for not disposing according to men's desert, or inquiring into it: for, says he, that great man who has a mind to help me, has as many to break through to come at me, as I have to come at him: therefore, he will conclude, that the man who would make a figure, especially in a military way, must get over all false modesty, and assist his patron against the importunity of other pretenders, by a proper assurance in his own vindication. He says it is a civil cowardice to be backward in asserting what you ought to expect, as it is a military fear to be slow in attacking when it is your duty. With this candour does the gentleman speak of himself and others. The same frankness runs through all his conversation. The military part of his life has furnished him with many adventures, in the relation of which he is very agreeable to the company; for he is never overbearing, though accustomed to command men in the utmost degree below him; nor ever too obsequious, from an habit of obeying men highly above him.

But, that our society may not appear a set of humourists[6], unacquainted with the gallantries and pleasures of the age, we have amongst us the gallant Will Honeycomb, a gentleman who, according to his years, should be in the decline of his life, but, having ever been very careful of his person, and always had a very easy fortune, time has made but a very little impression, either by wrinkles on his forehead, or traces on his brain. His person is well turned, of a good height. He is very ready at that sort of discourse with which men usually entertain women. He has all his life dressed very well, and remembers habits as others do men. He can smile when one speaks to him, and laughs easily. He knows the history of every mode, and can inform you from which of the French king's wenches our wives and daughters had this manner of curling their hair, that way of placing their hoods; whose frailty was covered by such a sort of petticoat, and whose vanity to show her foot made that part of the dress so short in such a year. In a word, all his conversation and knowledge have been in the female world. As other men of his age will take notice to you what such a minister said upon such and such an occasion, he will tell you when the Duke of Monmouth danced at court, such a woman was then smitten, another was taken with him at the head of his troops in the Park. In all these important relations, he has ever about the same time received a kind glance or a blow of a fan from some cele-

brated beauty, mother of the present Lord Such-a-one. This way of talking of his very much enlivens the conversation among us of a more sedate turn; and I find there is not one of the company, but myself, who rarely speak at all, but speaks of him as of that sort of man who is usually called a well-bred fine gentleman. To conclude his character, where women are not concerned, he is an honest worthy man.

I cannot tell whether I am to account him whom I am next to speak of, as one of our company; for he visits us but seldom, but when he does, it adds to every man else a new enjoyment of himself. He is a clergyman, a very philosophic man, of general learning, great sanctity of life, and the most exact good breeding. He has the misfortune to be of a very weak constitution; and consequently cannot accept of such cares and business as preferments in his function would oblige him to; he is therefore among divines what a chamber-councillor is among lawyers. The probity of his mind, and the integrity of his life, create him followers, as being eloquent or loud advances others. He seldom introduces the subject he speaks upon; but we are so far gone in years that he observes, when he is among us, an earnestness to have him fall on some divine topic, which he always treats with much authority, as one who has no interest in this world, as one who is hastening to the object of all his wishes, and conceives hope from his decays and infirmities. These are my ordinary companions.

—Steele, 1711

[6] I.e., eccentrics.

ALEXANDER POPE (1688-1744)

Alexander Pope, the chief of the neo-classical poets, was regarded by Dr. Johnson as the greatest of all English poets; his stock fell in the romantic nineteenth century; but in our century he has been re-established in critical favour and has been highly praised by such twentieth century poets as T. S. Eliot and Edith Sitwell.

Pope was born in London, the son of a Roman Catholic linen draper, but spent most of his early life in the country near Windsor. A sickly child, he was permanently deformed by an accident at the age of twelve, and hence had little formal education. He made up for this lack by voracious reading, and by the age of sixteen had attracted the attention of the playwright William Wycherley by the excellence of his verse. Wycherley introduced him to the literary society of London. At the age of twenty-one he won fame with his *Pastorals*, and two years later his *Essay on Criticism* appeared and earned the praise of Addison. *The Rape of the Lock* (1714), a delightful mock-epic lightly satirizing the affectations of fashionable society, consolidated his reputation. From this time until his death, his literary output was immense: he published very successful translations of Homer's *Iliad* and *Odyssey*, an annotated edition of Shakespeare, and many original works of his own including his most bitter satire *The Dunciad* (1728), his *Epistles* (1731-35), and *The Essay on Man* (1733) in which he attempted a systematic exposition of his views on man, society, and religion. From the death of his father in 1718 to his own death in 1744, Pope lived in a villa at Twickenham, where he cultivated an elaborate formal garden and played host to the most eminent and brilliant men of his time. Vain, sensitive, quick to wound and be wounded, Pope made many enemies but also many friends.

His production, in the light of his constant ill-health, was truly prodigious.

Inspired by the wit and regularity of Dryden, and by the lucidity and harmony of the ancient classics, Pope was perhaps the most deliberate craftsman in English poetic history. He subjected all his works to frequent revision, and was constantly seeking the most exact and concise form of expression. He wrote almost exclusively in the heroic couplet which Chaucer had introduced and Waller, Denham, and Dryden had re-popularized; within its narrow limits he managed to achieve amazing variety by slight adjustments of accent, rhythm, rhyme, and phrasing. He was a master phrase maker, and many of his lines have become proverbial. In thought he possessed—nor claimed—little originality: he aimed to write "what oft was thought, but ne'er so well expressed." In *The Essay on Man*, for example, he put forward the views of his friend Bolingbroke in particular and of the educated men of his time in general: especially the view that the universe (or "nature") is a vast, intricate, harmonious system and that man's task is not to understand or alter it but to find his proper place in it and adjust himself to it. A conscious moralist in verse, he boasted that "not in Fancy's maze he wandered long / But stooped to truth and moralized his song." The aim of his poems was similar to that of Addison's and Steele's essays: to entertain and instruct the middle class, to give it sensible precepts for the conduct of daily life. He was not capable of the expression of deep emotion, and only occasionally—in "Eloisa to Abelard," for example, and the "Elegy for an Unfortunate Lady"—even attempted it. His strengths were his conciseness, his irony, his wit, his satiric thrusts, his epigrammatic style, and his technical virtuosity.

FROM *An Essay on Criticism*

PART I

'Tis hard to say, if greater want of skill
Appear in writing or in judging ill;
But, of the two, less dang'rous is th' offence
To tire our patience, than mislead our sense.

Some few in that, but numbers err in this,
Ten censure wrong for one who writes amiss;
A fool might once himself alone expose,
Now one in verse makes many more in prose.
   'Tis with our judgments as our watches, none
Go just alike, yet each believes his own.   10
In poets as true genius is but rare,
True taste as seldom is the critic's share;
Both must alike from Heav'n derive their light,
These born to judge, as well as those to write.
Let such teach others who themselves excel,
And censure freely who have written well.
Authors are partial to their wit[1], 'tis true,
But are not critics to their judgment too?
   Yet if we look more closely, we shall find
Most have the seeds of judgment in their mind: 20
Nature affords at least a glimm'ring light;
The lines, though touch'd but faintly, are drawn right.
But as the slightest sketch, if justly trac'd,
Is by ill-colouring but the more disgrac'd,
So by false learning is good sense defac'd:
Some are bewilder'd in the maze of schools,
And some made coxcombs Nature meant but fools.
In search of wit these lose their common sense,
And then turn critics in their own defence:
Each burns alike, who can, or cannot write,   30
Or with a rival's, or an eunuch's spite.
All fools have still an itching to deride,
And fain would be upon the laughing side.
If Mævius[2] scribble in Apollo's spite,
There are, who judge still worse than he can write.
   Some have at first for wits, then poets past,
Turn'd critics next, and prov'd plain fools at last.
Some neither can for wits nor critics pass,
As heavy mules are neither horse nor ass.
Those half-learn'd witlings, num'rous in our isle,   40
As half-form'd insects on the banks of Nile;
Unfinish'd things, one knows not what to call,
Their generation's so equivocal:
To tell 'em, would a hundred tongues require,
Or one vain wit's, that might a hundred tire.
   But you who seek to give and merit fame,

[1]Imagination (not a form of humour); the ability to see a similarity between ideas.
[2]A minor Roman poet attacked by Virgil and Horace.

And justly bear a critic's noble name,
Be sure yourself and your own reach to know,
How far your genius, taste, and learning go;
Launch not beyond your depth, but be discreet,   50
And mark that point where sense and dullness meet.
   Nature to all things fix'd the limits fit,
And wisely curb'd proud man's pretending wit.
As on the land while here the ocean gains,
In other parts it leaves wide sandy plains;
Thus in the soul while memory prevails,
The solid pow'r of understanding fails;
Where beams of warm imagination play,
The memory's soft figures melt away.
One science only will one genius fit;   60
So vast is art, so narrow human wit:
Not only bounded to peculiar arts,
But oft in those confin'd to single parts.
Like kings we lose the conquests gain'd before,
By vain ambition still to make them more;
Each might his sev'ral province well command,
Would all but stoop to what they understand.
   First follow Nature, and your judgment frame
By her just standard, which is still the same:
Unerring Nature, still divinely bright,   70
One clear, unchang'd, and universal light,
Life, force, and beauty, must to all impart,
At once the source, and end, and test of art.
Art from that fund each just supply provides,
Works without show, and without pomp presides:
In some fair body thus th' informing soul
With spirits feeds, with vigour fills the whole,
Each motion guides, and ev'ry nerve sustains;
Itself unseen, but in th' effects, remains.
Some, to whom Heav'n in wit has been profuse,   80
Want as much more, to turn it to its use;
For wit and judgment often are at strife,
Though meant each other's aid, like man and wife.
'Tis more to guide, than spur the Muse's steed;
Restrain his fury, than provoke his speed;
The winged courser[3], like a gen'rous horse,
Shows most true mettle when you check his course.

        *   *   *

[3]Pegasus, the horse of the Muses.

PART II

Of all the causes which conspire to blind
Man's erring judgment, and misguide the mind,
What the weak head with strongest bias rules   90
Is Pride, the never-failing vice of fools.
Whatever Nature has in worth denied,
She gives in large recruits of needful pride;
For as in bodies, thus in souls, we find
What wants in blood and spirits, swell'd with wind:
Pride, where wit fails, steps in to our defence,
And fills up all the mighty void of sense.
If once right reason drives that cloud away,
Truth breaks upon us with resistless day.
Trust not yourself; but your defects to know,   100
Make use of ev'ry friend—and ev'ry foe.
    A little learning is a dang'rous thing;
Drink deep, or taste not the Pierian spring[4]:
There shallow draughts intoxicate the brain,
And drinking largely sobers us again.
Fired at first sight with what the Muse imparts,
In fearless youth we tempt the heights of arts,
While from the bounded level[5] of our mind
Short views we take, nor see the lengths behind[6];
But more advanc'd, behold with strange surprise   110
New distant scenes of endless science[7] rise!
So pleas'd at first the tow'ring Alps we try,
Mount o'er the vales, and seem to tread the sky,
Th' eternal snows appear already past,
And the first clouds and mountains seem the last;
But, those attain'd, we tremble to survey
The growing labours of the lengthen'd way,
Th' increasing prospect tires our wand'ring eyes,
Hills peep o'er hills, and Alps on Alps arise!
    A perfect judge will read each work of wit   120
With the same spirit that its author writ:
Survey the whole, nor seek slight faults to find
Where nature moves, and rapture warms the mind:
Nor lose, for that malignant dull delight,
The gen'rous pleasure to be charm'd with wit.
But in such lays as neither ebb, nor flow,
Correctly cold, and regularly low,
That shunning faults, one quiet tenour keep;

[4]The spring of the Muses on Mt. Helicon, here a symbol of learning.
[5]Restricted vision.   [6]Extent of territory still to be explored.   [7]Knowledge.

We cannot blame indeed—but we may sleep.
In wit, as nature, what affects our hearts   130
Is not th' exactness of peculiar parts;
'Tis not a lip, or eye, we beauty call,
But the joint force and full result of all.
Thus when we view some well-proportion'd dome[8],
(The world's just wonder, and ev'n thine, O Rome!)
No single parts unequally surprise,
All comes united to th' admiring eyes;
No monstrous height, or breadth, or length appear;
The whole at once is bold, and regular.

   Whoever thinks a faultless piece to see,   140
Thinks what ne'er was, nor is, nor e'er shall be.
In ev'ry work regard the writer's end,
Since none can compass more than they intend;
And if the means be just, the conduct true,
Applause, in spite of trivial faults, is due;
As men of breeding, sometimes men of wit,
T' avoid great errors, must the less commit:
Neglect the rules each verbal critic lays,
For not to know such trifles, is a praise.   150
Most critics, fond of some subservient art,
Still make the whole depend upon a part:
They talk of principles, but notions prize,
And all to one lov'd folly sacrifice.

*   *   *

PART III
*   *   *

   But where's the man, who counsel can bestow,
Still pleas'd to teach, and yet not proud to know?
Unbias'd, or by favour, or by spite;
Not dully prepossess'd, nor blindly right;
Though learn'd, well-bred; and though well-bred, sincere,
Modestly bold, and humanly severe: 160
Who to a friend his faults can freely show,
And gladly praise the merit of a foe?
Blest with a taste exact, yet unconfin'd;
A knowledge both of books and human kind:
Gen'rous converse; a soul exempt from pride;
And love to praise, with reason on his side?

*   *   *   1711

[8] The dome of St. Peter's.

FROM *An Essay on Man*

In Four Epistles, to H. St. John, Lord Bolingbroke

FROM EPISTLE I

Awake, my St. John[1]! leave all meaner things
To low ambition, and the pride of kings.
Let us (since life can little more supply
Than just to look about us and to die)
Expatiate free o'er all this scene of man;
A mighty maze! but not without a plan;
A wild, where weeds and flow'rs promiscuous shoot;
Or garden, tempting with forbidden fruit.
Together let us beat[2] this ample field,
Try what the open, what the covert yield;   10
The latent tracts, the giddy heights, explore
Of all who blindly creep, or sightless soar;
Eye Nature's walks, shoot folly as it flies,
And catch the manners living as they rise;
Laugh where we must, be candid where we can;
But vindicate the ways of God to man.
     I.   Say first, of God above, or man below,
What can we reason, but from what we know?
Of man, what see we but his station here,
From which to reason, or to which refer?   20
Through worlds unnumber'd though the God be known,
'Tis ours to trace him only in our own.
He, who through vast immensity can pierce,
See worlds on worlds compose one universe,
Observe how system into system runs,
What other planets circle other suns,
What varied being peoples ev'ry star,
May tell why Heav'n has made us as we are.
But of this frame the bearings, and the ties,
The strong connexions, nice dependencies,   30
Gradations just, has thy pervading soul
Look'd through? or can a part contain the whole?
     Is the great chain, that draws all to agree,
And drawn supports, upheld by God, or thee?

---

[1]Viscount Bolingbroke, the Tory Secretary of State, was accused of treason and fled
   England on the death of Queen Anne. He returned to England in 1723 and became a
   neighbour and intimate of Pope.
[2]Hunt over, or search for game.

II.   Presumptuous man! the reason wouldst thou find,
Why form'd so weak, so little, and so blind?
First, if thou canst, the harder reason guess,
Why form'd no weaker, blinder, and no less?
Ask of thy mother earth, why oaks are made
Taller or stronger than the weeds they shade?   40
Or ask of yonder argent fields above,
Why Jove's satellites[3] are less than Jove?
    Of systems possible, if 'tis confest
That Wisdom infinite must form the best,
Where all must full or not coherent be,
And all that rises, rise in due degree;
Then, in the scale of reas'ning life, 'tis plain,
There must be somewhere, such a rank as man:
And all the question (wrangle e'er so long)
Is only this, if God has plac'd him wrong?   50
    Respecting man, whatever wrong we call,
May, must be right, as relative to all.
In human works, though labour'd on with pain,
A thousand movements scarce one purpose gain;
In God's, one single can its end produce;
Yet serves to second too some other use.
So man, who here seems principal alone,
Perhaps acts second to some sphere unknown,
Touches some wheel, or verges to some goal;
'Tis but a part we see, and not a whole.   60
    When the proud steed shall know why man restrains
His fiery course, or drives him o'er the plains:
When the dull ox, why now he breaks the clod,
Is now a victim, and now Ægypt's God:
Then shall man's pride and dulness comprehend
His actions', passions', being's, use and end;
Why doing, suff'ring, check'd, impell'd; and why
This hour a slave, the next a deity.
    Then say not man's imperfect, Heav'n in fault;
Say rather, man's as perfect as he ought;   70
His knowledge measur'd to his state and place;
His time a moment, and a point his space.
If to be perfect in a certain sphere,
What matter, soon or late, or here or there?
The blest to day is as completely so,
As who began a thousand years ago.

[3]Satellite here has four syllables, as in the original Latin. The reference to Jove is to the planet,
   Jupiter.

VI.   What would this man? Now upward will he soar,
And little less than angel, would be more;
Now looking downwards, just as griev'd appears
To want the strength of bulls, the fur of bears.   80
Made for his use all creatures if he call,
Say what their use, had he the pow'rs of all?
Nature to these, without profusion, kind,
The proper organs, proper pow'rs assign'd;
Each seeming want compensated of course,
Here with degrees of swiftness, there of force;
All in exact proportion to the state;
Nothing to add, and nothing to abate.
Each beast, each insect, happy in its own:
Is Heav'n unkind to man, and man alone?   90
Shall he alone, whom rational we call,
Be pleas'd with nothing, if not bless'd with all?
     The bliss of man (could pride that blessing find)
Is not to act or think beyond mankind;
No pow'rs of body or of soul to share,
But what his nature and his state can bear.
Why has not man a microscopic eye?
For this plain reason, man is not a fly.
Say what the use, were finer optics giv'n,
T' inspect a mite, not comprehend the heav'n?   100
Or touch, if tremblingly alive all o'er,
To smart and agonize at ev'ry pore?
Or quick effluvia darting through the brain,
Die of a rose in aromatic pain?
If nature thunder'd in his op'ning ears,
And stunn'd him with the music of the spheres,
How would he wish that Heav'n had left him still
The whisp'ring zephyr, and the purling rill?
Who finds not Providence all good and wise,
Alike in what it gives, and what denies?   110

IX.   What if the foot, ordain'd the dust to tread,
Or hand, to toil, aspir'd to be the head?
What if the head, the eye, or ear repin'd
To serve mere engines to the ruling mind?
Just as absurd for any part to claim
To be another, in this gen'ral frame:
Just as absurd, to mourn the tasks or pains,
The great directing Mind of All ordains.

All are but parts of one stupendous whole,
Whose body Nature is, and God the soul;   120
That, chang'd through all, and yet in all the same;
Great in the earth, as in th' ethereal frame;
Warms in the sun, refreshes in the breeze,
Glows in the stars, and blossoms in the trees,
Lives through all life, extends through all extent,
Spreads undivided, operates unspent;
Breathes in our soul, informs our mortal part,
As full, as perfect, in a hair as heart:
As full, as perfect, in vile man that mourns,
As the rapt seraph that adores and burns: 130
To him no high, no low, no great, no small;
He fills, he bounds, connects, and equals all.

FROM EPISTLE II

    I. Know then thyself, presume not God to scan;
The proper study of mankind is man.
Placed on this isthmus of a middle state,
A being darkly wise, and rudely great:
With too much knowledge for the sceptic side,
With too much weakness for the stoic's pride,
He hangs between; in doubt to act, or rest;
In doubt to deem himself a god, or beast;   140
In doubt his mind or body to prefer;
Born but to die, and reas'ning but to err;
Alike in ignorance, his reason such,
Whether he thinks too little, or too much:
Chaos of thought and passion, all confus'd;
Still by himself abus'd, or disabus'd;
Created half to rise, and half to fall;
Great lord of all things, yet a prey to all;
Sole judge of truth, in endless error hurl'd:
The glory, jest, and riddle of the world!   150
    Go, wondrous creature! mount where science guides,
Go, measure earth, weigh air, and state the tides;
Instruct the planets in what orbs to run,
Correct old time, and regulate the sun;
Go, soar with Plato[4] to th' empyreal sphere,
To the first good, first perfect, and first fair;
Or tread the mazy round his follow'rs[5] trod,

[4]Greek philosopher, 427?-347? B.C., who thought all earthly things were mere shadows of
  eternal ideas.
[5]The neo-Platonists who thought truth was attained through mystic contemplation.

And quitting sense call imitating God;
As Eastern priests in giddy circles run,
And turn their heads to imitate the sun.   160
Go, teach Eternal Wisdom how to rule—
Then drop into thyself, and be a fool!

FROM EPISTLE IV

Come then, my friend[6]! my genius! come along,
Oh master of the poet, and the song!
And while the Muse now stoops, or now ascends,
To man's low passions, or their glorious ends,
Teach me, like thee, in various nature wise,
To fall with dignity, with temper rise;
Form'd by thy converse, happily to steer
From grave to gay, from lively to severe;   170
Correct with spirit, eloquent with ease,
Intent to reason, or polite to please.
Oh! while along the stream of time thy name
Expanded flies, and gathers all its fame,
Say, shall my little bark attendant sail,
Pursue the triumph, and partake the gale?
When statesmen, heroes, kings, in dust repose,
Whose sons shall blush their fathers were thy foes,
Shall then this verse to future age pretend
Thou wert my guide, philosopher, and friend?   180
That urg'd by thee, I turn'd the tuneful art
From sounds to things, from fancy to the heart;
For Wit's false mirror held up Nature's light;
Shew'd erring Pride, *whatever is, is right*;
That Reason, Passion, answer one great aim;
That true Self-Love and Social are the same;
That Virtue only makes our bliss below;
And all our Knowledge is, *ourselves to know*.

                                    1733-1734

---

[6]The reference is again to Pope's friend St. John (Viscount Bolingbroke). This passage is a summary of the thought of the whole poem.

SAMUEL JOHNSON (1709-1784)

Johnson was the dominant literary figure of the mid-eighteenth century, the great neo-classical critic as Pope had been the great neo-classical poet. But Johnson was not only a critic; he was an essayist, lexicographer, poet, novelist, biographer, and editor as well. Above all, he was a personality: a man of strong opinions, quick wit, and generous sympathies.

He was the son of a Lichfield bookseller, and was educated (but because of poverty did not complete his degree) at Oxford. He was briefly a schoolmaster and publisher's assistant; in 1737 he went to London with his former pupil, David Garrick, to seek success as a writer. In 1738 he published the verse satire *London*, in 1744 his *Life of Savage*, and in 1747 he issued the plan for his English Dictionary. Another verse satire, *The Vanity of Human Wishes*, and his tragedy *Irene*, appeared in 1749, and in the following year he founded *The Rambler*, a periodical which he largely wrote himself. The publication of his monumental dictionary in 1755 established his reputation, and he became the centre of a bril-

liant group including Joshua Reynolds, Oliver Goldsmith, and Edmund Burke. His novel *Rasselas* appeared in 1759; the portentous meeting with his future biographer, Boswell, occurred in 1763; his edition of Shakespeare was published in 1765; and his last important work, *The Lives of the Poets*, appeared at intervals during 1779 to 1781. Johnson had always been subject to fits of deep depression, and haunted by fears of death and insanity, but he died peacefully at the age of seventy-five and was buried in Westminster Abbey. Students who wish to know more of Johnson's life—of his marriage at twenty-six to a woman of forty, his many friendships, his eccentricities of appearance, speech, and conduct— are advised to read Boswell's biography.

In reading Johnson's criticism in the excerpts which follow, students should remember that he had very strong prejudices. As a biographer he was not always accurate; as a critic he was not always fair; but he was always trenchant and lively.

FROM Dryden

... Criticism, either didactic or defensive, occupies almost all his prose, except those pages which he has devoted to his patrons; but none of his prefaces were ever thought tedious. They have not the formality of a settled style, in which the first half of a sentence betrays the other. The clauses are never balanced, nor the periods modelled; every word seems to drop by chance, though it falls into its proper place. Nothing is cold or languid; the whole is airy, animated, and vigor-

ous: what is little, is gay; what is great, is splendid. He may be thought to mention himself too frequently; but while he forces himself upon our esteem, we cannot refuse him to stand high in his own. Everything is excused by the play of images and the sprightliness of expression. Though all is easy, nothing is feeble; though all seems careless, there is nothing harsh; and though since his earlier works more than a century has passed, they have nothing yet uncouth or obsolete.

He who writes much will not easily escape a manner, such a recurrence of particular modes as may be easily noted. Dryden is always "another and the same"; he does not exhibit a second time the same elegances in the same form, nor appears to have any art other than that of expressing with clearness what he thinks with vigour. His style could not easily be imitated, either seriously or ludicrously; for, being always equable and always varied, it has no prominent or discriminative characters. The beauty who is totally free from disproportion of parts and features, cannot be ridiculed by an overcharged resemblance.

From his prose, however, Dryden derives only his accidental and secondary praise; the veneration with which his name is pronounced by every cultivator of English literature is paid to him as he refined the language, improved the sentiments, and tuned the numbers of English poetry.

After about half a century of forced thoughts and rugged metre, some advances towards nature and harmony had been already made by Waller and Denham; they had shown that long discourses in rhyme grew more pleasing when they were broken into couplets, and that verse consisted not only in the number but the arrangement of syllables.

But though they did much, who can deny that they left much to do? Their works were not many, nor were their minds of very ample comprehension. More examples of more modes of composition were necessary for the establishment of regularity, and the introduction of propriety in word and thought.

Every language of a learned nation necessarily divides itself into diction scholastic and popular, grave and familiar, elegant and gross; and from a nice distinction of these different parts arises a great part of the beauty of style. But if we except a few minds, the favourites of nature, to whom their original rectitude was in the place of rules, this delicacy of selection was little known to our authors: our speech lay before them in a heap of confusion, and every man took for every purpose what chance might offer him.

There was therefore before the time of Dryden no poetical diction: no system of words at once refined from the grossness of domestic use, and free from the harshness of terms appropriated to particular arts. Words too familiar, or too remote, defeat the purpose of a poet. From those sounds which we hear on small or on coarse occasions, we do not easily receive strong impressions, or delightful images; and words to which we are nearly strangers, whenever they occur, draw that attention on themselves which they should transmit to things.

Those happy combinations of words which distinguish poetry from prose had been rarely attempted; we had few elegances or flowers of speech: the roses had not yet been plucked from the bramble, or different colours had not yet been joined to enliven one another.

It may be doubted whether Waller and Denham could have overborne the prejudices which had long prevailed, and which even then were sheltered by the protection of Cowley. The new versification, as it was called, may be considered as owing its establishment to Dryden; from whose time it is apparent that English poetry has had no tendency to relapse to its former savageness.

1781

FROM # Pope

[Pope] professed to have learned his poetry from Dryden whom, whenever an opportunity was presented, he praised through his whole life with unvaried liberality; and perhaps his character may receive some illustration if he be compared with his master. . . .

Pope was not content to satisfy; he desired to excel, and therefore always endeavoured to do his best: he did not court the candour, but dared the judgment of his reader, and, expecting no indulgence from others, he showed none to himself. He examined lines and words with minute and punctilious observation, and retouched every part with indefatigable diligence, till he had left nothing to be forgiven. . . .

In acquired knowledge, the superiority must be allowed to Dryden, whose education was more scholastic, and who before he became an author had been allowed more time for study, with better means of information. His mind has a larger range, and he collects his images and illustrations from a more extensive circumference of science. Dryden knew more of man in his general nature, and Pope in his local manners. The notions of Dryden were formed by comprehensive speculation, and those of Pope by minute attention. There is more dignity in the knowledge of Dryden, and more certainty in that of Pope.

Poetry was not the sole praise of either, for both excelled likewise in prose; but Pope did not borrow his prose from his predecessor. The style of Dryden is capricious and varied, that of Pope is cautious and uniform; Dryden obeys the motions of his own mind, Pope constrains his mind to his own rules of composition.

Dryden is sometimes vehement and rapid; Pope is always smooth, uniform, and gentle. Dryden's page is a natural field, rising into inequalities, and diversified by the varied exuberance of abundant vegetation; Pope's is a velvet lawn, shaven by the scythe, and levelled by the roller.

Of genius, that power which constitutes a poet; that quality without which judgment is cold and knowledge is inert; that energy which collects, combines, amplifies, and animates—the superiority must, with some hesitation, be allowed to Dryden. It is not to be inferred that of this poetical vigour Pope has only a little, because Dryden had more; for every other writer since Milton must give place to Pope; and even of Dryden it must be said, that if he has brighter paragraphs, he has not better poems. Dryden's performances were always hasty, either excited by some external occasion, or extorted by domestic necessity; he composed without consideration, and published without correction. What his mind could supply at call, or gather in one excursion, was all that he sought, and all that he gave. The dilatory caution of Pope enabled him to condense his sentiments, to multiply his images, and to accumulate all that study might produce, or chance might supply. If the flights of Dryden are higher, Pope continues longer on the wing. If of Dryden's fire the blaze is brighter, of Pope's the heat is more regular and constant. Dryden often surpasses expectation, and Pope never falls below it. Dryden is read with frequent astonishment, and Pope with perpetual delight.

1781

JAMES BOSWELL (1740-1795)

Boswell has always been famous as the biographer of Johnson, but in recent years his fame has been augmented by the discovery in Malahide Castle, near Dublin, of his manuscript journals, and their continuing publication in a series of volumes edited by Professor F. A. Pottle of Yale.

Boswell was born in Auchinleck, Ayrshire, the son of a Scottish judge, and was educated at the High School and University of Edinburgh. His profession was that of an advocate or lawyer, but he did a great deal of travelling. In 1763, on his way to the Continent, he passed through London and met Johnson; on the Continent itself he made the acquaintance of the French philosophers Rousseau and Voltaire; and on the island of Corsica he met the patriot General Paoli. His first published book was *An Account of Corsica* (1768). Between 1772 and Johnson's death in 1784 he made frequent trips from his Edinburgh home to London to be with Johnson and to collect material for his planned biography. In 1773 he and Johnson made a tour of the Hebrides, a journal of which he published in 1785. His life of Johnson appeared in 1791 and was at once recognized as a masterpiece.

The novelty of Boswell's biography is the extraordinary sense of intimacy which he achieves by the accumulation of small strokes of detail. That this was a deliberate innovation on his part is clear from this passage of a letter he wrote to his friend Temple: "I am absolutely certain that my mode of biography, which gives not only a history of Johnson's visible progress through the world, and of his publications, but a view of his mind, in his letters and conversations, is the most perfect that can be conceived, and will be more of a Life than any work that has ever yet appeared."

FROM The Life of Samuel Johnson, LL.D.

(THE YEAR 1747)

The year 1747 is distinguished as the epoch, when Johnson's arduous and important work, his *Dictionary* of the English Language, was announced to the world, by the publication of its Plan or *Prospectus*.

. . . The "Plan" was addressed to Philip Dormer, Earl of Chesterfield, then one of his Majesty's Principal Secretaries of State; a nobleman who was very ambitious of literary distinction, and who, upon being informed of the design, had expressed himself in terms very favourable to its success. There is, perhaps, in every thing of any consequence, a secret history which it would be amusing to know, could we have it authentically communicated. Johnson told me, "Sir, the way in which the plan of my Dictionary came to be inscribed to Lord Chesterfield, was this: I had neglected to write it by the time appointed. Dodsley suggested a desire to have it addressed to Lord Chesterfield. I laid hold of this as a pretext for delay, that it might be better done, and let Dodsley have his desire. I said to my friend, Dr. Bathurst, 'Now if any good comes of my addressing to Lord Chesterfield, it will be ascribed to deep policy,' when, in fact, it was only a casual excuse for laziness."

It is worthy of observation, that the "Plan" has not only the substantial merit of comprehension, perspicuity, and precision, but that the language of it is unexceptionably excellent; it being altogether free from that inflation of style, and those uncommon but apt and energetic words, which in some of his writings have been censured, with more petulance than justice; and never was there a more dignified strain of compliment than that in which he courts the attention of one who, he had been persuaded to believe, would be a respectable patron.

"With regard to questions of purity or propriety, (says he) I was once in doubt whether I should not attribute to myself too much in attempting to decide them, and whether my province was to extend beyond the proposition of the question, and the display of the suffrages on each side; but I have been since determined by your Lordship's opinion, to interpose my own judgement, and shall therefore endeavour to support what appears to me most consonant to grammar and reason." . . .

Dr. Adams[1] found him one day busy at his Dictionary, when the following dialogue ensued. "ADAMS. This is a great work, Sir. JOHNSON. Why, Sir, here is a shelf with Junius, and Skinner, and others; and there is a Welsh gentleman who has published a collection of Welsh proverbs, who will help me with the Welsh. ADAMS. But, Sir, how can you do this in three years? JOHNSON. Sir, thus it is. This is the proportion. Let me see; forty times forty is sixteen hundred. As three to sixteen hundred, so is the proportion of an Englishman to a Frenchman."[2] With so much ease and pleasantry could he talk of that prodigious labour which he had undertaken to execute.

. . . The Dictionary, we may believe, afforded Johnson full occupation this year. As it approached to its conclusion, he probably worked with redoubled vigour.

Lord Chesterfield, to whom Johnson had paid the high compliment of addressing to his Lordship the Plan of his Dictionary, had behaved to him in such a manner as to excite his contempt and indignation. The world has been for many years amused with a story confidently told, and as confidently repeated with additional circumstances, that a sudden disgust was taken by Johnson upon occasion of his having been one day kept long in waiting in his Lordship's antechamber, for which the reason assigned was, that he had company with him; and that at last, when the door opened, out walked Colley Cibber[3]; and that Johnson was so violently provoked when he found for whom he had been so long excluded, that he went away in a passion, and never would return. I remember having mentioned this story to George Lord Lyttelton, who told me he was very intimate with Lord Chesterfield; and holding it as a well-known truth, defended Lord Chesterfield by saying that "Cibber, who had been introduced familiarly by the backstairs, had probably not been there above ten minutes." It may seem strange even to entertain a doubt concerning a story so long and so widely current, and thus implicitly adopted, if not sanctioned, by the authority which I have mentioned: but Johnson himself assured me, that there was not the least foundation for it. He told me, that there never was any particular incident which produced a quarrel between Lord Chesterfield and him; but that his Lordship's continued neglect was the reason why he resolved to have no connexion with him. When the Dictionary was upon the eve of publication, Lord Chesterfield, who, it is

[1]Master of Pembroke College, Cambridge.
[2]The reference is to the project of a French dictionary to be produced over a period of forty years by the forty members of the French Academy.

[3]Colley Cibber (1671-1757), actor and dramatist.

said, had flattered himself with expectations that Johnson would dedicate the work to him, attempted, in a courtly manner, to soothe and insinuate himself with the Sage, conscious, as it should seem, of the cold indifference with which he had treated its learned author; and further attempted to conciliate him, by writing two papers in *The World* in recommendation of the work; and it must be confessed, that they contain some studied compliments, so finely turned, that if there had been no previous offence, it is probable that Johnson would have been highly delighted. Praise, in general, was pleasing to him; but by praise from a man of rank and elegant accomplishments, he was peculiarly gratified. . . .

This courtly device failed of its effect. Johnson, who thought that "all was false and hollow," despised the honeyed words, and was even indignant that Lord Chesterfield should, for a moment, imagine, that he could be the dupe of such an artifice. His expression to me concerning Lord Chesterfield, upon this occasion, was, "Sir, after making great professions, he had, for many years, taken no notice of me; but when my Dictionary was coming out, he fell a scribbling in *The World* about it. Upon which, I wrote him a letter expressed in civil terms, but such as might show him that I did not mind what he said or wrote, and that I had done with him."

This is that celebrated letter of which so much has been said, and about which curiosity has been so long excited, without being gratified. I for many years solicited Johnson to favour me with a copy of it, that so excellent a composition might not be lost to posterity. He delayed from time to time to give it me; till at last in 1781, when we were on a visit at Mr. Dilly's, at Southill in Bedfordshire, he was pleased to dictate it to me from memory. He afterwards found among his papers a copy of it which he had dictated to Mr. Baretti, with its title and corrections, in his own handwriting. This he gave to Mr. Langton, adding that if it were to come into print, he wished it to be from that copy. By Mr. Langton's kindness, I am enabled to enrich my work with a perfect transcript of what the world has so eagerly desired to see.

To the Right Honourable the Earl of Chesterfield

"My Lord,   February 7, 1755.

"I have been lately informed, by the proprietor of the World, that two papers, in which my Dictionary is recommended to the publick, were written by your Lordship. To be so distinguished, is an honour, which, being very little accustomed to favours from the great, I know not well how to receive, or in what terms to acknowledge.

"When, upon some slight encouragement, I first visited your Lordship, I was overpowered, like the rest of mankind, by the enchantment of your address, and could not forbear to wish that I might boast myself *Le vainqueur du vainqueur de la terre*:—that I might obtain that regard for which I saw the world contending; but I found my attendance so little encouraged, that neither pride nor modesty would suffer me to continue it. When I had once addressed your Lordship in publick, I had exhausted all the art of pleasing which a retired and uncourtly scholar can possess. I had done all that I could; and no man is well pleased to have his all neglected, be it ever so little.

"Seven years, my Lord, have now past, since I waited in your outward rooms, or was repulsed from your door; during which time I have been pushing on my work through difficulties, of which it is useless to complain, and have brought it, at last, to the verge of publication, without one act of assistance, one word of encouragement, or one smile of favour. Such treatment I did not expect, for I never had a Patron before.

"The shepherd in Virgil grew at last acquainted with Love, and found him a native of the rocks.

"Is not a Patron, my Lord, one who looks with unconcern on a man struggling for life in the water, and, when he has reached ground, encumbers him with help? The notice which you have been pleased to take of my labours, had it been early, had been kind; but it has been delayed till I am indifferent, and cannot enjoy it; till I am solitary, and cannot impart it; till I am known, and do not want it. I hope it is no very cynical asperity, not to confess obligations where no benefit has been received, or to be unwilling that the Publick should consider me as owing that to a Patron, which Providence has enabled me to do for myself.

"Having carried on my work thus far with so little obligation to any favourer of learning, I shall not be disappointed though I should conclude it, if less be possible, with less; for I have been long wakened from that dream of hope, in which I once boasted myself with so much exultation,

"My Lord,
"Your Lordship's most humble
"Most obedient servant,

"SAM. JOHNSON."

. . . The Dictionary, with a Grammar and History of the English Language, being now at length published, in two volumes folio, the world contemplated with wonder so stupendous a work achieved by one man, while other countries had thought such undertakings fit only for whole academies. Vast as his powers were, I cannot but think that his imagination deceived him, when he supposed that by constant application he might have performed the task in three years. Let the Preface be attentively perused, in which is given, in a clear, strong, and glowing style, a comprehensive, yet particular view of what he had done; and it will be evident, that the time he employed upon it was comparatively short. I am unwilling to swell my book with long quotations from what is in everybody's hands, and I believe there are few prose compositions in the English language that are read with more delight, or are more impressed upon the memory, than that preliminary discourse. One of its excellencies has always struck me with peculiar admiration; I mean the perspicuity with which he has expressed abstract scientific notions. As an instance of this, I shall quote the following sentence: "When the radical idea branches out into parallel ramification, how can a consecutive series be formed of senses in their own nature collateral?" We have here an example of what has been often said, and I believe with justice, that there is for every thought a certain nice adaptation of words which none other could equal, and which, when a man has been so fortunate as to hit, he has attained, in what particular case, the perfection of language.

. . . A few of his definitions must be admitted to be erroneous. Thus, Windward and Leeward, though directly of opposite meaning, are defined identically the same way; as to which inconsiderable specks it is enough to observe, that his Preface announces that he was aware there might be many such in so immense a work; nor was he at all disconcerted when an instance was pointed out to him. A lady once asked him how he came to define Pastern the knee of a horse: instead of making an elaborate defence, as she expected, he at once answered, "Ignorance, Madam, pure ignorance." His definition of Network has been often quoted with sportive malignity, as obscuring a thing in itself very plain. But to these frivolous censures no other answer is necessary than that with which we are furnished by his own Preface. "To explain, requires the use of terms less abstruse than that which is to be explained, and such terms cannot always be found. For as nothing can be proved but by supposing something intuitively known, and evident without proof, so nothing can be defined but by the use of words too plain to admit of definition. Sometimes easier words are changed into harder; as, burial, into sepulture or interment; dry, into desiccative; dryness, into siccity or aridity; fit, into paroxism, for, the easiest word, whatever it be, can never be translated into one more easy."

His introducing his own opinions, and even prejudices, under general definitions of words, while at the same time the original meaning of the words is not explained, as his Tory, Whig, Pension, Oats, Excise, and a few more, cannot be fully defended, and must be placed to the account of capricious and humorous indulgence. Talking to me upon this subject when we were at Ashbourne in 1777, he mentioned a still stronger instance of the predominance of his private feelings in the composition of this work, than any now to be found in it. "You know, Sir, Lord Gower forsook the old Jacobite interest. When I came to the *Renegado*, after telling that it meant 'one who deserts to the enemy, a revolter,' I added, Sometimes we say a GOWER. Thus it went to the press; but the printer had more wit than I, and struck it out."

Let it, however, be remembered, that this indulgence does not display itself only in sarcasm towards others, but sometimes in playful allusion to the notions commonly entertained of his own laborious task. Thus: "Grub-street, the name of a street in London, much inhabited by writers of small histories, dictionaries, and temporary poems; whence any mean production is called Grub-street."— "Lexicographer, a writer of dictionaries, a harmless drudge."

. . . He had spent, during the progress of the work, the money for which he had contracted to write his Dictionary. We have seen that the reward of his labour was only fifteen hundred and seventy-five pounds; and when the expense of amanuenses and paper, and other articles, are deducted, his clear profit was very inconsiderable. I once said to him, "I am sorry, Sir, you did not get more for your Dictionary." His answer was, "I am sorry too. But it was very well. The booksellers are generous liberal-minded men." He, upon all occasions, did ample justice to their character in this respect. He considered them as the patrons of literature; and, indeed, although they have eventually been considerable gainers by his Dictionary, it is to them that we owe its having been undertaken and carried through at the risk of great expense, for they were not absolutely sure of being indemnified. . . .

(THE YEAR 1763)

This is to me a memorable year; for in it I had the happiness to obtain the acquaintance of that extraordinary man whose memoirs I am now writing; an acquaintance which I shall ever esteem as one of the most fortunate circumstances in my life. Though then but two-and-twenty, I had for several years read his works with delight and instruction, and had the highest reverence for their authour, which had grown up in my fancy into a kind of mysterious veneration, by figuring to myself a state of solemn elevated abstraction, in which I supposed him to live in the immense metropolis of London.

. . . Mr. Thomas Davies, the actor, who then kept a bookseller's shop in Russel-street, Covent-garden, told me that Johnson was very much his friend, and came frequently to his house, where he more than once invited me to meet him: but by some unlucky accident or other he was prevented from coming to us. . . .

At last, on Monday the 16th of May, when I was sitting in Mr. Davies's back-parlour, after having drunk tea with him and Mrs. Davies, Johnson unexpectedly came into the shop; and Mr. Davies having perceived him through the glass-door in the room in which we were sitting, advancing towards us,—he announced his awful approach to me, somewhat in the manner of an actor in the part of Horatio, when he addresses Hamlet on the appearance of his father's ghost, "Look, my Lord, it comes." I found that I had a very perfect idea of Johnson's figure, from the portrait of him painted by Sir Joshua Reynolds soon after he had published his Dictionary, in the attitude of sitting in his easy chair in deep meditation; which was the first picture his friend did for him. . . . Mr. Davies mentioned my name, and respectfully introduced me to him. I was much agitated; and recollecting his prejudice against the Scotch, of which I had heard much, I said to Davies, "Don't tell where I come from." "From Scotland," cried Davies, roguishly. "Mr. Johnson, (said I) I do indeed come from Scotland, but I cannot help it." I am willing to flatter myself that I meant this as light pleasantry to soothe and conciliate him, and not as an humiliating abasement at the expense of my country. But however that might be, this speech was somewhat unlucky; for with that quickness of wit for which he was so remarkable, he seized the expression "come from Scotland," which I used in the sense of being of that country; and, as if I had said that I had come away from it, or left it, retorted, "That, Sir, I find is what a very great many of your countrymen cannot help." This stroke stunned me a good deal; and when we had sat down, I felt myself not a little embarrassed, and apprehensive of what might come next. He then addressed himself to Davies: "What do you think of Garrick? He has refused me an order for the play for Miss Williams, because he knows the house will be full, and that an order would be worth three shillings." Eager to take any opening to get into conversation with him, I ventured to say, "O, Sir, I cannot think Mr. Garrick would grudge such a trifle to you." "Sir (said he, with a stern look), I have known David Garrick longer than you have done: and I know no right you have to talk to me on the subject." Perhaps I deserved this check; for it was rather presumptuous in me, an entire stranger, to express any doubt of the justice of his animadversion upon his old acquaintance and pupil. I now felt myself much mortified, and began to think, that the hope which I had long indulged of obtaining his acquaintance was blasted. And, in truth, had not my ardour been uncommonly strong, and my resolution uncommonly persevering, so rough a reception might have deterred me forever from making any further attempts. Fortunately, however, I remained upon the field not wholly discomfited; and was soon rewarded by hearing some of his conversation, of which I preserved the following short minute, without marking the questions and observations by which it was produced.

"People (he remarked) may be taken in once, who imagine that an authour is greater in private life than other men. Uncommon parts required uncommon opportunities for their exertion.

"In barbarous society, superiority of parts is of real consequence. Great strength or great wisdom is of much value to an individual. But in more polished times there are people to do everything for money; and then there are a number of other superiorities, such as those of birth and fortune, and rank, that dissipate man's attention, and leave no extraordinary share of respect for personal and intellectual superiority. This is wisely ordered by Providence, to preserve some equality among mankind.

"Sir, this book (*The Elements of Criticism* which he had taken up,) is a pretty essay, and deserves to be held in some estimation, though much of it is chimerical."

Speaking of one who with more than ordinary boldness attacked publick measures and the royal family, he said, "I think he is safe from the law, but he is an abusive scoundrel; and instead of applying to my Lord Chief Justice to punish him, I would send half a dozen footmen and have him well ducked."

"The notion of liberty amuses the people of England, and helps to keep off the *tedium vitae*. When a butcher tells you that *his heart bleeds for his country*, he has, in fact, no uneasy feeling."

"Sheridan will not succeed at Bath with his oratory. Ridicule has gone down before him, and I doubt, Derrick is his enemy.

"Derrick may do very well, as long as he can outrun his character; but the moment his character gets up with him, it is all over."

It is, however, but just to record, that some years afterwards, when I reminded him of this sarcasm, he said, "Well, but Derrick has now got a character that he need not run away from."

I was highly pleased with the extraordinary vigour of his conversation, and regretted that I was drawn away from it by an engagement at another place. I had, for a part of the evening, been left alone with him, and had ventured to make an observation now and then, which he received very civilly; so that I was satisfied that though there was a roughness in his manner, there was no ill-nature in his disposition. Davies followed me to the door, and when I complained to him a little of the hard blows which the great man had given me, he kindly took upon him to console me by saying, "Don't be uneasy. I can see he likes you very well."

A few days afterwards I called on Davies, and asked him if he thought I might take the liberty of waiting on Mr. Johnson at his chambers in the Temple.

He said I certainly might, and that Mr. Johnson would take it as a compliment. So on Tuesday the 24th of May, after having been enlivened by the witty sallies of Messieurs Thornton, Wilkes, Churchill, and Lloyd[1], with whom I had passed the morning, I boldly repaired to Johnson. His Chambers were on the first floor of No. 1, Inner Temple Lane, and I entered them with an impression given me by the Reverend Dr. Blair, of Edinburgh, who had been introduced to him not long before, and described his having "found the Giant in his den"; an expression which, when I came to be pretty well acquainted with Johnson, I repeated to him, and he was diverted at this picturesque account of himself. Dr. Blair had been presented to him by Dr. James Fordyce. At this time the controversy concerning the pieces published by Mr. James Macpherson[2], as translations of Ossian, was at its height. Johnson had all along denied their authenticity; and, what was still more provoking to their admirers, maintained that they had no merit. The subject having been introduced by Dr. Fordyce, Dr. Blair, relying on the internal evidence of their antiquity, asked Dr. Johnson whether he thought any man of a modern age could have written such poems? Johnson replied, "Yes, Sir, many men, many women, and many children." Johnson at this time did not know that Dr. Blair had just published a Dissertation, not only defending their authenticity, but seriously ranking them with the poems of Homer and Virgil; and when he was afterwards informed of this circumstance,

[1]Minor writers of the period.
[2]In the 1760's, Macpherson (1736-1796) published a series of poems which he claimed (falsely) to be translations from the ancient Gaelic poet, Ossian.

he expressed some displeasure at Dr. Fordyce's having suggested the topick, and said, "I am not sorry that they got thus much for their pains. Sir, it was like leading one to talk of a book, when the authour is concealed behind the door."

He received me very courteously: but, it must be confessed, that his apartment, and furniture, and morning dress were sufficiently uncouth. His brown suit of cloaths looked very rusty: he had on a little old shrivelled unpowdered wig, which was too small for his head; his shirt-neck and knees of his breeches were loose; his black worsted stockings ill drawn up; and he had a pair of unbuckled shoes by way of slippers. But all these slovenly particularities were forgotten the moment that he began to talk. . . .

(THE YEAR 1784)

. . . Amidst the melancholy clouds which hung over the dying Johnson, his characteristical manner showed itself on different occasions . . .

A man whom he had never seen before was employed one night to sit up with him. Being asked next morning how he liked his attendant, his answer was, "Not at all, Sir. The fellow's an idiot. He is as awkward as a turn-spit when first put into the wheel, and as sleepy as a dormouse." . . .

He requested three things of Sir Joshua Reynolds: to forgive him thirty pounds which he had borrowed of him; to read the Bible; and never to use his pencil on Sunday. Sir Joshua readily acquiesced . . .

Johnson, with that native fortitude which, amidst all his bodily distress and mental sufferings, never forsook him, asked Dr. Brocklesby, as a man in whom he had confidence, to tell him plainly whether he would recover. "Give me (said he) a direct answer." The doctor having first asked him if he could bear the whole truth which way soever it might lead, and being answered that he could, declared that, in his opinion, he could not recover without a miracle. "Then (said Johnson) I will take no more physic, not even my opiates; for I have prayed that I may render up my soul to God unclouded." In this resolution he persevered, and, at the same time, used only the weakest kinds of sustenance. Being pressed by Mr. Windham to take somewhat more generous nourishment, lest too low a diet would have the very effect he dreaded, by debilitating his mind, he said, "I will take anything but inebriating sustenance." . . .

Having made his will on the 8th and 9th of December, and settled all his worldly affairs, he languished till Monday, the 13th of that month, when he expired about seven o'clock in the evening, with so little apparent pain that his attendants hardly perceived when his dissolution took place. . . .

A few days before his death, he had asked Sir John Hawkins, as one of his executors, where he should be buried; and on being answered, "Doubtless in Westminster Abbey," seemed to feel a satisfaction, very natural to a poet; and indeed in my opinion very natural to every man of any imagination, who has no family sepulcher in which he can be laid with his fathers. Accordingly, upon Monday, December 20, his remains were deposited in that noble and renowned edifice; and over his grave was placed a large blue flag-stone with this inscription:

SAMUEL JOHNSON LL.D.
Obit XIII die Decembris,
Anno Domini
M.DCC.LXXXIV.

AETATIS SUAE LXXV

His funeral was attended by a respectable number of his friends, particularly such of the members of the Literary Club as were then in town; and was also honoured with the presence of several of the Reverend Chapter of Westminster . . .

I trust I shall not be accused of affectation, when I declare, that I find myself unable to express all that I felt upon the loss of such a "guide, philosopher, and friend." I shall, therefore, not say one word of my own, but adopt those of an eminent friend, which he uttered with an abrupt felicity, superior to all studied compositions: "He has made a chasm, which not only nothing can fill up, but which nothing has a tendency to fill up. Johnson is dead. Let us go to the next best: there is nobody; no man can be said to put you in mind of Johnson."

1791

THOMAS GRAY (1716-1771)

The gradual transition from a neo-classical to a romantic type of poetry in the middle decades of the eighteenth century can be witnessed in the poetic development of Thomas Gray. His early poems lean towards neo-classicism in their formal language, their balanced phrasing, their moralizing, and their emotional restraint; his most famous single poem, the "Elegy Written in a Country Churchyard," is almost exactly balanced between the two tendencies; his later poems have more of the wildness, passion, and mystery of the romantic sensibility.

Gray was born in London and educated at Eton and Cambridge. After a journey to the Continent with his friend Horace Walpole, Gray returned to Cambridge where he spent the remainder of his life in study. In 1768 he was appointed Professor of History and Modern Languages at Cambridge. He was buried at Stoke Poges in the churchyard which forms the setting of his elegy.

A shy, studious, retiring man who, as Arnold put it, "never spoke out," Gray produced only a small number of poems. His first works appeared in 1742—his "Ode on Spring" and "Ode on a Distant Prospect of Eton College." The famous Elegy, published in 1751, established his fame as the leading poet of his period and led to his being offered the poet laureateship in 1757—an honour he characteristically declined. In his later years he became very interested in Icelandic and Celtic verse, and under such influences wrote his more impassioned poems, "The Fatal Sisters" and "The Descent of Odin." All his verse is marked by meticulous workmanship, precise observation, unity of mood, and memorable phrasing.

Elegy Written in a Country Churchyard

The curfew tolls the knell of parting day,
    The lowing herd winds slowly o'er the lea,
The plowman homeward plods his weary way,
    And leaves the world to darkness and to me.

Now fades the glimm'ring landscape on the sight,
    And all the air a solemn stillness holds,
Save where the beetle wheels his droning flight,
    And drowsy tinklings lull the distant folds;

Save that from yonder ivy-mantled tow'r
    The moping owl does to the moon complain   10
Of such as, wand'ring near her secret bow'r,
    Molest her ancient solitary reign.

Beneath those rugged elms, that yew-tree's shade,
    Where heaves the turf in many a mould'ring heap,
Each in his narrow cell for ever laid,
    The rude forefathers of the hamlet sleep.

The breezy call of incense-breathing Morn,
    The swallow twitt'ring from the straw-built shed,
The cock's shrill clarion, or the echoing horn,
    No more shall rouse them from their lowly bed.   20

For them no more the blazing hearth shall burn,
    Or busy housewife ply her evening care:
Nor children run to lisp their sire's return,
    Or climb his knees the envied kiss to share.

Oft did the harvest to their sickle yield,
    Their furrow oft the stubborn glebe has broke;
How jocund did they drive their team afield!
    How bow'd the woods beneath their sturdy stroke!

Let not Ambition mock their useful toil,
   Their homely joys, and destiny obscure;   30
Nor Grandeur hear with a disdainful smile,
   The short and simple annals of the poor.

The boast of heraldry, the pomp of pow'r,
   And all that beauty, all that wealth e'er gave,
Awaits alike th' inevitable hour.
   The paths of glory lead but to the grave.

Nor you, ye proud, impute to these the fault,
   If Mem'ry o'er their tomb no trophies raise,
Where thro' the long-drawn aisle and fretted vault
   The pealing anthem swells the note of praise.   40

Can storied urn or animated bust
   Back to its mansion call the fleeting breath?
Can Honour's voice provoke the silent dust,
   Or Flatt'ry soothe the dull cold ear of Death?

Perhaps in this neglected spot is laid
   Some heart once pregnant with celestial fire;
Hands, that the rod of empire might have sway'd,
   Or wak'd to ecstasy the living lyre.

But Knowledge to their eyes her ample page
   Rich with the spoils of time did ne'er unroll;   50
Chill Penury repress'd their noble rage,
   And froze the genial current of the soul.

Full many a gem of purest ray serene,
   The dark unfathom'd caves of ocean bear:
Full many a flow'r is born to blush unseen,
   And waste its sweetness on the desert air.

Some village-Hampden[1], that with dauntless breast
   The little tyrant of his fields withstood;
Some mute inglorious Milton here may rest,
   Some Cromwell[2] guiltless of his country's blood.   60

Th' applause of list'ning senates to command,
   The threats of pain and ruin to despise,
To scatter plenty o'er a smiling land,
   And read their hist'ry in a nation's eyes,

[1]John Hampden (1594-1643), a Puritan who was imprisoned for refusing to pay the obsolete tax of ship money to Charles I.   [2]Oliver Cromwell (1599-1658), the great opponent of Charles I and Lord Protector of England, 1653-1658.

Their lot forbade: nor circumscrib'd alone
    Their growing virtues, but their crimes confin'd;
Forbade to wade through slaughter to a throne,
    And shut the gates of mercy on mankind,

The struggling pangs of conscious truth to hide,
    To quench the blushes of ingenuous shame,   70
Or heap the shrine of Luxury and Pride
    With incense kindled at the Muse's flame.

Far from the madding crowd's ignoble strife,
    Their sober wishes never learn'd to stray;
Along the cool sequester'd vale of life
    They kept the noiseless tenor of their way.

Yet ev'n these bones from insult to protect,
    Some frail memorial still erected nigh,
With uncouth rhymes and shapeless sculpture deck'd,
    Implores the passing tribute of a sigh.   80

Their name, their years, spelt by th' unletter'd muse,
    The place of fame and elegy supply:
And many a holy text around she strews,
    That teach the rustic moralist to die.

For who to dumb Forgetfulness a prey,
    This pleasing anxious being e'er resign'd,
Left the warm precincts of the cheerful day,
    Nor cast one longing, ling'ring look behind?

On some fond breast the parting soul relies,
    Some pious drops the closing eye requires;   90
Ev'n from the tomb the voice of Nature cries,
    Ev'n in our ashes live their wonted fires.

For thee, who mindful of th' unhonour'd Dead
    Dost in these lines their artless tale relate;
If chance, by lonely contemplation led,
    Some kindred spirit shall inquire thy fate,

Haply some hoary-headed swain may say,
    "Oft have we seen him at the peep of dawn
Brushing with hasty steps the dews away
    To meet the sun upon the upland lawn.   100

"There at the foot of yonder nodding beech
    That wreathes its old fantastic roots so high,
His listless length at noontide would he stretch,
    And pore upon the brook that babbles by.

"Hard by yon wood, now smiling as in scorn,
    Mutt'ring his wayward fancies he would rove,
Now drooping, woeful wan, like one forlorn,
    Or craz'd with care, or cross'd in hopeless love.

"One morn I miss'd him on the custom'd hill,
    Along the heath and near his fav'rite tree;   110
Another came; nor yet beside the rill,
    Nor up the lawn, nor at the wood was he;

"The next with dirges due in sad array
    Slow thro' the church-way path we saw him borne.
Approach and read (for thou canst read) the lay,
    Grav'd on the stone beneath yon aged thorn."

THE EPITAPH

Here rests his head upon the lap of Earth
    A youth to Fortune and to Fame unknown.
Fair Science frown'd not on his humble birth,
    And Melancholy mark'd him for her own.   120

Large was his bounty, and his soul sincere,
    Heav'n did a recompense as largely send:
He gave to Mis'ry all he had, a tear,
    He gain'd from Heav'n ('twas all he wish'd) a friend.

No farther seek his merits to disclose,
    Or draw his frailties from their dread abode,
    (There they alike in trembling hope repose)
    The bosom of his Father and his God.

1742?-1750   1751

ROBERT BURNS (1759-1796)

Burns is one of those striking figures about whom legends and misconceptions seem inevitably to cluster. It is not correct to list him as another pre-Romantic English poet: he was a Scottish poet, the culmination of a national literary tradition that went back through Ramsay and Fergusson of the eighteenth century all the way to Henryson and Dunbar of the fifteenth century. Nor is it proper to think of him as an unlettered ploughman: from his father and a local schoolmaster he received a good basic education in literature and history. Another common misconception is to regard as his best such of Burns' non-dialect poems as "The Cotter's Saturday Night"; his more "corr ect" English poems are generally far inferior to his poems in dialect. Burns was primarily a Scottish lyric poet, who brought to fruition a long tradition of Scottish song; he was secondarily a Scottish satirist, who flayed the hypocrisy and cant of his self-righteous countrymen.

He was born at Alloway in Ayrshire, the son of a small farmer. He worked as a farm-labourer and then, unsuccessfully, as a farmer at Mossgiel in partnership with his brother. The publication of the Kilmarnock edition of his poems in 1786 made him famous and took him to Edinburgh, where he was a popular figure among the wits who then made Edinburgh one of the great intellectual centres of Europe. After another unsuccessful attempt at farming, Burns became an excise officer in the town of Dumfries. He suffered increasingly from physical pain, mental depression, and financial worries, and he died at the early age of thirty-seven.

A man of warm sympathies and strong passions, Burns had many love affairs and often acted in a manner that offended the piety of his Calvinist neighbours. But his gusto, his rollicking humour, his hearty love of life, his sympathy for the weak and the oppressed, and his hatred of all forms of sham more than compensated for his lapses from the strict path of propriety.

To a Mouse

ON TURNING HER UP IN HER NEST WITH
THE PLOUGH, NOVEMBER, 1785

Wee, sleekit[1], cowrin', tim'rous beastie,
O, what a panic's in thy breastie!
Thou need na start awa sae hasty
　　Wi' bickering brattle[2]!
I wad be laith to rin an' chase thee,
　　Wi' murdering pattle[3]!

I'm truly sorry man's dominion
Has broken nature's social union,
An' justifies that ill opinion
　　Which makes thee startle　10
At me, thy poor, earth-born companion
　　An' fellow mortal!

I doubt na, whyles[4], but thou may thieve;
What then? poor beastie, thou maun live!
A daimen icker in a thrave[5]
　　'S a sma' request;
I'll get a blessin' wi' the lave[6],
　　An' never miss 't!

Thy wee-bit housie, too, in ruin!
Its silly wa's the win's are strewin'!
An' naething, now, to big[7] a new ane,
　　O' foggage[8] green!
An' bleak December's win's ensuin',
　　Baith snell[9] an' keen!

Thou saw the fields laid bare an' waste,
An' weary winter comin' fast,

An' cozie here, beneath the blast,
　　Thou thought to dwell,
Till crash! the cruel coulter past
　　Out through thy cell.　30

That wee bit heap 'o leaves an' stibble,
Has cost thee monie a weary nibble!
Now thou's turned out, for a' thy trouble,
　　But house or hald[10],
To thole[11] the winter's sleety dribble,
　　An' cranreuch[12] cauld!

But Mousie, thou art no thy lane[13],
In proving foresight may be vain:
The best-laid schemes o' mice an' men
　　Gang aft agley[14],　40
An' lea'e us nought but grief an' pain,
　　For promised joy!

Still thou art blest, compared wi' me!
The present only toucheth thee:
But och! I backward cast my e'e,
　　On prospects drear!
An' forward, though I canna see,
　　I guess an' fear!
　　　　　　　　　　　　　1786

[10]*But house or hald.* Without a home.
[11]Endure.　　[12]Hoar frost.　　[13]Not alone.
[14]*Gang aft agley.* Often go wrong.

Ye Flowery Banks

Ye flowery banks o' bonnie Doon[1],
　　How can ye blume sae fair?
How can ye chant, ye little birds,
　　And I sae fu' o' care?

[1]Sleek.　　[2]Hurrying scamper.
[3]Spade for cleaning the plough.
[4]Sometimes.
[5]I.e., an occasional ear of grain in a shock.
[6]Rest.　　[7]Build.　　[8]Coarse grass.　　[9]Bitter.

[1] River in Ayrshire near which Burns was born.

Thou'll break my heart, thou bonie bird,
   That sings upon the bough;
Thou minds me o' the happy days,
   When my fause love was true.

Thou'll break my heart, thou bonie bird,
   That sings beside thy mate;   10
For sae I sat, and sae I sang,
   And wist na o' my fate.

Aft hae I rov'd by bonie Doon
   To see the wood-bine twine,
And ilka bird sang o' its luve,
   And sae did I o' mine.

Wi' lightsome heart I pu'd a rose
   Frae aff its thorny tree;
And my fause luver staw my rose
   But left the thorn wi' me.   20

1791   1808

Afton Water

Flow gently, sweet Afton[1], among thy green braes[2],
Flow gently, I'll sing thee a song in thy praise;
My Mary's asleep by thy murmuring stream,
Flow gently, sweet Afton, disturb not her dream.

Thou stock-dove, whose echo resounds thro' the glen,
Ye wild whistling blackbirds in yon thorny den,
Thou green-crested lapwing, thy screaming forbear,
I charge you disturb not my slumbering fair.

How lofty, sweet Afton, thy neighbouring hills,
Far mark'd with the courses of clear winding rills;   10
There daily I wander as noon rises high,
My flocks and my Mary's sweet cot in my eye.

How pleasant thy banks and green valleys below,
Where wild in the woodlands the primroses blow;
There oft, as mild Ev'ning weeps over the lea,
The sweet-scented birk shades my Mary and me.

Thy crystal stream, Afton, how lovely it glides,
And winds by the cot where my Mary resides,
How wanton thy waters her snowy feet lave,
As gathering sweet flowrets she stems thy clear wave.   20

Flow gently, sweet Afton, among thy green braes,
Flow gently, sweet river, the theme of my lays;
My Mary's asleep by thy murmuring stream,
Flow gently, sweet Afton, disturb not her dream.

1792

[1] A small river that flows into the Nith near New Cumnock.   [2] Hills.

Highland Mary[1]

Ye banks, and braes, and streams around
  The castle o' Montgomery,
Green be your woods and fair your flowers,
  Your waters never drumlie[2]!
There simmer first unfauld her robes,
  And there the langest tarry;
For there I took the last fareweel,
  O' my sweet Highland Mary.

How sweetly bloom'd the gay green birk,
  How rich the hawthorn's blossom,   10
As underneath their fragrant shade
  I clasp'd her to my bosom!
The golden hours, on angel wings,
  Flew o'er me and my dearie;
For dear to me as light and life,
  Was my sweet Highland Mary.

Wi' monie a vow and lock'd embrace
  Our parting was fu' tender;
And, pledging aft to meet again,
  We tore oursels asunder;   20
But O! fell death's untimely frost,
  That nipt my flower sae early!
Now green's the sod, and cauld's the clay,
  That wraps my Highland Mary!

O pale, pale now, those rosy lips,
  I aft hae kiss'd sae fondly!
And closed for aye the sparkling glance,
  That dwelt on me sae kindly!
And mould'ring now in silent dust,   30
  That heart that lo'ed me dearly!
But still within my bosom's core
  Shall live my Highland Mary.

[1]Mary Campbell, one of Burns' many sweet-
  hearts.   [2]Turbid.

1792   1799

WILLIAM BLAKE (1757-1827)

Blake was a true romantic in thought and style, but, because his work was scarcely known in his lifetime and had little influence until the late nineteenth century, he is not regarded as the founder of the English Romantic Movement.

Blake was born in Soho, London, the son of a hosier who was a disciple of the Swedish mystic, Swedenborg. Swedenborg held that God is Divine Man, Infinite Love, and Infinite Wisdom. Young Blake was greatly influenced by Swedenborg, and even as a boy saw visions as Swedenborg had done before him. At the age of fourteen Blake was apprenticed to an engraver, and thereafter made his living at that trade—or, rather, at that art, for Blake's engravings are of high artistic quality. Blake began to write poetry as a boy—"How sweet I roamed . . .," for example, was written when he was fourteen—and issued his first volume, *Poetical Sketches*, in 1783. Most of his books were not published in the ordinary way, but printed, engraved, and issued in small editions by himself. In this way he brought out many books: in 1789 *Songs of Innocence* and *The Book of Thel*, in 1791 *The French Revolution*

and *The Marriage of Heaven and Hell*, in 1793 *The Book of Ahania*, in 1797 *Vala* (afterwards named *The Four Zoas*), between 1803 and 1808 *Milton*, and between 1804 and 1820 *Jerusalem*. As can be seen from this long but incomplete list, Blake worked very hard, especially as he also illustrated many books by other writers, but he was always poor and neglected. Southey and others accused him of insanity, although Charles Lamb characteristically defended him. He died in 1827, by which time romanticism had become the vogue, but his work was little known even by poets like Wordsworth and Coleridge, and still less by the general public.

Scholars are still trying to interpret the more obscure passages of Blake's later verse, but the main outlines of his thought are fairly clear. There are, broadly speaking, two ways of looking at God and religion, ways which correspond roughly to those of the Old and the New Testaments. The Old Testament God, who in Blake's symbolic system became Urizen, was a God of vengeance, a jealous God, a God of restrictive commandments which are a series of "thou shalt not's." The New Testament God, on the other hand, as presented by Jesus Christ, is a God of love, mercy, and fulfillment, who wants us to "have life, and have it more abundantly." Blake stresses this creative, positive, energizing religion, and attacks the restrictive type. To him, the "marriage of heaven and hell" is the union of love with energy, which are the two great goods. All that lives, he asserts, is holy; that is, men, animals, plants, all living things, are part of the divine. Goodness, then, is not piety nor strictness, but the positive, passionate expression of love and reverence of all living things. To do evil is to restrict, confine, hate, be intolerant or authoritarian. It follows that Blake was a rebel, the friend of the French and American Revolutions, the foe of set creeds, tyrants, prisons, war, and all forms of selfishness and greed. In his early

poems these ideas were expressed in simple, childlike lyrics; in his later works they were expressed obscurely and symbolically in rhythmical chants that sometimes look more like prose than poetry; but the basic ideas were always the same.

Among the selections that follow are many poems in matched pairs from *Songs of Innocence* and *Songs of Experience*: the two "Introductions"; and "The Lamb" and "The Tyger"; "Holy Thursday (I) and (II)"; "The Divine Image" and "The Human Abstract." In Blake's later writings, he resolved these contrary perspectives by developing a theory in which innocence must pass through and comprehend the world of experience before reaching a third and higher state.

Song

How sweet I roam'd from field to field,
   And tasted all the summer's pride,
'Till I the prince of love beheld,
   Who in the sunny beams did glide!

He shew'd me lilies for my hair,
   And blushing roses for my brow;
He led me through his gardens fair,
   Where all his golden pleasures grow.

With sweet May dews my wings were wet,
   And Phœbus fir'd my vocal rage;
He caught me in his silken net,
   And shut me in his golden cage.

He loves to sit and hear me sing,
   Then, laughing, sports and plays with
      me;
Then stretches out my golden wing,
   And mocks my loss of liberty.

1783

Introduction to the Songs of Innocence

Piping down the valleys wild,
Piping songs of pleasant glee,
On a cloud I saw a child,
And he laughing said to me:

"Pipe a song about a Lamb!"
So I piped with merry cheer.
"Piper, pipe that song again";
So I piped: he wept to hear.

"Drop thy pipe, thy happy pipe;
Sing thy songs of happy cheer":   10
So I sung the same again,
While he wept with joy to hear.

"Piper, sit thee down and write
In a book, that all may read."
So he vanish'd from my sight,
And I pluck'd a hollow reed,

And I made a rural pen,
And I stain'd the water clear,
And I wrote my happy songs
Every child may joy to hear.   20

1789

The Lamb

Little Lamb, who made thee?
  Dost thou know who made thee?
Gave thee life, and bid thee feed
By the stream and o'er the mead;
Gave thee clothing of delight,
Softest clothing, woolly, bright;
Gave thee such a tender voice,
Making all the vales rejoice?
  Little Lamb, who made thee?
  Dost thou know who made thee?   10

Little Lamb, I'll tell thee,
  Little Lamb, I'll tell thee:
He is callèd by thy name,
For he calls himself a Lamb.
He is meek, and he is mild;
He became a little child.
I a child, and thou a lamb.
We are callèd by his name.
  Little Lamb, God bless thee!
  Little Lamb, God bless thee!   20

1789

Holy Thursday[1] [I]

'Twas on a Holy Thursday, their innocent faces clean,
The children walking two and two, in red and blue and green,
Grey-headed beadles walk'd before, with wands as white as snow,
Till into the high dome of Paul's they like Thames' waters flow.

O what a multitude they seem'd, these flowers of London town!
Seated in companies they sit with radiance all their own.
The hum of multitudes was there, but multitudes of lambs,
Thousands of little boys and girls raising their innocent hands.

Now like a mighty wind they raise to heaven the voice of song,
Or like harmonious thunderings the seats of Heaven among.
Beneath them sit the aged men, wise guardians of the poor;
Then cherish pity, lest you drive an angel from your door.

1789

[1]The Thursday of the week before Easter.

The Divine Image

To Mercy, Pity, Peace, and Love
All pray in their distress;
And to these virtues of delight
Return their thankfulness.

For Mercy, Pity, Peace, and Love
Is God, our father dear,
And Mercy, Pity, Peace, and Love
Is Man, his child and care.

For Mercy has a human heart,
Pity a human face,   10
And Love, the human form divine,
And Peace, the human dress.

Then every man, of every clime,[1]
That prays in his distress,
Prays to the human form divine,
Love, Mercy, Pity, Peace.

And all must love the human form,
In heathen, turk, or jew;
Where Mercy, Love, & Pity dwell
There God is dwelling too.   20
                                        1789

[1]Climate.

Introduction to the Songs of Experience

Hear the voice of the Bard!
Who Present, Past, and Future sees
Whose ears have heard
The Holy Word,
That walk'd among the ancient trees.[1]

Calling the lapsed Soul[2]
And weeping in the evening dew:
That might controll
The starry pole:
And fallen fallen light renew!   10

O Earth O Earth return!
Arise from out the dewy grass:
Night is worn,
And the morn
Rises from the slumberous mass.

Turn away no more:
Why wilt thou turn away
The starry floor
The wat'ry shore
Is giv'n thee till the break of day.   20
                                              1794

[1]When God spoke to Adam and Eve in Eden. Free to travel through time via his imagination, the Bard (poet) calls to the fallen soul and fallen earth to turn toward the light of vision and wonder—the world of the imagination God has given us.
[2]Lapsed, or fallen, since the expulsion from Eden.

The Tyger[1]

Tyger! Tyger! burning bright
In the forests of the night,
What immortal hand or eye
Could frame thy fearful symmetry?

In what distant deeps or skies
Burnt the fire of thine eyes?
On what wings dare he aspire?
What the hand dare seize the fire?

And what shoulder, and what art,
Could twist the sinews of thy heart,   10
And when thy heart began to beat,
What dread hand? and what dread feet?

What the hammer? what the chain?
In what furnace was thy brain?
What the anvil? what dread grasp
Dare its deadly terrors clasp?

When the stars threw down their spears,
And water'd heaven with their tears,
Did he smile his work to see?
Did he who made the Lamb make thee?

Tyger! Tyger! burning bright   21
In the forests of the night,
What immortal hand or eye,
Dare frame thy fearful symmetry?

1794

[1]This poem is the counterpart, in *Songs of Experience*, of "The Lamb" in *Songs of Innocence*. The tiger is the symbol of divine energy, as the lamb is the symbol of divine love. God is both energy and love.

Holy Thursday [II]

Is this a holy thing to see
In a rich and fruitful land,
Babes reduc'd to misery,
Fed with cold and usurous hand?

Is that trembling cry a song?
Can it be a song of joy?
And so many children poor?
It is a land of poverty!

And their sun does never shine,
And their fields are bleak and bare,
And their ways are fill'd with thorns:
It is eternal winter there.

For where-e'er the sun does shine,
And where-e'er the rain does fall,
Babe can never hunger there,
Nor poverty the mind appall.

1794

The Human Abstract[1]

Pity would be no more
If we did not make somebody Poor;
And Mercy no more could be
If all were as happy as we.

And mutual fear brings peace,
Till the selfish loves increase:
Then Cruelty knits a snare,
And spreads his baits with care.

He sits down with holy fears,
And waters the ground with tears;   10
Then Humility takes its root
Underneath his foot.

Soon spreads the dismal shade
Of Mystery over his head;
And the Catterpiller and Fly
Feed on the Mystery.

And it bears the fruit of Deceit,
Ruddy and sweet to eat;
And the Raven his nest has made
In its thickest shade.   20

The Gods of the earth and sea
Sought thro' Nature to find this Tree;
But their search was all in vain:
There grows one in the Human Brain.

1790-2   1794

[1]This poem is the matched opposite to "The Divine Image," from *Songs of Innocence*. Here cruelty, exploitation, selfishness and false humility replace the virtues of the earlier poem "Mercy, Pity, Peace and Love." These vices are represented as the seeds of the Tree of Mystery, which darkens and corrupts the natural world.

Auguries of Innocence

To see a world in a grain of sand
And a heaven in a wild flower,
Hold infinity in the palm of your hand
And eternity in an hour.

A robin redbreast in a cage
Puts all Heaven in a rage.
A dove house fill'd with doves and pigeons
Shudders Hell thro' all its regions.
A dog starv'd at his master's gate
Predicts the ruin of the state.   10
A horse misus'd upon the road
Calls to Heaven for human blood.
Each outcry of the hunted hare
A fibre from the brain does tear.
A skylark wounded in the wing,

A Cherubim does cease to sing.
The game cock clipp'd and arm'd for fight
Does the rising Sun affright.
Every wolf's and lion's howl
Raises from Hell a human soul.   20

*   *   *

He who respects the infant's faith
Triumphs over Hell and Death.
The child's toys and the old man's reasons
Are the fruits of the two seasons.
The questioner, who sits so sly,
Shall never know how to reply.
He who replies to words of doubt
Doth put the light of Knowledge out.
The strongest poison ever known

Came from Caesar's laurel crown. 30
Nought can deform the human race
Like to the armour's iron brace.
When gold and gems adorn the plow
To peaceful arts shall Envy bow.
A riddle, or the cricket's cry,
Is to doubt a fit reply.
The emmet's inch and eagle's mile
Make lame Philosophy to smile.
He who doubts from what he sees
Will ne'er believe, do what you please. 40
If the Sun and Moon should doubt,
They'd immediately go out.
To be in a passion you good may do,
But no good if a passion is in you.
The whore and gambler, by the state
Licens'd, build that nation's fate.
The harlot's cry from street to street,
Shall weave Old England's winding sheet.

The winner's shout, the loser's curse,
Dance before dead England's hearse. 50
Every night and every morn
Some to misery are born.
Every morn and every night
Some are born to sweet delight.
Some are born to sweet delight,
Some are born to endless night.
We are led to believe a lie
When we see not thro' the eye,
Which was born in a night to perish in a
     night,
When the Soul slept in beams of light. 60
God appears and God is light
To those poor souls who dwell in night,
But does a human form display
To those who dwell in realms of day.

c. 1800-1803?   1850

FROM *Milton*

A Poem in Two Books to Justify the
Ways of God to Men

PREFACE[1]

And did those feet in ancient time
Walk upon England's mountains green?
And was the holy Lamb of God
On England's pleasant pastures seen?

And did the Countenance Divine
Shine forth upon our clouded hills?
And was Jerusalem builded here
Among these dark Satanic mills?

Bring me my bow of burning gold:
Bring me my arrows of desire:
Bring me my spear: O clouds unfold!
Bring me my chariot of fire.

I will not cease from mental fight,
Nor shall my sword sleep in my hand
Till we have built Jerusalem,
In England's green and pleasant land.

1804

[1]Blake believed that the England in which he lived had been and could still be the Holy Land, and that it was the duty of Englishmen to restore their country to its ancient glory, to permit the Divine Countenance of Jesus to shine forth and pierce the gloom of hills clouded by error and the confusion and materialism symbolized by the "dark Satanic mills." This could be accomplished by heroic energy of mind.

1780   1790   1800

● Wordsworth and Coleridge: *Lyrical Ballads*

● Wordsworth: *The Prelude*

● Blake: *Jerusalem*

● Coleridge: *The Rime of the Ancient Mariner*

● Industrial Revolution

THE ROMANTIC PERIOD (1785-1836)

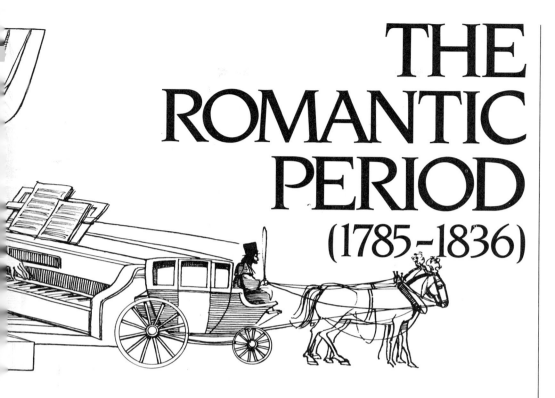

1820	1830	1840
		• First Reform Bill
• Byron: *Don Juan*		
• Shelley: *Prometheus Unbound*		
• Keats: *Lamia and Other Poems*		Reign of Queen Victoria •
• Lamb: *Essays of Elia*		

It is difficult to give precise dates for the Romantic Period of English literature. Some prefer to date it from the joint publication of Wordsworth's and Coleridge's volume *Lyrical Ballads* in 1798 to the First Reform Bill of 1832; but the death of Dr. Johnson in December 1784 more properly marks the end of one era, and the accession of Queen Victoria in 1836 the beginning of another. The important thing to remember is that romanticism in English literature did not abruptly begin or end. As we have seen, there were romantic qualities in various writers of the eighteenth century such as Thomson, Gray, Collins, Cowper, Burns, and Blake; and the great Victorians such as Tennyson, Browning, Arnold, Rossetti, Swinburne, and Morris were basically romantic artists too. But romanticism can be extended even further in both directions: the writers of the Elizabethan era had some romantic tendencies, and twentieth century writers such as Hardy, Housman, Yeats, D. H. Lawrence, and Dylan Thomas might be argued to be romantics also. The fact is that romanticism is a permanent element in all English literature; as Walter Pater put it, "Romanticism is rather a spirit which shows itself at all times in various degrees than the peculiarity of a time or school." Why, then, do we label this particular period in the late eighteenth and early nineteenth century romantic? Because during that period the romantic spirit was operative to an unusually high degree.

Not only is romanticism hard to date; it is also hard to define. So difficult is it to define that some critics have contended we should abandon the term altogether; but there is meaning in the term, though it is a complex and variable meaning. A glance at the origin and development of the term may help us to understand it more clearly.

The noun "romanticism" and the adjective "romantic" are derived from the Latin word *romanicus*, a dialect of Latin spoken by inhabitants of the western portions of the Roman Empire. From this word came *roman*, meaning something written in this dialect; and as the literature of these western portions such as Gaul (or France) came to concern itself with the deeds of heroes such as Charlemagne and King Arthur, tales of knighthood and courtly love or what we call the romances, *roman* came to mean writings fictional rather than historical like the epics, writings more concerned with feeling than with action, writings dealing in the strange, the fanciful, and the wonderful. Many of these qualities of the medieval romance, obviously, were revived in the Romantic Period; and it is interesting to notice how, in a strongly romantic literary era, enthusiasm for the life of the Middle Ages recurs.

The adjective "romantic" did not appear until the seventeenth century, when it meant "of a fabulous or fictitious character, having no foundation in fact." In the early eighteenth century it came to stand for a love of nature, a tendency towards sentimental melancholy, a delight in "enthusiasm" or strong feeling. Later in the eighteenth century new shades of meaning were added to the adjective: an interest in

231

the Middle Ages and especially its magical aspects, a taste for the horrible or gloomy or eerie, and a cult of eccentricity and irregularity.

Since the word contains all these shades of meaning, it is not surprising that a brief definition of it is almost impossible. Perhaps the short definition that comes closest to summing it up adequately is Theodore Watts-Dunton's phrase "the renaissance of wonder." After a century of attempts to give rational or scientific explanations of everything, men were happy to admit that the universe is after all a mysterious and wonderful place, that man himself in his complexity and variety is a wonderful being, that his physical environment is wonderful and fascinating, and that there is behind all physical appearances a mysterious and wonderful spiritual reality. Not all writers of the romantic period exhibit all the various tendencies which cluster about the word romantic, but they all do have in common this sense of wonder, this fascination with the mysterious.

The most fruitful approach is perhaps to list the major attributes of romanticism. The romantic writer believes in the creative imagination as at least a necessary complement to the critical intellect; he believes that feeling, intuition, and sensibility are important avenues to truth, as important—if not more important—than the common-sense or reason beloved by the writers of the Restoration and eighteenth century; he believes in the almost infinite potentialities of the individual human being instead of stressing man's limited role in an orderly, hierarchical universe as did Pope and Swift (this difference between the romantic and neo-classical outlook has been brilliantly summed up by the twentieth century critic T. E. Hulme, who said that to the neo-classicist man was a bucket, to the romantic a well); he believes in the maximum degree of political and moral freedom so that the individual may attain his maximum development; for this reason most romantics are radical in politics whereas most of the neo-classicists were conservative; the romantic writer is interested in the particular example rather than the general class, believing that each man's special insights are valuable, not merely the general principles of human nature; this interest in turn leads away from the neo-classical stress upon conformity and into a concern with the unique, the different, the abnormal, the eccentric; the romantic writer is not as preoccupied with the contemporary social scene as was the neo-classicist, but tends to interest himself in the distant in space; the romantic writer is interested in nature, not so much the nature of order and reason that charmed the neo-classicist as wild nature, the landscape which by its beauty or power or tumult arouses the sense of wonder or reverence or awe; finally, the romantic artist believes that new forms and styles are needed to reveal the new vision derived from inspiration and imagination; he therefore largely abandons the regular couplets cultivated so assiduously by the neo-classicists and branches out into a great variety of metrical forms.

These interests and attitudes were particularly conducive to poetic creation, and the Romantic Period is one of the great ages of English poetry. Wordsworth found delight and wonder in the simple natural objects of the Lake District of England; Coleridge went to the legendary and weird to find material with which to weave his mysterious imaginative fabrics; Sir Walter Scott found material for wonder in the legends of his native Scotland; Byron travelled around the Mediterranean countries in quest of wild nature and lawless men to celebrate in tumultuous verse; Shelley communed with his own untamed spirit and with the swift-moving winds and clouds, always seeking a glimpse of the ideal beauty which he believed to lie at the heart of reality; Keats steeped his senses in the beauty of the ancient world, of the natural world about him, or of women, in order to convey his vision of the mingled magic and melancholy of existence.

Prose fared less well. The new stress on personality and individuality brought intimacy to the essay, and in the hands of Charles Lamb, William Hazlitt, and Thomas De Quincey the personal, self-revealing essay reached perhaps its highest state of perfection. Literary criticism was also given a new direction by the romantic stress on sensibility and intuition and imagination, and Coleridge and Hazlitt in particular wrote criticism of Shakespeare and other writers that is more sensitive and exciting if less systematic and comprehensive than the criticism of Dryden and Johnson. But there is nothing in the non-fictional prose of the Romantic Period to equal its poetry, nor indeed to equal Swift's prose satires or Boswell's *Life of Johnson*.

Prose fiction did not flourish during the Romantic Period either. Romantic fiction sought to do what Romantic poetry did: to exploit the past for its fascination and mystery, and nature for its wonder and beauty. In the historical novels of Sir Walter Scott it approached a comparable success; but most of the fiction of the period was feeble and marginal when compared with the great eighteenth century novels of Defoe, Richardson, Fielding, and Sterne. Apart from Scott, only Jane Austen from this period is in the front rank of English novelists, and she was essentially a neo-classicist living out of her time. The typical romantic novel was the Gothic romance as practised by Mrs. Radcliffe, "Monk" Lewis, or Mary Shelley—a weird creation that is merely an object of curiosity today, in contrast with the enduring interest of the poetry of the period.

Drama was also a step-child of the Romantic Period. Long verse plays were written by Shelley and Byron, but whatever their value as poetry they have little value as drama—in fact, they were never intended for the stage. After the death of Sheridan, English drama went into virtual eclipse until the appearance of Ibsen in Norway in the late nineteenth century stimulated the modern revival associated particularly with George Bernard Shaw.

Since romantic literature was so much more individual and personal in its emphasis, there seems less need to stress the political and social background in discussing it. But it would be a mistake to leave the impression that this background did not affect the literature, or that the writers were not interested in it. Three great historical events had a tremendous influence upon the writers of this generation: the American Revolution, the French Revolution, and the Industrial Revolution. The first two, by showing the great changes that ordinary men could effect by united effort, confirmed the Romantic belief in human potentialities; and although the excesses to which the French Revolution in particular eventually went shocked and alienated its early sympathizers, most of the Romantics clung to the belief that in essence its effect would be a good and liberating one. If Wordsworth, for example, eventually came to modify his original enthusiasm for the French Revolution, he never lost his sympathy for its ideals. His later conservativism was not an acceptance of the *status quo*, but a plea for the restoration of ideals which he felt had been sacrificed in the new scramble for riches.

This scramble for riches, this growing materialism, was in large part the result of the Industrial Revolution. The Industrial Revolution, gradually replacing laborious hand manufacture by mass mechanical production, had three principal effects, only one of which the Romantics could approve. It made possible much cheaper goods and services, and to this extent benefited the ordinary man; but it destroyed much of the natural beauty of the English countryside and herded many of the erstwhile rural inhabitants into the slums of the new industrial towns; and it brought great wealth and power to those few men who owned the new means of production, and made them arrogant and greedy. The full effects of this process became more obvious in the Victorian period, but they were already visible enough in the early decades of the nineteenth century to bring protests from all the leading Romantic poets.

Politically and socially, then, the Romantic writers were non-conformists. They refused to see the American and French Revolutions as official England saw them: as the wicked works of wicked men. And they refused to hail the Industrial Revolution as the key to a new heaven on earth. Believing in the power of the individual, they held up the ideals of justice, equality, and liberty in an age which was showing all too evident signs of being ready to sacrifice these things on the altar of wealth.

WILLIAM WORDSWORTH (1770-1850)

Most of the qualities which we associate with romanticism can be found in Wordsworth: he writes of his own feelings, memories, and observations, rather than of politics or general questions of ethics; he stresses the role of the creative imagination and of intuitive wisdom; he finds food for wonder in the ordinary human being— a child, an old leech-gatherer, a girl in a harvest field; he supports the French Revolution when he thinks it is the friend of liberty, and turns against it when it threatens freedom; he writes feelingly of the beauties of the natural landscape rather than rationally of the laws of the natural universe; he discards the formal poetic diction of the eighteenth century and writes simply and naturally; he deserts the neo-classical couplet and restores blank verse, rhymed stanzas, the sonnet, and other lyrical forms to English verse. It is true that he has little interest in the Middle Ages, or in any distant times or places, and that he seldom writes of the wilder passions, but in all other respects he is a genuine romantic.

Wordsworth was born at Cockermouth, the son of an attorney, and was educated at Hawkshead Grammar School and St. John's College,

Cambridge. After graduation he spent a year in France, was greatly attracted to the doctrines of the French Revolution, and fell in love with a French girl, Annette Vallon. Shortly after his return to England, his country declared war on France, and Wordsworth was plunged into depression: he loved both England and France, and it was torture to see them at war; and he was unable to maintain contact with Annette, who bore his child out of wedlock. From this crisis of pessimism he was delivered by a prolonged stay in the country with his sister Dorothy, who encouraged his love of Nature. Communion with nature restored his spirit, and it is to this experience that we must attribute the almost religious reverence with which Wordsworth regarded nature. Wordsworth also owed much at this time to the friendship of Coleridge, with whom in 1798 he jointly published *Lyrical Ballads*. After a trip to Germany with Coleridge, Wordsworth settled in 1799 at Grasmere in the Lake District, and there, in Dove Cottage, he spent the rest of his life. In 1802 he married Mary Hutchinson, and in 1813 he was made distributor of stamps for Westmoreland. He held this post until 1842, when he was given a government pension; and he succeeded Robert Southey as poet laureate in 1843. He died at the age of eighty and was buried in Grasmere churchyard.

Wordsworth wrote poetry until the end of his long life, but almost all his best work was done in his youth, up to the year 1808. As he grew older, he became increasingly conservative and conventional. There is nothing conventional about his best verse, however: it has in a unique degree the power to evoke our response to the mystery, wonder, and comfort to be found in the familiar flowers of the field and in seemingly ordinary people and places. His plain, quiet, even style is ideally suited to his simple subject-matter and his homely wisdom.

FROM *The Prelude*[1]

or Growth of a Poet's Mind

BOOK FIRST—CHILDHOOD AND SCHOOL-TIME

When he had left the mountains and received
On his smooth breast the shadow of those towers[2]
That yet survive, a shattered monument
Of feudal sway, the bright blue river[3] passed
Along the margin of our terrace walk;
A tempting playmate whom we dearly loved.
Oh, many a time have I, a five years' child,
In a small mill-race severed from his stream,
Made one long bathing of a summer's day;
Basked in the sun, and plunged and basked again   10
Alternate, all a summer's day, or scoured
The sandy fields, leaping through flowery groves
Of yellow ragwort; or when rock and hill,
The woods, and distant Skiddaw's lofty height,
Were bronzed with deepest radiance, stood alone
Beneath the sky, as if I had been born
On Indian plains, and from my mother's hut
Had run abroad in wantonness, to sport,
A naked savage, in the thunder shower.

Fair seed-time had my soul, and I grew up   20
Fostered alike by beauty and by fear:
Much favoured in my birth-place, and no less
In that belovèd Vale[4] to which erelong
We were transplanted;— there were we let loose
For sports of wider range. Ere I had told
Ten birth-days, when among the mountain slopes
Frost, and the breath of frosty wind, had snapped
The last autumnal crocus, 'twas my joy

[1]The first version of "The Prelude" was completed in 1805, but not published until 1926.
This much-revised version of the poem was published just after Wordsworth's death in 1850.
[2]Cockermouth Castle.   [3]The Derwent.   [4]Esthwaite, where Hawkshead School was.

With store of springes[5] o'er my shoulder hung
To range the open heights where woodcocks run   30
Among the smooth green turf. Through half the night,
Scudding away from snare to snare, I plied
That anxious visitation;—moon and stars
Were shining o'er my head. I was alone,
And seemed to be a trouble to the peace
That dwelt among them. Sometimes it befell
In these night wanderings, that a strong desire
O'erpowered my better reason, and the bird
Which was the captive of another's toil
Became my prey; and when the deed was done   40
I heard among the solitary hills
Low breathings coming after me, and sounds
Of undistinguishable motion, steps
Almost as silent as the turf they trod.

Nor less, when spring had warmed the cultured vale,
Moved we as plunderers where the mother-bird
Had in high places built her lodge; though mean
Our object and inglorious, yet the end
Was not ignoble. Oh! when I have hung
Above the raven's nest, by knots of grass   50
And half-inch fissures in the slippery rock
But ill sustained, and almost (so it seemed)
Suspended by the blast that blew amain,
Shouldering the naked crag, oh, at that time
While on the perilous ridge I hung alone,
With what strange utterance did the loud dry wind
Blow through my ear! the sky seemed not a sky
Of earth—and with what motion moved the clouds!

Dust as we are, the immortal spirit grows
Like harmony in music; there is a dark   60
Inscrutable workmanship that reconciles
Discordant elements, makes them cling together
In one society. How strange, that all
The terrors, pains, and early miseries,
Regrets, vexations, lassitudes interfused
Within my mind, should e'er have borne a part,
And that a needful part, in making up
The calm existence that is mine when I
Am worthy of myself! Praise to the end!

⁵Snares or nooses.

Thanks to the means which Nature deigned to employ;   70
Whether her fearless visitings, or those
That came with soft alarm, like hurtless light
Opening the peaceful clouds; or she would use
Severer interventions, ministry
More palpable, as best might suit her aim.

    One summer evening (led by her) I found
A little boat tied to a willow tree
Within a rocky cave, its usual home.
Straight I unloosed her chain, and stepping in
Pushed from the shore. It was an act of stealth   80
And troubled pleasure, nor without the voice
Of mountain-echoes did my boat move on;
Leaving behind her still, on either side,
Small circles glittering idly in the moon,
Until they melted all into one track
Of sparkling light. But now, like one who rows,
Proud of his skill, to reach a chosen point
With unswerving line, I fixed my view
Upon the summit of a craggy ridge,
The horizon's utmost boundary; far above   90
Was nothing but the stars and the grey sky.
She was an elfin pinnace; lustily
I dipped my oars into the silent lake,
And, as I rose upon the stroke, my boat
Went heaving through the water like a swan;
When, from behind that craggy steep till then
The horizon's bound, a huge peak, black and huge,
As if with voluntary power instinct,
Upreared its head. I struck and struck again,
And growing still in stature the grim shape   100
Towered up between me and the stars, and still,
For so it seemed, with purpose of its own
And measured motion like a living thing,
Strode after me. With trembling oars I turned,
And through the silent water stole my way
Back to the covert of the willow tree;
There in her mooring-place I left my bark,—
And through the meadows homeward went, in grave
And serious mood; but after I had seen
That spectacle, for many days, my brain   110
Worked with a dim and undetermined sense
Of unknown modes of being; o'er my thoughts

There hung a darkness, call it solitude
Or blank desertion. No familiar shapes
Remained, no pleasant images of trees,
Of sea or sky, no colours of green fields;
But huge and mighty forms, that do not live
Like living men, moved slowly through the mind
By day, and were a trouble to my dreams.

    Wisdom and Spirit of the universe!   120
Thou Soul that art the eternity of thought,
That givest to forms and images a breath
And everlasting motion, not in vain
By day or star-light thus from my first dawn
Of childhood didst thou intertwine for me
The passions that build up our human soul;
Not with the mean and vulgar works of man,
But with high objects, with enduring things—
With life and nature—purifying thus
The elements of feeling and of thought,   130
And sanctifying, by such discipline,
Both pain and fear, until we recognise
A grandeur in the beatings of the heart.
Nor was this fellowship vouchsafed to me
With stinted kindness. In November days,
When vapours rolling down the valley made
A lonely scene more lonesome, among woods,
At noon and 'mid the calm of summer nights,
When, by the margin of the trembling lake,
Beneath the gloomy hills homeward I went   140
In solitude, such intercourse was mine;
Mine was it in the fields both day and night,
And by the waters, all the summer long.

    And in the frosty season, when the sun
Was set, and visible for many a mile
The cottage windows blazed through twilight gloom,
I heeded not their summons: happy time
It was indeed for all of us—for me
It was a time of rapture! Clear and loud
The village clock tolled six,—I wheeled about,   150
Proud and exulting like an untired horse
That cares not for his home. All shod with steel,

We hissed along the polished ice in games
Confederate, imitative of the chase
And woodland pleasures,—the resounding horn,
The pack loud chiming, and the hunted hare.
So through the darkness and the cold we flew,
And not a voice was idle; with the din
Smitten, the precipices rang aloud;
The leafless trees and every icy crag   160
Tinkled like iron; while far distant hills
Into the tumult sent an alien sound
Of melancholy not unnoticed, while the stars
Eastward were sparkling clear, and in the west
The orange sky of evening died away.
Not seldom from the uproar I retired
Into a silent bay, or sportively
Glanced sideway, leaving the tumultuous throng,
To cut across the reflex of a star
That fled, and, flying still before me, gleamed   170
Upon the glassy plain; and oftentimes,
When we had given our bodies to the wind,
And all the shadowy banks on either side
Came sweeping through the darkness, spinning still
The rapid line of motion, then at once
Have I, reclining back upon my heels,
Stopped short; yet still the solitary cliffs
Wheeled by me—even as if the earth had rolled
With visible motion her diurnal round!
Behind me did they stretch in solemn train,   180
Feebler and feebler, and I stood and watched
Till all was tranquil as a dreamless sleep.

   Ye Presences of Nature in the sky
And on the earth! Ye Visions of the hills!
And Souls of lonely places! can I think
A vulgar hope was yours when ye employed
Such ministry, when ye, through many a year
Haunting me thus among my boyish sports,
On caves and trees, upon the woods and hills,
Impressed, upon all forms, the characters   190
Of danger or desire; and thus did make
The surface of the universal earth,
With triumph and delight, with hope and fear,
Work like a sea? . . .

1799-1805   1850

Lines Composed a Few Miles above Tintern Abbey[1]

on Revisiting the Banks of the Wye during a Tour, July 13, 1798

Five years have past; five summers, with the length
Of five long winters! and again I hear
These waters, rolling from their mountain-springs
With a soft inland murmur.—Once again
Do I behold these steep and lofty cliffs,
That on a wild secluded scene impress
Thoughts of more deep seclusion; and connect
The landscape with the quiet of the sky.
The day is come when I again repose
Here, under this dark sycamore, and view   10
These plots of cottage-ground, these orchard-tufts,
Which at this season, with their unripe fruits,
Are clad in one green hue, and lose themselves
'Mid groves and copses.   Once again I see
These hedge-rows, hardly hedge-rows, little lines
Of sportive wood run wild: these pastoral farms,
Green to the very door; and wreaths of smoke
Sent up, in silence, from among the trees!
With some uncertain notice, as might seem
Of vagrant dwellers in the houseless woods,   20
Or of some Hermit's cave, where by his fire
The Hermit sits alone.
                    These beauteous forms,
Through a long absence, have not been to me
As is a landscape to a blind man's eye:
But oft, in lonely rooms, and 'mid the din
Of towns and cities, I have owed to them,
In hours of weariness, sensations sweet,
Felt in the blood, and felt along the heart;
And passing even into my purer mind,
With tranquil restoration:—feelings too   30
Of unremembered pleasure: such, perhaps,
As have no slight or trivial influence
On that best portion of a good man's life,
His little, nameless, unremembered, acts
Of kindness and of love.   Nor less, I trust,

[1]Tintern Abbey is a ruined monastery on the banks of the Wye in Monmouthshire.

To them I may have owed another gift,
Of aspect more sublime; that blessed mood,
In which the burthen of the mystery,
In which the heavy and the weary weight
Of all this unintelligible world,   40
Is lightened:—that serene and blessed mood,
In which the affections gently lead us on,—
Until, the breath of this corporeal frame
And even the motion of our human blood
Almost suspended, we are laid asleep
In body, and become a living soul:
While with an eye made quiet by the power
Of harmony, and the deep power of joy,
We see into the life of things.
                                                    If this
Be but a vain belief, yet, oh! how oft—   50
In darkness and amid the many shapes
Of joyless daylight; when the fretful stir
Unprofitable, and the fever of the world,
Have hung upon the beatings of my heart—
How oft, in spirit, have I turned to thee,
O sylvan Wye! thou wanderer thro' the woods,
How often has my spirit turned to thee!
    And now, with gleams of half-extinguished thought,
With many recognitions dim and faint,
And somewhat of a sad perplexity,   60
The picture of the mind revives again:
While here I stand, not only with the sense
Of present pleasure, but with pleasing thoughts
That in this moment there is life and food
For future years. And so I dare to hope,
Though changed, no doubt, from what I was when first
I came among these hills; when like a roe
I bounded o'er the mountains, by the sides
Of the deep rivers, and the lonely streams,
Wherever nature led: more like a man   70
Flying from something that he dreads, than one
Who sought the thing he loved. For nature then
(The coarser pleasures of my boyish days
And their glad animal movements all gone by)
To me was all in all.—I cannot paint
What then I was. The sounding cataract
Haunted me like a passion: the tall rock,

The mountain, and the deep and gloomy wood,
Their colours and their forms, were then to me
An appetite; a feeling and a love,   80
That had no need of a remoter charm,
By thought supplied, nor any interest
Unborrowed from the eye.—That time is past,
And all its aching joys are now no more,
And all its dizzy raptures. Not for this
Faint I, nor mourn nor murmur; other gifts
Have followed; for such loss, I would believe,
Abundant recompense. For I have learned
To look on nature, not as in the hour
Of thoughtless youth; but hearing oftentimes   90
The still sad music of humanity,
Nor harsh nor grating, though of ample power
To chasten and subdue.—And I have felt
A presence that disturbs me with the joy
Of elevated thoughts; a sense sublime
Of something far more deeply interfused,
Whose dwelling is the light of setting suns,
And the round ocean and the living air,
And the blue sky, and in the mind of man:
A motion and a spirit, that impels   100
All thinking things, all objects of all thought,
And rolls through all things. Therefore am I still
A lover of the meadows and the woods
And mountains; and of all that we behold
From this green earth; of all the mighty world
Of eye, and ear,—both what they half create,
And what perceive; well pleased to recognise
In nature and the language of the sense
The anchor of my purest thoughts, the nurse,
The guide, the guardian of my heart, and soul   110
Of all my moral being.
                                        Nor perchance,
If I were not thus taught, should I the more
Suffer my genial spirits to decay:
For thou art with me here upon the banks
Of this fair river; thou my dearest Friend,
My dear, dear Friend[2]; and in thy voice I catch
The language of my former heart, and read
My former pleasures in the shooting lights

[2]His sister, Dorothy Wordsworth.

Of thy wild eyes. Oh! yet a little while
May I behold in thee what I was once,   120
My dear, dear Sister! and this prayer I make,
Knowing that Nature never did betray
The heart that loved her; 'tis her privilege,
Through all the years of this our life, to lead
From joy to joy: for she can so inform
The mind that is within us, so impress
With quietness and beauty, and so feed
With lofty thoughts, that neither evil tongues,
Rash judgments, nor the sneers of selfish men,
Nor greetings where no kindness is, nor all   130
The dreary intercourse of daily life,
Shall e'er prevail against us, or disturb
Our cheerful faith, that all which we behold
Is full of blessings. Therefore let the moon
Shine on thee in thy solitary walk;
And let the misty mountain-winds be free
To blow against thee: and, in after years,
When these wild ecstasies shall be matured
Into a sober pleasure; when thy mind
Shall be a mansion for all lovely forms,   140
Thy memory be as a dwelling-place
For all sweet sounds and harmonies; oh! then,
If solitude, or fear, or pain, or grief,
Should be thy portion, with what healing thoughts
Of tender joy wilt thou remember me,
And these my exhortations! Nor, perchance—
If I should be where I no more can hear
Thy voice, nor catch from thy wild eyes these gleams
Of past existence—wilt thou then forget
That on the banks of this delightful stream   150
We stood together; and that I, so long
A worshipper of Nature, hither came
Unwearied in that service: rather say
With warmer love—oh! with far deeper zeal
Of holier love. Nor wilt thou then forget,
That after many wanderings, many years
Of absence, these steep woods and lofty cliffs,
And this green pastoral landscape, were to me
More dear, both for themselves and for thy sake!

1798   1798

She Dwelt among the Untrodden Ways

She dwelt among the untrodden ways
  Beside the springs of Dove,
A maid whom there were none to praise
  And very few to love:

A violet by a mossy stone
  Half hidden from the eye!
—Fair as a star, when only one
  Is shining in the sky.

    She lived unknown, and few could know
      When Lucy[1] ceased to be;
    But she is in her grave, and, oh,
      The difference to me!

1799   1800

[1]Probably an imaginary girl.

Composed upon Westminster Bridge
September 3, 1802

Earth has not anything to show more fair:
Dull would he be of soul who could pass by
A sight so touching in its majesty:
This City now doth, like a garment, wear
The beauty of the morning; silent, bare,
Ships, towers, domes, theatres, and temples lie
Open unto the fields, and to the sky;
All bright and glittering in the smokeless air.
Never did sun more beautifully steep
In his first splendour, valley, rock, or hill;
Ne'er saw I, never felt, a calm so deep!
The river glideth at his own sweet will:
Dear God! the very houses seem asleep;
And all that mighty heart is lying still!

1802   1807

Written in London, September, 1802

O Friend! I know not which way I must look
For comfort, being, as I am, opprest,
To think that now our life is only drest
For show; mean handy-work of craftsman, cook,
Or groom!—We must run glittering like a brook
In the open sunshine, or we are unblest:
The wealthiest man among us is the best:
No grandeur now in nature or in book
Delights us. Rapine, avarice, expense,
This is idolatry; and these we adore:

Plain living and high thinking are no more:
The homely beauty of the good old cause
Is gone; our peace, our fearful innocence,
And pure religion breathing household laws.

1802

1807

London, *1802*

Milton! thou shouldst be living at this hour:
England hath need of thee: she is a fen
Of stagnant waters: altar, sword, and pen,
Fireside, the heroic wealth of hall and bower,
Have forfeited their ancient English dower
Of inward happiness. We are selfish men;
Oh! raise us up, return to us again;
And give us manners, virtue, freedom, power.
Thy soul was like a Star, and dwelt apart:
Thou hadst a voice whose sound was like the sea:
Pure as the naked heavens, majestic, free,
So didst thou travel on life's common way,
In cheerful godliness; and yet thy heart
The lowliest duties on herself did lay.

1802

1807

FROM Preface

TO THE SECOND EDITION OF SEVERAL OF THE FOREGOING POEMS, PUBLISHED, WITH AN ADDITIONAL VOLUME, UNDER THE TITLE OF

Lyrical Ballads

The first volume of these poems has already been submitted to general perusal. It was published as an experiment, which, I hoped, might be of some use to ascertain how far, by fitting to metrical arrangement a selection of the real language of men in a state of vivid sensation, that sort of pleasure and that quantity of pleasure may be imparted, which a poet may rationally endeavour to impart.

I had formed no very inaccurate estimate of the probable effect of those poems: I flattered myself that they who should be pleased with them would read them with more than common pleasure; and, on the other hand, I was well aware that by those who should dislike them they would be read with more than common dislike. The result has differed from my expectation in this only, that a greater number have been pleased than I ventured to hope I should please.

Several of my friends are anxious for the success of these poems, from a belief that, if the views with which they were composed were indeed realized, a class of poetry would be produced, well adapted to interest mankind permanently, and not unimportant in the quality

and in the multiplicity of its moral relations; and on this account they have
advised me to prefix a systematic defence
of the theory upon which the poems were
written. But I was unwilling to undertake
the task, knowing that on this occasion
the reader would look coldly upon my
arguments, since I might be suspected of
having been principally influenced by
the selfish and foolish hope of *reasoning*
him into an approbation of these particular poems; and I was still more unwilling
to undertake the task, because adequately
to display the opinions, and fully to enforce the arguments, would require a
space wholly disproportionate to a preface. For, to treat the subject with the
clearness and coherence of which it is
susceptible, it would be necessary to give
a full account of the present state of the
public taste in this country, and to determine how far this taste is healthy or
depraved; which, again, could not be
determined without pointing out in what
manner language and the human mind
act and react on each other, and without
retracing the revolutions, not of literature
alone, but likewise of society itself. I have
therefore altogether declined to enter
regularly upon this defence; yet I am
sensible that there would be something
like impropriety in abruptly obtruding
upon the public, without a few words of
introduction, poems so materially different from those upon which general approbation is at present bestowed.

It is supposed that by the act of writing
in verse an author makes a formal engagement that he will gratify certain
known habits of association; that he not
only thus apprises the reader that certain
classes of ideas and expressions will be
found in his book, but that others will be
carefully excluded. This exponent or

symbol held forth by metrical language
must in different eras of literature have
excited very different expectations: for
example, in the age of Catullus[1], Terence[2],
and Lucretius[3], and that of Statius[4] or
Claudian[5], and in our own country, in the
age of Shakespeare and Beaumont and
Fletcher, and that of Donne and Cowley,
or Dryden, or Pope. I will not take upon
me to determine the exact import of the
promise which, by the act of writing in
verse, an author in the present day makes
to his reader; but it will undoubtedly
appear to many persons that I have not
fulfilled the terms of an engagement thus
voluntarily contracted. They who have
been accustomed to the gaudiness and
inane phraseology of many modern writers, if they persist in reading this book to
its conclusion, will, no doubt, frequently
have to struggle with feelings of strangeness and awkwardness; they will look
round for poetry, and will be induced to
inquire by what species of courtesy these
attempts can be permitted to assume that
title. I hope, therefore, the reader will not
censure me for attempting to state what
I have proposed to myself to perform;
and also (as far as the limits of a preface
will permit) to explain some of the chief
reasons which have determined me in the
choice of my purpose: that at least he
may be spared any unpleasant feeling of
disappointment, and that I myself may

[1]Roman lyric poet (84-54 B.C.) whom Wordsworth imitated in his youth.

[2]A Roman comic dramatist (190-159 B.C.).

[3]The Roman author (96-55 B.C.) of *De Rerum
Natura*, a famous philosophical poem. Wordsworth admired these writers for naturalness
and purity of style.

[4]Roman epic poet (A.D. 45-96), whose first
book *Thebaid* was translated by Alexander
Pope.

[5]A late Roman poet (A.D. 365-408) remarkable
for stylistic artificiality.

be protected from one of the most dishonorable accusations which can be brought against an author: namely, that of an indolence which prevents him from endeavoring to ascertain what is his duty, or, when his duty is ascertained, prevents him from performing it.

The principal object, then, proposed in these poems, was to choose incidents and situations from common life, and to relate or describe them throughout, as far as was possible, in a selection of language really used by men, and, at the same time, to throw over them a certain coloring of imagination, whereby ordinary things should be presented to the mind in an unusual aspect; and further, and above all, to make these incidents and situations interesting by tracing in them, truly though not ostentatiously, the primary laws of our nature, chiefly, as far as regards the manner in which we associate ideas in a state of excitement. Humble and rustic life was generally chosen, because in that condition the essential passions of the heart find a better soil in which they can attain their maturity, are less under restraint, and speak a plainer and more emphatic language; because in that condition of life our elementary feelings coexist in a state of greater simplicity, and, consequently, may be more accurately contemplated, and more forcibly communicated; because the manners of rural life germinate from those elementary feelings, and, from the necessary character of rural occupations, are more easily comprehended, and are more durable; and, lastly, because in that condition the passions of men are incorporated with the beautiful and permanent forms of nature. The language, too, of these men has been adopted (purified indeed from what appear to be its real defects, from all lasting and rational causes of dislike or disgust), because such men hourly communicate with the best objects from which the best part of language is originally derived; and because, from their rank in society and the sameness and narrow circle of their intercourse, being less under the influence of social vanity, they convey their feelings and notions in simple and unelaborated expressions. Accordingly, such a language, arising out of repeated experience and regular feelings, is a more permanent, and a far more philosophical language, than that which is frequently substituted for it by poets, who think that they are conferring honor upon themselves and their art in proportion as they separate themselves from the sympathies of men, and indulge in arbitrary and capricious habits of expression, in order to furnish food for fickle tastes and fickle appetites of their own creation.

*   *   *

Taking up the subject, then, upon general grounds, let me ask, what is meant by the word "poet"? What is a poet? To whom does he address himself? And what language is to be expected from him? He is a man speaking to men, a man, it is true, endowed with more lively sensibility, more enthusiasm and tenderness, who has a greater knowledge of human nature, and a more comprehensive soul, than are supposed to be common among mankind; a man pleased with his own passions and volitions, and who rejoices more than other men in the spirit of life that is in him, delighting to contemplate similar volitions and passions as manifested in the goings on of the universe, and habitually impelled to create them where he does not find them. To these qualities he has added a disposition to be affected more than any other men by absent things as if they were present; an ability of conjuring up in himself passions, which are indeed far from being the same as those produced by real events, yet (especially in those parts of the general sympathy which are pleasing and delightful) do more nearly resemble the passions produced by real events than anything which, from the motions of their own minds merely, other men are accustomed to feel in themselves —whence, and from practice, he has acquired a greater readiness and power in expressing what he thinks and feels, and especially those thoughts and feelings which, by his own choice, or from the structure of his own mind, arise in him without immediate external excitement.

But whatever portion of this faculty we may suppose even the greatest poet to possess, there cannot be a doubt that the language which it will suggest to him must often, in liveliness and truth, fall short of that which is uttered by men in real life under the actual pressure of those passions, certain shadows of which the poet thus produces, or feels to be produced, in himself.

However exalted a notion we would wish to cherish of the character of a poet, it is obvious that, while he describes and imitates passions, his employment is in some degree mechanical compared with the freedom and power of real and substantial action and suffering. So that it will be the wish of the poet to bring his feelings near to those of the persons whose feelings he describes, nay, for short spaces of time, perhaps, to let himself slip into an entire delusion, and even confound and identify his own feelings with theirs, modifying only the language which is thus suggested to him by a consideration that he describes for a particular purpose,

that of giving pleasure. Here, then, he will apply the principle of selection which has been already insisted upon. He will depend upon this for removing what would otherwise be painful or disgusting in the passion; he will feel that there is no necessity to trick out or to elevate nature; and the more industriously he applies this principle the deeper will be his faith that no words which *his* fancy or imagination can suggest will be to be compared with those which are the emanations of reality and truth.

But it may be said by those who do not object to the general spirit of these remarks that, as it is impossible for the poet to produce upon all occasions language as exquisitely fitted for the passion as that which the real passion itself suggests, it is proper that he should consider himself as in the situation of a translator, who does not scruple to substitute excellences of another kind for those which are unattainable by him; and endeavors occasionally to surpass his original, in order to make some amends for the general inferiority to which he feels he must submit. But this would be to encourage idleness and unmanly despair. Further, it is the language of men who speak of what they do not understand; who talk of poetry, as of a matter of amusement and idle pleasure; who will converse with us as gravely about a *taste* for poetry, as they express it, as if it were a thing as indifferent as a taste for rope dancing, or Frontiniac or sherry. Aristotle, I have been told, has said that poetry is the most philosophic of all writing; it is so: its object is truth, not individual and local, but general and operative; not standing upon external testimony, but carried alive into the heart by passion; truth which is its own testimony, which gives competence and confidence to the tribunal to which it appeals, and receives them from the same tribunal. Poetry is the image of man and nature. The obstacles which stand in the way of the fidelity of the biographer and historian, and of their consequent utility, are incalculably greater than those which are to be encountered by the poet who comprehends the dignity of his art. The poet writes under one restriction only, namely, the necessity of giving immediate pleasure to a human being possessed of that information which may be expected from him, not as a lawyer, a physician, a mariner, an astronomer, or a natural philosopher, but as a man. Except this one restriction, there is no object standing between the poet and the image of things; between this, and the biographer and historian, there are a thousand. . . .

1800

SAMUEL TAYLOR COLERIDGE (1772-1834)

Coleridge is sometimes pictured as a weakling who took drugs, wrote a few brilliant fragments of verse, and spent most of his life in idleness. He did take opium, but in those days it was popular as a pain-reliever; his output of verse was relatively small, but it was of surpassingly high quality; and in his later years he wrote a great amount of prose. He edited two periodicals, translated two long works by Schiller, wrote an autobiography (*Biographia Literaria*), a book of philosophical essays (*Aids to Reflection*), and three plays, compiled voluminous notebooks and was both the most influential literary critic of his generation and one of the most influential political theorists. All this was a truly amazing record for a man who was always in poor health.

Coleridge was the son of the vicar of Ottery St. Mary, Devon, and was educated at Christ's Hospital School and at Jesus College, Cambridge. At Cambridge, he became friendly with Robert Southey, and with him concocted the scheme of "pantisocracy," a form of communal living which they dreamed of establishing on the banks of the Susquehanna River. In 1795, Coleridge married Sara Fricker, and met Wordsworth. The two poets soon became close friends, and collaborated on *Lyrical Ballads* (1798). In 1798-1799, Coleridge visited Germany; from 1804 to 1806, he was secretary to the British governor of Malta, returning to England in poor health and a prey to opium. After several years of great physical and mental suffering he put himself, in 1816, in the hands of a kindly doctor, James Gillman. Gillman's residence at Highgate became Coleridge's home for the remaining nineteen years of his life, and there he produced his most notable prose works.

Coleridge's poetry is chiefly distinguished by its atmospheric power, melodic subtlety, and strong visual and other sensory effects. His prose, and especially his literary criticism, reveals a mind sensitive and subtle, capable of making and defending the finest distinctions.

Kubla Khan

OR, A VISION IN A DREAM

In Xanadu[1] did Kubla Khan[2]
A stately pleasure-dome decree:
Where Alph, the sacred river, ran
Through caverns measureless to man
Down to a sunless sea.

[1] A region in Tartary, which stretched from Eastern Europe to Asia in the thirteenth and fourteenth centuries and was ruled by the Mongols.
[2] Kubla Khan (1214-1294) was the Mongol conqueror of China and grandson of Genghis Khan.

So twice five miles of fertile ground
With walls and towers were girdled round:
And there were gardens bright with sinuous rills.
Where blossomed many an incense-bearing tree;
And here were forests ancient as the hills,   10
Enfolding sunny spots of greenery.

But oh! that deep romantic chasm which slanted
Down the green hill athwart a cedarn cover!
A savage place! as holy and enchanted
As e'er beneath a waning moon was haunted
By woman wailing for her demon-lover!
And from this chasm, with ceaseless turmoil seething.
As if this earth in fast thick pants were breathing,
A mighty fountain momently was forced:
Amid whose swift half-intermitted burst   20
Huge fragments vaulted like rebounding hail,
Or chaffy grain beneath the thresher's flail:
And 'mid these dancing rocks at once and ever
It flung up momently the sacred river.
Five miles meandering with a mazy³ motion
Through wood and dale the sacred river ran,
Then reached the caverns measureless to man,
And sank in tumult to a lifeless ocean:
And 'mid this tumult Kubla heard from far
Ancestral voices prophesying war!   30

   The shadow of the dome of pleasure
   Floated midway on the waves;
   Where was heard the mingled measure
   From the fountain and the caves.
It was a miracle of rare device,
A sunny pleasure-dome with caves of ice!

   A damsel with a dulcimer⁴
   In a vision once I saw:
   It was an Abyssinian maid,
   And on her dulcimer she played,   40
   Singing of Mount Abora⁵.
   Could I revive within me
   Her symphony and song,
   To such a deep delight 'twould win me,

³Intricately winding.   ⁴A stringed instrument.   ⁵Possibly Mount Amara in Abyssinia, but more probably a composite or imaginary name.

That with music loud and long,
I would build that dome in air,
That sunny dome! those caves of ice!
And all who heard should see them there,
And all should cry, Beware! Beware!
His flashing eyes, his floating hair! 50
Weave a circle round him thrice,
And close your eyes with holy dread,
For he on honey-dew⁶ hath fed,
And drunk the milk of Paradise.

1797 1816

⁶A sweet fluid secreted by certain plants and insects.

FROM *Christabel*¹

PART I

'Tis the middle of night by the castle
    clock,
And the owls have awakened the crowing
    cock;
Tu—whit!——Tu—whoo!
And hark, again! the crowing cock,
How drowsily it crew.
Sir Leoline, the Baron rich,
Hath a toothless mastiff bitch;
From her kennel beneath the rock
She maketh answer to the clock,
Four for the quarters, and twelve for the
    hour; 10
Ever and aye, by shine and shower,
Sixteen short howls, not over loud;
Some say, she sees my lady's shroud.

Is the night chilly and dark?
The night is chilly, but not dark.
The thin gray cloud is spread on high,
It covers but not hides the sky.

¹"Christabel" was never finished, although there is a second part which is not printed here. Geraldine herself is obviously an evil creature—a witch or demon—as can be seen by the various references to her unwillingness to praise the Virgin, the moaning of the dog, the flickering of the fire, and so on.

The moon is behind, and at the full;
And yet she looks both small and dull.
The night is chill, the cloud is gray: 20
'Tis a month before the month of May,
And the Spring comes slowly up this way.

The lovely lady, Christabel,
Whom her father loves so well,
What makes her in the wood so late,
A furlong from the castle gate?
She had dreams all yesternight
Of her own betrothèd knight;
And she in the midnight wood will pray
For the weal of her lover that's far away.

She stole along, she nothing spoke, 31
The sighs she heaved were soft and low,
And naught was green upon the oak
But moss and rarest mistletoe:
She kneels beneath the huge oak tree,
And in silence prayeth she.

The lady sprang up suddenly,
The lovely lady, Christabel!
It moaned as near, as near can be,
But what it is she cannot tell.— 40
On the other side it seems to be,
Of the huge, broad-breasted, old oak tree.

The night is chill; the forest bare;
Is it the wind that moaneth bleak?
There is not wind enough in the air
To move away the ringlet curl
From the lovely lady's cheek—
There is not wind enough to twirl
The one red leaf, the last of its clan,
That dances as often as dance it can,   50
Hanging so light, and hanging so high,
On the topmost twig that looks up at the
    sky.

Hush, beating heart of Christabel!
Jesu, Maria, shield her well!
She folded her arms beneath her cloak,
And stole to the other side of the oak.
       What sees she there?

There she sees a damsel bright,
Drest in a silken robe of white,
That shadowy in the moonlight shone:
The neck that made that white robe
    wan,   61
Her stately neck, and arms were bare;
Her blue-veined feet unsandal'd were,
And wildly glittered here and there
The gems entangled in her hair.
I guess, 'twas frightful there to see
A lady so richly clad as she—
Beautiful exceedingly!

Mary mother, save me now!
(Said Christabel,) And who art thou?   70

The lady strange made answer meet,
And her voice was faint and sweet:—
Have pity on my sore distress,
I scarce can speak for weariness:
Stretch forth thy hand, and have no fear!
Said Christabel, How camest thou here?
And the lady, whose voice was faint and
    sweet,
Did thus pursue her answer meet:—

My sire is of a noble line,
And my name is Geraldine: 80
Five warriors seized me yestermorn,
Me, even me, a maid forlorn:
They choked my cries with force and
    fright,
And tied me on a palfrey white.
The palfrey was as fleet as wind,
And they rode furiously behind.

They spurred amain, their steeds were
    white:
And once we crossed the shade of night.
As sure as Heaven shall rescue me,
I have no thought what men they be;   90
Nor do I know how long it is
(For I have lain entranced I wis)
Since one, the tallest of the five,
Took me from the palfrey's back,
A weary woman, scarce alive.
Some muttered words his comrades spoke:
He placed me underneath this oak;
He swore they would return with haste;
Whither they went I cannot tell—
I thought I heard, some minutes past, 100
Sounds as of a castle bell.
Stretch forth thy hand (thus ended she),
And help a wretched maid to flee.

Then Christabel stretched forth her hand,
And comforted fair Geraldine:
O well, bright dame! may you command
The service of Sir Leoline;
And gladly our stout chivalry
Will he send forth and friends withal
To guide and guard you safe and free
Home to your noble father's hall.   111

She rose: and forth with steps they passed
That strove to be, and were not, fast.
Her gracious stars the lady blest,
And thus spake on sweet Christabel;
All our household are at rest,
The hall as silent as the cell;

Sir Leoline is weak in health,
And may not well awakened be,
But we will move as if in stealth,   120
And I beseech your courtesy,
This night, to share your couch with me.

They crossed the moat, and Christabel
Took the key that fitted well;
A little door she opened straight,
All in the middle of the gate;
The gate that was ironed within and
   without,
Where an army in battle array had
   marched out.
The lady sank, belike through pain,
And Christabel with might and main
Lifted her up, a weary weight,   131
Over the threshold of the gate:
Then the lady rose again,
And moved, as she were not in pain.

So free from danger, free from fear,
They crossed the court: right glad they
   were.
And Christabel devoutly cried
To the lady by her side,
Praise we the Virgin all divine
Who hath rescued thee from thy distress!
Alas, alas! said Geraldine,   141
I cannot speak for weariness.
So free from danger, free from fear,
They crossed the court: right glad they
   were.

Outside her kennel, the mastiff old
Lay fast asleep, in moonshine cold.
The mastiff old did not awake,
Yet she an angry moan did make!
And what can ail the mastiff bitch?
Never till now she uttered yell   150
Beneath the eye of Christabel.
Perhaps it is the owlet's scritch:
For what can ail the mastiff bitch?

They passed the hall, that echoes still,
Pass as lightly as you will!
The brands were flat, the brands were
   dying,
Amid their own white ashes lying;
But when the lady passed, there came
A tongue of light, a fit of flame;
And Christabel saw the lady's eye,   160
And nothing else saw she thereby,
Save the boss of the shield of Sir Leoline
   tall,
Which hung in a murky old niche in the
   wall.
O softly tread, said Christabel,
My father seldom sleepeth well.

Sweet Christabel her feet doth bare,
And jealous of the listening air
They steal their way from stair to stair,
Now in glimmer, and now in gloom,
And now they pass the Baron's room, 170
As still as death, with stifled breath!
And now have reached her chamber
   door;
And now doth Geraldine press down
The rushes of the chamber floor.

The moon shines dim in the open air,
And not a moonbeam enters here.
But they without its light can see
The chamber carved so curiously,
Carved with figures strange and sweet,
All made out of the carver's brain,   180
For a lady's chamber meet:
The lamp with twofold silver chain
Is fastened to an angel's feet.

The silver lamp burns dead and dim;
But Christabel the lamp will trim.
She trimmed the lamp, and made it
   bright,
And left it swinging to and fro,
While Geraldine, in wretched plight,
Sank down upon the floor below.

O weary lady, Geraldine, 190
I pray you, drink this cordial wine!
It is a wine of virtuous powers;
My mother made it of wild flowers.

And will your mother pity me,
Who am a maiden most forlorn?
Christabel answered—Woe is me!
She died the hour that I was born.
I have heard the grey-haired friar tell
How on her death-bed she did say,
That she should hear the castle-bell 200
Strike twelve upon my wedding-day.
O mother dear! that thou wert here!
I would, said Geraldine, she were!

But soon with altered voice, said she—
"Off, wandering mother! Peak and pine!
I have power to bid thee flee."
Alas! what ails poor Geraldine?
Why stares she with unsettled eye?
Can she the bodiless dead espy?
And why with hollow voice cries she, 210
"Off, woman, off! this hour is mine—
Though thou her guardian spirit be,
Off, woman, off! 'tis given to me."

Then Christabel knelt by the lady's side,
And raised to heaven her eyes so blue—
Alas! said she, this ghastly ride—
Dear lady! it hath wildered you!
The lady wiped her moist cold brow,
And faintly said, "'tis over now!"

Again the wild-flower wine she drank:
Her fair large eyes 'gan glitter bright, 221
And from the floor whereon she sank,
The lofty lady stood upright:
She was most beautiful to see,
Like a lady of a far countree.

And thus the lofty lady spake—
"All they who live in the upper sky,
Do love you, holy Christabel!
And you love them, and for their sake

And for the good which me befel, 230
Even I in my degree will try,
Fair maiden, to requite you well.
But now unrobe yourself; for I
Must pray, ere yet in bed I lie."

Quoth Christabel, So let it be!
And as the lady bade, did she.
Her gentle limbs did she undress,
And lay down in her loveliness.

But through her brain of weal and woe
So many thoughts moved to and fro, 240
That vain it were her lids to close;
So half-way from the bed she rose,
And on her elbow did recline
To look at the lady Geraldine.

Beneath the lamp the lady bowed,
And slowly rolled her eyes around;
Then drawing in her breath aloud,
Like one that shuddered, she unbound
The cincture from beneath her breast;
Her silken robe, and inner vest, 250
Dropt to her feet, and full in view,
Behold! her bosom and half her side—
A sight to dream of, not to tell!
O shield her! shield sweet Christabel!

Yet Geraldine nor speaks nor stirs;
Ah! what a stricken look was hers!
Deep from within she seems half-way
To lift some weight with sick assay,
And eyes the maid and seeks delay;
Then suddenly, as one defied, 260

Collects herself in scorn and pride,
And lay down by the Maiden's side!—
And in her arms the maid she took,
Ah well-a-day!
And with low voice and doleful look
These words did say:
"In the touch of this bosom there worketh
a spell,

Which is lord of thy utterance Christabel!
Thou knowest to-night, and wilt know
    to-morrow,
This mark of my shame, this seal of my
    sorrow;   270
        But vainly thou warrest,
          For this is alone in
        Thy power to declare,
          That in the dim forest
        Thou heard'st a low moaning,
And found'st a bright lady, surpassingly
    fair;
And dist bring her home with thee in love
    and in charity,
To shield her and shelter her from the
    damp air."

THE CONCLUSION TO PART I

It was a lovely sight to see
The lady Christabel, when she   280
Was praying at the old oak tree.
        Amid the jaggèd shadows
        Of mossy leafless boughs,
        Kneeling in the moonlight,
        To make her gentle vows;
Her slender palms together prest,
Heaving sometimes on her breast;
Her face resigned to bliss or bale—
Her face, oh call it fair not pale,
And both blue eyes more bright than
    clear,   290
Each about to have a tear.

With open eyes (ah woe is me!)
Asleep, and dreaming fearfully,
Fearfully dreaming, yet, I wis,
Dreaming that alone, which is—
O sorrow and shame! Can this be she,

The lady, who knelt at the old oak tree?
And lo! the worker of these harms,
That holds the maiden in her arms,
Seems to slumber still and mild,   300
As a mother with her child.

A star hath set, a star hath risen,
O Geraldine! since arms of thine
Have been the lovely lady's prison.
O Geraldine! one hour was thine—
Thou'st had thy will! By tairn and rill,
The night-birds all that hour were still.
But now they are jubilant anew,
From cliff and tower, tu—whoo! tu—
    whoo!
Tu—whoo! tu—whoo! from wood and
    fell!   310

And see! the lady Christabel
Gathers herself from out her trance;
Her limbs relax, her countenance
Grows sad and soft; the smooth thin lids
Close o'er her eyes; and tears she sheds—
Large tears that leave the lashes bright!
And oft the while she seems to smile
As infants at a sudden light!

Yea, she doth smile, and she doth weep,
Like a youthful hermitess,   320
Beauteous in a wilderness,
Who, praying always, prays in sleep.
And, if she move unquietly,
Perchance, 'tis but the blood so free
Comes back and tingles in her feet.
No doubt, she hath a vision sweet.
What if her guardian spirit 'twere,
What if she knew her mother near?
But this she knows, in joys and woes,
That saints will aid if men will call: 330
For the blue sky bends over all!

1797   1816

The Rime of the Ancient Mariner

IN SEVEN PARTS

Facile credo, plures esse Naturas invisibiles quam visibiles in rerum universitate. Sed horum omnium familiam quis nobis enarrabit? et gradus et cognationes et discrimina et singulorum munera? Quid agunt? quae loca habitant? Harum rerum notitiam semper ambivit ingenium humanum, nunquam attigit. Juvat, interea, non diffiteor, quandoque in animo, tanquam in tabula, majoris et melioris mundi imaginem contemplari : ne mens assuefacta hodiernae vitae minutiis se contrahat nimis, et tota subsidat in pusillas cogitationes. Sed veritati interea invigilandum est, modusque servandus, ut certa ab incertis, diem a nocte, distinguamus.—T. BURNET, *Archaeol. Phil.* p. 68[1]

ARGUMENT

How a Ship having passed the Line was driven by storms to the cold Country towards the South Pole; and how from thence she made her course to the tropical Latitude of the Great Pacific Ocean; and of the strange things that befell; and in what manner the Ancyent Marinere came back to his own Country.

PART I

An ancient Mariner meeteth three Gallants bidden to a wedding-feast, and detaineth one.	IT is an ancient Mariner, And he stoppeth one of three, 'By thy long grey beard and glittering eye, Now wherefore stopp'st thou me?

The Bridegroom's doors are opened wide,
And I am next of kin;
The guests are met, the feast is set:
May'st hear the merry din.'

He holds him with his skinny hand,
'There was a ship,' quoth he.   10
'Hold off! unhand me, grey-beard loon!'
Eftsoons[2] his hand dropt he.

The Wedding-Guest is spellbound by the eye of the old seafaring man, and constrained to hear his tale.	He holds him with his glittering eye— The Wedding-Guest stood still, And listens like a three years' child: The Mariner hath his will.

The Wedding-Guest sat on a stone:
He cannot choose but hear;

[1]*Latin epigraph*: "I readily believe that there are more invisible than visible Natures in the universe. But who will explain for us the family of all these beings, and the ranks and relations and distinguishing features and functions of each? What do they do? What places do they inhabit? The human mind has always sought the knowledge of these things, but never attained it. Meanwhile I do not deny that it is helpful sometimes to contemplate in the mind, as on a tablet, the image of a greater and better world, lest the intellect, habituated to the petty things of daily life, narrow itself and sink wholly into trivial thoughts. But at the same time, we must be watchful for the truth and keep a sense of proportion, so that we may distinguish the certain from the uncertain, day from night."

[2]At once.

And thus spake on that ancient man,
The bright-eyed Mariner.   20

'The ship was cheered, the harbour cleared,
Merrily did we drop

The Mariner tells how
the ship sailed south-
ward with a good
wind and fair weather,
till it reached the line.

Below the kirk,[3] below the hill,
Below the lighthouse top.

The Sun came up upon the left,
Out of the sea came he!
And he shone bright, and on the right
Went down into the sea.

Higher and higher every day,
Till over the mast at noon—'[4]   30
The Wedding-Guest here beat his breast,
For he heard the loud bassoon.

The Wedding-Guest
heareth the bridal
music; but the Mari-
ner continueth his
tale.

The bride hath paced into the hall,
Red as a rose is she;
Nodding their heads before her goes
The merry minstrelsy.

The Wedding-Guest he beat his breast,
Yet he cannot choose but hear;
And thus spake on that ancient man,
The bright-eyed Mariner.   40

The ship driven by a
storm toward the
south pole.

'And now the STORM-BLAST came, and he
Was tyrannous and strong:
He struck with his o'ertaking wings,
And chased us south along.

With sloping masts and dipping prow,
As who pursued with yell and blow
Still treads the shadow of his foe,
And forward bends his head,
The ship drove fast, loud roared the blast,
And southward aye we fled.   50

And now there came both mist and snow,
And it grew wondrous cold:
And ice, mast-high, came floating by.
As green as emerald.

And through the drifts the snowy clifts[5]

---

[3]Church.
[4]The ship had reached the Equator (the "line").
[5]Cliffs.

The land of ice, and
of fearful sounds
where no living thing
was to be seen.

Did send a dismal sheen:
Nor shapes of men nor beasts we ken—
The ice was all between.

The ice was here, the ice was there,
The ice was all around: 60
It cracked and growled, and roared and howled,
Like noises in a swound!⁶

Till a great sea-bird,
called the Albatross,
came through the
snow-fog, and was re-
ceived with great joy
and hospitality.

At length did cross an Albatross,
Thorough the fog it came;
As if it had been a Christian soul,
We hailed it in God's name.

It ate the food it ne'er had eat,
And round and round it flew.
The ice did split with a thunder-fit;
The helmsman steered us through!   70

And lo! the Albatross
proveth a bird of good
omen, and followeth
the ship as it returned
northward through
fog and floating ice.

And a good south wind sprung up behind;
The Albatross did follow,
And every day, for food or play,
Came to the mariner's hollo!

In mist or cloud, on mast or shroud,⁷
It perched for vespers nine;
Whiles all the night, through fog-smoke white,
Glimmered the white Moon-shine.'

The ancient Mariner
inhospitably killeth
the pious bird of good
omen.

'God save thee, ancient Mariner!
From the fiends, that plague thee thus!—   80
Why look'st thou so?'—With my cross-bow
I shot the ALBATROSS.

PART II

The Sun now rose upon the right:⁸
Out of the sea came he,
Still hid in mist, and on the left
Went down into the sea.

And the good south wind still blew behind,
But no sweet bird did follow,
Nor any day for food or play
Came to the mariners' hollo!   90

⁶Swoon.
⁷Rope supporting the mast.
⁸Having rounded Cape Horn, the ship heads north into the Pacific.

His shipmates cry out against the ancient Mariner, for killing the bird of good luck.

And I had done a hellish thing,
And it would work 'em woe:
For all averred, I had killed the bird
That made the breeze to blow.
Ah wretch! said they, the bird to slay,
That made the breeze to blow!

But when the fog cleared off, they justify the same, and thus make themselves accomplices in the crime.

Nor dim nor red, like God's own head,
The glorious Sun uprist:
Then all averred, I had killed the bird
That brought the fog and mist.
'Twas right, said they, such birds to slay,
That bring the fog and mist.

100

The fair breeze continues; the ship enters the Pacific Ocean, and sails northward, even till it reaches the Line.

The fair breeze blew, the white foam flew,
The furrow followed free;
We were the first that ever burst
Into that silent sea.

The ship hath been suddenly becalmed.

Down dropt the breeze, the sails dropt down,
'Twas sad as sad could be;
And we did speak only to break
The silence of the sea!

110

All in a hot and copper sky,
The bloody Sun, at noon,
Right up above the mast did stand,
No bigger than the Moon.

Day after day, day after day,
We stuck, nor breath nor motion;
As idle as a painted ship
Upon a painted ocean.

And the Albatross begins to be avenged.

Water, water, every where,
And all the boards did shrink;
Water, water, every where,
Nor any drop to drink.

120

The very deep did rot: O Christ!
That ever this should be!
Yea, slimy things did crawl with legs
Upon the slimy sea.

About, about, in reel and rout
The death-fires[9] danced at night;

[9]*St. Elmo's fire.* Atmospheric electricity on a ship's rigging, believed by the superstitious sailor to portend disaster.

The water, like a witch's oils,
Burnt green, and blue and white.   130

And some in dreams assuréd were
Of the Spirit that plagued us so;
Nine fathom deep he had followed us
From the land of mist and snow.

A Spirit had followed them; one of the invisible inhabitants of this planet, neither departed souls nor angels; concerning whom the learned Jew, Josephus, and the Platonic Constantinopolitan, Michael Psellus, may be consulted. They are very numerous, and there is no climate or element without one or more.

And every tongue, through utter drought,
Was withered at the root;
We could not speak, no more than if
We had been choked with soot.

The shipmates, in their sore distress, would fain throw the whole guilt on the ancient Mariner: in sign whereof they hang the dead sea-bird round his neck.

Ah! well a-day! what evil looks
Had I from old and young!   140
Instead of the cross, the Albatross
About my neck was hung.

PART III

There passed a weary time. Each throat
Was parched, and glazed each eye.
A weary time! a weary time!
How glazed each weary eye,
When looking westward, I beheld
A something in the sky.

The ancient Mariner beholdeth a sign in the element afar off.

At first it seemed a little speck,
And then it seemed a mist;   150
It moved and moved, and took at last
A certain shape, I wist.

A speck, a mist, a shape, I wist![10]
And still it neared and neared:
As if it dodged a water-sprite,
It plunged and tacked and veered.

As its nearer approach, it seemeth him to be a ship; and at a dear ransom he freeth his speech from the bonds of thirst.

With throats unslaked, with black lips baked,
We could nor laugh nor wail;
Through utter drought all dumb we stood!
I bit my arm, I sucked the blood,   160
And cried, A sail! a sail!

With throats unslaked, with black lips baked,
Agape they heard me call:

A flash of joy;

Gramercy![11] they for joy did grin,

[10] Knew.
[11] From the French *grand-merci* ("great thanks").

And all at once their breath drew in,
As they were drinking all.

And horror follows.
For can it be a ship
that comes onward
without wind or tide?

See! See! (I cried) she tacks no more!
Hither to work us weal;[12]
Without a breeze, without a tide,
She steadies with upright keel!   170

The western wave was all a-flame.
The day was well nigh done!
Almost upon the western wave
Rested the broad bright Sun;
When that strange shape drove suddenly
Betwixt us and the Sun.

It seemeth him but
the skeleton of a ship.

And straight the Sun was flecked with bars,
(Heaven's Mother send us grace!)
As if through a dungeon-grate he peered
With broad and burning face.   180

And its ribs are seen
as bars on the face of
the setting Sun.

Alas! (thought I, and my heart beat loud)
How fast she nears and nears!
Are those *her* sails that glance in the Sun,
Like restless gossameres?[13]

The Spectre-Woman
and her Deathmate,
and no other on board
the skeleton ship.

Are those *her* ribs through which the Sun
Did peer, as through a grate?
And is that Woman in her crew?
Is that a DEATH? and are there two?
Is DEATH that woman's mate?

Like vessel, like crew!
Death and Life-in-
Death have diced for
the ship's crew, and
she (the latter) win-
neth the ancient Mari-
ner.

Her lips were red, *her* looks were free,   190
Her locks were yellow as gold:
Her skin was as white as leprosy,
The Night-mare LIFE-IN-DEATH was she,
Who thicks man's blood with cold.

The naked hulk alongside came,
And the twain were casting dice;
'The game is done! I've won! I've won!'
Quoth she, and whistles thrice.

No twilight within the
courts of the Sun.

The Sun's rim dips; the stars rush out:
At one stride comes the dark;   200
With far-heard whisper, o'er the sea,
Off shot the spectre-bark.

[12]Benefit.
[13]Filmy cobwebs.

At the rising of the
Moon,

We listened and looked sideways up!
Fear at my heart, as at a cup,
My life-blood seemed to sip!
The stars were dim, and thick the night,
The steersman's face by his lamp gleamed white;
From the sails the dew did drip—

Till clomb above the eastern bar
The hornéd Moon, with one bright star   210
Within the nether tip.[14]

One after another,

One after one, by the star-dogged Moon,
Too quick for groan or sigh,
Each turned his face with a ghastly pang,
And cursed me with his eye.

His shipmates drop
down dead.

Four times fifty living men,
(And I heard nor sigh nor groan)
With heavy thump, a lifeless lump,
They dropped down one by one.

But Life-in-Death
begins her work on
the ancient Mariner.

The souls did from their bodies fly,—   220
They fled to bliss or woe!
And every soul, it passed me by,
Like the whizz of my cross-bow!

PART IV

The Wedding-Guest
feareth that a Spirit is
talking to him;

'I fear thee, ancient Mariner!
I fear thy skinny hand!
And thou art long, and lank, and brown,
As is the ribbed sea-sand.

I fear thee and thy glittering eye,
And thy skinny hand, so brown.'—

But the ancient Mari-
ner assureth him of
his bodily life, and
proceedeth to relate
his horrible penance.

Fear not, fear not, thou Wedding-Guest!   230
This body dropt not down.

Alone, alone, all, all alone,
Alone on a wide wide sea!
And never a saint took pity on
My soul in agony.

He despiseth the crea-
tures of the calm,

The many men, so beautiful!
And they all dead did lie:
And a thousand thousand slimy things
Lived on; and so did I.

[14]Omen of impending evil.

And envieth that *they*
should live, and so
many lie dead.

I looked upon the rotting sea, 240
And drew my eyes away;
I looked upon the rotting deck,
And there the dead men lay.

I looked to heaven, and tried to pray;
But or ever a prayer had gusht,
A wicked whisper came, and made
My heart as dry as dust.

I closed my lids, and kept them close,
And the balls like pulses beat;
For the sky and the sea, and the sea and the sky 250
Lay like a load on my weary eye,
And the dead were at my feet.

But the curse liveth
for him in the eye of
the dead men.

The cold sweat melted from their limbs,
Nor rot nor reek did they:
The look with which they looked on me
Had never passed away.

An orphan's curse would drag to hell
A spirit from on high;
But oh! more horrible than that
Is the curse in a dead man's eye! 260
Seven days, seven nights, I saw that curse,
And yet I could not die.

In his loneliness and
fixedness he yearneth
towards the journey-
ing Moon, and the
stars that still sojourn,
yet still move onward;
and every where the
blue sky belongs to
them, and is their ap-
pointed rest, and their
native country and
their own natural
homes, which they
enter unannounced,
as lords that are cer-
tainly expected and
yet there is a silent joy
at their arrival.

The moving Moon went up the sky,
And no where did abide:
Softly she was going up,
And a star or two beside—

Her beams bemocked the sultry main,
Like April hoar-frost spread;
But where the ship's huge shadow lay,
The charmèd water burnt alway 270
A still and awful red.

By the light of the
Moon he beholdeth
God's creatures of the
great calm.

Beyond the shadow of the ship,
I watched the water-snakes:
They moved in tracks of shining white,
And when they reared, the elfish light
Fell off in hoary flakes.

Within the shadow of the ship
I watched their rich attire:
Blue, glossy green, and velvet black,
They coiled and swam; and every track 280

Was a flash of golden fire.

Their beauty and
their happiness.

O happy living things! no tongue
Their beauty might declare:
A spring of love gushed from my heart,
And I blessed them unaware:
Sure my kind saint took pity on me,
And I blessed them unaware.

He blesseth them in
his heart.

The self-same moment I could pray;
And from my neck so free
The Albatross fell off, and sank   290
Like lead into the sea.

The spell begins to
break.

PART V

Oh sleep! it is a gentle thing,
Beloved from pole to pole!
To Mary Queen the praise be given!
She sent the gentle sleep from Heaven,
That slid into my soul.

By grace of the holy
Mother, the ancient
Mariner is refreshed
with rain.

The silly[15] buckets on the deck,
That had so long remained,
I dreamt that they were filled with dew;
And when I awoke, it rained.   300

My lips were wet, my throat was cold,
My garments all were dank;
Sure I had drunken in my dreams,
And still my body drank.

I moved, and could not feel my limbs:
I was so light—almost
I thought that I had died in sleep,
And was a blessèd ghost.

He heareth sounds
and seeth strange
sights and commo-
tions in the sky and
the element.

And soon I heard a roaring wind:
It did not come anear;   310
But with its sound it shook the sails,
That were so thin and sere.

The upper air burst into life!
And a hundred fire-flags sheen,[16]
To and fro they were hurried about!
And to and fro, and in and out,
The wan stars danced between.

[15]Blessed, happy—the original meaning of silly.
[16]Refers to Aurora Australis, the Southern Lights.

And the coming wind did roar more loud,
And the sails did sigh like sedge;
And the rain poured down from one black cloud; 320
The Moon was at its edge.

The thick black cloud was cleft, and still
The Moon was at its side:
Like waters shot from some high crag,
The lightning fell with never a jag,
A river steep and wide.

The bodies of the ship's crew are in-spired [inspirited, *S.L.*] and the ship moves on;

The loud wind never reached the ship,
Yet now the ship moved on!
Beneath the lightning and the Moon
The dead men gave a groan. 330

They groaned, they stirred, they all uprose,
Nor spake, nor moved their eyes;
It had been strange, even in a dream,
To have seen those dead men rise.

The helmsman steered, the ship moved on;
Yet never a breeze up-blew;
The mariners all 'gan work the ropes,
Where they were wont to do;
They raised their limbs like lifeless tools—
We were a ghastly crew. 340

The body of my brother's son
Stood by me, knee to knee:
The body and I pulled at one rope,
But he said nought to me.

But not by the souls of the men, nor by dae-mons of earth or mid-dle air, but by a blessed troop of an-gelic spirits, sent down by the invocation of the guardian saint.

'I fear thee, ancient Mariner!'
Be calm, thou Wedding-Guest!
'Twas not those souls that fled in pain,
Which to their corses[17] came again,
But a troop of spirits blest:

For when it dawned—they dropped their arms, 350
And clustered round the mast;
Sweet sounds rose slowly through their mouths,
And from their bodies passed.

Around, around, flew each sweet sound,
Then darted to the Sun;
Slowly the sounds came back again,
Now mixed, now one by one.

[17]Corpses.

Sometimes a-dropping from the sky
I heard the sky-lark sing;
Sometimes all little birds that are,   360
How they seemed to fill the sea and air
With their sweet jargoning![18]

And now 'twas like all instruments,
Now like a lonely flute;
And now it is an angel's song,
That makes the heavens be mute.

It ceased; yet still the sails made on
A pleasant noise till noon,
A noise like of a hidden brook   370
In the leafy month of June,
That to the sleeping woods all night
Singeth a quiet tune.

Till noon we quietly sailed on,
Yet never a breeze did breathe:
Slowly and smoothly went the ship,
Moved onward from beneath.

The lonesome Spirit
from the south-pole
carries on the ship as
far as the Line, in obe-
dience to the angelic
troop, but still re-
quireth vengeance.

Under the keel nine fathom deep,
From the land of mist and snow,
The spirit slid: and it was he
That made the ship to go.   380
The sails at noon left off their tune,
And the ship stood still also.

The Sun, right up above the mast,
Had fixed her to the ocean:
But in a minute she 'gan stir,
With a short uneasy motion—
Backwards and forwards half her length
With a short uneasy motion.

Then like a pawing horse let go,
She made a sudden bound: 390
It flung the blood into my head,
And I fell down in a swound.

The Polar Spirit's fel-
low daemons, the in-
visible inhabitants of
the element, take part
in his wrong; and two
of them relate, one to
the other, that pen-
ance long and heavy

How long in that same fit I lay,
I have not to declare;
But ere my living life returned,
I heard and in my soul discerned
Two voices in the air.

[18]Warbling, in Middle English.

for the ancient Mari-
ner hath been ac-
corded to the Polar
Spirit, who returneth

'Is it he?' quoth one, 'Is this the man?
By him who died on cross,
With his cruel bow he laid full low   400
The harmless Albatross.

The spirit who bideth by himself
In the land of mist and snow,
He loved the bird that loved the man
Who shot him with his bow.'

The other was a softer voice,
As soft as honey-dew:
Quoth he, 'The man hath penance done,
And penance more will do.'

PART VI

FIRST VOICE

'But tell me, tell me! speak again,   410
Thy soft response renewing—
What makes that ship drive on so fast?
What is the ocean doing?'

SECOND VOICE

'Still as a slave before his lord,
The ocean hath no blast;
His great bright eye most silently
Up to the Moon is cast—

If he may know which way to go;
For she guides him smooth or grim.
See, brother, see! how graciously   420
She looketh down on him.'

FIRST VOICE

The Mariner hath
been cast into a
trance; for the angelic
power causeth the ves-
sel to drive northward
faster than human life
could endure.

'But why drives on that ship so fast,
Without or wave or wind?'

SECOND VOICE

'The air is cut away before,
And closes from behind.

Fly, brother, fly! more high, more high!
Or we shall be belated:
For slow and slow that ship will go,
When the Mariner's trance is abated.'

The supernatural mo-
tion is retarded; the
Mariner awakes, and
his penance begins
anew.

I woke, and we were sailing on   430
As in a gentle weather:
'Twas night, calm night, the moon was high;
The dead men stood together.

All stood together on the deck,
For a charnel-dungeon fitter:
All fixed on me their stony eyes,
That in the Moon did glitter.

The pang, the curse, with which they died,
Had never passed away:
I could not draw my eyes from theirs,   440
Nor turn them up to pray.

The curse is finally ex-
piated.

And now this spell was snapt: once more
I viewed the ocean green,
And looked far forth, yet little saw
Of what had else been seen—

Like one, that on a lonesome road
Doth walk in fear and dread,
And having once turned round walks on,
And turns no more his head;
Because he knows, a frightful fiend   450
Doth close behind him tread.

But soon there breathed a wind on me,
Nor sound nor motion made:
Its path was not upon the sea,
In ripple or in shade.

It raised my hair, it fanned my cheek
Like a meadow-gale of spring—
It mingled strangely with my fears,
Yet it felt like a welcoming.

Swiftly, swiftly flew the ship,   460
Yet she sailed softly too:
Sweetly, sweetly blew the breeze—
On me alone it blew.

And the ancient Mari-
ner beholdeth his na-
tive country.

Oh! dream of joy! is this indeed
The light-house top I see?
Is this the hill? is this the kirk?
Is this mine own countree?

We drifted o'er the harbour-bar,
And I with sobs did pray—

O let me be awake, my God!   470
Or let me sleep alway.

The harbour-bay was clear as glass,
So moothly it was strewn!
And on the bay the moonlight lay,
And the shadow of the Moon.

The rock shone bright, the kirk no less,
That stands above the rock:
The moonlight steeped in silentness
The steady weathercock.

And the bay was white with silent light,   480
Till rising from the same,
Full many shapes, that shadows were,
In crimson colours came.

The angelic spirits leave the dead bodies,

And appear in their own forms of light.

A little distance from the prow
Those crimson shadows were:
I turned my eyes upon the deck—
Oh, Christ! what saw I there!

Each corse lay flat, lifeless and flat,
And, by the holy rood![19]
A man all light, a seraph-man,[20]   490
On every corse there stood.

This seraph-band, each waved his hand:
It was a heavenly sight!
They stood as signals to the land,
Each one a lovely light;

This seraph-band, each waved his hand,
No voice did they impart—
No voice; but oh! the silence sank
Like music on my heart.

But soon I heard the dash of oars,   500
I heard the Pilot's cheer;
My head was turned perforce away
And I saw a boat appear.

The Pilot and the Pilot's boy,
I heard them coming fast:
Dear Lord in Heaven! it was a joy
The dead men could not blast.

[19]Cross.
[20]*seraph*. Highest of the angels.

I saw a third—I heard his voice:
It is the Hermit good!
He singeth loud his godly hymns   510
That he makes in the wood.
He'll shrieve my soul, he'll wash away
The Albatross's blood.

PART VII

The Hermit of the
Wood,

This Hermit good lives in that wood
Which slopes down to the sea.
How loudly his sweet voice he rears!
He loves to talk with marineres
That come from a far countree.

He kneels at morn, and noon, and eve—
He hath a cushion plump: 520
It is the moss that wholly hides
The rotted old oak-stump.

The skiff-boat neared: I heard them talk,
'Why, this is strange, I trow!
Where are those lights so many and fair,
That signal made but now?'

Approacheth the ship
with wonder.

'Strange, by my faith!' the Hermit said—
'And they answered not our cheer!
The planks looked warped! and see those sails,
How thin they are and sere!   530
I never saw aught like to them,
Unless perchance it were

Brown skeletons of leaves that lag
My forest-brook along;
When the ivy-tod[21] is heavy with snow,
And the owlet whoops to the wolf below,
That eats the she-wolf's young.'

'Dear Lord! it hath a fiendish look—
(The Pilot made reply)
I am a-feared'—'Push on, push on!'   540
Said the Hermit cheerily.

The boat came closer to the ship,
But I nor spake nor stirred;
The boat came close beneath the ship,
And straight a sound was heard.

[21]Clump of ivy.

The ship suddenly
sinketh.

Under the water it rumbled on,
Still louder and more dread:
It reached the ship, it split the bay;
The ship went down like lead.

The ancient Mariner
is saved in the Pilot's
boat.

Stunned by that loud and dreadful sound,   550
Which sky and ocean smote,
Like one that hath been seven days drowned
My body lay afloat;
But swift as dreams, myself I found
Within the Pilot's boat.

Upon the whirl, where sank the ship,
The boat spun round and round;
And all was still, save that the hill
Was telling of the sound.

I moved my lips—the Pilot shrieked   560
And fell down in a fit;
The holy Hermit raised his eyes,
And prayed where he did sit.

I took the oars: the Pilot's boy,
Who now doth crazy go,
Laughed loud and long, and all the while
His eyes went to and fro.
'Ha! ha!' quoth he, 'full plain I see,
The Devil knows how to row.'

And now, all in my own countree,   570
I stood on the firm land!
The Hermit stepped forth from the boat,
And scarcely he could stand.

The ancient Mariner
earnestly entreateth
the Hermit to shrieve
him; and the penance
of life falls on him.

'O shrieve me, shrieve me, holy man!'
The Hermit crossed his brow.
'Say quick,' quoth he, 'I bid thee say—
What manner of man art thou?'

Forthwith this frame of mine was wrenched
With a woful agony,
Which forced me to begin my tale;   580
And then it left me free.

And ever and anon
through out his future
life an agony con-
straineth him to travel
from land to land;

Since then, at an uncertain hour,
That agony returns:
And till my ghastly tale is told,
This heart within me burns.

I pass, like night, from land to land;

I have strange power of speech;
That moment that his face I see,
I know the man that must hear me:
To him my tale I teach.   590

What loud uproar bursts from that door!
The wedding-guests are there:
But in the garden-bower the bride
And bride-maids singing are:
And hark the little vesper bell,
Which biddeth me to prayer!

O Wedding-Guest! this soul hath been
Alone on a wide wide sea:
So lonely 'twas, that God himself
Scarce seemed there to be.   600

O sweeter than the marriage-feast,
'Tis sweeter far to me,
To walk together to the kirk
With a goodly company!—

To walk together to the kirk,
And all together pray,
While each to his great Father bends,
Old men, and babes, and loving friends
And youths and maidens gay!

And to teach, by his
own example, love   Farewell, farewell! but this I tell   .   610
and reverence to all   To thee, thou Wedding-Guest!
things that God made   He prayeth well, who loveth well
and loveth.   Both man and bird and beast.

He prayeth best, who loveth best
All things both great and small;
For the dear God who loveth us,
He made and loveth all.

The Mariner, whose eye is bright,
Whose beard with age is hoar,
Is gone: and now the Wedding-Guest   620
Turned from the bridegroom's door.

He went like one that hath been stunned,
And is of sense forlorn:[22]
A sadder and a wiser man,
He rose the morrow morn.

1797-1816   1798-1817

[22]Forsaken.

FROM Lectures on Shakespeare

THE CHARACTER OF HAMLET

The seeming inconsistencies in the conduct and character of Hamlet have long exercised the conjectural ingenuity of critics; and, as we are always loth to suppose that the cause of defective apprehension is in ourselves, the mystery has been too commonly explained by the very easy process of setting it down as in fact inexplicable, and by resolving the phenomenon into a misgrowth or *lusus* of the capricious and irregular genius of Shakespeare. The shallow and stupid arrogance of these vulgar and indolent decisions I would fain do my best to expose. I believe the character of Hamlet may be traced to Shakespeare's deep and accurate science in mental philosophy. Indeed, that this character must have some connection with the common fundamental laws of our nature may be assumed from the fact that Hamlet has been the darling of every country in which the literature of England has been fostered. In order to understand him, it is essential that we should reflect on the constitution of our own minds. Man is distinguished from the brute animals in proportion as thought prevails over sense: but in the healthy processes of the mind, a balance is constantly maintained between the impressions from outward objects and the inward operations of the intellect—for if there be an overbalance in the contemplative faculty, man thereby becomes the creature of mere meditation, and loses his natural power of action. Now one of Shakespeare's modes of creating characters is, to conceive any one intellectual or moral faculty in morbid excess, and then to place himself, Shakespeare, thus mutilated or diseased, under given circumstances. In Hamlet he seems to have wished to exemplify the moral necessity of a due balance between our attention to the objects of our senses, and our meditation on the workings of our minds—an *equilibrium* between the real and imaginary worlds. In Hamlet this balance is disturbed: his thoughts, and the images of his fancy, are far more vivid than his actual perceptions, and his very perceptions, instantly passing through the *medium* of his contemplations, acquire, as they pass, a form and a colour not naturally their own. Hence we see a great, an almost enormous, intellectual activity, and a proportionate aversion to real action consequent upon it, with all its symptoms and accompanying qualities. This character Shakespeare places in circumstances, under which it is obliged to act on the spur of the moment:—Hamlet is brave and careless of death; but he vacillates from sensibility, and procrastinates from thought, and loses the power of action in the energy of resolve. Thus it is that this tragedy presents a direct contrast to that of "Macbeth"; the one proceeds with the utmost slowness, the other with a crowded and breathless rapidity.

The effect of this overbalance of the imaginative power is beautifully illustrated in the everlasting broodings and superfluous activities of Hamlet's mind, which, unseated from its healthy relation, is constantly occupied with the world within, and abstracted from the world without—giving substance to shadows, and throwing a mist over all commonplace actualities. It is the nature of thought to be indefinite; definiteness belongs to external imagery alone. Hence it is that the sense of sublimity arises, not from the sight of an outward object, but from the beholder's reflection upon it;— not from the sensuous impression, but from the imaginative reflex. Few have seen a celebrated waterfall without feeling something akin to disappointment; it is only subsequently that the image comes back full into the mind, and brings with it a train of grand or beautiful associations. Hamlet feels this; his senses are in a state of trance, and he looks upon external things as hieroglyphics. His soliloquy, "O! that this too too solid flesh would melt . . ." springs from that craving after the indefinite—for that which is not—which most easily besets men of genius; and the self-delusion common to this temper of mind is finely exemplified in the character which Hamlet gives of himself:

> It cannot be
> But I am pigeon-liver'd, and lack gall
> To make oppression bitter.

He mistakes the seeing his chains for the breaking them, delays action till action is of no use, and dies the victim of mere circumstance and accident.   1808

CHARLES LAMB (1775-1834)

Lamb was an essayist, critic, dramatist, novelist, and poet, but it is primarily as the most delightful familiar essayist in the language that he is remembered.

He was born in London, the son of a lawyer's clerk, and educated at Christ's Hospital School, where he formed a life-long friendship with Coleridge. From 1789 to 1792 he was a clerk in the South Sea House, and then transferred to a clerkship in India House. He lived a life of great self-sacrifice, giving up his plans for marriage in order to care for his sister Mary ("Cousin Bridget" of the essays), who was subject to fits of insanity. His first publications were a book of poems and a romantic novel, both appearing in 1798. He then tried his hand at playwriting, producing *John Woodvil*, a tragedy, and *Mr. H.*, a farce, but had little success. Fame and a degree of fortune came in 1807 when he and his invalid sister collaborated on the children's classic, *Tales from Shakespeare*. Other children's books followed, and an edition of the Elizabethan dramatists to which Lamb contributed brilliant critical introductions. In 1818 he began to contribute to the *London Magazine* the famous "Essays of Elia," which appeared in book form in two series, 1823 and 1833. He retired on pension from India House in 1825, and died on December 29, 1834.

As an essayist, Lamb carried on the tradition of the informal or familiar essay initiated in English by Addison and Steele, but made it (as we should expect of a member of the romantic generation) more personal, more self-revealing, more emotional, and more whimsical. He reveals his personality to us with disarming frankness, seeking not to impress us with his superiority but rather slightly exaggerating his own faults and foibles. As a critic, he did much to revive interest in the minor Elizabethan dramatists and to stimulate a more subtle and sensitive approach to Shakespeare.

Old China

I have an almost feminine partiality for old china. When I go to see any great house, I inquire for the china-closet, and next for the picture gallery. I cannot defend the order of preference, but by saying that we have all some taste or other, of too ancient a date to admit of our remembering distinctly that it was an acquired one. I can call to mind the first play, and the first exhibition, that I was taken to; but I am not conscious of a time when china jars and saucers were introduced into my imagination.

I have no repugnance then—why should

I now have?—to those little, lawless, azure-tinctured grotesques, that, under the notion of men and women, float about, uncircumscribed by any element, in that world before perspective—a china tea-cup.

I like to see my old friends—whom distance cannot diminish—figuring up in the air (so they appear to our optics), yet on *terra firma* still—for so we must in courtesy interpret that speck of deeper blue—which the decorous artist, to prevent absurdity, had made to spring up beneath their sandals.

I love the men with women's faces, and the women, if possible, with still more womanish expressions.

Here is a young and courtly Mandarin, handing tea to a lady from a salver—two miles off. See how distance seems to set off respect! And here the same lady, or another—for likeness is identity on tea-cups—is stepping into a little fairy boat, moored on the hither side of this calm garden river, with a dainty mincing foot, which in a right angle of incidence (as angles go in our world) must infallibly land her in the midst of a flowery mead—a furlong off on the other side of the same strange stream!

Farther on—if far or near can be predicated of their world—see horses, tree, pagodas, dancing the hays[1].

Here—a cow and rabbit couchant, and co-extensive—so objects show, seen through the lucid atmosphere of fine Cathay.

I was pointing out to my cousin last evening, over our Hyson[2] (which we are old-fashioned enough to drink unmixed still of an afternoon), some of these *speciosa miracula*[3] upon a set of extra-

ordinary old blue china (a recent purchase) which we were now for the first time using; and could not help remarking, how favourable circumstances had been to us of late years, that we could afford to please the eye sometimes with trifles of this sort—when a passing sentiment seemed to overshade the brows of my companion. I am quick at detecting these summer clouds in Bridget.

"I wish the good old times would come again," she said, "when we were not quite so rich. I do not mean that I want to be poor; but there was a middle state"—so she was pleased to ramble on—"in which I am sure we were a great deal happier. A purchase is but a purchase, now that you have money enough and to spare. Formerly it used to be a triumph. When we coveted a cheap luxury (and oh! how much ado I had to get you to consent in those times!)—we were used to have a debate two or three days before, and to weigh the *for* and *against*, and think what we might spare it out of, and what saving we could hit upon that should be an equivalent. A thing was worth buying then, when we felt the money that we paid for it.

"Do you remember the brown suit, which you made to hang upon you, till all your friends cried shame upon you, it grew so thread-bare—and all because of the folio Beaumont and Fletcher, which you dragged home late at night from Barker's in Covent Garden? Do you remember how we eyed it for weeks before we could make up our minds to the purchase, and had not come to a determination till it was near ten o'clock of the Saturday night, when you set off from Islington, fearing you should be too late—and when the old bookseller with some grumbling opened his shop, and by the

[1]An old English dance.　　[2]A green tea.
[3]Beautiful wonders.

twinkling taper (for he was settling bed-wards) lighted out the relic from his dusty treasures—and when you lugged it home, wishing it were twice as cumbersome—and when you presented it to me—and when we were exploring the perfectness of it (*collating*, you called it)—and while I was repairing some of the loose leaves with paste, which your impatience would not suffer to be left till daybreak—was there no pleasure in being a poor man? Or can those neat black clothes which you wear now, and are so careful to keep brushed, since we have become rich and finical, give you half the honest vanity with which you flaunted it about in that overworn suit—your old corbeau[4]—for four or five weeks longer than you should have done, to pacify your conscience for the mighty sum of fifteen—or sixteen shillings was it?—a great affair we thought it then—which you had lavished on the old folio. Now you can afford to buy any book that pleases you, but I do not see that you ever bring me home any nice old purchases now.

"When you came home with twenty apologies for laying out a less number of shillings upon that print after Leonardo, which we christened the 'Lady Blanch'; when you looked at the purchase, and thought of the money—and thought of the money, and looked again at the picture—was there no pleasure in being a poor man? Now, you have nothing to do but to walk in Colnaghi's[5], and buy a wilderness of Leonardos. Yet do you?

"Then, do you remember our pleasant walks to Enfield, and Potter's Bar, and Waltham, when we had a holiday—holidays, and all other fun, are gone, now we are rich—and the little hand-basket in

which I used to deposit our day's fare of savory cold lamb and salad—and how you would pry about at noontide for some decent house where we might go in and produce our store—only paying for the ale that you must call for—and speculate upon the looks of the landlady, and whether she was likely to allow us a tablecloth—and wish for such another honest hostess as Izaak Walton has described many a one on the pleasant banks of the Lea, when he went a-fishing—and sometimes they would look grudgingly upon us—but we had cheerful looks still for one another, and would eat our plain food savorily, scarcely grudging Piscator[6] his Trout Hall? Now,—when we go out a day's pleasuring, which is seldom, moreover, we *ride* part of the way—and go into a fine inn, and order the best of dinners, never debating the expense—which, after all, never has half the relish of those chance country snaps, when we were at the mercy of uncertain usage and a precarious welcome.

"You are too proud to see a play anywhere now but in the pit. Do you remember where it was we used to sit, when we saw the 'Battle of Hexham' and the 'Surrender of Calais'[7], and Bannister and Mrs. Bland in the 'Children in the Wood'[8]—when we squeezed out our shillings a-piece to sit three or four times in a season in the one-shilling gallery—where you felt all the time that you ought not to have brought me—and more strongly I felt obligation to you for having brought me—and the pleasure was the better for a little shame—and when the curtain drew up, what cared we for our place in the house, or what mattered it where we

---

[4]Very dark green.   [5]A London print shop.

[6]A character in Walton's *Compleat Angler*, who met with Venator at Trout Hall.
[7]Comedies by George Colman (1762-1836).
[8]A comedy by Thomas Morton (1764-1838).

were sitting, when our thoughts were with Rosalind in Arden, or with Viola at the Court of Illyria? You used to say that the Gallery was the best place of all for enjoying a play socially—that the relish of such exhibitions must be in proportion to the infrequency of going—that the company we met there, not being in general readers of plays, were obliged to attend the more, and did attend, to what was going on, on the stage, because a word lost would have been a chasm which it was impossible for them to fill up. With such reflections we consoled our pride then—and I appeal to you, whether, as a woman, I met generally with less attention and accommodation than I have done since in more expensive situations in the house? The getting in indeed, and the crowding up those inconvenient staircases, was bad enough—but there was still a law of civility to woman recognized to quite as great an extent as we ever found in the other passages—and how a little difficulty overcome heightened the snug seat and the play, afterwards! Now we can only pay our money and walk in. You cannot see, you say, in the galleries now. I am sure, we saw, and heard too, well enough then—but sight and all, I think, is gone with our poverty.

"There was the pleasure in eating strawberries, before they became quite common—in the first dish of peas, while they were yet dear—to have them for a nice supper, a treat. What treat can you have now? If we were to treat above our means, it would be selfish and wicked. It is very little more that we allow ourselves beyond what the actual poor can get at, that makes what I call a treat—when two people, living together as we have done, now and then indulge themselves in a cheap luxury, which both like;

while each apologizes, and is willing to take both halves of the blame to his single share. I see no harm in people making much of themselves in that sense of the word. It may give them a hint how to make much of others. But now—what I mean by the word—we never do make much of ourselves. None but the poor can do it. I do not mean the veriest poor of all, but persons as we were, just above poverty.

"I know what you were going to say, that it is mighty pleasant at the end of the year to make all meet—and much ado we used to have every thirty-first night of December to account for our exceedings—many a long face did you make over your puzzled accounts, and in contriving to make it out how we had spent so much—or that we had not spent so much—or that it was impossible we should spend so much next year—and still we found our slender capital decreasing, but then—betwixt ways, and projects, and compromises of one sort or another, and talk of curtailing this charge, and doing without that for the future—and the hope that youth brings, and laughing spirits (in which you were never poor till now), we pocketed up our loss, and in conclusion, with 'lusty brimmers' (as you used to quote it out of 'hearty cheerful Mr. Cotton'[9] as you called him), we used to welcome in the 'coming guest.' Now we have no reckoning at all at the end of the old year—no flattering promises about the new year doing better for us."

Bridget is so sparing of her speech on most occasions, that when she gets into a rhetorical vein, I am careful how I interrupt it. I could not help, however, smiling at the phantom of wealth which

[9]Charles Cotton (1630-1687), poet and friend of Walton, in a poem "The New Year."

her dear imagination had conjured up out of a clear income of a poor hundred pounds a year. "It is true we were happier when we were poorer, but we were also younger, my cousin. I am afraid we must put up with the excess, for if we were to shake the superflux into the sea, we should not much mend ourselves. That we had much to struggle with as we grew up together, we have reason to be most thankful. It strengthened and knit our compact closer. We could never have been what we have been to each other, if we had always had the sufficiency which you now complain of. The resisting power —those natural dilations of the youthful spirit, which circumstances cannot straiten —with us are long since passed away. Competence to age is supplementary youth, a sorry supplement indeed, but I fear the best that is to be had. We must ride, where we formerly walked: live better, and lie softer—and shall be wise to do so—than we had means to do in those good old days you speak of. Yet could those days return—could you and I once more walk our thirty miles a day—could Bannister and Mrs. Bland again be young, and you and I be young to see

them—could the good old one-shilling gallery days return—they are dreams, my cousin, now—but could you and I at this moment, instead of this quiet argument, by our well-carpeted fireside, sitting on this luxurious sofa—be once more struggling up those inconvenient staircases, pushed about and squeezed, and elbowed by the poorest rabble of poor gallery scramblers—could I once more hear those anxious shrieks of yours—and the delicious 'Thank God, we are safe,' which always followed when the topmost stair, conquered, let in the first light of the whole cheerful theatre down beneath us—I know not the fathom line that ever touched a descent so deep as I would be willing to bury more wealth in than Croesus had, or the great Jew R----[10] is supposed to have, to purchase it. And now do just look at that merry little Chinese waiter holding an umbrella, big enough for a bed-tester, over the head of that pretty insipid half Madonna-ish chit of a lady in that very blue summer-house."

1823

[10]Nathan Mayer Rothschild (1777-1836), founder of the English branch of the famous European banking house.

WILLIAM HAZLITT (1778-1830)

Hazlitt did not possess Lamb's subtlety and sensitivity as an essayist and critic, but he had greater energy and force. His gusto—his hearty delight in life and literature—makes him one of the most refreshing of English prose writers.

He was born at Maidstone, Kent, the son of a Unitarian minister, and was himself educated for that ministry. His meeting with Coleridge in 1798, however, interested him in art and literature as a career. For several years he studied painting, but decided that his talent was not sufficient and turned to writing. He published his *Essay on the Principles of Human Action* in 1805, and thereafter became a frequent contributor of articles on politics, philosophy,

and drama to various magazines and newspapers. The best of his books of literary criticism—*On the English Poets*, *On the English Comic Writers*, and *On the Dramatic Literature of the Age of Elizabeth*—appeared successively in 1818, 1819, and 1820. He went on to publish *Table Talk* (1822), *The Spirit of the Age* (1825), and biographies of Napoleon and Titian. Hazlitt was a man of quick temper and strong opinions, and this led to the breakdown of both of his marriages and to many controversies with his contemporaries. But he was also an honest and vigorous man, and these are the chief virtues that inform his lively prose.

FROM My First Acquaintance with Poets

My father was a Dissenting Minister at W-----m[1] in Shropshire; and in the year 1798 (the figures that compose that date are to me like the "dreaded name of Demogorgon"[2]) Mr. Coleridge came to Shrewsbury, to succeed Mr. Rowe in the spiritual charge of a Unitarian congregation there. He did not come till late on the Saturday afternoon before he was to preach; and Mr. Rowe, who himself went down to the coach in a state of anxiety and expectation, to look for the arrival of his successor, could find no one at all answering the description but a round-faced man in a short black coat (like a shooting jacket) which hardly seemed to have been made for him, but who seemed to be talking at a great rate to his fellow-passengers. Mr. Rowe had scarce returned to give an account of his disappointment, when the round-faced man in black entered, and dissipated all doubts on the subject, by beginning to talk. He did not cease while he stayed; nor has he since, that I know of. He held the good town of Shrewsbury in delightful suspense for three weeks that he remained there, "fluttering the proud Salopians like an eagle in a dove-cote"[3]; and the Welsh mountains that skirt the horizon with their tempestuous confusion, agree to have heard no such mystic sounds since the days of

High-born Hoel's harp or soft Llewellyn's lay![4]

As we passed along between W-----m and Shrewsbury, and I eyed their blue tops seen through the wintry branches, or the red rustling leaves of the sturdy oak-trees by the roadside, a sound was in my ears as of a Siren's song; I was stunned, startled with it, as from deep sleep; but I had no notion then that I should ever be able to express my admiration to others in motley imagery or quaint allusion, till the light of his genius shone into my soul, like the sun's rays glittering in the puddles of the road. I was at that time dumb, inarticulate, helpless, like a worm by the wayside, crushed, bleeding, lifeless; but now, bursting from the deadly bands that bound them,

With Styx nine times round them,[5]

my ideas float on winged words, and as they expand their plumes, catch the golden light of other years. My soul has indeed remained in its original bondage, dark obscure, with longings infinite and unsatisfied; my heart, shut up in the prison-house of this rude clay, has never found, nor will it ever find, a heart to speak to; but that my understanding also did not remain dumb and brutish, or at length found a language to express itself, I owe to Coleridge. But this is not to my purpose.

My father lived ten miles from Shrewsbury, and was in the habit of exchanging visits with Mr. Rowe, and with Mr. Jenkins of Whitchurch (nine miles farther on) according to the custom of Dissenting Ministers in each other's neighbourhood. A line of communication is thus established, by which the flame of civil and religious liberty is kept alive, and nourished its smouldering fire unquenchable, like the fires in the Agamemnon of Aeschylus, placed at different stations,

---

[1]The village of Wem, near Shrewsbury.
[2]See *Paradise Lost*, II, 964-965.
[3]See *Coriolonus*, V, vi: 115-116.
[4]Gray, "The Bard," 1. 28.

[5]Pope, "Ode on St. Cecilia's Day," 1. 91.

that waited for ten long years to announce with their blazing pyramids the destruction of Troy. Coleridge had agreed to come over to see my father, according to the courtesy of the country, as Mr. Rowe's probable successor; but in the meantime I had gone to hear him preach the Sunday after his arrival. A poet and a philosopher getting up into a Unitarian pulpit to preach the Gospel, was a romance in these degenerate days, a sort of revival of the primitive spirit of Christianity, which was not to be resisted.

It was in January, 1798, that I rose one morning before daylight, to walk ten miles in the mud, and went to hear this celebrated person preach. Never, the longest day I have to live, shall I have such another walk as this cold, raw, comfortless one, in the winter of the year 1798. *Il y a des impressions que ni le temps ni les circonstances peuvent effacer. Dusse-je vivre des siècles entiers, le doux temps de ma jeunesse ne peut renaître pour moi, ni s'effacer jamais dans ma mémoire.*[6] When I got there, the organ was playing the 100th Psalm, and when it was done, Mr. Coleridge rose and gave out his text, "And he went up into the mountain to pray, HIMSELF, ALONE." As he gave out this text, his voice "rose like a steam of rich distilled perfumes,"[7] and when he came to the two last words, which he pronounced loud, deep, and distinct, it seemed to me, who was then young, as if the sounds had echoed from the bottom of the human heart, and as if that prayer might have floated in solemn silence through the universe. The idea of St. John came into mind, "of one crying in the wilderness, who had his loins girt about, and whose food was locusts and wild honey." The preacher

then launched into his subject, like an eagle dallying with the wind. The sermon was upon peace and war; upon church and state—not their alliance, but their separation—on the spirit of the world and the spirit of Christianity, not as the same, but as opposed to one another. He talked of those who had "inscribed the cross of Christ on banners dripping with human gore." He made a poetical and pastoral excursion—and to show the fatal effects of war, drew a striking contrast between the simple shepherd boy, driving his team afield, or sitting under the hawthorn, piping to his flock, "as though he should never be old," and the same poor country lad, crimped, kidnapped, brought into town, made drunk at an alehouse, turned into a wretched drummer-boy, with his hair sticking on end with powder and pomatum, a long cue at his back, and tricked out in the loathsome finery of the profession of blood.

Such were the notes our once-loved poet sung.[8]

And for myself, I could not have been more delighted if I had heard the music of the spheres. Poetry and Philosophy had met together. Truth and Genius had embraced, under the eye and with sanction of Religion. This was even beyond my hopes. I returned home well satisfied. The sun that was still laboring pale and wan through the sky, obscured by thick mists, seemed an emblem of the good cause; and the cold dank drops of dew that hung half melted on the beard of the thistle, had something genial and refreshing in them; for there was a spirit of hope and youth in all nature, that turned everything into good. The face of nature

[6]From Rousseau, *Confessions*, Part II.
[7]Milton, "Comus," l. 556.

[8]Pope, "Epistle to Robert Earl of Oxford" l. 1.

had not then the brand of Jus Divinum on it:

Like to that sanguine flower inscribed with woe.[9]

On the Tuesday following, the half-inspired speaker came. I was called down into the room where he was, and went half-hoping, half-afraid. He received me very graciously, and I listened for a long time without uttering a word. I did not suffer in his opinion by my silence. "For those two hours," he afterwards was pleased to say, "he was conversing with W.H.'s forehead!" His appearance was different from what I had anticipated from seeing him before. At a distance, and in the dim light of the chapel, there was to me a strange wildness in his aspect, a dusky obscurity, and I thought him pitted with the small-pox. His complexion was at that time clear, and even bright—

As are the children of yon azure sheen.[10]

His forehead was broad and high, light as if built of ivory, with large projecting eyebrows, and his eyes rolling beneath them like a sea with darkened lustre. "A certain tender bloom his face o'er-spread,"[11] a purple tinge as we see it in the pale thoughtful complexions of the Spanish portrait-painters, Murillo and Velasquez. His mouth was gross, voluptuous, open, eloquent; his chin good-humoured and round; but his nose, the rudder of the face, the index of the will, was small, feeble, nothing—like what he has done. It might seem that the genius of his face as from a height surveyed and projected him (with sufficient capacity and huge aspiration) into the world unknown of thought and imagination,

with nothing to support or guide his veering purpose, as if Columbus had launched his adventurous course for the New World in a scallop, without oars or compass. So at least I comment on it after the event. Coleridge in his person was rather above the common size, inclining to the corpulent, or like Lord Hamlet, "somewhat fat and pursy." His hair (now, alas! grey) was then black and glossy as the raven's, and fell in smooth masses over his forehead. This long pendulous hair is peculiar to enthusiasts, to those whose minds tend heavenward; and is traditionally inseparable (though of a different colour) from the pictures of Christ. It ought to belong, as a character, to all who preach Christ crucified, and Coleridge was at that time one of those!

It was curious to observe the contrast between him and my father, who was a veteran in the cause, and then declining into the vale of years. He had been a poor Irish lad, carefully brought up by his parents, and sent to the University of Glasgow (where he studied under Adam Smith) to prepare him for his future destination. It was his mother's proudest wish to see her son a Dissenting Minister. So if we look back to past generations (as far as eye can reach) we see the same hopes, fears, wishes, followed by the same disappointments, throbbing in the human heart; and so we may see them (if we look forward) rising up forever, and disappearing, like vapourish bubbles, in the human breast! After being tossed about from congregation to congregation in the heats of the Unitarian controversy, and squabbles about the American war, he had been relegated to an obscure village, where he was to spend the last thirty years of his life, far from the only

[9]"Lycidas" 1. 106.
[10]Thomson, *Castle of Indolence*, II, 1. 33.
[11]*Castle of Indolence*, I, 1. 57.

converse that he loved, the talk about disputed texts of Scripture and the cause of civil and religious liberty. Here he passed his days, repining but resigned, in the study of the Bible, and the perusal of the Commentators—huge folios, not easily got through, one of which would outlast a winter! Why did he pore on these from morn to night (with the exception of a walk in the fields or a turn in the garden to gather broccoli-plants or kidney-beans of his own rearing, with no small degree of pride and pleasure)? Here were "no figures nor no fantasies"[12]— neither poetry nor philosophy—nothing to dazzle, nothing to excite modern curiosity; but to his lack-luster eyes there appeared, within the pages of the ponderous, unwieldy, neglected tomes, the sacred name of JEHOVAH in Hebrew capitals: pressed down by the weight of the style, worn to the last fading thinness of the understanding, there were glimpses, glimmering notions of the patriarchal wanderings, with palm-trees hovering in the horizon, and processions of camels at the distance of three thousand years; there was Moses with the Burning Bush, the number of the Twelve Tribes, types, shadows, glosses on the law and the prophets; there were discussions (dull enough) on the age of Methuselah, a mighty speculation! there were outlines, rude guesses at the shape of Noah's Ark and of the riches of Solomon's Temple; questions as to the date of the creation, predictions of the end of all of the creation, predictions of the end of all things; the great lapses of time, the strange mutations of the globe were unfolded with the voluminous leaf, as it turned over; and though the soul might slumber with an hieroglyphic veil of inscrutable mysteries

[12]*Julius Caesar*, II, i, 1. 231.

drawn over it, yet it was in a slumber ill-exchanged for all the sharpened realities of sense, wit, fancy, or reason. My father's life was comparatively a dream; but it was a dream of infinity and eternity, of death, the resurrection, and a judgment to come!

No two individuals were ever more unlike than were the host and his guest. A poet was to my father a sort of nondescript: yet whatever added grace to the Unitarian cause was to him welcome. He could hardly have been more surprised or pleased, if our visitor had worn wings. Indeed, his thoughts had wings; and as the silken sounds rustled round our little wainscoted parlour, my father threw back his spectacles over his forehead, his white hairs mixing with its sanguine hue; and a smile of delight beamed across his rugged cordial face, to think that Truth had found a new ally in Fancy! Besides, Coleridge seemed to take considerable notice of me, and that of itself was enough. He talked very familiarly, but agreeably, and glanced over a variety of subjects. At dinner-time he grew more animated, and dilated in a very edifying manner on Mary Wollstonecraft[13] and Mackintosh.[14] The last, he said, he considered (on my father's speaking of his *Vindiciae Galicae* as a capital performance) as a clever scholastic man—a master of the topics,—or as the ready warehouseman of letters, who knew exactly where to lay his hand on what he wanted, though the goods were not his own. He thought him no match for Burke,[15] either

[13]English author (1759-1797), champion of women's rights.
[14]Sir James Mackintosh (1765-1832), Scottish philosopher and historian.
[15]Edmund Burke (1729-1797), English parliamentarian and opponent of the French Revolution.

in style or matter. Burke was a metaphysician, Mackintosh a mere logician. Burke was an orator (almost a poet) who reasoned in figures, because he had an eye for nature: Mackintosh on the other hand, was a rhetorician, who had only an eye to commonplaces. On this I ventured to say that I had always entertained a great opinion of Burke, and that (as far as I could find) the speaking of him with contempt might be made the test of a vulgar democratical mind. This was the first observation I ever made to Coleridge, and he said it was a very just and striking one. I remember the leg of Welsh mutton and the turnips on the table that day had the finest flavour imaginable. Coleridge added that Mackintosh and Tom Wedgwood[16] (of whom, however, he spoke highly) had expressed a very indifferent opinion of his friend Mr. Wordsworth, on which he remarked to them—"He strides on so far before you, that he dwindles in the distance!" Godwin[17] had once boasted to him of having carried on an argument with Mackintosh for three hours with dubious success; Coleridge told him—"If there had been a man of genius in the room, he would have settled the question in five minutes." He asked me if I had ever seen Mary Wollstonecraft, and I said, I had once for a few moments, and that she seemed to me to turn off Godwin's objections to something she advanced with quite a playful, easy air. He replied, that "this was only one instance of the ascendancy which people of imagination exercised over those of mere intellect." He did not rate Godwin very high

(this was caprice or prejudice, real or affected) but he had a great idea of Mrs. Wollstonecraft's powers of conversation, none at all of her talent for bookmaking. We talked a little about Holcroft.[18] He had been asked if he was not much struck with him, and he said he thought himself in more danger of being struck by him. I complained that he would not let me get on at all, for he required a definition of even the commonest word, exclaiming, "What do you mean by a sensation, Sir?" "What do you mean by an idea?" This Coleridge said, was barricading the road to truth:—it was setting up a turnpike-gate at every step we took. I forget a great number of things, many more than I remember; but the day passed off pleasantly, and the next morning Mr. Coleridge was to return to Shrewsbury. When I came down to breakfast, I found that he had just received a letter from his friend T. Wedgwood, making him an offer of £150 a year if he chose to waive his present pursuit, and devote himself entirely to the study of poetry and philosophy. Coleridge seemed to make up his mind to close with this proposal in the act of tying on one of his shoes. It threw an additional damp on his departure. It took the wayward enthusiast quite from us to cast him into Deva's winding vales, or by the shores of old romance. Instead of living at ten miles distance, of being the pastor of a Dissenting congregation at Shrewsbury, he was henceforth to inhabit the Hill of Parnassus, to be a Shepherd on the Delectable Mountains. Alas! I knew not the way thither, and felt very little gratitude for Mr. Wedgwood's bounty. I was presently relieved from the dilemma; for Mr. Coleridge, asking for a pen and

[16]Tom Wedgwood (1771-1805), of the famous Wedgwood pottery family, and a generous patron of Coleridge.

[17]William Godwin (1756-1836), English political theorist, husband of Mary Wollstonecraft and father of Mary Shelley.

[18]Thomas Holcroft (1745-1809), dramatist and novelist of radical sympathies.

ink, and going to a table to write something on a bit of card, advanced towards me with undulating step, and giving me the precious document, said that that was his address, Mr. Coleridge, Nether Stowey, Somersetshire; and that he should be glad to see me there in a few weeks' time, and, if I chose, would come halfway to meet me. I was not less surprised than the shepherd boy (this simile is to be found in Cassandra) when he sees a thunderbolt fall close at his feet. I stammered out my acknowledgments and acceptance of this offer (I thought Mr. Wedgwood's annuity a trifle to it) as well as I could; and this mighty business being settled, the poet-preacher took leave, and I accompanied him six miles on the road. It was a fine morning in the middle of winter, and he talked the whole way. The scholar in Chaucer is described as going

. . . sounding on his way.

So Coleridge went on his. In digressing, in dilating, in passing from subject to subject, he appeared to me to float in air, to slide on ice. He told me in confidence (going along) that he should have preached two sermons before he accepted the situation at Shrewsbury, one on Infant Baptism, the other on the Lord's Supper, shewing that he could not administer either, which would have effectually disqualified him for the object in view. I observed that he continually crossed me on the way by shifting from one side of the footpath to the other. This struck me as an odd movement; but I did not at that time connect it with any instability of purpose or involuntary change of principle, as I have done since. He seemed unable to keep on in a straight line. He spoke slightingly of Hume[19]

(whose Essay on Miracles he said was stolen from an objection started in one of South's sermons—Credat Judaeus Apella![20]). I was not very much pleased at this account of Hume, for I had just been reading, with infinite relish, that completest of all metaphysical chokepears, his Treatise on Human Nature, to which the Essays, in point of scholastic subtlety and close reasoning, are mere elegant trifling, light summer-reading. Coleridge even denied the excellence of Hume's general style, which I think betrayed a want of taste or candor. He, however, made me amends by the manner in which he spoke of Berkeley[21]. He dwelt particularly on his Essay on Vision as a masterpiece of analytical reasoning. So it undoubtedly is. He was exceedingly angry with Dr. Johnson for striking the stone with his foot, in allusion to this author's Theory of Matter and Spirit, and saying, "Thus I confute him, Sir." Coleridge drew a parallel (I don't know how he brought about the connection) between Bishop Berkeley and Tom Paine[22]. He said the one was an instance of a subtle, the other of an acute mind, than which no two things could be more distinct. The one was a shop-boy's quality, the other the characteristic of a philosopher. He considered Bishop Butler[23] as a true philosopher, a profound and conscientious thinker, a genuine reader of nature and of his own mind. He did not speak of his Analogy, but of his Sermons at the Rolls' Chapel, of which I had never heard. Coleridge somehow always contrived to

[19]David Hume (1711-1776), Scottish philosopher and historian.

[20]*Let the Jew Appela believe it.* (Homer, Satires, I, v, 100).

[21]George Berkeley (1685-1757), philosopher who argued that things exist only when they are perceived.

[22]Tom Paine (1737-1809), political theorist.

[23]Joseph Butler (1692-1752), bishop and theologian.

prefer the unknown to the known. In this instance he was right. The Analogy is a tissue of sophistry, of wire-drawn, theological special-pleading; the Sermons (with the Preface to them) are in a fine vein of deep, matured reflection, a candid appeal to our observation of human nature, without pedantry and without bias. I told Coleridge I had written a few remarks, and was sometimes foolish enough to believe that I had made a discovery on the same subject (the Natural Disinterestedness of the Human Mind)— and I tried to explain my view of it to Coleridge, who listened with great willingness, but I did not succeed in making myself understood. I sat down to the task shortly afterwards for the twentieth time, got new pens and paper, determined to make clear work of it, wrote a few meager sentences in the skeleton-style of a mathematical demonstration, stopped halfway down the second page; and, after trying in vain to pump up any words, images, notions, apprehensions, facts, or observations, from that gulph of abstraction in which I had plunged myself for four or five years preceding, gave up the attempt as labour in vain, and shed tears of helpless despondency on the blank unfinished paper. I can write fast enough now. Am I better than I was then? Oh no! One truth discovered, one pang of regret at not being able to express it, is better than all the fluency and flippancy in the world. Would that I could go back to what I then was! Why can we not revive past times as we can revisit old places? If I had the quaint Muse of Sir Philip Sidney to assist me, I would write a Sonnet to the Road between W-----m and Shrewsbury, and immortalize every step of it by some fond enigmatical conceit. I would swear that the very milestone had ears, and that

Harmer-hill stooped with all its pines, to listen to a poet, as he passed! I remember but one other topic of discourse in this walk. He mentioned Paley[24], praised the naturalness and clearness of his style, but condemned his sentiments, thought him a mere time-serving casuist, and said that "the fact of his work on Moral and Political Philosophy being made a text-book in our Universities was a disgrace to the national character." We parted at the six-mile stone; and I returned homeward, pensive but much pleased. I had met with unexpected notice from a person, whom I believed to have been prejudiced against me. "Kind and affable to me had been his condescension, and should be honored ever with suitable regard."[25] He was the first poet I had known, and he certainly answered to that inspired name. I had heard a great deal of his powers of conversation, and was not disappointed. In fact, I never met with anything at all like them, either before or since. I could easily credit the accounts which were circulated of his holding forth to a large party of ladies and gentlemen, an evening or two before, on the Berkeleian Theory, when he made the whole material universe look like a transparency of fine words; and another story (which I believe he has somewhere told himself) of his being asked to a party at Birmingham, of his smoking tobacco and going to sleep after dinner on a sofa, where the company found him to their no small surprise, which was increased to wonder when he started up of a sudden, and rubbing his eyes, looked about him, and launched into a three-hours' description of the third heaven, of which he had

[24]William Paley (1743-1805), theologian and philosopher.
[25]Paraphrased from *Paradise Lost*, viii, 11. 648-650.

had a dream, very different from Mr. Southey's Vision of Judgment, and also from that other Vision of Judgment, which Mr. Murray, the Secretary of the Bridge Street Junto, has taken into his especial keeping![26]

On my way back, I had a sound in my ears, it was the voice of Fancy: I had a light before me, it was the face of Poetry. The one still lingers there, the other has not quitted my side! Coleridge in truth met me halfway on the ground of philosophy, or I should not have been won over to his imaginative creed. I had an uneasy, pleasurable sensation all the time, till I was to visit him. During those months the chill breath of winter gave me a welcoming; the vernal air was balm and inspiration to me. The golden sunsets, the silver star of evening, lighted me on my way to new hopes and prospects. I was to visit Coleridge in the spring. This circumstance was never absent from my thoughts, and mingled with all my feelings. I wrote to him at the time proposed, and received an answer postponing my intended visit for a week or two, but very cordially urging me to complete my promise then. This delay did not damp, but rather increased my ardor. In the meantime I went to Llangollen Vale, by way of initiating myself in the mysteries of natural scenery; and I must say I was enchanted with it. I had been reading Coleridge's description of England, in his fine Ode on the Departing Year, and I applied it, *con amore*, to the objects before me. That valley was to me (in a manner) the cradle of a new existence: in the river that winds through it, my spirit was baptized in the waters of Helicon![27]

1823

[26]This is a reference to Byron's parody of Southey's *Vision of Judgment.* For publishing this, Leigh Hunt was prosecuted by Charles Murray, solicitor to the Constitutional Association for Opposing Disloyal and Seditious Principles.

[27]Mount Helicon is the abode of the Muses.

LORD BYRON (1788-1824)

On the Continent, Byron was regarded as the greatest of the English romantics, and "Byronism" became almost a synonym for romanticism. At home his reputation was never as high, partly because of the bad taste left by the scandals of his personal life, and partly because of the slipshod technique of much of his verse. Both as man and poet, he was a curiously mixed being. He could be haughty, impetuous, cruel, and cynical; but he was also capable of humility, a genuine sympathy for the poor, and a sincere devotion to liberty. Matthew Arnold perhaps best summed up his strengths and weaknesses as a poet when he wrote: "Byron has not a great artist's profound and patient skill . . . But he has a wonderful power of vividly conceiving a single incident, a single situation; of throwing himself upon it, grasping it as if it were real and he saw and felt it, and of making us see and feel it too."

Byron was born in London, the son of Captain John Byron, and inherited the title of Baron at the age of ten as the result of the death of his cousin. He was educated at Harrow and Trinity College, Cambridge, and from 1809 to 1811 travelled through the Mediterranean area. His verse travelogue of this tour, the first two cantos of *Childe Harold's Pilgrimage*, was published in 1812 and brought him immediate fame. He followed up this success with six long narrative poems set in the Near East, and their exotic settings and characters made them very popular. In 1815 Byron married Anne Isabella Milbanke, but their temperaments were incompatible and they separated within a year. Byron was rumoured to be in love with his half-sister

Augusta, and left England forever in 1816 under a cloud of scandal. Thereafter he lived mainly in Italy, seeing much of the Shelleys, having many short-lived love affairs and one prolonged one with the Countess Guiccioli, and turning out a steady stream of poems and verse dramas including *Manfred* (1817), *Don Juan* (1819-24), *Cain* (1821), and *The Vision of Judgment* (1821). In 1823 Byron joined the Greeks in their fight for independence, and he died of fever at Missolonghi in April, 1824.

Byron's verse is usually marked by energy and incisiveness rather than by its melodic beauty, but some of his lyrics, such as "She Walks in Beauty," combine beauty of sound with tenderness of feeling. Although in certain moods he made fun of the nature cult of his fellow-romantics, he had a quick response to natural beauty, especially nature in its wilder aspects. He also had a shrewd insight into character, and a gift for describing scenes of rapid action. An admirer of Pope, he also could write satire effectively, as his poems *English Bards and Scotch Reviewers*, *Don Juan*, and *The Vision of Judgment* abundantly demonstrate.

She Walks in Beauty

She walks in Beauty, like the night
  Of cloudless climes and starry skies;
And all that's best of dark and bright
  Meet in her aspect and her eyes:
Thus mellow'd to that tender light
  Which Heaven to gaudy day denies.

One shade the more, one ray the less,
  Had half impair'd the nameless grace
Which waves in every raven tress,
  Or softly lightens o'er her face;

Where thoughts serenely sweet express
  How pure, how dear their dwelling-
    place.

And on that cheek, and o'er that brow,
  So soft, so calm, yet eloquent,
The smiles that win, the tints that glow,
  But tell of days in goodness spent,
A mind at peace with all below,
  A heart whose love is innocent!

1814   1815

The Destruction of Sennacherib

The Assyrian came down like the wolf on the fold,
And his cohorts were gleaming in purple and gold;
And the sheen of their spears was like stars on the sea,
When the blue wave rolls nightly on deep Galilee.

Like the leaves of the forest when Summer is green,
That host with their banners at sunset were seen;
Like the leaves of the forest when Autumn hath blown,
That host on the morrow lay withered and strown.[1]

[1] Strewn.

For the Angel of Death spread his wings on the blast,
And breathed in the face of the foe as he passed;   10
And the eyes of the sleepers waxed deadly and chill,
And their hearts but once heaved, and for ever grew still!

And there lay the steed with his nostril all wide,
But through it there rolled not the breath of his pride;
And the foam of his gasping lay white on the turf,
And cold as the spray of the rock-beating surf.

And there lay the rider distorted and pale,
With the dew on his brow, and the rust on his mail;
And the tents were all silent, the banners alone,
The lances unlifted, the trumpet unblown.   20

And the widows of Ushur[2] are loud in their wail,
And the idols are broke in the temple of Baal,[3]
And the might of the Gentile,[4] unsmote by the sword,
Hath melted like snow in the glance of the Lord!

1815

[2] Assyria.
[3] An Assyrian god.
[4] One who is a stranger to Hebrew beliefs—here, Sennacherib.

On This Day I Complete My Thirty-Sixth Year

MISSOLONGHI, JANUARY 22, 1824

'Tis time this heart should be unmoved,
  Since others it hath ceased to move:
Yet, though I cannot be beloved,
    Still let me love!

My days are in the yellow leaf;
  The flowers and fruits of love are gone;
The worm, the canker, and the grief
    Are mine alone!

The fire that on my bosom preys
  Is lone as some volcanic isle;   10
No torch is kindled at its blaze—
    A funeral pile.

The hope, the fear, the jealous care,
  The exalted portion of the pain

And power of love, I cannot share,
    But wear the chain.

But 't is not *thus*—and 't is not *here*—
  Such thoughts should shake my soul,
    nor *now*,
Where glory decks the hero's bier,
    Or binds his brow.   20

The sword, the banner, and the field,
  Glory and Greece, around me see!
The Spartan,[1] borne upon his shield,
    Was not more free.

[1] *Spartan, borne . . . shield.* The exhortation of the wives and mothers of Spartan warriors going to battle was that they return with their shields, or on them.

Awake! (not Greece—she *is* awake!)
  Awake, my spirit! Think through *whom*
Thy life-blood tracks its parent lake,
  And then strike home!

Tread those reviving passions down,
  Unworthy manhood!—unto thee   30
Indifferent should the smile or frown
  Of beauty be.

Jan. 22, 1824

If thou regret'st thy youth, *why live?*
  The land of honorable death
Is here:—up to the field, and give
  Away thy breath!

Seek out—less often sought than found—
  A soldier's grave, for thee the best;
Then look around, and choose thy ground,
  And take thy rest.   40

1824

So We'll Go No More A-Roving

So we'll go no more a-roving
  So late into the night,
Though the heart be still as loving,
  And the moon be still as bright.

For the sword outwears its sheath,[1]
  And the soul wears out the breast,
And the heart must pause to breathe,
  And Love itself have rest.

Though the night was made for loving,
  And the day returns too soon,   10
Yet we'll go no more a-roving
  By the light of the moon.

1817

1836

[1] In a letter of February 1817, which also contains this poem, Byron wrote, "I find 'the sword wearing out the scabbard' though I have but just turned the corner of twenty-nine."

PERCY BYSSHE SHELLEY (1792-1822)

Shelley was born at Field Place, Sussex, and educated at Eton and Oxford. He was expelled from the university in 1811 for writing an atheistic pamphlet, and in the same year impetuously married the sixteen-year-old Harriet Westbrook. He left Harriet in 1814 to elope to the Continent with Mary Godwin, whom he married in 1816 after Harriet had committed suicide. On the Continent he became friendly with Byron, with whom he spent the summer of 1816 in Switzerland writing, among other poems, "The Hymn to Intellectual Beauty." After a brief stay in England, he and Mary moved to Italy in 1818. On July 8, 1822, he was drowned while sailing off the Italian coast. He was buried in the Protestant cemetery in Rome.

Shelley was the most purely lyrical of all the English romantics. His verse has a poignant intensity, a soaring, lilting quality that at its worst leads to shrillness and declamation but at its best to memorable melodic effects. The speed of his verse is partly accounted for by his choice of very active words such as "rolling," "sped," and "driven," partly by his frequent use of hyphenated words such as "sleep-unsheltered" and "eagle-baffling," and partly by his many images of nature in motion such as floating clouds, dancing waves, and driving winds.

His thought matched his style. He was the idealist of idealists, believing that love and beauty were the supreme powers in the universe —that man if free would naturally choose these values but that he is presently thwarted by corrupt social forces, that nature is the embodiment of love, beauty, and liberty, and that eventually these forces will triumph and usher in a paradise in which Man, Nature, and God live together in perfect harmony. These ideas are given most complete expression in his long verse drama, *Prometheus Unbound*, but they are at least in the background of all his poems. Like most idealists, Shelley was often plunged into melancholy by the failure of reality to match his ideals.

Stanzas Written in Dejection, Near Naples

The sun is warm, the sky is clear,
    The waves are dancing fast and bright,
Blue isles and snowy mountains wear
    The purple noon's transparent might,
    The breath of the moist earth is light,
Around its unexpanded buds;
    Like many a voice of one delight,
    The winds, the birds, the ocean floods,
The City's voice itself, is soft like Solitude's.

I see the Deep's untrampled floor   10
    With green and purple seaweeds strown;
I see the waves upon the shore,
    Like light dissolved in star-showers, thrown:
    I sit upon the sands alone,—
The lightning of the noontide ocean
    Is flashing round me, and a tone
    Arises from its measured motion,
How sweet! did any heart now share in my emotion.

Alas! I have nor hope nor health,
    Nor peace within nor calm around,   20
Nor that content surpassing wealth
    The sage in meditation found,
    And walked with inward glory crowned—
Nor fame, nor power, nor love, nor leisure.
    Others I see whom these surround—

Smiling they live, and call life pleasure;
To me that cup has been dealt in another measure.

Yet now despair itself is mild,
  Even as the winds and waters are;
I could lie down like a tired child,
  And weep away the life of care   30
    Which I have borne and yet must bear,
Till death like sleep might steal on me,
  And I might feel in the warm air
My cheek grow cold, and hear the sea
Breathe o'er my dying brain its last monotony.

Some might lament that I were cold,
  As I, when this sweet day is gone,
Which my lost heart, too soon grown old,
  Insults with this untimely moan;   40
    They might lament—for I am one
Whom men love not,—and yet regret,
  Unlike this day, which, when the sun
Shall on its stainless glory set,
Will linger, though enjoyed, like joy in memory yet.

1818
                                       1824

Ozymandias

I met a traveler from an antique land
Who said: Two vast and trunkless legs of stone
Stand in the desert . . . Near them, on the sand,
Half sunk, a shattered visage lies, whose frown,
And wrinkled lip, and sneer of cold command,
Tell that its sculptor well those passions read

Which yet survive, stamped on these lifeless things,
The hand that mocked them, and the heart that fed:[1]
And on the pedestal these words appear:
"My name is Ozymandias, king of kings: 10
Look on my works, ye Mighty, and despair!"
Nothing beside remains. Round the decay
Of that colossal wreck, boundless and bare
The lone and level sands stretch far away.

1817
                                       1818

[1]The passions sculptured in stone survive the hand of the sculptor who had mocked them (mocked here means both the original sense of *imitation* and that of *derision*), as well as the heart of Ozymandias, which had been their source.

Ode to the West Wind

I

O Wild West Wind, thou breath of Autumn's being,
Thou, from whose unseen presence the leaves dead
Are driven, like ghosts from an enchanter fleeing,

Yellow, and black, and pale, and hectic red,
Pestilence-striken multitudes: O thou,
Who chariotest to their dark wintry bed

The wingèd seeds, where they lie cold and low,
Each like a corpse within its grave, until
Thine azure sister of the Spring shall blow

Her clarion o'er the dreaming earth, and fill   10
(Driving sweet buds like flocks to feed in air)
With living hues and odours plain and hill:

Wild Spirit, which art moving everywhere;
Destroyer and preserver; hear, O, hear!

II

Thou on whose stream, 'mid the steep sky's commotion,
Loose clouds like earth's decaying leaves are shed,
Shook from the tangled boughs of Heaven and Ocean,

Angels of rain and lightning: there are spread
On the blue surface of thine aëry surge,
Like the bright hair uplifted from the head   20

Of some fierce Maenad[1], even from the dim verge
Of the horizon to the zenith's height,
The locks of the approaching storm.   Thou dirge

Of the dying year, to which this closing night
Will be the dome of a vast sepulchre,
Vaulted with all thy congregated might

Of vapours, from whose solid atmosphere
Black rain, and fire, and hail will burst: O, hear!

---

[1] A Bacchante or female follower of Bacchus.

III

Thou who didst waken from his summer dreams
The blue Mediterranean, where he lay,   30
Lulled by the coil of his crystàlline streams,

Beside a pumice isle in Baiae's bay,
And saw in sleep old palaces and towers
Quivering within the wave's intenser day,

All overgrown with azure moss and flowers
So sweet, the sense faints picturing them! Thou
For whose path the Atlantic's level powers

Cleave themselves into chasms, while far below
The sea-blooms and the oozy woods which wear
The sapless foliage of the ocean, know   40

Thy voice, and suddenly grow gray with fear,
And tremble and despoil themselves: O, hear!

IV

If I were a dead leaf thou mightest bear;
If I were a swift cloud to fly with thee;
A wave to pant beneath thy power, and share

The impulse of thy strength, only less free
Than thou, O uncontrollable! If even
I were as in my boyhood, and could be

The comrade of thy wanderings over Heaven,
As then, when to outstrip thy skiey speed   50
Scarce seemed a vision; I would ne'er have striven

As thus with thee in prayer in my sore need.
Oh, lift me as a wave, a leaf, a cloud!
I fall upon the thorns of life! I bleed!

A heavy weight of hours has chained and bowed
One too like thee: tameless, and swift, and proud.

V

Make me thy lyre, even as the forest is:
What if my leaves are falling like its own!
The tumult of thy mighty harmonies

Will take from both a deep, autumnal tone,   60
Sweet though in sadness.   Be thou, Spirit fierce,
My spirit!   Be thou me, impetuous one!

Drive my dead thoughts over the universe
Like withered leaves to quicken a new birth!
And, by the incantation of this verse,

Scatter, as from an unextinguished hearth
Ashes and sparks, my words among mankind!
Be through my lips to unawakened earth

The trumpet of a prophecy!   O, Wind,
If Winter comes, can Spring be far behind?   70

1819   1820

The Cloud

I bring fresh showers for the thirsting flowers,
    From the seas and the streams;
I bear light shade for the leaves when laid
    In their noonday dreams.
From my wings are shaken the dews that waken
    The sweet buds every one,
When rocked to rest on their mother's breast,
    As she dances about the sun.
I wield the flail of the lashing hail,
    And whiten the green plains under,   10
And then again I dissolve it in rain,
    And laugh as I pass in thunder.

I sift the snow on the mountains below,
    And their great pines groan aghast;
And all the night 'tis my pillow white,
    While I sleep in the arms of the blast.
Sublime on the towers of my skiey bowers,
    Lightning my pilot sits;
In a cavern under is fettered the thunder,
    It struggles and howls at fits;   20
Over earth and ocean, with gentle motion,
    This pilot is guiding me,

Lured by the love of the genii that move
    In the depths of the purple sea;
Over the rills, and the crags, and the hills,
    Over the lakes and the plains,
Wherever he dream, under mountain or stream,
    The Spirit he loves remains;
And I all the while bask in Heaven's blue smile,
    Whilst he is dissolving in rains.   30

The sanguine Sunrise, with his meteor eyes,
    And his burning plumes outspread,
Leaps on the back of my sailing rack[1],
    When the morning star shines dead;
As on the jag of a mountain crag,
    Which an earthquake rocks and swings,
An eagle alit one moment may sit
    In the light of its golden wings.
And when Sunset may breathe, from the lit sea beneath,
    Its ardours of rest and of love,   40
And the crimson pall of eve may fall
    From the depth of Heaven above,
With wings folded I rest, on mine aëry nest,
    As still as a brooding dove.

That orbèd maiden with white fire laden,
    Whom mortals call the Moon,
Glides glimmering o'er my fleece-like floor,
    By the midnight breezes strewn;
And wherever the beat of her unseen feet,
    Which only the angels hear,   50
May have broken the woof of my tent's thin roof,
    The stars peep behind her and peer;
And I laugh to see them whirl and flee,
    Like a swarm of golden bees,
When I widen the rent in my wind-built tent,
    Till the calm rivers, lakes, and seas,
Like strips of the sky fallen through me on high,
    Are each paved with the moon and these.

[1]A mass of clouds.

I bind the Sun's throne with a burning zone,
    And the Moon's with a girdle of pearl;   60
The volcanoes are dim, and the stars reel and swim,
    When the whirlwinds my banner unfurl.
From cape to cape, with a bridge-like shape,
    Over a torrent sea,
Sunbeam-proof, I hang like a roof,
    The mountains its columns be.
The triumphal arch through which I march
    With hurricane, fire, and snow,
When the Powers of the air are chained to my chair,
    Is the million-coloured bow;   70
The sphere-fire above its soft colours wove,
    While the moist Earth was laughing below.

I am the daughter of Earth and Water,
    And the nursling of the Sky;
I pass through the pores of the ocean and shores;
    I change, but I cannot die.
For after the rain when with never a stain
    The pavilion of Heaven is bare,
And the winds and sunbeams with their convex gleams
    Build up the blue dome of air,   80
I silently laugh at my own cenotaph,
    And out of the caverns of rain,
Like a child from the womb, like a ghost from the tomb,
    I arise and unbuild it again.

      1820

To a Skylark

Hail to thee, blithe Spirit!
    Bird thou never wert,
That from Heaven, or near it,
    Pourest thy full heart
In profuse strains of unpremeditated art.

Higher still and higher
    From the earth thou springest
Like a cloud of fire;
    The blue deep thou wingest,
And singing still dost soar, and soaring ever singest.   **10**

In the golden lightning
　　Of the sunken Sun,
O'er which the clouds are bright'ning,
　　Thou dost float and run;
Like an unbodied joy whose race is just begun.

The pale purple even
　　Melts around thy flight;
Like a star of Heaven,
　　In the broad daylight
Thou art unseen, but yet I hear thy shrill delight,   20

Keen as are the arrows
　　Of that silver sphere,
Whose intense lamp narrows
　　In the white dawn clear
Until we hardly see—we feel that it is there.

All the earth and air
　　With thy voice is loud,
As, when Night is bare,
　　From one lonely cloud
The moon rains out her beams, and Heaven is overflowed.   30

What thou art we know not;
　　What is most like thee?
From rainbow clouds there flow not
　　Drops so bright to see
As from thy presence showers a rain of melody.

Like a poet hidden
　　In the light of thought,
Singing hymns unbidden,
　　Till the world is wrought
To sympathy with hopes and fears it heeded not: 40

Like a high-born maiden
　　In a palace-tower,
Soothing her love-laden
　　Soul in secret hour
With music sweet as love, which overflows her bower;

Like a glow-worm golden
　　In a dell of dew,
Scattering unbeholden
　　Its aëreal hue
Among the flowers and grass, which screen it from the view: 50

Like a rose embowered
    In its own green leaves,
By warm winds deflowered
    Till the scent it gives
Makes faint with too much sweet those heavy-wingèd thieves:

Sound of vernal showers
    On the twinkling grass,
Rain-awakened flowers,
    All that ever was
Joyous, and clear, and fresh, thy music doth surpass: 60

Teach us, Sprite or Bird,
    What sweet thoughts are thine:
I have never heard
    Praise of love or wine
That panted forth a flood of rapture so divine.

Chorus Hymeneal,
    Or triumphal chaunt,
Matched with thine would be all
    But an empty vaunt,
A thing wherein we feel there is some hidden want.   70

What objects are the fountains
    Of thy happy strain?
What fields, or waves, or mountains?
    What shapes of sky or plain?
What love of thine own kind? what ignorance of pain?

With thy clear keen joyance
    Languor cannot be:
Shadow of annoyance
    Never came near thee:
Thou lovest—but ne'er knew love's sad satiety.   80

Waking or asleep,
    Thou of death must deem
Things more true and deep
    Than we mortals dream,
Or how could thy notes flow in such a crystal stream?

We look before and after,
    And pine for what is not:
Our sincerest laughter
    With some pain is fraught;
Our sweetest songs are those that tell of saddest thought.   90

Yet if we could scorn
  Hate, and pride, and fear;
If we were things born
  Not to shed a tear,
I know not how thy joy we ever should come near.

Better than all measures
  Of delightful sound,
Better than all treasures
  That in books are found,
Thy skill to poet were, thou scorner of the ground!   100

Teach me half the gladness
  That thy brain must know,
Such harmonious madness
  From my lips would flow
The world should listen then, as I am listening now.

                    1820

JOHN KEATS (1795-1821)

Keats is the most concrete and sensuous of the English romantics. Whereas Byron's verse characteristically gallops and Shelley's soars, Keats' loiters to take in all the sensuous details of a scene. And whereas beauty for Shelley is an intellectual thing, an idea or ideal, for Keats it is the concrete sense-impression, the rich scent or bright colour or sweet taste of the immediate object. Although his letters prove that he shared the liberal political ideals of his fellow-romantics, his poetry is a poetry of sensations rather than of thoughts. In its mellifluousness it reminds us of Spenser, in its density of texture of Milton, in its aptness of phrasing and fertility of imagery of Shakespeare. Had he lived longer Keats might have become the greatest of English poets, for his verse was constantly improving through his short poetic career of some five years. As it is, his odes are perhaps the finest in the language.

Keats was the son of a livery stable keeper in a London suburb, and was largely self-educated. He qualified by apprenticeship as a surgeon, but having made the acquaintance of Leigh Hunt, Hazlitt, and Shelley he decided to devote himself wholly to a literary career. His first poems appeared in Hunt's liberal magazine, *The Examiner*, in 1816, and his first book, *Poems*, in 1817. These early efforts attracted little notice, but *Endymion* (1818) was bitterly attacked by reviewers. These hostile reviews, the death of his brother Thomas, his unrequited love for Fanny Brawne, and the growing symptoms of tuberculosis in himself combined to plunge him into frequent fits of melancholy. Often his poems reiterate the theme that delight and melancholy are closely interwoven, that only those most sensitive to beauty know the full sadness of beauty's brevity. He continued to write, however, and in 1820 brought out *Lamia and Other Poems*, which included some of his best work such as "The Eve of St. Agnes," "Ode to a Nightingale," and "Ode on a Grecian Urn." This book was praised by the critics, but Keats' health was deteriorating rapidly. To seek relief, he went to Italy in 1821, died shortly afterwards, and was buried in the Protestant cemetery in Rome.

On First Looking into Chapman's Homer

Much have I travell'd in the realms of gold,
    And many goodly states and kingdoms seen;
    Round many western islands have I been
Which bards in fealty to Apollo hold.
Oft of one wide expanse had I been told
    That deep-brow'd Homer ruled as his demesne;
    Yet did I never breathe its pure serene
Till I heard Chapman speak out loud and bold:
Then felt I like some watcher of the skies
    When a new planet swims into his ken[1];
Or like stout Cortez[2] when with eagle eyes
    He star'd at the Pacific—and all his men
Look'd at each other with a wild surmise—
    Silent, upon a peak in Darien.

1816   1817

[1] *Then felt I . . . his ken.* Keats may have had in mind Sir William Herschel's discovery of Uranus in 1781.
[2] It was really Balboa, not Cortez, who first crossed the isthmus to the Pacific. Keats had confused two passages in Robertson's *History of America.*

When I Have Fears That I May Cease to Be

When I have fears that I may cease to be
    Before my pen has glean'd my teeming brain,
Before high-pilèd books, in charact'ry,
    Hold like rich garners the full ripen'd grain;
When I behold, upon the night's starr'd face,
    Huge cloudy symbols of a high romance,
And think that I may never live to trace
    Their shadows, with the magic hand of chance;
And when I feel, fair creature of an hour,
    That I shall never look upon thee more,
Never have relish in the faery power
    Of unreflecting love;—then on the shore
Of the wide world I stand alone, and think
Till love and fame to nothingness do sink.

1818   1848

The Eve of St. Agnes

St. Agnes' Eve[1]—Ah, bitter chill it was!
The owl, for all his feathers, was a-cold;
The hare limped trembling through the frozen grass,
And silent was the flock in woolly fold:
Numb were the Beadsman's[2] fingers, while he told
His rosary, and while his frosted breath,
Like pious incense from a censer old,
Seemed taking flight for heaven, without a death,
Past the sweet Virgin's picture, while his prayer he saith.

His prayer he saith, this patient, holy man;   10
Then takes his lamp, and riseth from his knees,
And back returneth, meagre, barefoot, wan,
Along the chapel aisle by slow degrees:
The sculptured dead, on each side, seem to freeze,
Emprisoned in black, purgatorial rails:
Knights, ladies, praying in dumb orat'ries[3].
He passeth by; and his weak spirit fails
To think how they may ache in icy hoods and mails.

Northward he turneth through a little door,
And scarce three steps, ere Music's golden tongue 20
Flattered to tears this aged man and poor;
But no—already had his deathbell rung;
The joys of all his life were said and sung:
His was harsh penance on St. Agnes' Eve:
Another way he went, and soon among
Rough ashes sat he for his soul's reprieve,
And all night kept awake, for sinners' sake to grieve.

That ancient Beadsman heard the prelude soft;
And so it chanced, for many a door was wide,
From hurry to and fro. Soon, up aloft,   30
The silver, snarling trumpets 'gan to chide:
The level chambers, ready with their pride,
Were glowing to receive a thousand guests:
The carvèd angels, ever eager-eyed,
Stared, where upon their heads the cornice rests,
With hair blown back, and wings put cross-wise on their breasts.

[1]January 20 was supposed to be the coldest day of the year.
[2]A beadsman was, literally, a *praying* man.
[3]An oratory is a small chapel for prayer, "dumb" because occupied by the sculptured figures
 of the knights and ladies buried there.

At length burst in the argent revelry,
With plume, tiara, and all rich array,
Numerous as shadows haunting faerily
The brain, new stuffed, in youth, with triumphs gay   40
Of old romance. These let us wish away,
And turn, sole-thoughted, to one Lady there,
Whose heart had brooded, all that wintry day,
On Love, and winged St. Agnes' saintly care,
As she had heard old dames full many times declare.

They told her how, upon St. Agnes' Eve[4],
Young virgins might have visions of delight,
And soft adorings from their loves receive
Upon the honeyed middle of the night,
If ceremonies due they did aright;   50
As, supperless to bed they must retire,
And couch supine their beauties, lily white;
Nor look behind, nor sideways, but require
Of Heaven with upward eyes for all that they desire.

Full of this whim was thoughtful Madeline:
The music, yearning like a God in pain,
She scarcely heard: her maiden eyes divine,
Fixed on the floor, saw many a sweeping train
Pass by—she heeded not at all: in vain
Came many a tiptoe, amorous cavalier,   60
And back retired; not cooled by high disdain,
But she saw not: her heart was otherwhere:
She sighed for Agnes' dreams, the sweetest of the year.

She danced along with vague, regardless eyes,
Anxious her lips, her breathing quick and short:
The hallowed hour was near at hand: she sighs
Amid the timbrels, and the thronged resort
Of whisperers in anger, or in sport;
'Mid looks of love, defiance, hate, and scorn,
Hoodwinked with faery fancy; all amort,   70
Save to St. Agnes and her lambs unshorn,
And all the bliss to be before to-morrow morn.

So, purposing each moment to retire,
She lingered still. Meantime, across the moors,
Had come young Porphyro, with heart on fire
For Madeline. Beside the portal doors,

[4]During the Middle Ages the legend grew up that, if she observed certain conditions, a maiden might dream of her future husband on the night before St. Agnes' Day.

Buttressed from moonlight, stands he, and implores
All saints to give him sight of Madeline,
But for one moment in the tedious hours,
That he might gaze and worship all unseen;   80
Perchance speak, kneel, touch, kiss—in sooth such things have been.

He ventures in: let no buzzed whisper tell:
All eyes be muffled, or a hundred swords
Will storm his heart, Love's fev'rous citadel:
For him, those chambers held barbarian hordes,
Hyena foemen, and hot-blooded lords,
Whose very dogs would execrations howl
Against his lineage: not one breast affords
Him any mercy, in that mansion foul,
Save one old beldame, weak in body and in soul.   90

Ah, happy chance! the agèd creature came,
Shuffling along with ivory-headed wand,
To where he stood, hid from the torch's flame,
Behind a broad hall-pillar, far beyond
The sound of merriment and chorus bland:
He startled her; but soon she knew his face,
And grasped his fingers in her palsied hand,
Saying, "Mercy, Porphyro! hie thee from this place!
They are all here to-night, the whole blood-thirsty race!

"Get hence! get hence! there's dwarfish Hildebrand;   100
He had a fever late, and in the fit
He cursèd thee and thine, both house and land:
Then there's that old Lord Maurice, not a whit
More tame for his gray hairs—Alas me! flit!
Flit like a ghost away."—"Ah, Gossip dear,
We're safe enough; here in this arm-chair sit,
And tell me how"—"Good Saints! not here, not here;
Follow me, child, or else these stones will be thy bier."

He followed through a lowly archèd way,
Brushing the cobwebs with his lofty plume;   110
And as she muttered "Well-a—well-a-day!"
He found him in a little moonlight room,
Pale, latticed, chill, and silent as a tomb.
"Now tell me where is Madeline," said he,
"O tell me, Angela, by the holy loom
Which none but secret sisterhood may see,
When they St. Agnes' wool are weaving, piously."

"St. Agnes! Ah! it is St. Agnes' Eve—
Yet men will murder upon holy days:
Thou must hold water in a witch's sieve,   120
And be liege-lord of all the Elves and Fays,
To venture so: it fills me with amaze
To see thee, Porphyro!—St. Agnes' Eve!
God's help! my lady fair the conjuror plays
This very night: good angels her deceive!
But let me laugh awhile, I've mickle time to grieve."

Feebly she laugheth in the languid moon,
While Porphyro upon her face doth look,
Like puzzled urchin on an agèd crone
Who keepeth closed a wond'rous riddle-book,   130
As spectacled she sits in chimney nook.
But soon his eyes grew brilliant, when she told
His lady's purpose; and he scarce could brook
Tears, at the thought of those enchantments cold,
And Madeline asleep in lap of legends old.

Sudden a thought came like a full-blown rose,
Flushing his brow, and in his painèd heart
Made purple riot: then doth he propose
A stratagem, that makes the beldame start:
"A cruel man and impious thou art: 140
Sweet lady, let her pray, and sleep, and dream
Alone with her good angels, far apart
From wicked men like thee. Go, go! I deem
Thou canst not surely be the same that thou didst seem."

"I will not harm her, by all saints I swear,"
Quoth Porphyro: "O may I ne'er find grace
When my weak voice shall whisper its last prayer,
If one of her soft ringlets I displace,
Or look with ruffian passion in her face:
Good Angela, believe me by these tears;   150
Or I will, even in a moment's space,
Awake, with horrid shout, my foemen's ears,
And beard them, though they be more fanged than wolves and bears."

"Ah! why wilt thou affright a feeble soul?
A poor, weak, palsy-stricken, churchyard thing,
Whose passing-bell may ere the midnight toll;
Whose prayers for thee, each morn and evening,

Were never missed."—Thus plaining, doth she bring
A gentler speech from burning Porphyro;
So woeful, and of such deep sorrowing,   160
That Angela gives promise she will do
Whatever he shall wish, betide her weal or woe.

Which was, to lead him, in close secrecy,
Even to Madeline's chamber, and there hide
Him in a closet, of such privacy
That he might see her beauty unespied,
And win perhaps that night a peerless bride,
While legioned faeries paced the coverlet,
And pale enchantment held her sleepy-eyed.
Never on such a night have lovers met,   170
Since Merlin paid his Demon all the monstrous debt.

"It shall be as thou wishest," said the Dame:
"All cates and dainties shall be storèd there
Quickly on this feast-night: by the tambour frame
Her own lute thou wilt see: no time to spare,
For I am slow and feeble, and scarce dare
On such a catering trust my dizzy head.
Wait here, my child, with patience; kneel in prayer
The while: Ah! thou must needs the lady wed,
Or may I never leave my grave among the dead."   180

So saying, she hobbled off with busy fear.
The lover's endless minutes slowly passed;
The dame returned, and whispered in his ear
To follow her; with agèd eyes aghast
From fright of dim espial. Safe, at last,
Through many a dusky gallery, they gain
The maiden's chamber, silken, hushed, and chaste;
Where Porphyro took covert, pleased amain.
His poor guide hurried back with agues in her brain.

Her falt'ring hand upon the balustrade,   190
Old Angela was feeling for the stair,
When Madeline, St. Agnes' charmèd maid,
Rose, like a missioned spirit, unaware:
With silver taper's light, and pious care,
She turned, and down the agèd gossip led
To a safe level matting. Now prepare,
Young Porphyro, for gazing on that bed;
She comes, she comes again, like ring-dove frayed and fled.

Out went the taper as she hurried in;
Its little smoke, in pallid moonshine, died: 200
She closed the door, she panted, all akin
To spirits of the air, and visions wide:
No uttered syllable, or, woe betide!
But to her heart, her heart was voluble,
Paining with eloquence her balmy side;
As though a tongueless nightingale should swell
Her throat in vain, and die, heart-stifled, in her dell.

A casement high and triple-arched there was,
All garlanded with carven imag'ries
Of fruits, and flowers, and bunches of knot-grass,   210
And diamonded with panes of quaint device,
Innumerable of stains and splendid dyes,
As are the tiger-moth's deep-damasked wings;
And in the midst, 'mong thousand heraldries,
And twilight saints, and dim emblazonings,
A shielded scutcheon blushed with blood of queens and kings.

Full on this casement shone the wintry moon,
And threw warm gules on Madeline's fair breast,
As down she knelt for heaven's grace and boon;
Rose-bloom fell on her hands, together prest,   220
And on her silver cross soft amethyst,
And on her hair a glory, like a saint:
She seemed a splendid angel, newly drest,
Save wings, for heaven:—Porphyro grew faint:
She knelt, so pure a thing, so free from mortal taint.

Anon his heart revives: her vespers done,
Of all its wreathèd pearls her hair she frees;
Unclasps her warmèd jewels one by one;
Loosens her fragrant boddice; by degrees
Her rich attire creeps rustling to her knees: 230
Half-hidden, like a mermaid in sea-weed,
Pensive awhile she dreams awake, and sees,
In fancy, fair St. Agnes in her bed,
But dares not look behind, or all the charm is fled.

Soon, trembling in her soft and chilly nest,
In sort of wakeful swoon, perplexed she lay,
Until the poppied warmth of sleep oppressed
Her soothèd limbs, and soul fatigued away;

Flown, like a thought, until the morrow-day;
Blissfully havened both from joy and pain;   240
Clasped like a missal where swart Paynims pray;
Blinded alike from sunshine and from rain,
As though a rose should shut, and be a bud again.

Stol'n to this paradise, and so entranced,
Porphyro gazed upon her empty dress,
And listened to her breathing, if it chanced
To wake into a slumb'rous tenderness;
Which when he heard, that minute did he bless,
And breathed himself: then from the closet crept,
Noiseless as fear in a wide wilderness,   250
And over the hushed carpet, silent, stept,
And 'tween the curtains peeped, where, lo!—how fast she slept.

Then by the bed-side, where the faded moon
Made a dim, silver twilight, soft he set
A table, and, half anguished, threw thereon
A cloth of woven crimson, gold, and jet:—
O for some drowsy Morphean amulet!
The boisterous, midnight, festive clarion,
The kettle-drum, and far-heard clarinet,
Affray his ears, though but in dying tone:—   260
The hall-door shuts again, and all the noise is gone.

And still she slept an azure-lidded sleep,
In blanchèd linen, smooth, and lavendered,
While he from forth the closet brought a heap
Of candied apple, quince, and plum, and gourd;
With jellies soother than the creamy curd,
And lucent syrops, tinct with cinnamon;
Manna and dates, in argosy transferred
From Fez; and spicèd dainties, every one,
From silken Samarcand to cedared Lebanon.   270

These delicates he heaped with glowing hand
On golden dishes and in baskets bright
Of wreathèd silver: sumptuous they stand
In the retired quiet of the night,
Filling the chilly room with perfume light.—
"And now, my love, my seraph fair, awake!
Thou art my heaven, and I thine eremite:
Open thine eyes, for meek St. Agnes' sake,
Or I shall drowse beside thee, so my soul doth ache."

Thus whispering, his warm, unnervèd arm   280
Sank in her pillow. Shaded was her dream
By the dusk curtains:—'twas a midnight charm
Impossible to melt as icèd stream:
The lustrous salvers in the moonlight gleam;
Broad golden fringe upon the carpet lies:
It seemed he never, never could redeem
From such a steadfast spell his lady's eyes;
So mused awhile, entoiled in woofèd phantasies.

Awakening up, he took her hollow lute,—
Tumultuous,—and, in chords that tenderest be,   290
He played an ancient ditty, long since mute,
In Provence called "La belle dame sans mercy":
Close to her ear touching the melody;—
Wherewith disturbed, she uttered a soft moan:
He ceased—she panted quick—and suddenly
Her blue affrayèd eyes wide open shone:
Upon his knees he sank, pale as smooth-sculptured stone.

Her eyes were open, but she still beheld,
Now wide awake, the vision of her sleep:
There was a painful change, that nigh expelled   300
The blisses of her dream so pure and deep
At which fair Madeline began to weep,
And moan forth witless words with many a sigh;
While still her gaze on Porphyro would keep;
Who knelt, with joinèd hands and piteous eye,
Fearing to move or speak, she looked so dreamingly.

"Ah, Porphyro!" said she, "but even now
Thy voice was at sweet tremble in mine ear,
Made tunable with every sweetest vow;
And those sad eyes were spiritual and clear: 310
How changed thou art! how pallid, chill, and drear!
Give me that voice again, my Porphyro,
Those looks immortal, those complainings dear!
Oh leave me not in this eternal woe,
For if thou diest, my Love, I know not where to go."

Beyond a mortal man impassioned far
At these voluptuous accents, he arose,
Ethereal, flushed, and like a throbbing star
Seen mid the sapphire heaven's deep repose;

Into her dream he melted, as the rose   320
Blendeth its odour with the violet,—
Solution sweet: meantime the frost-wind blows
Like Love's alarum pattering the sharp sleet
Against the window-panes; St. Agnes' moon hath set.

'Tis dark: quick pattereth the flaw-blown sleet:
"This is no dream, my bride, my Madeline!"
'Tis dark: the icèd gusts still rave and beat:
"No dream, alas! alas! and woe is mine!
Porphyro will leave me here to fade and pine.—
Cruel! what traitor could thee hither bring?   330
I curse not, for my heart is lost in thine,
Though thou forsakest a deceivèd thing;—
A dove forlorn and lost with sick unprunèd wing."

"My Madeline! sweet dreamer! lovely bride!
Say, may I be for aye thy vassal blest?
Thy beauty's shield, heart-shaped and vermeil dyed?
Ah, silver shrine, here will I take my rest
After so many hours of toil and quest,
A famished pilgrim,—saved by miracle.
Though I have found, I will not rob thy nest   340
Saving of thy sweet self; if thou think'st well
To trust, fair Madeline, to no rude infidel.

"Hark! 'tis an elfin-storm from faery land,
Of haggard seeming, but a boon indeed:
Arise—arise! the morning is at hand;—
The bloated wassailers will never heed:—
Let us away, my love, with happy speed;
There are no ears to hear, or eyes to see,—
Drowned all in Rhenish and the sleepy mead:
Awake! arise! my love, and fearless be,   350
For o'er the southern moors I have a home for thee."

She hurried at his words, beset with fear,
For there were sleeping dragons all around,
At glaring watch, perhaps, with ready spears—
Down the wide stairs a darkling way they found.—
In all the house was heard no human sound.
A chain-drooped lamp was flick'ring by each door;
The arras, rich with horseman, hawk, and hound,
Fluttered in the besieging wind's uproar;
And the long carpets rose along the gusty floor.   360

They glide, like phantoms, into the wide hall,
Like phantoms, to the iron porch, they glide;
Where lay the Porter, in uneasy sprawl,
With a huge empty flagon by his side:
The wakeful bloodhound rose, and shook his hide,
But his sagacious eye an inmate owns:
By one, and one, the bolts full easy slide:—
The chains lie silent on the footworn stones;—
The key turns, and the door upon its hinges groans.

And they are gone: aye, ages long ago   370
These lovers fled away into the storm.
That night the Baron dreamt of many a woe,
And all his warrior-guests, with shade and form
Of witch, and demon, and large coffin-worm,
Were long be-nightmared. Angela the old
Died palsy-twitched, with meagre face deform;
The Beadsman after thousand aves told,
For aye unsought-for slept among his ashes cold.

1819   1820

Ode on a Grecian Urn

I

THOU still unravish'd bride of quietness,
    Thou foster-child of silence and slow time,
Sylvan historian, who canst thus express
    A flowery tale more sweetly than our rhyme:
What leaf-fring'd legend haunts about thy shape
    Of deities or mortals, or of both,
        In Tempe or the dales of Arcady?
    What men or gods are these? What maidens loth?
What mad pursuit? What struggle to escape?
        What pipes and timbrels? What wild ecstasy?   10

II

Heard melodies are sweet, but those unheard
    Are sweeter; therefore, ye soft pipes, play on;
Not to the sensual ear, but, more endear'd,
    Pipe to the spirit ditties of no tone:
Fair youth, beneath the trees, thou canst not leave
    Thy song, nor ever can those trees be bare;

Bold Lover, never, never canst thou kiss,
  Though winning near the goal—yet, do not grieve;
    She cannot fade, though thou hast not thy bliss,
    For ever wilt thou love, and she be fair!   20

III

Ah, happy, happy boughs! that cannot shed
  Your leaves, nor ever bid the Spring adieu;
And, happy melodist, unwearied,
  For ever piping songs for ever new;
More happy love! more happy, happy love!
  For ever warm and still to be enjoy'd,
    For ever panting, and for ever young;
All breathing human passion far above,
  That leaves a heart high-sorrowful and cloy'd,
    A burning forehead, and a parching tongue.   30

IV

Who are these coming to the sacrifice?
  To what green altar, O mysterious priest,
Lead'st thou that heifer lowing at the skies,
  And all her silken flanks with garlands drest?
What little town by river or sea shore,
  Or mountain-built with peaceful citadel,
    Is emptied of this folk, this pious morn?
And, little town, thy streets for evermore
  Will silent be; and not a soul to tell
    Why thou art desolate, can e'er return.   40

V

O Attic shape! Fair attitude! with brede
  Of marble men and maidens overwrought,
With forest branches and the trodden weed;
  Thou, silent form, dost tease us out of thought
As doth eternity: Cold Pastoral!
  When old age shall this generation waste,
    Thou shalt remain, in midst of other woe
Than ours, a friend to man, to whom thou say'st,
  'Beauty is truth, truth beauty,'—that is all
    Ye know on earth, and all ye need to know.   50

1820

To Autumn

Season of mists and mellow fruitfulness,
   Close bosom-friend of the maturing sun;
Conspiring with him how to load and bless
   With fruit the vines that round the thatch-eves run;
To bend with apples the moss'd cottage-trees,
   And fill all fruit with ripeness to the core;
     To swell the gourd, and plump the hazel shells
   With a sweet kernel; to set budding more,
And still more, later flowers for the bees,
Until they think warm days will never cease,   10
     For Summer has o'er-brimm'd their clammy cells.

Who hath not seen thee oft amid thy store?
   Sometimes whoever seeks abroad may find
Thee sitting careless on a granary floor,
   Thy hair soft-lifted by the winnowing wind;
Or on a half-reap'd furrow sound asleep,
   Drows'd with the fume of poppies, while thy hook
     Spares the next swath and all its twinèd flowers:
And sometimes like a gleaner thou dost keep
   Steady thy laden head across a brook;   20
   Or by a cyder-press, with patient look,
     Thou watchest the last oozings hours by hours.

Where are the songs of Spring? Ay, where are they?
   Think not of them, thou hast thy music too,—
While barrèd clouds bloom the soft-dying day,
   And touch the stubble-plains with rosy hue;
Then in a wailful choir the small gnats mourn
   Among the river sallows[1], borne aloft
     Or sinking as the light wind lives or dies;
And full-grown lambs loud bleat from hilly bourn;   30
   Hedge-crickets sing; and now with treble soft
   The red-breast whistles from a garden-croft;
     And gathering swallows twitter in the skies.

1819   1820

[1]Willows on the river bank.

1830

1840

1850

● Tennyson: *Poems*

Darwin: *Origin of the Spec*

● Browning: *Pauline*

● Poe: *The Cask of Amontillado*

● Tennyson: *In Memoriam*

● Arnold: *Poems*

Whitman: *Leaves of Grass* ●

● Thoreau: *Wald*

● D. Rossetti: *My Sister's Sleep*

THE
VICTORIAN
PERIOD
(1837–1901)

1870	1880	1900
		Queen Victoria's Diamond Jubilee •
• British North America Act		• G. D. Roberts: *Orion and Other Poems*
• Browning: *The Ring and the Book*		Founding of Labour Party •
		Carmen: *Songs from Vagabondia* •
	D. C. Scott: *The Magic House and Other Poems* •	
	Lampman: *Among the Millet* •	

The literature of the Victorian Period was in some respects a continuation of the literature of the Romantic Period. The romantic emphases on individualism, liberty, natural scenery, and the emotions were all continued, but they were chastened and subdued; they were, in short, domesticated. They were domesticated in several senses of that word: they were tamed, made tractable and respectable, made fit for family reading. Domesticity is a key word for the Victorian Period: it was the great era of the home, the family, the domestic virtues (see, for example, their terminology: the Family Bible, magazines such as *Household Words* and *The Woman's Home Companion* and the *Family Herald*). Thus Tennyson has much of the colourfulness and sensuousness of Keats, but none of Keats' excesses; Browning has much of Shelley's exhilaration and idealism but little of Shelley's revolutionary passion; Arnold has Wordsworth's calm contemplativeness, but little of his mystical ecstasy. Another way of putting it might be to say that Victorian literature modifies romantic feeling with a tincture of eighteenth-century common-sense, romantic exuberance with a tincture of neo-classical restraint.

Another strong similarity between the Romantic and Victorian literary periods was their common opposition to materialism, to the preoccupation with material wealth and material progress. The Industrial Revolution was accelerated in Victorian times, and England was growing more and more wealthy at the top and more and more poverty-stricken at the bottom. The chief unifying factor in Victorian literature is the revulsion it expresses against the ugliness, arrogance, and vulgarity bred of the new wealth. Dickens' sympathetic portrayals of the poor and satirical attacks upon the harsh employers such as Mr. Gradgrind; Tennyson's caustic comments on the arrogance of the newly rich in poems such as "Locksley Hall" or "Maud"; Arnold's satirical labelling of upper class Englishmen as "barbarians" and of middle class Englishmen as "philistines"; Thackeray's lampooning of social snobbery; Morris's pleas for the old values of craftsmanship as against the mechanized ugliness of the new mass-production methods: all these actions stem from the same basic dissatisfaction with the impact of the Industrial Revolution upon English society. If the Victorian writers seem rather timid and half-hearted to us in their attacks, a little too ready to compromise, we should recognize that they were fighting against an enemy far more entrenched than we can easily imagine. The citizen of today's Welfare State owes much to the protests of Victorian writers against the tyranny of wealth.

It has recently been fashionable to jeer at Victorianism, and there is much in the period that deserves our ridicule. It was an age of snobbery, of prudery (even the legs of a table must be referred to as limbs, lest the former word excite lascivious thoughts), and of frequent hypocrisy and humbug. But if we indict the age, we should not indict the writers of the age, for they were all almost as critical of it as we are. Nor should we forget that Victorian society had many difficult problems to solve, and that it made much progress towards their solution.

It is impossible in an introduction of this length to do justice to the complex problems that beset the Victorian age, and any brief summary is bound to distort and oversimplify. There was the problem we have already glanced at: how to take advantage of the positive benefits of the Industrial Revolution and yet to mitigate its evil effects of unsanitary labour conditions, ugly factories and smoke-clouded towns, over-powerful employers and under-paid employees. This problem was not altogether solved, but certain developments did much to make our more equable and just society possible: the various Factory Acts setting minimum wage rates and maximum working hours, the successive Reform Bills extending the franchise to more and more members of the population, the Education Acts of 1870 and 1891 extending free education to all, and the growth of socialist thought signalized by the development of the Fabian movement in the eighties and nineties and the foundation of the Labour Party in 1900.

Another important Victorian problem concerned religious belief, and particularly the conflict between religion and science. We have seen that as early as the seventeenth century the rise of rationalism and science had led to the dismissal of some elements of religion as mere superstition; in the eighteenth century, Christianity, as Swift brilliantly demonstrated in some of his prose satires, was becoming for many merely lip-service, and even some of the clergy had little genuine faith in anything except the human reason; in the nineteenth century science had made such huge strides that many felt that it was merely a matter of time until science explained everything and religion could be quietly forgotten. The scientific examination of the Bible, known as the Higher Criticism, made it appear that that hitherto sacred book had some curious inconsistencies; Darwin's *Origin of the Species* (1859), suggesting that man had evolved from ape-like creatures over long centuries of time, made the Genesis story of Adam and Eve look, to some, like a fairy-tale. It is easy for us, with the benefit of hindsight, to see that most of these conclusions were illogical and premature and that there is no necessary conflict between religious insight and scientific truth; to the Victorians these shocks were immediate and urgent and very unsettling. Various expedients were tried: some sought in evangelical fervour to renew their devotion to Christian ideals; others, such as John Henry Newman, sought support in the ancient rituals and traditions of the Church, and became either Anglo-Catholics or Roman Catholics; others, such as Charles Kingsley, laid less stress on the supernatural, liturgical aspects of Christianity and stressed rather its humanitarian aspects, its ideals of the brotherhood of man and of humble service to others; some, such as Thomas Henry Huxley, the essayist, declared themselves agnostics, arguing that man could not know whether or not there was a God; a few, such as Charles Bradlaugh, became outright atheists and declared their opposition to all forms of religious belief. But no thinking person could ignore the problem; the efforts of Tennyson and Browning to buttress the traditional Christian beliefs in such things as immortality, and the effort of Arnold to find a substitute for religion in poetry and culture, were attempts to provide comfort for a deeply anxious populace.

Another important Victorian problem was that of the British Empire. The bravery of English sailors and soldiers, and the enterprise of English merchant adventurers, had built up a great overseas empire—in America, in India, in Africa, and in the Pacific—in the seventeenth and eighteenth centuries. Already, in the American Revolution of 1776-83, one large segment of that Empire had split away; in the Victorian period there was restlessness in Canada, India, Ireland, and parts of Africa. Should England seek to hang on to the Empire by brute force, or should she give the colonies concessions which might quiet them for a while but allow them eventually to drift away from her? There were extremists who wanted to rule with an iron hand, and other extremists who wanted to get rid of the colonies entirely. Here again the Victorians made a large measure of progress towards a solution. Lord Durham's Report on Canada in 1838, and the British North America Act of 1867, set a pattern of enlightened colonial administration by which the modern Commonwealth has gradually developed. The pattern was not always followed—the Indian Mutiny and the Boer War are reminders of the real blunders that were sometimes made—but it did become the basic design of British policy. Something more admirable than the triumph of brute force was symbolized by the pageant of Imperial splendour that marked Queen Victoria's Diamond Jubilee in 1897.

This development of English civilization abroad, of course, meant that English literature was no longer confined to England. The American colonies had had the beginnings of a literature well before the Revolution; early in the nineteenth century Washington Irving, by tales such as "The Legend of Sleepy Hollow" and "Rip Van Winkle," had won an international audience; and in the Victorian period American authors such as Emerson, Thoreau, Poe, Longfellow, Hawthorne, Twain, and Whitman were almost as well-known in England as Tennyson and Dickens. Canada, emerging as a unified nation only in 1867, almost a century later than the U.S.A., was naturally slower in producing authors of international rank; but early in the Victorian period Thomas Chandler Haliburton's humorous portrayals of Sam Slick crossed the Atlantic, and by the end of the period many Englishmen were reading the novels of Gilbert Parker and the poems of such young Canadians as Charles G. D. Roberts, Bliss Carman, Archibald Lampman, and Duncan Campbell Scott.

The detailed stories of American and Canadian literature cannot be told here. The thoughtful student will see many parallels between these literatures and that of England in the Victorian Period: in all three the romantic emphasis on individualism, natural scenery, and emotion are uppermost. American and Canadian place-names and distinctive landscape features give a special flavour; and some problems, such as the slavery issue that produced the American Civil War, are peculiar to one country. But for all three there is more in common than in contrast; the problems of an industrial society are reflected as clearly in Emerson and Lampman as in Dickens and Arnold; for all there is the issue of religious belief in a scientific age; for all there is the problem of controlling material pride in a period of rapid material expansion.

ENGLISH LITERATURE

ALFRED, LORD TENNYSON (1809-1892)

Tennyson was the most representative and most popular poet of the Victorian age. He expressed most fully its moral earnestness, its religious doubts, its mingled fears and hopes about the advance of science and democracy. His contemporaries saw him as a great philosophic poet, a great narrative poet, and a great lyrical poet. Only the last of these claims has stood the test of time. Tennyson was fond of preaching, but had nothing very new or striking to say, and his narratives are weak in characterization and slow in action. But he could express emotion, especially melancholy emotions of grief and loss and loneliness, in lines that are musical and memorable; and he did have a quick eye for the beauty of landscape and a strong sense of atmosphere.

Tennyson was one of twelve children of a Lincolnshire rector, and published his first book of poems in collaboration with his brother Charles at the age of seventeen. He attended Louth Grammar School and Trinity College, Cambridge. At Cambridge he formed a close friendship with Arthur Henry Hallam, whose death he was to mourn in the famous elegy, *In Memoriam* (1850), and published his second book of verse, *Poems, Chiefly Lyrical* (1830). In 1832 he published a third volume, *Poems*, which contained some of his best works such as "Oenone" and "The Lady of Shalott" but was savagely attacked by the *Quarterly Review* as the production of a "namby-pamby poet." The death of Hallam in 1833 combined with this hostile review to plunge Tennyson into severe melancholy, and for ten years he published nothing. He re-appeared before the public with two volumes in 1842, however—*English Idylls* and *Poems*—and from then on his reputation was secure. In 1850 he was named Poet Laureate in succession to Wordsworth, in 1853 acquired a large country estate on the Isle of Wight, in 1855 was honoured by a doctorate from Oxford, and in 1883 received a peerage from Queen Victoria. In these latter years he was a national institution, the object of deferential visits from all the great men of his time. His later poetry, however, was increasingly conservative, moralistic, and complacent.

The Lady of Shalott

PART I

On either side the river lie
Long fields of barley and of rye,
That clothe the wold and meet the sky;
And thro' the field the road runs by
　　To many-tower'd Camelot[1];
And up and down the people go,
Gazing where the lilies blow
Round an island there below,
　　The island of Shalott.

Willows whiten, aspens quiver,　　　　10
Little breezes dusk and shiver

Thro' the wave that runs for ever
By the island in the river
　　Flowing down to Camelot.
Four grey walls, and four grey towers,
Overlook a space of flowers,
And the silent isle imbowers
　　The Lady of Shalott.

By the margin, willow veil'd,
Slide the heavy barges trail'd　　　　20
By slow horses; and unhail'd
The shallop flitteth silken-sail'd
　　Skimming down to Camelot:

[1]The capital of Arthur's kingdom, probably in Wales.

But who hath seen her wave her hand?
Or at the casement seen her stand?
Or is she known in all the land,
    The Lady of Shalott?

Only reapers, reaping early
In among the bearded barley,
Hear a song that echoes cheerly   30
From the river winding clearly,
    Down to tower'd Camelot:
And by the moon the reaper weary,
Piling sheaves in uplands airy,
Listening, whispers " 'Tis the fairy
    Lady of Shalott."

PART II

There she weaves by night and day
A magic web with colours gay.
She has heard a whisper say,
A curse is on her if she stay   40
    To look down to Camelot.
She knows not what the curse may be,
And so she weaveth steadily,
And little other care hath she,
    The Lady of Shalott.

And moving thro' a mirror clear
That hangs before her all the year,
Shadows of the world appear.
There she sees the highway near
    Winding down to Camelot: 50
There the river eddy whirls,
And there the surly village-churls,
And the red cloaks of market girls,
    Pass onward from Shalott.

Sometimes a troop of damsels glad,
An abbot on an ambling pad,
Sometimes a curly shepherd-lad,
Or long-hair'd page in crimson clad,
    Goes by to tower'd Camelot;
And sometimes thro' the mirror blue   60

The knights come riding two and two:
She hath no loyal knight and true,
    The Lady of Shalott.

But in her web she still delights
To weave the mirror's magic sights,
For often thro' the silent nights
A funeral, with plumes and lights
    And music, went to Camelot:
Or when the moon was overhead,
Came two young lovers lately wed: 70
"I am half sick of shadows," said
    The Lady of Shalott.

PART III

A bow-shot from her bower-eaves,
He rode between the barley-sheaves,
The sun came dazzling thro' the leaves,
And flamed upon the brazen greaves
    Of bold Sir Lancelot.
A red-cross knight for ever kneel'd
To a lady in his shield,
That sparkled on the yellow field,   80
    Beside remote Shalott.

The gemmy bridle glitter'd free,
Like to some branch of stars we see
Hung in the golden Galaxy.
The bridle bells rang merrily
    As he rode down to Camelot:
And from his blazon'd baldric slung
A mighty silver bugle hung,
And as he rode his armour rung,
    Beside remote Shalott.   90

All in the blue unclouded weather
Thick-jewell'd shone the saddle-leather,
The helmet and the helmet-feather
Burn'd like one burning flame together,
    As he rode down to Camelot.

As often thro' the purple night,
Below the starry clusters bright,
Some bearded meteor, trailing light,
        Moves over still Shalott.

His broad clear brow in sunlight glow'd;
On burnish'd hooves his war-horse trode;
From underneath his helmet flow'd   102
His coal-black curls as on he rode,
        As he rode down to Camelot.
From the bank and from the river
He flash'd into the crystal mirror,
"Tirra lirra," by the river
        Sang Sir Lancelot.

She left the web, she left the loom,
She made three paces thro' the room,
She saw the water-lily bloom,   111
She saw the helmet and the plume,
        She look'd down to Camelot.
Out flew the web and floated wide;
The mirror crack'd from side to side;
"The curse is come upon me," cried
        The Lady of Shalott.

PART IV

In the stormy east-wind straining,
The pale yellow woods were waning,
The broad stream in his banks
        complaining,   120
Heavily the low sky raining
        Over tower'd Camelot;
Down she came and found a boat
Beneath a willow left afloat,
And round about the prow she wrote
        The Lady of Shalott.

And down the river's dim expanse
Like some bold seër in a trance,
Seeing all his own mischance—
With a glassy countenance   130
        Did she look to Camelot.

And at the closing of the day
She loosed the chain, and down she lay;
The broad stream bore her far away,
        The Lady of Shalott.

Lying, robed in snowy white
That loosely flew to left and right—
The leaves upon her falling light—
Thro' the noises of the night   139
        She floated down to Camelot:
And as the boat-head wound along
The willowy hills and fields among,
They heard her singing her last song,
        The Lady of Shalott.

Heard a carol, mournful, holy,
Chanted loudly, chanted lowly,
Till her blood was frozen slowly,
And her eyes were darken'd wholly,
        Turn'd to tower'd Camelot.
For ere she reach'd upon the tide   150
The first house by the water-side,
Singing in her song she died,
        The Lady of Shalott.

Under tower and balcony,
By garden-wall and gallery,
A gleaming shape she floated by,
Dead-pale between the houses high,
        Silent into Camelot.
Out upon the wharfs they came,   159
Knight and burgher, lord and dame,
And round the prow they read her name,
        The Lady of Shalott.

Who is this? and what is here?
And in the lighted palace near
Died the sound of royal cheer;
And they cross'd themselves for fear,
        All the knights at Camelot:
But Lancelot mused a little space;
He said, "She has a lovely face;
God in his mercy lend her grace,   170
        The Lady of Shalott."

                                    1832

Ulysses[1]

It little profits that an idle king,
By this still hearth, among these barren crags,
Matched with an aged wife, I mete and dole[2]
Unequal laws unto a savage race,
That hoard, and sleep, and feed, and know not me.
I cannot rest from travel; I will drink
Life to the lees. All times I have enjoyed
Greatly, have suffered greatly, both with those
That loved me, and alone; on shore, and when
Through scudding drifts the rainy Hyades[3]   10
Vexed the dim sea. I am become a name;
For always roaming with a hungry heart
Much have I seen and known—cities of men
And manners, climates, councils, governments,
Myself not least, but honored of them all—
And drunk delight of battle with my peers,
Far on the ringing plains of windy Troy.
I am a part of all that I have met;
Yet all experience is an arch wherethrough
Gleams that untraveled world whose margin fades   20
Forever and forever when I move.
How dull it is to pause, to make an end,
To rust unburnished, not to shine in use!
As though to breathe were life! Life piled on life
Were all too little, and of one to me
Little remains; but every hour is saved
From that eternal silence, something more,
A bringer of new things; and vile it were
For some three suns to store and hoard myself,
And this gray spirit yearning in desire   30
To follow knowledge like a sinking star.
Beyond the utmost bound of human thought.

This is my son, mine own Telemachus,
To whom I leave the scepter and the isle—
Well-loved of me, discerning to fulfill
This labor, by slow prudence to make mild

---

[1]In "Ulysses," the poet pictures the hero of Homer's *Odyssey*, in old age, urging a band of followers to set off on a voyage of exploration. Tennyson stated that the poem expressed his own "need of going forward and braving the struggle of life."
[2]Measure out rewards and punishments.
[3]Driving rain showers; the Hyades is a group of stars whose rising is said to presage rain.

A rugged people, and through soft degrees
Subdue them to the useful and the good.
Most blameless is he, centered in the sphere
Of common duties, decent not to fail   40
In offices of tenderness, and pay
Meet adoration to my household gods,
When I am gone. He works his work, I mine.

   There lies the port; the vessel puffs her sail;
There gloom the dark, broad seas. My mariners,
Souls that have toiled, and wrought, and thought with me—
That ever with a frolic welcome took
The thunder and the sunshine, and opposed
Free hearts, free foreheads—you and I are old;
Old age hath yet his honor and his toil.   50
Death closes all; but something ere the end,
Some work of noble note, may yet be done,
Not unbecoming men that strove with Gods,
The lights begin to twinkle from the rocks;
The long day wanes; the slow moon climbs; the deep
Moans round with many voices. Come, my friends,
'Tis not too late to seek a newer world.
Push off, and sitting well in order smite
The sounding furrows; for my purpose holds
To sail beyond the sunset, and the baths   60
Of all the western stars, until I die.
It may be that the gulfs will wash us down;
It may be we shall touch the Happy Isles,[4]
And see the great Achilles, whom we knew.
Though much is taken, much abides; and though
we are not now that strength which in old days
Moved earth and heaven, that which we are, we are—
One equal temper of heroic hearts,
Made weak by time and fate, but strong in will   70
To strive, to seek, to find, and not to yield.

1833   1842

---

[4]The islands of the Blessed or Elysium, where heroes enjoyed life after death in Greek mythology.

from *In Memoriam*[1]

XXVII

I envy not in any moods
  The captive void of noble rage,
  The linnet born within the cage,
That never knew the summer woods:

I envy not the beast that takes
  His license in the field of time,
  Unfetter'd by the sense of crime,
To whom a conscience never wakes;

Nor, what may count itself as blest,
  The heart that never plighted troth
  But stagnates in the weeds of sloth;
Nor any want-begotten rest.   12

I hold it true, whate'er befall;
  I feel it, when I sorrow most;
  'Tis better to have loved and lost
Than never to have loved at all.

LIV

Oh, yet we trust that somehow good
  Will be the final goal of ill,
To pangs of nature, sins of will,
Defects of doubt, and taints of blood;

That nothing walks with aimless feet;
  That not one life shall be destroy'd,
  Or cast as rubbish to the void,
When God hath made the pile complete;

That not a worm is cloven in vain;
  That not a moth with vain desire   10
  Is shrivell'd in a fruitless fire,
Or but subserves another's gain.

Behold, we know not anything;
  I can but trust that good shall fall
  At last—far off—at last, to all,
And every winter change to spring.

So runs my dream: but what am I?
  An infant crying in the night:
  An infant crying for the light:
And with no language but a cry.

XCVI

You say, but with no touch of scorn,
  Sweet-hearted, you, whose light-blue eyes
  Are tender over drowning flies,
You tell me, doubt is Devil-born.

I know not: one indeed I knew
  In many a subtle question versed,
  Who touch'd a jarring lyre at first,
But ever strove to make it true:

Perplext in faith, but pure in deeds,
  At last he beat his music out.   10
  There lives more faith in honest doubt,
Believe me, than in half the creeds.

He fought his doubts and gather'd strength,
  He would not make his judgment blind,
  He faced the spectres of the mind
And laid them: thus he came at length

To find a stronger faith his own;

---

[1]An elegy composed of 131 sections or separate poems and written in memory of Arthur Henry Hallam, a brilliant young Cambridge friend of Tennyson's and the fiancé of Tennyson's sister. In the elegy, Tennyson not only expresses his grief but also his struggle to preserve his faith in a just and loving God and in a morally ordered universe.

And Power was with him in the night,
Which makes the darkness and the
    light,
And dwells not in the light alone,   20

But in the darkness and the cloud,
  As over Sinai's peaks of old,
  While Israel made their gods of gold,
Altho' the trumpet blew so loud.

CXXIV

That which we dare invoke to bless;
  Our dearest faith; our ghastliest doubt;
  He, They, One, All; within, without;
The Power in darkness whom we guess;

I found Him not in world or sun,
  Or eagle's wing, or insect's eye;
  Nor thro' the questions men may try
The petty cobwebs we have spun:

If e'er when faith had fall'n asleep,
  I heard a voice, "believe no more," 10
  And heard an ever-breaking shore
That tumbled in the Godless deep,

A warmth within the breast would melt
  The freezing reason's colder part,
  And like a man in wrath the heart
Stood up and answer'd, "I have felt."

No, like a child in doubt and fear:
  But that blind clamour made me wise;
  Then was I as a child that cries,
But, crying, knows his father near;   20

And what I am beheld again
  What is, and no man understands;
  And out of darkness came the hands
That reach thro' nature, moulding men.

CXXVI

Love is and was my Lord and King,
  And in his presence I attend
  To hear the tidings of my friend,
Which every hour his couriers bring.

Love is and was my King and Lord,
  And will be, tho' as yet I keep
  Within the court on earth, and sleep
Encompass'd by his faithful guard,

And hear at times a sentinel
  Who moves about from place to
    place,   10
  And whispers to the worlds of space,
In the deep night, that all is well.

1833-1850   1850

Crossing the Bar [1]

Sunset and evening star,
  And one clear call for me!
And may there be no moaning of the bar, [2]
  When I put out to sea,

But such a tide as moving seems asleep,
  Too full for sound and foam,
When that which drew from out the
    boundless deep
  Turns again home.

[1] Written in the poet's eighty-first year.
[2] *moaning of the bar*. Mournful sound the ocean makes beating upon a sand bar.

Twilight and evening bell,
   And after that the dark!   10
And may there be no sadness of farewell,
   When I embark;

For though from out our bourne[3] of Time
   and Place
The flood may bear me far,
I hope to see my Pilot face to face
   When I have crossed the bar.

                     1889

[3]Boundary.

ROBERT BROWNING (1812-1889)

Although Tennyson and Browning were the leading poets of their age, they differed widely in their styles and attitudes. Tennyson's style was smooth and mellifluous, Browning's rough and explosive; Tennyson was most successful in creating a melancholy mood, Browning a mood of aggressive optimism; Tennyson cautioned against the longing for impossible perfection and counselled moderation, whereas Browning urged his readers to reach for the ungraspable and to gamble on extremes. In spite of these differences, however, they were both characteristic Victorian spokesmen by virtue of their moral earnestness, their individualism, their humanism, and their determination to buttress by reason the traditional religious beliefs.

Browning was the son of a well-to-do banker who encouraged his son's interest in art and literature. Privately educated, Browning published his first poem, *Pauline*, at the age of twenty-one. By 1846 he had published three more volumes of verse and a tragedy, *Strafford*, but had won little fame. In that year he eloped to Italy with Elizabeth Barrett, and the fifteen years he spent in Italy up to Elizabeth's death in 1861 were the happiest of his life. Fame, however, came slowly: *Men and Women* (1855) was hailed by the discriminating, but not by the general public; and it was not until after his return to England, and the publication of *Dramatis Personae* in 1864 and *The Ring and the Book* in 1868-9, that he was finally recognized as second only to Tennyson in the hierarchy of Victorian poets. Like Tennyson, he became in the last two decades of his life a national celebrity. Browning Clubs were founded to study his often obscure later verse. He died in Venice and was buried in Westminster Abbey.

Regarded as a great thinker by his contemporaries, Browning is valued today for his psychological insight and his technical skill. Delighting in the world, imperfect as it is, he delights in the people who seek by various means to answer its challenge. The clues to successful living, in his view, are courage, devotion, and selfless love; and if these virtues do not bring their reward in this life, they will hereafter. Technically, his chief innovations were the dramatic monologue, in which a character exposes himself in a speech addressed to a silent listener, and the use of a highly condensed, allusive language which matches the speed of excited conversation or of impassioned thought.

My Last Duchess

FERRARA

That's my last Duchess painted on the wall,
Looking as if she were alive.   I call
That piece a wonder, now: Frà Pandolf's hands
Worked busily a day, and there she stands.
Will 't please you sit and look at her?   I said
"Frà Pandolf" by design, for never read
Strangers like you that pictured countenance,
The depth and passion of its earnest glance,
But to myself they turned (since none puts by
The curtain I have drawn for you, but I)   10
And seemed as they would ask me, if they durst,
How such a glance came there; so, not the first
Are you to turn and ask thus.   Sir, 'twas not
Her husband's presence only, called that spot
Of joy into the Duchess' cheek: perhaps
Frà Pandolf chanced to say, "Her mantle laps
Over my Lady's wrist too much," or "Paint
Must never hope to reproduce the faint
Half-flush that dies along her throat": such stuff
Was courtesy, she thought, and cause enough   20
For calling up that spot of joy.   She had
A heart . . . how shall I say? . . . too soon made glad,
Too easily impressed; she liked whate'er
She looked on, and her looks went everywhere.
Sir, 'twas all one!   My favour at her breast,
The dropping of the daylight in the West,
The bough of cherries some officious fool
Broke in the orchard for her, the white mule
She rode with round the terrace—all and each
Would draw from her alike the approving speech,   30
Or blush, at least.   She thanked men,—good; but thanked
Somehow . . . I know not how . . . as if she ranked
My gift of a nine-hundred-years-old name
With anybody's gift.   Who'd stoop to blame
This sort of trifling?   Even had you skill
In speech—(which I have not)—to make your will
Quite clear to such an one, and say, "Just this
Or that in you disgusts me; here you miss,
Or there exceed the mark"—and if she let
Herself be lessoned so, nor plainly set   40
Her wits to yours, forsooth, and made excuse,

—E'en then would be some stooping; and I chuse
Never to stoop.   Oh, sir, she smiled, no doubt,
Whene'er I passed her; but who passed without
Much the same smile?   This grew; I gave commands;
Then all smiles stopped together.   There she stands
As if alive.   Will 't please you rise?   We'll meet
The company below, then.   I repeat,
The Count your Master's known munificence
Is ample warrant that no just pretence   50
Of mine for dowry will be disallowed;
Though his fair daughter's self, as I avowed
At starting, is my object.   Nay, we'll go
Together down, Sir!   Notice Neptune, though,
Taming a sea-horse, thought a rarity,
Which Claus of Innsbruck cast in bronze for me!

                                                1842

Home Thoughts, from Abroad[1]

Oh, to be in England
Now that April's there,
And whoever wakes in England
Sees, some morning, unaware,
That the lowest boughs and the brushwood sheaf
Round the elm tree bole are in tiny leaf,
While the chaffinch sings on the orchard bough
In England—now!

And after April, when May follows,
And the whitethroat builds, and all the swallows!   10
Hark, where my blossomed pear tree in the hedge
Leans to the field and scatters on the clover
Blossoms and dewdrops—at the bent spray's edge—
That's the wise thrush! he sings each song twice over,
Lest you should think he never could recapture
The first fine careless rapture!
And though the fields look rough with hoary dew,
All will be gay when noontide wakes anew
The buttercups, the little children's dower
—Far brighter than this gaudy melon flower!   20

                                                1845

[1]Written while the poet lived in Italy.

Love among the Ruins

Where the quiet-coloured end of evening smiles,
    Miles and miles
On the solitary pastures where our sheep
    Half-asleep
Tinkle homeward thro' the twilight, stray or stop
    As they crop—
Was the site once of a city great and gay,
    (So they say)
Of our country's very capital, its prince
    Ages since   10
Held his court in, gathered councils, wielding far
    Peace or war.

Now—the country does not even boast a tree,
    As you see,
To distinguish slopes of verdure, certain rills
    From the hills
Intersect and give a name to, (else they run
    Into one)
Where the domed and daring palace shot its spires
    Up like fires   20
O'er the hundred-gated circuit of a wall
    Bounding all,
Made of marble, men might march on nor be prest
    Twelve abreast.

And such plenty and perfection, see, of grass
    Never was!
Such a carpet as, this summer-time, o'er-spreads
    And embeds
Every vestige of the city, guessed alone,
    Stock or stone—   30
Where a multitude of men breathed joy and woe
    Long ago;
Lust of glory pricked their hearts up, dread of shame
    Struck them tame;
And that glory and that shame alike, the gold
    Bought and sold.

Now,—the single little turret that remains
    On the plains,
By the caper[1] overrooted, by the gourd

---

[1] A low prickly shrub.

Overscored, 40
While the patching houseleek's[2] head of blossom winks
    Through the chinks—
Marks the basement whence a tower in ancient time
    Sprang sublime,
And a burning ring, all round, the chariots traced
    As they raced,
And the monarch and his minions and his dames
    Viewed the games.

And I know, while thus the quiet-coloured eve
    Smiles to leave
To their folding, all our many-tinkling fleece 50
    In such peace,
And the slopes and rills in undistinguished grey
    Melt away—
That a girl with eager eyes and yellow hair
    Waits me there
In the turret whence the charioteers caught soul
    For the goal,
When the king looked, where she looks now, breathless, dumb
    Till I come. 60

But he looked upon the city, every side,
    Far and wide,
All the mountains topped with temples, all the glades'
    Colonnades,
All the causeys, bridges, aqueducts,—and then,
    All the men!
When I do come, she will speak not, she will stand,
    Either hand
On my shoulder, give her eyes the first embrace
    Of my face, 70
Ere we rush, ere we extinguish sight and speech
    Each on each.

In one year they sent a million fighters forth
    South and North,
And they built their gods a brazen pillar high
    As the sky,
Yet reserved a thousand chariots in full force—
    Gold, of course.

[2]A climbing plant with pink flowers.

Oh heart! oh blood that freezes, blood that burns!
    Earth's returns   80
For whole centuries of folly, noise and sin!
    Shut them in,
With their triumphs and their glories and the rest!
    Love is best.

        1855

Prospice[1]

Fear death?—to feel the fog in my throat,
    The mist in my face,
When the snows begin, and the blasts denote
    I am nearing the place,
The power of the night, the press of the storm,
    The post of the foe;
Where he stands, the Arch Fear in a visible form,
    Yet the strong man must go:
For the journey is done and the summit attained,
    And the barriers fall,   10
Though a battle's to fight ere the guerdon[2] be gained,
    The reward of it all.
I was ever a fighter, so—one fight more,
    The best and the last!

I would hate that death bandaged my eyes, and forbore,[3]
    And bade me creep past.
No! let me taste the whole of it, fare like my peers
    The heroes of old,
Bear the brunt, in a minute pay glad life's arrears
    Of pain, darkness and cold.   20
For sudden the worst turns the best to the brave,
    The black minute's at end,
And the elements' rage, the fiend-voices that rave,
    Shall dwindle, shall blend,
Shall change, shall become first a peace out of pain,
    Then a light, then thy breast,
O thou soul of my soul![4] I shall clasp thee again,
    And with God be the rest!

        1864

[1]Meaning "Look Forward."
[2]Reward.
[3]Injured only that much.
[4]Browning's wife.

MATTHEW ARNOLD (1822-1888)

Arnold's literary career divides into two roughly equal parts: for the twenty years prior to 1867 he was primarily a poet; for the remaining twenty years after 1867 he was a prose essayist, writing literary and social criticism.

He was the son of Thomas Arnold, famous headmaster of Rugby School, and was educated at Rugby and Oxford. From 1851 to 1883 he was Inspector of Schools for the British government, and from 1857 to 1866 was Professor of Poetry at Oxford. He made several visits to the Continent, and a lecture tour of North America in 1883-4. His first volume of poems, *The Strayed Reveller*, appeared in 1849; *Empedocles on Etna* was published in 1852 and *Poems* (including "The Scholar-Gipsy") in 1853; his last volume, *New Poems*, appeared in 1867. In prose, the most important of his books were *Essays in Criticism* (1865 and 1888) and *Culture and Anarchy* (1869).

Both in his poetry and his prose, Arnold was a quiet, scholarly critic of a vulgar age. He yearned to retreat like the Scholar-Gipsy into some idyllic haven, but instead he courageously faced his age and challenged its values with persistent questions. He promulgated an ideal for human life which might best be summed up in the word "serenity": he believed that there is a basic stability and order in the cosmos, but that we lose contact with it through our restless scramble for wealth and power. He therefore attacked his age for its materialism, its Macaulayesque worship of machines and progress. The solution he advocated was not to retreat to the past, but to move confidently into the future armed with culture. He felt that the shrill protests of romantics such as Shelley and Byron were ultimately of little value, and that we should learn to possess our souls in patience and seek to mend things by slow and unspectacular means such as education and criticism.

Shakespeare

Others abide our question.   Thou art free.
We ask and ask—Thou smilest and art still,
Out-topping knowledge.   For the loftiest hill,
Who to the stars uncrowns his majesty,

Planting his steadfast footsteps in the sea,
Making the heaven of heavens his dwelling-place,
Spares but the cloudy border of his base
To the foil'd searching of mortality;

And thou, who didst the stars and sunbeams know,
Self-school'd, self-scann'd, self-honour'd, self-secure,
Didst tread on earth unguess'd at.—Better so!

All pains the immortal spirit must endure,
All weakness which impairs, all griefs which bow,
Find their sole speech in that victorious brow.

1849

To Marguerite—Continued[1]

Yes! in the sea of life enisled,
With echoing straits between us thrown,
Dotting the shoreless watery wild,
We mortal millions live *alone*.
The islands feel the enclasping flow,
And then their endless bounds they know.[2]

But when the moon their hollows lights,
And they are swept by balms of spring,
And in their glens, on starry nights,
The nightingales divinely sing;   10
And lovely notes, from shore to shore,
Across the sounds and channels pour—

Oh! then a longing like despair
Is to their farthest caverns sent;
For surely once, they feel, we were
Parts of a single continent!
Now round us spreads the watery plain—
Oh might our marges meet again!

Who ordered that their longing's fire
Should be, as soon as kindled, cooled? 20
Who renders vain their deep desire?—
A God, a God their severance ruled!
And bade betwixt their shores to be
The unplumbed, salt, estranging sea.

1849   1852

[1] Addressed to a girl Arnold met in Switzerland in the late 1840s.
[2] Compare this poem with John Donne's "Meditation XVII": "No man is an island, entire of itself;
    every man is a piece of the continent, a part of the main, ..."

Dover Beach

The sea is calm to-night.
The tide is full, the moon lies fair
Upon the straits;—on the French coast the light
Gleams and is gone; the cliffs of England stand,
Glimmering and vast, out in the tranquil bay.
Come to the window, sweet is the night-air!
Only, from the long line of spray
Where the sea meets the moon-blanched land,
Listen! you hear the grating roar
Of pebbles which the waves draw back, and fling,   10
At their return, up the high strand,
Begin, and cease, and then again begin,
With tremulous cadence slow, and bring
The eternal note of sadness in.

Sophocles long ago
Heard it on the Aegean, and it brought
Into his mind the turbid ebb and flow
Of human misery; we
Find also in the sound a thought,
Hearing it by this distant northern sea.   20

The Sea of Faith
Was once, too, at the full, and round earth's shore
Lay like the folds of a bright girdle furled.
But now I only hear
Its melancholy, long, withdrawing roar,
Retreating, to the breath
Of the night-wind, down the vast edges drear
And naked shingles of the world.

Ah, love, let us be true
To one another! for the world, which seems   30
To lie before us like a land of dreams,
So various, so beautiful, so new,
Hath really neither joy, nor love, nor light,
Nor certitude, nor peace, nor help for pain;
And we are here as on a darkling plain
Swept with confused alarms of struggle and flight,
Where ignorant armies clash by night.

                                                              1867

DANTE GABRIEL ROSSETTI (1828-1882)

Rossetti began his career as a painter, and the painter's eye for colour and form is always evident in his poetry. As a painter, he founded the Pre-Raphaelite Brotherhood, a group which sought to restore the simplicity and directness of medieval art as it existed before Raphael. This yearning for the Middle Ages is also seen in his poetry, much of which is set in the Middle Ages and uses the ballad form. Like Arnold, Rossetti was repelled by the vulgar materialism of the Victorian age, but chose the alternative of retreat to an imagined past which Arnold rejected. In his escapism, Rossetti may be said to represent a decadent form of romanticism. Nevertheless, he left us a few poems that are brilliant evocations of the past, and a sonnet sequence, "The House of Life," which movingly presents his half-sensual, half-mystical view of love.

Rossetti was the son of a professor of Italian at King's College, London, and the brother of Christina Rossetti, who is regarded by many critics as the best woman poet of the age. Repelled by his father's intense interest in politics,

Rossetti turned to painting. Together with Ford Madox Brown, Holman Hunt, and John Millais he founded the Pre-Raphaelite Brotherhood in 1848. The brotherhood launched a magazine, *The Germ*, to spread its views, and in its pages in 1850 appeared the first of Rossetti's poems, "My Sister's Sleep" and "The Blessed Damozel." In 1850, also, he met Elizabeth Siddal, who became his model and, in 1860, his wife; her sudden death in 1862 plunged him into melancholy from which he never fully recovered. Feeling that he was in some way responsible for her death—she died of an overdose of laudanum—he buried the manuscripts of his poems with her and went into virtual seclusion. He finally recovered the manuscripts from her grave, and published them as *Poems* in 1870. They were an instant success, but a bitter attack on them by Robert Buchanan in 1871, and Rossetti's own nervous maladies, largely prevented their author from enjoying their success. A second volume, *Ballads and Sonnets*, appeared in 1881 shortly before Rossetti's death.

My Sister's Sleep

She fell asleep on Christmas Eve.
  At length the long-ungranted shade
  Of weary eyelids overweigh'd
The pain nought else might yet relieve.

Our mother, who had leaned all day
  Over the bed from chime to chime,
  Then raised herself for the first time,
And as she sat her down, did pray.

Her little work-table was spread
  With work to finish.   For the glare 10
  Made by her candle, she had care
To work some distance from the bed.

Without, there was a cold moon up,
  Of winter radiance sheer and thin;
  The hollow halo it was in
Was like an icy crystal cup.

Through the small room, with subtle
      sound
  Of flame, by vents the fireshine drove
  And reddened.   In its dim alcove
The mirror shed a clearness round.   20

I had been sitting up some nights,
  And my tired mind felt weak and blank;
  Like a sharp strengthening wine it
      drank
The stillness and the broken lights.

Twelve struck.   That sound, by
      dwindling years
  Heard in each hour, crept off; and then
  The ruffled silence spread again,
Like water that a pebble stirs.

Our mother rose from where she sat:
  Her needles, as she laid them down,
  Met lightly, and her silken gown   31
Settled: no other noise than that.

"Glory unto the Newly Born!"
  So, as said angels, she did say;
  Because we were in Christmas Day,
Though it would still be long till morn.

Just then in the room over us
  There was a pushing back of chairs,
  As some who had sat unawares   39
So late, now heard the hour, and rose.

With anxious softly-stepping haste
  Our mother went where Margaret lay,
  Fearing the sounds o'erhead—should
      they
Have broken her long watched-for rest!

She stooped an instant, calm, and turned;
  But suddenly turned back again;
  And all her features seemed in pain
With woe, and her eyes gazed and
      yearned.

For my part, I but hid my face,
  And held my breath, and spoke no
      word: 50
  There was none spoken; but I heard
The silence for a little space.

Our mother bowed herself and wept:
  And both my arms fell, and I said,
  "God knows I knew that she was dead."
And there, all white, my sister slept.

Then kneeling, upon Christmas morn
  A little after twelve o'clock,
  We said, ere the first quarter struck,
"Christ's blessing on the newly born!"   60

1847   1850

The Blessed Damozel

The blessed damozel leaned out
  From the gold bar of heaven;
Her eyes were deeper than the depth
  Of waters stilled at even;
She had three lilies in her hand,
  And the stars in her hair were seven.

Her robe, ungirt from clasp to hem,
  No wrought flowers did adorn,
But a white rose of Mary's gift,
  For service meetly worn;   10
Her hair that lay along her back
  Was yellow like ripe corn.

Herseemed she scarce had been a day
  One of God's choristers;
The wonder was not yet quite gone
  From that still look of hers;
Albeit, to them she left, her day
  Had counted as ten years.

(To one, it is ten years of years.
  . . . Yet now, and in this place,   20
Surely she leaned o'er me—her hair
  Fell all about my face. . . .
Nothing: the autumn fall of leaves.
  The whole year sets apace.)

It was the rampart of God's house
  That she was standing on;
By God built over the sheer depth
  The which is space begun;
So high, that looking downward thence
  She scarce could see the sun.   30

It lies in heaven, across the flood
  Of ether, as a bridge.
Beneath, the tides of day and night
  With flame and darkness ridge
The void, as low as where this earth
  Spins like a fretful midge.

Around her, lovers, newly met
  'Mid deathless love's acclaims,
Spoke evermore among themselves
  Their heart-remembered names;   40
And the souls mounting up to God
  Went by her like thin flames.

And still she bowed herself and stooped
  Out of the circling charm;
Until her bosom must have made
  The bar she leaned on warm,
And the lilies lay as if asleep
  Along her bended arm.

From the fixed place of heaven she saw
  Time, like a pulse, shake fierce   50
Through all the worlds. Her gaze still
    strove
  Within the gulf to pierce
Its path; and now she spoke as when
  The stars sang in their spheres.

The sun was gone now; the curled moon
  Was like a little feather
Fluttering far down the gulf; and now
  She spoke through the still weather.
Her voice was like the voice the stars
  Had when they sang together.   60

(Ah sweet! Even now, in that bird's song,
  Strove not her accents there,
Fain to be hearkened? When those bells
  Possessed the mid-day air,
Strove not her steps to reach my side
  Down all the echoing stair?)

"I wish that he were come to me,
  For he will come," she said.
"Have I not prayed in heaven?—on
    earth,
  Lord, Lord, has he not prayed?   70
Are not two prayers a perfect strength?
  And shall I feel afraid?

"When round his head the aureole clings,
   And he is clothed in white,
I'll take his hand and go with him
   To the deep wells of light;
As unto a stream we will step down,
   And bathe there in God's sight.

"We two will stand beside that shrine,
   Occult, withheld, untrod,   80
Whose lamps are stirred continually
   With prayers sent up to God;
And see our old prayers, granted, melt
   Each like a little cloud.

"We two will lie in the shadow of
   That living mystic tree
Within whose secret growth the Dove
   Is sometimes felt to be,
While every leaf that His plumes touch
   Saith His name audibly.   90

"And I myself will teach to him,
   I myself, lying so,
The songs I sing here; which his voice
   Shall pause in, hushed and slow,
And find some knowledge at each pause,
   Or some new thing to know."

(Alas! We two, we two, thou say'st!
   Yea, one wast thou with me
That once of old. But shall God lift
   To endless unity   100
The soul whose likeness with thy soul
   Was but its love for thee?)

"We two," she said, "will seek the groves
   Where the lady Mary is,
With her five handmaidens, whose names
   Are five sweet symphonies,
Cecily, Gertrude, Magdalen,
   Margaret, and Rosalys.

"Circlewise sit they, with bound locks
   And foreheads garlanded;   110
Into the fine cloth, white like flame
   Weaving the golden thread,
To fashion the birth-robes for them
   Who are just born, being dead.

"He shall fear, haply, and be dumb:
   Then will I lay my cheek
To his, and tell about our love,
   Not once abashed or weak;
And the dear Mother will approve
   My pride, and let me speak.   120

"Herself shall bring us, hand in hand,
   To Him round whom all souls
Kneel, the clear-ranged unnumbered
      heads
   Bowed with their aureoles;
And angels meeting us shall sing
   To their citherns and citoles.

"There will I ask of Christ the Lord
   Thus much for him and me:—
Only to live as once on earth
   With love,—only to be,   130
As then awhile, forever now
   Together, I and he."

She gazed and listened and then said,
   Less sad of speech than mild,—
"All this is when he comes." She ceased.
   The light thrilled towards her, filled
With angels in strong level flight.
   Her eyes prayed, and she smiled.

(I saw her smile.) But soon their path
   Was vague in distant spheres: 140
And then she cast her arms along
   The golden barriers,
And laid her face between her hands,
   And wept. (I heard her tears.)

1847   1850

FROM *The House of Life*

THE SONNET

A Sonnet is a moment's monument,—
   Memorial from the Soul's eternity
   To one dead deathless hour. Look that it be,
Whether for lustral rite or dire portent,
Of its own arduous fulness reverent:
   Carve it in ivory or in ebony,
   As Day or Night may rule; and let Time see
Its flowering crest impearled and orient.

A Sonnet is a coin: its face reveals
   The soul,—its converse, to what Power 'tis due:—
Whether for tribute to the august appeals
   Of Life, or dower in Love's high retinue,
It serve; or 'mid the dark wharf's cavernous breath,
In Charon's palm it pay the toll to Death.

1881

XIX. SILENT NOON

Your hands lie open in the long fresh grass,—
   The finger-points look through like rosy blooms:
   Your eyes smile peace. The pasture gleams and glooms
'Neath billowing skies that scatter and amass.
All round our nest, far as the eye can pass,
   Are golden kingcup-fields with silver edge
   Where the cow-parsley skirts the hawthorn hedge.
'Tis visible silence, still as the hour-glass.

Deep in the sun-searched growths the dragon-fly
Hangs like a blue thread loosened from the sky:—
   So this wing'd hour is dropt to us from above.
Oh! clasp we to our hearts, for deathless dower,
This close-companioned inarticulate hour
   When twofold silence was the song of love.

1870

LXVI. THE HEART OF THE NIGHT

From child to youth; from youth to arduous man;
   From lethargy to fever of the heart;
   From faithful life to dream-dowered days apart;
From trust to doubt; from doubt to brink of ban;—
Thus much of change in one swift cycle ran
   Till now. Alas, the soul!—how soon must she
   Accept her primal immortality,—
The flesh resume its dust whence it began?

O Lord of work and peace! O Lord of life!
  O Lord, the awful Lord of will! though late,
  Even yet renew this soul with duteous breath:
That when the peace is garnered in from strife,
  The work retrieved, the will regenerate,
  This soul may see thy face, O Lord of death!

1881

CHRISTINA ROSSETTI (1830-1894)

The sister of Dante Gabriel Rossetti, Christina Rossetti suffered as a result of two painfully broken engagements. Her quiet life was dedicated to church and charity projects, and to the care of relatives.

In 1862, she published *Goblin Market and Other Poems*, the first collection in the Pre-Raphaelite style to gain public recognition. This was followed by *The Prince's Progress* in 1866, *Sing Songs* in 1872, and *A Pageant and Other Poems* in 1881. A volume of *New Poems* appeared in 1896, after her death.

Rossetti's work ranges from poems of fantasy and verse for children to religious poetry, which makes up the bulk of her writing. Her poems are marked by a high degree of technical perfection, and are pervaded by a spiritual, melancholy atmosphere.

Song

When I am dead, my dearest,
  Sing no sad songs for me;
Plant thou no roses at my head,
  Nor shady cypress tree.
Be the green grass above me
  With showers and dewdrops wet;
And if thou wilt, remember,
  And if thou wilt, forget.

I shall not see the shadows,
  I shall not feel the rain;   10
I shall not hear the nightingale
  Sing on as if in pain.
And dreaming through the twilight
  That doth not rise nor set,
Haply I may remember,
  And haply may forget.

1848

1862

GERARD MANLEY HOPKINS (1844-1889)

Hopkins lived in the Victorian period, but his poetry only became known after World War I as a result of the edition of his work published by his friend Robert Bridges in 1918. Since that time, he has exercised a profound influence on English poetry by virtue of the novelty of his style and the passionate intensity of his thought. His technical experiments take the forms of (a) "sprung rhythm," by which an accented syllable is given great impact by being joined with a group of several unaccented syllables, (b) the use of hyphenated words to heighten the effect of breathless energy or passion, (c) the omission of relative pronouns and of all but the most essential words, for the same purpose, and (d) the occasional employment of "run-over rhymes," in which the rhyme is attained by joining the end of one line with the beginning of the next. His thought, remarkable for its intensity rather than its originality, consists mainly in an ecstatic delight in the beauty of God's creation or of an equally passionate grief for the transience of that beauty.

Hopkins was educated at Highgate School and Balliol College, Oxford. Like Newman before him, he came in contact at the university with those who leaned towards Catholicism, and in 1866 he was converted to the Church of Rome. He became a member of the Order of Jesus in 1868, and was appointed Professor of Greek in Dublin University in 1884. None of his poems were published in his lifetime; they were merely included in letters addressed to his few close friends.

God's Grandeur

The world is charged with the grandeur of God.
  It will flame out, like shining from shook foil;
  It gathers to a greatness, like the ooze of oil
Crushed. Why do men then now not reck his rod?
Generations have trod, have trod, have trod;
  And all is seared with trade; bleared, smeared with toil;
  And wears man's smudge and shares man's smell: the soil
Is bare now, nor can foot feel, being shod.

And for all this, nature is never spent;
  There lives the dearest freshness deep down things;
And though the last lights off the black West went
  Oh, morning, at the brown brink eastward, springs—
Because the Holy Ghost over the bent
  World broods with warm breast and with ah! bright wings.

1877   1918

The Windhover

TO CHRIST OUR LORD

I caught this morning morning's minion, king-
  dom of daylight's dauphin, dapple-dawn-drawn Falcon, in his riding
Of the rolling level underneath him steady air, and striding

High there, how he rung upon the rein of a wimpling wing
In his ecstasy! then off, off forth on swing,
  As a skate's heel sweeps smooth on a bow-bend: the hurl and gliding
  Rebuffed the big wind. My heart in hiding
Stirred for a bird,—the achieve of, the mastery of the thing!

Brute beauty and valor and act, oh, air, pride, plume, here
  Buckle! And the fire that breaks from thee then, a billion
Times told lovelier, more dangerous, O my chevalier!

  No wonder of it: sheer plod makes plough down sillion
Shine, and blue-bleak embers, ah my dear,
  Fall, gall themselves, and gash gold-vermilion.

1877   1918

Pied Beauty

  Glory be to God for dappled things—
    For skies of couple-color as a brinded cow;
      For rose-moles all in stipple upon trout that swim;
  Fresh-firecoal chestnut-falls; finches' wings;
    Landscape plotted and pieced—fold, fallow, and plough;
      And all trades, their gear and tackle and trim.

  All things counter, original, spare, strange;
    Whatever is fickle, freckled (who knows how?)
      With swift, slow; sweet, sour; adazzle, dim;
  He fathers-forth whose beauty is past change:
                                        Praise him.

1877   1918

Inversnaid

    This darksome burn, horseback brown,
    His rollrock highroad roaring down,
    In coop and in comb the fleece of his foam
    Flutes and low to the lake falls home.

A windpuff-bonnet of fawn-froth
Turns and twindles over the broth
Of a pool so pitchblack, fell-frowning,
It rounds and rounds Despair to drowning.

Degged with dew, dappled with dew
Are the groins of the braes that the brook treads through,
Wiry heathpacks, flitches of fern,
And the beadbonny ash that sits over the burn.

What would the world be, once bereft
Of wet and of wildness? Let them be left,
O let them be left, wildness and wet;
Long live the weeds and the wilderness yet.

1881   1918

AMERICAN LITERATURE

RALPH WALDO EMERSON (1803-1882)

Emerson and Thoreau are the chief glories of the cultural flowering of New England in the middle decades of the nineteenth century. They were also the leaders of the Transcendentalist movement which launched that experiment in communal and contemplative living, Brook Farm, published the magazine known as *The Dial*, and promulgated a set of basic convictions about the nature of life. These convictions may be summarized as the belief in a spiritual force or "oversoul" which directs, pervades, and transcends the material world, the belief that man must seek contact with this spiritual force through contemplation and communion with Nature, and the belief that having established this contact he must rely upon his own intuitions concerning it and thus be as free as possible from external authority of any kind. In their opposition to materialism and conformity Emerson and Thoreau played much the same role in nineteenth century America as Arnold played in Victorian England.

Emerson was born in Boston, the son of a Unitarian minister, and was educated at the Boston Latin School and at Harvard. From 1829 to 1832 he was minister of the Second Unitarian Church in Boston, but finding that he could not accept all the doctrines and practices of his church he resigned the pastorate, made a tour of Europe, and in 1835 began in Boston his career as a public lecturer. A year later he published his first essay *Nature*, and founded the Transcendentalist Club. His collected *Essays* were published in 1844, *Poems* in 1846, *Representative Men* in 1850, and *English Traits* in 1856. From this point on his work declined sharply in quality, although he lived until 1882. In his best work Emerson combined the practical, shrewd common-sense of the Yankee with the wisdom and mystical ecstasy of the visionary. His style, similarly, is a mixture of the colloquial and the learned, of the homely metaphor and the scholarly allusion.

Days[1]

Daughters of Time, the hypocritic Days,
Muffled and dumb like barefoot dervishes,
And marching single in an endless file,
Bring diadems and fagots in their hands.
To each they offer gifts after his will,
Bread, kingdoms, stars, and sky that holds them all.
I, in my pleachèd garden, watched the pomp,
Forgot my morning wishes, hastily
Took a few herbs and apples, and the Day
Turned and departed silent. I, too late,
Under her solemn fillet saw the scorn.

1851?   1867

[1]In his essay "Works and Days," Emerson writes: "The days are ever divine, as to the first
Aryans. They come and go like muffled and veiled figures, sent from a distant friendly party; but
they say nothing, and if we do not use the gifts they bring, they carry them as silently away."

FROM Self-Reliance

I read the other day some verses written by an eminent painter which were original and not conventional. The soul always hears an admonition in such lines, let the subject be what it may. The sentiment they instil is of more value than any thought they may contain. To believe your own thought, to believe that what is true for you in your private heart is true for all men,—that is genius. Speak your latent conviction, and it shall be the universal sense; for the inmost in due time becomes the outmost, and our first thought is rendered back to us by the trumpets of the Last Judgment. Familiar as the voice of the mind is to each, the highest merit we ascribe to Moses, Plato, and Milton is that they set at naught books and traditions, and spoke not what men, but what *they* thought. A man should learn to detect and watch that gleam of light which flashes across his mind from within, more than the lustre of the firmament of bards and sages. Yet he dismisses without notice his thought, because it is his. In every work of genius we recognize our own rejected thoughts; they come back to us with a certain alienated majesty. Great works of art have no more affecting lesson for us than this. They teach us to abide by our spontaneous impression with good-humored inflexibility then most when the whole cry of voices is on the other side. Else tomorrow a stranger will say with masterly good sense precisely what we have thought and felt all the time, and we shall be forced to take with shame our own opinion from another.

There is a time in every man's education when he arrives at the conviction that envy is ignorance; that imitation is suicide; that he must take himself for better for worse as his portion; that though the wide universe is full of good, no kernel of nourishing corn can come to him but through his toil bestowed on that plot of ground which is given to him to till. The power which resides in him is new in nature, and none but he knows what that is which he can do, nor does he know until he has tried. Not for nothing one face, one character, one fact, makes much impression on him and another none. This sculpture in the memory is not without pre-established harmony. The eye was placed where one ray should fall, that it might testify of that particular ray. We but half express ourselves, and are ashamed of that divine idea which each of us represents. It may be safely trusted as proportionate and of good issues, so it be faithfully imparted, but God will not have his work made manifest by cowards. A man is relieved and gay when he has put his heart into his work and done his best; but what he has said or done otherwise shall give him no peace. It is a deliverance which does not deliver. In the attempt his genius deserts him; no muse befriends; no invention, no hope.

Trust thyself: every heart vibrates to that iron string. Accept the place the divine providence has found for you, the society of your contemporaries, the connection of events. Great men have always done so, and confided themselves childlike to the genius of their age, betraying their perception that the absolutely trustworthy was seated at their heart, working through their hands, predominating in all their being. And we are now men, and must accept in the highest mind the same transcendent destiny; and not minors and invalids in a protected corner, not cowards fleeing before a revolution, but guides, redeemers, and benefactors, obeying the Almighty effort and advancing on Chaos and the Dark.

What pretty oracles nature yields us on this text in the face and behavior of children, babes, and even brutes! That divided and rebel mind, that distrust of a sentiment because our arithmetic has computed the strength and means opposed to our purpose, these have not. Their mind being whole, their eye is as yet unconquered, and when we look in their faces we are disconcerted. Infancy conforms to nobody; all conform to it; so that one babe commonly makes four or five out of the adults who prattle and play to it. So God has armed youth and puberty and manhood no less with its own piquancy and charm, and made it enviable and gracious and its claims not to be put by, if it will stand by itself. Do not think the youth has no force, because he cannot speak to you and me. Hark! in the next room his voice is sufficiently clear and emphatic. It seems he knows how to speak to his contemporaries. Bashful or bold then, he will know how to make us seniors very unnecessary.

The nonchalance of boys who are sure of a dinner, and would disdain as much as a lord to do or say aught to conciliate one, is the healthy attitude of human nature. A boy is in the parlor what the pit is in the playhouse; independent, irresponsible, looking out from his corner on such people and facts as pass by, he tries and sentences them on their merits, in the swift, summary ways of boys, as good, bad, interesting, silly, eloquent, troublesome. He cumbers himself never about consequences, about interests; he gives an independent, genuine verdict. You must court him; he does not court you. But the man is as it were clapped into gaol by his consciousness. As soon as he has once acted or spoken with *éclat* he is a committed person, watched by the sympathy or the hatred of hundreds whose affections must now enter into his account. There is no Lethe for this. Ah, that he could pass again into his neutrality! Who can thus avoid all pledges and, having observed, observe again from the same unaffected, unbiassed, unbribable, unaffrighted innocence,—must always be formidable. He would utter opinions on all passing affairs, which being seen to be not private but necessary, would sink like darts into the ear of men and put them in fear.

These are the voices which we hear in solitude, but they grow faint and inaudible as we enter into the world. Society everywhere is in conspiracy against the manhood of every one of its members. Society is a joint-stock company, in which the members agree, for the better securing of his bread to each shareholder, to surrender the liberty and culture of the eater. The virtue in most request is conformity. Self-reliance is its aversion. It loves not realities and creators, but names and customs.

Whoso would be a man, must be a nonconformist. He who would gather immortal palms must not be hindered by the name of goodness, but must explore if it be goodness. Nothing is at last sacred but the integrity of your own mind. Absolve you to yourself, and you shall have the suffrage of the world. I remember an answer which when quite young I was prompted to make to a valued adviser who was wont to importune me with the dear old doctrines of the church. On my saying, "What have I to do with the sacredness of traditions, if I live wholly from within?" my friend suggested,—"But these impulses may be from below, not from above." I replied,

"They do not seem to me to be such; but if I am the Devil's child, I will live then from the Devil." No law can be sacred to me but that of my nature. Good and bad are but names very readily transferable to that or this; the only right is what is after my constitution: the only wrong what is against it. A man is to carry himself in the presence of all opposition as if everything were titular and ephemeral but he. I am ashamed to think how easily we capitulate to badges and names, to large societies and dead institutions. Every decent and well-spoken individual affects and sways me more than is right. I ought to go upright and vital, and speak the rude truth in all ways. If malice and vanity wear the coat of philanthropy, shall that pass? If an angry bigot assumes this bountiful cause of Abolition[1], and comes to me with his last news from Barbados[2], why should I not say to him, "Go love thy infant; love thy woodchopper; be good-natured and modest; have that grace; and never varnish your hard, uncharitable ambition with this incredible tenderness for black folk a thousand miles off. Thy love afar is spite at home." Rough and graceless would be such a greeting, but truth is handsomer than the affectation of love. Your goodness must have some edge to it,—else it is none. The doctrine of hatred must be preached, as the counteraction of the doctrine of love, when that pules and whines. I shun father and mother and wife and brother when my genius calls me. I would write on the lintels of the doorpost, *Whim.* I hope it is somewhat better than whim at last, but

[1] The movement for the abolition of slavery.
[2] An island of the West Indies. Presumably the person referred to was more interested in the welfare of negroes in the West Indies than in his own family and neighbours.

we cannot spend the day in explanation. Expect me not to show cause why I seek or why I exclude company. Then again, do not tell me, as a good man did today, of my obligation to put all poor men in good situations. Are they *my* poor? I tell thee, thou foolish philanthropist, that I grudge the dollar, the dime, the cent I give to such men as do not belong to me and to whom I do not belong. There is a class of persons to whom by all spiritual affinity I am bought and sold; for them I will go to prison if need be; but your miscellaneous popular charities; the education at college of fools; the building of meeting-houses to the vain end to which many now stand; alms to sots, and the thousand-fold Relief Societies;—though I confess with shame I sometimes succumb and give the dollar, it is a wicked dollar, which by and by I shall have the manhood to withhold.

Virtues are, in the popular estimate, rather the exception than the rule. There is the man *and* his virtues. Men do what is called a good action, as some piece of courage or charity, much as they would pay a fine in expiation of daily non-appearance on parade. Their works are done as an apology or extenuation of their living in the world,—as invalids and the insane pay a high board. Their virtues are penances. I do not wish to expiate, but to live. My life is for itself and not for a spectacle. I much prefer that it should be of a lower strain, so it be genuine and equal, than that it should be glittering and unsteady. I wish it to be sound and sweet, and not to need diet and bleeding. I ask primary evidence that you are a man and refuse this appeal from the man to his actions. I know that for myself it makes no difference whether I do or forbear those actions which are reckoned excellent. I cannot consent to pay for a privilege where I have intrinsic right. Few and mean as my gifts may be, I actually am, and do not need for my own assurance or the assurance of my fellows any secondary testimony.

What I must do is all that concerns me, not what the people think. This rule, equally arduous in actual and in intellectual life, may serve for the whole distinction between greatness and meanness. It is the harder because you will always find those who think they know what is your duty better than you know it. It is easy in the world to live after the world's opinion; it is easy in solitude to live after our own; but the great man is he who in the midst of the crowd keeps with perfect sweetness the independence of solitude. . . .

1841

NATHANIEL HAWTHORNE (1804-1864)

Although he too was a New Englander, for a time a neighbour of Emerson and Thoreau in Concord, and even invested in the Brook Farm venture, Hawthorne could not accept the optimistic, liberal doctrines of Transcendentalism. The tradition of New England Puritanism had a stronger hold upon him, and although he rebelled against most of its ideas and practices, he could never escape its gloomy sense of sin, its morbid fascination with guilt.

Hawthorne was born in Salem, Mass., the son of a sea-captain of that port. From 1821 to 1825 he attended Bowdoin College in Maine, and for the next fourteen years lived in Salem, working for two years in the customs house and thereafter writing stories for magazines. His first novel, *Fanshawe* (1828) was a failure, but he fared much better with his first book of short stories, *Twice-Told Tales* (1837). From 1839 to 1841 he served in the Boston Custom House, then lived briefly at Brook Farm, and in 1842 married Sophia Peabody and set up house in Concord. He returned to Salem in 1846, and there wrote his masterpiece, *The Scarlet Letter* (1850). He was American Consul in Liverpool, England, from 1853 to 1857, from 1857 to 1860 lived in various parts of Italy and England, and returned to Salem in 1860. He died while on a visit to New Hampshire in 1864.

The two most striking characteristics of Hawthorne's writings are his deep moral earnestness and his highly developed sense of form. He is an introspective writer, continually probing the consciences of his characters and finding the unpardonable sin in pride and whatever alienates us from our fellow-men. In technique he makes much use of symbolism, and of the imagery of light and shade; his style is pure and lucid, and all his stories and novels have a symmetrical structure and a rich sense of mood.

The Ambitious Guest

One September night a family had gathered round their hearth and piled it high with the drift-wood of mountain streams, the dry cones of the pine, and the splintered ruins of great trees that had come crashing down the precipice. Up the chimney roared the fire, and brightened the room with its broad blaze. The faces of the father and mother had a sober gladness; the children laughed; the eldest daughter was the image of Happiness at seventeen; and the aged grandmother, who sat knitting in the warmest place, was the image of Happiness grown old. They had found the "herb, heart's-ease," in the bleakest spot of all New England. This family were situated in the Notch of the White Hills, where the wind was sharp throughout the year, and pitilessly cold in the winter—giving their cottage all its fresh inclemency, before it descended on the valley of the Saco. They dwelt in a cold spot and a dangerous one; for a mountain towered above their heads, so steep, that the stones would often rumble down its sides, and startle them at midnight.

The daughter had just uttered some simple jest, that filled them all with mirth, when the wind came through the Notch, and seemed to pause before their cottage—rattling the door, with a sound of wailing and lamentation, before it passed into the valley. For a moment it saddened them, though there was nothing unusual in the tones. But the family were glad again, when they perceived that the latch was lifted by some traveller, whose footsteps had been unheard amid the dreary blast which heralded his approach, and wailed as he was entering, and went moaning away from the door.

Though they dwelt in such a solitude, these people held daily converse with the world. The romantic pass of the Notch is a great artery, through which the life-blood in internal commerce is continually throbbing, between Maine on one side, and the Green Mountains and the shores of the St. Lawrence on the other. The stagecoach always drew up before the door of the cottage. The wayfarer, with no companion but his staff, paused here to exchange a word, that the sense of loneliness might not utterly overcome him, ere he could pass through the cleft of the mountain, or reach the first house in the valley. And here the teamster, on his way to Portland market, would put up for the night; and, if a bachelor, might sit an hour beyond the usual bed-time, and steal a kiss from the mountain maid at parting. It was one of those primitive taverns where the traveller pays only for food and lodging, but meets with a homely kindness, beyond all price. When the footsteps were heard, therefore, between the outer door and the inner one, the whole family rose up, grandmother, children, and all, as if about to welcome some one who belonged to them, and whose fate was linked with theirs.

The door was opened by a young man. His face at first wore the melancholy expression, almost despondency, of one who travels a wild and bleak road at nightfall and alone, but soon brightened up when he saw the kindly warmth of his reception. He felt his heart spring forward to meet them all, from the old woman, who wiped a chair with her apron, to the little child that held out its arms to him. One glance and smile placed the stranger on a footing of innocent familiarity with the eldest daughter.

"Ah, this fire is the right thing!" cried he; "especially when there is such a pleasant circle round it. I am quite benumbed; for the Notch is just like the pipe of a great pair of bellows; it has blown a terrible blast in my face, all the way from Bartlett."

"Then you are going towards Vermont?" said the master of the house, as he helped to take a light knapsack off the young man's shoulder.

"Yes; to Burlington, and far enough beyond," replied he. "I meant to have been at Ethan Crawford's tonight; but a pedestrian lingers along such a road as this. It is no matter; for, when I saw this good fire, and all your cheerful faces, I felt as if you had kindled it on purpose for me, and were waiting my arrival. So I shall sit down among you, and make myself at home."

The frank-hearted stranger had just drawn his chair to the fire, when something like a heavy footstep was heard without, rushing down the steep side of the mountain, as with long and rapid strides, and taking such a leap, in passing the cottage, as to strike the opposite precipice. The family held their breath, because they knew the sound, and their guest held his by instinct.

"The old mountain has thrown a stone at us, for fear we should forget him," said the landlord, recovering himself. "He sometimes nods his head, and threatens to come down; but we are old neighbours, and agree together pretty well, upon the whole. Besides, we have a sure place of refuge hard by, if he should be coming in good earnest."

Let us now suppose the stranger to have finished his supper of bear's meat; and, by his natural felicity of manner, to have placed himself on a footing of kindness with the whole family, so that they talked as freely together as if he belonged to their mountain brood. He was of a proud, yet gentle spirit—haughty and reserved among the rich and great; but ever ready to stoop his head to the lowly cottage-door, and be like a brother or a son at the poor man's fireside. In the household of the Notch he found warmth and simplicity of feeling, the pervading intelligence of New England, and a poetry of native growth, which they had gathered, when they little thought of it, from the mountain peaks and chasms, and at the very threshold of their romantic and dangerous abode. He had travelled far and alone; his whole life, indeed, had been a solitary path; for, with the lofty caution of his nature, he had kept himself apart from those who might otherwise have been his companions. The family, too, though so kind and hospitable, had that consciousness of unity among themselves, and separation from the world at large, which, in every domestic circle, should still keep a holy place where no stranger may intrude. But, this evening, a prophetic sympathy impelled the refined and educated youth to pour out his heart before the simple mountaineers, and constrained them to answer him with the same free confidence. And thus it should have been. Is not the kindred of a common fate a closer tie than that of birth?

The secret of the young man's character was a high and abstracted ambition. He could have borne to live an undistinguished life, but not to be forgotten in the grave. Yearning desire had been transformed into hope; and hope, long cherished, had become like a certainty, that, obscurely as he journeyed now, a glory was to beam on all his pathway—though, not perhaps, while he was treading it. But, when posterity should gaze back into the gloom of what was now the present, they would trace the brightness of his footsteps, brightening as meaner glories faded, and confess that a gifted one had passed from his cradle to his tomb, with none to recognize him.

"As yet," cried the stranger, his cheek glowing and his eye flashing with enthusiasm, "as yet, I have done nothing. Were I to vanish from the earth tomorrow, none would know so much of me as you; that a nameless youth came up, at nightfall, from the valley of the Saco, and opened his heart to you in the evening, and passed through the Notch, by sunrise, and was seen no more. Not a soul would ask—'Who was he?—Whither did the wanderer go?' But I cannot die till I have achieved my destiny. Then let Death come! I shall have built my monument!"

There was a continual flow of natural emotion, gushing forth amid abstracted reverie, which enabled the family to understand this young man's sentiments, though so foreign from their own. With quick sensibility of the ludicrous, he blushed at the ardour into which he had been betrayed.

"You laugh at me," said he, taking the eldest daughter's hand, and laughing himself. "You think my ambition as nonsensical as if I were to freeze myself to death on the top of Mount Washington, only that people might spy at me from the country round about. And truly, that would be a noble pedestal for a man's statue!"

"It is better to sit here by this fire," answered the girl, blushing, "and be comfortable and contented, though nobody thinks about us."

"I suppose," said her father, after a fit of musing, "there is something natural in what the young man says; and if my mind had been turned that way, I might have felt just the same. It is strange, wife, how this talk has set my head running on things that are pretty certain never to come to pass."

"Perhaps they may," observed the wife. "Is the man thinking what he will do when he is a widower?"

"No, no!" cried he, repelling the idea with reproachful kindness. "When I think of your death, Esther, I think of mine too. But I was wishing we had a good farm, in Bartlett, or Bethlehem, or Littleton, or some other township round the White Mountains; but not where they could tumble on our heads. I should want to stand well with my neighbours, and be called 'Squire,' and sent to General Court for a term or two; for a plain honest man may do as much good there as a lawyer. And when I should be grown quite an old man, and you an old woman, so as not to be long apart, I might die happy enough in my bed, and leave you all crying around me. A slate gravestone would suit me as well as a marble one—with just my name and age, and a verse of a hymn, and something to let people know that I lived an honest man and died a Christian."

"There now!" exclaimed the stranger; "it is our nature to desire a monument, be it slate, or marble, or a pillar of granite, or a glorious memory in the universal heart of man."

"We're in a strange way tonight," said the wife, with tears in her eyes. "They say it's a sign of something when folks' minds go a-wandering so. Hark to the children!"

They listened accordingly. The younger children had been put to bed in another room, but with an open door between, so that they could be heard talking busily among themselves. One and all seemed to have caught the infection from the fireside circle, and were outvying each other in wild stories and childish projects of what they would do, when they came to be men and women. At length, a little boy, instead of addressing his brothers and sisters, called out to his mother.

"I'll tell you what I wish, mother," cried he. "I want you and father and grandma'm, and all of us, and the stranger too, to start right away, and go and take a drink out of the basin of the Flume!"

Nobody could help laughing at the child's notion of leaving a warm bed, and dragging them from a cheerful fire, to visit the basin of the Flume—a brook, which tumbles over the precipice, deep within the Notch. The boy had hardly spoken, when a wagon rattled along the road, and stopped a moment before the door. It appeared to contain two or three men, who were cheering their hearts with the rough chorus of a song, which resounded in broken notes, between the cliffs, while the singers hesitated whether to continue their journey, or put up here for the night.

"Father," said the girl, "they are calling you by name."

But the good man doubted whether they had really called him, and was unwilling to show himself too solicitous of gain, by inviting people to patronize his house. He therefore did not hurry to the door; and the lash being soon applied, the travellers plunged into the Notch, still singing and laughing, though their music came back drearily from the heart of the mountain.

"There, mother!" cried the boy, again. "They'd have given us a ride to the Flume."

Again they laughed at the child's pertinacious fancy for a night ramble. But it happened that a light cloud passed over the daughter's spirit; she looked gravely into the fire, and drew a breath that was almost a sigh. It forced its way, in spite of a little struggle to repress it. Then starting and blushing, she looked quickly round the circle, as if they had caught a glimpse into her bosom. The stranger asked what she had been thinking of.

"Nothing," answered she, with a downcast smile. "Only I felt lonesome just then."

"Oh, I have always had a gift of feeling what is in other people's hearts," said he, half seriously. "Shall I tell the secrets of yours? For I know what to think when a young girl shivers by a warm hearth, and complains of lonesomeness at her mother's side. Shall I put these feelings into words?"

"They would not be a girl's feelings any longer, if they could be put into words," replied the mountain nymph, laughing, but avoiding his eye.

All this was said apart. Perhaps a germ of love was springing in their hearts, so pure that it might blossom in paradise, since it could not be matured on earth; for women worship such gentle dignity as his; and the proud, contemplative, yet kindly soul is oftenest captivated by simplicity like hers. But, while they spoke softly, and he was watching the happy sadness, the lightsome shadows, the shy yearnings of a maiden's nature, the wind, through the Notch, took a deeper and drearier sound. It seemed, as the fanciful stranger said, like the choral strain of the spirits of the blast, who, in old Indian times, had their dwelling among these mountains, and made their heights and recesses a sacred region. There was a wail along the road, as if a funeral were passing. To chase away the gloom, the family threw pine-branches on their fire, till the dry leaves crackled, and the flame arose, discovering once again a scene of peace and humble happiness. The light hovered about them fondly, and caressed them all. There were the little faces of the children peeping from their bed apart, and here the father's frame of strength, the mother's subdued and careful mien, the highbrowed youth, the budding girl, and the good old grandam, still knitting in the warmest place. The aged woman looked up from her task, and, with fingers ever busy, was the next to speak.

"Old folks have their notions," said she, "as well as young ones. You've been wishing and planning, and letting your heads run on one thing and another, till you've set my mind a-wandering too. Now what should an old woman wish for when she can go but a step or two before she comes to her grave? Children, it will haunt me night and day till I tell you."

"What is it, mother?" cried the husband and wife at once.

Then the old woman, with an air of mystery, which drew the circle closer round the fire, informed them that she had provided her grave-clothes some years before—a nice linen shroud, a cap with a muslin ruff, and everything of a finer sort than she had worn since her wedding-day. But this evening an old superstition had strangely recurred to her. It used to be said, in her younger days, that if anything were amiss with a corpse, if only the ruff were not smooth, or the cap did not set right, the corpse, in the coffin and beneath the clods, would strive to put up its cold hands and arrange it. The bare thought made her nervous.

"Don't talk so, grandmother!" said the girl, shuddering.

"Now," continued the old woman, with singular earnestness, yet smiling strangely at her own folly, "I want one of you, my children—when your mother is dressed, and in the coffin—I want one of you to hold a looking-glass over my face. Who knows but I may take a glimpse at myself, and see whether all's right?"

"Old and young, we dream of graves and monuments," murmured the stranger youth. "I wonder how mariners feel when the ship is sinking, and they, unknown and undistinguished, are to be buried together in the ocean—that wide and nameless sepulchre!"

For a moment the old woman's ghastly

conception so engrossed the minds of her hearers, that a sound, abroad in the night, rising like the roar of a blast, had grown broad, deep, and terrible before the fated group were conscious of it. The house, and all within it, trembled; the foundations of the earth seemed to be shaken, as if this awful sound were the peal of the last trump. Young and old exchanged one wild glance, and remained an instant, pale, affrighted, without utterance, or power to move. Then the same shriek burst simultaneously from all their lips.

"The Slide! the Slide!"

The simplest words must intimate, but not portray, the unutterable horror of the catastrophe. The victims rushed from their cottage and sought refuge in what they deemed a safer spot—where, in contemplation of such an emergency, a sort of barrier had been reared. Alas! They had quitted their security and fled right into the pathway of destruction. Down came the whole side of the mountain in a cataract of ruin. Just before it reached the house the stream broke into two branches, shivering not a window there, but overwhelming the whole vicinity, blocked up the road and annihilated everything in its dreadful course. Long ere the thunder of that great Slide had ceased to roar among the mountains, the mortal agony had been endured, and the victims were at peace. Their bodies were never found.

The next morning the light smoke was seen stealing from the cottage chimney up the mountain-side. Within, the fire was yet smouldering on the hearth, and the chairs in a circle around it, as if the inhabitants had but gone forth to view the devastation of the Slide, and would shortly return to thank Heaven for their miraculous escape. All had left separate tokens, by which those who had known the family were made to shed a tear for each. Who has not heard their name? The story has been told far and wide, and will for ever be a legend of these mountains. Poets have sung their fate.

There were circumstances which led some to suppose that a stranger had been received into the cottage on this awful night, and had shared the catastrophe of all its inmates. Others denied that there were sufficient grounds for such a conjecture. Woe for the high-souled youth, with his dream of Earthly Immortality! His name and person utterly unknown; his history, his way of life, his plans—a mystery never to be solved; his death and his existence equally a doubt! Whose was the agony of that death-moment?

1835

EDGAR ALLAN POE (1809-1849)

Poe is one of those literary figures who are more important for their influence on others than in their own right. His tightly plotted, highly atmospheric short stories created a vogue for that form, and he is thus entitled to be called the father of the modern short story; his stories of crime, mystery, and detection provided the basic model for almost all subsequent detective fiction; and his trance-like poems were hailed in France and influenced such members of the Symbolist school as Mallarmé and Verlaine. Moreover his work in both prose and poetry testifies to the international vogue of romanticism, for it illustrates clearly the cult of eccentricity and the taste for the morbid and diseased which were among the chief aspects of that movement.

Poe was born in Boston, Mass., the child of

travelling actors. Left an orphan as a small boy, he was brought up by foster parents in Richmond, Virginia. He was educated at Stoke Newington in England and at the University of Virginia, served briefly in the American army, and was the editor of various American literary magazines. In 1835 he married his thirteen-year-old cousin, Virginia Clemm; she was always delicate, and died at the age of twenty-six. Poe himself frequently drank to excess and suffered from nervous disorders. He died in mysterious circumstances in Baltimore on October 7, 1849.

The Raven

Once upon a midnight dreary, while I pondered, weak and weary,
Over many a quaint and curious volume of forgotten lore—
While I nodded, nearly napping, suddenly there came a tapping,
As of some one gently rapping, rapping at my chamber door.
" 'Tis some visitor," I muttered, "tapping at my chamber door—
 Only this and nothing more."

Ah, distinctly I remember it was in the bleak December;
And each separate dying ember wrought its ghost upon the floor.
Eagerly I wished the morrow;—vainly I had sought to borrow
From my books surcease of sorrow—sorrow for the lost Lenore—   10
For the rare and radiant maiden whom the angels name Lenore—
 Nameless here for evermore.

And the silken, sad, uncertain rustling of each purple curtain
Thrilled me—filled me with fantastic terrors never felt before;
So that now, to still the beating of my heart, I stood repeating
" 'Tis some visitor entreating entrance at my chamber door;—
 This it is and nothing more."

Presently my soul grew stronger; hesitating then no longer,
"Sir," said I, "or Madam, truly your forgiveness I implore;
But the fact is I was napping, and so gently you came rapping,   20
And so faintly you came tapping, tapping at my chamber door,
That I scarce was sure I heard you"—here I opened wide the door;—
 Darkness there and nothing more.

Deep into that darkness peering, long I stood there wondering, fearing,
Doubting, dreaming dreams no mortal ever dared to dream before;
But the silence was unbroken, and the stillness gave no token,
And the only word there spoken was the whispered word, "Lenore!"
This I whispered, and an echo murmured back the word "Lenore!"
 Merely this and nothing more.

Back into the chamber turning, all my soul within me burning,   30
Soon again I heard a tapping somewhat louder than before.
"Surely," said I, "surely that is something at my window lattice;
Let me see, then, what thereat is, and this mystery explore—
Let my heart be still a moment and this mystery explore;—
    'Tis the wind and nothing more!"

Open here I flung the shutter, when, with many a flirt and flutter
In there stepped a stately Raven of the saintly days of yore.
Not the least obeisance made he; not a minute stopped or stayed he;
But, with mien of lord or lady, perched above my chamber door—
Perched upon a bust of Pallas just above my chamber door—   40
    Perched, and sat, and nothing more.

Then this ebony bird beguiling my sad fancy into smiling,
By the grave and stern decorum of the countenance it wore,
"Though thy crest be shorn and shaven, thou," I said, "art sure no craven,
Ghastly grim and ancient Raven wandering from the Nightly shore—
Tell me what thy lordly name is on the Night's Plutonian shore!"
    Quoth the Raven, "Nevermore."

Much I marvelled this ungainly fowl to hear discourse so plainly,
Though its answer little meaning—little relevancy bore;
For we cannot help agreeing that no living human being   50
Ever yet was blessed with seeing bird above his chamber door—
Bird or beast upon the sculptured bust above his chamber door,
    With such name as "Nevermore."

But the Raven, sitting lonely on the placid bust, spoke only
That one word, as if his soul in that one word he did outpour.
Nothing farther then he uttered—not a feather then he fluttered—
Till I scarcely more than muttered "Other friends have flown before—
On the morrow he will leave me, as my hopes have flown before."
    Then the bird said "Nevermore."

Startled at the stillness broken by reply so aptly spoken,   60
"Doubtless," said I, "what it utters is its only stock and store
Caught from some unhappy master whom unmerciful Disaster
Followed fast and followed faster till his songs one burden bore—
Till the dirges of his Hope that melancholy burden bore
    Of "Never—nevermore!"

But the Raven still beguiling all my fancy into smiling,
Straight I wheeled a cushioned seat in front of bird, and bust and door;
Then, upon the velvet sinking, I betook myself to linking
Fancy unto fancy, thinking what this ominous bird of yore—
What this grim, ungainly, ghastly, gaunt, and ominous bird of yore   70
    Meant in croaking "Nevermore."

Thus I sat engaged in guessing, but no syllable expressing
To the fowl whose fiery eyes now burned into my bosom's core;
This and more I sat divining, with my head at ease reclining
On the cushion's velvet lining that the lamplight gloated o'er,
But whose velvet violet lining with the lamplight gloating o'er,
　　She shall press, ah, nevermore!

Then, methought, the air grew denser, perfumed from an unseen censer
Swung by Seraphim whose foot-falls tinkled on the tufted floor.
"Wretch," I cried, "thy God hath lent thee—by these angels he hath sent the
Respite—respite and nepenthe from thy memories of Lenore;　　81
Quaff, oh quaff this kind nepenthe and forget this lost Lenore!"
　　Quoth the Raven "Nevermore."

"Prophet!" said I, "thing of evil! prophet still, if bird or devil!—
Whether Tempter sent, or whether tempest tossed thee here ashore,
Desolate yet all undaunted, on this desert land enchanted—
On this home by Horror haunted—tell me truly, I implore—
Is there—is there balm in Gilead?—tell me—tell me, I implore!"
　　Quoth the Raven "Nevermore."

"Prophet!" said I, "thing of evil—prophet still, if bird or devil!　　90
By that Heaven that bends above us—by that God we both adore—
Tell this soul with sorrow laden if, within the distant Aidenn,
It shall clasp a sainted maiden whom the angels name Lenore—
Clasp a rare and radiant maiden whom the angels name Lenore."
　　Quoth the Raven "Nevermore."

"Be that word our sign of parting, bird or fiend!" I shrieked, upstarting—
"Get thee back into the tempest and the Night's Plutonian shore!
Leave no black plume as a token of that lie thy soul hath spoken!
Leave my loneliness unbroken!—quit the bust above my door!
Take thy beak from out my heart, and take thy form from off my door!" 100
　　Quoth the Raven "Nevermore."

And the Raven, never flitting, still is sitting, still is sitting
On the pallid bust of Pallas just above my chamber door;
And his eyes have all the seeming of a demon's that is dreaming,
And the lamp-light o'er him streaming throws his shadow on the floor;
And my soul from out that shadow that lies floating on the floor
　　Shall be lifted—nevermore!

1845

The Cask of Amontillado

The thousand injuries of Fortunato I had borne as I best could, but when he ventured upon insult I vowed revenge. You, who so well know the nature of my soul, will not suppose, however, that I gave utterance to a threat. *At length* I would be avenged; this was a point definitely settled—but the very definitiveness with which it was resolved precluded the idea of risk. I must not only punish but punish with impunity. A wrong is unredressed when retribution overtakes its redresser. It is equally unredressed when the avenger fails to make himself felt as such to him who has done the wrong.

It must be understood that neither by word nor deed had I given Fortunato cause to doubt my good will. I continued, as was my wont, to smile in his face, and he did not perceive that my smile *now* was at the thought of his immolation.

He had a weak point—this Fortunato —although in other regards he was a man to be respected and even feared. He prided himself on his connoisseurship in wine. Few Italians have the true virtuoso[1] spirit. For the most part their enthusiasm is adopted to suit the time and opportunity, to practise imposture upon the British and Austrian *millionaires*. In painting and gemmary[2], Fortunato, like his countrymen, was a quack, but in the matter of old wines he was sincere. In this respect I did not differ from him materially;—I was skilful in the Italian vintages myself, and bought largely whenever I could.

It was about dusk, one evening during the supreme madness of the carnival season, that I encountered my friend. He accosted me with excessive warmth, for he had been drinking much. The man wore motley. He had on a tight-fitting parti-striped dress, and his head was surmounted by the conical cap and bells. I was so pleased to see him that I thought I should never have done wringing his hand.

I said to him—"My dear Fortunato, you are luckily met. How remarkably well you are looking today. But I have received a pipe[3] of what passes for Amontillado[4], and I have my doubts."

"How?" said he. "Amontillado? A pipe? Impossible! And in the middle of the carnival!"

"I have my doubts," I replied; "and I was silly enough to pay the full Amontillado price without consulting you in the matter. You were not to be found, and I was fearful of losing a bargain."

"Amontillado!"

"I have my doubts."

"Amontillado!"

"And I must satisfy them."

"Amontillado!"

"As you are engaged, I am on my way to Luchresi. If any one has a critical turn it is he. He will tell me——"

"Luchresi cannot tell Amontillado from Sherry."

"And yet some fools will have it that his taste is a match for your own."

"Come, let us go."

"Whither?"

"To your vaults."

"My friend, no; I will not impose upon your good nature. I perceive you have an engagement. Luchresi—"

[1] A skilled practitioner, an expert.
[2] The science of gems.

[3] A small barrel.
[4] A sweet sherry coming from Montilla, in Spain.

"I have no engagement;—come."

"My friend, no. It is not the engagement, but the severe cold with which I perceive you are afflicted. The vaults are insufferably damp. They are encrusted with nitre."

"Let us go, nevertheless. The cold is merely nothing. Amontillado! You have been imposed upon. And as for Luchresi he cannot distinguish Sherry from Amontillado."

Thus speaking, Fortunato possessed himself of my arm; and putting on a mask of black silk and drawing a *roquelaire*[5] closely about my person, I suffered him to hurry me to my palazzo.

There were no attendants at home; they had absconded to make merry in honour of the time. I had told them that I should not return until the morning, and had given them explicit orders not to stir from the house. These orders were sufficient, I well knew, to insure their immediate disappearance, one and all, as soon as my back was turned.

I took from their sconces two flambeaux[6], and giving one to Fortunato, bowed him through several suites of rooms to the archway that led into the vaults. I passed down a long and winding staircase, requesting him to be cautious as he followed. We came at length to the foot of the descent, and stood together upon the damp ground of the catacombs of the Montresors.

The gait of my friend was unsteady, and the bells upon his cap jingled as he strode.

"The pipe," he said.

"It is farther on," said I; "but observe the white web-work which gleams from these cavern walls."

[5]A cloak.
[6]Torches.

He turned towards me, and looked into my eyes with two filmy orbs that distilled the rheum of intoxication.

"Nitre?" he asked, at length.

"Nitre," I replied. "How long have you had that cough?"

"Ugh! ugh! ugh!—ugh! ugh! ugh!— ugh! ugh! ugh!—ugh! ugh! ugh!—ugh! ugh! ugh!"

My poor friend found it impossible to reply for many minutes.

"It is nothing," he said, at last.

"Come," I said, with decision, "we will go back; your health is precious. You are rich, respected, admired, beloved; you are happy, as once I was. You are a man to be missed. For me it is no matter. We will go back; you will be ill, and I cannot be responsible. Besides, there is Luchresi—"

"Enough," he said; "the cough is a mere nothing; it will not kill me. I shall not die of a cough."

"True—true," I replied; "and, indeed, I had no intention of alarming you unnecessarily—but you should use all proper caution. A draught of this Medoc will defend us from the damps."

Here I knocked off the neck of a bottle which I drew from a long row of its fellows that lay upon the mould.

"Drink," I said, presenting him the wine.

He raised it to his lips with a leer. He paused and nodded to me familiarly, while his bells jingled.

"I drink," he said, "to the buried that repose around us."

"And I to your long life."

He again took my arm, and we proceeded.

"These vaults," he said, "are extensive."

"The Montresors," I replied, "were a great and numerous family."

"I forget your arms."

"A huge human foot d'or, in a field azure; the foot crushes a serpent rampant whose fangs are imbedded in the heel."

"And the motto?"

" 'Nemo me impune lacessit[7].' "

"Good!" he said.

The wine sparkled in his eyes and the bells jingled. My own fancy grew warm with the Medoc. We had passed through long walls of piled skeletons, with casks and puncheons intermingling, into the inmost recesses of the catacombs. I paused again, and this time I made bold to seize Fortunato by an arm above the elbow.

"The nitre!" I said: "see, it increases. It hangs like moss upon the vaults. We are below the river's bed. The drops of moisture trickle among the bones. Come, we will go back ere it is too late. Your cough—"

"It is nothing," he said; "let us go on. But first, another draught of the Medoc."

I broke and reached him a flagon of De Grâve. He emptied it at a breath. His eyes flashed with a fierce light. He laughed and threw the bottle upwards with a gesticulation I did not understand.

I looked at him in surprise. He repeated the movement—a grotesque one.

"You do not comprehend?" he said.

"Not I," I replied.

"Then you are not of the brotherhood."

"How?"

"You are not of the masons."

"Yes, yes," I replied, "yes, yes."

"You? Impossible! A mason?"

"A mason," I replied.

"A sign," he said, "a sign."

"It is this," I answered, producing from beneath the folds of my *roquelaire* a trowel.

[7]"No one can harm me with impunity."

"You jest," he exclaimed, recoiling a few paces. "But let us proceed to the Amontillado."

"Be it so," I said, replacing the tool beneath the cloak and again offering him my arm. He leaned upon it heavily. We continued our route in search of the Amontillado. We passed through a range of low arches, descended, passed on, and descending again, arrived at a deep crypt, in which the foulness of the air caused our flambeaux rather to glow than flame.

At the most remote end of the crypt there appeared another less spacious. Its walls had been lined with human remains, piled to the vault overhead, in the fashion of the great catacombs of Paris. Three sides of this interior crypt were still ornamented in this manner. From the fourth side the bones had been thrown down, and lay promiscuously upon the earth, forming at one point a mound of some size. Within the wall thus exposed by the displacing of the bones, we perceived a still interior crypt or recess, in depth about four feet, in width three, in height six or seven. It seemed to have been constructed for no especial use within itself, but formed merely the interval between two of the colossal supports of the roof of the catacombs, and was backed by one of their circumscribing walls of solid granite.

It was in vain that Fortunato, uplifting his dull torch, endeavoured to pry into the depth of the recess. Its termination the feeble light did not enable us to see.

"Proceed," I said; "herein is the Amontillado. As for Luchresi—"

"He is an ignoramus," interrupted my friend, as he stepped unsteadily forward, while I followed immediately at his heels. In an instant he had reached the extremity of the niche, and finding his progress arrested by the rock, stood stupidly bewildered. A moment more and I had fettered him to the granite. In its surface were two iron staples, distant from each other about two feet, horizontally. From one of these depended a short chain, from the other a padlock. Throwing the links about his waist, it was but the work of a few seconds to secure it. He was too much astounded to resist. Withdrawing the key I stepped back from the recess.

"Pass your hand," I said, "over the wall; you cannot help feeling the nitre. Indeed, it is *very* damp. Once more let me *implore* you to return. No? Then I must positively leave you. But I must first render you all the little attentions in my power."

"The Amontillado!" ejaculated my friend, not yet recovered from his astonishment.

"True," I replied; "the Amontillado."

As I said these words I busied myself among the pile of bones of which I have before spoken. Throwing them aside, I soon uncovered a quantity of building stone and mortar. With these materials and with the aid of my trowel, I began vigorously to wall up the entrance of the niche.

I had scarcely laid the first tier of the masonry when I discovered that the intoxication of Fortunato had in a great measure worn off. The earliest indication I had of this was a low moaning cry from the depth of the recess. It was *not* the cry of a drunken man. There was then a long and obstinate silence. I laid the second tier, and the third, and the fourth; and then I heard the furious vibrations of the chain. The noise lasted for several minutes, during which, that I might hearken to it with the more satisfaction, I ceased my labours and sat down upon the bones.

When at last the clanking subsided, I resumed the trowel, and finished without interruption the fifth, the sixth, and the seventh tier. The wall was now nearly upon a level with my breast. I again paused, and holding the flambeaux over the mason-work, threw a few feeble rays upon the figure within.

A succession of loud and shrill screams, bursting suddenly from the throat of the chained form, seemed to thrust me violently back. For a brief moment I hesitated, I trembled. Unsheathing my rapier, I began to grope with it about the recess; but the thought of an instant reassured me. I placed my hand upon the solid fabric of the catacombs, and felt satisfied. I reapproached the wall; I replied to the yells of him who clamoured. I re-echoed, I aided, I surpassed them in volume and in strength. I did this, and the clamourer grew still.

It was now midnight, and my task was drawing to a close. I had completed the eighth, the ninth, and the tenth tier. I had finished a portion of the last and the eleventh; there remained but a single stone to be fitted and plastered in. I struggled with its weight; I placed it partially in its destined position. But now there came from out the niche a low laugh that erected the hairs up on my head. It was succeeded by a sad voice, which I had difficulty in recognizing as that of the noble Fortunato. The voice said—

"Ha! ha! ha!—he! he! he!—a very good joke, indeed—an excellent jest. We will have many a rich laugh about it at the palazzo—he! he! he!—over our wine —he! he! he!"

"The Amontillado!" I said.

"He! he! he!—he!—he! he!—yes, the Amontillado. But is it not getting late?

Will not they be awaiting us at the palazzo, the Lady Fortunato and the rest? Let us be gone."

"Yes," I said, "let us be gone."

"For the love of God, Montresor!"

"Yes," I said, "for the love of God!"

But to these words I hearkened in vain for a reply. I grew impatient. I called aloud—

"Fortunato!"

No answer. I called again—

"Fortunato!"

No answer still. I thrust a torch through the remaining aperture and let it fall within. There came forth in return only a jingling of the bells. My heart grew sick; it was the dampness of the catacombs that made it so. I hastened to make an end of my labour. I forced the last stone into its position; I plastered it up. Against the new masonry I re-erected the old rampart of bones. For the half of a century no mortal has disturbed them. *In pace requiescat*[8]!

1846

[8] "May he rest in peace!"

HENRY DAVID THOREAU (1817-1862)

Thoreau embodied all that is finest in American civilization: its individualism, its devotion to liberty, its idealism, its sturdy common sense. And whereas Emerson preached the doctrines of Transcendentalism, Thoreau tested them in practice: he went to live in a hut at Walden Pond to prove that solitude and communion with Nature do bring spiritual insight; he refused to pay his poll tax to a government that sanctioned war and slavery; he reduced his material goods and needs to a minimum and lived instead a life rich in spiritual values.

Thoreau was born at Concord, Mass., and educated at Harvard. After graduation, he began an association with Emerson that lasted throughout his life. Like Emerson, he made his career that of a public lecturer, delivering his first lecture at Concord in 1838. In March of 1845 he retired to Walden Pond, where he lived until September 6, 1847. It was during this period that he spent a night in jail for refusing to pay his taxes. He made several expeditions into the Maine woods, and in 1850 visited Canada, but unlike his friend Emerson he never went to Europe. His masterpiece, *Walden*, was published in 1854. His health began to fail in the following year, but in spite of that he took a prominent part in the agitation to end slavery in the South. He died in 1862, at the age of forty-five.

Thoreau's prose is a remarkably economical and lucid expression of his liberal principles. His words are a fascinating mixture of the homely and the learned, his phrases are neat and pungent, his sentences condensed and firmly built. Of his poems, he himself said that they were "of a homespun kind, well-woven, but indifferently cut." They are plain, not very musical, but packed with detailed observation and moral insight.

FROM # Walden

. . . When first I took up my abode in the woods, that is, began to spend my nights as well as days there, which, by accident, was on Independence Day, or the Fourth of July, 1845, my house was not finished for winter, but was merely a defence against the rain, without plastering or chimney, the walls being of rough, weatherstained boards, with wide chinks, which made it cool at night. The upright white hewn studs and freshly planed door and window casings gave it a clean and airy look, especially in the morning, when its timbers were saturated with dew, so that I fancied that by noon some sweet gum would exude from them. To my imagination it retained throughout the day more or less of this auroral character, reminding me of a certain house on a mountain which I had visited a year before. This was an airy and unplastered cabin, fit to entertain a travelling god, and where a goddess might trail her garments. The winds which passed over my dwelling were such as sweep over the ridges of mountains, bearing the broken strains, or celestial parts only, of terrestrial music. The morning wind forever blows, the poem of creation is uninterrupted: but few are the ears that hear it. Olympus is but the outside of the earth everywhere.

The only house I had been the owner of before, if I except a boat, was a tent, which I used occasionally when making excursions in the summer, and this is still rolled up in my garret; but the boat, after passing from hand to hand, has gone down the stream of time. With this more substantial shelter about me, I had made some progress toward settling in the world. This frame, so slightly clad, was a sort of crystallization around me, and reacted on the builder. It was suggestive somewhat as a picture in outlines. I did not need to go outdoors to take the air, for the atmosphere within had lost none of its freshness. It was not so much within-doors as behind a door where I sat, even in the rainiest weather. The Harivansa[1] says, "An abode without birds is like a meat without seasoning." Such was not my abode, for I found myself suddenly neighbour to the birds; not by having imprisoned one, but having caged myself near them. I was not only nearer to some of those which commonly frequent

[1] A Sanskrit epic poem of the fifth century A.D. Thoreau and Emerson were both interested in Eastern and Near Eastern religious literature.

the garden and the orchard, but to those wilder and more thrilling songsters of the forest which never, or rarely, serenade a villager,—the wood thrush, the veery, the scarlet tanager, the field sparrow, the whip-poor-will, and many others.

I was seated by the shore of a small pond, about a mile and a half south of the village of Concord and somewhat higher than it, in the midst of an extensive wood between that town and Lincoln, and about two miles south of that our only field known to fame, Concord Battle Ground; but I was so low in the woods that the opposite shore, half a mile off, like the rest, covered with wood, was my most distant horizon. For the first week, whenever I looked out on the pond it impressed me like a tarn high upon the side of a mountain, its bottom far above the surface of other lakes, and, as the sun arose, I saw it throwing off its nightly clothing of mist, and here and there, by degrees, its soft ripples or its smooth reflecting surface was revealed, while the mists, like ghosts, were stealthily withdrawing in every direction into the woods, as at the breaking up of some nocturnal conventicle. The very dew seemed to hang upon the trees later into the day than usual, as on the sides of mountains.

This small lake was of most value as a neighbour in the intervals of a gentle rain-storm in August, when, both air and water being perfectly still, but the sky overcast, mid-afternoon had all the serenity of evening, and the wood thrush sang around, and was heard from shore to shore. A lake like this is never smoother than at such a time; and the clear portion of the air above it being shallow and darkened by clouds, the water, full of light and reflections, becomes a lower heaven itself so much the more important.

From a hill-top near by, where the wood had been recently cut off, there was a pleasing vista southward across the pond, through a wide indentation in the hills which form the shore there, where their opposite sides sloping toward each other suggested a stream flowing out in that direction through a wooded valley, but stream there was none. That way I looked between and over the near green hills to some distant and higher ones on the horizon, tinged with blue. Indeed, by standing on tiptoe I could catch a glimpse of some of the peaks of the still bluer and more distant mountain ranges in the northwest, those true-blue coins from heaven's own mint, and also of some portion of the village. But in other directions, even from this point, I could not see over or beyond the woods which surrounded me. It is well to have some water in your neighbourhood, to give buoyancy to and float the earth. One value even of the smallest well is that when you look into it you see that the earth is not continent but insular. This is as important as that it keeps butter cool. When I looked across the pond from this peak toward the Sudbury meadows, which in time of flood I distinguished elevated perhaps by a mirage in their seething valley, like a coin in a basin, all the earth beyond the pond appeared like a thin crust insulated and floated even by this small sheet of intervening water, and I was reminded that this on which I dwelt was but *dry land*.

Though the view from my door was still more contracted, I did not feel crowded or confined in the least. There was pasture enough for my imagination. The low shrub oak plateau to which the opposite shore arose stretched away toward the prairies of the West and the steppes of Tartary, affording ample room for all the roving families of men. "There are none happy in the world but beings who enjoy freely a vast horizon," said Damodara[2], when his herds required new and larger pastures.

Both place and time were changed, and I dwelt nearer to those parts of the universe and to those eras in history which had most attracted me. Where I lived was as far off as many a region viewed nightly by astronomers. We are wont to imagine rare and delectable places in some remote and more celestial corner of the system, behind the constellation of Cassiopeia's Chair, far from noise and disturbance. I discovered that my house actually had its site in such a withdrawn, but forever new and unprofaned, part of the universe. If it were worth the while to settle in those parts near to the Pleiades or the Hyades[3], to Aldebaran or Altair[4], then I was really there, or at an equal remoteness from the life which I had left behind, dwindled and twinkling with as fine a ray to my nearest neighbour, and to be seen only in moonless nights by him. Such was that part of creation where I had squatted;

There was a shepherd that did live,
  And held his thoughts as high
As where the mounts whereon his flocks
  Did hourly feed him by.

What should we think of the shepherd's life if his flocks always wandered to higher pastures than his thoughts?

Every morning was a cheerful invitation to make my life of equal simplicity, and I may say innocence, with Nature herself. I have been as sincere a worshipper of Aurora[5] as the Greeks. I got

[2]The Hindu divinity, Krishna.
[3]*Pleiades, Hyades*, constellations.
[4]*Aldebaran, Altair*, bright stars.
[5]The Greek goddess of dawn.

up early and bathed in the pond; that was a religious exercise, and one of the best things which I did. They say that characters were engraven on the bathing tub of King Tching-thang to this effect: "Renew thyself completely each day; do it again, and again, and forever again." I can understand that. Morning brings back the heroic ages. I was as much affected by the faint hum of a mosquito making its invisible and unimaginable tour through my apartment at earliest dawn, when I was sitting with door and windows open, as I could be by any trumpet that ever sang of fame. It was Homer's requiem; itself an Iliad and Odyssey in the air, singing its own wrath and wanderings. There was something cosmical about it; a standing advertisement, till forbidden, of the everlasting vigor and fertility of the word. The morning, which is the most memorable season of the day, is the awakening hour. Then there is least somnolence in us: and for an hour, at least, some part of us awakes which slumbers all the rest of the day and night. Little is to be expected of that day, if it can be called a day, to which we are not awakened by our Genius, but by the mechanical nudgings of some servitor, are not awakened by our own newly acquired force and aspirations from within, accompanied by the undulations of celestial music, filling the air—to a higher life than we fell asleep from; and thus the darkness bear its fruit, and prove itself to be good, no less than the light. That man who does not believe that each day contains an earlier, more sacred, and auroral hour than he has yet profaned, has despaired of life, and is pursuing a descending and darkening way. After a partial cessation of his sensuous life, the soul of man, or its organs rather, are reinvigorated each day, and his Genius tries again what noble life it can make. All memorable events, I should say, transpire in morning time and in a morning atmosphere. The Vedas[6] say, "All intelligences awake with the morning." Poetry and art, and the fairest and most memorable of the actions of men, date from such an hour. All poets and heroes, like Memnon[7], are the children of Aurora, and emit their music at sunrise. To him whose elastic and vigorous thought keeps pace with the sun, the day is a perpetual morning. It matters not what the clocks say or the attitudes and labours of men. Morning is when I am awake and there is a dawn in me. Moral reform is the effort to throw off sleep. Why is it that men give so poor an account of their day if they have not been slumbering? They are not such poor calculators. If they had not been overcome with drowsiness, they would have performed something. The millions are awake enough for physical labour; but only one in a million is awake enough for effective intellectual exertion, only one in a hundred millions to a poetic or divine life. To be awake is to be alive. I have never yet met a man who was quite awake. How could I have looked him in the face?

We must learn to reawaken and keep ourselves awake, not by mechanical aids, but by an infinite expectation of the dawn, which does not forsake us in our soundest sleep. I know of no more encouraging fact than the unquestionable ability of man to elevate his life by a conscious endeavour. It is something to be able to paint a particular picture, or to carve a statue, and so to make a few objects

[6] The sacred literature of the Hindus.
[7] Son of Aurora; his statue is reputed to emit a harp-like sound at sunrise.

beautiful; but it is far more glorious to carve and paint the very atmosphere and medium through which we look, which morally we can do. To affect the quality of the day, that is the highest of arts. Every man is tasked to make his life, even in its details, worthy of the contemplation of his most elevated and critical hour. If we refused, or rather used up, such paltry information as we get, the oracles would distinctly inform us how this might be done.

I went to the woods because I wished to live deliberately, to front only the essential facts of life, and see if I could not learn what it had to teach, and not, when I came to die, discover that I had not lived. I did not wish to live what was not life, living is so dear; nor did I wish to practise resignation, unless it was quite necessary. I wanted to live deep and suck out all the marrow of life, to live so sturdily and Spartan-like as to put to rout all that was not life, to cut a broad swath and shave close, to drive life into a corner, and reduce it to its lowest terms, and, if it proved to be mean, why then to get the whole and genuine meanness of it, and publish its meanness to the world; or if it were sublime, to know it by experience, and be able to give a true account of it in my next excursion. For most men, it appears to me, are in a strange uncertainty about it, whether it is of the devil or of God, and have *somewhat hastily* concluded that it is the chief end of man here to "glorify God and enjoy him forever." . . .

1854

WALT WHITMAN (1819-1892)

Whitman was in many respects the embodiment of the ideal American poet whom Emerson had envisioned in his essay "The Poet": one who addressed himself directly to the life about him, celebrated the regions and occupations of America, and used the stuff of American speech. Whitman recognized his debt to Emerson, and said "I was simmering, simmering, simmering; Emerson brought me to a boil." Both Whitman and Emerson loved America, were champions of individual liberty, and regarded the poet as prophet. But Whitman was more earthy than Emerson: there is a joy in physical life and love in Whitman's writings that makes Emerson's seem pallid and desiccated in comparison. In rolling chants that resemble the psalms of the Bible rather than the orthodox metres of English poetry, Whitman celebrates life in all its aspects: labour and laziness, sensuality and mysticism, lonely contemplation and group excitement.

Whitman was born of a poor Quaker family on a farm on Long Island. He began to earn his own living at the age of eleven, and was successively an office boy, a school teacher, and a newspaper reporter and editor. His first published work was a temperance tract in the form of a novel: *Franklin Evans* (1842). In 1855 he published the first edition of his verse masterpiece, *Leaves of Grass*, the title of which symbolized his belief in growth, equality, freedom, and hope. The book was ridiculed by most critics, largely ignored by the general public, but hailed with enthusiasm by Emerson. Emerson's view prevailed: the book had gone through eight editions by 1882 and has been in steady demand ever since. During the American Civil War, Whitman served as a volunteer nurse in an army hospital in Washington, and remained there after the war as a civil servant. He suffered the first of a series of paralytic strokes in 1873, and died in 1892.

Critical opinion is still sharply divided about the merits of Whitman's verse. Some critics dismiss him as a barbarian; others claim that in his sense of cosmic unity he is fit to set beside Dante and Shakespeare.

Song of Myself

I celebrate myself, and sing myself,
And what I assume you shall assume,
For every atom belonging to me as good belongs to you.

I loafe and invite my soul,
I lean and loafe at my ease observing a spear of summer grass.

My tongue, every atom of my blood, form'd from this soil, this air,
Born here of parents born here from parents the same, and their parents the same,
I, now thirty-seven years old in perfect health begin,
Hoping to cease not till death.

Creeds and schools in abeyance,   10
Retiring back a while sufficed at what they are, but never forgotten,
I harbor for good or bad, I permit to speak at every hazard,
Nature without check with original energy . . .

A child said *What is the grass?* fetching it to me with full hands;
How could I answer the child? I do not know what it is any more than he.

I guess it must be the flag of my disposition, out of hopeful green stuff woven.

Or I guess it is the handkerchief of the Lord,
A scented gift and remembrancer designedly dropt,
Bearing the owner's name someway in the corners, that we may see and remark, and
     say *Whose?*

Or I guess the grass is itself a child, the produced babe of the vegetation.   20

Or I guess it is a uniform hieroglyphic,
And it means, Sprouting alike in broad zones and narrow zones,
Growing among black folks as among white,
Kanuck, Tuckahoe, Congressman, Cuff, I give them the same, I receive them the
     same.

And now it seems to me the beautiful uncut hair of graves.

Tenderly will I use you curling grass,
It may be you transpire from the breasts of young men,
It may be if I had known them I would have loved them,
It may be you are from old people, or from offspring taken soon out of their mothers'
     laps,
And here you are the mothers' laps.   30

This grass is very dark to be from the white heads of old mothers,
Darker than the colorless beards of old men,
Dark to come from under the faint red roofs of mouths.

O I perceive after all so many uttering tongues,
And I perceive they do not come from the roofs of mouths for nothing.
I wish I could translate the hints about the dead young men and women,
And the hints about old men and mothers, and the offspring taken soon out of their
    laps.

What do you think has become of the young and old men?
And what do you think has become of the women and children?

They are alive and well somewhere,   40
The smallest sprout shows there is really no death,
And if ever there was it led forward life, and does not wait at the end to arrest it,
And ceas'd the moment life appear'd.

All goes onward and outward, nothing collapses,
And to die is different from what any one supposed, and luckier. . . .

                                                                1855

Pioneers! O Pioneers!

                Come my tan-faced children,
Follow well in order, get your weapons ready,
Have you your pistols? have you your sharp-edged axes?
                Pioneers! O pioneers!

                For we cannot tarry here,
We must march my darlings, we must bear the brunt of danger,
We the youthful sinewy races, all the rest on us depend,
                Pioneers! O pioneers!

                O you youths, Western youths,
So impatient, full of action, full of manly pride and friendship,   10
Plain I see you Western youths, see you tramping with the foremost,
                Pioneers! O pioneers!

                Have the elder races halted?
Do they droop and end their lesson, wearied over there beyond the seas?
We take up the task eternal, and the burden and the lesson,
                Pioneers! O pioneers!

All the past we leave behind,
We debouch upon a newer mightier world, varied world,
Fresh and strong the world we seize, world of labour and the march,
    Pioneers! O pioneers! 20

    We detachments steady throwing,
Down the edges, through the passes, up the mountains steep,
Conquering, holding, daring, venturing as we go the unknown ways,
    Pioneers! O pioneers!

    We primeval forests felling,
We the rivers stemming, vexing we and piercing deep the mines within,
We the surface broad surveying, we the virgin soil upheaving,
    Pioneers! O pioneers!

    Colorado men are we,
From the peaks gigantic, from the great sierras and the high plateaus, 30
From the mine and from the gully, from the hunting trail we come,
    Pioneers! O pioneers!

    From Nebraska, from Arkansas,
Central inland race are we, from Missouri, with the continental blood intervein'd,
All the hands of comrades clasping, all the Southern, all the Northern,
    Pioneers! O pioneers!

    O resistless restless race!
O beloved race in all! O my breast aches with tender love for all!
O I mourn and yet exult, I am rapt with love for all,
    Pioneers! O pioneers! 40

    Raise the mighty mother mistress,
Waving high the delicate mistress, over all the starry mistress, (bend your heads all,)
Raise the fang'd and warlike mistress, stern, impassive, weapon'd mistress,
    Pioneers! O pioneers!

    See my children, resolute children,
By those swarms upon our rear we must never yield or falter,
Ages back in ghostly millions frowning there behind us urging,
    Pioneers! O pioneers!

    On and on the compact ranks,
With accessions ever waiting, with the places of the dead quickly fill'd, 50
Through the battle, through defeat, moving yet and never stopping,
    Pioneers! O pioneers!

O to die advancing on!
Are there some of us to droop and die? has the hour come?
Then upon the march we fittest die, soon and sure the gap is fill'd,
    Pioneers! O pioneers!

All the pulses of the world,
Falling in they beat for us, with the Western movement beat,
Holding single or together, steady moving to the front, all for us,
    Pioneers! O pioneers!   60

Life's involv'd and varied pageants,
All the forms and shows, all the workmen at their work,
All the seamen and the landsmen, all the masters with their slaves,
    Pioneers! O pioneers!

All the hapless silent lovers,
All the prisoners in the prisons, all the righteous and the wicked,
All the joyous, all the sorrowing, all the living, all the dying,
    Pioneers! O pioneers!

I too with my soul and body,
We, a curious trio, picking, wandering on our way,   70
Through these shores amid the shadows, with the apparitions pressing,
    Pioneers! O pioneers!

Lo, the darting bowling orb!
Lo, the brother orbs around, all the clustering suns and planets,
All the dazzling days, all the mystic nights with dreams,
    Pioneers! O pioneers!

These are of us, they are with us,
All for primal needed work, while the followers there in embryo wait behind,
We to-day's procession heading, we the route for travel clearing,
    Pioneers! O pioneers!   80

O you daughters of the West!
O you young and elder daughters! O you mothers and you wives!
Never must you be divided, in our ranks you move united,
    Pioneers! O pioneers!

Minstrels latent on the prairies!
(Shrouded bards of other lands, you may rest, you have done your work),
Soon I hear you coming warbling, soon you rise and tramp amid us,
    Pioneers! O pioneers!

Not for delectations sweet,
Not the cushion and the slipper, not the peaceful and the studious,   90
Not the riches safe and palling, not for us the tame enjoyment,
    Pioneers! O pioneers!

Do the feasters gluttonous feast?
Do the corpulent sleepers sleep? Have they lock'd and bolted doors?
Still be ours the diet hard, and the blanket on the ground,
        Pioneers! O pioneers!

Has the night descended?
Was the road of late so toilsome? did we stop discouraged nodding on our way?
Yet a passing hour I yield you in your tracks to pause oblivious,
        Pioneers! O pioneers!   100

Till with sound of trumpet,
Far, far off the daybreak call—hark! how loud and clear I hear it wind,
Swift! to the head of the army!—swift! spring to your places,
        Pioneers! O pioneers!

           1865

O Captain! My Captain![1]

O Captain! my Captain! our fearful trip is done,
The ship has weather'd every rack, the prize we sought is won,
The port is near, the bells I hear, the people all exulting,
While follow eyes the steady keel, the vessel grim and daring;
    But O heart! heart! heart!
    O the bleeding drops of red,
      Where on the deck my Captain lies,
      Fallen cold and dead.

O Captain! my Captain! rise up and hear the bells;
Rise up—for you the flag is flung—for you the bugle trills,   10
For you bouquets and ribbon'd wreaths—for you the shores a-crowding,
For you they call, the swaying mass, their eager faces turning;
    Here Captain! dear father!
    This arm beneath your head!
      It is some dream that on the deck,
      You've fallen cold and dead.

My Captain does not answer, his lips are pale and still,
My father does not feel my arm, he has no pulse nor will,
The ship is anchor'd safe and sound, its voyage closed and done,
From fearful trip the victor ship comes in with object won;   20
    Exult O shores, and ring O bells!
    But I with mournful tread,
      Walk the deck my Captain lies,
      Fallen cold and dead.

           1865

[1]This poem is an elegy to Abraham Lincoln, whom Whitman greatly admired.

EMILY DICKINSON (1830-1886)

Although Walt Whitman and Emily Dickinson were contemporaries, and although they have in common the fact that they were once disdained and are now world-famous, their poetry was very different. Whitman was an expansive optimist in his verse, who celebrated his new country in long sweeping lines; Emily Dickinson was a shy introvert who dealt primarily with her own moods and mystical insights in short, chiselled lyrics. Rather than rushing us along on a tide of enthusiastic rhetoric, her poems invite us to stop and think about the quiet secrets of the human heart and about the complexity of apparently simple things.

Emily Dickinson was born on December 10, 1830, in Amherst, Massachusetts, the daughter of a lawyer who was also the treasurer of Amherst College. She had little schooling outside her own home, and much of her life was spent in caring for her invalid mother; during the last twenty years of her life she never left the family house and garden. Dickinson's chief contact with the outside world came through letters: she was a voluminous correspondent, and her letters are witty, frank, and acutely perceptive. She began to write poetry in her early twenties, but she made no effort to publish her poems, and it was not until four years after her death in 1886 that the first book of her poems appeared. This book was made possible by her sister Lavinia, who after Dickinson's death found the manuscripts in her room: poems scribbled on scraps of paper, newspaper margins, the backs of envelopes, nearly all with corrections and alternative readings. The first book was followed by several others, and by the beginning of World War I Dickinson was recognized as one of the best poets America had produced.

I Taste a Liquor Never Brewed

I taste a liquor never brewed—
From Tankards scooped in Pearl—
Not all the Frankfort Berries
Yield such an Alcohol!

Inebriate of Air—am I—
And Debauchee of Dew—
Reeling—through endless summer days—
From inns of Molten Blue—

When "Landlords" turn the drunken bee
Out of the Foxglove's door—
When Butterflies—renounce their
        "drams"—
I shall but drink the more!

Till Seraphs swing their snowy Hats—
And Saints—to windows run—
To see the little Tippler
From Manzanilla come!

1860   1861

After Great Pain, a Formal Feeling Comes

After great pain, a formal feeling comes—
The Nerves sit ceremonious, like Tombs—
The stiff Heart questions was it He, that
        bore,
And Yesterday, or Centuries before?

The Feet, mechanical, go round—
A Wooden way
Of Ground, or Air, or Ought—
Regardless grown,
A Quartz contentment, like a stone—

This is the Hour of Lead—
Remembered, if outlived,
As Freezing persons, recollect the Snow—
First—Chill—then Stupor—then the
        letting go—

1862   1929

"Heaven"—Is What I Cannot Reach!

"Heaven"—is what I cannot reach!
The Apple on the Tree—
Provided it do hopeless—hang—
That—"Heaven" is—to Me!

The Colour, on the Cruising Cloud—
The interdicted Land—
Behind the Hill—the House behind—
There—Paradise—is found!

Her teazing Purples—Afternoons—
The credulous—decoy—
Enamoured—of the Conjuror—
That spurned us—Yesterday!

1861   1896

There's Been a Death, in the Opposite House

There's been a Death, in the Opposite
      House,
As lately as Today—
I know it, by the numb look
Such Houses have—alway—

The Neighbours rustle in and out—
The Doctor—drives away—
A Window opens like a Pod—
Abrupt—mechanically—

Somebody flings a Mattress out—
The Children hurry by—
They wonder if it died—on that—
I used to—when a Boy—

The Minister—goes stiffly in—
As if the House were His—
And He owned all the Mourners—now—
And little Boys—besides

And then the Milliner—and the Man
Of the Appalling Trade—
To take the measure of the House—
There'll be that Dark Parade—

Of Tassels—and of Coaches—soon—
It's easy as a Sign—
The Intuition of the News—
In just a Country Town—

1862   1896

This Is My Letter to the World

This is my letter to the World
That never wrote to Me—
The simple News that Nature told—
With tender Majesty

Her Message is committed
To Hands I cannot see—
For love of Her—Sweet—countrymen—
Judge tenderly—of Me

1862   1890

I Like to See It Lap the Miles

I like to see it lap the Miles—
And lick the Valleys up—
And stop to feed itself at Tanks—
And then—prodigious step

Around a Pile of Mountains—
And supercilious peer
In Shanties—by the sides of Roads—
And then a Quarry pare

To fit its ribs and crawl between
Complaining all the while
In horrid—hooting stanza—
Then chase itself down Hill—

And neigh like Boanerges—
Then—prompter than a Star
Stop—docile and omnipotent
At its own stable door—

1862   1891

Because I Could Not Stop for Death

Because I could not stop for Death—
He kindly stopped for me—
The Carriage held but just Ourselves—
And Immortality.

We slowly drove—He knew no haste
And I had put away
My labour and my leisure too,
For His Civility—

We passed the School, where Children
strove
At Recess—in the Ring—
We passed the Fields of Gazing Grain—
We passed the Setting Sun—

Or rather—He passed Us—
The Dews drew quivering and chill—
For only Gossamer, my Gown—
My Tippet—only Tulle—

We paused before a House that seemed
A Swelling of the Ground—
The Roof was scarcely visible—
The Cornice—in the Ground—

Since then—'tis Centuries—and yet
Feels shorter than the Day
I first surmised the Horses Heads
Were toward Eternity—
1863   1890

I Never Saw a Moor

I never saw a Moor—
I never saw the Sea—
Yet know I how the Heather looks
And what a Billow be.

I never spoke with God
Nor visited in Heaven—
Yet certain am I of the spot
As if the Checks were given—
1865   1890

The Wind Begun to Knead the Grass

The Wind begun to knead the Grass—
As Women do a Dough—
He flung a Hand full at the Plain—
A Hand full at the Sky—
The Leaves unhooked themselves from
Trees—
And started all abroad—
The Dust did scoop itself like Hands—
And throw away the Road—
The Wagons quickened on the Street—
The Thunders gossiped low—
The Lightning showed a Yellow Head—
And then a livid Toe—
The Birds put up the Bars to Nests—
The Cattle flung to Barns—
Then came one drop of Giant Rain—
And then, as if the Hands
That held the Dams—had parted hold—
The Waters Wrecked the Sky—
But overlooked my Father's House—
Just Quartering a Tree—
1864   1891

The Brain—Is Wider Than the Sky

The Brain—is wider than the Sky—
For—put them side by side—
The one the other will contain
With ease—and You—beside—

The Brain is deeper than the sea—
For—hold them—Blue to Blue—
The one the other will absorb—
As Sponges—Buckets—do

The Brain is just the weight of God—
For—Heft them—Pound for Pound—
And they will differ—if they do—
As Syllable from Sound—
1862   1896

There Is No Frigate Like a Book

There is no Frigate like a Book
To take us Lands away
Nor any Coursers like a Page
Of prancing Poetry—
This Travel may the poorest take
Without offence of Toll—
How frugal is the Chariot
That bears the Human soul.

1873   1894

How Happy Is the Little Stone

How happy is the little Stone
That rambles in the Road alone,
And doesn't care about Careers
And Exigencies never fears—
Whose Coat of elemental Brown
A passing Universe put on,
And independent as the Sun
Associates or glows alone,
Fulfilling absolute Decree
In casual simplicity—

1882   1891

My Life Closed Twice Before Its Close

My life closed twice before its close;
It yet remains to see
If Immortality unveil
A third event to me,

So huge, so hopeless to conceive
As these that twice befell.
Parting is all we know of heaven,
And all we need of hell.   1896

MARK TWAIN (1835-1910)

Of Mark Twain, the greatest American humourist, Stephen Leacock, the greatest Canadian humourist, wrote: "If Mark Twain did not create American humour, he at least took it over and made something of it. He did for it what Shakespeare did for the English drama, and what Milton did for hell. He 'put it on the map.' He shaped it into a form of thought, a way of looking at things, and hence a mode or kind of literature." And it is as the father of a distinctive American humour, and the creator of such unforgettable characters as Tom Sawyer and Huck Finn, that Twain has won his place in the hearts of millions. There was, however, another aspect to Twain's personality: he was passionately devoted to peace and liberty, he had intense religious doubts, and in his later years he became very disillusioned with the human race because of its wars, greed, and intolerance.

"Mark Twain" was a pseudonym for Samuel Langhorne Clemens. He was born of a poor pioneer family in Florida, Missouri, grew up at Hannibal on the bank of the Mississippi, and began work at an early age in a printing shop. For a few years he was a river pilot, then went out west to the pioneer territory of Nevada where he became a journalist in the frontier mining town of Virginia City. It was as a journalist in San Francisco in the eighteen-sixties that he began to attract national attention; and the basis of his literary reputation was laid in 1865 with the publication of *Jim Smiley and His Jumping Frog*. Within a few years the publication of *The Innocents Abroad* (1869), *The Adventures of Tom Sawyer* (1876), and *Huckleberry Finn* (1885) made him an international celebrity. His books sold well, and he was much in demand as a lecturer, but rash investments brought him to bankruptcy in 1894. His last years were also saddened by the illnesses of his two daughters. He died in 1910.

Twain was the great literary representative of the American frontier—unconventional, profane, realistic, boisterous, democratic, touched with crudity and coarseness but basically tender-hearted. His easy colloquial style is the fitting garment of his thought.

The Celebrated Jumping Frog of Calaveras County

In compliance with the request of a friend of mine, who wrote me from the East, I called on good-natured, garrulous old Simon Wheeler, and inquired after my friend's friend, *Leonidas W. Smiley*, as requested to do, and I hereunto append the result. I have a lurking suspicion that *Leonidas W. Smiley* is a myth; that my friend never knew such a personage; and that he only conjectured that, if I asked old Wheeler about him, it would remind him of his infamous *Jim Smiley*, and he would go to work and bore me nearly to death with some infernal reminiscence of him as long and tedious as it should be useless to me. If that was the design, it certainly succeeded.

I found Simon Wheeler dozing comfortably by the bar-room stove of the old, dilapidated tavern in the ancient mining camp of Angel's, and I noticed that he was fat and bald-headed, and had an expression of winning gentleness and simplicity upon his tranquil countenance. He roused up and gave me good-day. I told him a friend of mine had commissioned me to make some inquiries about a cherished companion of his boyhood named *Leonidas W. Smiley—Rev. Leonidas W. Smiley*—a young minister of the Gospel, who he had heard was at one time a resident of Angel's Camp. I added that if Mr. Wheeler could tell me anything about this Rev. Leonidas W. Smiley, I would feel under many obligations to him.

Simon Wheeler backed me into a corner and blockaded me there with his chair, and then sat me down and reeled off the monotonous narrative which follows this paragraph. He never smiled, he never frowned, he never changed his voice from the gentle-flowing key to which he tuned the slightest suspicion of enthusiasm; but all through the interminable narrative there ran a vein of impressive earnestness and sincerity, which showed me plainly that, so far from his imagining that there was anything ridiculous or funny about his story, he regarded it as a really important matter, and admired its two heroes as men of transcendent genius in *finesse*. To me, the spectacle of a man drifting serenely along through such a queer yarn without ever smiling, was exquisitely absurd. As I said before, I asked him to tell me what he knew of Rev. Leonidas W. Smiley, and he replied as follows. I let him go on in his own way, and never interrupted him once:

There was a feller here once by the name of *Jim* Smiley, in the winter of '49 —or may be it was in the spring of '50—I don't recollect exactly, somehow, though what makes me think it was one or the other is because I remember the big flume wasn't finished when he first came to the camp; but any way, he was the curiosest man about always betting on any thing that turned up you ever see, if he could get any body to bet on the other side; and if he couldn't, he'd change sides. Any way that suited the other man would suit him—any way just so's he got a bet, *he* was satisfied. But still he was lucky; uncommon lucky; he most always come out winner. He was always ready and laying for a chance; there couldn't be no solitary thing mentioned but that feller'd offer to bet on it, and take any side you please, as I was just telling you. If there was a horserace, you'd find him flush, or you'd find him busted at the end of it; if there was a dogfight, he'd bet on it; if there was a catfight, he'd bet on it; if there was a chicken-fight, he'd bet on it; why, if there was two birds setting on a fence, he would bet you which one would fly first; or if there was a camp-meeting, he would be there reg'lar, to bet on Parson Walker, which he judged to be the best exhorter about there, and so he was, too, and a good man. If he ever seen a straddle-bug start to go anywheres, he would bet you how long it would take him to get wherever he was going to, and if you took him up, he would follow that straddle-bug to Mexico but what he would find out where he was bound for and how long he was on the road. Lots of the boys here has seen that Smiley, and can tell you about him. Why, it never made no difference to *him*—he would bet on *any* thing—the dangdest feller. Parson Walker's wife laid very sick once, for a good while, and it seemed as if they warn't going to save her; but one morning he come in, and Smiley asked how she was, and he said she was considerable better—thank the Lord for his inf'nit mercy—and coming on so smart that, with the blessing of Prov'dence she'd get well yet; and Smiley, before he thought, says, "Well, I'll risk two-and-a-half that she won't any way."

Thish-yer Smiley had a mare—the boys called her the fifteen-minute nag but that was only in fun, you know, because, of course, she was faster than that—and he used to win money on that horse, for all she was so slow and always had the asthma, or the distemper, or the consumption, or something of that kind. They used to give her two or three hundred yards start, and then pass her under way; but always at the fag-end of the race she'd get excited and desperate-like, and come cavorting and straddling up, and scattering her legs around limber, sometimes in the air, and sometimes out to one side amongst the fences, and kicking up m-o-r-e dust, and raising m-o-r-e racket with her coughing and sneezing and blowing her nose—and always fetch up at the stand just about a neck ahead, as near as you could cypher it down.

And he had a little small bull pup, that to look at him you'd think he wa'n't worth a cent, but to set around and look ornery, and lay for a chance to steal something. But as soon as money was up on him, he was a different dog; his under-jaw'd begin to stick out like the fo'castle of a steamboat, and his teeth would uncover, and shine savage like the furnaces. And a dog might tackle him, and bully-rag him, and bite him, and throw him over his shoulder two or three times, and Andrew Jackson—which was the name of the pup—Andrew Jackson would never let on but what *he* was satisfied, and hadn't expected nothing else—and the bets being doubled and doubled on the other side all the time, till the money was all up; and then all of a sudden he would grab that other dog jest by the j'int of his hind leg and freeze to it—not chaw, you understand, but only jest grip and hang on till they throwed up the sponge, if it was a year. Smiley always come out winner on that pup, till he harnessed a dog once that didn't have no hind legs, because they'd been sawed off by a circular saw, and when the thing had gone along far enough, and the money was all up, and he come to make a snatch for his pet holt, he saw in a minute how he'd been imposed on, and how the other dog had him in the door, so to speak, and he 'peard surprised, and then looked sorter discouraged-like, and didn't try no more to win the fight, and so he got shucked out bad. He give Smiley a look, as much as to say his heart was broke, and it was *his* fault, for putting up a dog that hadn't no hind legs for him to take holt of, which was his main dependence in a fight, and then he limped off a piece and laid down and died. It was a good pup, was that Andrew Jackson, and would have made a name for hisself if he'd lived, for the stuff was in him, and he had genius—I know it, because he hadn't had no opportunity to speak of, and it don't stand to reason that a dog could make such a fight as he could under them circumstances, if he hadn't no talent. It always makes me feel sorry when I think of that last fight of his'n, and the way it turned out.

Well, thish-yer Smiley had rat-terriers, and chicken cocks, and tom-cats, and all them kind of things, till you couldn't rest, and you couldn't fetch nothing for him to bet on but he'd match you. He ketched a frog one day, and took him home, and said he cal'klated to edercate him; and so he never done nothing for three months but set in his back yard and learn that frog to jump. And you bet he *did* learn him, too. He'd give him a little punch behind, and the next minute you'd see that frog whirling in the air like a doughnut—see him turn one summerset, or may be a couple, if he got a good start, and come down flat-footed and all right, like a cat. He got him up so in the matter of catching flies, and kept him in practice so constant, that he'd nail a fly every time as far as he could see him. Smiley said all a frog wanted was education, and he could do most anything—and I believe him. Why, I've

seen him set Dan'l Webster down here on this floor—Dan'l Webster was the name of the frog—and sing out, "Flies, Dan'l flies!" and quickern' you could wink, he'd spring straight up, and snake a fly off'n the counter there, and flop down on the floor again as solid as a gob of mud, and fall to scratching the side of his head with his hind foot as indifferent as if he hadn't no idea he'd been doin' any more'n any frog might do. You never see a frog so modest and straightfor'ard as he was, for all he was so gifted. And when it come to fair and square jumping on a dead level, he could get over more ground at one straddle than any animal of his breed you ever see. Jumping on a dead level was his strong suit, you understand; and when it come to that, Smiley would ante up money on him as long as he had a red. Smiley was monstrous proud of his frog, and well he might be, for fellers that had travelled and been everywheres, all said he laid over any frog that ever *they* see.

Well Smiley kept the beast in a little lattice box, and he used to fetch him down town sometimes and lay for a bet. One day a feller—a stranger in the camp, he was—come across him with his box, and says:

"What might it be that you've got in the box?"

And Smiley says, sorter indifferent like, "It might be a parrot, or it might be a canary, may be, but it ain't—it's only just a frog."

And the feller took it, and looked at it careful, and turned it round this way and that, and says, "H'm—so 'tis. Well, what's *he* good for?"

"Well," Smiley says, easy and careless, "he's good enough for *one* thing, I should judge—he can outjump any frog in Calaveras county."

The feller took the box again, and took another long, particular look, and give it back to Smiley, and says, very deliberate, "Well, I don't see no p'ints about that frog that's any better'n any other frog."

"May be you don't," Smiley says. "May be you understand frogs, and may be you don't understand 'em; may be you've had experience, and may be you an't only a amature, as it were. Any ways, I've got *my* opinion, and I'll risk forty dollars he can outjump any frog in Calaveras county."

And the feller studied a minute, and then says, kinder sad like, "Well, I'm only a stranger here, and I ain't got no frog, but if I had a frog, I'd bet you."

And then Smiley says, "That's all right—that's all right— if you'll hold my box a minute, I'll go and get you a frog." And so the feller took the box, and put up his forty dollars along with Smiley's, and set down to wait.

So he set there a good while thinking and thinking to hisself, and then he got the frog out and prized his mouth open and took a teaspoon and filled him full of quail shot—filled him pretty near up to his chin—and set him on the floor. Smiley he went to the swamp and slopped around in the mud for a long time, and finally he ketched a frog, and fetched him in, and give him to this feller and says:

"Now, if you're ready, set him alongside of Dan'l, with his fore-paws just even with Dan'l, and I'll give the word." Then he says, "one—two—three—jump!" and him and the feller touched up the frogs from behind, and the new frog hopped off, but Dan'l give a heave, and

hysted up his shoulders—so—like a Frenchman, but it want no use—couldn't budge; he was planted as solid as an anvil, and he couldn't no more stir than if he was anchored out. Smiley was a good deal surprised, and he was disgusted, too, but he didn't have no idea what the matter was, of course.

The feller took the money and started away; and when he was going out of the door, he sorter jerked his thumb over his shoulders—this way—at Dan'l, and says again, very deliberate, "Well *I* don't see no p'ints about that frog that's any better'n any other frog."

Smiley stood scratching his head and looking down at Dan'l a long time, and at last he says, "I wonder what in the nation that frog throw'd off for—I wonder if there ain't something the matter with him—he 'pears to look mighty baggy, somehow." And he ketched Dan'l by the nap of the neck and lifted him up and says, "Why, blame my cats, if he don't weigh five pound!" and turned him upside down, and he belched out a double handful of shot. And then he see how it was, and he was the maddest man—he set the frog down and took out after that feller, but he never ketched him. And—

(Here Simon Wheeler heard his name called from the front yard, and got up to see what was wanted.) And turning to me as he moved away, he said: "Just set where you are, stranger, and rest easy—I ain't going to be gone a second."

But by your leave, I did not think that a continuation of the history of the enterprising vagabond *Jim* Smiley would be likely to afford me much information concerning the Rev. *Leonidas W.* Smiley, and so I started away.

At the door I met the sociable Wheeler returning, and he buttonholed me and recommenced:

"Well, thish-yer Smiley had a yaller one-eyed cow that didn't have no tail, only jest a short stump like a bannanner, and—"

"Oh! hang Smiley and his afflicted cow!" I muttered, good-naturedly, and bidding the old gentleman good-day, I departed.

1865

CANADIAN LITERATURE

CHARLES G. D. ROBERTS (1860-1943)

Although colonial Canada had produced minor poets such as Charles Sangster and Charles Heavysege, and internationally known prose writers such as John Richardson and Thomas Chandler Haliburton, it is really Charles G. D. Roberts who most deserves the title of "father of Canadian literature." Born on the eve of Confederation, he was the leader of the "Group of the Sixties" which included Bliss Carman, Archibald Lampman, Duncan Campbell Scott, Wilfred Campbell, Frederick George Scott, and others, and which gave to the young Dominion its first significant poetry. He also wrote novels and short stories, one of the first histories of Canada, and a variety of descriptive and critical essays.

Roberts was born at Douglas, N.B., spent part of his boyhood at Westcock near Sackville, and was educated at the Fredericton Collegiate School and at the University of New Brunswick. He taught school briefly, was editor for a few months of *The Week* in Toronto, and from 1885 to 1895 was professor of English and French at King's College, Windsor, N.S. In 1897 he went to New York City as a magazine editor, and from 1907 to 1925 made London, England, his headquarters. He returned to Canada in 1925, settling in Toronto and being recognized as the dean of Canadian letters. He was knighted for his literary services in 1935, and died on November 26, 1943.

Roberts began his literary career by publishing *Orion and Other Poems* in 1880. There followed several other volumes of poetry, some novels, and many volumes of short stories concerned chiefly with animal life. In both poetry and prose, his chief talent was for the detailed observation and description of landscape. He had a great familiarity with the woods and their animal inhabitants, and could describe their appearance and behaviour sensitively and accurately. When he tried to philosophize, or to deal with the relations between human beings, he was less successful.

Tantramar[1] *Revisited*

Summers and summers have come, and gone with the flight of the swallow;
Sunshine and thunder have been, storm, and winter, and frost;
Many and many a sorrow has all but died from remembrance,
Many a dream of joy fall'n in the shadow of pain.
Hands of chance and change have marred, or moulded, or broken,
Busy with spirit or flesh, all I most have adored;
Even the bosom of Earth is strewn with heavier shadows,—
Only in these green hills, aslant to the sea, no change!

[1]The Tantramar is an area of low-lying land on the borders of Nova Scotia and New Brunswick, near Sackville, N.B.

Here where the road that has climbed from the inland valleys and woodlands,
Dips from the hill-tops down, straight to the base of the hills,—   10
Here, from my vantage-ground, I can see the scattering houses,
Stained with time, set warm in orchards, meadows, and wheat,
Dotting the broad bright slopes outspread to southward and eastward,
Wind-swept all day long, blown by the south-east wind.

Skirting the sunbright uplands stretches a riband of meadow,
Shorn of the labouring grass, bulwarked well from the sea,
Fenced on its seaward border with long clay dikes from the turbid
Surge and flow of the tides vexing the Westmoreland shores.
Yonder, toward the left, lie broad the Westmoreland marshes,—
Miles on miles they extend, level, and grassy, and dim,   20
Clear from the long red sweep of flats to the sky in the distance,
Save for the outlying heights, green-rampired Cumberland Point;
Miles on miles outrolled, and the river-channels divide them,—
Miles on miles of green, barred by the hurtling gusts.

Miles on miles beyond the tawny bay is Minudie.
There are the low blue hills; villages gleam at their feet.
Nearer a white sail shines across the water, and nearer
Still are the slim, grey masts of fishing boats dry on the flats.
Ah, how well I remember those wide red flats, above tide-mark,
Pale with scurf of the salt, seamed and baked in the sun!   30
Well I remember the piles of blocks and ropes, and the net-reels
Wound with the beaded nets, dripping and dark from the sea!
Now at this season the nets are unwound; they hang from the rafters
Over the fresh-stowed hay in upland barns, and the wind
Blows all day through the chinks, with streaks of sunlight, and sways them
Softly at will; or they lie heaped in the gloom of a loft.

Now at this season the reels are empty and idle; I see them
Over the lines of the dikes, over the gossiping grass.
Now at this season they swing in the long strong wind, thro' the lonesome
Golden afternoon, shunned by the foraging gulls.   40
Near about sunset the crane will journey homeward above them;
Round them, under the moon, all the calm night long,
Winnowing soft grey wings of marsh-owls wander and wander,
Now to the broad, lit marsh, now to the dusk of the dike.
Soon, thro' their dew-wet frames, in the live keen freshness of morning,
Out of the teeth of the dawn blows back the awakening wind.
Then, as the blue day mounts, and the low-shot shafts of the sunlight
Glance from the tide to the shore, gossamers jewelled with dew
Sparkle and wave, where late sea-spoiling fathoms of drift-net,
Myriad-meshed, uploomed sombrely over the land.   50

Well I remember it all. The salt, raw scent of the margin;
While, with men at the windlass, groaned each reel, and the net,
Surging in ponderous lengths, uprose and coiled in its station;
Then each man to his home,—well I remember it all!

Yet, as I sit and watch, this present peace of the landscape,—
Stranded boats, these reels empty and idle, the hush,
One grey hawk slow-wheeling above yon cluster of haystacks,—
More than the old-time stir this stillness welcomes me home.

Ah, the old-time stir, how once it stung me with rapture,—
Old-time sweetness, the winds freighted with honey and salt!   60
Yet will I stay my steps and not go down to the marshland,—
Muse and recall far off, rather remember than see,—
Lest on too close sight I miss the darling illusion,
Spy at their task even here the hands of chance and change.

1883   1886

The Sower

A brown, sad-coloured hillside, where the soil
Fresh from the frequent harrow, deep and fine,
Lies bare; no break in the remote sky-line,
Save where a flock of pigeons streams aloft,
Startled from feed in some low-lying croft,
Or far-off spires with yellow of sunset shine;
And here the Sower, unwittingly divine,
Exerts the silent forethought of his toil.
Alone he treads the glebe, his measured stride
Dumb in the yielding soil; and though small joy
Dwell in his heavy face, as spreads the blind
Pale grain from his dispensing palm aside,
This plodding churl grows great in his employ;—
Godlike, he makes provision for mankind.

1886

The Potato Harvest

A high bare field, brown from the plough, and borne
Aslant from sunset; amber wastes of sky
Washing the ridge; a clamour of crows that fly
In from the wide flats where the spent tides mourn
To yon their rocking roosts in pines wind-torn;

A line of grey snake-fence, that zigzags by
A pond, and cattle; from the homestead nigh
The long deep summonings of the supper horn.
Black on the ridge, against that lonely flush,
A cart, and stoop-necked oxen; ranged beside
Some barrels; and the day-worn harvest-folk,
Here emptying their baskets, jar the hush
With hollow thunders.   Down the dusk hillside
Lumbers the wain; and day fades out like smoke.

1886

Ice

When Winter scourged the meadow and the hill
And in the withered leafage worked his will,
The water shrank, and shuddered, and stood still,—
Then built himself a magic house of glass,
Irised with memories of flowers and grass,
Wherein to sit and watch the fury pass.

1898

"The Young Ravens That Call upon Him"

It was just before dawn, and a greyness was beginning to trouble the dark about the top of the mountain.

Even at that cold height there was no wind. The veil of cloud that hid the stars hung but a hand-breadth above the naked summit. To eastward the peak broke away sheer, beetling in a perpetual menace to the valleys and the lower hills. Just under the brow, on a splintered and creviced ledge, was the nest of the eagles.

As the thick dark shrank down the steep like a receding tide, and the greyness reached the ragged heap of branches forming the nest, the young eagles stirred uneasily under the loose droop of the mother's wings. She raised her head and peered about her, slightly lifting her wings as she did so; and the nestlings, complaining at the chill air that came in upon their unfledged bodies, thrust themselves up amid the warm feathers of her thighs. The male bird, perched on a jutting fragment beside the nest, did not move. But he was awake. His white, narrow, flat-crowned head was turned to one side, and his yellow eye, under its straight, fierce lid, watched the pale streak that was growing along the distant eastern sea-line.

The great birds were racked with hunger. Even the nestlings, to meet the petitions of whose gaping beaks they stinted themselves without mercy, felt meagre and uncomforted. Day after day the parent birds had fished almost in vain; day after day their wide and tireless hunting had brought them scant reward. The schools of alewives, mackerel, and herring seemed to shun their shores that spring. The rabbits seemed to have fled from all the coverts about their mountain.

The mother eagle, larger and of mightier wing than her mate, looked as if she had met with misadventure. Her plumage was disordered. Her eyes, fiercely and restlessly anxious, at moments grew dull as if with exhaustion. On the day before, while circling at her viewless height above a lake far inland, she had marked a huge lake-trout, basking near the surface of the water. Dropping upon it with half-closed, hissing wings, she had fixed her talons in its back. But the fish had proved too powerful for her. Again and again it had dragged her under water, and she had almost been drowned before she could unloose the terrible grip of her claws. Hardly, and late, had she beaten her way back to the mountain-top.

And now the pale streak in the east grew ruddy. Rust-red stains and purple, crawling fissures began to show on the rocky face of the peak. A piece of scarlet cloth, woven among the faggots of the nest, glowed like new blood in the increasing light. And presently a wave of rose appeared to break and wash down over the summit, as the rim of the sun came above the horizon.

The male eagle stretched his head far out over the depth, lifted his wings and screamed harshly, as if in greeting of the day. He paused a moment in that position, rolling his eye upon the nest. Then his head went lower, his wings spread wider, and he launched himself swiftly and smoothly into the abyss of air as a swimmer glides into the sea. The female watched him, a faint wraith of a bird darting through the gloom, till presently, completing his mighty arc, he rose again into the full light of the morning. Then on level, almost moveless wing, he sailed away toward the horizon.

As the sun rose higher and higher, the darkness began to melt on the tops of the lower hills and to diminish on the slopes of the upland pastures, lingering in the valleys as the snow delays there in spring. As point by point the landscape uncovered itself to his view, the eagle shaped his flight into a vast circle, or rather into a series of stupendous loops. His neck was stretched toward the earth, in the intensity of his search for something to ease the bitter hunger of his nestlings and his mate.

Not far from the sea, and still in darkness, stood a low, round hill or swelling upland. Bleak and shelterless, whipped by every wind that the heavens could let loose, it bore no bush but an occasional juniper scrub. It was covered with mossy hillocks, and with a short grass, meagre but sweet. There in the chilly gloom, straining her ears to catch the lightest footfall of approaching peril, but hearing only the hushed thunder of the surf, stood a lonely ewe over the lamb to which she had given birth in the night.

Having lost the flock when the pangs

of travail came upon her, the unwonted solitude filled her with apprehension. But as soon as the first feeble bleating of the lamb fell upon her ear, everything was changed. Her terrors all at once increased ten-fold—but they were for her young, not for herself; and with them came a strange boldness such as her heart had never known before. As the little weakling shivered against her side, she uttered low, short bleats and murmurs of tenderness. When an owl hooted in the woods across the valley, she raised her head angrily and faced the sound, suspecting a menace to the young. When a mouse scurried past her, with a small, rustling noise amid the withered mosses of the hillock, she stamped fiercely, and would have charged had the intruder been a lion.

When the first grey of dawn descended over the pasture, the ewe feasted her eyes with the sight of the trembling little creature, as it lay on the wet grass. With gentle nose she coaxed it and caressed it, till presently it struggled to its feet, and, with its pathetically awkward legs spread wide apart to preserve its balance, it began to nurse. Turning her head as far around as she could, the ewe watched its every motion with soft murmurings of delight.

And now that wave of rose, which had long ago washed the mountain and waked the eagles, spread tenderly across the open pasture. The lamb stopped nursing; and the ewe, moving forward two or three steps, tried to persuade it to follow her. She was anxious that it should as soon as possible learn to walk freely, so they might together rejoin the flock. She felt that the open pasture was full of dangers.

The lamb seemed afraid to take so many steps. It shook its ears and bleated piteously. The mother returned to its side, caressed it anew, pushed it with her nose, and again moved away a few feet, urging it to go with her. Again the feeble little creature refused, bleating loudly. At this moment there came a terrible hissing rush out of the sky, and a great form fell upon the lamb. The ewe wheeled and charged madly; but at the same instant the eagle, with two mighty buffetings of his wings, rose beyond her reach and soared away toward the mountain. The lamb hung limp from his talons; and with piteous cries the ewe ran beneath, gazing upward, and stumbling over the hillocks and juniper bushes.

In the nest of the eagles there was content. The pain of their hunger appeased, the nestlings lay dozing in the sun, the neck of one resting across the back of the other. The triumphant male sat erect upon his perch, staring out over the splendid world that displayed itself beneath him. Now and again he half lifted his wings and screamed joyously at the sun. The mother bird, perched upon a limb on the edge of the nest, busily rearranged her plumage. At times she stooped her head into the nest to utter over her sleeping eaglets a soft chuckling noise, which seemed to come from the bottom of her throat.

But hither and thither over the round bleak hill wandered the ewe, calling for her lamb, unmindful of the flock, which had been moved to other pastures.

1896

BLISS CARMAN (1861-1929)

A first cousin of Charles Roberts, Bliss Carman earned the greatest international reputation of any Canadian poet. He was born in Fredericton, N.B., and educated at the Collegiate School, the University of New Brunswick, Edinburgh, and Harvard. At Harvard he was greatly influenced by Josiah Royce, the idealistic philosopher, by Francis Child, the great authority on ballads, and by Richard Hovey, a young poet with whom he collaborated on his most popular volume of verse, *Songs from Vagabondia* (1894). For a few years after giving up his studies in English at Harvard, Carman worked on various American magazines, but for most of his life he devoted himself entirely to writing poetry and some prose essays. A bachelor, he had no home of his own, and lived in various parts of the United States and Canada with friends. His most permanent headquarters were in New Canaan, Connecticut, where he lived with his friends, Dr. and Mrs. King. He died in New Canaan and was buried in Forest Hill cemetery in his native Fredericton.

Carman's reputation is not as great as it once was. He was not a clear or deep thinker, his verse was often careless and repetitive, and he wrote too easily and too much. But the best of his work lives by virtue of his mastery of mood and music. He could write lines which haunt the memory by their magic suggestiveness, their melodic beauty, and their visual accuracy.

Low Tide on Grand Pré

The sun goes down, and over all
  These barren reaches by the tide
Such unelusive glories fall,
  I almost dream they yet will bide
  Until the coming of the tide.

And yet I know that not for us,
  By any ecstasy of dream,
He lingers to keep luminous
  A little while the grievous steam,
  Which frets, uncomforted of dream—

A grievous steam, that to and fro   11
  Athrough the fields of Acadie
Goes wandering, as if to know
  Why one beloved face should be
  So long from home and Acadie.

Was it a year or lives ago
  We took the grasses in our hands,
And caught the summer flying low
  Over the waving meadow lands,   19
  And held it there between our hands?

The while the river at our feet—
  A drowsy inland meadow steam—
At set of sun the after-heat
  Made running gold, and in the gleam
  We freed our birch upon the stream.

There down along the elms at dusk
  We lifted dripping blade to drift,
Through twilight scented fine like musk,
  Where night and gloom awhile uplift,
  Nor sunder soul and soul adrift.   30

And that we took into our hands
  Spirit of life or subtler thing—
Breathed on us there, and loosed the bands
  Of death, and taught us, whispering,
  The secret of some wonder-thing.

Then all your face grew light, and seemed
  To hold the shadow of the sun;
The evening faltered, and I deemed
  That time was ripe, and years had done
  Their wheeling underneath the sun.   40

So all desire and all regret,
  And fear and memory, were naught;
One to remember or forget
  The keen delight our hands had caught;
  Morrow and yesterday were naught.

The night has fallen, and the tide . . . .
  Now and again comes drifting home,
Across these aching barrens wide,
  A sigh like driven wind or foam:
  In grief the flood is bursting home.   50

1893

And then my heart beat once and broke
  To hear the sweeping rain forebode
Some ruin in the April world,
  Between the woodside and the road.

Tonight can bring no healing now;
  The calm of yesternight is gone;
Surely the wind is but the wind,
  And I a broken waif thereon.   20

1893

A Windflower

Between the roadside and the wood,
  Between the dawning and the dew,
A tiny flower before the sun,
  Ephemeral in time, I grew.

And there upon the trail of spring,
  Not death nor love nor any name
Known among men in all their lands
  Could blur the wild desire with shame.

But down my dayspan of the year
  The feet of straying winds came by;   10
And all my trembling soul was thrilled
  To follow one lost mountain cry.

A Vagabond Song

There is something in the autumn that is native to my blood—
Touch of manner, hint of mood;
And my heart is like a rhyme,
With the yellow and the purple and the crimson keeping time.

The scarlet of the maples can shake me like a cry
Of bugles going by.
And my lonely spirit thrills
To see the frosty asters like a smoke upon the hills.

There is something in October sets the gypsy blood astir;
We must rise and follow her,   10
When from every hill of flame
She calls and calls each vagabond by name.

              1896

Vestigia

I took a day to search for God,
And found Him not. But as I trod
By rocky ledge, through woods untamed,
Just where one scarlet lily flamed,
I saw His footprint in the sod.

Then suddenly, all unaware,
Far off in the deep shadows, where
A solitary hermit thrush
Sang through the holy twilight hush—
I heard His voice upon the air. 10

And even as I marvelled how
God gives us Heaven here and now,
In a stir of wind that hardly shook
The poplar leaves beside the brook—
His hand was light upon my brow.

At last with evening as I turned
Homeward, and thought what I had learned
And all that there was still to probe—
I caught the glory of His robe
Where the last fires of sunset burned. 20

    Back to the world with quickening start
    I looked and longed for any part
    In making saving Beauty be . . .
    And from that kindling ecstasy
    I knew God dwelt within my heart.

              1921

ARCHIBALD LAMPMAN (1861-1899)

Lampman was the most dedicated craftsman and the most patient observer in the Group of the Sixties. His best poems record with minute accuracy, and with an almost mystical sense of the cycle of life, the natural scenes and seasons of Ontario and Quebec. A second group, not quite as successful but still memorable, express his dissatisfaction with the commercial and industrial society of late nineteenth century Canada. A great admirer of Matthew Arnold, Lampman sought serenity, and he found it in the country and in the full round of the seasons;

in the city, and above all in the factories of the city, he saw a nightmare world which was the very antithesis of serenity.

Like Charles Roberts, Lampman was the son of an Anglican rector. His boyhood was spent in various small Ontario towns, and he was educated at the Cobourg Collegiate Institute, Trinity College School, and Trinity College, Toronto. As an undergraduate he read Roberts' *Orion* and was moved to emulation. In 1883 he entered the Post Office Department at Ottawa, where he remained as a rather reluctant clerk until his death. In Ottawa he formed a close friendship with Duncan Campbell Scott, with whom he went on many canoe trips in the Ottawa region. He had always been a delicate and rather melancholy person, and he died in February, 1899, at the early age of thirty-eight. The two books published in his lifetime were *Among the Millet* (1888) and *Lyrics of Earth* (1893); a third book was in preparation at the time of his death. His collected poems, together with a long and helpful introduction, were published after his death by Duncan Campbell Scott.

Heat

From plains that reel to southward, dim,
    The road runs by me white and bare;
Up the steep hill it seems to swim
    Beyond, and melt into the glare.
Upward half-way, or it may be
    Nearer the summit, slowly steals
A hay-cart, moving dustily
    With idly clacking wheels.

By his cart's side the wagoner
    Is slouching slowly at his ease,   10
Half-hidden in the windless blur
    Of white dust puffing to his knees.
This wagon on the height above,
    From sky to sky on either hand,
Is the sole thing that seems to move
    In all the heat-held land.

Beyond me in the fields the sun
    Soaks in the grass and hath his will;
I count the marguerites one by one;
    Even the buttercups are still.   20
On the brook yonder not a breath
    Disturbs the spider or the midge.
The water-bugs draw close beneath
    The cool gloom of the bridge.

Where the far elm-tree shadows flood
    Dark patches in the burning grass,
The cows, each with her peaceful cud,
    Lie waiting for the heat to pass.
From somewhere on the slope near by
    Into the pale depth of the noon   30
A wandering thrush slides leisurely
    His thin revolving tune.

In intervals of dreams I hear
    The cricket from the droughty ground;
The grasshoppers spin into mine ear
    A small innumerable sound.
I lift mine eyes sometimes to gaze:
    The burning sky-line blinds my sight:
The woods far off are blue with haze:
    The hills are drenched in light.   40

And yet to me not this or that
    Is always sharp or always sweet;
In the sloped shadow of my hat
    I lean at rest, and drain the heat;
Nay more, I think some blessèd power
    Hath brought me wandering idly here:
In the full furnace of this hour
    My thoughts grow keen and clear.

1888

In November

With loitering step and quiet eye,
Beneath the low November sky,
I wandered in the woods, and found
A clearing, where the broken ground
Was scattered with black stumps and
    briers,
And the old wreck of forest fires.
It was a bleak and sandy spot,
And, all about, the vacant plot
Was peopled and inhabited
By scores of mulleins long since dead. 10
A silent and forsaken brood
In that mute opening of the wood,
So shrivelled and so thin they were,
So grey, so haggard, and austere,
Not plants at all they seemed to me,
But rather some spare company
Of hermit folk, who long ago,
Wandering in bodies to and fro,
Had chanced upon this lonely way,
And rested thus, till death one day   20
Surprised them at their compline prayer,
And left them standing lifeless there.
There was no sound about the wood
Save the wind's secret stir. I stood
Among the mullein-stalks as still
As if myself had grown to be
One of their sombre company,
A body without wish or will.
And as I stood, quite suddenly,
Down from a furrow in the sky   30
The sun shone out a little space
Across that silent sober place,
Over the sand heaps and brown sod,
The mulleins and dead goldenrod,
And passed beyond the thickets grey,
And lit the fallen leaves that lay,
Level and deep within the wood,
A rustling yellow multitude.
And all around me the thin light,
So sere, so melancholy bright,   40
Fell like the half-reflected gleam

Or shadow of some former dream;
A moment's golden reverie
Poured out on every plant and tree
A semblance of weird joy, or less,
A sort of spectral happiness;
And I, too, standing idly there,
With muffled hands in the chill air,
Felt the warm glow about my feet,
And shuddering betwixt cold and heat,
Drew my thoughts closer, like a cloak, 51
While something in my blood awoke,
A nameless and unnatural cheer,
A pleasure secret and austere.

                                    1893

A Sunset at Les Eboulements

Broad shadows fall. On all the mountain
    side
The scythe-swept fields are silent. Slowly
    home
By the long beach the high-piled hay-
    carts come,
Splashing the pale salt shallows. Over
    wide
Fawn-coloured wastes of mud the slipping
    tide,
Round the dun rocks and wattled fisher-
    ies,
Creeps murmuring in. And now by twos
    and threes,
O'er the slow spreading pools with clam-
    orous chide,
Belated crows from strip to strip take
    flight.
Soon will the first star shine; yet ere the
    night
Reach onward to the pale-green dis-
    tances,
The sun's last shaft beyond the grey
    sea-floor
Still dreams upon the Kamouraska shore,
And the long line of golden villages.

                                    1900

The City of the End of Things

Beside the pounding cataracts
Of midnight streams unknown to us
'Tis builded in the leafless tracts
And valleys huge of Tartarus.
Lurid and lofty and vast it seems;
It hath no rounded name that rings,
But I have heard it called in dreams
The City of the End of Things.

Its roofs and iron towers have grown
None knoweth how high within the night,
But in its murky streets far down   11
A flaming terrible and bright
Shakes all the stalking shadows there,
Across the walls, across the floors,
And shifts upon the upper air
From out a thousand furnace doors;
And all the while an awful sound
Keeps roaring on continually,
And crashes in the ceaseless round
Of a gigantic harmony.   20
Through its grim depths re-echoing
And all its weary height of walls,
With measured roar and iron ring,
The inhuman music lifts and falls.
Where no thing rests and no man is,
And only fire and night hold sway;
The beat, the thunder and the hiss
Cease not, and change not, night nor day.
And moving at unheard commands,
The abysses and vast fires between,   30
Flit figures that with clanking hands
Obey a hideous routine;
They are not flesh, they are not bone,
They see not with the human eye,
And from their iron lips is blown
A dreadful and monotonous cry;
And whoso of our mortal race
Should find that city unaware,
Lean Death would smite him face to face,

And blanch him with its venomed air: 40
Or caught by the terrific spell,
Each thread of memory snapt and cut,
His soul would shrivel and its shell
Go rattling like an empty nut.

It was not always so, but once,
In days that no man thinks upon,
Fair voices echoed from its stones,
The light above it leaped and shone:
Once there were multitudes of men,
That built that city in their pride,   50
Until its might was made, and then
They withered age by age and died.
But now of that prodigious race,
Three only in an iron tower,
Set like carved idols face to face,
Remain the masters of its power;
And at the city gate a fourth,
Gigantic and with dreadful eyes,
Sits looking toward the lightless north,
Beyond the reach of memories;   60
Fast rooted to the lurid floor,
A bulk that never moves a jot,
In his pale body dwells no more,
Or mind or soul,—an idiot!
But sometime in the end those three
Shall perish and their hands be still,
And with the master's touch shall flee
Their incommunicable skill.
A stillness absolute as death
Along the slacking wheels shall lie,   70
And flagging at a single breath,
The fires shall moulder out and die.
The roar shall vanish at its height,
And over that tremendous town
The silence of eternal night
Shall gather close and settle down.
All its grim grandeur, tower and hall,
Shall be abandoned utterly,

And into rust and dust shall fall
From century to century; 80
Nor ever living thing shall grow,
Nor trunk of tree, nor blade of grass;
No drop shall fall, no wind shall blow,

Nor sound of any foot shall pass:
Alone of its accursèd state,
One thing the hand of Time shall spare,
For the grim Idiot at the gate
Is deathless and eternal there.

1900

DUNCAN CAMPBELL SCOTT (1862-1947)

The fourth member of the Canadian Group of the Sixties, Scott resembles the rest of the group in his strong interest in landscape, but tends to deal with more wild and rugged parts of the country than they. He also differs from them in his interest in and knowledge of Indian life: many of his best poems are narratives in which Indians are the leading characters.

These differences are accounted for largely by the circumstances of Scott's life. Born in Ottawa, the son of a Methodist minister, he entered the Department of Indian Affairs at the age of eighteen, and remained there, eventually as its head, for almost half a century. As an official of this department, he made many journeys into the more remote parts of Canada, and naturally came to know much of Indian life and legend. Beginning with *The Magic House and Other*

Poems in 1893, Scott produced eight volumes of poetry, two books of short stories, and two biographies. He also collected and edited the poems of his friend, Archibald Lampman. His own poems and stories usually involve violence, but violence which is eventually controlled. The essence of Scott's view of the world seems to be a vision of a battle-ground where nature is in conflict with itself, man in conflict with nature, and man in conflict with man. But he does not leave it at that. Out of the conflict emerges, whether soon or late, peace and beauty. He has faith in the ultimate rightness of things . . . and in man's capacity to endure. The final note of Scott's work is not that of storm but of the silence that follows the storm, is not despair but serenity.

The Voice and the Dusk

The slender moon and one pale star,
   A rose-leaf and a silver bee
From some god's garden blown afar
   Go down the gold deep tranquilly.

Within the south there rolls and grows
   A mighty town with tower and spire,
From a cloud bastion masked with rose
   The lightning flashes diamond fire.

The purple-martin darts about
   The purlieus of the iris fen; 10
The king-bird rushes up and out,
   He screams and whirls and screams again.

A thrush is hidden in a maze
   Of cedar buds and tamarac bloom,
He throws his rapid flexile phrase,
   A flash of emeralds in the gloom.

A voice is singing from the hill
  A happy love of long ago;
Ah! tender voice, be still, be still,
  'Tis sometimes better not to know. 20

The rapture from the amber height
  Floats tremblingly along the plain,
Where in the reeds with fairy light
  The lingering fireflies gleam again.

Buried in dingles more remote,
  Or drifted from some ferny rise,
The swooning of the golden throat
  Drops in the mellow dusk and dies.

A soft wind passes lightly drawn,
  A wave leaps silverly and stirs   30
The rustling sedge, and then is gone
  Down the black cavern in the firs.

                                        1893

The Forsaken

I

Once in the winter
Out on a lake
In the heart of the north-land,
Far from the Fort
And far from the hunters,
A Chippewa woman
With her sick baby,
Crouched in the last hours
Of a great storm.
Frozen and hungry,   10
She fished through the ice
With a line of the twisted
Bark of the cedar,
And a rabbit-bone hook
Polished and barbed;
Fished with the bare hook
All through the wild day,
Fished and caught nothing;
While the young chieftain
Tugged at her breasts,   20
Or slept in the lacings
Of the warm *tikanagan*.

All the lake-surface
Streamed with the hissing
Of millions of iceflakes
Hurled by the wind;
Behind her the round
Of a lonely island
Roared like a fire
With the voice of the storm   30
In the deeps of the cedars.
Valiant, unshaken,
She took of her own flesh,
Baited the fish-hook,
Drew in a grey-trout,
Drew in his fellows,
Heaped them beside her,
Dead in the snow.
Valiant, unshaken,
She faced the long distance,   40
Wolf-haunted and lonely,
Sure of her goal
And the life of her dear one:

Tramped for two days,
On the third in the morning,
Saw the strong bulk
Of the Fort by the river,
Saw the wood-smoke

Hang soft in the spruces,
Heard the keen yelp   50
Of the ravenous huskies
Fighting for whitefish:
Then she had rest.

II

Years and years after,
When she was old and withered,
When her son was an old man
And his children filled with vigour,
They came in their northern tour on the verge of winter,
To an island in a lonely lake.
There one night they camped, and on the morrow   60
Gathered their kettles and birch-bark,
Their rabbit-skin robes and their mink-traps,
Launched their canoes and slunk away through the islands,
Left her alone forever,
Without a word of farewell,
Because she was old and useless,
Like a paddle broken and warped,
Or a pole that was splintered.
Then, without a sigh,
Valiant, unshaken,   70
She smoothed her dark locks under her kerchief,
Composed her shawl in state,
Then folded her hands ridged with sinews and corded with veins,
Folded them across her breasts spent with the nourishing of children,
Gazed at the sky past the tops of the cedars,
Saw two spangled nights arise out of the twilight,
Saw two days go by filled with the tranquil sunshine,
Saw, without pain, or dread, or even a moment of longing:
Then on the third great night there came thronging and thronging
Millions of snowflakes out of a windless cloud;   80
They covered her close with a beautiful crystal shroud,
Covered her deep and silent.

But in the frost of the dawn,
Up from the life below,
Rose a column of breath
Through a tiny cleft in the snow,
Fragile, delicately drawn,
Wavering with its own weakness,
In the wilderness a sign of the spirit
Persisting still in the sight of the sun　　　　　　　　　　90
Till day was done.
Then all light was gathered up by the hand of God and hid in His breast,
Then there was born a silence deeper than silence,
Then she had rest.

　　　　　　　　　　　　　　　　　　　　　　1905

1900   **1920**   **1940**

● Hardy: *Wessex Poems*   ● Yeats: *Sailing to Byzantium*   ● Birney

                    ● Frost: *Poems*   ● D. H. Lawrence: *Birds, Beasts and Flowers*

                                    ● Freud: *General Introduction to Psychoanalysis*

● Housman: *A Shropshire Lad*   ● Thomas: *Eighteen Poems*

            ● Leacock: *Literary Lapses*

                ● Joyce: *Dubliners*   ● Hemingway: *A Farewell to Arms*

                            ● Mansfield: *The Garden Party*   F. R. Scott: *Overture* ●

                ● Eliot: *The Love Song of J. Alfred Prufrock*

            ● Sandburg: *Chicago*   ● Grove: *Fruits of the Earth*

THE TWENTIETH CENTURY

1960   1980   2000

- Callaghan: *Stories*

- Layton: *Red Carpet for the Sun*

- Laurence: *The Stone Angel*

- Atwood: *The Circle Game*

In many ways the literature and general intellectual outlook of the present century have represented a reaction against the Victorian period. For all their doubts and problems, most Victorians felt secure in their belief in progress; we, on the other hand, have been obsessed with the notion of decline, afraid that our Western civilization might follow other civilizations into eclipse. The Victorian period, with the brief exceptions of the Crimean War and the Boer War, was a long era of peace; ours has seen two world wars on an unprecedented scale, several small wars, and the perpetual fear of new wars. Victoria's reign, also, was a period of almost uninterrupted prosperity and economic expansion; our century has witnessed the great depression of the thirties, and we shall never be quite free of the fear of its recurrence. It is no wonder that the fundamental optimism of the Victorians has given way in our period to what W. H. Auden has called "the age of anxiety."

There is a similar difference in our attitudes towards science. Most of the Victorians welcomed scientific advance as an unmixed blessing; we have seen that science is as capable of creating the hydrogen bomb as penicillin, the tank as the tractor, and so we have a curiously ambivalent attitude to the scientist, seeing him as half-saint, half-monster. The difference can be seen by contrasting the Victorian Thomas Henry Huxley with his twentieth century grandson, Aldous Huxley. The grandfather saw science as the key to progress; Aldous Huxley, in novels such as *Brave New World* and *Ape and Essence*, has warned us that science may be the key to our destruction.

There has also been a great change in our economic thinking. Until the last decade or two of the Victorian period, laissez-faire capitalism was the order of the day; government was not to interfere with the economy, which instead was to be magically regulated by the law of supply and demand. In our century, public opinion and the pressure of events such as the world wars and the depression have forced governments to interfere more and more in the economy, to regulate more and more closely wages, hours of work, prices, monopolistic practices, and so on. Various forms of social security—unemployment insurance, old age pensions, public health schemes—have transformed the heavily individualist Victorian economy into a more collectivist economy.

Similarly, we have changed our conception of human nature. To the Victorians, as to the men of the eighteenth century, man was essentially a rational being, needing only education and opportunity to make him act in a reasonable and "civilized" manner. For us, because of the revelations of great psychologists such as Freud and Jung, and because of the frightening practical demonstrations we have had in the acts of dictatorial lunatics such as Hitler and in the mass hysteria of his followers, man seems much less tidy a being, much more irrational in his nature, much less easy to civilize.

This new view of man, which stresses his animality rather than his rationality and doubts his capacity to improve himself unaided, has led many leading thinkers of our century to return to religious faith. T. S. Eliot, W. H. Auden, Aldous Huxley, Theodore Dreiser—all these leading writers eventually came to feel that man's real hope is not in communism or rationalism or liberalism but in God, not in self-assertion but in self-surrender to the divine will.

In one respect, however, there has been great continuity between the Victorian period and our own: the struggle to control materialism. The Industrial Revolution has continued with even greater rapidity in our century, as machines and gadgets have proliferated on every side. Like the Victorians, we have been tempted to make a god of material progress, to equate happiness with the possession of the greatest possible number of the latest goods and appliances. Practically all the great writers of our century—Yeats, Lawrence, Eliot, Auden, Huxley, Dreiser, Sinclair Lewis, Thomas Wolfe, to mention but a few—have attacked this preoccupation with what Lawrence called "the bitch-goddess, Success." Perhaps the most direct and damning indictments in England and America, respectively, have been Aldous Huxley's *Brave New World* and Sinclair Lewis's *Babbitt*; but in the selections in this text the theme can be seen clearly in the short stories of D. H. Lawrence and Katherine Mansfield and the poems of T. S. Eliot.

In form and style, twentieth century literature has been much more daring and experimental than that of the Victorian period. Probably because of the rapid changes in other spheres of life, writers have felt that they must seek new forms to express the new world of the combustion engine, the movies, the radio, and atomic energy. They have often incorporated techniques from these other media into their work: the movie in particular has had a strong influence on literary technique, producing or encouraging such devices as the flashback, montage, close-up, and fade-out. In their choice of words, twentieth century writers have tried to get away from "literary language" or "poetic diction" and use the speech of contemporary society; for their metaphors and similes, they have drawn upon the machine and appliances which are part of our everyday experience; in their rhythms they have tried to catch something of the restless speed at which twentieth century life is lived. Made aware by Freud of the various levels of consciousness, they have tried to portray man more fully by transcribing his innermost thoughts (in the so-called "stream of consciousness" technique) as well as his words and rational motives. Some of these experiments have led to mere obscurity or strangeness, but most of them have been justified by the greater realism of the resultant portrayals.

A search for greater realism is perhaps the best way to sum up the tendency of contemporary literature. In England, novelists in the late nineteenth century became aware of the depth and honesty of French realistic fiction as practised by Flaubert, Zola, and De Maupassant, and came to feel that Victorians like Thackeray and Dickens had been merely scratching the surface. As a result, English novelists such as George Moore, Arnold Bennett, and Joseph Conrad produced their painstaking studies of human life around the turn of the century. D. H. Lawrence, James Joyce, and Virginia Woolf, in turn, felt that Moore and Bennett in particular had still not gone deep enough, and in their own novels they tried to probe the most secret recesses of the mind.

The poet had similar ambitions. In the last decade of the nineteenth century, Hardy, Housman, and Yeats began a revolution against the optimism of Tennyson and Browning: they revealed in their predominantly bitter poetry that all is *not* right with the world, and that the vague comfort offered by Tennyson and Browning was not enough. The Georgian poets, of the period just prior to and during World War I, tried to find alternative and traditional comfort in the beauties of the English landscape; but the poetry of T. S. Eliot, which dominated the nineteen-twenties, made their work appear thin and shallow. Eliot set out to show the full and tragic dilemma of modern man, and in *The Waste Land* (1923) in particular, succeeded brilliantly; having shown the dilemma, he proceeded to show the way to escape it, by a return to traditional Christianity. But to the young poets of the thirties—W. H. Auden, Cecil Day-Lewis, Stephen Spender—Eliot's solution seemed inadequate. They felt that the problem was not so much a spiritual as a social and economic one, and so they pictured the horrors of war, unemployment and Fascism, and recommended a socialist or communist state as the best means of overcoming them. Dylan Thomas, the Welsh poet who dominated the nineteen-forties and fifties, in his turn felt that the problem was deeper than either a traditional religion or a new political system could solve, that man must accept and indeed glory in his part in a recurrent cycle of birth, growth, decay, and death. For all their differences of style and thought, these writers had in common the ambition not to be misled by illusions, but rather to see life steadily and see it whole, to face up honestly to all its complexity and difficulty.

Similar patterns of development can be seen in the twentieth century literature of the United States and Canada. American novelists such as Theodore Dreiser, Sinclair Lewis, Ernest Hemingway, John Dos Passos, William Faulkner, Thomas Wolfe, James Farrell, and more recently, Truman Capote and J. D. Salinger sought to show the real pressures of an industrial society upon the individual, to discard illusions and reveal an America that has much poverty as well as much wealth, much cruelty as well as much kindness, much strife and bitterness and suffering as well as the pursuit of freedom and happiness on which Americans have prided themselves. A similar impulse led Carl Sandburg to write poems such as "Chicago," Robert Frost to write his realistic sketches of New England life, Edwin Arlington Robinson and Edgar Lee Masters to write their poems of frustrated, tormented individuals, and Robinson Jeffers his violent poems of passion and cruelty between men and women.

In Canada, the new realism was, understandably, slow in developing. The poetic movement which had begun in the eighteen-eighties lost most of its impetus in the early twentieth century, and it was not until after the First World War that the realistic narratives of E. J. Pratt, and the social satires of the Montreal School of F. R. Scott, A. J. M. Smith, and A. M. Klein, re-invigorated Canadian poetry. In the nineteen-thirties and early forties Canada had a school of social protest poetry similar to the Spender-Auden-Lewis group in England, the leading representatives being Dorothy Livesay, Earle Birney, Anne Marriott, P. K. Page, and Patrick Anderson. After World War II, a new wave of realism brought the down-to-earth poetry of Irving Layton, and the clever, mordant tragi-comedies of James Reaney. Many other poets wrote clear-eyed, unsentimental accounts of life in various parts of the country—Raymond Souster of Toronto, for example, Louis Dudek and Miriam Waddington of Montreal, Fred Cogswell and Alden Nowlan of New Brunswick. In the sixties and seventies, a new generation of poets brought unheralded popularity to Canadian poetry. Represented here are such diverse artists as the hypnotic Leonard Cohen and the colloquial Alden Nowlan; works range in scope from John Newlove's wide, open wilderness to Michael Ondaatje's human miniatures.

Realistic fiction in Canada also got its start after World War I. Up to that time the Canadian novel had been almost exclusively in the form of the historical romance, such as William Kirby's *Golden Dog* (1877) or Gilbert Parker's *Seats of the Mighty* (1896), or of the regional idyll, such as the novels of Ralph Connor, L. M. Montgomery, and Marian Keith. After the war came Frederick Philip Grove's honest, detailed portrayals of pioneer life in the West, Morley Callaghan's sensitive stories of life in our eastern cities, and, in the forties and fifties, the searching sociological novels of Hugh MacLennan and the deftly satirical work of Ethel Wilson and Robertson Davies. Both the perceptive, finely-crafted novels of Margaret Laurence and the witty, satirical novels of Mordecai Richler dominated fiction during the sixties. In the last decade, Canadian women writers have moved into the foreground; Alice Munro, the author of probing, evocative studies of women, is one of many promising novelists to gain prominence in the seventies. As Margaret Atwood's novels meet receptive foreign audiences, she is now widely recognized as Canada's foremost novelist. To mention the many Canadian writers omitted from this anthology would merely lead to further omissions; included here are works by many internationally recognized Canadian writers who have made the past two decades the most vital in the nation's literary history.

As is to be expected in view of the many upheavals of the twentieth century, the literature of our time is predominantly grim and fearful, though it is often lightened by "the feather-pate of folly," which, as Housman says, "bears the falling sky." Its chief strength is its unremitting honesty, its refusal to compromise or offer merely illusory comfort. As Thomas Hardy put it, "if a way to the better there be, it deserves a full look at the worst," and it is in that courageous spirit that most twentieth-century literature has been written.

ENGLISH LITERATURE

THOMAS HARDY (1840-1928)

Thomas Hardy had the unique honour of being a leading novelist of one century and a leading poet of another. He began to write poetry in the 1860's, but gave it up for fiction. Between 1871 and 1896 he produced a series of novels and short stories that constituted the greatest achievement in fiction of the late Victorian period. He then returned to his first love, poetry, and won recognition as one of the chief English poets of the twentieth century. His poetry and fiction have much in common: they both stress the tragic aspects of life and react against Victorian optimism by calling attention to the suffering and injustice that exist in the world; they are both primarily concerned with rustic and small town life in the southwestern ("Wessex") area of England; they are both strongly architectural in form, solidly and harmoniously built; and they are both distinguished above all by their depth and honesty of observation and insight.

Hardy was the son of a stonemason, and was born in the village of Higher Bockhampton, Dorset. Denied the opportunity of attending university, he educated himself by wide reading. He was apprenticed to an architect, and won a prize for the excellence of his designs, but deserted architecture for literature after the success of his first novel, *Desperate Remedies* (1871). Among his other novels were *The Return of the Native* (1878), *Tess of the D'Urbervilles* (1891), and *Jude the Obscure* (1896). Attacks on the alleged indecency of the latter two novels led him to return to poetry. As a poet, Hardy published seven volumes of short poems beginning with *Wessex Poems* in 1898, and a long verse-drama *The Dynasts* (1904-1908).

Hap

If but some vengeful god would call to me
From up the sky, and laugh: "Thou suffering thing,
Know that thy sorrow is my ecstasy,
That thy love's loss is my hate's profiting!"
Then would I bear it, clench myself, and die,
Steeled by the sense of ire unmerited;
Half-eased in that a Powerfuller than I
Had willed and meted me the tears I shed.

But not so. How arrives it joy lies slain,
And why unblooms the best hope ever sown?
—Crass Casualty obstructs the sun and rain,
And dicing Time for gladness casts a moan . . .
These purblind Doomsters had as readily strown
Blisses about my pilgrimage as pain.

1866   1898

Neutral Tones

We stood by a pond that winter day,
And the sun was white, as though chidden of God,
And a few leaves lay on the starving sod;
   —They had fallen from an ash, and were gray.

Your eyes on me were as eyes that rove
Over tedious riddles of years ago;
And some words played between us to and fro
   On which lost the more by our love.

The smile on your mouth was the deadest thing
Alive enough to have strength to die;
And a grin of bitterness swept thereby
   Like an ominous bird a-wing. . . .

Since then, keen lessons that love deceives,
And wrings with wrong, have shaped to me
Your face, and the God-curst sun, and a tree,
   And a pond edged with grayish leaves.

1867   1898

The Man He Killed

"Had he and I but met
   By some old ancient inn,
We should have sat us down to wet
   Right many a nipperkin![1]

"But ranged as infantry,
   And staring face to face,
I shot at him as he at me,
   And killed him in his place.

"I shot him dead because—
   Because he was my foe,   10
Just so: my foe of course he was;
   That's clear enough; although

"He thought he'd 'list, perhaps,
   Off-hand like—just as I—
Was out of work—had sold his traps[2]—
   No other reason why.

"Yes; quaint and curious war is!
   You shoot a fellow down
You'd treat if met where any bar is,
   Or help to half-a-crown."[3]   20

                                   1902

[1]A half-pint of ale.
[2]Simple personal belongings.
[3]English coin, worth about fifty cents in Hardy's day.

The Darkling Thrush

I leant upon a coppice gate
    When Frost was spectre-gray,
And Winter's dregs made desolate
    The weakening eye of day.
The tangled bine-stems scored the sky
    Like strings of broken lyres,
And all mankind that haunted nigh
    Had sought their household fires.

The land's sharp features seemed to be
    The Century's corpse outleant,   10
His crypt the cloudy canopy,
    The wind his death-lament.
The ancient pulse of germ and birth
    Was shrunken hard and dry,
And every spirit upon earth
    Seemed fervourless as I.

At once a voice arose among
    The bleak twigs overhead
In a full-hearted evensong
    Of joy illimited;   20
An aged thrush, frail, gaunt, and small,
    In blast-beruffled plume,
Had chosen thus to fling his soul
    Upon the growing gloom.

So little cause for carolings
    Of such ecstatic sound
Was written on terrestrial things
    Afar or nigh around,
That I could think there trembled through
    His happy good-night air   30
Some blessèd Hope, whereof he knew
    And I was unaware.

1900   1902

A Plaint to Man[1]

When you slowly emerged from the den
    of Time,
And gained percipience as you grew,
And fleshed you fair out of shapeless
    slime,

Wherefore, O Man, did there come to you
The unhappy need of creating me—
A form like your own—for praying to?

My virtue, power, utility,
Within my maker must all abide,
Since none in myself can ever be,

One thin as a phasm on a lantern-slide 10
Shown forth in the dark upon some dim
    sheet,
And by none but its showman vivified.

"Such a forced device," you may say,
    "is meet
For easing a loaded heart at whiles:
Man needs to conceive of a mercy-seat

Somewhere above the gloomy aisles
Of this wailful world, or he could not bear
The irk no local hope beguiles."

—But since I was framed in your first
    despair
The doing without me has had no play 20
In the minds of men when shadows scare;

And now that I dwindle day by day
Beneath the deicide eyes of seers
In a light that will not let me stay,

And to-morrow the whole of me
    disappears,
The truth should be told, and the fact be
    faced
That had best been faced in earlier years:

The fact of life with dependence placed
On the human heart's resource alone,
In brotherhood bonded close and graced

With loving-kindness fully blown,   31
And visioned help unsought, unknown.

[1]In this poem, God is imagined as speaking to
Man.

1909-10   1914

The Year's Awakening

How do you know that the pilgrim track
Along the belting zodiac
Swept by the sun in his seeming rounds
Is traced by now to the Fishes' bounds
And into the Ram, when weeks of cloud
Have wrapt the sky in a clammy shroud,
And never as yet a tinct of spring
Has shown in the Earth's apparelling;
  O vespering bird, how do you know,
    How do you know?   10

How do you know, deep underground,
Hid in your bed from sight and sound,
Without a turn in temperature,
With weather life can scarce endure,
That light has won a fraction's strength,
And day put on some moments' length,
Whereof in merest rote will come,
Weeks hence, mild airs that do not numb,
  O crocus root, how do you know,
    How do you know?   20

1910   1914

The Blinded Bird

So zestfully canst thou sing?
And all this indignity,
With God's consent, on thee!
Blinded ere yet a-wing
By the red-hot needle thou[1],
I stand and wonder how
So zestfully thou canst sing!

Resenting not such wrong,
Thy grievous pain forgot,
Eternal dark thy lot,   10
Groping thy whole life long,
After that stab of fire,
Enjailed in pitiless wire;
Resenting not such wrong!

Who hath charity? This bird.
Who suffereth long and is kind,
Is not provoked, though blind
And alive ensepulchred?
Who hopeth, endureth all things?
Who thinketh no evil, but sings?   20
Who is divine? This bird.

1917

[1]An automatic nervous reaction makes a bird
  sing when its eyes are pierced by a red-hot
  needle.

The Oxen

Christmas Eve, and twelve of the clock.
  "Now they are all on their knees[1],"
An elder said as we sat in a flock
  By the embers in hearthside ease.

We pictured the meek mild creatures where
  They dwelt in their strawy pen,
Nor did it occur to one of us there
  To doubt they were kneeling then.

So fair a fancy few would weave
  In these years! Yet, I feel,
If someone said on Christmas Eve,
  "Come; see the oxen kneel,

"In the lonely barton by yonder coomb
  Our childhood used to know,"
I should go with him in the gloom,
  Hoping it might be so.

1915   1917

[1]There is a legend that at midnight on Christmas
  Eve cattle kneel in their pens as a tribute to
  Jesus.

In Time of "The Breaking of Nations"

(JEREMIAH li, 20)

Only a man harrowing clods
  In a slow silent walk
With an old horse that stumbles and nods
  Half asleep as they stalk.

Only thin smoke without flame
  From the heaps of couch-grass;
Yet this will go onward the same
  Though Dynasties pass.

Yonder a maid and her wight
  Come whispering by:
War's annals will fade into night
  Ere their story die.

1915   1917

A. E. HOUSMAN (1859-1936)

Housman's poetry expresses much the same tragic view of life as Hardy's, but in a more facile and light-hearted style. His outlook is best summed up in his own line "the feather-pate of folly bears the falling sky." He attempts to ward off the sense of impending disaster with the shield of irony and wit. His poems are brief, rhythmical, epigrammatic, and neatly turned, but they do not have Hardy's weight and substance.

Housman attended St. John's College, Oxford, worked for a few years as a civil servant, and then was successively professor of Latin in the universities of London and Cambridge. He was one of the leading classical scholars of this century, and Greek and Latin poetry had considerable influence in shaping his own terse poetic style. He published only two slim volumes of verse, *A Shropshire Lad* (1896) and *Last Poems* (1922).

Loveliest of Trees

Loveliest of trees, the cherry now
Is hung with bloom along the bough,
And stands about the woodland ride,
Wearing white for Eastertide.

Now, of my threescore years and ten,
Twenty will not come again,
And take from seventy springs a score,
It only leaves me fifty more.

And since to look at things in bloom
Fifty springs are little room,
About the woodlands I will go
To see the cherry hung with snow.

1896

Is My Team Ploughing

"Is my team ploughing,
   That I was used to drive
And hear the harness jingle
   When I was man alive?"

Ay, the horses trample,
   The harness jingles now;
No change though you lie under
   The land you used to plough.

"Is football playing
   Along the river shore,   10
With lads to chase the leather,
   Now I stand up no more?"

Ay, the ball is flying,
   The lads play heart and soul;
The goal stands up, the keeper
   Stands up to keep the goal.

"Is my girl happy,
   That I thought hard to leave,
And has she tired of weeping
   As she lies down at eve?"   20

Ay, she lies down lightly,
   She lies not down to weep:
Your girl is well contented.
   Be still, my lad, and sleep.

"Is my friend hearty,
   Now I am thin and pine,
And has he found to sleep in
   A better bed than mine?"

Yes, lad, I lie easy,
   I lie as lads would choose;   30
I cheer a dead man's sweetheart—
   Never ask me whose.

1896

When I Was One-and-Twenty

When I was one-and-twenty
   I heard a wise man say,
"Give crowns and pounds and guineas[1]
   But not your heart away;
Give pearls away and rubies
   But keep your fancy free."
But I was one-and-twenty,
   No use to talk to me.

When I was one-and-twenty
   I heard him say again,   10
"The heart out of the bosom
   Was never given in vain;
'Tis paid with sighs a plenty
   And sold for endless rue."[2]
And I am two-and-twenty,
   And oh, 'tis true, 'tis true.

1896

[1]*crowns . . . guineas.* British coins.
[2]Regret, sorrow.

To an Athlete Dying Young

The time you won your town the race
We chaired you through the market place;
Man and boy stood cheering by,
And home we brought you shoulder-high.

Today, the road all runners come,
Shoulder-high we bring you home,
And set you at your threshold down,
Townsman of a stiller town.

Smart lad, to slip betimes away
From fields where glory does not stay   10
And early though the laurel[1] grows
It withers quicker than the rose.

Eyes the shady night has shut
Cannot see the record cut,[2]
And silence sounds no worse than cheers
After earth has stopped the ears:

Now you will not swell the rout
Of lads that wore their honors out,
Runners whom renown outran
And the name died before the man.   20

So set, before its echoes fade,
The fleet foot on the sill of shade,[3]
And hold to the low lintel[4] up
The still-defended challenge cup.

And round that early-laureled head
Will flock to gaze the strengthless dead,
And find unwithered on its curls
The garland briefer than a girl's.

1896

[1] A laurel wreath, the customary award for victorious athletes.
[2] Beaten.
[3] Doorway of death.
[4] Beam at the top of a doorway.

When Smoke Stood Up from Ludlow

When smoke stood up from Ludlow,
    And mist blew off from Teme,
And blithe afield to ploughing
    Against the morning beam
    I strode beside my team,

The blackbird in the coppice
    Looked out to see me stride,
And hearkened as I whistled
    The trampling team beside,
    And fluted and replied: 10

"Lie down, lie down, young yeoman;
    What use to rise and rise?
Rise man a thousand mornings
    Yet down at last he lies,
    And then the man is wise."

I heard the tune he sang me,
    And spied his yellow bill;
I picked a stone and aimed it
    And threw it with a will:
    Then the bird was still.   20

Then my soul within me
    Took up the blackbird's strain,
And still beside the horses
    Along the dewy lane
    It sang the song again:

"Lie down, lie down, young yeoman;
    The sun moves always west;
The road one treads to labor
    Will lead one home to rest,
    And that will be the best."   30

1896

The Chestnut Casts His Flambeaux[1]

The chestnut casts his flambeaux, and the flowers
    Stream from the hawthorn on the wind away,
The doors clap to, the pane is blind with showers.
    Pass me the can, lad; there's an end of May.

There's one spoilt spring to scant our mortal lot,
    One season ruined of our little store.
May will be fine next year as like as not:
    Oh ay, but then we shall be twenty-four.

We for a certainty are not the first
    Have sat in taverns while the tempest hurled   10
Their hopeful plans to emptiness, and cursed
    Whatever brute and blackguard made the world.

It is in truth iniquity on high
    To cheat our sentenced souls of aught they crave,
And mar the merriment as you and I
    Fare on our long fool's-errand to the grave.

Iniquity it is; but pass the can.
    My lad, no pair of kings our mothers bore;
Our only portion is the estate of man:
    We want the moon, but we shall get no more.   20

[1] A reference to the torch-like shape and flame-like colour of the chestnut blossoms.

If here to-day the cloud of thunder lours
To-morrow it will hie on far behests;
The flesh will grieve on other bones than ours
Soon, and the soul will mourn in other breasts.

The troubles of our proud and angry dust
Are from eternity, and shall not fail.
Bear them we can, and if we can we must.
Shoulder the sky, my lad, and drink your ale.

1922

WILLIAM BUTLER YEATS (1865-1939)

Yeats is considered by many critics to be the finest poet of this century. He began his poetic career in the eighties and nineties of the last century, writing mainly soft, sad, dreamy poems about the Irish past; in the first two decades of this century he turned to a much plainer, tougher, and more realistic poetry of frustrated love and social criticism; in the last two decades of his life he wrote powerful, gaily bitter poems about the problems of old age, the relations between soul and body, and the plight of the artist in a decadent society. In spite of these changes of style and subject, there was a hard core of consistency in Yeats' work: his style was always resonant, musical, and disciplined; his chief values were always art, love, human dignity, and spiritual vision.

Yeats was the son of the painter John Butler Yeats, and was born in Dublin on June 13, 1865. He spent much of his childhood in County Sligo, where he acquired his interest in Irish folklore. From the age of nine to fifteen he lived with his parents in London, where he attended the Godolphin School. The years from fifteen to twenty-one were spent mainly in Dublin, attending the Erasmus Smith School and the Metropolitan School of Art. In the late eighties and nineties he lived in London, writing poetry, associating with poets of the Rhymers' Club such as Lionel Johnson, Arthur Symons, and Ernest Dowson, and interesting himself in spiritualism and Irish nationalist movements. Back in Dublin at the turn of the century, he helped to found the Abbey Theatre, wrote plays for production there, and in every way sought to develop the cultural life of his native country. His services to the nation were recognized in 1922 when he was elected to the senate of the Irish Free State, and his services to the world a year later when he was awarded the Nobel Prize for literature. He died on January 28, 1939, on the French Riviera, and was buried in the little cemetery at Rocquebrune. After the war his body was brought back for burial at Drumcliff, near Sligo, Ireland, in accordance with his wishes; see "Under Ben Bulben."

When You Are Old

When you are old and grey and full of sleep,
And nodding by the fire, take down this book,
And slowly read, and dream of the soft look
Your eyes had once, and of their shadows deep;

How many loved your moments of glad grace,
And loved your beauty with love false or true;
But one man loved the pilgrim soul in you,
And loved the sorrows of your changing face.

And bending down beside the glowing bars
Murmur, a little sadly, how love fled
And paced upon the mountains overhead
And hid his face amid a crowd of stars.

1893

Red Hanrahan's Song about Ireland[1]

The old brown thorn trees break in two high over Cummen Strand,
Under a bitter black wind that blows from the left hand;
Our courage breaks like an old tree in a black wind and dies,
But we have hidden in our hearts the flame out of the eyes
Of Cathleen, the daughter of Houlihan.

The wind has bundled up the clouds high over Knocknarea,
And thrown the thunder on the stones for all that Maeve can say.
Angers that are like noisy clouds have set our hearts abeat;
But we have all bent low and low and kissed the quiet feet
Of Cathleen, the daughter of Houlihan.

The yellow pool has overflowed high up on Clooth-na-Bare,
For the wet winds are blowing out of the clinging air;
Like heavy flooded waters our bodies and our blood:
But purer than a tall candle before the Holy Rood
Is Cathleen, the daughter of Houlihan.

1897

[1]Red Hanrahan was a roistering Irishman whom Yeats created as a character in his short stories. Cathleen is here a symbol of Ireland. The place-names are all Irish.

The Song of Wandering Aengus[1]

I went out to the hazel wood,
Because a fire was in my head,
And cut and peeled a hazel wand,
And hooked a berry to a thread;
And when white moths were on the wing,
And moth-like stars were flickering out,
I dropped the berry in a stream
And caught a little silver trout.

When I had laid it on the floor
I went to blow the fire aflame, 10
But something rustled on the floor,
And some one called me by my name:

It had become a glimmering girl
With apple blossom in her hair
Who called me by my name and ran
And faded through the brightening air.

Though I am old with wandering
Through hollow lands and hilly lands,
I will find out where she has gone,
And kiss her lips and take her hands; 20
And walk among long dappled grass,
And pluck till time and times are done
The silver apples of the moon,
The golden apples of the sun.

1899

[1]This poem is based upon an Irish legend of Aengus, who once had a vision of perfect beauty and spent the rest of his life wandering in search of a second glimpse.

September, 1913

What need you, being come to sense,
But fumble in a greasy till
And add the halfpence to the pence
And prayer to shivering prayer, until
You have dried the marrow from the
    bone;
For men were born to pray and save:
Romantic Ireland's dead and gone,
It's with O'Leary[1] in the grave.

Yet they were of a different kind,
The names that stilled your childish play,
They have gone about the world like
    wind,   11
But little time had they to pray
For whom the hangman's rope was spun,
And what, God help us, could they save?
Romantic Ireland's dead and gone,
It's with O'Leary in the grave.

Was it for this the wild geese[2] spread
The grey wing upon every tide;
For this that all that blood was shed,
For this Edward Fitzgerald died,   20
And Robert Emmet and Wolfe Tone,
All that delirium of the brave?
Romantic Ireland's dead and gone,
It's with O'Leary in the grave.

Yet could we turn the years again,
And call those exiles as they were
In all their loneliness and pain,
You'd cry, "Some woman's yellow hair
Has maddened every mother's son":   29
They weighed so lightly what they gave.
But let them be, they're dead and gone,
They're with O'Leary in the grave.

                                        1914

[1] John O'Leary, the Fenian leader, for many
years a friend of Yeats.

[2] A reference to Irish rebels and patriots who
refused to accept England's rule of Ireland.
Fitzgerald, Emmet, and Tone were all such
rebels.

The Wild Swans at Coole[1]

The trees are in their autumn beauty,
The woodland paths are dry,
Under the October twilight the water
Mirrors a still sky;
Upon the brimming water among the
    stones
Are nine-and-fifty swans.

The nineteenth autumn has come upon
    me
Since I first made my count;
I saw, before I had well finished,
All suddenly mount   10
And scatter wheeling in great broken
    rings
Upon their clamorous wings.

I have looked upon those brilliant crea-
    tures,
And now my heart is sore.
All's changed since I, hearing at
    twilight,
The first time on this shore,
The bell-beat of their wings above my
    head,
Trod with a lighter tread.

Unwearied still, lover by lover,
They paddle in the cold,   20
Companionable streams or climb
    the air;
Their hearts have not grown old;

[1] Coole Park, country house of Lady Gregory, Irish playwright and close friend of Yeats.

Passion or conquest, wander where they
   will,
Attend upon them still.

But now they drift on the still water
Mysterious, beautiful;

Among what rushes will they build,
By what lake's edge or pool
Delight men's eyes when I awake some
   day
To find they have flown away?   30

1919

Sailing to Byzantium[1]

That is no country for old men. The young
In one another's arms, birds in the trees
(Those dying generations) at their song,
The salmon-falls, the mackerel-crowded seas,
Fish, flesh, or fowl, commend all summer long
Whatever is begotten, born, and dies.
Caught in that sensual music, all neglect
Monuments of unaging intellect.

An aged man is but a paltry thing,
A tattered coat upon a stick, unless   10
Soul clap its hands and sing, and louder sing
For every tatter in its mortal dress;
Nor is there singing school but studying
Monuments of its own magnificence;
And therefore I have sailed the seas and come
To the holy city of Byzantium.

O sages, standing in God's holy fire
As in the gold mosaic of a wall,
Come from the holy fire, perne in a gyre,
And be the singing-masters of my soul.   20
Consume my heart away—sick with desire
And fastened to a dying animal
It knows not what it is—and gather me
Into the artifice of eternity.

Once out of nature I shall never take
My bodily form from any natural thing,
But such a form as Grecian goldsmiths make
Of hammered gold and gold enamelling
To keep a drowsy emperor awake;
Or set upon a golden bough to sing   30
To lords and ladies of Byzantium
Of what is past, or passing, or to come.   1928

[1]The city later known as Constantinople. It was the capital of the eastern portion of the Roman Empire from 395 A.D. to 1453, and was distinguished by its artistic development, especially in architecture. Yeats always used Byzantium as the symbol of a society wholeheartedly devoted to art.

Among School Children

I walk through the long schoolroom questioning,
A kind old nun in a white hood replies;
The children learn to cipher and to sing,
To study reading-books and history,
To cut and sew, be neat in everything
In the best modern way—the children's eyes
In momentary wonder stare upon
A sixty year old smiling public man[1].

I dream of a Ledæan[2] body, bent
Above a sinking fire, a tale that she   10
Told of a harsh reproof, or trivial event
That changed some childish day to tragedy—
Told, and it seemed that our two natures blent
Into a sphere from youthful sympathy,
Or else, to alter Plato's parable[3],
Into the yolk and white of the one shell.

And thinking of that fit of grief or rage
I look upon one child or t'other there
And wonder if she stood so at that age—
For even daughters of the swan can share   20
Something of every paddler's heritage—
And had that color upon cheek or hair;
And thereupon my heart is driven wild:
She stands before me as a living child.

Her present image floats into the mind—
Did quattrocento finger fashion it[4]
Hollow of cheek as though it drank the wind
And took a mess of shadows for its meat?
And I though never of Ledæan kind
Had pretty plumage once—enough of that,   30
Better to smile on all that smile, and show
There is a comfortable kind of old scarecrow.

[1]A reference to Yeats' role as Irish senator.
[2]Leda, a beautiful girl with whom Jupiter fell in love; he took the form of a swan to
  approach her. The actual person referred to here is probably Maud Gonne.
[3]Plato suggested that man and woman were originally one being; they broke apart and
  have subsequently always attempted to reunite.
[4]*quattrocento finger*, etc.—a reference to late medieval Italian painters, who painted thin
  and shadowy saints, martyrs, etc.

What youthful mother, a shape upon her lap
Honey of generation had betrayed,
And that must sleep, shriek, struggle to escape
As recollection or the drug decide,
Would think her son, did she but see that shape
With sixty or more winters on its head,
A compensation for the pang of his birth,
Or the uncertainty of his setting forth?   40

Plato thought nature but a spume that plays
Upon a ghostly paradigm of things[5];
Solider Aristotle played the taws
Upon the bottom of a king of kings[6];
World-famous golden-thighed Pythagoras
Fingered upon a fiddle stick or strings
What a star sang and careless Muses heard[7]:
Old clothes upon old sticks to scare a bird.

Both nuns and mothers worship images,
But those the candles light are not as those   50
That animate a mother's reveries,
But keep a marble or a bronze repose.
And yet they too break hearts—O Presences
That passion, piety, or affection knows,
And that all heavenly glory symbolize—
O self-born mockers of man's enterprise;

Labour is blossoming or dancing where
The body is not bruised to pleasure soul,
Nor beauty born out of its own despair,
Nor blear-eyed wisdom out of midnight oil.   60
O chestnut tree, great rooted blossomer,
Are you the leaf, the blossom, or the bole?
O body swayed to music, O brightening glance,
How can we know the dancer from the dance[8]?

                                                1928

[5]A reference to Plato's theory that ideas are more real than material things.
[6]A reference to Aristotle's theory of the first cause.
[7]Pythagoras explained the universe in terms of mathematics and music.
[8]In this final stanza, Yeats expresses his mature philosophy of a rounded life in which body
    and soul, physical beauty and spiritual wisdom, are seen not to be antagonistic or
    exclusive, but complementary parts of a single whole.

JAMES JOYCE (1882-1941)

James Joyce is one of the most influential figures in twentieth century fiction. He did not invent the stream of consciousness technique, which seeks to reveal character by recording the successive images which flow through the mind, but he developed it more fully than any other writer. He also did much to establish the use of symbols in fiction: in the story that follows, for example, Araby is not merely an actual fair but the symbol of that exotic world of fancy for which the boy vainly yearns. Joyce has also been influential as a stylist: he wrote his fiction in a cadenced prose which varied most skilfully to suit the changing moods of the story.

Since there is a strong autobiographical element in most of Joyce's work, a knowledge of his life is important. He was born in Dublin in 1882 and grew up while the Irish literary revival associated with Yeats, Synge, Lady Gregory, A. E. (George Russell), and others was in its heyday; although he officially dissociated himself from it, he was stimulated by it. He was educated at Clongowes Wood School, Belvedere College, and University College, Dublin. These were all Jesuit institutions, and again, although he later broke with the Church, the training he there received in the Thomistic philosophy left a deep imprint upon his mind. From 1904 onward Joyce spent most of his time in Trieste (1904-1914), in Zurich (1914-1919), and in Paris (1919-1940). The last months of his life were spent in Zurich, where he fled at the collapse of France in 1940. He died, after an intestinal operation, on January 13, 1941. For many years he had been almost totally blind.

Joyce's first book, a slim volume of verse called *Chamber Music*, appeared in 1907. His short stories, *Dubliners*, were published in 1914, and his first novel, *Portrait of the Artist as a Young Man*, appeared in 1916. The two great experimental novels of his maturity, *Ulysses* and *Finnegans Wake*, appeared respectively in 1922 and 1939.

Araby

North Richmond Street, being blind, was a quiet street except at the hour when the Christian Brothers' School set the boys free. An uninhabited house of two stories stood at the blind end, detached from its neighbours in a square ground. The other houses of the street, conscious of decent lives within them, gazed at one another with brown imperturbable faces.

The former tenant of our house, a priest, had died in the back drawing-room. Air, musty from having been long enclosed, hung in all the rooms, and the waste room behind the kitchen was littered with old useless papers. Among these I found a few paper-covered books, the pages of which were curled and damp: *The Abbot*, by Walter Scott, *The Devout Communicant*, and *The Memoirs of Vidocq*. I liked the last best because its leaves were yellow. The wild garden behind the house contained a central apple-tree and a few straggling bushes, under one of which I found the late tenant's rusty bicycle-pump. He had been a very charitable priest; in his will he had left all his money to institutions and the furniture of his house to his sister.

When the short days of winter came, dusk fell before we had well eaten our dinners. When we met in the street the houses had grown sombre. The space of sky above us was the colour of ever-changing violet, and towards it the lamps of the street lifted their feeble lanterns. The cold air stung us and we played till our bodies glowed. Our shouts echoed in the silent street. The career of our play brought us through the dark muddy lanes behind the houses, where we ran the gauntlet of the rough tribes from the cottages, to the back doors of the dark dripping gardens where odours arose from the ashpits, to the dark odorous stables where a coachman smoothed and combed the horse or shook music from the buckled harness. When we returned to the street, light from the kitchen windows had filled the areas. If my uncle was seen turning the corner, we hid in the shadow until we had seen him safely housed. Or if Mangan's sister came out on the doorstep to call her brother in to his tea, we watched her from our shadow peer up and down the street. We waited to see whether she would remain or go in and, if she remained, we left our shadow and walked up to Mangan's steps resignedly. She was waiting for us, her figure defined by the light from the half-opened door. Her brother always teased her before he obeyed, and I stood by the railings looking at her. Her dress swung as she moved her body, and the soft rope of her hair tossed from side to side.

Every morning I lay on the floor in the front parlour watching her door. The blind was pulled down to within an inch of the sash so that I could not be seen. When she came out on the doorstep my heart leaped. I ran to the hall, seized my books and followed her. I kept her brown figure always in my eye and, when we came near the point at which our ways diverged, I quickened my pace and passed her. This happened morning after morning. I had never spoken to her except for a few casual words, and yet her name was like a summons to all my foolish blood.

Her image accompanied me even in places the most hostile to romance. On Saturday evenings when my aunt went marketing I had to go to carry some of the parcels. We walked through the flaring streets, jostled by drunken men and bargaining women, amid the curses of labourers, the shrill litanies of shopboys who stood on guard by the barrels of pigs' cheeks, the nasal chanting of street-singers, who sang a *come-all-you* about O'Donovan Rossa, or a ballad about the troubles in our native land. These noises converged in a single sensation of life for me: I imagined that I bore my chalice safely through a throng of foes. Her name sprang to my lips at moments in strange prayers and praises which I myself did not understand. My eyes were often full of tears (I could not tell why) and at times a flood from my heart seemed to pour itself out into my bosom. I thought little of the future. I did not know whether I would ever speak to her or not or, if I spoke to her, how I could tell her of my confused adoration. But my body was like a harp and her words and gestures were like fingers running upon the wires.

One evening I went into the back drawing-room in which the priest had died. It was a dark rainy evening and there was no sound in the house. Through one of the broken panes I heard the rain impinge upon the earth, the fine incessant needles of water playing in the sodden beds. Some distant lamp or lighted window gleamed below me. I was thankful that I could see so little. All my senses seemed to desire to veil themselves and, feeling that I was about to slip from them, I pressed the palms of my hands together until they trembled, murmuring: "*O love! O love!*" many times.

At last she spoke to me. When she addressed the first words to me I was so confused that I did not know what to answer. She asked me was I going to *Araby*. I forgot whether I answered yes or no. It would be a splendid bazaar; she said she would love to go.

"And why can't you?" I asked.

While she spoke she turned a silver bracelet round and round her wrist. She could not go, she said, because there would be a retreat that week in her convent. Her brother and two other boys were fighting for their caps, and I was alone at the railings. She held one of the spikes, bowing her head towards me. The light from the lamp opposite our door caught the white curve of her neck, lit up her hair that rested there and, falling, lit up the hand upon the railing. It fell over one side of her dress and caught the white border of a petticoat, just visible as she stood at ease.

"It's well for you," she said.

"If I go," I said, "I will bring you something."

What innumerable follies laid waste my waking and sleeping thoughts after that evening! I wished to annihilate the tedious intervening days. I chafed against the work of school. At night in my bedroom and by day in the classroom her image came between me and the page I strove to read. The syllables of the word *Araby* were called to me through the silence in which my soul luxuriated and cast an Eastern enchantment over me. I asked for leave to go to the bazaar on Saturday night. My aunt was surprised, and hoped it was not some Freemason affair. I answered few questions in class. I watched my master's face pass from amiability to sternness; he hoped I was not beginning to idle. I could not call my wandering thoughts together. I had hardly any patience with the serious work of life which, now that it stood between me and my desire, seemed to me child's play, ugly monotonous child's play.

On Saturday morning I reminded my uncle that I wished to go to the bazaar in the evening. He was fussing at the hall-stand, looking for the hat-brush, and answered me curtly:

"Yes, boy, I know."

As he was in the hall I could not go into the front parlour and lie at the window. I left the house in bad humour and walked slowly towards the school. The air was pitilessly raw and already my heart misgave me.

When I came home to dinner my uncle had not yet been home. Still it was early. I sat staring at the clock for some time and, when its ticking began to irritate me, I left the room. I mounted the staircase and gained the upper part of the house. The high, cold, empty, gloomy rooms liberated me and I went from room to room singing. From the front window I saw my companions playing below in the street. Their cries reached me weakened and indistinct and, leaning my forehead against the cool glass, I looked over at the dark house where she lived. I may have stood there for an hour, seeing nothing but the brown-clad figure cast by my imagination, touched discreetly by the lamplight at the curved neck, at the hand upon the railings and at the border below the dress.

When I came downstairs again I found Mrs. Mercer sitting at the fire. She was an old, garrulous woman, a pawnbroker's widow, who collected used stamps for some pious purpose. I had to endure the gossip of the tea-table. The meal was prolonged beyond an hour and still my uncle did not come. Mrs. Mercer stood up to go: she was sorry she couldn't wait any longer, but it was after eight o'clock and she did not like to be out late, as the night air was bad for her. When she was gone I began to walk up and down the room, clenching my fists. My aunt said:

"I'm afraid you may put off your bazaar for this night of Our Lord."

At nine o'clock I heard my uncle's latchkey in the hall door. I heard him talking to himself and heard the hallstand rocking when it had received the weight of his overcoat. I could interpret these signs. When he was midway through his dinner I asked him to give me the money to go to the bazaar. He had forgotten.

"The people are in bed and after their first sleep now," he said.

I did not smile. My aunt said to him energetically:

"Can't you give him the money and let him go? You've kept him late enough as it is."

My uncle said he was very sorry he had forgotten. He said he believed in the old saying: "All work and no play makes Jack a dull boy." He asked me where I was going and, when I had told him a second time, he asked me did I know *The Arab's Farewell to His Steed*. When I left the kitchen he was about to recite the opening lines of the piece to my aunt.

I held a florin[1] tightly in my hand as I strode down Buckingham Street towards the station. The sight of the streets thronged with buyers and glaring with gas recalled to me the purpose of my journey. I took my seat in a third-class carriage of a deserted train. After an intolerable delay the train moved out of the station slowly. It crept onward among ruinous houses and over the twinkling river. At Westland Row Station a crowd of people pressed to the carriage doors;

[1] A two-shilling piece, roughly equivalent to fifty cents.

but the porters moved them back, saying that it was a special train for the bazaar. I remained alone in the bare carriage. In a few minutes the train drew up beside an improvised wooden platform. I passed out on to the road and saw by the lighted dial of a clock that it was ten minutes to ten. In front of me was a large building which displayed the magical name.

I could not find any sixpenny entrance and, fearing that the bazaar would be closed, I passed in quickly through a turnstile, handing a shilling to a weary-looking man. I found myself in a big hall girded at half its height by a gallery. Nearly all the stalls were closed and the greater part of the hall was in darkness. I recognized a silence like that which pervades a church after a service. I walked into the centre of the bazaar timidly. A few people were gathered about the stalls which were still open. Before a curtain, over which the words *Café Chantant* were written in coloured lamps, two men were counting money on a salver. I listened to the fall of the coins.

Remembering with difficulty why I had come, I went over to one of the stalls and examined porcelain vases and flow-ered tea-sets. At the door of the stall a young lady was talking and laughing with two young gentlemen. I remarked their English accents and listened vaguely to their conversation.

"O, I never said such a thing!"

"O, but you did!"

"O, but I didn't!"

"Didn't she say that?"

"Yes. I heard her."

"O, there's a . . . fib!"

Observing me, the young lady came over and asked me did I wish to buy anything. The tone of her voice was not encouraging; she seemed to have spoken to me out of a sense of duty. I looked humbly at the great jars that stood like eastern guards at either side of the dark entrance to the stall and murmured:

"No, thank you."

The young lady changed the position of one of the vases and went back to the two young men. They began to talk of the same subject. Once or twice the young lady glanced at me over her shoulder.

I lingered before her stall, though I knew my stay was useless, to make my interest in her wares seem the more real. Then I turned away slowly and walked down the middle of the bazaar. I allowed the two pennies to fall against the sixpence in my pocket. I heard a voice call from one end of the gallery that the light was out. The upper part of the hall was now completely dark.

Gazing up into the darkness I saw myself as a creature driven and derided by vanity; and my eyes burned with anguish and anger.

1914

VIRGINIA WOOLF (1882-1941)

Virginia Woolf's life span corresponded almost exactly with that of James Joyce, and as a novelist she was in some respects his feminine counterpart. Like Joyce, and partly because of his example, she used the stream of consciousness technique, aided in breaking up the tidy pattern of the "well-made novel" of the late nineteenth century to make way for a more flexible form, and shifted the emphasis from the social realism of writers such as Arnold Bennett, H. G. Wells, and John Galsworthy to psychological realism, the exploration of the inner life. There was, however, a great difference in tone between Woolf and Joyce: she was a much quieter, gentler, more urbane writer, but lacked his robustness and humour. She also differed from Joyce in that she wrote almost as many books of literary criticism as of fiction. As a critic, she was sensitive, original, humourous, and penetrating: hers was the type of criticism we call impressionistic, since what she wrote is not scholarly or systematic but the straightforward expression of her personal reactions to a book.

Virginia Woolf was the daughter of Sir Leslie Stephen, the well-known Cambridge don and literary critic. She grew up in a cultured home, read widely, and came naturally to the profession of literature. In 1912 she married Leonard Woolf, a writer on political and economic subjects, and with him founded the Hogarth Press. Her home in London became the rendezvous of a brilliant group of intellectuals including the biographer Lytton Strachey, the novelist E. M. Forster, and the art critic Roger Fry. Her first two novels, *The Voyage Out* (1915) and *Night and Day* (1919), were fairly conventional exercises, but her third, *Jacob's Room* (1922), used the stream of consciousness and other experimental devices and attracted wide interest. In 1925 she published one of her best novels, *Mrs. Dalloway*, and her first book of criticism, *The Common Reader*. Her later novels included *To the Lighthouse* (1927), *Orlando* (1928), *The Waves* (1931), *The Years* (1937), and *Between the Acts* (1941). Her later criticism appeared in *The Second Common Reader* (1932), *The Death of the Moth* (1942), *The Moment* (1947), and *The Captain's Death Bed* (1950). The last three of these books were edited and published after her death by her husband; always subject to bouts of nervous depression, and hating war, Woolf committed suicide by drowning early in 1941, shortly after her house had been bombed in the blitz.

In "Shakespeare's Sister," a persuasive criticism of men's attitude toward women through the ages, Woolf raises many of the points argued by feminists today.

Shakespeare's Sister

Perhaps now it would be better to give up seeking for the truth, and receiving on one's head an avalanche of opinion hot as lava, discolored as dishwater. It would be better to draw the curtains; to shut out distractions; to light the lamp; to narrow the enquiry and to ask the historian, who records not opinions but facts, to describe under what conditions women lived, not throughout the ages, but in England, say in the time of Elizabeth.

For it is a perennial puzzle why no woman wrote a word of that extraordinary literature when every other man, it seemed, was capable of song or sonnet. What were the conditions in which women lived, I asked myself; for fiction, imaginative work that is, is not dropped like a pebble upon the ground, as science may be; fiction is like a spider's web, attached ever so lightly perhaps, but still attached to life at all four corners. Often the attachment is scarcely perceptible; Shakespeare's plays, for instance, seem to hang there complete by themselves. But when the web is pulled askew, hooked up at the edge, torn in the middle, one remembers that these webs are not spun in midair by incorporeal creatures, but are the work of suffering human beings, and are attached to grossly material things, like health and money and the houses we live in.

I went, therefore, to the shelf where the histories stand and took down one of the latest, Professor Trevelyan's *History of England*.[1] Once more I looked up Women, found "position of," and turned to the pages indicated. "Wife-beating," I read, "was a recognized right of man, and was practiced without shame by high as well as low. . . . Similarly," the historian goes on, "the daughter who refused to marry the gentleman of her parents' choice was liable to be locked up, beaten and flung about the room, without any shock being inflicted on public opinion. Marriage was not an affair of personal affection, but of family avarice, particularly in the 'chivalrous' upper classes. . . . Betrothal often took place while one or both of the parties was in the cradle, and marriage when they were scarcely out of the nurses' charge." That was about 1470, soon after Chaucer's time. The next reference to the position of women is some two hundred years later, in the time of the Stuarts. "It was still the exception for women of the upper and middle class to choose their own husbands, and when the husband had been assigned, he was lord and master, so far at least as law and custom could make him. Yet even so," Professor Trevelyan concludes, "neither Shakespeare's women nor those of authentic seventeenth-century memoirs, like the Verneys and the Hutchinsons, seem wanting in personality and character." Certainly, if we consider it, Cleopatra must have had a way with her; Lady Macbeth, one would suppose, had a will of her own; Rosalind,[2] one might conclude, was an attractive girl. Professor Trevelyan is speaking no more than the truth when he remarks that Shakespeare's women do not seem wanting in personality and character. Not being a historian, one might go even further and say that women have burnt like beacons in all the works of all the poets from the beginning of time—Clytemnes-

[1] George M. Trevelyan (1876-1962) was a noted English historian.
[2] All three women are characters from Shakespeare's plays; Rosalind appears in *As You Like It*.

tra, Antigone, Cleopatra, Lady Macbeth, Phèdre, Cressida, Rosalind, Desdemona, the Duchess of Malfi,[3] among the dramatists; then among the prose writers: Millamant, Clarissa, Becky Sharp, Anna Karenine, Emma Bovary, Madame de Guermantes[4]—the names flock to mind, nor do they recall women "lacking in personality and character." Indeed, if woman had no existence save in the fiction written by men, one would imagine her a person of the utmost importance; very various; heroic and mean; splendid and sordid; infinitely beautiful and hideous in the extreme; as great as a man, some think even greater. But this is woman in fiction. In fact, as Professor Trevelyan points out, she was locked up, beaten and flung about the room.

A very queer, composite being thus emerges. Imaginatively she is of the highest importance; practically she is completely insignificant. She pervades poetry from cover to cover; she is all but absent from history. She dominates the lives of kings and conquerors in fiction; in fact she was the slave of any boy whose parents forced a ring upon her finger. Some of the most inspired words, some of the most profound thoughts in literature fall from her lips; in real life she could hardly read, could scarcely spell, and was the property of her husband.

It was certainly an odd monster that one made up by reading the historians first and the poets afterwards—a worm winged like an eagle; the spirit of life and beauty in a kitchen chopping up suet. But these monsters, however amusing to the imagination, have no existence in fact. What one must do to bring her to life was to think poetically and prosaically at one and the same moment, thus keeping in touch with fact—that she is Mrs. Martin, aged thirty-six, dressed in blue, wearing a black hat and brown shoes; but not losing sight of fiction either—that she is a vessel in which all sorts of spirits and forces are coursing and flashing perpetually. The moment, however, that one tries this method with the Elizabethan woman, one branch of illumination fails; one is held up by the scarcity of facts. One knows nothing detailed, nothing perfectly true and substantial about her. History scarcely mentions her. And I turned to Professor Trevelyan again to see what history meant to him. I found by looking at his chapter headings that it meant—

"The Manor Court and the Methods of Openfield Agriculture . . . The Cistercians and Sheep-farming . . . The Crusades . . . The University . . . The House of Commons . . . The Hundred Years' War . . . The Wars of the Roses . . . The Renaissance Scholars . . . The Dissolution of the Monasteries . . . Agrarian and Religious Strife . . . The Origin of English Sea-power . . . The Armada . . ." and so on. Occasionally an individual woman is mentioned, an Elizabeth, or a Mary; a queen or a great lady. But by no possible means could middle-class women with nothing but brains and character at their command have taken part in any one of the great move-

---

[3]Names refer to characters from plays by the great Greek dramatists Sophocles and Euripides (Clytemnestra, Antigone); the French neo-classical playwright Racine (Phèdre); Shakespeare (Cleopatra, Lady Macbeth, Cressida, Rosalind, and Desdemona) and Shakespeare's contemporary, John Webster (Duchess of Malfi).

[4]Creations of various great prose writers: William Congreve (Millamant); Samuel Richardson (Clarissa); W. M. Thackeray (Becky Sharp); Leo Tolstoy (Anna Karenine); Gustave Flaubert (Emma Bovary) and Marcel Proust (Madame de Guermantes).

ments which, brought together, constitute the historian's view of the past. Nor shall we find her in any collection of anecdotes. Aubrey[5] hardly mentions her. She never writes her own life and scarcely keeps a diary; there are only a handful of her letters in existence. She left no plays or poems by which we can judge her. What one wants, I thought—and why does not some brilliant student at Newnham or Girton[6] supply it?—is a mass of information; at what age did she marry; how many children had she as a rule; what was her house like; had she a room to herself; did she do the cooking; would she be likely to have a servant? All of these facts lie somewhere, presumably, in parish registers and account books; the life of the average Elizabethan woman must be scattered about somewhere, could one collect it and make a book of it. It would be ambitious beyond my daring, I thought, looking about the shelves for books that were not there, to suggest to the students of those famous colleges that they should re-write history, though I own that it often seems a little queer as it is, unreal, lop-sided; but why should they not add a supplement to history? calling it, of course, by some inconspicuous name so that women might figure there without impropriety? For one often catches a glimpse of them in the lives of the great, whisking away into the background, concealing, I sometimes think, a wink, a laugh, perhaps a tear. And, after all, we have lives enough of Jane Austen; it scarcely seems necessary to consider again the influence of the tragedies of Joanna Baillie[7] upon the poetry of Edgar Allan Poe; as for myself, I should not mind if the homes and haunts of Mary Russell Mitford[8] were closed to the public for a century at least. But what I find deplorable, I continued, looking about the bookshelves again, is that nothing is known about women before the eighteenth century. I have no model in my mind to turn about this way and that. Here am I asking why women did not write poetry in the Elizabethan age, and I am not sure how they were educated; whether they were taught to write; whether they had sitting-rooms to themselves; how many women had children before they were twenty-one; what, in short, they did from eight in the morning till eight at night. They had no money evidently; according to Professor Trevelyan they were married whether they liked it or not before they were out of the nursery; at fifteen or sixteen very likely. It would have been extremely odd, even upon this showing, had one of them suddenly written the plays of Shakespeare, I concluded, and I thought of that old gentleman, who is dead now, but was a bishop, I think, who declared that it was impossible for any woman, past, present, or to come, to have the genius of Shakespeare. He wrote to the papers about it. He also told a lady who applied to him for information that cats do not as a matter of fact go to heaven, though they have, he added, souls of a sort. How much thinking those old gentlemen used to save one! How the borders of ignorance shrank back at their approach! Cats do not go to heaven. Women cannot write the plays of Shakespeare.

Be that as it may, I could not help think-

[5]John Aubrey (1626-1697), an English antiquarian.
[6]*Newnham or Girton.* Women's colleges at Cambridge University in England.
[7]*Joanna Baillie.* Scottish poet and dramatist (1762-1851), who influenced Poe.
[8]*Mary Russell Mitford.* English novelist and dramatist (1787-1855), now fallen out of favour.

ing, as I looked at the works of Shakespeare on the shelf, that the bishop was right at least in this; it would have been impossible, completely and entirely, for any woman to have written the plays of Shakespeare in the age of Shakespeare. Let me imagine, since facts are so hard to come by, what would have happened had Shakespeare had a wonderfully gifted sister, called Judith, let us say. Shakespeare himself went, very probably—his mother was an heiress—to the grammar school, where he may have learnt Latin—Ovid, Virgil and Horace[9]—and the elements of grammar and logic. He was, it is well known, a wild boy who poached rabbits, perhaps shot a deer, and had, rather sooner than he should have done, to marry a woman in the neighborhood, who bore him a child rather quicker than was right. That escapade sent him to seek his fortune in London. He had, it seemed a taste for the theatre; he began by holding horses at the stage door. Very soon he got work in the theatre, became a successful actor, and lived at the hub of the universe, meeting everybody, knowing everybody, practising his art on the boards, exercising his wits in the streets, and even getting access to the palace of the queen. Meanwhile his extraordinarily gifted sister, let us suppose, remained at home. She was as adventurous, as imaginative, as agog to see the world as he was. But she was not sent to school. She had no chance of learning grammar and logic, let alone of reading Horace and Virgil. She picked up a book now and then, one of her brother's perhaps, and read a few pages. But then her parents came in and told her to mend the stockings or mind the stew and not moon about with books and papers. They would

have spoken sharply but kindly, for they were substantial people who knew the conditions of life for a woman and loved their daughter—indeed, more likely than not she was the apple of her father's eye. Perhaps she scribbled some pages up in an apple loft on the sly, but was careful to hide them or set fire to them. Soon, however, before she was out of her teens, she was to be betrothed to the son of a neighboring wool-stapler. She cried out that marriage was hateful to her, and for that she was severely beaten by her father. Then he ceased to scold her. He begged her instead not to hurt him, not to shame him in this matter of her marriage. He would give her a chain of beads or a fine petticoat, he said; and there were tears in his eyes. How could she disobey him? How could she break his heart? The force of her own gift alone drove her to it. She made up a small parcel of her belongings, let herself down by a rope one summer's night and took the road to London. She was not seventeen. The birds that sang in the hedge were not more musical than she was. She had the quickest fancy, a gift like her brother's, for the tune of words. Like him, she had a taste for the theatre. She stood at the stage door; she wanted to act, she said. Men laughed in her face. The manager—a fat, loose-lipped man—guffawed. He bellowed something about poodles dancing and women acting—no woman, he said, could possibly be an actress. He hinted—you can imagine what. She could get no training in her craft. Could she even seek her dinner in a tavern or roam the streets at midnight? Yet her genius was for fiction and lusted to feed abundantly upon the lives of men and women and the study of their ways. At

---

[9]Poets of ancient Rome.

last—for she was very young, oddly like Shakespeare the poet in her face, with the same grey eyes and rounded brows—at last Nick Greene the actor-manager took pity on her; she found herself with child by that gentleman and so—who shall measure the heat and violence of the poet's heart when caught and tangled in a woman's body?— killed herself one winter's night and lies buried at some cross-roads where the omnibuses[10] now stop outside the Elephant and Castle.[11]

That, more or less, is how the story would run, I think, if a woman in Shakespeare's day had had Shakespeare's genius. But for my part, I agree with the deceased bishop, if such he was—it is unthinkable that any woman in Shakespeare's day should have had Shakespeare's genius. For genius like Shakespeare's is not born among laboring, uneducated, servile people. It was not born in England among the Saxons and the Britons. It is not born today among the working classes. How, then, could it have been born among women whose work began, according to Professor Trevelyan, almost before they were out of the nursery, who were forced to it by their parents and held to it by all the power of law and custom? Yet genius of a sort must have existed among women as it must have existed among the working classes. Now and again an Emily Brontë or a Robert Burns blazes out and proves its presence. But certainly it never got itself on to paper. When, however, one reads of a witch being ducked, of a woman possessed by devils, of a wise woman selling herbs, or even of a very remarkable man who had a mother, then I think we are on the track of a lost novelist, a suppressed poet, of some mute and inglorious Jane Austen, some Emily Brontë who dashed her brains out on the moor or mopped and mowed about the highways crazed with the torture that her gift had put her to. Indeed, I would venture to guess that Anon, who wrote so many poems without signing them, was often a woman. It was a woman Edward Fitzgerald,[12] I think, suggested who made the ballads and the folksongs, crooning them to her children, beguiling her spinning with them, or the length of the winter's night.

1929

---

[10]Buses.
[11]A British pub.
[12]English poet and translator (1809-1883).

D. H. LAWRENCE (1885-1930)

D. H. Lawrence was one of the most versatile artists of this, or indeed of any, century, being an accomplished novelist, short story writer, essayist, poet, and painter. He was born at Eastwood, a small mining town in Nottinghamshire, on September 11, 1885. His father was a coal-miner, and his mother an ex-schoolteacher. At the age of thirteen the young Lawrence won a scholarship to Nottingham High School. After leaving high school he worked briefly for a firm of surgical goods manufacturers in Nottingham, and then became a pupil teacher in his native town. To complete his teacher's qualifications, he enrolled at University College, Nottingham, and while there began his first novel, *The White Peacock* (1911). He taught school at Croydon for a few months, but turned to writing as a full-time occupation. After two years of travel on the continent he returned to England and married Frieda von Richthofen in July, 1914. Lawrence was called up several times during World War I, but was always rejected for service on medical grounds. After the war he and his wife travelled

extensively in Europe, Australia, and the United States. Lawrence died of tuberculosis on March 2, 1930, and was buried at Vence in the south of France.

In all forms of artistic expression, Lawrence's work is marked by its freshness of vision and its dynamic energy. The characters in his fiction are tremendously alive, pulsating sources of attraction and repulsion; and he can invest with the same vitality birds, animals, vegetation, and places. He calls for a renewed recognition of the importance of the instinctive life of the whole man as against the tendency of modern civilization to value only the intellect and material possessions.

The essay that follows appeared first in *The Athenaeum* of April 11, 1919, and in book form in *Phoenix* (1936). It is perhaps significant that it was written in the first spring after World War I.

The poems are from *Birds, Beasts, and Flowers* (1923).

Whistling of Birds

The frost held for many weeks, until the birds were dying rapidly. Everywhere in the fields and under the hedges lay the ragged remains of lapwings, starlings, thrushes, redwings, innumerable ragged bloody cloaks of birds, when the flesh was eaten by invisible beasts of prey.

Then, quite suddenly, one morning, the change came. The wind went to the south, and came off the sea warm and soothing. In the afternoon there were gleams of sunshine, and the doves began, without interval, slowly and awkwardly to coo. The doves were cooing, though with a laboured sound, as if they were

still winter-stunned. Nevertheless, all the afternoon they continued their noise, in the mild air, before the frost had thawed off the road. At evening the wind blew gently, still gathering a bruising quality of frost from the hard earth. Then, in the yellow-gleamy sunset, wild birds began to whistle faintly in the blackthorn thickets of the stream-bottom.

It was startling and almost frightening after the heavy silence of frost. How could they sing at once, when the ground was thickly strewn with the torn carcasses of birds? Yet out of the evening came the uncertain, silvery sounds that made one's soul start alert, almost with fear. How could the little silver bugles sound the rally so swiftly, in the soft air, when the earth was yet bound? Yet the birds continued their whistling, rather dimly and brokenly, but throwing the threads of silver, germinating noise into the air.

It was almost a pain to realize, so swiftly, the new world. *Le monde est mort. Vive le monde!*[1] But the birds omitted even the first part of the announcement, their cry was only a faint, blind, fecund *vive!*

There is another world. The winter is gone. There is a new world of spring. The voice of the turtle is heard in the land. But the flesh shrinks from so sudden a transition. Surely the call is premature while the clods are still frozen, and the ground is littered with the remains of wings! Yet we have no choice. In the bottoms of impenetrable blackthorn, each evening and morning now, out flickers a whistling of birds.

Where does it come from, the song? After so long a cruelty, how can they make it up so quickly? But it bubbles through them, they are like little well-heads, little fountain-heads whence the spring trickles and bubbles forth. It is not of their own doing. In their throats the new life distils itself into sound. It is the rising of silvery sap of a new summer, gurgling itself forth.

All the time, whilst the earth lay choked and killed and winter-mortified, the deep undersprings were quiet. They only wait for the ponderous encumbrance of the old order to give way, yield in the thaw, and there they are, a silver realm at once. Under the surge of ruin, unmitigated winter, lies the silver potentiality of all blossom. One day the black tide must spend itself and fade back. Then all-suddenly appears the crocus, hovering triumphant in the rear, and we know the order has changed, there is a new regime, sound of a new *vive! vive!*

It is no use any more to look at the torn remnants of birds that lie exposed. It is no longer any use remembering the sullen thunder of frost and the intolerable pressure of cold upon us. For whether we will or not, they are gone. The choice is not ours. We may remain wintry and destructive for a little longer, if we wish it, but the winter is gone out of us, and willy-nilly our hearts sing a little at sunset.

Even whilst we stare at the ragged horror of the birds scattered broadcast, part-eaten, the soft, uneven cooing of the pigeon ripples from the outhouses, and there is a faint silver whistling in the bushes come twilight. No matter, we stand and stare at the torn and unsightly ruins, we watch the weary, mutilated columns of winter retreating under our eyes. Yet in our ears are the silver bugles of a new creation advancing on us from behind, we hear the rolling of the soft and happy drums of the doves.

We may not choose the world. We have hardly any choice for ourselves. We follow with our eyes the bloody and horrid line of march of extreme winter, as it passes away. But we cannot hold back the spring. We cannot make the birds silent, prevent the bubbling of the wood-pigeons. We cannot stay the fine world of silver-fecund creation from gathering itself and taking place upon us. Whether we will or no, the daphne tree

[1] An allusion to the formula used when the King dies: "The King is dead! Long live the King!" Literally, "The world is dead. Live the world!"

will soon be giving off perfume, the lambs dancing on two feet, the celandines will twinkle all over the ground, there will be a new heaven and new earth.

For it is in us, as well as without us. Those who can may follow the columns of winter in their retreat from the earth. Some of us, we have no choice, the spring is within us, the silver fountain begins to bubble under our breast, there is gladness in spite of ourselves. And on the instant we accept the gladness! The first day of change, out whistles an unusual interrupted paean, a fragment that will augment itself imperceptibly. And this in spite of the extreme bitterness of the suffering, in spite of the myriads of torn dead.

Such a long, long winter, and the frost only broke yesterday. Yet it seems, already we cannot remember it. It is strangely remote, like a far-off darkness. It is as unreal as a dream in the night. This is the morning of reality, when we are ourselves. This is natural and real, the glimmering of a new creation that stirs in us and about us. We know there was winter, long, fearful. We know the earth was strangled and mortified, we know the body of life was torn and scattered broadcast. But what is this retrospective knowledge? It is something extraneous to us, extraneous to this that we are now. And what we are, and what, it seems, we always have been, is this quickening lovely silver plasm of pure creativity. All the mortification and tearing, ah yes, it was upon us, encompassing us. It was like a storm or a mist or a falling from a height. It was entangled with us, like bats in our hair, driving us mad. But it was never really our innermost self. Within, we were always apart, we were this, this

limpid fountain of silver, then quiescent, rising and breaking now into the flowering.

It is strange, the utter incompatibility of death with life. Whilst there is death, life is not to be found. It is all death, one overwhelming flood. And then a new tide rises, and it is all life, a fountain of silvery blissfulness. It is one or the other. We are for life, or we are for death, one or the other, but never in our essence both at once.

Death takes us, and all is torn redness, passing into darkness. Life rises, and we are faint fine jets of silver running out to blossom. All is incompatible with all. There is the silver-speckled, incandescent-lovely thrush, whistling pipingly his first song in the blackthorn thicket. How is he to be connected with the bloody feathered unsightliness of the thrush-remnants just outside the bushes? There is no connexion. They are not to be referred the one to the other. Where one is, the other is not. In the kingdom of death the silvery song is not. But where there is life, there is no death. No death whatever, only silvery gladness, perfect, the other-world.

The blackbird cannot stop his song, neither can the pigeon. It takes place in him, even though all his race was yesterday destroyed. He cannot mourn, or be silent, or adhere to the dead. Of the dead he is not, since life has kept him. The dead must bury their dead. Life has now taken hold on him and tossed him into the new ether of a new firmament, where he bursts into song as if he were combustible. What is the past, those others, now he is tossed clean into the new, across the untranslatable difference?

In his song is heard the first brokenness

and uncertainty of the transition. The transit from the grip of death into new being is a death from death, in its sheer metempsychosis, a dizzy agony. But only for a second, the moment of trajectory, the passage from one state to another, from the grip of death to the liberty of newness. In a moment he is a kingdom of wonder, singing at the centre of a new creation.

The bird did not hang back. He did not cling to his death and his dead. There is no death, and the dead have buried their dead. Tossed into the chasm between two worlds, he lifted his wings in dread, and found himself carried on the impulse.

We are lifted to be cast away into the new beginning. Under our hearts the fountain surges, to toss us forth. Who can thwart the impulse that comes upon us? It comes from the unknown upon us, and it behooves us to pass delicately and exquisitely upon the subtle new wind from heaven, conveyed like birds in unreasoning migrations from death to life.

1919

1936

Snake

A snake came to my water-trough
On a hot, hot day, and I in pyjamas for the heat,
To drink there.

In the deep, strange-scented shade of the great dark carob-tree
I came down the steps with my pitcher
And must wait, must stand and wait, for there he was at the trough
    before me.

He reached down from a fissure in the earth-wall in the gloom
And trailed his yellow-brown slackness soft-bellied down, over the edge of
    the stone trough
And rested his throat upon the stone bottom,
And where the water had dripped from the tap, in a small clearness,   10
He sipped with his straight mouth,
Softly drank through his straight gums, into his slack long body,
Silently.

Someone was before me at my water-trough,
And I, like a second comer, waiting.

He lifted his head from his drinking, as cattle do,
And looked at me vaguely, as drinking cattle do,
And flickered his two-forked tongue from his lips, and mused a moment,
And stooped and drank a little more,
Being earth-brown, earth-golden from the burning bowels of the earth   20
On the day of Sicilian July, with Etna smoking.

The voice of my education said to me
He must be killed,
For in Sicily the black, black snakes are innocent, the gold are venomous.

And voices in me said, If you were a man
You would take a stick and break him now, and finish him off.

But must I confess how I liked him,
How glad I was he had come like a guest in quiet, to drink at my
          water-trough
And depart peaceful, pacified, and thankless,
Into the burning bowels of this earth?   30

Was it cowardice, that I dared not kill him?
Was it perversity, that I longed to talk to him?
Was it humility, to feel so honoured?
I felt so honoured.

And yet those voices:
If you were not afraid, you would kill him!

And truly I was afraid, I was most afraid,
But even so, honoured still more
That he should seek my hospitality
From out the dark door of the secret earth.   40

He drank enough
And lifted his head, dreamily, as one who has drunken,
And flickered his tongue like a forked night on the air, so black,
Seeming to lick his lips,
And looked around like a god, unseeing, into the air,
And slowly turned his head,
And slowly, very slowly, as if thrice adream,
Proceeded to draw his slow length curving round
And climb again the broken bank of my wall-face.

And as he put his head into that dreadful hole,   50
And as he slowly drew up, snake-easing his shoulders, and entered farther,
A sort of horror, a sort of protest against his withdrawing into that
    horrid black hole,
Deliberately going into the blackness, and slowly drawing himself after,
Overcame me now his back was turned.

I looked round, I put down my pitcher,
I picked up a clumsy log
And threw it at the water-trough with a clatter.

I think it did not hit him,
But suddenly that part of him that was left behind convulsed in
    undignified haste,
Writhed like lightning, and was gone   60
Into the black hole, the earth-lipped fissure in the wall-front,
At which, in the intense still noon, I stared with fascination.

And immediately I regretted it.
I thought how paltry, how vulgar, what a mean act!
I despised myself and the voices of my accursed human education.
And I thought of the albatross,
And I wished he would come back, my snake.

For he seemed to me again like a king,
Like a king in exile, uncrowned in the underworld,
Now due to be crowned again.   70

And so, I missed my chance with one of the lords
Of life.
And I have something to expiate;
A pettiness.

1921?
                                           1923

Humming-Bird

I can imagine, in some otherworld
Primeval-dumb, far back
In that most awful stillness, that only gasped and hummed,
Humming-birds raced down the avenues.

Before anything had a soul,
While life was a heave of Matter, half inanimate,
This little bit chipped off in brilliance
And went whizzing through the slow, vast, succulent stems.

I believe there were no flowers then,
In the world where the humming-bird flashed ahead of creation.
I believe he pierced the slow vegetable veins with his long beak.

Probably he was big
As mosses, and little lizards, they say, were once big.
Probably he was a jabbing, terrifying monster.

We look at him through the wrong end of the long telescope of Time,
Luckily for us.

1920?   1923

Kangaroo

In the northern hemisphere
Life seems to leap at the air, or skim under the wind
Like stags on rocky ground, or pawing horses, or springy scut-tailed rabbits.

Or else rush horizontal to charge at the sky's horizon,
Like bulls or bisons or wild pigs.

Or slip like water slippery towards its ends,
As foxes, stoats, and wolves, and prairie dogs.

Only mice, and moles, and rats, and badgers, and beavers, and perhaps bears
Seem belly-plumbed to the earth's mid-navel.
Or frogs that when they leap come flop, and flop to the centre of the earth.   10

But the yellow antipodal Kangaroo, when she sits up,
Who can unseat her, like a liquid drop that is heavy, and just touches earth.

The downward drip
The down-urge
So much denser than cold-blooded frogs.

Delicate mother Kangaroo
Sitting up there rabbit-wise, but huge, plump-weighted,
And lifting her beautiful slender face, oh! so much more gently and finely lined
    than a rabbit's, or than a hare's,
Lifting her face to nibble at a round white peppermint drop which she loves,
    sensitive mother Kangaroo.

Her sensitive, long, pure-bred face.   20
Her full antipodal eyes, so dark,
So big and quiet and remote, having watched so many empty dawns in silent
    Australia.

Her little loose hands, and drooping Victorian shoulders.
And then her great weight below the waist, her vast pale belly
With a thin young yellow little paw hanging out, and straggle of a long thin ear,
    like ribbon,
Like a funny trimming to the middle of her belly, thin little dangle of an immature
    paw, and one thin ear.

Her belly, her big haunches
And, in addition, the great muscular python-stretch of her tail.

There, she shan't have any more peppermint drops.   29
So she wistfully, sensitively sniffs the air, and then turns, goes off in slow sad leaps

On the long flat skis of her legs,
Steered and propelled by that steel-strong snake of a tail.
Stops again, half turns, inquisitive to look back.
While something stirs quickly in her belly, and a lean little face comes out, as from
    a window,
Peaked and a bit dismayed,
Only to disappear again quickly away from the sight of the world, to snuggle down
    in the warmth,
Leaving the trail of a different paw hanging out.

Still she watches with eternal, cocked wistfulness!
How full her eyes are, like the full, fathomless, shining eyes of an Australian black-boy
Who has been lost so many centuries on the margins of existence!   40
She watches with insatiable wistfulness.
Untold centuries of watching for something to come,
For a new signal from life, in that silent lost land of the South.

Where nothing bites but insects and snakes and the sun, small life.
Where no bull roared, no cow ever lowed, no stag cried, no leopard screeched, no
    lion coughed, no dog barked,
But all was silent save for parrots occasionally, in the haunted blue bush.

Wistfully watching, with wonderful liquid eyes.
And all her weight, all her blood, dripping sack-wise down towards the earth's centre,
And the live little-one taking in its paw at the door of her belly.   49

Leap then, and come down on the line that draws to the earth's deep, heavy centre.

1922?   1923

KATHERINE MANSFIELD (1888-1923)

Katherine Mansfield was one of the most sensitive and talented practitioners of the short story in this century. She was born in Wellington, New Zealand, her real name being Kathleen Mansfield Beauchamp. She was educated at Queen's College, London, where she was editor of the college magazine. Her first career was that of a cellist, but she gave up music for writing. Mansfield's short stories began to appear in the magazines just before World War I, bringing her to the attention of the editor and critic, John Middleton Murry, whom she eventually married. With Murry and D.H. Lawrence she collaborated in founding a literary magazine, *The Signature.* The publication of *Bliss and Other Stories* in 1920 established her reputation, and it was confirmed by *The Garden Party* (1922). Her health, however, was rapidly deteriorating, and she died of tuberculosis at the age of thirty-five, in a French sanitarium to which she had gone in

the hope of effecting a cure. *The Dove's Nest* appeared in the year of her death, and *Something Childish* in 1924. Her letters and journals have been published subsequently by her husband.

The core of almost all of Mansfield's stories is her compassion for the poor, the lonely, or the outsider, and her contempt for the over-rich, the smug, and the snobbish. She finds her material in the ordinary lives of ordinary people, and by closely observing their reactions to the little crises of everyday life makes us aware of the intense feelings involved in them. She can take an object such as a fur neck-piece or a doll's house and make it a symbol of human yearning or pride. Like all genuine works of art, her stories are at once particular and universal; they are true to their own place and time, but true also of all places and times. Their quiet delicacy and irony of style enhance their sense of truth.

The Doll's House

When dear old Mrs. Hay went back to town after staying with the Burnells she sent the children a doll's house. It was so big that the carter and Pat carried it into the courtyard, and there it stayed, propped up on two wooden boxes beside the feed-room door. No harm could come to it; it was summer. And perhaps the smell of paint would have gone off by the time it had to be taken in. For, really, the smell of paint coming from that doll's house ("Sweet of old Mrs. Hay, of course; most sweet and generous!")— but the smell of paint was quite enough to make anyone seriously ill, in Aunt Beryl's opinion. Even before the sacking was taken off. And when it was . . .

There stood the doll's house, a dark, oily, spinach green, picked out with bright yellow. Its two solid little chim-

neys, glued on to the roof, were painted red and white, and the door, gleaming with yellow varnish, was like a little slab of toffee. Four windows, real windows, were divided into panes by a broad streak of green. There was actually a tiny porch, too, painted yellow, with big lumps of congealed paint hanging along the edge.

But perfect, perfect little house! Who could possibly mind the smell? It was part of the joy, part of the newness.

"Open it quickly, someone!"

The hook at the side was stuck fast. Pat pried it open with his penknife, and the whole house front swung back, and— there you were, gazing at one and the same moment into the drawing-room and the dining-room, the kitchen and the two bedrooms. That is the way for a house to open! Why don't all houses open like that? How much more exciting than peering through the slit of a door into a mean little hall with a hatstand and two umbrellas! That is—isn't it?—what you long to know about a house when you put your hand on the knocker. Perhaps it is the way God opens houses at the dead of night when He is taking a quiet turn with an angel. . . .

"O-oh!" The Burnell children sounded as though they were in despair. It was too marvellous; it was too much for them. They had never seen anything like it in their lives. All the rooms were papered. There were pictures on the walls, painted on the paper, with gold frames complete. Red carpets covered all the floors except the kitchen; red plush chairs in the drawing-room, green in the dining-room; tables, beds with real bedclothes, a cradle, a stove, a dresser with tiny plates and one big jug. But what Kezia liked more than anything, what she liked frightfully, was the lamp. It stood in the middle of the dining-room table, an exquisite little amber lamp with a white globe. It was even filled all ready for lighting, though, of course, you couldn't light it. But there was something inside that looked like oil and moved when you shook it.

The father and mother dolls, who sprawled very stiff as though they had fainted in the drawing-room, and their two little children asleep upstairs, were really too big for the doll's house. They didn't look as though they belonged. But the lamp was perfect. It seemed to smile at Kezia, to say, "I live here." The lamp was real.

The Burnell children could hardly walk to school fast enough the next morning. They burned to tell everybody, to describe, to—well—to boast about their doll's house before the school-bell rang.

"I'm to tell," said Isabel, "because I'm the eldest. And you two can join in after. But I'm to tell first."

There was nothing to answer. Isabel was bossy, but she was always right, and Lottie and Kezia knew too well the powers that went with being eldest. They brushed through the thick buttercups at the road edge and said nothing.

"And I'm to choose who's to come and see it first. Mother said I might."

For it had been arranged that while the doll's house stood in the courtyard they might ask the girls at school, two at a time, to come and look. Not to stay to tea, of course, or to come traipsing through the house. But just to stand quietly in the courtyard while Isabel pointed out the beauties, and Lottie and Kezia looked pleased. . . .

But hurry as they might, by the time they had reached the tarred palings of the boys' playground the bell had begun to jangle. They only just had time to whip off their hats and fall into line before the roll was called. Never mind. Isabel tried to make up for it by looking very important and mysterious and by whispering behind her hand to the girls near her, "Got something to tell you at playtime."

Playtime came and Isabel was surrounded. The girls of her class nearly fought to put their arms round her, to walk away with her, to beam flatteringly, to be her special friend. She held quite a court under the huge pine trees at the side of the playground. Nudging, giggling together, the little girls pressed up close. And the only two who stayed outside the ring were the two who were always outside, the little Kelveys. They knew better than to come anywhere near the Burnells.

For the fact was, the school the Burnell children went to was not at all the kind of place their parents would have chosen if there had been any choice. But there was none. It was the only school for miles. And the consequence was all the children of the neighbourhood, the judge's little girls, the doctor's daughters, the store-keeper's children, the milkman's, were forced to mix together. Not to speak of there being an equal number of rude, rough, little boys as well. But the line had to be drawn somewhere. It was drawn at the Kelveys. Many of the children, including the Burnells, were not allowed even to speak to them. They walked past the Kelveys with their heads in the air, and as they set the fashion in all matters of behaviour, the Kelveys were shunned by everybody. Even the teacher had a special voice for them, and a special smile for the other children when Lil Kelvey came up to her desk with a bunch of dreadfully common-looking flowers.

They were the daughters of a spry, hard-working little washerwoman, who went about from house to house by the day. This was awful enough. But where was Mr. Kelvey? Nobody knew for certain. But everybody said he was in prison. So they were the daughters of a washerwoman and a gaolbird. Very nice company for other people's children! And they looked it. Why Mrs. Kelvey made them so conspicuous was hard to understand. The truth was they were dressed in "bits" given to her by the people for whom she worked. Lil, for instance, who was a stout, plain child, with big freckles, came to school in a dress made from a green art-serge table-cloth of the Burnells, with red plush sleeves from the Logans' curtains. Her hat, perched on top of her high fore-head, was a grown-up woman's hat, once the property of Miss Leckie, the post-mistress. It was turned up at the back and trimmed with a large scarlet quill. What a little guy she looked! It was impossible not to laugh. And her little sister, our Else, wore a long white dress, rather like a nightgown, and a pair of little boy's boots. But whatever our Else wore she would have looked strange. She was a tiny wishbone of a child, with cropped hair and enormous, solemn eyes—a little white owl. Nobody had ever seen her smile; she scarcely ever spoke. She went through life holding on to Lil, with a piece of Lil's skirt screwed up in her hand. Where Lil went, our Else followed. In the playground, on the road going to and from school, there was Lil marching in front and our Else holding on behind. Only when she wanted anything, or when she was out of breath, our Else gave Lil a tug, a twitch, and Lil stopped and turned round. The Kelveys never failed to understand each other.

Now they hovered at the edge; you couldn't stop them listening. When the little girls turned round and sneered, Lil, as usual, gave her silly, shamefaced smile, but our Else only looked.

And Isabel's voice, so very proud, went telling. The carpet made a great sensation, but so did the beds with real bedclothes, and the stove with an oven door.

When she finished Kezia broke in. "You've forgotten the lamp, Isabel."

"Oh, yes," said Isabel, "and there's a teeny little lamp, all made of yellow glass, with a white globe that stands on the dining-room table. You couldn't tell it from a real one."

"The lamp's best of all," cried Kezia. She thought Isabel wasn't making half enough of the little lamp. But nobody paid any attention. Isabel was choosing the two who were to come back with them that afternoon and see it. She chose Emmie Cole and Lena Logan. But when the others knew they were all to have a chance, they couldn't be nice enough to Isabel. One by one they put their arms round Isabel's waist and walked her off. They had something to whisper to her, a secret. "Isabel's *my* friend."

Only the little Kelveys moved away forgotten; there was nothing for them to hear.

Days passed, and as more children saw the doll's house, the fame of it spread. It became the one subject, the rage. The one question was, "Have you seen Burnell's doll's house? Oh, ain't it lovely!" "Haven't you seen it? Oh, I say!"

Even the dinner hour was given up to talking about it. The little girls sat under the pines eating their thick mutton sandwiches and big slabs of johnny cake spread with butter. While always, as near as they could get, sat the Kelveys, our Else holding on to Lil, listening too, while they chewed their jam sandwiches out of a newspaper soaked with large red blobs.

"Mother," said Kezia, "can't I ask the Kelveys just once?"

"Certainly not, Kezia."

"But why not?"

"Run away Kezia; you know quite well why not."

At last everybody had seen it except them. On that day the subject rather flagged. It was the dinner hour. The children stood together under the pine trees, and suddenly, as they looked at the Kelveys eating out of their paper, always by themselves, always listening, they wanted to be horrid to them. Emmie Cole started the whisper.

"Lil Kelvey's going to be a servant when she grows up."

"O-oh, how awful!" said Isabel Burnell, and she made eyes at Emmie.

Emmie swallowed in a very meaning way and nodded to Isabel as she'd seen her mother do on these occasions.

"It's true—it's true—it's true," she said.

Then Lena Logan's little eyes snapped. "Shall I ask her?" she whispered.

"Bet you don't," said Jessie May.

"Pooh, I'm not frightened," said Lena. Suddenly she gave a little squeal and danced in front of the other girls. "Watch! Watch me! Watch me now!" said Lena. And sliding, gliding, dragging one foot, giggling behind her hand, Lena went over to the Kelveys.

Lil looked up from her dinner. She wrapped the rest quickly away. Our Else stopped chewing. What was coming now?

"Is it true you're going to be a servant when you grow up, Lil Kelvey?" shrilled Lena.

Dead silence. But instead of answering, Lil only gave her silly, shamefaced smile. She didn't seem to mind the question at all. What a sell for Lena! The girls began to titter.

Lena couldn't stand that. She put her hands on her hips; she shot forward. "Yah, yer father's in prison!" she hissed, spitefully.

This was such a marvellous thing to have said that the little girls rushed away in a body, deeply, deeply excited, wild with joy. Someone found a long rope, and they began skipping. And never did they skip so high, run in and out so fast, or do such daring things as on that morning.

In the afternoon Pat called for the Burnell children with the buggy and they drove home. There were visitors. Isabel and Lottie, who liked visitors, went upstairs to change their pinafores. But Kezia thieved out at the back. Nobody was about; she began to swing on the big white gates of the courtyard. Presently, looking along the road, she saw two little dots. They grew bigger, they were coming towards her. Now she could see that they were the Kelveys. Kezia stopped swinging. She slipped off the gate as if she was going to run away. Then she hesitated. The Kelveys came nearer, and beside them walked their shadows, very long, stretching right across the road with their heads in the buttercups. Kezia clambered back on the gate; she had made up her mind; she swung out.

"Hullo," she said to the passing Kelveys.

They were so astounded that they stopped. Lil gave her silly smile. Our Else stared.

"You can come and see our doll's house if you want to," said Kezia, and she dragged one toe on the ground. But at that Lil turned red and shook her head quickly.

"Why not?" asked Kezia.

Lil gasped, then she said, "Your ma told our ma you wasn't to speak to us."

"Oh, well," said Kezia. She didn't know what to reply. "It doesn't matter. You can come and see our doll's house all the same. Come on. Nobody's looking."

But Lil shook her head still harder.

"Don't you want to?" asked Kezia.

Suddenly there was a twitch, a tug at Lil's skirt. She turned around. Our Else was looking at her with big, imploring eyes; she was frowning; she wanted to go. For a moment Lil looked at our Else, very doubtfully. But then our Else twitched her skirt again. She started forward. Kezia led the way. Like two little stray cats they followed across the courtyard to where the doll's house stood.

"There it is," said Kezia.

There was a pause. Lil breathed loudly, almost snorted; our Else was still as stone.

"I'll open it for you," said Kezia kindly. She undid the hook and they looked inside.

"There's the drawing-room and the dining-room, and that's the—"

"Kezia!"

Oh, what a start they gave!

It was Aunt Beryl's voice. They turned round. At the back door stood Aunt Beryl, staring as if she couldn't believe what she saw.

"How dare you ask the little Kelveys into the courtyard?" said her cold, furious voice. "You know as well as I do, you're not allowed to talk to them. Run away, children, run away at once. And don't come back again," said Aunt Beryl. And she stepped into the yard and shooed them out as if they were chickens.

"Off you go immediately!" she called, cold and proud.

They did not need telling twice. Burning with shame, shrinking together, Lil huddling along like her mother, our Else, dazed, somehow they crossed the big courtyard and squeezed through the white gate.

"Wicked, disobedient little girl!" said Aunt Beryl bitterly to Kezia, and she slammed the doll's house to.

The afternoon had been awful. A letter had come from Willie Brent, a terrifying, threatening letter, saying if she did not meet him that evening in Pulman's

Bush, he'd come to the front door and ask the reason why! But now that she had frightened those little rats of Kelvey's and given Kezia a good scolding, her heart felt lighter. That ghastly pressure was gone. She went back to the house humming.

When the Kelveys were well out of sight of Burnells', they sat down to rest on a big red drainpipe by the side of the road. Lil's cheeks were still burning; she took off the hat with the quill and held it on her knee. Dreamily they looked over the hay paddocks, past the creek, to the group of wattles where Logan's cows stood waiting to be milked. What were their thoughts?

Presently our Else nudged up close to her sister. But now she had forgotten the cross lady. She put out a finger and stroked her sister's quill; she smiled her rare smile.

"I seen the little lamp!" she said, softly.

Then both were silent once more.

1923

W.H. AUDEN (1907-1973)

W.H. Auden was born in 1907 in York, England. During his three years at Oxford, he issued his first volume, *Poems*, which his friend Stephen Spender published on a hand press. Auden was one of a group of young British poets who became known in the 1930s as the left-wing school—a group which also included Stephen Spender, Cecil Day-Lewis and Louis MacNeice. Reaching adulthood at a time of great economic depression, these poets could not accept the religious passivity which T.S. Eliot had advocated in his lines

Teach us to care and not to care
Teach us to sit still . . .

Auden, Spender and the rest said in effect: "Teach us to care more and more about poverty, unemployment and war; teach us how to stand up and do something." They sought solutions to the urgent problems of their time in the teachings of Marx and Freud, and were all at one time or another drawn to the idea of a communist revolution as the only way out of economic stagnation and drift towards war. Their poems were poems of warning and exhortation, written in contemporary idiom, using images drawn from an urban and industrial society.

Auden wrote and travelled throughout the 1930s, visiting Iceland, Spain and China (the latter two were involved in wars and political strife at the time). The curious shifts of communist policy at the outbreak of World War II disillusioned him with communism, and he moved to America in 1939, turning from political matters to a broader view of human experience. His last years were divided between America and Austria. He left behind an impressive body of work, including poems, prose, drama and opera libretti.

Auden is a poet of understatement, a disenchanter—in other words, an anti-romantic. He celebrates the value of love while underlining its transience and uncertainty (as in "Lay Your Sleeping Head, My Love"). He asserts the importance of poetry while denying it has any influence outside the world of poetry itself. His later poems focus on a Christian view of experience, but his piety is much more earthy and straightforward than T.S. Eliot's.

Lay Your Sleeping Head, My Love

Lay your sleeping head, my love,
Human on my faithless arm;

Time and fevers burn away
Individual beauty from
Thoughtful children, and the grave
Proves the child ephemeral:
But in my arms till break of day
Let the living creature lie,
Mortal, guilty, but to me
The entirely beautiful.   10

Soul and body have no bounds:
To lovers as they lie upon
Her tolerant enchanted slope
In their ordinary swoon,
Grave the vision Venus sends[1]
Of supernatural sympathy,
Universal love and hope;
While an abstract insight wakes
Among the glaciers and the rocks
The hermit's carnal ecstasy.[2]   20

Certainty, fidelity
On the stroke of midnight pass[3]
Like vibrations of a bell
And fashionable madmen raise
Their pedantic boring cry:
Every farthing of the cost,
All the dreaded cards foretell,
Shall be paid, but from this night
Not a whisper, not a thought,
Not a kiss nor look be lost.   30

Beauty, midnight, vision dies:
Let the winds of dawn that blow
Softly round your dreaming head
Such a day of welcome show
Eye and knocking heart may bless,
Find our mortal world enough;[4]

[1]Venus, the goddess of Love, gives to lovers a vision of "supernatural sympathy," in which the body and soul of man and woman achieve true union. This swoon is "ordinary" because it is available to all.
[2]In a uniting of opposites, the religious hermit discovers abstract truths through sensory deprivation and solitude.
[3]There is no absolute knowledge or faithfulness among human beings—"to err is human."
[4]We must cherish this transitory, faithless love that has been given us; we must learn to find this "mortal world" and "human love" enough.

Noons of dryness find you fed
By the involuntary powers,
Nights of insult let you pass
Watched by every human love.   40
                                                     1937

Musée des Beaux Arts [1]

About suffering they were never wrong.
The Old Masters: how well they understood
Its human position; how it takes place
While someone else is eating or opening a window or just walking dully along;
How, when the aged are reverently, passionately waiting
For the miraculous birth, there always must be

Children who did not specially want it to happen, skating
On a pond at the edge of the wood:
They never forgot
That even the dreadful martyrdom must run its course   10
Anyhow in a corner, some untidy spot
Where the dogs go on with their doggy life and the torturer's horse
Scratches its innocent behind on a tree.

In Breughel's *Icarus* [2], for instance: how everything turns away
Quite leisurely from the disaster; the ploughman may
Have heard the splash, the forsaken cry,
But for him it was not an important failure; the sun shone
As it had to on the white legs disappearing into the green
Water; and the expensive delicate ship that must have seen
Something amazing, a boy falling out of the sky,
Had somewhere to get to and sailed calmly on.   20
                                                                        1938

[1]"Museum of Fine Arts."
[2]In Greek mythology Icarus flew on wings made of feathers and wax, but soared too close to the
   sun, fell into the ocean and drowned. Painting this subject, Pieter Brueghel (1520-1569)
   portrayed the scene with many bystanders unaware of Icarus's fatal fall. The painting is
   housed in the Musées Royaux des Beaux Arts, Brussels.

Their Lonely Betters

As I listened from a beach-chair in the shade
To all the noises that my garden made,
It seemed to me only proper that words
Should be withheld from vegetables and birds.

A robin with no Christian name ran through
The Robin-Anthem which was all it knew,
And rustling flowers for some third party waited
To say which pairs, if any, should get mated.

Not one of them was capable of lying,
There was not one which knew that it was dying   10
Or could have with a rhythm or a rhyme
Assumed responsibility for time.

Let them leave language to their lonely betters
Who count some days and long for certain letters;
We, too, make noises when we laugh or weep:
Words are for those with promises to keep.

                                                        1950

DYLAN THOMAS (1914-1953)

Dylan Thomas has been the most prominent and controversial English poet of the period since World War II. He became a legend in his own life-time, and interest in his personality and his poetry has increased rather than diminished since his premature death. Gifted with an expressive voice, he owed his fame in part to the vogue of recorded poetry in our time, and records of his poetry, and indeed of his prose, have circulated widely on both sides of the Atlantic. His verse is difficult, but even when it is not fully understood it has such power and melody that it attracts interest and admiration.

Thomas was born at Swansea in South Wales, the son of a teacher of English in the local Grammar (or High) School. He attended that school himself but was an indifferent pupil: when told to work harder he always replied that he had no need to do so, since he was going to be a poet! True to his promise, he made writing and broadcasting his full-time career after leaving school, and published his first book of verse, *Eighteen Poems* (1934), before he was twenty. He also wrote short stories, a humorous autobiography entitled *Portrait of the Artist as a Young Dog* (1940), film scripts, radio plays, and an unfinished novel, *Adventures in the Skin Trade*, parts of which were published in 1941 and 1953. He frequently read his poems over the radio and to live audiences in England, Canada, and the United States. He died while on a visit to the United States—in New York City in November, 1953.

Critical opinion is still divided about the merits of Thomas's poetry. Some have described it as "the most absolute poetry that has been written in our time." Others have said that reading it is like taking an "unconducted tour of Bedlam." His concentrated symbols and his distortions of syntax make for difficult reading, but the melody of his verse and its strength of personal emotion often carry us through. Unlike the social realist poets of the thirties, he cares little for politics and is a thorough-going romantic. He is at his best in a poem such as "Fern Hill," where his memories of his own boyhood, and his sense of the continuity and inevitability of decay and death, are expressed directly and powerfully. His most profound insight is of the unity of life and death, of growth and decay, of the continuous cycle of being in which all created things revolve.

The Force That Through the Green Fuse Drives the Flower

The force that through the green fuse drives the flower
Drives my green age; that blasts the roots of trees
Is my destroyer.
And I am dumb to tell the crooked rose
My youth is bent by the same wintry fever.

The force that drives the water through the rocks
Drives my red blood; that dries the mouthing streams
Turns mine to wax.
And I am dumb to mouth unto my veins
How at the mountain spring the same mouth sucks.   10

The hand that whirls the water in the pool
Stirs the quicksand; that ropes the blowing wind
Hauls my shroud sail.
And I am dumb to tell the hanging man
How of my clay is made the hangman's lime.

The lips of time leech to the fountain head;
Love drips and gathers, but the fallen blood
Shall calm her sores.
And I am dumb to tell a weather's wind
How time has ticked a heaven round the stars.   20

And I am dumb to tell the lover's tomb
How at my sheet goes the same crooked worm.

                                        1934

And Death Shall Have No Dominion

And death shall have no dominion.
Dead men naked they shall be one
With the man in the wind and the west moon;
When their bones are picked clean and the clean bones gone,
They shall have stars at elbow and foot;
Though they go mad they shall be sane,
Though they sink through the sea they shall rise again;
Though lovers be lost love shall not;
And death shall have no dominion.

And death shall have no dominion.   10
Under the windings of the sea
They lying long shall not die windily;
Twisting on racks when sinews give way,
Strapped to a wheel, yet they shall not break;
Faith in their hands shall snap in two,
And the unicorn evils run them through;
Split all ends up they shan't crack;
And death shall have no dominion.

And death shall have no dominion.
No more may gulls cry at their ears   20
Or waves break loud on the seashores;
Where blew a flower may a flower no more
Lift its head to the blows of the rain;
Though they be mad and dead as nails,
Heads of the characters hammer through daisies;
Break in the sun till the sun breaks down,
And death shall have no dominion.

                                                                          1936

Poem in October

It was my thirtieth year to heaven
Woke to my hearing from harbour and neighbour wood
    And the mussel pooled and the heron
        Priested shore
    The morning beckon
With water praying and call of seagull and rook
And the knock of sailing boats on the net webbed wall
    Myself to set foot
        That second
In the still sleeping town and set forth.   10

    My birthday began with the water-
Birds and the birds of the winged trees flying my name
    Above the farms and the white horses
        And I rose
    In rainy autumn
And walked abroad in a shower of all my days.
High tide and the heron dived when I took the road
    Over the border
        And the gates
Of the town closed as the town awoke.   20

A springful of larks in a rolling
Cloud and the roadside bushes brimming with whistling
   Blackbirds and the sun of October
      Summery
   On the hill's shoulder,
Here were fond climates and sweet singers suddenly
Come in the morning where I wandered and listened
   To the rain wringing
      Wind blow cold
In the wood faraway under me.   30

   Pale rain over the dwindling harbour
And over the sea wet church the size of a snail
   With its horns through mist and the castle
      Brown as owls
   But all the gardens
Of spring and summer were blooming in the tall tales
Beyond the border and under the lark-full cloud.
   There could I marvel
      My birthday
Away but the weather turned around.   40

   It turned away from the blithe country
And down the other air and the blue altered sky
   Streamed again a wonder of summer
      With apples
   Pears and red currants
And I saw in the turning so clearly a child's
Forgotten mornings when he walked with his mother
   Through the parables
      Of sun light
And the legends of the green chapels   50

   And the twice told fields of infancy
That his tears burned my cheeks and his heart moved in mine.
   These were the woods the river and sea
      Where a boy
   In the listening
Summertime of the dead whispered the truth of his joy
To the trees and the stones and the fish in the tide.
   And the mystery
      Sang alive
Still in the water and singing birds.   60

And there could I marvel my birthday
Away but the weather turned around. And the true
  Joy of the long dead child sang burning
    In the sun.
  It was my thirtieth
Year to heaven stood there then in the summer noon
Though the town below lay leaved with October blood.
  O may my heart's truth
    Still be sung
On this high hill in a year's turning.   70

                                              1946

A Refusal to Mourn the Death, by Fire, of a Child in London

Never until the mankind making
Bird beast and flower
Fathering and all humbling darkness
Tells with silence the last light breaking
And the still hour
Is come of the sea tumbling in harness

And I must enter again the round
Zion of the water bead
And the synagogue of the ear of corn
Shall I let pray the shadow of a sound   10
Or sow my salt seed
In the least valley of sackcloth to mourn

The majesty and burning of the child's death.
I shall not murder
The mankind of her going with a grave truth
Nor blaspheme down the stations of the breath
With any further
Elegy of innocence and youth.

Deep with the first dead lies London's daughter,
Robed in the long friends,   20
The grains beyond age, the dark veins of her mother,
Secret by the unmourning water
Of the riding Thames.
After the first death, there is no other.

                                              1946

Fern Hill

Now as I was young and easy under the apple boughs
About the lilting house and happy as the grass was green,
   The night above the dingle starry,
     Time let me hail and climb
   Golden in the heydays of his eyes,
And honoured among wagons I was prince of the apple towns
And once below a time I lordly had the trees and leaves
     Trail with daisies and barley
   Down the rivers of the windfall light.

And as I was green and carefree, famous among the barns   10
About the happy yard and singing as the farm was home,
   In the sun that is young once only,
     Time let me play and be
   Golden in the mercy of his means,
And green and golden I was huntsman and herdsman, the calves
Sang to my horn, the foxes on the hills barked clear and cold,
     And the sabbath rang slowly
   In the pebbles of the holy streams.

All the sun long it was running, it was lovely, the hay
Fields high as the house, the tunes from the chimneys, it was air   20
   And playing, lovely and watery
     And fire green as grass.
   And nightly under the simple stars
As I rode to sleep the owls were bearing the farm away,
All the moon long I heard, blessed among stables, the nightjars
     Flying with the ricks, and the horses
     Flashing into the dark.

And then to awake, and the farm, like a wanderer white
With the dew, come back, the cock on his shoulder: it was all
   Shining, it was Adam and maiden,   30
     The sky gathered again
   And the sun grew round that very day.
So it must have been after the birth of the simple light
In the first, spinning place, the spellbound horses walking warm
   Out of the whinnying green stable
     On to the fields of praise.

And honoured among foxes and pheasants by the gay house
Under the new made clouds and happy as the heart was long,
   In the sun born over and over,
     I ran my heedless ways,   40
   My wishes raced through the house-high hay
And nothing I cared, at my sky blue trades, that time allows
In all his tuneful turning so few and such morning songs
   Before the children green and golden
     Follow him out of grace,

Nothing I cared, in the lamb white days, that time would take me
Up to the swallow thronged loft by the shadow of my hand,
   In the moon that is always rising,
     Nor that riding to sleep
   I should hear him fly with the high fields   50
And wake to the farm forever fled from the childless land.
Oh as I was young and easy in the mercy of his means,
   Time held me green and dying
   Though I sang in my chains like the sea.

1943   1946

Do Not Go Gentle into That Good Night[1]

Do not go gentle into that good night,
Old age should burn and rave at close of day;
Rage, rage against the dying of the light.

Though wise men at their end know dark is right,
Because their words had forked no lightning they
Do not go gentle into that good night.

Good men, the last wave by, crying how bright
Their frail deeds might have danced in the green bay,
Rage, rage against the dying of the light.

Wild men who caught and sang the sun in flight,   10
And learn, too late, they grieved it on its way,
Do not go gentle into that good night.

Grave men, near death, who see with blinding sight
Blind eyes could blaze like meteors and be gay,
Rage, rage against the dying of the light.

[1] This poem was written during the final illness of Thomas's father, D. J. Thomas.

And you, my father, there on the sad height,
Curse, bless, me now with your fierce tears, I pray.
Do not go gentle into that good night.
Rage, rage against the dying of the light.

1951

Memories of Christmas

One Christmas was so much like another, in those years, around the sea town corner now, and out of all sound except the distant speaking of the voices I sometimes hear a moment before sleep, that I can never remember whether it snowed for six days and six nights when I was twelve or whether it snowed for twelve days and twelve nights when I was six; or whether the ice broke and the skating grocer vanished like a snow man through a white trap-door on that same Christmas Day that the mince-pies finished Uncle Arnold and we tobogganed down the seaward hill, all the afternoon, on the best tea-tray, and Mrs. Griffiths complained, and we threw a snowball at her niece, and my hands burned so, with the heat and the cold, when I held them in front of the fire, that I cried for twenty minutes and then had some jelly.

All the Christmases roll down the hill towards the Welsh-speaking sea, like a snowball growing whiter and bigger and rounder, like a cold and headlong moon bundling down the sky that was our street; and they stop at the rim of the ice-edged, fish-freezing waves, and I plunge my hands in the snow and bring out whatever I can find; holly or robins or pudding, squabbles and carols and oranges and tin whistles, and the fire in the front room, and bang go the crackers, and holy, holy, holy, ring the bells, and the glass bells shaking on the tree, and Mother Goose, and Struwelpeter—oh! the baby-burning flames and the clacking scissorman!—Billy Bunter and Black Beauty, Little Women and Boys who have three helpings, Alice and Mrs. Potter's badgers, penknives, teddy-bears —named after a Mr. Theodore Bear, their inventor, or father, who died recently in the United States—mouth-organs, tin-soldiers, and blancmange, and Auntie Bessie playing "Pop Goes the Weasel" and "Nuts in May" and "Oranges and Lemons" on the untuned piano in the parlour all through the thimble-hiding musical-chairing blind-man's-buffing party at the end of the never-to-be-forgotten day at the end of the unremembered year.

In goes my hand into that wool-white bell-tongued ball of holidays resting at the margin of the carol-singing sea, and out come Mrs. Prothero and the firemen.

It was on the afternoon of the day of Christmas Eve, and I was in Mrs. Prothero's garden, waiting for cats, with her son Jim. It was snowing. It was always snowing at Christmas; December, in my memory, is white as Lapland, though there were no reindeers. But there were cats. Patient, cold, and callous, our hands wrapped in socks, we waited to snowball the cats. Sleek and long as jaguars and terrible-whiskered, spitting and snarling they would slink and sidle over the white backgarden walls, and the lynx-eyes hunters, Jim and I, fur-capped and moccasined trappers from Hudson's Bay off Eversley Road, would hurl our deadly snowballs at the green of their eyes. The wise cats never appeared. We were so still, Eskimo-footed arctic marksmen in the muffling silence of the eternal snows—eternal, ever since Wednesday—that we never heard Mrs. Prothero's first cry from her igloo at the bottom of the garden. Or, if we heard it at all, it was, to us, like the far-off challenge of our enemy and prey, the neighbour's Polar Cat. But soon the voice grew louder. "Fire!" cried Mrs. Prothero, and she beat the dinner-gong. And we ran down the garden, with the snowballs in our arms, towards the house, and smoke, indeed, was pouring out of the dining-room, and the gong was bombilating, and Mrs. Prothero was announcing ruin like a town-crier in Pompeii. This was better than all the cats in Wales standing on the wall in a row. We bounded into the house, laden with snowballs, and stopped at the open door of the smoke-filled room. Something was burning all right; perhaps it was Mr. Prothero, who always slept there after midday dinner with a newspaper over his face; but he was standing in the middle of the room, saying "A fine Christmas!" and smacking at the smoke with a slipper.

"Call the fire-brigade," cried Mrs. Prothero as she beat the gong.

"They won't be there," said Mr. Prothero, "it's Christmas."

There was no fire to be seen, only clouds of smoke and Mr. Prothero standing in the middle of them, waving his slipper as though he were conducting.

"Do something," he said.

And we threw all our snowballs into the smoke—I think we missed Mr. Prothero—and ran out of the house to the telephone-box.

"Let's call the police as well," Jim said.

"And the ambulance."

"And Ernie Jenkins, he likes fires."

But we only called the fire-brigade, and soon the fire-engine came and three tall men in helmets brought a hose into the house and Mr. Prothero got out just in time before they turned it on. Nobody could have had a noisier Christmas Eve. And when the firemen turned off the hose and were standing in the wet and smoky room, Jim's aunt, Miss Prothero, came downstairs and peered in at them. Jim and I waited, very quietly, to hear what she would say to them. She said the right thing, always. She looked at the three tall firemen in their shining helmets, standing among the smoke and cinders and dissolving snowballs, and she said: "Would you like something to read?"

Now out of that bright white snowball of Christmas gone comes the stocking, the stocking of stockings, that hung at the foot of the bed with the arm of a golliwog dangling over the top and small bells ringing in the toes. There was a company, gallant and scarlet but never nice to taste though I always tried when very young, of belted and busbied and musketed lead soldiers so soon to lose their heads and legs in the wars on the kitchen table after the tea-things, the mince-pies, and the cakes that I helped to make by stoning the raisins and eating them, had been cleared away; and a bag of moist and many-coloured jelly-babies and a folded flag and a false nose and a tram-conductor's cap and a machine that punched tickets and rang a bell; never a catapult; once, by a mistake that no one could explain, a little hatchet; and a rubber buffalo, or it may have been a horse, with a yellow head and haphazard legs; and a celluloid duck that made, when you pressed it, a most unducklike noise, a mewing moo that an ambitious cat might make who wishes to be a cow; and a painting-book in which I could make the grass, the trees, the sea, and the animals any colour I pleased: and still the dazzling sky-blue sheep are grazing in the red field under a flight of rainbow-beaked and pea-green birds.

Christmas morning was always over before you could say Jack Frost. And look! Suddenly the pudding was burning! Bang the gong and call the fire-brigade and the book-loving firemen! Someone found the silver threepenny-bit with a currant on it; and the some-one was always Uncle Arnold. The motto in my cracker read:

Let's all have fun this Christmas Day,
Let's play and sing and shout hooray!

and the grown-ups turned their eyes towards the ceiling and Auntie Bessie, who had already been frightened, twice, by a clockwork mouse, whimpered at the sideboard and had some elderberry wine. And someone put a glass bowl full of nuts on the littered table, and my uncle said, as he said once every year: "I've got a shoe-nut here. Fetch me a shoe-horn to open it, boy."

And dinner was ended.

And I remember that on the afternoon of Christmas Day, when the others sat around the fire and told each other that this was nothing, no, nothing, to the great snowbound and turkey-proud yule-log-crackling holly-berry-bedizened and kissing-under-the-mistletoe Christmas when they were children, I would go out, school-capped and gloved and mufflered, with my bright new boots squeaking, into the white world on to the seaward hill, to call on Jim and Dan and Jack and to walk with them through the silent snow-scape of our town.

We went padding through the streets, leaving huge deep footprints in the snow, on the hidden pavements.

"I bet people'll think there's been hippoes."

"What would you do if you saw a hippo coming down Terrace Road?"

"I'd go like this, bang! I'd throw him over the railings and roll him down the hill and then I'd tackle him under the ear and he'd wag his tail . . ."

"What would you do if you saw two hippoes . . . ?"

Iron-flanked and bellowing he-hippoes clanked and blundered and battered through the scudding snow towards us as we passed by Mr. Daniel's house.

"Let's post Mr. Daniel a snowball through his letterbox."

"Let's write things in the snow."

"Let's write 'Mr. Daniel looks like a spaniel' all over his lawn."

"Look," Jack said, "I'm eating snow-pie."

"What's it taste like?"

"Like snow-pie," Jack said.

Or we walked on the white shore.

"Can the fishes see it's snowing?"

"They think it's the sky falling down."

The silent one-clouded heavens drifted on to the sea.

"All the old dogs have gone."

Dogs of a hundred mingled makes yapped in the summer at the sea-rim and yelped at the trespassing mountains of the waves.

"I bet St. Bernards would like it now."

And we were snowblind travellers lost on the north hills, and the great dew-lapped dogs, with brandy-flasks round their necks, ambled and shambled up to us, baying "Excelsior."

We returned home through the deso-late poor seafacing streets where only a few children fumbled with bare red fingers in the thick wheel-rutted snow and cat-called after us, their voices fading away, as we trudged uphill, into the cries of the dock-birds and the hooters of ships out in the white and whirling bay.

Bring out the tall tales now that we told by the fire as we roasted chestnuts and the gaslight bubbled low. Ghosts with their heads under their arms trailed their chains and said "whooo" like owls in the long nights when I dared not look over my shoulder; wild beasts lurked in the cubby-hole under the stairs where the gas-meter ticked. "Once upon a time," Jim said, "there were three boys, just like us, who got lost in the dark in the snow, near Bethesda Chapel, and this is what happened to them. . . ." It was the most dreadful happening I had ever heard.

And I remember that we went singing carols once, a night or two before Christmas Eve, when there wasn't the shaving of a moon to light the secret, white-flying streets. At the end of a long road was a drive that led to a large house, and we stumbled up the darkness of the drive that night, each one of us afraid, each one holding a stone in his hand in case, and all of us too brave to say a word. The wind made through the drive-trees noises as of old and unpleasant and maybe web-footed men wheezing in caves. We reached the black bulk of the house.

"What shall we give them?" Dan whispered.

" 'Hark the Herald'? 'Christmas comes but Once a Year'?"

"No," Jack said: "We'll sing 'Good King Wenceslas.' I'll count three."

One, two, three, and we began to sing, our voices high and seemingly distant in the snow-felted darkness round the house that was occupied by nobody we knew. We stood close together, near the dark door.

> Good King Wenceslas looked out
> On the Feast of Stephen.

And then a small, dry voice, like the voice of someone who has not spoken for a long time, suddenly joined our singing: a small, dry voice from the other side of the door: a small, dry voice through the keyhole. And when we stopped running we were outside our house; the front room was lovely and bright; the gramophone was playing; we saw the red and white balloons hanging from the gas-bracket; uncles and aunts sat by the fire; I thought I smelt our supper being fried in the kitchen. Everything was good again, and Christmas shone through all the familiar town.

"Perhaps it was a ghost," Jim said.

"Perhaps it was trolls," Dan said, who was always reading.

"Let's go in and see if there's any jelly left," Jack said. And we did that.

1954

AMERICAN LITERATURE

ROBERT FROST (1875-1963)

The promise of the first half of the nineteenth century in American poetry was not fulfilled in the latter half. Emerson, Thoreau, Longfellow, Whittier, Bryant, Poe, and above all Whitman had laid the foundations of what promised to be a great national poetry, but American poetry from 1860 to 1910 (with the single exception of Emily Dickinson, whose work was scarcely known in her lifetime) was pallid and lifeless, or crude and coarse, by comparison. It was not until the eve of World War I that American poetry had a new start; and then it came with a rush. The work of Edwin Arlington Robinson, Edgar Lee Masters, Vachel Lindsay, Carl Sandburg, Robert Frost, T. S. Eliot, Ezra Pound, Robinson Jeffers, Amy Lowell, Archibald McLeish, and Edna St. Vincent Millay began to appear almost simultaneously, and excited the poetry-loving public with its strength, novelty, and skill.

All of the above poets might well claim a place in an anthology such as this, but considerations of space have led us to choose the three most outstanding and variously representative figures: Frost, Sandburg, and Eliot. Frost may be said to represent New England, and to revive the tradition initiated by Emerson and Thoreau; Sandburg to represent the Middle West, and the tradition of Whitman; and T. S. Eliot to represent the new cosmopolitanism of twentieth century culture, the attempt to establish a new classicism in literature, and the new experimental techniques in poetry designed to cope with the complexities of psychology and sociology in our time.

Frost is unmistakably the voice of New England, portraying in his verse its scenery, rural life, homespun wisdom, folk speech, and folk ways. Both a realist and an idealist, he is aware of the suffering, frustration, and pathos of life, but asserts human dignity, endurance, and possible triumph. Democratic, humanistic, and at times mystical, he expounds a positive but profound view of life. In technique he is relatively conservative, preferring to embroider variations upon the traditional patterns rather than to invent new ones. The most striking quality of his style is his use of speech rhythms. "All poetry," he writes, "is the reproduction of the tones of actual speech."

Robert Frost was born in San Francisco, March 26, 1875, but grew up in Lawrence, Mass. After graduation from high school he was a millworker, teacher, and reporter before entering Harvard in 1897. Leaving Harvard after two years, he was a farmer and teacher in Derry, New Hampshire, until 1912 when he sold his farm and moved to England. In England he published his first two books of verse. After his return from England in 1915, he divided his time between farming in New Hampshire and teaching in various colleges and universities, mainly Amherst and Harvard. During the last years of his life he was much in demand as a reader of his own poetry, and he made perhaps his most famous appearance as a reader at the inauguration of President John F. Kennedy.

The Pasture

I'm going out to clean the pasture spring;
I'll only stop to rake the leaves away
(And wait to watch the water clear, I may):
I sha'n't be gone long.—You come too.

I'm going out to fetch the little calf
That's standing by the mother. It's so young,

It totters when she licks it with her tongue.
I sha'n't be gone long.—You come too.

1914

Mending Wall

Something there is that doesn't love a wall,
That sends the frozen-ground-swell under it,
And spills the upper boulders in the sun;
And makes gaps even two can pass abreast.
The work of hunters is another thing:
I have come after them and made repair
Where they have left not one stone on a stone,
But they would have the rabbit out of hiding,
To please the yelping dogs. The gaps I mean,
No one has seen them made or heard them made,   10
But at spring mending-time we find them there.
I let my neighbour know beyond the hill;
And on a day we meet to walk the line
And set the wall between us once again.
We keep the wall between us as we go.
To each the boulders that have fallen to each.
And some are loaves and some so nearly balls
We have to use a spell to make them balance:
"Stay where you are until our backs are turned!"
We wear our fingers rough with handling them.   20
Oh, just another kind of out-door game,
One on a side. It comes to little more:
There where it is we do not need the wall:
He is all pine and I am apple orchard.
My apple trees will never get across
And eat the cones under his pines, I tell him.
He only says, "Good fences make good neighbours."
Spring is the mischief in me, and I wonder   30
If I could put a notion in his head:
"*Why* do they make good neighbours? Isn't it
Where there are cows? But here there are no cows.
Before I built a wall I'd ask to know
What I was walling in or walling out,
And to whom I was like to give offence.
Something there is that doesn't love a wall,
That wants it down." I could say "Elves" to him,
But it's not elves exactly, and I'd rather
He said it for himself. I see him there   40

Bringing a stone grasped firmly by the top
In each hand, like an old stone savage armed.
He moves in darkness as it seems to me,
Not of woods only and the shade of trees.
He will not go behind his father's saying,
And he likes having thought of it so well
He says again, "Good fences make good neighbours."

1914

Birches

When I see birches bend to left and right
Across the lines of straighter dark trees,
I like to think some boy's been swinging them.
But swinging doesn't bend them down to stay
As ice storms do. Often you must have seen them
Loaded with ice a sunny winter morning
After a rain. They click upon themselves
As the breeze rises, and turn many-colored
As the stir cracks and crazes their enamel.
Soon the sun's warmth makes them shed crystal shells   10
Shattering and avalanching on the snow crust—
Such heaps of broken glass to sweep away
You'd think the inner dome of heaven had fallen.
They are dragged to the withered bracken by the load,
And they seem not to break; though once they are bowed
So low for long, they never right themselves:
You may see their trunks arching in the woods
Years afterwards, trailing their leaves on the ground
Like girls on hands and knees that throw their hair
Before them over their heads to dry in the sun.   20
But I was going to say when Truth broke in
With all her matter of fact about the ice storm,
I should prefer to have some boy bend them
As he went out and in to fetch the cows—
Some boy too far from town to learn baseball,
Whose only play was what he found himself,
Summer or winter, and could play alone.
One by one he subdued his father's trees
By riding them down over and over again
Until he took the stiffness out of them,   30
And now one but hung limp, not one was left

For him to conquer. He learned all there was
To learn about not launching out too soon
And so not carrying the tree away
Clear to the ground. He always kept his poise
To the top branches, climbing carefully
With the same pains you use to fill a cup
Up to the brim, and even above the brim.
Then he flung outward, feet first, with a swish,
Kicking his way down through the air to the ground.   40
So was I once myself a swinger of birches.
And so I dream of going back to be.
It's when I'm weary of considerations,
And life is too much like a pathless wood
Where your face burns and tickles with the cobwebs
Broken across it, and one eye is weeping
From a twig's having lashed across it open.
I'd like to get away from earth awhile
And then come back to it and begin over.
May no fate willfully misunderstand me   50
And half grant what I wish and snatch me away
Not to return. Earth's the right place for love:
I don't know where it's likely to go better.
I'd like to go by climbing a birch tree,
And climb black branches up a snow-white trunk
Toward heaven, till the tree could bear no more,
But dipped its top and set me down again.
That would be good both going and coming back.
One could do worse than be a swinger of birches.

1915

'Out, Out—'[1]

The buzz-saw snarled and rattled in the yard
And made dust and dropped stove-length sticks of wood,
Sweet-scented stuff when the breeze drew across it.
And from there those that lifted eyes could count
Five mountain ranges one behind the other
Under the sunset far into Vermont.

---

[1]The title is taken from the famous soliloquy in Shakespeare's *Macbeth*: "Out, out, brief candle!
Life's but a walking shadow, a poor player/That struts and frets his hour upon the stage/And
then is heard no more . . ."

And the saw snarled and rattled, snarled and rattled,
As it ran light, or had to bear a load.
And nothing happened: day was all but done.
Call it a day, I wish they might have said   10
To please the boy by giving him the half hour
That a boy counts so much when saved from work.
His sister stood beside them in her apron
To tell them 'Supper.' At the word, the saw,
As if to prove saws knew what supper meant,
Leaped out at the boy's hand, or seemed to leap—
He must have given the hand. However it was,
Neither refused the meeting. But the hand!
The boy's first outcry was a rueful laugh,
As he swung toward them holding up the hand   20
Half in appeal, but half as if to keep
The life from spilling. Then the boy saw all—
Since he was old enough to know, big boy
Doing a man's work, though a child at heart—
He saw all spoiled. 'Don't let him cut my hand off—
The doctor, when he comes. Don't let him, sister!'
So, But the hand was gone already.
The doctor put him in the dark of ether.
He lay and puffed his lips out with his breath.
And then—the watcher at his pulse took fright.
No one believed. They listened at his heart.
Little—less—nothing!—and that ended it.
No more to build on there. And they, since they
Were not the one dead, turned to their affairs.

1916

Fire and Ice

Some say the world will end in fire,
Some say in ice.
From what I've tasted of desire
I hold with those who favour fire.
But if it had to perish twice,

I think I know enough of hate
To say that for destruction ice
Is also great
And would suffice.

1923

Stopping by Woods on a Snowy Evening

Whose woods these are I think I know
His house is in the village, though;
He will not see me stopping here
To watch his woods fill up with snow.

My little horse must think it queer
To stop without a farmhouse near
Between the woods and frozen lake
The darkest evening of the year.

He gives his harness bells a shake
To ask if there is some mistake.   10
The only other sound's the sweep
Of easy wind and downy flake.

The woods are lovely, dark and deep.
But I have promises to keep,
And miles to go before I sleep,
And miles to go before I sleep.[1]

                                                                    1923

---

[1] Frost intended the repetition of the line to suggest a somnolent dreaminess in the speaker.

CARL SANDBURG (1878-1967)

If Frost is the voice of New England, Sandburg is the voice of the American mid-west: his poetry is strong, energetic, crude at some moments, sentimental at others. He celebrates the great open plains and corn fields of Illinois and Wisconsin, the skyscrapers and factories of Chicago, and the farmers, truck-drivers, steel-workers, and stenographers who populate them. He looks to the future, dismisses the past as a bucket of ashes, glories in the new and the daring, despises conservativism and timidity. His central idea is his faith in the common man: he has an almost mystical faith in the people. His poems are written in free verse that owes much to the example of Whitman, and in a similarly colloquial language.

Sandburg was born of Swedish immigrant parents in Galesburg, Illinois, January 6, 1878. As a youth, he engaged in a great variety of manual occupations such as truck-driver, dishwasher, and house-painter. From 1898 to 1902 he attended Lombard College in Galesburg, then travelled for a while, worked as organizer for the Social-Democrat party in Wisconsin, was secretary of the first Socialist mayor of Milwaukee, and became an editorial writer for the Chicago Daily News. His first recognition as a poet came in 1914, when a group of his poems including "Chicago" appeared in Harriett Monroe's magazine, Poetry. He went on to publish many books of verse and a monumental biography of Abraham Lincoln. He also travelled extensively as a lecturer, reader of poetry, and singer of folk songs until his death in 1967.

Chicago

Hog Butcher for the World,
Tool Maker, Stacker of Wheat,
Player with Railroads and the Nation's
　　　　Freight Handler;
Stormy, husky, brawling,
City of the Big Shoulders:

They tell me you are wicked and I believe them, for I have seen your painted women
　　under the gas lamps luring the farm boys.
And they tell me you are crooked and I answer: Yes, it is true I have seen the gunman
　　kill and go free to kill again.
And they tell me you are brutal and my reply is: On the faces of women and children
　　I have seen the marks of wanton hunger.
And having answered so I turn once more to those who sneer at this my city, and I
　　give them back the sneer and say to them:
Come and show me another city with lifted head singing so proud to be alive and
　　coarse and strong and cunning.　　　　　　　　　　　　　　　　　　　　　　10
Flinging magnetic curses amid the toil of piling job on job, here is a tall bold slugger
　　set vivid against the little soft cities;
Fierce as a dog with tongue lapping for action, cunning as a savage pitted against the
　　wilderness,
　　　　　　　　　　Bareheaded,
　　　　　　　　　　Shoveling,
　　　　　　　　　　Wrecking,
　　　　　　　　　　Planning,
　　　　　　　　　　Building, breaking, rebuilding,

Under the smoke, dust all over his mouth, laughing with white teeth,
Under the terrible burden of destiny laughing as a young man laughs,
Laughing even as an ignorant fighter laughs who has never lost a battle,　　　　20
Bragging and laughing that under his wrist is the pulse, and under his ribs the heart
　　of the people,
　　　　　　　　　　Laughing!
Laughing the stormy, husky, brawling laughter of Youth, half-naked, sweating, proud
　　to be Hog Butcher, Tool Maker, Stacker of Wheat, Player with Railroads, and
　　Freight Handler to the Nation.

　　　　　　　　　　　　　　　　　　　　　　　　　1916

Caboose Thoughts

It's going to come out all right—do you know?
The sun, the birds, the grass—they know.
They get along—and we'll get along.

Some days will be rainy and you will sit waiting
And the letter you wait for won't come,
And I will sit watching the sky tear off grey and grey
And the letter I wait for won't come.

There will be ac-ci-dents.
I know ac-ci-dents are coming.
Smash-ups, signals wrong, washouts, trestles rotten,   10
Red and yellow ac-ci-dents.
But somehow and somewhere the end of the run
The train gets put together again
And the caboose and the green tail lights
Fade down the right of way like a new white hope.

I never heard a mockingbird in Kentucky
Spilling its heart in the morning.
I never saw the snow on Chimborazo.
It's a high white Mexican hat, I hear.

I never had supper with Abe Lincoln,   20
Nor a dish of soup with Jim Hill[1].

But I've been around.
I know some of the boys here who can go a little.
I knows girls good for a burst of speed any time.

I heard Williams and Walker
Before Walker died in the bughouse.

I knew a mandolin player
Working in a barber shop in an Indiana town,
And he thought he had a million dollars.

I knew a hotel girl in Des Moines.   30
She had eyes; I saw her and said to myself
The sun rises and the sun sets in her eyes.
I was her steady and her heart went pit-a-pat.
We took away the money for a prize waltz at a Brotherhood dance.
She had eyes; she was safe as the bridge over the Mississippi at Burlington;
    I married her.

Last summer we took the cushions going west.
Pike's Peak is a big old stone, believe me.
It's fastened down; something you can count on.

[1]American labour leader.

It's going to come out all right—do you know?   40
The sun, the birds, the grass—they know.
They get along—and we'll get along.

1918

Prayers of Steel

Lay me on an anvil, O God.
Beat me and hammer me into a crowbar.
Let me pry loose old walls.
Let me lift and loosen old foundations.
Lay me on an anvil, O God.
Beat me and hammer me into a steel spike.
Drive me into the girders that hold a skyscraper together.
Take red-hot rivets and fasten me into the central girders.
Let me be the great nail holding a skyscraper through blue nights into white stars.

1918

Cool Tombs

When Abraham Lincoln was shoveled into the tombs, he forgot the copperheads and
the assassin . . . in the dust, in the cool tombs.

And Ulysses Grant lost all thought of con men and Wall Street, cash and collateral
turned ashes . . . in the dust, in the cool tombs.

Pocahontas' body, lovely as a poplar, sweet as a red haw in November or a pawpaw
in May, did she wonder? does she remember? . . . in the dust, in the cool tombs?

Take any streetful of people buying clothes and groceries, cheering a hero or throwing
confetti and blowing tin horns . . . tell me if the lovers are losers . . . tell me if any
get more than the lovers . . . in the dust . . . in the cool tombs.

1918

T. S. ELIOT (1888-1965)

T. S. Eliot has probably been the most influential American man of letters of our century. As poet, critic, and dramatist he has set high standards and, appealing at first only to an intellectual minority, has gradually won wide acceptance.

Eliot was born in St. Louis, Missouri, of an old New England family. Graduating with a B.A. from Harvard in 1909, he continued post-graduate studies in philosophy and languages at Harvard, at the Sorbonne in Paris, in Germany, and at Merton College, Oxford. From 1914 onwards, he made his home in England, although he made frequent visits to the United States. In England he was temporarily a bank clerk and teacher before turning to literary journalism on *The Egoist*, *The Athenaeum*, *Times Literary Supplement*, and his own very influential magazine, *The Criterion* (1922-1938). In 1925 he became associated with the publishing house now known as Faber and Faber, of which he was a director. In 1927 he became a British subject and a member of the Church of England, announcing his position as that of a classicist in literature, a royalist in politics, and an Anglo-Catholic in religion.

Eliot's condensed, witty, impersonal, and urban-centred verse marked a sharp break with the tradition of romantic love and nature poetry that had been dominant for over a century, and soon became influential in England, the United States, and Canada. His own work has progressed from the light, bored, disillusioned verse of *Prufrock* (1917), through the near-despair of "Gerontion" and "The Hollow Men" and *The Waste Land* (1923), to the positive affirmation of Christian faith and humility of *Ash Wednesday* (1930) and *The Four Quartets* (1943)—or roughly, to use his own terminology, from boredom through horror to glory. His poetic methods, however, have remained quite consistent. His writing at first seems difficult and obscure because he is trying to say new things in a new way; he is an allusive poet, quoting or paraphrasing from other writers to enlarge the scope of his own verse; he is fond of the device of contrast, juxtaposing the past with the present, the sublime with the ridiculous, the rich with the poor, or the elegant with the vulgar; he writes in free verse rather than regular metres in order to permit quick transitions of mood; he often uses myths or rituals as frameworks for his poems in order to give them universality; and he makes much use of symbols such as water, fire, and rocks as a means of quickly suggesting his meaning. In reading his poetry, one must be sensitive and alert; but if one makes the effort, it is well rewarded.

As a critic, Eliot has done much to restore interest in Jacobean drama, the metaphysical poetry of Donne and his followers, and the poetry of Dryden: in general, in literature that combines intelligence with passion. As a dramatist, he has attempted, not with complete success, to revive poetic drama.

The Love Song of J. Alfred Prufrock

S'io credesse che mia risposta fosse
A persona che mai tornasse al mondo,
Questa fiamma staria senza piu scosse.
Ma perciocche giammai di questo fondo
Non torno vivo alcun, s'i'odo il vero,
Senza tema d'infamia ti rispondo[1].

Let us go then, you and I,
When the evening is spread out against the sky
Like a patient etherized upon a table;
Let us go, through certain half-deserted streets,
The muttering retreats

[1]These lines are from Dante's *Inferno*, an early fourteenth century poem, part of the larger *Divina Commedia*. Guido is in this passage accounting for his presence in Hell, and says in effect, "If I thought my reply were to someone who could return to the world, I should say no more; but since I understand that no one ever returned alive from these depths, without shame I answer you." The suggestion is that Prufrock is also living in a kind of hell—and that we are too!

Of restless nights in one-night cheap hotels
And sawdust restaurants with oyster-shells:
Streets that follow like a tedious argument
Of insidious intent
To lead you to an overwhelming question . . .
Oh, do not ask, "What is it?"
Let us go and make our visit.

In the room the women come and go
Talking of Michelangelo.

The yellow fog that rubs its back upon the window-panes,
The yellow smoke that rubs its muzzle on the window-panes
Licked its tongue into the corners of the evening,
Lingered upon the pools that stand in drains,
Let fall upon its back the soot that falls from chimneys,
Slipped by the terrace, made a sudden leap,
And seeing that it was a soft October night,
Curled once about the house, and fell asleep.

And indeed there will be time
For the yellow smoke that slides along the street,
Rubbing its back upon the window-panes;
There will be time, there will be time
To prepare a face to meet the faces that you meet;
There will be time to murder and create,
And time for all the works and days of hands
That lift and drop a question on your plate;
Time for you and time for me,
And time yet for a hundred indecisions,
And for a hundred visions and revisions,
Before the taking of a toast and tea.

In the room the women come and go
Talking of Michelangelo.

And indeed there will be time
To wonder, "Do I dare?" and, "Do I dare?"
Time to turn back and descend the stair,
With a bald spot in the middle of my hair—
(They will say: "How his hair is growing thin!")
My morning coat, my collar mounting firmly to the chin,
My necktie rich and modest, but asserted by a simple pin—
(They will say: "But how his arms and legs are thin!")

10

20

30

40

Do I dare
Disturb the universe?
In a minute there is time
For decisions and revisions which a minute will reverse.

For I have known them all already, known them all: 50
Have known the evenings, mornings, afternoons,
I have measured out my life with coffee spoons;
I know the voices dying with a dying fall
Beneath the music from a farther room.
        So how should I presume?

And I have known the eyes already, known them all—
The eyes that fix you in a formulated phrase,
And when I am formulated, sprawling on a pin,
When I am pinned and wriggling on the wall,   60
Then how should I begin
To spit out all the butt-ends of my days and ways?
        And how should I presume?

And I have known the arms already, known them all—
Arms that are braceleted and white and bare
(But in the lamplight, downed with light brown hair!)
Is it perfume from a dress
That makes me so digress?
Arms that lie along a table, or wrap about a shawl.
        And should I then presume?   70
And how should I begin?

                        *   *   *

Shall I say, I have gone at dusk through narrow streets
And watched the smoke that rises from the pipes
Of lonely men in shirt-sleeves, leaning out of windows? . . .

I should have been a pair of ragged claws
Scuttling across the floors of silent seas.

                        *   *   *

And the afternoon, the evening, sleeps so peacefully!
Smoothed by long fingers,
Asleep . . . tired . . . or it malingers,
Stretched on the floor, here beside you and me.
Should I, after tea and cakes and ices,   80
Have the strength to force the moment to its crisis?
But though I have wept and fasted, wept and prayed,

Though I have seen my head (grown slightly bald) brought in upon a platter,
I am no prophet—and here's no greater matter;
I have seen the moment of my greatness flicker,
And I have seen the eternal Footman hold my coat, and snicker.
And in short, I was afraid.

And would it have been worth it, after all,
After the cups, the marmalade, the tea,   90
Among the porcelain, among some talk of you and me,
Would it have been worth while,
To have bitten off the matter with a smile,
To have squeezed the universe into a ball
To roll it toward some overwhelming question,
To say: 'I am Lazarus, come from the dead,

Come back to tell you all, I shall tell you all'—
If one, settling a pillow by her head,
    Should say: "That is not what I meant at all;
    That is not it, at all."   100

And would it have been worth it, after all,
Would it have been worth while,
After the sunsets and the dooryards and the sprinkled streets,
After the novels, after the teacups, after the skirts that trail along the floor—
And this, and so much more?—
It is impossible to say just what I mean!
But as if a magic lantern threw the nerves in patterns on a screen:
Would it have been worth while
If one, settling a pillow or throwing off a shawl,   110
And turning toward the window, should say:
    "That is not it at all,
    That is not what I meant, at all."

                    *   *   *

No! I am not Prince Hamlet, nor was meant to be;
Am an attendant lord, one that will do
To swell a progress, start a scene or two,
Advise the prince; no doubt, an easy tool,
Deferential, glad to be of use,
Politic, cautious, and meticulous;
Full of high sentence, but a bit obtuse;   120
At times, indeed, almost ridiculous—
Almost, at times, the Fool.

I grow old . . . I grow old . . .

I shall wear the bottoms of my trousers rolled.

Shall I part my hair behind? Do I dare to eat a peach?
I shall wear white flannel trousers, and walk upon the beach.
I have heard the mermaids singing, each to each.

I do not think that they will sing to me.

I have seen them riding seaward on the waves
Combing the white hair of the waves blown back   130
When the wind blows the water white and black.

We have lingered in the chambers of the sea
By sea-girls wreathed with seaweed red and brown
Till human voices wake us, and we drown.

1917

The Hollow Men
A penny for the old guy[1]

I

We are the hollow men
We are the stuffed men
Leaning together
Headpiece filled with straw. Alas!
Our dried voices, when
We whisper together
Are quiet and meaningless
As wind in dry grass
Or rats' feet over broken glass
In our dry cellar.   10

Shape without form, shade without color,
Paralyzed force, gesture without motion;

Those who have crossed
With direct eyes, to death's other King-
dom
Remember us—if at all—not as lost
Violent souls, but only
As the hollow men
The stuffed men.

II

Eyes I dare not meet in dreams
In death's dream kingdom   20
These do not appear:
There, the eyes are
Sunlight on a broken column
There, is a tree swinging
And voices are
In the wind's singing
More distant and more solemn
Than a fading star.

Let me be no nearer
In death's dream kingdom   30
Let me also wear
Such deliberate disguises
Rat's skin, crowskin, crossed staves
In a field
Behaving as the wind behaves
No nearer—

Not that final meeting
In the twilight kingdom.

[1]A saying used by English children on Guy Fawkes Night (Nov. 5), when they make a dummy
of the traitor and ask for treats, much as Canadian children do on Hallowe'en.

III

This is the dead land
This is cactus land 40
Here the stone images
Are raised, here they receive
The supplication of a dead man's hand
Under the twinkle of a fading star.

Is it like this
In death's other kingdom
Waking alone
At the hour when we are
Trembling with tenderness
Lips that would kiss 50
Form prayers to broken stone.

IV

The eyes are not here
There are no eyes here
In this valley of dying stars
In this hollow valley
This broken jaw of our lost kingdoms

In this last of meeting places
We grope together
And avoid speech
Gathered on this beach of the tumid river

Sightless, unless 61
The eyes reappear
As the perpetual star
Multifoliate rose
Of death's twilight kingdom
The hope only
Of empty men.

V

Here we go round the prickly pear
Prickly pear prickly pear
Here we go round the prickly pear 70
At five o'clock in the morning.

Between the idea
And the reality
Between the motion
And the act
Falls the Shadow

For Thine is the Kingdom

Between the conception
And the creation
Between the emotion 80
And the response
Falls the Shadow

Life is very long

Between the desire
And the spasm
Between the potency
And the existence
Between the essence
And the descent
Falls the Shadow 90

For Thine is the Kingdom

For Thine is
Life is
For Thine is the

This is the way the world ends
This is the way the world ends
This is the way the world ends
Not with a bang but a whimper.

1925

JAMES THURBER (1894-1961)

James Thurber, considered by many to be the greatest American humorist of this century, was born in Columbus, Ohio. He attended Ohio State University and then turned to journalism. He worked first for the Columbus *Dispatch*, went to France and contributed to the Paris edition of the Chicago *Tribune*, and really found himself as a writer when he returned to New York in 1926 and became one of the brilliant contribu-tors to Harold Ross's *New Yorker* magazine. Thurber's writings, like the drawings with which he frequently illustrated his works, combine in an intriguing way a sense of absurdity and a sense of pathos. As in the story that follows, the frustrated little man who dreams of great ful-fillment is a comic figure—but he is also a pathetic if not a tragic one.

The Secret Life of Walter Mitty

"We're going through!" The Comman-der's voice was like thin ice breaking. He wore his full-dress uniform, with the heavily braided white cap pulled down rakishly over one cold grey eye. "We can't make it, sir. It's spoiling for a hurricane, if you ask me." "I'm not asking you, Lieutenant Berg," said the Commander. "Throw on the power lights! Rev her up to 8,500! We're going through!" The pounding of the cylinders increased: ta-pocketa-pocketa-pocketa-pocketa. The Commander stared at the ice forming on the pilot window. He walked over and twisted a row of com-plicated dials. "Switch on No. 8 auxili-ary!" he shouted. "Switch on No. 8 auxiliary!" repeated Lieutenant Berg. "Full strength in No. 3 turret!" shouted the Commander. "Full strength in No. 3 turret!" The crew, bending to their various tasks in the huge, hurtling, eight-engined Navy hydroplane, looked at each other and grinned. "The Old Man'll get us through," they said to one another. "The Old Man ain't afraid of Hell!" . . .

"Not so fast! You're driving too fast!" said Mrs. Mitty. "What are you driving so fast for?"

"Hmm?" said Walter Mitty. He looked at his wife, in the seat beside him, with shocked astonishment. She seemed grossly unfamiliar, like a strange woman who had yelled at him in a crowd. "You were up to fifty-five," she said. "You know I don't like to go more than forty. You were up to fifty-five." Walter Mitty drove on toward Waterbury in silence, the roaring of the SN202 through the worst storm in twenty years of Navy flying fading in the remote, intimate air-ways of his mind. "You're tensed up again," said Mrs. Mitty. "It's one of your days. I wish you'd let Dr. Renshaw look you over."

Walter Mitty stopped the car in front of the building where his wife went to have her hair done. "Remember to get those overshoes while I'm having my hair done," she said. "I don't need over-shoes," said Mitty. She put her mirror back into her bag. "We've been all through that," she said, getting out of the car. "You're not a young man any longer." He raced the engine a little. "Why don't you wear your gloves? Have you lost your gloves?" Walter Mitty reached into a pocket and brought out the gloves. He put them on, but after she had turned and gone into the build-ing and he had driven on to a red light, he took them off again. "Pick it up, brother!" snapped a cop as the light changed, and Mitty hastily pulled on his gloves and lurched ahead. He drove around the streets aimlessly for a time, and then he drove past the hospital on his way to the parking lot.

. . . "It's the millionaire banker, Wellington McMillan," said the pretty nurse. "Yes?" said Walter Mitty, removing his gloves slowly. "Who has the case?" "Dr. Renshaw and Dr. Benbow, but there are two specialists here, Dr. Remington from New York and Mr. Pritchard-Mitford from London. He flew over." A door opened down a long, cool corridor and Dr. Renshaw came out. He looked distraught and haggard. "Hello, Mitty," he said. "We're having the devil's own time with McMillan, the millionaire banker and close personal friend of Roosevelt. Obstreosis of the ductal tract. Tertiary. Wish you'd take a look at him." "Glad to," said Mitty.

In the operating room there were whispered introductions: "Dr. Remington, Dr. Mitty. Mr. Pritchard-Mitford, Dr. Mitty." "I've read your book on streptothricosis," said Pritchard-Mitford, shaking hands. "A brilliant performance, sir." "Thank you," said Walter Mitty. "Didn't know you were in the States, Mitty," grumbled Remington. "Coals to Newcastle, bringing Mitford and me up here for a tertiary." "You are very kind," said Mitty. A huge machine, connected to the operating table, with many tubes and wires, began at this moment to go pocketa-pocketa-pocketa. "The new anesthetizer is giving way!" shouted an interne. "There is no one in the East who knows how to fix it!" "Quiet, man!" said Mitty, in a low, cool voice. He sprang to the machine, which was now going pocketa-pocketa-queep-pocketa-queep.

He began fingering delicately a row of glistening dials. "Give me a fountain pen!" he snapped. Someone handed him a fountain pen. He pulled a faulty piston out of the machine and inserted the pen in its place. "That will hold for ten minutes," he said. "Get on with the operation." A nurse hurried over and whispered to Renshaw, and Mitty saw the man turn pale. "Coreopsis has set in," said Renshaw nervously. "If you would take over, Mitty?" Mitty looked at him and at the craven figure of Benbow, who drank, and at the two great specialists. "If you wish," he said. They slipped a white gown on him; he adjusted a mask and drew on thin gloves; nurses handed him shining . . .

"Back it up, Mac! Look out for that Buick!" Walter Mitty jammed on the brakes. "Wrong lane, Mac," said the parking-lot attendant, looking at Mitty closely. "Gee. Yeh," muttered Mitty. He began cautiously to back out of the lane marked "Exit Only." "Leave her sit there," said the attendant. "I'll put her away." Mitty got out of the car. "Hey, better leave the keys." "Oh," said Mitty, handing the man the ignition key. The attendant vaulted into the car, backed it up with insolent skill, and put it where it belonged.

They're so damn cocky, thought Walter Mitty, walking along Main Street; they think they know everything. Once he had tried to take his chains off, outside New Milford, and he had got them wound around the axles. A man had had to come out in a wrecking car and unwind them, a young, grinning garageman. Since then Mrs. Mitty always made him drive to a garage to have the chains taken off. The next time, he thought, I'll wear my right arm in a sling; they won't grin at me then. I'll have my right arm in a sling and they'll see I couldn't possibly take the chains off myself. He kicked at the slush on the sidewalk. "Overshoes," he said to himself, and he began looking for a shoe store.

When he came out into the street again, with the overshoes in a box under his arm, Walter Mitty began to wonder what the other thing was his wife had told him to get. She had told him twice, before they set out from their house for Waterbury. In a way he hated these weekly trips to town—he was always getting something wrong. Kleenex, he thought, Squibb's, razor blades? No. Toothpaste, toothbrush, bicarbonate, carborundum, initiative and referendum? He gave it up. But she would remember it. "Where's the what's-its-name?" she would ask. "Don't tell me you forgot the what's-its-name." A newsboy went by shouting something about the Waterbury trial.

. . . "Perhaps this will refresh your memory." The District Attorney suddenly thrust a heavy automatic at the quiet figure on the witness stand. "Have you ever seen this before?" Walter Mitty took the gun and examined it expertly. "This is my Webley-Vickers 50.80," he said calmly. An excited buzz ran around the courtroom. The judge rapped for order. "You are a crack shot with any sort of firearms I believe?" said the District Attorney, insinuatingly. "Objection!" shouted Mitty's attorney. "We have shown that the defendant could not have fired the shot. We have shown that he wore his right arm in a sling on the night of the fourteenth of July." Walter Mitty raised his hand briefly and the bickering attorneys were stilled. "With any known make of gun," he said evenly, "I could

have killed Gregory Fitzhurst at three hundred feet with my left hand." Pandemonium broke loose in the courtroom. A woman's scream rose above the bedlam and suddenly a lovely, dark-haired girl was in Walter Mitty's arms. The District Attorney struck at her savagely. Without rising from his chair, Mitty let the man have it on the point of the chin. "You miserable cur!" . . .

"Puppy biscuit," said Walter Mitty. He stopped walking and the buildings of Waterbury rose up out of the misty courtroom and surrounded him again. A woman who was passing laughed. "He said 'Puppy biscuit'," she said to her companion. "That man said 'Puppy biscuit' to himself." Walter Mitty hurried on. He went into an A. & P., not the first one he came to but a smaller one farther up the street. "I want some biscuit for small, young dogs," he said to the clerk. "Any special brand, sir?" The greatest pistol shot in the world thought a moment. "It says 'Puppies Bark for It' on the box," said Walter Mitty.

His wife would be through at the hairdresser's in fifteen minutes, Mitty saw in looking at his watch, unless they had trouble drying it; sometimes they had trouble drying it. She didn't like to get to the hotel first; she would want him to be there waiting for her as usual. He found a big leather chair in the lobby, facing a window, and he put the overshoes and the puppy biscuit on the floor beside it. He picked up an old copy of *Liberty* and sank down into the chair. "Can Germany Conquer the World Through the Air?" Walter Mitty looked at the pictures of bombing planes and of ruined streets.

. . . "The cannonading has got the wind up in young Raleigh, sir," said the sergeant. Captain Mitty looked up at him through tousled hair. "Get him to bed," he said wearily. "With the others. I'll fly alone." "But you can't sir," said the sergeant anxiously. "It takes two men to handle that bomber and the Archies are pounding hell out of the air. Von Richtan's circus is between here and Saulier." "Somebody's got to get that ammunition dump," said Mitty. "I'm going over. Spot of brandy?" He poured a drink for the sergeant and one for himself. War thundered and whined around the dugout and battered at the door. There was a rending of wood and splinters flew through the room. "A bit of a near thing," said Captain Mitty carelessly. "The box barrage is closing in," said the sergeant. "We only live once Sergeant," said Mitty, with his faint, fleeting smile. "Or do we?" He poured another brandy and tossed it off. "I never see a man could hold his brandy like you, sir," said the sergeant. "Begging your pardon, sir." Captain Mitty stood up and strapped on his huge Webley-Vickers automatic. "It's forty kilometers through hell, sir," said the sergeant. Mitty finished one last brandy. "After all," he said softly "what isn't?" The pounding of the cannon increased; there was the rat-tat-tatting of machine guns, and from somewhere came the menacing pocketa-pocketa-pocketa of the new flame-throwers. Walter Mitty walked to the door of the dugout humming "Auprès de Ma Blonde." He turned and waved to the sergeant. "Cheerio!" he said . . .

Something struck his shoulder. "I've been looking all over this hotel for you," said Mrs. Mitty. "Why do you have to hide in this old chair? How did you expect me to find you?" "Things close in," said Walter Mitty vaguely. "What?" Mrs. Mitty said. "Did you get the what's-its-name? The puppy biscuit? What's in that box?" "Overshoes," said Mitty. "Couldn't you have put them on in the store?" "I was thinking," said Walter Mitty. "Does it ever occur to you that I am sometimes thinking?" She looked at him. "I'm going to take your temperature when I get you home," she said.

They went out through the revolving doors that made a faintly derisive whistling sound when you pushed them. It was two blocks to the parking lot. At the drugstore on the corner she said, "Wait here for me. I forgot something. I won't be a minute." She was more than a minute. Walter Mitty lighted a cigarette. It began to rain, rain with sleet in it. He stood up against the wall of the drugstore, smoking . . . He put his shoulders back and his heels together. "To hell with the handkerchief," said Walter Mitty scornfully. He took one last drag on his cigarette and snapped it away. Then, with that faint, fleeting smile playing about his lips, he faced the firing squad; erect and motionless, proud and disdainful, Walter Mitty the Undefeated, inscrutable to the last.

1939

WILLIAM FAULKNER (1897-1962)

Faulkner is considered by many critics to be the most profound and powerful American novelist of this century. He was born in New Albany, Mississippi, of a family which had heroic memories of the Old South but had been reduced to genteel poverty by the Civil War between the states. The devastating effect of the Civil War on the morale of the South forms the subject-matter of many of his novels. During World War I Faulkner joined the Royal Canadian Air

Force rather than fight with the "Yankees." He returned to Oxford, Mississippi, after the War, studied briefly at the state university there, and soon began to write. His books include *The Sound and the Fury* (1929), *As I Lay Dying* (1930), *Sanctuary* (1931), *Light in August* (1932), *Absalom! Absalom!* (1936), *Go Down Moses and Other Stories* (1942), *Intruder in the Dust* (1948), and *Collected Stories* (1950). In 1950 he was awarded the Nobel Prize for literature "for his forceful and independently artistic contribution to modern American fiction."

Faulkner's violent and frequently tragic stories often led to the charge of morbidity and pessimism, but the Nobel Prize speech which follows, and indeed a sensitive reading of his works, reveal that he had faith in man's ability to endure and to prevail.

Remarks upon Receiving the Nobel Prize

I feel that this award was not made to me as a man but to my work—a life's work in the agony and sweat of the human spirit, not for glory and least of all for profit, but to create out of the materials of the human spirit something which did not exist before. So this award is only mine in trust. It will not be difficult to find a dedication for the money part of it commensurate with the purpose and significance of its origin. But I would like to do the same with the acclaim too, by using this moment as a pinnacle from which I might be listened to by the young men and women already dedicated to the same anguish and travail, among whom is already that one who will some day stand here where I am standing.

Our tragedy today is a general and universal physical fear so long sustained by now that we can even bear it. There are no longer problems of the spirit. There is only the question: when will I be blown up? Because of this, the young man or woman writing today has forgotten the problems of the human heart in conflict with itself which alone can make good writing because only that is worth writing about, worth the agony and the sweat.

He must learn them again. He must teach himself that the basest of all things is to be afraid; and, teaching himself that, forget it forever, leaving no room in his workshop for anything but the old verities and truths of the heart, the old universal truths lacking which any story is ephemeral and doomed—love and honour and pity and pride and compassion and sacrifice. Until he does so he labours under a curse. He writes not of love but of lust, of defeats in which nobody loses anything of value, of victories without hope and worst of all without pity or compassion. His griefs grieve on no universal bones, leaving no scars. He writes not of the heart but of the glands.

Until he relearns these things he will write as though he stood among and watched the end of man. I decline to accept the end of man. It is easy enough to say that man is immortal simply because he will endure; that when the last ding-dong of doom has clanged and faded from the last worthless rock hanging tideless in the last red and dying evening, that even then there will still be one more sound: that of his puny inexhaustible voice, still talking. I refuse to accept this. I believe that man will not merely endure: he will prevail. He is immortal, not because he alone among creatures has an inexhaustible voice, but because he has a soul, a spirit capable of compassion and sacrifice and endurance. The poet's, the writer's, duty is to write about these things. It is his privilege to help man endure by lifting his heart, by reminding him of the courage and honour and hope and pride and compassion and pity and sacrifice which have been the glory of his past. The poet's voice need not merely be the record of man, it can be one of the props, the pillars to help him endure and prevail.

1950

ERNEST HEMINGWAY (1898-1961)

Hemingway was the most distinguished American short story writer of this century, and the novelist who most fully combined popular appeal and critical acclaim. His sparse, clipped style, his emphasis on the manly virtues of strength and courage, and his gift for realistic dialogue, suggestive description of persons and places, and the narration of rapid and often violent action, made him the most widely known and frequently imitated American prose writer of his generation.

Hemingway was born in Oak Park, Illinois, the son of a doctor. Graduating from high school in 1917, he went to the war in Europe as an ambulance driver, transferred to the Italian infantry, and was wounded and invalided home. In 1920, he became a reporter for the Toronto Star, and was sent by that paper as a foreign correspondent to the Near East. In 1921 he moved to Paris, where he lived for several years and was associated with Ezra Pound, Gertrude Stein, James Joyce, and other expatriates. His first novel, The Sun Also Rises (1926), described a group of such expatriates in France and Spain, and expressed the futility, boredom, and disillusionment of the so-called "lost generation" who grew up under the shadow of World War I. His Farewell to Arms, a love story set in Italy during that war, appeared in 1929 and established his reputation. During the nineteen-thirties Hemingway spent much time in Spain and Africa: the books Death in the Afternoon (1932) and For Whom the Bell Tolls (1940) reflect his Spanish experiences, The Green Hills of Africa and some of his best short stories his African ones. In his later life, Hemingway made his home in Cuba. His later novels, with the exception of The Old Man and The Sea (1953), were less successful. His short stories appeared in many magazines and anthologies, and in five separate volumes. He died of a gunshot wound, after a period of ill-health, in 1961.

In Another Country

In the fall the war was always there, but we did not go to it any more. It was cold in the fall in Milan and the dark came very early. Then the electric lights came on, and it was pleasant along the streets looking in the windows. There was much game hanging outside the shops, and the snow powdered in the fur of the foxes and the wind blew their tails. The deer hung stiff and heavy and empty, and small birds blew in the wind and the wind turned their feathers. It was a cold fall and the wind came down from the mountains.

We were all at the hospital every afternoon, and there were different ways of walking across the town through the dusk to the hospital. Two of the ways were alongside canals, but they were long. Always, though, you crossed a bridge across a canal to enter the hospital. There was a choice of three bridges. On one of them a woman sold roasted chestnuts. It was warm, standing in front of her charcoal fire, and the chestnuts were warm afterward in your pocket. The hospital was very old and very beautiful, and you entered through a gate and walked across a courtyard and out a gate on the other side. There were usually funerals starting from the courtyard. Beyond the old hospital were the new brick pavilions, and there we met every afternoon and were all very polite and interested in what was the matter, and sat in the machines that were to make so much difference.

The doctor came up to the machine where I was sitting and said: "What did you like best to do before the war? Did you practise a sport?"

I said: "Yes, football."

"Good," he said. "You will be able to play football again better than ever."

My knee did not bend and the leg dropped straight from the knee to the ankle without a calf, and the machine was to bend the knee and make it move as in riding a tricycle. But it did not bend yet, and instead the machine lurched when it came to the bending part. The doctor said: "That will all pass. You are a fortunate young man. You will play football again like a champion."

In the next machine was a major who had a little hand like a baby's. He winked at me when the doctor examined his hand, which was between two leather straps that bounced up and down and flapped the stiff fingers, and said: "And will I too play football, captain-doctor?" He had been a very great fencer, and before the war the greatest fencer in Italy.

The doctor went to his office in a back room and brought a photograph which showed a hand that had been withered almost as small as the major's, before it had taken a machine course, and after was a little larger. The major held the photograph with his good hand and looked at it very carefully. "A wound?" he asked.

"An industrial accident," the doctor said.

"Very interesting, very interesting," the major said, and handed it back to the doctor.

"You have confidence?"

"No," said the major.

There were three boys who came each day who were about the same age I was. They were all three from Milan, and one of them was to be a lawyer, and one was to be a painter, and one had intended to be a soldier, and after we were finished with the machines, sometimes we walked back together to the Café Cova, which was next door to the Scala. We walked the short way through the communist quarter because we were four together. The people hated us because we were officers, and from a wine-shop some one called out, "A basso gli ufficiali!" as we passed. Another boy who walked with us sometimes and made us five wore a black silk handkerchief across his face because he had no nose then and his face was to be rebuilt. He had gone out to the front from the military academy and been wounded within an hour after he had gone into the front line for the first time. They rebuilt his face, but he came from a very old family and they could never get the nose exactly right. He went to

South America and worked in a bank. But this was a long time ago, and then we did not any of us know how it was going to be afterward. We only knew then that there was always the war, but that we were not going to it any more.

We all had the same medals, except the boy with the black silk bandage across face, and he had not been at the front long enough to get any medals. The tall boy with a very pale face who was to be a lawyer had been a lieutenant of Arditi and had three medals of the sort we each had only one of. He had lived a very long time with death and was a little detached. We were all a little detached, and there was nothing that held us together except that we met every afternoon at the hospital. Although, as we walked to the Cova through the tough part of town, walking in the dark, with light and singing coming out of the wine-shops, and sometimes having to walk into the street when the men and women would crowd together on the sidewalk so that we would have had to jostle them to get by, we felt held together by there being something that had happened that they, the people who disliked us, did not understand.

We ourselves all understood the Cova, where it was rich and warm and not too brightly lighted, and noisy and smoky at certain hours, and there were always girls at the tables and the illustrated papers on a rack on the wall. The girls at the Cova were very patriotic, and I found that the most patriotic people in Italy were the café girls—and I believe they are still patriotic.

The boys at first were very polite about my medals and asked me what I had done to get them. I showed them the papers, which were written in very beautiful language and full of *fratellanza* and *abnegazione*, but which really said, with the adjectives removed, that I had been given the medals because I was an American. After that their manner changed a little toward me, although I was their friend against outsiders. I was a friend, but I was never really one of them after they had read the citations, because it had been different with them and they had done very different things to get their medals. I had been wounded, it was true; but we all knew that being wounded, after all, was really an accident. I was never ashamed of the ribbons, though, and sometimes, after the cocktail hour, I would imagine myself having done all the things they had done to get their medals; but walking home at night through the empty streets with the cold wind and all the shops closed, trying to keep near the street lights, I knew that I would never have done such things, and I was very much afraid to die, and often lay in bed at night by myself, afraid to die and wondering how I would be when I went back to the front again.

The three with the medals were like hunting-hawks; and I was not a hawk, although I might seem a hawk to those who had never hunted; they, the three, knew better and so we drifted apart. But I stayed good friends with the boy who had been wounded his first day at the front, because he would never know now how he would have turned out; so he could never be accepted either, and I liked him because I thought perhaps he would not have turned out to be a hawk either.

The major, who had been the great fencer, did not believe in bravery, and spent much time while we sat in the machines correcting my grammar. He had complimented me on how I spoke Italian, and we talked together very easily. One day I had said that Italian seemed such an easy language to me that I could not take a great interest in it; everything was so easy to say. "Ah, yes," the major said. "Why, then, do you not take up the use of grammar?" So we took up the use of grammar, and soon Italian was such a difficult language that I was afraid to talk to him until I had the grammar straight in my mind.

The major came very regularly to the hospital. I do not think he ever missed a day, although I am sure he did not believe in the machines. There was a time when none of us believed in the machines, and one day the major said it was all nonsense. The machines were new then and it was we who were to prove them. It was an idiotic idea, he said, "a theory, like another." I had not learned my grammar, and he said I was a stupid impossible disgrace, and he was a fool to have bothered with me. He was a small man and he sat straight up in his chair with his right hand thrust into the machine and looked straight ahead at the wall while the straps thumped up and down with his fingers in them.

"What will you do when the war is over if it is over?" he asked me. "Speak grammatically!"

"I will go to the States."

"Are you married?"

"No, but I hope to be."

"The more of a fool you are," he said.

He seemed very angry. "A man must not marry."

"Why, Signor Maggiore?"

"Don't call me 'Signor Maggiore.' "

"Why must not a man marry?"

"He cannot marry. He cannot marry," he said angrily. "If he is to lose everything, he should not place himself in a position to lose that. He should not place himself in a position to lose. He should find things he cannot lose."

He spoke very angrily and bitterly, and looked straight ahead while he talked.

"But why should he necessarily lose it?"

"He'll lose it," the major said. He was looking at the wall. Then he looked down at the machine and jerked his little hand out from between the straps and slapped it hard against his thigh. "He'll lose it," he almost shouted. "Don't argue with me!" Then he called to the attendant who ran the machines. "Come and turn this damned thing off."

He went back into the other room for the light treatment and the massage. Then I heard him ask the doctor if he might use his telephone and he shut the door. When he came back into the room, I was sitting in another machine. He was wearing his cape and had his cap on, and he came directly toward my machine and put his arm on my shoulder.

"I am so sorry," he said, and patted me on the shoulder with his good hand. "I would not be rude. My wife has just died. You must forgive me."

"Oh—" I said, feeling sick for him. "I am so sorry."

He stood there biting his lower lip. "It is very difficult," he said. "I cannot resign myself."

He looked straight past me and out through the window. Then he began to cry. "I am utterly unable to resign myself," he said and choked. And then crying, his head up looking at nothing, carrying himself straight and soldierly, with tears on both his cheeks and biting his lips, he walked past the machines and out the door.

The doctor told me that the major's wife, who was very young and whom he had not married until he was definitely invalided out of the war, had died of pneumonia. She had been sick only a few days. No one expected her to die. The major did not come to the hospital for three days. Then he came at the usual hour, wearing a black band on the sleeve of his uniform When he came back, there were large framed photographs around the wall, of all sorts of wounds before and after they had been cured by the machines. In front of the machine the major used were three photographs of hands like his that were completely restored. I do not know where the doctor got them. I always understood we were the first to use the machines. The photographs did not make much difference to the major because he only looked out of the window.

1927

1927

CANADIAN LITERATURE

STEPHEN LEACOCK (1869-1944)

Stephen Leacock was born in Hampshire, England, but came to Canada as a boy of seven. He was educated at Upper Canada College, the University of Toronto, and the University of Chicago, from which he obtained his Ph.D. in 1903. For many years he was Professor of Economics at McGill University in Montreal. His summers were spent mainly at Orillia, Ontario, where there is now a shrine to his memory.

Leacock wrote a number of serious books on economics, politics, and history, but it was as a humorist that he established a world-wide reputation. He published many books of humour, beginning with *Literary Lapses* in 1910. Perhaps the best of his comic books are *Sunshine Sketches of A Little Town* (1912), a nostalgic and whimsical but sometimes gently satirical study of small town life, and *Arcadian Adventures with the Idle Rich* (1914), a more hostile but still extremely funny commentary on the wealthy denizens of a large North American city.

The sketch which follows, perhaps his most well-known, is from *Literary Lapses*, 1910.

My Financial Career

When I go into a bank I get rattled. The clerks rattle me; the wickets rattle me; the sight of the money rattles me; everything rattles me.

The moment I cross the threshold of a bank and attempt to transact business there, I become an irresponsible idiot.

I knew this beforehand, but my salary had been raised to fifty dollars a month and I felt that the bank was the only place for it.

So I shambled in and looked timidly round at the clerks. I had an idea that a person about to open an account must needs consult the manager.

I went up to a wicket marked "Accountant." The accountant was a tall, cool devil. The very sight of him rattled me. My voice was sepulchral.

"Can I see the manager?" I said, and added solemnly, "alone." I don't know why I said "alone."

"Certainly," said the accountant, and fetched him.

The manager was a grave, calm man. I held my fifty-six dollars clutched in a crumpled ball in my pocket.

"Are you the manager?" I said. God knows I didn't doubt it.

"Yes," he said.

"Can I see you," I asked, "alone?" I didn't want to say "alone" again, but without it the thing seemed self-evident.

The manager looked at me in some alarm. He felt that I had an awful secret to reveal.

"Come in here," he said, and led the way to a private room. He turned the key in the lock.

"We are safe from interruption here," he said; "sit down."

We both sat down and looked at each other. I found no voice to speak.

"You are one of Pinkertons'[1] men, I presume," he said.

He had gathered from my mysterious manner that I was a detective. I knew what he was thinking, and it made me worse.

"No, not from Pinkerton's," I said, seeming to imply that I came from a rival agency.

"To tell the truth," I went on, as if I had been prompted to lie about it, "I am not a detective at all. I have come to open an account. I intend to keep all my money in this bank."

The manager looked relieved but still serious; he concluded now that I was a son of Baron Rothschild or a young Gould.

"A large account, I suppose," he said.

"Fairly large," I whispered, "I propose to deposit fifty-six dollars now and fifty dollars a month regularly."

The manager got up and opened the door. He called to the accountant.

"Mr. Montgomery," he said unkindly loud, "this gentlemen is opening an account; he will deposit fifty-six dollars. Good morning."

I rose.

A big iron door stood open at the side of the room.

"Good morning," I said, and stepped into the safe.

"Come out," said the manager coldly, and showed me the other way.

I went up to the accountant's wicket and poked the ball of money at him with a quick convulsive movement as if I were doing a conjuring trick.

My face was ghastly pale.

---

[1] A detective agency established in the United States in the nineteenth century.

"Here," I said, "deposit it." The tone of the words seemed to mean, "Let us do this painful thing while the fit is on us."

He took the money and gave it to another clerk.

He made me write the sum on a slip and sign my name in a book. I no longer knew what I was doing. The bank swam before my eyes.

"Is it deposited?" I asked in a hollow, vibrating voice.

"It is," said the accountant.

"Then I want to draw a cheque."

My idea was to draw out six dollars of it for present use. Someone gave me a cheque book through a wicket and someone else began telling me how to write it out. The people in the bank had the impression that I was an invalid millionaire. I wrote something on the cheque and thrust it in at the clerk. He looked at it.

"What! are you drawing it all out again?" he asked in surprise. Then I realized that I had written fifty-six instead of six. I was too far gone to reason now. I had a feeling that it was impossible to explain the thing. All the clerks had stopped writing to look at me.

Reckless with misery, I made a plunge.

"Yes, the whole thing."

"You withdraw your money from the bank?"

"Every cent of it."

"Are you not going to deposit any more?" said the clerk, astonished.

"Never."

An idiot hope struck me that they might think something had insulted me while I was writing the cheque and that I had changed my mind. I made a wretched attempt to look like a man with a fearfully quick temper.

The clerk prepared to pay the money.

"How will you have it?" he said.

"What?"

"How will you have it?"

"Oh"—I caught his meaning and answered without even trying to think—"in fifties."

He gave me a fifty-dollar bill.

"And the six?" he asked dryly.

"In sixes," I said.

He gave it to me and I rushed out.

As the big door swung behind me I caught the echo of a roar of laughter that went up to the ceiling of the bank. Since then I bank no more. I keep my money in cash in my trousers' pocket and my savings in silver dollars in a sock.

1910

FREDERICK PHILIP GROVE (1871-1948)

Frederick Philip Grove was born near the Russo-Polish border while his parents were travelling to their home in southern Sweden. Most of his childhood and youth was spent either in Sweden at the family home, or in various cities of Europe where his mother travelled in search of art and entertainment. After the death of his mother in 1887, he made a journey through Russia and on to the Far East, attended briefly the universities in Paris, Rome, and Munich, and in 1892 came to North America as a tourist. Stranded in Toronto by the bankruptcy and death of his father, he was compelled to make his living by a series of menial jobs. For some twenty years he was an itinerant harvest hand in the American and Canadian West, and began to write his novels during the winters. In 1912 he became a schoolteacher in Manitoba, in which province he lived until 1929. In that year he came to Ontario, and after a year or two in Ottawa with a publishing firm settled on a farm near Simcoe, where he lived until his death.

Grove wrote about a dozen novels, of which eight were published: *Settlers of the Marsh* (1925), *A Search for America* (1927), *Our Daily Bread* (1928), *The Yoke of Life* (1930), *Fruits of the Earth* (1933), *Two Generations* (1939), *The Master of the Mill* (1944), and *Consider Her Ways* (1947). He also wrote three volumes of essays, an autobiography entitled *In Search of Myself* (1946), and several short stories. Most of Grove's writings consist of honest, realistic accounts of rural life in the prairie provinces of Canada; the story which follows illustrates the accuracy with which he observed the people, the climate, and the natural scenery of that region. "Snow" first appeared in the *Queen's Quarterly*, Spring, 1932.

Snow

Towards morning the blizzard had died down, though it was still far from daylight. Stars without number blazed in the dark-blue sky which presented that brilliant and uncompromising appearance always characterizing, on the northern plains of America, those nights in the dead of winter when the thermometer dips to its lowest levels.

In the west, Orion was sinking to the horizon. It was between five and six o'clock.

In the bush-fringe of the Big Marsh, sheltered by thick but bare bluffs of aspens, stood a large house, built of logs, whitewashed, solid—such as a settler who is still single would put up only when he thinks of getting married. It, too, looked ice-cold, frozen in the night. Not a breath stirred where it stood; a thin thread of whitish smoke, reaching up to the level of the tree-tops, seemed to be suspended into the chimney rather than to issue from it.

Through the deep snow of the yard, newly packed, a man was fighting his way to the door. Arrived there, he knocked and knocked, first tapping with his knuckles, then hammering with his fists.

Two, three minutes passed. Then a sound awoke in the house, as of somebody stirring, getting out of bed.

The figure on the door-slab—a medium-sized, slim man in sheepskin and high rubber boots into which his trousers were tucked, with the ear-flaps of his cap pulled down—stood and waited, bent over, hands thrust into the pockets of the short coat, as if he wished to shrink into the smallest possible space so as to offer the smallest possible surface to the attack of the cold. In order to get rid of the dry, powdery snow which filled every crease of his foot-gear and trousers, he stamped his feet. His chin was drawn deep into the turned-up collar on whose points his breath had fallen in the form of a thick layer of hoarfrost.

At last a bolt was drawn inside.

The face of a man peered out, just discernible in the starlight.

Then the door was opened; in ominous silence the figure from the outside entered, still stamping its feet.

Not a word was spoken till the door had been closed. Then a voice sounded through the cold and dreary darkness of the room.

"Redcliff hasn't come home. He went to town about noon and expected to get back by midnight. We're afraid he's lost."

The other man, quite invisible in the dark, had listened, his teeth chattering with the cold. "Are you sure he started out from town?"

"Well," the newcomer answered hesitatingly, "one of the horses came into the yard."

"One of his horses?"

"Yes, one of those he drove. The woman worked her way to my place to get help."

The owner of the house did not speak again. He went, in the dark, to the door in the rear and opened it. There, he groped about for matches and, finding them, lighted a lamp. In the room stood a big stove, a coal-stove of the self-feeder type; but the fuel used was wood. He opened the drafts and shook the grate clear of ashes; there were two big blocks of spruce in the fire-box, smouldering away for the night. In less than a minute they blazed up.

The newcomer entered, blinking in the light of the lamp, and looked on. Before many minutes the heat from the stove began to tell.

"I'll call Bill," the owner of the house said. He was himself of medium height or only slightly above it, but of enormous breadth of shoulder: a figure built for lifting loads. By his side the other man looked small, weakly, dwarfed.

He left the room and, returning through the bare, cold hall in front, went upstairs.

A few minutes later a tall, slender, well-built youth bolted into the room where the newcomer was waiting. Bill, Carroll's hired man, was in his underwear and carried his clothes, thrown in a heap over his arm. Without loss of time, but jumping, stamping, swinging his arms, he began at once to dress.

He greeted the visitor. "Hello, Mike! What's that Abe tells me? Redcliff got lost?"

"Seems that way," said Mike listlessly.

"By gringo," Bill went on, "I shouldn't wonder. In that storm! I'd have waited in town! Wouldn't catch me going out in that kind of weather!"

"Didn't start till late in the afternoon," Mike Sobotski said in his shivering way.

"No. And didn't last long, either," Bill agreed while he shouldered into his overalls. "But while she lasted . . ."

At this moment Abe Carroll, the owner of the farm, re-entered, with sheepskin, fur cap, and long woollen scarf on his arm. His deeply lined, striking, square face bore a settled frown while he held the inside of his sheepskin to the stove, to warm it up. Then, without saying a word, he got deliberately into it.

Mike Sobotski still stood bent over, shivering, though he had opened his coat and, on his side of the stove, was catching all the heat it afforded.

Abe, with the least motion needed to complete dressing, made for the door. In passing Bill, he flung out an elbow which touched the young man's arm, "Come on," he said; and to the other, pointing to the stove, "Close the drafts."

A few minutes later a noise as of rearing and snorting horses in front of the house...

Mike, buttoning up his coat and pulling his mitts over his hand, went out.

They mounted three unsaddled horses. Abe leading, they dashed through the new drifts in the yard and out through the gate to the road. Here, where the shelter of the bluffs screening the house was no longer effective, a light but freshening breeze from the north-west made itself felt as if fine little knives were cutting into the flesh of their faces.

Abe dug his heels into the flank of his rearing mount. The horse was unwilling to obey his guidance, for Abe wanted to leave the road and to cut across wild land to the south-west.

The darkness was still inky black, though here and there, where the slope of the drifts slanted in the right direction, starlight was dimly reflected from the snow. The drifts were six, eight, in places ten feet high; and the snow was once more crawling up their flanks, it was so light and fine. It would fill the tracks in half an hour. As the horses plunged through, the crystals dusted up in clouds, flying aloft over horses and riders.

In less than half an hour they came to a group of two little buildings, of logs, that seemed to squat on their haunches in the snow. Having entered the yard through a gate, they passed one of the buildings and made for the other, a little stable; their horses snorting, they stopped in its lee.

Mike dismounted, throwing the halter-shank of his horse to Bill. He went to the house, which stood a hundred feet or so away. The shack was even smaller than the stable, twelve by fifteen feet perhaps. From its flue-pipe a thick, white plume of smoke blew to the south-east.

Mike returned with a lantern; the other two sprang to the ground; and they opened the door to examine the horse which the woman had allowed to enter.

The horse was there, still excited, snorting at the leaping light and shadows from the lantern, its eyes wild, its nostrils dilated. It was covered with white frost and fully harnessed, though its traces were tied up to the back-band.

"He let him go," said Mike, taking in these signs. "Must have stopped and unhitched him."

"Must have been stuck in a drift," Bill said, assenting.

"And tried to walk it," Abe added.

For a minute or so they stood silent, each following his own gloomy thoughts. Weird, luminous little clouds issued fitfully from the nostrils of the horse inside.

"I'll get the cutter," Abe said at last.

"I'll get it," Bill volunteered. "I'll take the drivers along. We'll leave the filly here in the stable."

"All right."

Bill remounted, leading Abe's horse. He disappeared into the night.

Abe and Mike, having tied the filly and the other horse in their stalls, went out, closed the door, and turned to the house.

There, by the light of a little coal-oil lamp, they saw the woman sitting at the stove, pale, shivering, her teeth a-chatter, trying to warm her hands, which were cold with fever, and looking with lack-lustre eyes at the men as they entered.

The children were sleeping; the oldest, a girl, on the floor, wrapped in a blanket and curled up like a dog; four others in one narrow bed, with hay for a mattress, two at the head, two at the foot; the baby on, rather than in, a sort of cradle made of a wide board slung by thin ropes to the pole-roof of the shack.

The other bed was empty and unmade. The air was stifling from a night of exhalations.

"We're going to hunt for him," Mike said quietly. "We've sent for a cutter. He must have tried to walk."

The woman did not answer. She sat and shivered.

"We'll take some blankets," Mike went on. "And some whisky if you've got any in the house."

He and Abe were standing by the stove, opposite the woman, and warming their hands, their mitts held under their armpits.

The woman pointed with a look to a home-made little cupboard nailed to the wall and apathetically turned back to the stove. Mike went, opened the door of the cupboard, took a bottle from it, and slipped it into the pocket of his sheepskin. Then he raised the blankets from the empty bed, rolled them roughly into a bundle, dropped it, and returned to the stove where, with stiff fingers, he fell to rolling a cigarette.

Thus they stood for an hour or so.

Abe's eye was fastened on the woman. He would have liked to say a word of comfort, of hope. What was there to be said?

She was the daughter of a German settler in the bush, some six or seven miles north-east of Abe's place. Her father, an oldish, unctuous, bearded man, had, some ten years ago, got tired of the hard life in the bush where work meant clearing, picking stones, and digging stumps. He had sold his homestead and bought a prairie-farm, half a section, on crop-payments, giving notes for the equipment which he needed to handle the place. He had not been able to make it a "go." His bush farm had fallen back on his hands; he had lost his all and returned to the place. He had been counting on the help of his two boys—big, strapping young fellows—who were to clear much land and to raise crops which would lift the debt. But the boys had refused to go back to the bush; they could get easy work in town. Ready money would help. But the ready money had melted away in their hands. Redcliff, the old people's son-in-law, had been their last hope. They were on the point of losing even their bush farm. Here they might perhaps still have found a refuge for their old age —though Redcliff's homestead lay on the sand-flats bordering on the marsh where the soil was thin, dreadfully thin; it drifted when the scrub-brush was cleared off. Still, with Redcliff living, this place had been a hope. What were they to do if he was gone? And this woman, hardly more than a girl, in spite of her six children!

The two, tiny, square windows of the shack began to turn grey.

At last Abe, thinking he heard a sound, went to the door and stepped out. Bill was there; the horses were shaking the snow out of their pelts; one of them was pawing the ground.

Once more Abe opened the door and gave Mike a look for a signal. Mike gathered the bundle of blankets into his arms, pulled on his mitts, and came out.

Abe reached for the lines, but Bill objected.

"No. Let me drive. I found something."

And as soon as the two older men had climbed in, squeezing into the scant space on the seat, he clicked his tongue.

"Get up there!" he shouted, hitting the horses' backs with his lines. And with a leap they darted away.

Bill turned, heading back to the Carroll farm. The horses plunged, reared, snorted, and then, throwing their heads, shot along in a gallop, scattering snow-slabs right and left and throwing wing-waves of the fresh, powdery snow, especially on the lee side. Repeatedly they tried to turn into the wind, which they were cutting at right angles. But Bill plied the whip and guided them expertly.

Nothing was visible anywhere; nothing but the snow in the first grey of dawn. Then, like enormous ghosts, or like evanescent apparitions, the trees of the bluff were adumbrated behind the lingering veils of the night.

Bill turned to the south, along the straight trail which bordered Abe Carroll's farm. He kept looking out sharply to right and left. But after a while he drew his galloping horses in.

"Whoa!" he shouted, tearing at the lines in seesaw fashion. And when the rearing horses came to a stop, excited and breathless, he added, "I've missed it." He turned.

"What is it?" Abe asked.

"The other horse," Bill answered. "It must have had the scent of our yard. It's dead . . . frozen stiff."

A few minutes later he pointed to a huge white mound on top of a drift to the left. "That's it," he said, turned the horses into the wind, and stopped.

To the right, the bluffs of the farm slowly outlined themselves in the morning greyness.

The two older men alighted and, with their hands, shovelled the snow away. There lay the horse, stiff and cold, frozen into a rock-like mass.

"Must have been here a long while," Abe said.

Mike nodded. "Five, six hours." Then he added, "Couldn't have had the smell of the yard. Unless the wind has turned."

"It has," Abe answered and pointed to a fold in the flank of the snow-drift which indicated that the present drift had been superimposed on a lower one whose longitudinal axis ran to the north-east.

For a moment longer they stood and pondered.

Then Abe went back to the cutter and reached for the lines. "I'll drive," he said.

Mike climbed in.

Abe took his bearings, looking for landmarks. They were only two or three hundred feet from his fence. That enabled him to estimate the exact direction of the breeze. He clicked his tongue. "Get up!"

And the horses, catching the infection of a dull excitement, shot away. They went straight into the desert of drifts to the west, plunging ahead without any trail, without any landmark in front to guide them.

They went for half an hour, an hour, and longer.

None of the three men said a word. Abe knew the sandflats better than any other; Abe reasoned better than they. If anyone could find the missing man, it was Abe.

Abe's thoughts ran thus. The horse had gone against the wind. It would never have done so without good reason; that reason could have been no other than a scent to follow. If that was so, however, it would have gone in as straight a line as it could. The sand-flats stretched away to the south-west for sixteen miles with not a settlement, not a farm but Redcliff's. If Abe managed to strike that line of scent, it must take him to the point where the horse had started.

Clear and glaring, with an almost indifferent air, the sun rose to their left.

And suddenly they saw the wagon-box of the sleigh sticking out of the snow ahead of them.

Abe stopped, handed Bill the lines, and got out. Mike followed. Nobody said a word.

The two men dug the tongue of the vehicle out of the snow and tried it. This was part of the old, burnt-over bush land south of the sand-flats. The sleigh was tightly wedged in between several charred stumps which stuck up through the snow. That was the reason why the man had unhitched the horses and turned them loose. What else, indeed, could he have done?

The box was filled with a drift which, toward the tail-gate, was piled high, for there three bags of flour were standing on end and leaning against a barrel half-filled with small parcels the interstices between which were packed with mealy snow.

Abe waded all around the sleigh, reconnoitering; and as he did so, wading at the height of the upper-edge of the wagon-box, the snow suddenly gave way beneath him; he broke in; the drift was hollow.

A suspicion took hold of him; with a few quick reaches of his arm he demolished the roof of the drift all about.

And there, in the hollow, lay the man's body as if he were sleeping, a quiet expression as of painless rest on his face. His eyes were closed; a couple of bags were wrapped about his shoulders. Apparently he had not even tried to walk! Already chilled to the bone, he had given in to that desire for rest, for shelter at any price, which overcomes him who is doomed to freeze.

Without a word the two men carried him to the cutter and laid him down in the snow.

Bill, meanwhile, had unhitched the horses and was hooking them to the tongue of the sleigh. The two others looked on in silence. Four times the horses sprang, excited because Bill tried to make them pull with a sudden twist. The sleigh did not stir.

"Need an axe," Mike said at last, "to cut the stumps. We'll get the sleigh later."

Mike hitched up again and turned the cutter. The broken snow-drifts through which they had come gave the direction. Then they laid the stiff, dead body across the floor of their vehicle, leaving the side-doors open, for it protruded both ways. They themselves climbed up on the seat and crouched down, so as not to put their feet on the corpse.

Thus they returned to Abe Carroll's farm where, still in silence, they deposited the body in the granary.

That done, they stood for a moment as if in doubt. Then Bill unhitched the horses and took them to the stable to feed.

"I'll tell the woman," said Mike. "Will you go tell her father?"

Abe nodded. "Wait for breakfast," he added.

It was ten o'clock; and none of them had eaten since the previous night.

On the way to Altmann's place in the bush, drifts were no obstacles to driving. Drifts lay on the marsh, on the open sand-flats.

Every minute of the time Abe, as he drove along, thought of that woman in the shack: the woman, alone, with six children, and with the knowledge that her man was dead.

Altmann's place in the bush looked the picture of peace and comfort: a large log-house of two rooms. Window frames and doors were painted green. A place to stay with, not to leave . . .

When Abe knocked, the woman, whom he had seen but once in his life, at the sale where they had lost their possessions, opened the door—an enormously fat woman, overflowing her clothes. The man, tall, broad, with a long rolling beard, now grey, stood behind her, peering over her shoulder. A visit is an event in the bush!

"Come in," he said cheerfully when he saw Abe. "What a storm that was!"

Abe entered the kitchen which was also dining- and living-room. He sat down on the chair which was pushed forward for him and looked at the two old people, who remained standing.

Suddenly, from the expression of his face, they anticipated something of his message. No use dissembling.

"Redcliff is dead," he said. "He was frozen to death last night on his way home from town."

The two old people also sat down; it looked as if their knees had given way beneath them. They stared at him, dumbly, a sudden expression of panic fright in their eyes.

"I thought you might want to go to your daughter," Abe added sympathetically.

The man's big frame seemed to shrink as he sat there. All the unctuousness and the conceit of the handsome man dwindled out of his bearing. The woman's eyes had already filled with tears.

Thus they remained for two, three minutes.

Then the woman folded her fat, pudgy hands; her head sank low on her breast; and she sobbed, "God's will be done!"

1932

E. J. PRATT (1882-1964)

Edwin John Pratt is the leading Canadian poet of this century. Coming to prominence in the nineteen-twenties, at about the same time as the Montreal Group of Smith, Scott, and Klein, he pursued an independent path, writing verse which is neither aggressively modernist nor smugly reactionary. He won most popular acclaim for his long narrative poems, many of them set at sea, such as "The Cachalot" (1926), *The Roosevelt and the Antinoe* (1930), *The Titanic* (1935) and *Brébeuf and His Brethren* (1940), but he also wrote many subtle short lyrics, character sketches, satires, and meditative poems His energy, high spirits, humour, and his admiration for physical and mental courage are his most obvious characteristics; but beneath the deceptively simple surface of his verse lies a complex but consistent philosophy of life. This philosophy may best be briefly described as Christian humanism: man finds his highest expression in Christ-like acts of self-sacrificing love, but is always in danger of relapsing into barbaric savagery. Pratt sees man, in other words, as delicately balanced between the temple and the cave, saintliness and savagery.

Pratt was born on February 4, 1882, at Western Bay, Newfoundland. He intended to follow in his father's footsteps as a Methodist minister, and in 1907 entered Victoria College, Toronto, to begin his ministerial training. Although he successfully completed this training, he chose to become a university professor rather than a preacher, and from 1919 to the early nineteen-fifties was a member of the Department of English at Victoria. He won many honours for his poetry: the Governor-General's Medal on several occasions, honorary degrees from several universities, and the companionship of the Order of St. Michael and St. George from King George VI.

The Shark

He seemed to know the harbour,
So leisurely he swam;
His fin,
Like a piece of sheet-iron,
Three-cornered,
And with knife-edge,
Stirred not a bubble
As it moved
With its base-line on the water.

His body was tubular   10
And tapered
And smoke-blue,
And as he passed the wharf
He turned,
And snapped at a flat-fish

That was dead and floating.
And I saw the flash of a white throat,
And a double row of white teeth,
And eyes of metallic grey,
Hard and narrow and slit.   20

Then out of the harbour,
With that three-cornered fin
Shearing without a bubble the water
Lithely,
Leisurely,
He swam—
That strange fish,
Tubular, tapered, smoke-blue,
Part vulture, part wolf,
Part neither—for his blood was cold.   30

1923

From Stone to Steel

From stone to bronze, from bronze to
    steel
Along the road-dust of the sun,
Two revolutions of the wheel
From Java[1] to Geneva[2] run.

The snarl Neanderthal[3] is worn
Close to the smiling Aryan[4] lips,
The civil polish of the horn
Gleams from our praying finger tips.

[1]Here used as a symbol of savagery and violence.
[2]Here used as a symbol of civilization and the search for international peace (Geneva was the headquarters of the League of Nations between World War I and World War II).
[3]A form of primitive man.
[4]A sarcastic allusion to Hitler's theory of the superiority of the Aryan race.

The evolution of desire
Has but matured a toxic wine,   10
Drunk long before its heady fire
Reddened Euphrates or the Rhine[5].

Between the temple and the cave
The boundary lies tissue-thin:
The yearlings still the altars crave
As satisfaction for a sin.

The road goes up, the road goes down—
Let Java or Geneva be—
But whether to the cross or crown,
The path lies through Gethsemane[6].   20

[5]References to ancient and modern battles.
[6]Where Christ suffered the agony in the Garden.
   The suggestion is that man must always
   undergo deep suffering.

                                                    1932

Come Away, Death

Willy-nilly, he comes or goes, with the clown's logic,
Comic in epitaph, tragic in epithalamium,
And unseduced by any mused rhyme.
However blow the winds over the pollen,
Whatever the course of the garden variables,
He remains the constant,
Ever flowering from the poppy seeds.

There was a time he came in formal dress,
Announced by Silence tapping at the panels
In deep apology.   10
A touch of chivalry in his approach,
He offered sacramental wine,
And with acanthus leaf
And petals of the hyacinth
He took the fever from the temples
And closed the eyelids,
Then led the way to his cool longitudes
In the dignity of the candles.

His medieval grace is gone—
Gone with the flame of the capitals   20
And the leisured turn of the thumb
Leafing the manuscripts,

Gone with the marbles
And the Venetian mosaics,
With the bend of the knee
Before the rose-strewn feet of the Virgin.
The paternosters of his priests,
Committing clay to clay,
Have rattled in their throats
Under the gride of his traction tread.   30

One night we heard his footfall—one September night—
In the outskirts of a village near the sea.
There was a moment when the storm
Delayed its fist, when the surf fell
Like velvet on the rocks—a moment only;
The strangest lull we ever knew!
A sudden truce among the oaks
Released their fratricidal arms;
The poplars straightened to attention
As the winds stopped to listen   40
To the sound of a motor drone—

And then the drone was still.
We heard the tick-tock on the shelf
And the leak of valves in our hearts.
A calm condensed and lidded
As at the core of a cyclone ended breathing.
This was the Monologue of Silence
Grave and unequivocal.

What followed was a bolt
Outside the range and target of the thunder,   50
And human speech curved back upon itself
Through Druid runways and the Piltdown scarps,
Beyond the stammers of the Java caves,
To find its origins in hieroglyphs
On mouths and eyes and cheeks
Etched by a foreign stylus never used
On the outmoded page of the Apocalypse.

                                                          1943

The Truant

"What have you there?" the great Panjandrum said
To the Master of the Revels who had led
A bucking truant with a stiff backbone
Close to the foot of the Almighty's throne.

"Right Reverend, most adored,
And forcibly acknowledged Lord
By the keen logic of your two-edged sword!
This creature has presumed to classify
Himself—a biped, rational, six feet high
And two feet wide; weighs fourteen stone;   10
Is guilty of a multitude of sins.
He has abjured his choric origins,
And like an undomesticated slattern,
Walks with tangential step unknown
Within the weave of the atomic pattern.
He has developed concepts, grins
Obscenely at your Royal bulletins,
Possesses what he calls a will
Which challenges your power to kill."

"What is his pedigree?"   20

"The base is guaranteed, your Majesty—
Calcium, carbon, phosphorus, vapour
And other fundamentals spun
From the umbilicus of the sun,
And yet he says he will not caper
Around your throne, nor toe the rules
For the ballet of the fiery molecules."
"His concepts and denials—scrap them, burn them—
To the chemists with them promptly."

                                        "Sire,   30
The stuff is not amenable to fire.
Nothing but their own kind can overturn them.
The chemists have sent back the same old story—
'With our extreme gelatinous apology,
We beg to inform your Imperial Majesty,
Unto whom be dominion and power and glory,
There still remains that strange precipitate
Which has the quality to resist
Our oldest and most trusted catalyst.
It is a substance we cannot cremate   40
By temperatures known to our Laboratory.' "
And the great Panjandrum's face grew dark—
"I'll put those chemists to their annual purge,

And I myself shall be the thaumaturge[1]
To find the nature of this fellow's spark.
Come, bring him nearer by yon halter rope:
I'll analyze him with the cosmoscope."

Pulled forward with his neck awry,
The little fellow six feet short,
Aware he was about to die,   50
Committed grave contempt of court
By answering with a flinchless stare
The Awful Presence seated there.

The ALL HIGH swore until his face was black.
He called him a coprophagite,[2]
A *genus homo*, egomaniac,[3]
Third cousin to the family of worms,
A sporozoan[4] from the ooze of night,
Spawn of a spavined troglodyte:[5]
He swore by all the catalogue of terms   60
Known since the slang of carboniferous Time.
He said that he could trace him back
To pollywogs and earwigs in the slime.
And in his shrillest tenor he began
Reciting his indictment of the man,
Until he closed upon this capital crime—
"You are accused of singing out of key,
(A foul unmitigated dissonance)
Of shuffling in the measures of the dance,
Then walking out with that defiant, free   70
Toss of your head, banging the doors,
Leaving a stench upon the jacinth floors.
You have fallen like a curse
On the mechanics of my Universe.

"Herewith I measure out your penalty—
Hearken while you hear, look while you see:
I send you now upon your homeward route
Where you shall find
Humiliation for your pride of mind.
I shall make deaf the ear, and dim the eye,   80
Put palsy in your touch, make mute
Your speech, intoxicate your cells and dry
Your blood and marrow, shoot

[1]Magician.   [2]One who feeds on filth.   [3]One who is obsessed with himself.
[4]One of a group of parasites.   [5]A cave man.

Arthritic needles through your cartilage,
And having parched you with old age,
I'll pass you wormwise through the mire;
And when your rebel will
Is mouldered, all desire
Shrivelled, all your concepts broken,
Backward in dust I'll blow you till   90
You join my spiral festival of fire.
Go, Master of the Revels—I have spoken."

And the little *genus homo*, six feet high,
Standing erect, countered with this reply—
"You dumb insouciant invertebrate,
You rule a lower than a feudal state—
A realm of flunkey decimals that run,
Return; return and run; again return,
Each group around its little sun,
And every sun a satellite.   100
There they go by day and night,
Nothing to do but run and burn,
Taking turn and turn about,
Light-year in and light-year out,
Dancing, dancing in quadrillions,
Never leaving their pavilions.

"Your astronomical conceit
Of bulk and power is anserine.[6]
Your ignorance so thick,
You did not know your own arithmetic.
We flung the graphs about your flying feet;   110
We measured your diameter—
Merely a line
Of zeros prefaced by an integer.
Before we came
You had no name.
You did not know direction or your pace;
We taught you all you ever knew
Of motion, time, and space.
We healed you of your vertigo
And put you in our kindergarten show,   120
Perambulated you through prisms, drew

[6]Gooselike, hence silly or stupid.

Your mileage through the Milky Way,
Lassoed your comets when they ran astray,
Yoked Leo, Taurus, and your team of Bears
To pull our kiddy cars of inverse squares.

"Boast not about your harmony,
Your perfect curves, your rings
Of *pure and endless light*[7]—'Twas we
Who pinned upon your Seraphim their wings,
And when your brassy heavens rang   130
With joy that morning while the planets sang
Their choruses of archangelic lore,
'Twas we who ordered the notes upon their score
Out of our winds and strings.
Yes! all your shapely forms
Are ours—parabolas of silver light,
Those blueprints of your spiral stairs
From nadir depth to zenith height,
Coronas, rainbows after storms,
Auroras on your eastern tapestries   140
And constellations over western seas.

"And when, one day, grown conscious of your age,
While pondering an eolith,
We turned a human page
And blotted out a cosmic myth
With all its baby symbols to explain
The sunlight in Apollo's eyes,
Our rising pulses and the birth of pain,
Fear, and that fern-and-fungus breath
Stalking our nostrils to our caves of death—   150
That day we learned how to anatomize
Your body, calibrate your size
And set a mirror up before your face
To show you what you really were—a rain
Of dull Lucretian[8] atoms crowding space,
A series of concentric waves which any fool
Might make by dropping stones within a pool,
Or an exploding bomb forever in flight
Bursting like hell through Chaos and Old Night.

---

[7] *your rings of pure and endless light.* A reference to Henry Vaughan's poem "The World."
Vaughan (1622-95) was one of the metaphysical poets. "The World" begins:
I saw eternity the other night/Like a great ring of pure and endless light.   See page 172.
[8] Lucretius (99-55 B.C.) was a Roman poet in whose *De Rerum Natura* an atomic theory of
the universe is put forward

"You oldest of the hierarchs   160
Composed of electronic sparks,
We grant you speed,
We grant you power, and fire
That ends in ash, but we concede
To you no pain nor joy nor love nor hate,
No final tableau of desire,
No causes won or lost, no free
Adventure at the outposts—only
The degradation of your energy
When at some late   170
Slow number of your dance your sergeant-major Fate
Will catch you blind and groping and will send
You reeling on that long and lonely
Lockstep of your wave-lengths towards your end.

"We who have met
With stubborn calm the dawn's hot fusillades;
Who have seen the forehead sweat
Under the tug of pulleys on the joints,
Under the liquidating tally
Of the cat-and-truncheon bastinades;   180
Who have taught our souls to rally
To mountain horns and the sea's rockets
When the needle ran demented through the points;
We who have learned to clench
Our fists and raise our lightless sockets
To morning skies after the midnight raids,
Yet cocked our ears to bugles on the barricades,
And in cathedral rubble found a way to quench
A dying thirst within a Galilean valley—
No! by the Rood, we will not join your ballet."   190

                                                    1943

ETHEL WILSON (1890-1980)

Ethel Wilson was born in Port Elizabeth, South Africa, and spent her early childhood in England. In 1898, after the death of her parents, she moved to Vancouver to live with her maternal grandmother; she spent the remainder of her life there except for four years at an English boarding-school (1901-1905). In 1921 she married the distinguished physician, Dr. Wallace Wilson.

It was not until 1937, when she was almost fifty, that Wilson began to publish prose fiction, but she was soon recognized as a fine novelist. *Hetty Dorval* (1947) was followed by *The Innocent Traveller* (1949), *The Equations of Love* (1952), *Swamp Angel* (1954) and *Love and Salt-Water* (1956); her short stories were collected in *Mrs. Golightly and Other Stories* (1961). She has been the recipient of several awards and honorary degrees including the Lorne Pierce Medal in 1964.

Wilson is a quiet and unpretentious writer; her style is gentle and straightforward, but her shrewd observations and unobtrusive symbolism constantly probe the profundities of life. The natural environment of British Columbia, rendered with graphic accuracy, is often an active participant in her work, and her emphasis is on the inter-relationships of human beings and the value of Christian virtues such as charity, honesty, and humility.

The Window

The great big window must have been at least twenty-five feet wide and ten feet high. It was constructed in sections divided by segments of something that did not interfere with the view; in fact the eye bypassed these divisions and looked only at the entrancing scenes beyond. The window, together with a glass door at the western end, composed a bland shallow curve and formed the entire transparent north-west (but chiefly north) wall of Mr. Willy's living-room.

Upon his arrival from England Mr. Willy had surveyed the various prospects of living in the quickly growing city of Vancouver with the selective and discarding characteristics which had enabled him to make a fortune and retire all of a sudden from business and his country in his advanced middle age. He settled immediately upon the very house. It was a small old house overlooking the sea between Spanish Banks and English Bay. He knocked out the north wall and made the window. There was nothing particular to commend the house except that it faced immediately on the seashore and the view. Mr. Willy had left his wife and her three sisters to play bridge together until death should overtake them in England. He now paced from end to end of his living-room, that is to say from east to west, with his hands in his pockets, admiring the northern view. Sometimes he stood with his hands behind him looking through the great glass window, seeing the wrinkled or placid sea and the ships almost at his feet and beyond the sea the mountains, and seeing sometimes his emancipation. His emancipation drove him into a dream, and sea sky mountain swam before him, vanished, and he saw with immense release his wife in still another more repulsive hat. He did not know, nor would he have cared, that much discussion went on in her world, chiefly in the afternoons, and that he was there alleged to have deserted her. So he had, after providing well for her physical needs which were all the needs of which she was capable. Mrs. Willy went on saying '. . . and he would come home my dear and never speak a word I can't tell you my dear how frightful it was night after night I might say for *years* I simply can't tell you . . .' No, she could not tell but she did, by day and night. Here he was at peace, seeing out of the window the crimped and wrinkled sea and the ships which passed and passed each other, the seabirds and the dream-inducing sky.

At the extreme left curve of the window an island appeared to slope into the sea. Behind this island and to the north, the mountains rose very high. In the summer time the mountains were soft, deceptive in their innocency, full of crags and crevasses and *arêtes*[1] and danger. In the winter they lay magnificent, white and much higher, it seemed, than in the summer time. They tossed, static, in almost visible motion against the sky, inhabited only by eagles and—so a man had told Mr. Willy, but he didn't believe this man—by

---

[1]A sharp-crested ridge in rugged mountains.

mountain sheep and some cougars, bears, wild cats and, certainly, on the lower slopes, deer, and now a ski camp far out of sight. Mr. Willy looked at the mountains and regretted his past youth and his present wealth. How could he endure to be old and rich and able only to look at these mountains which in his youth he had not known and did not climb. Nothing, now, no remnant of his youth would come and enable him to climb these mountains. This he found hard to believe, as old people do. He was shocked at the newly realized decline of his physical powers which had proved good enough on the whole for his years of success, and by the fact that now he had, at last, time and could not swim (heart), climb mountains (heart and legs), row a boat in a rough enticing sea (call that old age). These things have happened to other people, thought Mr. Willy, but not to us, now, who have been so young, and yet it will happen to those who now are young.

Immediately across the water were less spectacular mountains, pleasant slopes which in winter time were covered with invisible skiers. Up the dark mountain at night sprang the lights of the ski-lift, and ceased. The shores of these mountains were strung with lights, littered with lights, spangled with lights, necklaces, bracelets, constellations, far more beautiful as seen through this window looking across the dark water than if Mr. Willy had driven his car across the Lions' Gate Bridge and westwards among those constellations which would have disclosed a shopping centre, people walking in the streets, street lights, innumerable cars and car lights like anywhere else and, up the slopes, peoples' houses. Then, looking back to the south across the dark water towards his own home and the great lighted window which he could not distinguish so far away, Mr. Willy would see lights again, a carpet of glitter thrown over the slopes of the city.

Fly from one shore to the other, fly and fly back again, fly to a continent or to an island, but you are no better off than if you stayed all day at your own window (and such a window), thought Mr. Willy pacing back and forth, then into the kitchen to put the kettle on for a cup of tea which he will drink beside the window, back for a glass of whisky, returning in time to see a cormorant flying level with the water, not an inch too high not an inch too low, flying out of sight. See the small ducks lying on the water, one behind the other, like beads on a string. In the mornings Mr. Willy drove into town to see his investment broker and perhaps to the bank or round the park. He lunched, but not at a club. He then drove home. On certain days a woman called Mrs. Ogden came in to 'do' for him. This was his daily life, very simple, and a routine was formed whose pattern could at last be discerned by an interested observer outside the window.

One night Mr. Willy beheld a vast glow arise behind the mountains. The Arctic world was obviously on fire—but no, the glow was not fire glow, flame glow. The great invasion of colour that spread up and up the sky was not red, was not rose, but of a synthetic cyclamen[2] colour. This cyclamen glow remained steady from mountain to zenith and caused ·Mr. Willy, who had never seen the Northern Lights, to believe that these were not Northern Lights but that something had occurred for which one must be prepared. After about an hour, flanges of green as of putrefaction[3], and a melodious yellow arose and spread. An hour later the Northern Lights faded, leaving Mr. Willy small and alone.

Sometimes as, sitting beside the window, he drank his tea, Mr. Willy thought that never-

[2]Bright pink flowers of the primrose.
[3]Decomposition of organic matter.

theless it is given to few people to be as happy (or contented, he would say) as he was, at his age, too. In his life of decisions, men, pressures, more men, antagonisms, fusions, fissions and Mrs. Willy, in his life of hard success, that is, he had sometimes looked forward but so vaguely and rarely to a time when he would not only put this life down: he would leave it. Now he had left it and here he was by his window. As time went on, though, he had to make an effort to summon this happiness, for it seemed to elude him. Sometimes a thought or a shape (was it), gray, like wood ash that falls in pieces when it is touched, seemed to be behind his chair, and this shape teased him and communicated to him that he had left humanity behind, that a man needs humanity and that if he ceases to be in touch with man and is not in touch with God, he does not matter. You do not matter any more, said the spectre, like wood ash before it fell to pieces, because you are no longer in touch with any one and so you do not exist. You are in a vacuum and so you are nothing. Then Mr. Willy, at first uneasy, became satisfied again for a time after being made uneasy by the spectre. A storm would get up and the wind, howling well, would lash the window sometimes carrying the salt spray from a very high tide which it flung against the great panes of glass. That was a satisfaction to Mr. Willy and within him something stirred and rose and met the storm and effaced the spectre and other phantoms which were really vague regrets. But the worst that happened against the window was that from time to time a little bird, sometimes but not often a seabird, flung itself like a stone against the strong glass of the window and fell, killed by the passion of its flight. This grieved Mr. Willy, and he could not sit unmoved when the bird flew at the clear glass and was met by death. When this happened, he arose from his chair, opened the glass door at the far end of the window, descended three or four steps, and sought in the grasses for the body of the bird. But the bird was dead, or it was dying, its small bones were smashed, its head was broken, its beak split, it was killed by the rapture of its flight. Only once Mr. Willy found the bird a little stunned and picked it up. He cupped the bird's body in his hands and carried it into the house.

Looking up through the grasses at the edge of the rough terrace that descended to the beach, a man watched him return into the house, carrying the bird. Still looking obliquely through the grasses the man watched Mr. Willy enter the room and vanish from view. Then Mr. Willy came again to the door, pushed it open, and released the bird which flew away, who knows where. He closed the door, locked it, and sat down on the chair facing east beside the window and began to read his newspaper. Looking over his paper he saw, to the east, the city of Vancouver deployed over rising ground with low roofs and high buildings and at the apex the tall Electric Building which at night shone like a broad shaft of golden light.

This time, as evening drew on, the man outside went away because he had other business.

Mr. Willy's investment broker was named Gerald Wardho. After a time he said to Mr. Willy in a friendly but respectful way 'Will you have lunch with me at the Club tomorrow?' and Mr. Willy said he would. Some time later Gerald Wardho said 'Would you like me to put you up at the Club?'

Mr. Willy considered a little the life which he had left and did not want to re-enter and also the fact that he had only last year resigned his memberships in three clubs, so he said 'That's very good of you, Wardho, but I think not. I'm enjoying things as they are. It's a novelty, living in a vacuum . . . I like it, for a time anyway.'

'Yes, but,' said Gerald Wardho, 'you'd be some time on the waiting list. It wouldn't hurt—'

'No,' said Mr. Willy, 'no.'

Mr. Willy had, Wardho thought, a distinguished appearance or perhaps it was an affable accustomed air, and so he had. When Mrs. Wardho said to her husband 'Gerry, there's not an extra man in this town and I need a man for Saturday,' Gerald Wardho said 'I know a man. There's Willy.'

Mrs. Wardho said doubtfully 'Willy? Willy who? Who's Willy?'

Her husband said 'He's fine, he's okay, I'll ask Willy.'

'How old is he?'

'About a hundred . . . but he's okay.'

'Oh-h-h,' said Mrs. Wardho, 'isn't there anyone anywhere unattached young any more? Does he play bridge?'

'I'll invite him, I'll find out,' said her husband, and Mr. Willy said he'd like to come to dinner.

'Do you care for a game of bridge, Mr. Willy?' asked Gerald Wardho.

'I'm afraid not,' said Mr. Willy kindly but firmly. He played a good game of bridge but had no intention of entering servitude again just yet, losing his freedom, and being enrolled as what is called a fourth. Perhaps later; not yet. 'If you're having bridge I'll come another time. Very kind of you Wardho.'

'No no no,' said Gerald Wardho, 'there'll only be maybe a table of bridge for anyone who wants to play. My wife would be disappointed.'

'Well thank you very much. Black tie?'

'Yes, Black tie,' said Gerald Wardho.

And so, whether he would or no, Mr. Willy found himself invited to the kind of evening parties to which he had been accustomed and which he had left behind, given by people younger and more animated than himself, and he realized that he was on his way to becoming old odd man out. There was a good deal of wood ash at these parties—that is, behind him the spectre arose, falling to pieces when he looked at it, and said So this is what you came to find out on this coast, so far from home, is it, or is there something else. What else is there? The spectre was not always present at these parties but sometimes awaited him at home and said these things.

One night Mr. Willy came home from an evening spent at Gerald Wardho's brother-in-law's house, a very fine house indeed. He had left lights burning and began to turn out the lights before he went upstairs. He went into the living-room and before turning out the last light gave a glance at the window which had in the course of the evening behaved in its accustomed manner. During the day the view through the window was clear or cloudy, according to the weather or the light or absence of light in the sky; but there it was—the view—never quite the same though, and that is owing to the character of oceans or of any water, great or small, and of light. Both water and light have so great an effect on land observed on any scene, rural urban or wilderness, that one begins to think that life, that a scene, is an illusion produced by influences such as water and light. At all events, by day the window held this fine view as in a frame, and the view was enhanced by ships at sea of all kinds, but never was the sea crowded, and by birds, clouds, and even aeroplanes in the sky—no people to spoil this fine view. But as evening approached, and moonless night, all the view (illusion again) vanished slowly. The window, which was not illusion, only the purveyor of illusion, did not vanish, but became a mirror which reflected against the blackness every detail of the shallow living-room. Through this clear reflection of the whole room, distant lights from across the water intruded, and so chains of light were thrown across the reflected mantlepiece, or a picture, or a human face, enhancing it. When Mr. Willy had left his house to dine at Gerald Wardho's brother-in-law's house the view through the window was placidly clear, but when he returned at 11:30 the window was dark and the room was reflected from floor to ceiling against the blackness. Mr. Willy saw himself entering the room like a stranger, looking at first debonair with such a gleaming shirt front and then—as he approached himself—a little shabby, his hair perhaps. He advanced to the window and stood looking at himself with the room in all its detail behind him.

Mr. Willy was too often alone, and spent far too much time in that space which lies between the last page of the paper or the turning-off of the radio in surfeit, and sleep. Now as he stood at the end of the evening and the beginning of the night, looking at himself and the room behind himself, he admitted that the arid feeling which he had so often experienced lately was probably what is called loneliness. And yet he did not want another woman in his life. It was a long time since he had seen a woman whom he wanted to take home or even to see again. Too much smiling. Men were all right, you talked to them about the market, the emergence of the Liberal Party, the impossibility of arriving anywhere with those people while that fellow was in office, nuclear war (instant hells opened deep in everyone's mind and closed again), South Africa where Mr. Willy was born, the Argentine where Mr. Wardho's brother-in-law had spent many years—and then everyone went home.

Mr. Willy, as the months passed by, was dismayed to find that he had entered an area of depression unknown before, like a tundra, and he was a little frightened of this tundra. Returning from the dinner party he did not at once turn out the single last light and go upstairs. He sat down on a chair beside the window and at last bowed his head upon his hands. As he sat there, bowed, his thoughts went very stiffly (for they had not had much exercise in that direction throughout his life) to some area that was not tundra but was that area where there might be some meaning in creation which Mr. Willy supposed must be the place where some people seemed to find a God, and perhaps a personal God at that. Such theories, or ideas, or passions had never been of interest to him, and if he had thought of such theories, or ideas, or passions he would have dismissed them as invalid and having no bearing on life as it is lived, especially when one is too busy. He had formed the general opinion that people who hold such beliefs were either slaves to an inherited convention, hypocrites, or nit-wits. He regarded such people without interest, or at least he thought them negligible as he returned to the exacting life in hand. On the whole, though, he did not like them. It is not easy to say why Mr. Willy thought these people were hypocrites or nit-wits because some of them, not all, had a strong religious faith, and why he was not a hypocrite or nit-wit because he had not a strong religious faith; but there it was.

As he sat on and on looking down at the carpet with his head in his hands he did not think of these people, but he underwent a strong shock of recognition. He found himself looking this way and that way out of his aridity for some explanation or belief beyond the non-explanation and non-belief that had always been sufficient and had always been his, but in doing this he came up against a high and strong almost visible wall of concrete or granite, set up between him and a religious belief. This wall had, he thought, been built by him through the period of his long life, or perhaps he was congenitally[4] unable to have a belief; in that case it was no fault of his and there was no religious belief possible to him. As he sat there he came to have the conviction that the absence of a belief which extended beyond the visible world had something to do with his malaise[5]; yet the malaise might possibly be cirrhosis of the liver or a sort of delayed male menopause. He recognized calmly that death was as inevitable as tomorrow morning or even tonight and he had a rational absence of fear of death. Nevertheless his death (he knew) had begun, and had begun— what with his awareness of age and this malaise of his—to assume a certainty that it had not had before. His death did not trouble him as much as the increasing tastelessness of living in this tundra of mind into which a belief did not enter.

The man outside the window had crept up through the grasses and was now watching Mr. Willy from a point rather behind him. He was a morose man and strong. He had served two terms for robbery with violence. When he worked, he worked up the coast. Then he came to town and if he did not get into trouble it was through no fault of his own. Last summer he had lain there and, rolling over, had looked up through the grasses and into, only just into the room where this guy was who seemed to live alone. He seemed to be a rich guy because he wore good close and hadn't he got this great big window and— later, he discovered—a high price car. He had lain in the grasses and because his thoughts always turned that way, he tried to figger out how he could get in there. Money was the only thing that was any good to him and maybe the old guy didn't keep money or even carry it but he likely did. The man thought quite a bit about Mr. Willy and then went up the coast and when he came down again he remembered the great big window and one or two nights he went around and about the place and figgered how he'd work it. The doors was all locked, even that glass door. That was easy enough to break but he guessed he'd go in without warning when the old guy was there so's he'd have a better chance of getting something off of him as well. Anyways he wouldn't break in, not that night, but if nothing else offered he'd do it sometime soon.

Suddenly Mr. Willy got up, turned the light out, and went upstairs to bed. That was Wednesday.

On Sunday he had his first small party. It seemed inevitable if only for politeness. Later he would have a dinner party if he still felt sociable and inclined. He invited the Wardhos and their in-laws and some other couples. A Mrs. Lessways asked if she might bring her aunt and he said yes. Mrs. Wardho said might she bring her niece who was arriving on Saturday to meet her fiancé who was due next week from Hong Kong, and the Wardhos were going to give the two young people a quiet wedding, and Mr. Willy said Please do. Another couple asked if they could bring another couple.

Mr. Willy, surveying his table, thought that Mrs. Ogden had done well. 'Oh I'm glad

---

[4]Existing or dating from birth.
[5]An indefinite sense of ill-being or lack of health.

you think so,' said Mrs. Ogden, pleased. People began to arrive. 'Oh!' they exclaimed without fail, as they arrived, 'what a beautiful view!' Mrs. Lessways' aunt who had blue hair fell delightedly into the room, turning this way and that way, acknowledging smiles and tripping to the window. 'Oh,' she cried turning to Mr. Willy in a fascinating manner, 'isn't that just lovely! Edna says you're quite a recluse! I'm sure I don't blame you! Don't you think that's the loveliest view Edna . . . oh how d'you do how d'you do, isn't that the loveliest view? . . .' Having paid her tribute to the view she turned away from the window and did not see it again. The Aunt twirled a little bag covered with irridescent beads on her wrist. 'Oh!' and 'Oh!' she exclaimed, turning, 'my dear how *lovely* to see you! I didn't even know you were back! Did you have a good time?' She reminded Mr. Willy uneasily of his wife. Mr. and Mrs. Wardho arrived accompanied by their niece Sylvia.

A golden girl, thought Mr. Willy taking her hand, but her young face surrounded by sunny curls was stern. She stood, looking from one to another, not speaking, for people spoke busily to each other and the young girl stood apart, smiling only when need be and wishing that she had not had to come to the party. She drifted to the window and seemed (and was) forgotten. She looked at the view as at something seen for the first and last time. She inscribed those notable hills on her mind because had she not arrived only yesterday? And in two days Ian would be here and she would not see them again.

A freighter very low laden emerged from behind a forest and moved slowly into the scene. So low it was that it lay like an elegant black line upon the water with great bulkheads below. Like an iceberg, thought Sylvia, and her mind moved along with the freighter bound for foreign parts. Someone spoke to her and she turned. 'Oh thank you!' she said for her cup of tea.

Mr. Willy opened the glass door and took with him some of the men who had expressed a desire to see how far his property ran. 'You see, just a few feet, no distance,' he said.

After a while day receded and night came imperceptibly on. There was not any violence or reflected sunset tonight and mist settled down on the view with only distant dim lights aligning the north shore. Sylvia, stopping to respond to ones and twos, went to the back of the shallow room and sat down behind the out-jut of the fireplace where a wood fire was burning. Her mind was on two levels. One was all Ian and the week coming, and one—no thicker than a crust on the surface—was this party and all these people talking, the Aunt talking so busily that one might think there was a race on, or news to tell. Sylvia, sitting in the shadow of the corner and thinking about her approaching lover, lost herself in this reverie, and her lips, which had been so stern, opened slightly in a tender smile. Mr. Willy who was serving drinks from the dining-room where Mrs. Ogden had left things ready, came upon her and, struck by her beauty, saw a different sunny girl. She looked up at him. She took her drink from him with a soft and tender smile that was grateful and happy and was only partly for him. He left her, with a feeling of beauty seen.

Sylvia held her glass and looked towards the window. She saw, to her surprise, so quickly had black night come, that the end of the room which had been a view was now a large black mirror which reflected the glowing fire, the few lights, and the people unaware of the view, its departure, and its replacement by their own reflections behaving to each other like people at a party. Sylvia watched Mr. Willy who moved amongst them, taking a glass and bringing a glass. He was removed from the necessities, now, of conversation, and looked very sad. Why does he look sad, she wondered and was young enough to think, he shouldn't look sad, he is well off. She took time off to like Mr. Willy and to feel sorry that he seemed melancholy.

People began to look at their watches and say goodbye. The Aunt redoubled her vivacity. The women all thanked Mr. Willy for his tea party and for the beautiful beautiful view. They gave glances at the window but there was no view.

When all his guests had gone, Mr. Willy, who was an orderly man, began to collect glasses and take them into the kitchen. In an armchair lay the bag covered with iridescent beads belonging to the Aunt. Mr. Willy picked it up and put in on a table, seeing the blue hair of the Aunt. He would sit down and smoke for a while. But he found that when, lately, he sat down in the evening beside the window and fixed his eyes upon the golden shaft of the Electric Building, in spite of his intention of reading or smoking his thoughts turned towards this subject of belief which now teased him, eluded, yet compelled him. He was brought up, every time, against the great stone wall, how high, how wide he knew, but not how thick. If he could, in some way, break through this wall which bounded the area of his aridity and his comprehension, he knew without question that there was a light (not darkness) beyond, and that this light could in some way come through to him and alleviate the sterility and lead him, lead him. If there were some way, even some conventional way—although he did not care for convention—he would take it in order to break the wall down and reach the light so that it would enter his life; but he did not know the way. So fixed did Mr. Willy become in contemplation that he looked as though he were graven in stone.

Throughout the darkened latter of the tea party, the man outside had lain or crouched near the window. From the sands, earlier, he had seen Mr. Willy open the glass door and go outside, followed by two or three men. They looked down talking, and soon went inside again together. The door was closed. From anything the watcher knew, it was not likely that the old guy would turn and lock the door when he took the other guys in. He'd just close it, see?

As night came on the man watched the increased animation of the guests preparing for departure. Like departing birds they moved here and there in the room before taking flight. The man was impatient but patient because when five were left, then three, then no-one but the old guy who lived in the house, he knew his time was near. (How gay and how meaningless the scene had been, of these well-dressed persons talking and talking, like some kind of a show where nothing happened—or so it might seem, on the stage of the lighted room from the pit of the dark shore.)

The watcher saw the old guy pick up glasses and take them away. Then he came back into the room and looked around. He took something out of a chair and put it on a table. He stood still for a bit, and then he found some kind of paper and sat down in the chair facing eastward. But the paper drooped in his hand and then it dropped to the floor as the old guy bent his head and then he put his elbows on his knees and rested his head in his hands as if he was thinking, or had some kind of a headache.

The watcher, with a sort of joy and a feeling of confidence that the moment had come, moved strongly and quietly to the glass door. He turned the handle expertly, slid inside, and slowly closed the door so that no draught should warn his victim. He moved cat-like to the back of Mr. Willy's chair and quickly raised his arm. At the selfsame moment that he raised his arm with a short blunt weapon in his hand, he was aware of the swift movement of another person in the room. The man stopped still, his arm remained high, every fear was aroused. He turned instantly and saw a scene clearly enacted beside him in the dark mirror of the window. At the moment and shock of turning, he drew a sharp intake of breath and it was this that Mr. Willy heard and that caused him to look up and around and see in the dark mirror the intruder, the danger, and the victim who was himself. At that still moment, the telephone rang shrilly, twice as loud in that still moment, on a small table near him.

It was not the movement of the figure in the dark mirror, it was not the bell ringing close at hand and insistently, it was an irrational and stupid fear lest his action, reproduced visibly beside him in the mirror, was being faithfully registered in some impossible way that filled the intruder with fright. The telephone rang shrilly, Mr. Willy now facing him, the play enacted beside him, and this irrational momentary fear caused him to turn and bound towards the door, to escape into the dark, banging the glass door with a clash behind him. When he got well away from the place he was angry—everything was always against him, he never had no luck, and if he hadn'ta lost his head it was a cinch he coulda done it easy.

'Damn you!' shouted Mr. Willy in a rage, with his hand on the telephone, 'you might have broken it! Yes?' he said into the telephone, moderating the anger that possessed him and continuing within himself a conversation that said It was eighteen inches away, I was within a minute of it and I didn't know, it's no use telephoning the police but I'd better do that, it was just above me and I'd have died not knowing. 'Yes? Yes?' he said impatiently, trembling a little.

'Oh,' said a surprised voice, 'it *is* Mr. Willy, isn't it? Just for a minute it didn't sound like you Mr. Willy that was the *loveliest* party and what a *lovely* view and I'm sorry to be such a nuisance I kept on ringing and ringing because I thought you couldn't have gone out so soon' (tinkle tinkle) 'and you couldn't have gone to bed so soon but I do believe I must have left my little bead bag it's not the *value* but . . .' Mr. Willy found himself shaking more violently now, not only with death averted and the rage of the slammed glass door but with the powerful thoughts that had usurped him and were interrupted by the dangerous moment which was now receding, and the tinkling voice on the telephone.

'I have it here. I'll bring it tomorrow,' he said shortly. He hung up the telephone and at the other end the Aunt turned and exclaimed 'Well if he isn't the rudest man I never was treated like that in my whole life d'you know what he . . .'

Mr. Willy was in a state of abstraction.

He went to the glass door and examined it. It was intact. He turned the key and drew the shutter down. Then he went back to the telephone in this state of abstraction. Death or near-death was still very close, though receding. It seemed to him at that moment that a crack had been coming in the great wall that shut him off from the light but perhaps he was wrong. He dialled the police, perfunctorily[6] not urgently. He knew that before him lay the hardest work of his life—in his life but out of his country. He must in some way and soon break the great wall that shut him off from whatever light there might be. Not for fear of death oh God not for fear of death but for fear of something else.

1958   1961

---

[6]Routinely, mechanically.

F. R. SCOTT (1899-   )

Francis Reginald Scott is Canada's best-known satirical poet, although satire is not his only poetic vein. He was one of the members of the Montreal group of poets who introduced "modernist" verse to Canada in the nineteen-twenties through the pages of the *McGill Fortnightly Review*, the *Canadian Forum*, and the *Canadian Mercury*. The other leading members of the group were A. J. M. Smith, A. M. Klein, and Leo Kennedy. They reacted against the romantic love and nature lyrics of the Group of the Sixties to write realistic, witty, or passionate poems about modern urban life. If they wrote of nature or love, as they occasionally did, it was in a tighter, sparser, more disciplined and disillusioned way than their romantic predecessors. In the nineteen-thirties and forties, this group felt the influence of depression and war, and of the response to these things of the Auden-Spender group in England, and wrote poems of social protest and social idealism.

F. R. Scott was born on August 1, 1899, in Quebec City, and was the son of the Reverend Frederick George Scott, an Anglican clergyman and minor poet. Educated at Bishop's College, Oxford, and McGill, Scott became professor of civil law at McGill in 1928. He has taken an active part in Canadian politics, having been one of the founders in the early thirties of both the League for Social Reconstruction and the Co-operative Commonwealth Federation. In 1940 to 1941 he was a Guggenheim Fellow at Harvard, and in 1952 a United Nations technical assistance representative in Burma. He has written several books on political and legal matters, and is an expert on the Canadian constitution. He has also played a prominent role in the literary life of Canada, having been associated with a great many literary magazines from the *McGill Fortnightly Review* to *Tamarack Review*, organized the Canadian Writers' Conference of 1955, and encouraged a host of young poets. His own verse has appeared in many magazines, several anthologies, and in the volumes *Overture* (1945), *Events and Signals* (1954), *The Eye of the Needle* (1956), *Signature* (1965) and *The Dance Is One* (1973).

The Canadian Authors Meet[1]

Expansive puppets percolate self-unction
Beneath a portrait of the Prince of Wales.
Miss Crotchet's muse has somehow failed to function,
Yet she's a poetess. Beaming, she sails

From group to chattering group, with such a dear
Victorian saintliness, as is her fashion,
Greeting the other unknowns with a cheer—
Virgins of sixty who still write of passion.

The air is heavy with "Canadian" topics,
And Carman, Lampman, Roberts, Campbell, Scott   10
Are measured for their faith and philanthropics,
Their zeal for God and King, their earnest thought.

[1]This poem was inspired by Scott's attendance at a Canadian Authors' Association meeting. The association had been founded in 1921 to develop Canadian literature, but its tendency to over-rate Canadian books and writers, in keeping with the fervid nationalism of that time, irritated many critics.

The cakes are sweet, but sweeter is the feeling
That one is mixing with the *literati*;
It warms the old and melts the most congealing.
Really, it is a most delightful party.

Shall we go round the mulberry bush, or shall
We gather at the river, or shall we
Appoint a poet laureate this Fall,
Or shall we have another cup of tea? 20

O Canada, O Canada, Oh can
A day go by without new authors springing
To paint the native maple, and to plan
More ways to set the selfsame welkin ringing?

1927 1936

Saturday Sundae

The triple-decker and the double-cone
I side-swipe swiftly, suck the coke-straws dry
Ride toadstool seat beside the slab of morgue—
Sweet corner drug-store, sweet pie in the sky.

Him of the front-flap apron, him I sing,
The counter-clockwise clerk in underalls.
Swing low, sweet chocolate, Oh swing, swing,
While cheek by juke the jitter chatter falls.

I swivel on my axle and survey
The latex tintex kotex cutex land. 10
Soft kingdoms sell for dimes, Life Pic Look Click
Inflate the male with conquest girly grand.

My brothers and my sisters, two by two,
Sit sipping succulence and sighing sex.
Each tiny adolescent universe
A world the vested interests annex.

Such bread and circuses these times allow,
Opium most popular, life so small and slick,
Perhaps with candy is the new world born
And cellophane shall wrap the heretic. 20

1945

Flux

Under the constant impact, the swift response.
We leap from crumbling footholds, gulfs below,
Or like the Arctic male seeking a pole
Traverse the sea-lanes when the floes touch.
Trained to the tram-line and the office walk
The week-end outing and the game of bridge
Little avails us now the trim routine.

Refugees of the mind load their loved bric-a-brac
Glass gew-gaws and their little tea-set faiths
On the piled ox-cart of tradition; make for the rear.   10
This self-imprisonment obstructs the roads
And only the mobile heart allows escape.

Now from each corner of their settled ways
Egos draw to the mass, millions move.
Robot men swarm in their steel shells
Over the crust of seven continents.
There's naught for me and you, only for us.

Strip for this venture forth, my pretty man.
Props and property are caving in.
The roar of masonry and smothered towns,   20
Ice-cap solitudes on money-marts
And four winds out of untested skies—
This is the thunder of the still small voice.

And if the ultimate I, the inner mind,
The only shelter proof against attack,
Sustain these days, carry this banner out
To the clumsy dawn: A green seed
Lies on the ground, under a leafless tree.

                                        1945

Conflict

When I see the falling bombs
Then I see defended homes.
Men above and men below
Die to save the good they know.

Through the wrong the bullets prove
Shows the bravery of love.
Pro and con have single stem
Half a truth dividing them.

Between the dagger and the breast
The bond is stronger than the beast. 10
Prison, ghetto, flag and gun
Mark the craving for the One.

Persecution's cruel mouth
Shows a twisted love of truth.
Deeper than the rack and rope
Lies the double human hope.

My good, your good, good we seek
Though we turn no other cheek.
He who slays and he who's slain
Like in purpose, like in pain.   20

Who shall bend to single plan
The narrow sacrifice of man?
Find the central human urge
To make a thousand roads converge?

1945

Tourist Time

This fat woman in canvas knickers
Gapes seriously at everything.
We might be a city of the dead
Or cave men
Instead of simple town folk.
We have nothing to show
That can't be seen better somewhere else,
Yet for this woman the wonder ceases not.

Madam, the most extraordinary thing in
    this town
Is the shape of your legs.

O communication!
O rapid transit!

1945

A. J. M. SMITH (1902-1980)

A native of Montreal, A. J. M. Smith attended McGill University in that city, and later, the University of Edinburgh. While a student in Montreal, he and F. R. Scott began to write in a witty and *imagist* manner, introducing a new tone into Canadian poetry. Together they established the *McGill Fortnightly Review* as a medium for modernist poetry. Smith spent most of his life as an English professor at Michigan State University, returning to Montreal whenever possible. He died on November 21, 1980.

Smith's poetry is characterized by precision of language, metaphysical wit, and restraint of emotion. All of his poems, although relatively few in number, are marked by an intense accuracy and an energy generated by the language itself; he speaks in exact images, usually of mythology, nature or love.

News of the Phoenix, his first collection, won the Governor-General's Award in 1943. *A Sort of Ecstasy* followed in 1954 and *The Classic Shade*, his selected poems, appeared in 1978.

The Lonely Land

Cedar and jagged fir
uplift sharp barbs
against the gray
and cloud-piled sky;
and in the bay
blown spume and windrift
and thin, bitter spray
snap
at the whirling sky;
and the pine trees   10
lean one way.

A wild duck calls
to her mate,
and the ragged
and passionate tones
stagger and fall,
and recover,
and stagger and fall,
on these stones—
are lost   20
in the lapping of water
on smooth, flat stones.

This is a beauty
of dissonance,
this resonance
of stony strand,
this smoky cry
curled over a black pine
like a broken
and wind-battered branch   30
when the wind
bends the tops of the pines
and curdles the sky
from the north.

This is the beauty
of strength
broken by strength
and still strong.

          1943

News of the Phoenix [1]

They say the Phoenix is dying, some say dead.
Dead without issue is what one messange said,
But that has been suppressed, officially denied.

I think myself the man who sent it lied.
In any case, I'm told, he has been shot,
As a precautionary measure, whether he did or not.

          1943

[1] A legendary bird which, according to one account, lived five hundred years, burned itself to ashes on a pyre, then rose youthfully from the ashes to live again.

Sea Cliff

Wave on wave
and green on rock
and white between

the splash and black
the crash and hiss
of the feathery fall,
the snap and shock
of the water wall
and the wall of rock:
after—   10
after the ebb-flow,
wet rock,
high—
high over the slapping green,
water sliding away
and the rock abiding,
new rock riding
out of the spray.

                                      1943

The Archer[1]

Bend back thy bow, O Archer, till the string
Is level with thine ear, thy body taut,
Its nature art, thyself thy statue wrought
Of marble blood, thy weapon the poised wing
Of coiled and acquiline Fate. Then, loosening, fling
The hissing arrow like a burning thought
Into the empty sky that smokes as the hot
Shaft plunges to the bullseye's quenching ring.

So for a moment, motionless, serene,
Fixed between time and time, I aim and wait;   10
Nothing remains for breath now but to waive
His prior claim and let the barb fly clean
Into the heart of what I know and hate—
That central black, the ringed and targeted grave.

                                      1943

[1]A symbol of the artist, originating in the Greek play *Philoctetes*, by Sophocles.

MORLEY CALLAGHAN (1903-   )

Morley Callaghan is the best short story writer and one of the best novelists Canada has produced. His short stories are in the great modern tradition of that form, a tradition which includes Hawthorne and Chekov, Joyce and Mansfield, Anderson and Hemingway, to name but a few. Like all these writers he is interested in the fine shades of psychology, the choice of the exact revealing word, a style that gets its effects by under- rather than by over-statement, the trivial accidents and disappointments of everyday life—interested in these things rather than in the tightly knit plots, the surprising or violent episodes which characterize the romantic short stories of Poe and his followers. But Callaghan is not simply part of a tradition. His own special note is a Christian sensibility, a rich compassion and tenderness for the poor, the suffering, the lonely, the outcasts. His novels especially— *Such Is My Beloved* (1934), for example, *More Joy*

in Heaven (1937), or *The Loved and the Lost* (1953) —concern themselves with the plight of the alien, the outsider, the man who does not fit the orthodox patterns of society.

Callaghan was born in Toronto in 1903, and is a graduate of St. Michael's College and of Osgoode Hall. After graduation he was a reporter on the Toronto *Star* and met a fellow-reporter on that paper, Ernest Hemingway. Hemingway encouraged Callaghan's interest in the short story, and the latter was soon publishing stories in the leading literary magazines. He lived briefly in Paris in the late twenties, but since his marriage to Loretto Dee in 1929 he has made his home in Toronto. His first novel, *Strange Fugitive*, was published in 1928, and his first book of short stories, *A Native Argosy*, in 1929. His collected *Stories* were published in 1959.

The Blue Kimono

It was hardly more than dawn when George woke up so suddenly. He lay wide awake listening to a heavy truck moving slowly on the street below; he heard one truck-driver shout angrily to another; he heard a hundred small street sounds multiplying and rolling with the motion of the city awakening.

For many mornings in the last six months George had lain awake waiting to hear all the noises of people preparing to go to work, the noises of doors slamming, of women taking in the milk, of cars starting, and sometimes, later on in the morning, he had wondered where all these people went when they hurried out briskly with so much assurance.

Each morning he awakened a little earlier and was wide awake at once. But this time he was more restless than ever and he thought with despair, "We're unlucky, that's it. We've never had any luck since we've come here. There's something you can't put your hands on working to destroy us. Everything goes steadily against us from bad to worse. We'll never have any luck. I can feel it. We'll starve before I get a job."

Then he realized that his wife, Marthe, was no longer in the bed beside him. He looked around the room that seemed so much larger and so much emptier in that light and he thought, "What's the matter with Marthe? Is it getting that she can't sleep?" Sitting up, he peered uneasily into the room's dark corners. There was a light coming from the kitchenette. As he got out of bed slowly, with his thick hair standing up straight all over his head, and reached for his slippers and dressing-gown, the notion that something mysterious and inexorable was working to destroy them was so strong in him that he suddenly wanted to stand in front of his wife and shout in anger, "What can I do? You tell me something to do. What's the use of me going out to the streets today. I'm going to sit down here and wait, day after day." That time when they had first got married and were secure now seemed such a little far-away forgotten time.

In his eagerness to make his wife feel the bad luck he felt within him, he went striding across the room, his old, shapeless slippers flapping on the floor, his dressing-gown only half pulled on, looking in that dim light like someone huge, reckless, and full of sudden savage impulse, who wanted to pound a table and shout. "Marthe, Marthe," he called, "what's the matter with you? Why are you up at this time?"

She came into the room carrying their two-year-old boy. "There's nothing the matter with me," she said. "I got up when I heard Walter crying." She was a small, slim, dark woman with black hair hanging on her shoulders, a thin eager face, and large soft eyes, and as she walked over to the window with the boy she swayed her body as though she were humming to him. The light from the window was now a little stronger. She sat there in her old blue kimono holding the boy tight and feeling his head with her hand.

"What's the matter with him?" George said.

"I don't know. I heard him whimpering, so I got up. His head felt so hot."

"Is there anything I can do?" he said.

"I don't think so."

She seemed so puzzled, so worried and aloof from even the deepest bitterness within him, that George felt impatient, as if it were her fault that the child was sick. For a while he watched her rocking back and forth, making always the same faint humming sound, with the stronger light showing the deep frown on her face, and he couldn't seem to think of the child at all. He wanted to speak with sympathy, but he burst out, "I had to get up because I couldn't go on with my own thoughts. We're unlucky, Marthe. We haven't had a day's luck since we've come to this city. How much longer can this go on before they throw us out on the street? I tell you we never should have come here."

She looked up at him indignantly. He couldn't see the fierceness in her face because her head was against the window light. Twice he walked the length of the room, then he stood beside her, looking down at the street. There was now traffic and an increasing steady hum of motion. He felt chilled and his fingers grasped at the collar of his dressing-gown, pulling it across his chest. "It's cold here, and you can imagine what it'll be like in winter," he said. And when Marthe again did not answer, he said sullenly, "You wanted us to come here. You wanted us to give up what we had and come to a bigger city where there were bigger things ahead. Where we might amount to something because of my fine education and your charming manner. You thought we didn't have enough ambition, didn't you?"

"Why talk about it now, George?"

"I want you to see what's happened to us."

"Say I'm responsible. Say anything you wish."

"All right. I'll tell you what I feel in my bones. Luck is against us. Something far stronger than our two lives is working against us. I was thinking about it when I woke up. I must have been thinking about it all through my sleep."

"We've been unlucky, but we've often had a good time, haven't we?" she said.

"Tell me honestly, have we had a day's luck since we got married?" he said brutally.

"I don't know," she said with her head down. Then she looked up suddenly, almost pleading, but afraid to speak.

The little boy started to whimper and then sat up straight, pushing away the blanket his mother tried to keep around him. When she insisted on covering him, he began to fight and she had a hard time holding him till suddenly he was limp in her arms, looking around the darkened room with the bright wonder that comes in a child's fevered eyes.

George watched Marthe trying to soothe the child. The morning light began to fall on her face, making it seem a little leaner, a little narrower and so dreadfully worried. A few years ago everybody used to speak about her extraordinary smile, about the way the lines around her mouth were shaped for laughter, and they used to say, too, that she had a mysterious, tapering, Florentine face. Once a man had said to George, "I remember clearly the first time I met your wife. I said to myself, 'Who is the lady with that marvellous smile?'"

George was now looking at this face as though it belonged to a stranger. He could think of nothing but the shape of it. There were so many angles in that light; it seemed so narrow. "I used to think it was beautiful. It doesn't look beautiful. Would anybody say it was beautiful?" he thought, and yet these thoughts had nothing to do with his love for her.

In some intuitive way she knew that he was no longer thinking of his bad luck, but was thinking of her, so she said patiently, "Walter seems to have quite a fever, George." Then he stopped walking and touched Walter's head, which was very hot.

"Here, let me hold him a while and you get something," he said. "Get him some aspirin."

"I'll put it in orange juice, if he'll take it," she said.

"For God's sake, turn on the light, Marthe," he called. "This ghastly light is getting on my nerves."

He tried talking to his son while Marthe was away. "Hello, Walter, old boy, what's the matter with you? Look at me, big boy, say something bright to your old man." But the little boy shook his head violently, stared vacantly at the wall a moment, and then tried to bury his face in his father's shoulder. So George, looking disconsolately around the cold room, felt that it was more barren than ever.

Marthe returned with the orange juice and the aspirin. They both began to coax Walter to take it. They pretended to be drinking it themselves, made ecstatic noises with their tongues as though it were delicious and kept it up till the boy cried, "Orange, orange, me too," with an unnatural animation. His eyes were brilliant. Then he swayed as if his spine were made of putty and fell back in his mother's arms.

"We'd better get a doctor in a hurry, George," Marthe said.

"Do you think it's that bad?"

"Look at him," she said, laying him on the bed. "I'm sure he's very sick. You don't want to lose him, do you?" and she stared at Walter, who had closed his eyes and was sleeping.

As Marthe in her fear kept looking up at George, she was fingering her old blue kimono, drawing it tighter around her to keep her warm. The kimono had been of a Japanese pattern adorned with clusters of brilliant flowers sewn in silk. George had given it to her at the time of their marriage; now he stared at it, torn as it was at the arms, with pieces of old padding hanging out at the hem, with the light-coloured lining showing through in many places, and he remembered how, when the kimono was new, Marthe used to make the dark hair across her forehead into bangs, fold her arms across her breasts, with her

wrists and hands concealed in the sleeve folds, and go around the room in the bright kimono, taking short, prancing steps, pretending she was a Japanese girl.

The kimono now was ragged and gone; it was gone, he thought, like so many bright
dreams and aspirations they had once had in the beginning, like so many fine resolutions
he had sworn to accomplish, like so many plans they had made and hopes they had
cherished.

"Marthe, in God's name," he said suddenly, "the very first money we get, even if we just
have enough to put a little down, you'll have to get a decent dressing-gown. Do you
hear?"

She was startled. Looking up at him in bewilderment, she swallowed hard, then turned
her eyes down again.

"It's terrible to have to look at you in that thing," he muttered.

After he had spoken in this way he was ashamed, and he was able to see for the first
time the wild terrified look on her face as she bent over Walter.

"Why do you look like that?" he asked. "Hasn't he just got a little fever?"

"Did you see the way he held the glass when he took the orange juice?"

"No, I didn't notice."

"His hand trembled. Earlier, when I first went to him, and gave him a drink I noticed
the strange trembling in his hand."

"What does it mean?" he said, awed by the fearful way she was whispering.

"His body seemed limp and he could not sit up either. Last night I was reading about
such symptoms in the medical column in the paper. Symptoms like that with a fever are
symptoms of infantile paralysis."

"Where's the paper?"

"Over there on the table."

George sat down and began to read the bit of newspaper medical advice very calmly;
over and over he read it, very calmly. Marthe had described the symptoms accurately; but
in a stupid way he could not get used to the notion that his son might have such a dreadful
disease. So he remained there calmly for a long time.

And then he suddenly realized how they had been dogged by bad luck; he
realized how surely everything they loved was being destroyed day by day and he jumped
up and cried out, "We'll have to get a doctor." And as if he realized to the full what was
inevitably impending, he cried out, "You're right, Marthe, he'll die. That child will die.
It's the luck that's following us. Then it's over. Everything's over. I tell you I'll curse the
day I ever saw the light of the world. I'll curse the day we ever met and ever married. I'll
smash everything I can put my hands on in this world."

"George, don't go on like that. You'll bring something dreadful down on us," she whispered in terror.

"What else can happen? What else can happen to us worse than this?"

"Nothing, nothing, but please don't go on saying it, George."

Then they both bent down over Walter and they took turns putting their hands on his
head. "What doctor will come to us at this house when we have no money?" he kept muttering. "We'll have to take him to a hospital." They remained kneeling together, silent for
a long time, almost afraid to speak.

Marthe said suddenly, "Feel, feel his head. Isn't it a little cooler?"

"What could that be?"

"It might be the aspirin working on him."

So they watched, breathing steadily together while the child's head gradually got cooler. Their breathing and their silence seemed to waken the child, for he opened his eyes and stared at them vaguely. "He must be feeling better," George said. "See the way he's looking at us."

"His head does feel a lot cooler."

"What could have been the matter with him, Marthe?"

"It might have been a chill. Oh, I hope it was only a chill."

"Look at him, if you please. Watch me make the rascal laugh."

With desperate eagerness George rushed over to the table, tore off a sheet of newspaper, folded it into a thin strip about eight inches long and twisted it like a cord. Then he knelt down in front of Walter and cried, "See, see," and thrust the twisted paper under his own nose and held it with his upper lip while he wiggled it up and down. He screwed up his eyes diabolically. He pressed his face close against the boy's.

Laughing, Walter put out his hand. "Le me," he said. So George tried to hold the paper moustache against Walter's lip. But that was no good. Walter pushed the paper away and said, "You, you."

"I think his head is cool now," Marthe said. "Maybe he'll be all right."

She got up and walked away from the bed, over to the window with her head down. Standing up, George went to follow her, but his son shouted tyrannically so he had to kneel down and hold the paper moustache under his nose and say, "Look here, look, Walter."

Marthe was trying to smile as she watched them. She took one deep breath after another, as though she would never succeed in filling her lungs with air. But even while she stood there, she grew troubled. She hesitated, she lowered her head and wanted to say, "One of us will find work of some kind, George," but she was afraid.

"I'll get dressed now," she said quietly, and she started to take off her kimono.

As she took off the kimono and was holding it on her arm, her face grew full of deep concern. She held the kimono up so the light shone on the gay silken flowers. Sitting down in the chair, she spread the faded silk on her knee and looked across the room at her sewing basket which was on the dresser by the mirror. She fumbled patiently with the lining, patting the places that were torn; and suddenly she was sure she could draw the torn parts together and make it look bright and new.

"I think I can fix it up so it'll look fine, George," she said.

"Eh," he said. "What are you bothering with that for?" Then he ducked down to the floor again and wiggled his paper moustache fiercely at the child.

1959

EARLE BIRNEY (1904-   )

Earle Birney has written two novels and several volumes of poetry, and has become well-known in Canada as a provocative public speaker and radio and television personality. His work both in prose and poetry has been concerned for the most part with the paramount social issues of his own place and time, and he is likely to be remembered as the most lively chronicler of and commentator upon Canadian life in his generation. His first novel, *Turvey* (1949), is an amusing and ironic account of a private soldier's adventures and misadventures in World War II, and his second, *Down the Long Table* (1955), is a more serious but less successful chronicle of the great depression of the nineteen-thirties. His poems have been published in many volumes including: *David and Other Poems* (1942), *Now Is Time* (1945), *The Strait of Anian* (1948), *Trial of a City* (1952), *Ice, Cod, Bell, and Stone* (1962), *Rag and Bone Shop* (1971) and *Collected Poems* (1975).

Dr. Birney was born on May 13, 1904, in Calgary, Alberta, and spent his childhood in the central Alberta bush and in the mountain resort village of Banff. At the age of fourteen he was taken by his parents to Creston, British Columbia, and most of his subsequent life has been spent in that province. He graduated from the University of British Columbia in 1926, and was subsequently a graduate student in English at the University of Toronto and University of California and an instructor at the University of Utah. In 1936 he obtained his doctorate from the University of Toronto, and became a lecturer in the Department of English there and literary editor of the magazine *Canadian Forum*. During World War II he served in Canada and Europe with the Canadian Army, and soon after the end of hostilities was appointed professor of English in the University of British Columbia.

David

I

David and I that summer cut trails on the Survey,
All week in the valley for wages, in air that was steeped
In the wail of mosquitoes, but over the sunalive weekends
We climbed, to get from the ruck of the camp, the surly

Poker, the wrangling, the snoring under the fetid
Tents, and because we had joy in our lengthening coltish
Muscles, and mountains for David were made to see over,
Stairs from the valleys and steps to the sun's retreats.

II

Our first was Mount Gleam. We hiked in the long afternoon
To a curling lake and lost the lure of the faceted
Cone in the swell of its sprawling shoulders. Past
The inlet we grilled our bacon, the strips festooned

On a poplar prong, in the hurrying slant of the sunset.
Then the two of us rolled in the blanket while round us the cold
Pines thrust at the stars. The dawn was a floating
Of mists till we reached to the slopes above timber, and won

10

To snow like fire in the sunlight. The peak was upthrust
Like a fist in a frozen ocean of rock that swirled
Into valleys the moon could be rolled in. Remotely unfurling
Eastward the alien prairie glittered. Down through the dusty   20

Skree on the west we descended, and David showed me
How to use the give of shale for giant incredible
Strides. I remember, before the larches' edge,
That I jumped a long green surf of juniper flowing

Away from the wind, and landed in gentian and saxifrage
Spilled on the moss. Then the darkening firs
And the sudden whirring of water that knifed down a fern-hidden
Cliff and splashed unseen into mist in the shadows.

III

One Sunday on Rampart's arête[1] a rainsquall caught us,
And passed, and we clung by our blueing fingers and bootnails   30
An endless hour in the sun, not daring to move
Till the ice had steamed from the slate. And David taught me

How time on a knife-edge can pass with the guessing of fragments
Remembered from poets, the naming of strata beside one,
And matching of stories from schooldays . . . We crawled astride
The peak to feast on the marching ranges flagged

By the fading shreds of the shattered stormcloud. Lingering
There it was David who spied to the south, remote
And unmapped, a sunlit spire on Sawback, an overhang
Crooked like a talon. David named it the Finger.   40

That day we chanced on the skull and the splayed white ribs
Of a mountain goat underneath a cliff, caught tight
On a rock. Around were the silken feathers of kites.
And that was the first I knew that a goat could slip.

IV

And then Inglismaldie. Now I remember only
The long ascent of the lonely valley, the live
Pine spirally scarred by lightning, the slicing pipe
Of invisible pika[2], and great prints, by the lowest

---

[1]A sharp mountain spur or ridge.   [2]Small hare-like mammals without tails.

Snow, of a grizzly. There it was too that David
Taught me to read the scroll of coral in limestone   50
And the beetle-seal in the shale of ghostly trilobites[3],
Letters delivered to man from the Cambrian waves.

V

On Sundance we tried from the col[4] and the going was hard.
The air howled from our feet to the smudged rocks
And the papery lake below. At an outthrust we balked
Till David clung with his left to a dint in the scarp[5],

Lobbed the iceaxe over the rocky lip,
Slipped from his holds and hung by the quivering pick,
Twisted his long legs up into space and kicked
To the crest. Then grinning, he reached with his freckled wrist   60

And drew me up after. We set a new time for that climb.
That day returning we found a robin gyrating
In grass, wing-broken. I caught it to tame but David
Took and killed it, and said, "Could you teach it to fly?"

VI

In August, the second attempt, we ascended The Fortress.
By the forks of the Spray we caught five trout and fried them
Over a balsam fire. The woods were alive
With the vaulting of mule-deer and drenched with clouds all the morning,

Till we burst at noon to the flashing and floating round
Of the peaks. Coming down we picked in our hats the bright   70
And sunhot raspberries, eating them under a mighty
Spruce, while a marten moving like quicksilver scouted us.

VII

But always we talked of the Finger on Sawback, unknown
And hooked, till the first afternoon in September we slogged
Through the musky woods, past a swamp that quivered with frog-song,
And camped by a bottle-green lake. But under the cold

Breath of the glacier sleep would not come, the moonlight
Etching the Finger. We rose and trod past the feathery
Larch, while the stars went out, and the quiet heather
Flushed, and the skyline pulsed with the surging bloom   80

---

[3]Extinct marine anthropods, related to crabs and turtles.
[4]A depression between two mountains.   [5]A steep slope.

Of incredible dawn in the Rockies. David spotted
Bighorns across the moraine and sent them leaping
With yodels the ramparts redoubled and rolled to the peaks,
And the peaks to the sun. The ice in the morning thaw

Was a gurgling world of crystal and cold blue chasms,
And seracs[6] that shone like frozen saltgreen waves.
At the base of the Finger we tried once and failed. Then David
Edged to the west and discovered the chimney; the last

Hundred feet we fought the rock and shouldered and kneed
Our way for an hour and made it. Unroping we formed   90
A cairn on the rotting tip. Then I turned to look north
At the glistening wedge of giant Assiniboine, heedless

Of handhold. And one foot gave. I swayed and shouted.
David turned sharp and reached out his arm and steadied me
Turning again with a grin and his lips ready
To jest. But the strain crumbled his foothold. Without

A gasp he was gone. I froze to the sound of grating
Edge-nails and fingers, the slither of stones, the lone
Second of silence, the nightmare thud. Then only
The wind and the muted beat of unknowing cascades.   100

                                 VIII

Somehow I worked down the fifty impossible feet
To the ledge, calling and getting no answer but echoes
Released in the cirque[7], and trying not to reflect
What an answer would mean. He lay still, with his lean

Young face upturned and strangely unmarred, but his legs
Splayed beneath him, beside the final drop,
Six hundred feet sheer to the ice. My throat stopped
When I reached him, for he was alive. He opened his grey

Straight eyes and brokenly murmured "over . . . over."
And I, feeling beneath him a cruel fang   110
Of the ledge thrust in his back, but not understanding,
Mumbled stupidly, "Best not to move," and spoke

Of his pain. But he said, "I can't move. . . . If only I felt
Some pain." Then my shame stung the tears to my eyes

---

[6]A large block into which glacier ice breaks in passing down steep inclines.
[7]A circular valley with steep walls.

As I crouched, and I cursed myself, but he cried,
Louder, "No, Bobbie! Don't ever blame yourself.

I didn't test my foothold." He shut the lids
Of his eyes to the stare of the sky, while I moistened his lips
From our water flask and tearing my shirt into strips
I swabbed the shredded hands. But the blood slid   120

From his side and stained the stone and the thirsting lichens,
And yet I dared not lift him up from the gore
Of the rock. Then he whispered, "Bob, I want to go over!"
This time I knew what he meant and I grasped for a lie

And said, "I'll be back here by midnight with ropes
And men from the camp and we'll cradle you out." But I knew
That the day and the night must pass and the cold dews
Of another morning before such men unknowing

The ways of mountains could win to the chimney's top.
And then, how long? And he knew . . . and the hell of hours   130
After that, if he lived till we came, roping him out.
But I curled beside him and whispered, "The bleeding will stop.

You can last." He said only, "Perhaps. . . . For what? A wheelchair,
Bob?" His eyes brightening with fever upbraided me.
I could not look at him more and said, "Then I'll stay
With you." But he did not speak, for the clouding fever.

I lay dazed and stared at the long valley,
The glistening hair of a creek on the rug stretched
By the firs, while the sun leaned round and flooded the ledge,
The moss, and David still as a broken doll.

I hunched to my knees to leave, but he called and his voice   140
Now was sharpened with fear. "For Christ's sake push me over!
If I could move. . . . Or die. . . ." The sweat ran from his forehead,
But only his head moved. A kite was buoying

Blackly its wings over the wrinkled ice.
The purr of a waterfall rose and sank with the wind.
Above us climbed the last joint of the Finger
Beckoning bleakly the wide indifferent sky.

Even then in the sun it grew cold lying there. . . . And I knew
He had tested his holds. It was I who had not. . . . I looked
At the blood on the ledge, and the far valley. I looked
At last in his eyes. He breathed, "I'd do it for you, Bob."   150

IX

I will not remember how nor why I could twist
Up the wind-devilled peak, and down through the chimney's empty
Horror, and over the traverse alone. I remember
Only the pounding fear I would stumble on It

When I came to the grave-cold maw of the bergschrund[8] . . . reeling
Over the sun-cankered snowbridge, shying the caves
In the névé[9] . . . the fear, and the need to make sure It was there
On the ice, the running and falling and running, leaping

Of gaping greenthroated crevasses, alone and pursued   160
By the Finger's lengthening shadow. At last through the fanged
And blinding seracs I slid to the milky wrangling
Falls at the glacier's snout, through the rocks piled huge

On the humped moraine, and into the spectral larches,
Alone. By the glooming lake I sank and chilled
My mouth but I could not rest and stumbled still
To the valley, losing my way in the ragged marsh.

I was glad of the mire that covered the stains, on my ripped
Boots, of his blood, but panic was on me, the reek
Of the bog, the purple glimmer of toadstools obscene   170
In the twilight. I staggered clear to a fire waste, tripped

And fell with a shriek on my shoulder. It somehow eased
My heart to know I was hurt, but I did not faint
And I could not stop while over me hung the range
Of the Sawback. In blackness I searched for the trail by the creek

And found it. . . . My feet squelched a slug and horror
Rose again in my nostrils. I hurled myself
Down the path. In the woods behind some animal yelped.
Then I saw the glimmer of tents and babbled my story.

I said that he fell straight to the ice where they found him,   180
And none but the sun and incurious clouds have lingered
Around the marks of that day on the ledge of the Finger,
That day, the last of my youth, on the last of our mountains.

                                                                        1942

---

[8]A crevasse at the head of a glacier.   [9]Granular snow found on the upper part of a mountain.

Slug in Woods

For eyes he waves greentipped
taut horns of slime. They dipped,
hours back, across a reef,
a salmonberry leaf.
Then strained to grope past fin
of spruce. Now eyes suck in
as through the hemlock butts
of his day's ledge there cuts
a vixen chipmunk. Stilled
is he—green mucus chilled,   10
or blotched and soapy stone,
pinguid[1] in moss, alone.
Hours on, he will resume
his silver scrawl, illume
his palimpsest[2], emboss

his diver's line across
that waving green illim-
itable seafloor. Slim
young jay his sudden shark;
the wrecks he skirts are dark   20
and fungussed firlogs, whom
spirea sprays emplume,
encoral. Dew his shell,
while mounting boles foretell
of isles in dappled air
fathoms above his care.
Azygous[3] muted life,
himself his viscid[4] wife,
foodward he noses cold beneath his sea.
So spends a summer's jasper century. 30
1942

[1]Fatty, oily.
[2]A manuscript or parchment which has been written on several times after erasures.

[3]Occurring singly, not in pairs.
[4]Glutinous, sticky.

Anglosaxon Street[1]

Dawndrizzle ended,   dampness steams from
blotching brick and   blank plasterwaste.
Faded housepatterns,   hoary and finicky,
unfold stuttering,   stick like a phonograph.
Over the eaves and   over dank roofs
peep giraffetowers,   pasted planless
against grey sky,   great dronecliffs
like cutouts for kids,   clipped in two dimensions. . . .

Here is a ghetto   gotten for goyim,
O with care denuded   of nigger and kike.   10
No coonsmell rankles,   reeks only cellarrot,
attar of carexhaust,   catcorpse and cookinggrease.
Imperial hearts   heave in this haven.
Cracks across windows   are welded with slogans;
There'll Always Be An England   enhances geraniums,
and *V*'s for a *Victory*   vanquish the housefly.

[1]Birney, who is a specialist in Old and Middle English, has modelled the form of this poem on the alliterative poetry written in Anglo-Saxon times, and has deliberately used certain archaic words such as *farded* (laden with bundles) and such "kennings" (condensed metaphors) as *wheelboat* (streetcar) and *alehall* (tavern).

Ho! with climbing sun,   heading from cocoons,
go bleached beldames,   garnished in bargainbasements,
festooned with shoppingbags,   farded, flatarched,
bigthewed Saxonwives,   stepping over buttrivers,   20
waddling back to suckle   smallfry, wienerladen.

Hoy! with sunslope,   shrieking over hydrants,
flood from learninghall.   the lean fingerlings,
Nordic, nobblecheeked,   not all clean of nose,
leaping Commando-wise   into leprous lanes.

What! after whistleblow,   spewed from wheelboat,
after daylong doughtiness,   dire handplay
in sewertrench or sandpit,   come Saxonthegns,
Junebrown Jutekings,   jawslack for meat.

Sit after supper   on smeared doorstops,   30
not humbly swearing   hatedeeds on Huns,
profiteers, politicians,   pacifists and Jews.

Canada: Case History

This is the case of a high-school land,
deadset in adolescence,
loud treble laughs and sudden fists,
bright cheeks, the gangling presence.
This boy is wonderful at sports
and physically quite healthy;
he's taken to church on Sunday still
and keeps his prurience stealthy.
He doesn't like books except about bears,
collects new coins and model planes,   10
and never refuses a dare.
His Uncle spoils him with candy, of course,
yet shouts him down when he talks at table.
You will note he's got some of his French mother's look.
though he's not so witty and no more stable.
He's really much more like his father and yet
if you say so he'll pull a great face.
He wants to be different from everyone else
and daydreams of winning the global race.
Parents unmarried and living abroad,   20

relatives keen to bag the estate,
schizophrenia not excluded,
will he learn to grow up before it's too late?

1948

Vancouver Lights

About me the night   moonless   wimples[1] the mountains
wraps ocean   land   air   and mounting
sucks at the stars   The city   throbbing below
webs the sable peninsula   The golden
strands overleap the seajet   by bridge and buoy
vault the shears of the inlet   climb the woods
toward me   falter   and halt   Across to the firefly
haze of a ship on the gulf's erased horizon
roll the lambent[2] spokes of a lighthouse

Through the feckless[3] years we have come to the time   10
when to look on this quilt of lamps is a troubling delight
Welling from Europe's bog   through Africa flowing
and Asia   drowning the lonely lumes[4] on the oceans
tiding up over Halifax   now to this winking
outpost comes flooding the primal ink

On this mountain's brutish forehead with terror of space
I stir   of the changless night and the stark ranges
of nothing   pulsing down from beyond and between
the fragile planets   We are a spark beleaguered
by darkness   this twinkle we make in a corner of emptiness   20
how shall we utter our fear that the black Experimentress
will never in the range of her microscope find it?   Our Phoebus[5]
himself is a bubble that dries on Her slide   while the Nubian[6]
wears for an evening's whim a necklace of nebulae[7]

Yet we must speak   we the unique glowworms
Out of the waters and rocks of our little world
we conjured these flames   hooped these sparks
by our will   From blankness and cold we fashioned stars

[1]To cover with a veil.
[2]Flickering, softly radiant.
[3]Irresponsible, careless.
[4]Lights.
[5]Phoebus Apollo, Greek god of the sun.
[6]A black-skinned native of Nubia, in Africa—hence, the night.
[7]Galaxies.

to our size   and signalled Aldebaran[8]
This must we say   whoever may be to hear us   30
if murk devour   and none weave again in gossamer:

                              These rays were ours
we made and unmade them   Not the shudder of continents
doused us   the moon's passion   nor crash of comets
In the fathomless heat of our dwarfdom   our dream's combustion
we contrived the power   the blast that snuffed us
No one bound Prometheus[9]   Himself he chained
and consumed his own bright liver   O stranger
Plutonian[10]   descendant   or beast in the stretching night—
there was light   40
1941   1966

[8]A red star of the highest magnitude—the brightest star in the Hyades.
[9]A titan in Greek mythology who gave man the use of fire and was punished by the gods—as he was
    chained to a rock, a vulture came and plucked out his liver. The gift of fire is often seen as a sym-
    bol of knowledge and civilization.
[10]An inhabitant of Pluto, or Hades, the underworld in Greek mythology. Also, the most distant
    planet.

HUGH MACLENNAN (1907-   )

Born in Cape Breton, Hugh MacLennan was educated in the classics at Dalhousie, Oxford, and Princeton Universities. He is currently Professor Emeritus of English at McGill University in Montreal.

MacLennan dominated the Canadian literary scene in the forties and fifties, receiving five Governor General's Awards. His first novel, *Barometer Rising* (1941) is still widely read today, while critics agree that *Two Solitudes* (1945) and *Each Man's Son* (1951) are his finest works. Written at the age of seventy-four, his seventh novel, *Voices in Time* (1981) has received critical acclaim.

Praised for his skill in descriptive writing, MacLennan's novels explore national themes and settings from a peculiarly Canadian point of view. His several volumes of essays are marked by profound insights into the character and development of Canada.

Scotchman's Return

Whenever I stop to think about it, the knowledge that I am three-quarters Scotch, and Highland at that, seems like a kind of doom from which I am too Scotch even to think of praying for deliverance. I can thank my father for this last-ditch neurosis. He was entirely Scotch; he was a living specimen of a most curious heritage. In spite of his medical knowledge, which was large; in spite of his quick nervous vitality and tireless energy, he was never able to lay to rest the beasties which went bump in his mind at three o'clock in the morning. It mattered nothing that he was a third-generation Canadian who had never seen the Highlands before he visited them on leave in the First World War. He never needed to go there to understand whence he came or what he was. He was neither a Scot nor yet was he Scottish; he never used those genteel appellations which now are supposed to be *de rigueur*[1]. He was simply Scotch. All the perplexity and doggedness of the race was in him, its loneliness, tenderness and affection, its deceptive vitality, its quick flashes of violence, its dog-whistle sensitivity to sounds to which Anglo-Saxons are stone-deaf, its incapacity to tell its heart to foreigners save in terms foreigners do not comprehend, its resigned indifference to whether they comprehend or not. "It's not easy being Scotch," he told me more than once. To which I suppose another Scotchman might say: "It wasn't meant to be."

So far as I could tell, my father found it almost impossible to believe that anyone not Scotch is entirely real. Yet at the same time, buried in the fastnesses of his complex mind, was the contradictory notion that if a Scotchman ever amounts to anything important, he will not be any too real, either, for some beastie will come along and spoil him. As engineers keeping the ships going, as captains serving the owners of the lines, as surgeons, teachers, clergymen and the like, as loyal seconds-in-command—in these niches the Scotch might expect to fare well. But you seldom found them on the summit, and if by reason of an accident one them got there, something bad was pretty sure to happen. When Ramsay Macdonald became the first man with a Mac in his name to become a British Prime Minister, my father shook his head gloomily over Macdonald's picture on the front page of the paper, and when I asked him why, he said: "He won't do." He had an overweening[2] admiration for the English so long as they stayed in England, and for the Royal Navy above all other English institutions. Indeed, one of his motives for becoming a doctor was an idea in the back of his youthful mind that as a surgeon he might become an R.N. officer. But he was no light Anglophile[3]. I well remember a summer afternoon in the mid-twenties when a British squadron paid Halifax a courtesy call, and better still do I remember that the two leading ships were *H.M.S. Hood* and *H.M.S. Repulse*. As my father at that time was doing some work in the military hospital, he was called to perform an emergency operation on an officer of the *Repulse*, and the Commander of the ship later invited him to tea in the wardroom. He took me along, and as I also was brought up to love the Royal Navy, this was a great thrill to me. It turned out to be an experience almost traumatic.

No sooner had we taken our seats in the wardroom than the officer-of-the-watch entered resplendent in the dress of the day and carrying his cocked hat under his arm. He laid the hat beside him on the table, nodded to a steward for his tea, glanced at us, and when he saw we were civilians and natives, his lips parted in an expression of disdain in which, to quote a famous English author who has noted such expressions as carefully as Shelley the lips of Ozymandias[4], delicacy had no part. Ignoring my father, this officer inclined his eyes vaguely in my direction and said: "D'you live here?" "Yes, sir," I replied. "Beastly place," was his comment and then he fell silent. So did everyone else.

After several minutes the silence was broken by the racket of an R.C.A.F. training biplane stunting over the harbour and the arrogant disdain on the face of the former of-

[1]Prescribed or required by fashion, etiquette or custom.
[2]Immoderate, exaggerated.
[3]Lover of the English.
[4]See P. 291.

ficer-of-the-watch was replaced by something very like a flush of anger. "So you have those wretched things over here, too?" he asked my father accusingly. I noted with some pride that my father did not reply to this officer, but instead turned to another man who had been embarrassed by his colleague's behaviour, and asked mildly if the development of aircraft had made it necessary for the Navy to alter its battle tactics. This officer was beginning to reply in some detail when the officer-of-the-watch interrupted: "Do you," he asked my father, "seriously believe that a wretched little gnat like that aircraft could possibly threaten a ship like this?"

No, it was not a successful tea party, nor did it last much longer. My father rose as soon as he felt it courteous to do so, we were escorted to the ladder and handed down into the launch, and as the launch drove through the fog my father was informatively silent. After a while he said, as though excusing the officer's rudeness: "Of course, the weather has been depressing here and they've come up from New York." But before the launch touched the jetty he added: "All the same, he shouldn't have said that." I understood then that my father had not felt himself snubbed, but that the Scotch in him had been gravely concerned by the officer's *hubris*[5] concerning the air force. A beastie had been alerted to keep a special eye on that slim, powerful but extremely vulnerable battlecruiser which was the last brain-child of the ferocious Admiral Jackie Fisher, the ship which Winston Churchill later described as having the brilliance and the fragility one is apt to associate with the children of very old men. Years later in the terrible December of 1941, when the news came from Malaya, I recalled that afternoon aboard *Repulse* with a thrill of sheer horror.

My father was also the reason why I never visited the Highlands when I was a student in the Old Country. Nor did he think I should have done so. "You'll see them one of these days," he said. And he added as an afterthought: "If you're spared and well." And he added as another afterthought: "When you do see them you'll understand." Naturally he did not tell me what I would understand, assuming I would know, but this comment did nothing to foment a desire in me to travel north of the Highland Line.

But we can't escape ourselves forever, and more of ourselves than we choose to admit is the accumulated weight of our ancestors. As I grew older the thought of the Highlands began to haunt me, and in the summer of 1958, after having lived for a long time under a great strain, I decided to get a change and sail to England on a freight ship. I landed in Manchester and of course went south, but after spending a week in London, I went north on the train to Edinburgh and on a Monday morning I found myself in a car-rental agency in the Haymarket making a deal for a Vauxhall.

Ahead of me was the only American I saw in the Old Country that year who behaved as Europeans desire Americans to behave abroad. After complaining about the tastelessness of British food, the harshness and skiddiness of British toilet paper and the absurdity of driving on the left-hand side of the road, he finally came to the topic of the Edinburgh Sabbath which he had just survived.

"Do you realize," he said to the car dealer, "that in the United States there's not even a village as quiet as this town was yesterday?"

The Scotchman looked up at him, inwardly gratified but outwardly glum.

"Ay!" he said, and assumed incorrectly that the American understood that both himself

[5]Exaggerated pride.

and his country had been rebuked.

When he turned to me after the American had departed, and had identified my nationality by my driving licence, he allowed himself the luxury of an irrelevant comment.

"Ye appear to have deeficult neighbours," he said.

"Perhaps you have difficult neighbours, too?"

"Ay!" he said, and seemed pleased, for an instant later he said "Ay" again.

More or less secure in the Vauxhall I headed north for Stirling and the Highland Line, and after a night by Loch Katrine struck north by Balquhidder, mistook my road to Glencoe and went too far west, and soon found myself beside Loch Awe. I also found myself, with some surprise and mortification, unwilling to perceive any beauty in this region because Loch Awe is in Campbell country, and in the near past of several centuries ago, the Campbell chiefs had been an anathema[6] to the less successful clans they pillaged.

The roads in the Highlands, as those will know who have travelled them, are not only so narrow that in most sections two baby Austins are unable to pass, they are also infested with livestock. Sheep fall asleep on their narrow shoulders and cars must stop again and again while bullocks make up their minds whether or not to move out of the way. The roads were built by some English general, I think his name was Wade, who had the eighteenth-century English notion that if he built roads the communications between the clans would improve. Only lately have General Wade's roads been hard-topped, and never have they been widened except at regular intervals where cars may turn out to allow approaching cars to pass. They are adequately marked if you are familiar with them, but I was not familiar with them and again lost my way. I went into the pub of a hamlet to ask where I was and discovered behind the bar an elderly gentleman with white hair and the demeanour of a Presbyterian elder, and beside the bar three workmen silently sipping ale.

"What's the name of this place?" I asked the publican[7].

"The Heather and Bull," he said.

"I meant, what's this community?"

"Mostly Protestant," he said, "but in recent years wi' a small smattering of Roman Catholics." He turned to one of the workmen: "John, how many Catholics now?"

"About eighteen percent. Going on for twenty."

"They're risin' fast," said a third man.

"Ay!" said the publican. And turning to me has asked when I had left Canada.

"How on earth did you guess I'm a Canadian?"

"You are not English, that is certain, and you are not American. You still have some of the voice." He put out his hand: "God bless you!"

We talked of Scotland, Canada and theology and I forgot what I had intended to ask him. An hour later, when I shook his hand and received my directions, his noble face was as solemn as a memory from childhood.

"You will be disappointed," he warned me. "Scotland is full of nothing but Irish now. Och, we have no dignity left."

An Anglo-Saxon or an American might assume a racial situation from this remark, but

---

[6]A bane or curse.

[7]Licensee of a public house.

it was the sort of thing I grew up with, the sort of remark I have made myself, in different connotations, all my life. Its meaning was clear to me if to nobody else. The old gentleman was unburdening himself of a beastie which had nothing whatever to do with the Catholics, the Irish or with anything, possibly, that he himself could put into words.

The next day I was in the true north of Scotland among the sheep, the heather, the whin[8], the mists and the homes of the vanished races. Such sweeps of emptiness I never saw in Canada before I went to the Mackenzie River later in that same summer. But this Highland emptiness, only a few hundred miles above the massed population of England, is a far different thing from the emptiness of our own Northwest Territories. Above the sixtieth parallel in Canada you feel that nobody but God has ever been there before you, but in a deserted Highland glen you feel that everyone who ever mattered is dead and gone. Those glens are the most hauntingly lovely sights I have ever seen: they are vaster, more moving, more truly vacated than the southern abbeys ruined by Henry VIII. They are haunted by the lost loves and passions of a thousand years. Later that summer on the lower reaches of the Mackenzie, after talking to an Athabascan Indian with Celtic eyes and the name of McPherson, I remembered the wild loneliness of Lochaber and it occurred to me that only a man from a country as lonely and ghost-ridden as the Highlands could have had the insane determination to paddle a canoe through the Rocky Mountains and down La Grande Rivière-en-bas to the Beaufort Sea, and that nothing was more in the life-style of the Highlander than Alexander Mackenzie's feat in searching for the Northwest Passage in a canoe. After an achievement of incredible boldness and endurance, what, after all, did this Highlander find but nothing?

Yet, as a by-product, he and others like him surely found much of Canada, even though one of them, solitary on the Qu'Appelle or the Saskatchewan, admitting the grandeur of the woods and prairies of the New World, sang from a broken heart that he was an exile from his native land, and while making possible the existence of a country so vast that Scotland would be lost in it, regretted his inability to wield a claymore[9] in defence of a barren glen presided over by an imbecile chief. The exiled Irish never forgave their landlords, but the exiled Highlanders pined for the scoundrel Pretender[10], and even regretted the proprietors who preferred sheep to humanity, enclosed their own people and drove them starving across the western ocean with such an uncomprehended yearning in their souls that some of them ended up in log cabins along the Athabasca and on the shores of James Bay.

In the parish of Kintail, whence some of my own people were driven a century and a half ago, I was told there are now barely four hundred inhabitants. In my ancestors' days there were more than twelve thousand.

"Where are they?" the minister said when I asked him. "Where indeed but in Canada? And some in Australia and New Zealand of course, but most of them in Canada."

With them they brought—no doubt of this—that nameless haunting guilt they never understood, and the feeling of failure, and the loneliness of all the warm-hearted, not very intelligent folk so outmoded by the Anglo-Saxon success that they knew they were

[8]Furze, a spiny shrub.
[9]A large, two-edged sword, formerly used by Scottish Highlanders.
[10]James Stuart, the pretender or claimant to the English throne.

helpless unless they lived as the Anglo-Saxons did, failures unless they learned to feel (or not to feel at all) as the Anglo-Saxons ordained. Had my father been clairvoyant when he told me I would understand when I went to the Highlands?

I'm not sure that I do understand or ever will understand what he wanted me to know. But one evening watching a rainbow form over Loch Leven, the mists drop down the hills into rain, then watching the sky rent open and such a tumult of golden light pour forth that the mountains themselves moved and were transfigured, still moved and then were lifted up until they ceased to be mountains and turned themselves into an abstraction of sheer glory and gold—watching this I realized, or thought I did, why these desperate people had endured so long against the civilization of the south. Unlike Ulysses, they had failed to stop their ears when the sirens sang, and the sirens that sing in the Highlands, suddenly and when you least expect to hear them, have voices more dangerously beguiling than any in the Aegaean Isles. Beauty is nearly the most dangerous thing on earth, and those who love her too much, or look too deeply into her eyes, they pay the price for her, which often is an empty stomach and a life of misunderstanding.

So it was here, though an economist would point out that the land is barren and that in the early days the people lacked education and civilized techniques. But this practical attitude merely begs the question of why the people stayed so long: stayed, in fact, until they were driven out. These mountains are almost as useless to the cultivator as the upper reaches of the Laurentian Shield. The Gaelic tongue sounds soft and lovely, but compared with English and French it is a primitive means of communication. The ancestors of almost a quarter of modern Canada never did, and in their native glens they never could, develop even the rudiments of an urban culture. When they made the acquaintance of the English this must have sorely troubled their conscience, for they were religious, they were Christianized after a fashion, and the parable that meant most to them was the Parable of the Talents. Only a few of their chiefs could possibly be called intelligent, and the conduct of the chiefs of their only really successful clan (it shall be nameless here, though every Highlander knows the one I have in mind) was of the crafty peasant sort, the more base because it exploited the loyalty of a people who were already enslaved by their own conception of honour. But though these chiefs did well for themselves, they only became rich and famous after they had conspired with the English enemy. No leader, not even a genius, could have raised in the terrain of the Highlands a civilization capable of competing with England's. Yet the Highlanders held on to the glens; incredibly they held on to them until the end of the eighteenth century. Often I have said to myself that my grandfathers three times removed lived in a culture as primitive as Homer's, and last summer in the Highlands I knew that they really had.

Driving south through Glencoe where the Campbells massacred the Macdonalds, I remembered the first time I met Angus L. Macdonald, who then was Premier of Nova Scotia and previously had been Canada's Minister for the Navy. With a suddenness that would have been startling to anyone but another clansman, Mr. Macdonald turned to me in a company of people and from the depths of a mutual empathy he said: "To be a Celt is never to be far from tears."

But we Celts are withal a mercurial[11] people also; our sorrowful moods pass like the

---

[11]Moody, unpredictable.

mists on the braes and the sunlight strikes through when we least expect it. A week later I was in the most fatally civilized country in the world, Sweden, waiting for a Pan-American Clipper to take me home.

Just as I belong to the last Canadian generation raised with a Highland nostalgia, so also do I belong to the last which regards a trans-Atlantic flight as a miracle. When I was a boy I saw the first tiny plane to fly the ocean, the American seaplane N.C.4, which took a very long time moving by stages from Halifax to Sydney, to Bonavista Bay, to the Azores and finally to Lisbon. Eight years later plane after plane set out on non-stop ventures and disappeared into the sea.

Now, eating a filet mignon and sipping champagne in the supreme luxury of this Pan-American aircraft, I looked down on the waste of seas which, together with the mountains of British Columbia, had divided the clansmen from their homes over a century ago. Sitting there idle I felt an unwarranted lift of joy and omnipotent power. The plane nuzzled into the stratospheric wind, she rolled as slowly and surely as a shark speeding through the water in which it was born, she went so fast that though she left Stockholm as late as 4.30 in the afternoon it was still bright daylight when she put down in a rainstorm in Keflavik. She took on fuel and set out again, I slept for an hour or two, wakened to a change in the propeller pitch and learned we were circling Gander, which as usual was buried in fog. After an hour the pilot said over the intercom:

"The weather in Gander has deteriorated to zero-zero. We are now proceeding to New York. We will arrive in Idlewild at 7.40 Eastern Daylight Time. We will arrive on schedule."

Here, of course, was the supreme triumph of the civilization which, in wrecking the clansmen, had made it possible for me to think of Canada as home. The plane tore through the fog, the stewardess brought a delicious breakfast, and just as I was sipping my coffee the sun broke dazzlingly through the window into the cabin. I looked out and there, in a semi-circle of sunshine, the only sunshine apparently in the whole northern hemisphere at that particular moment, lay Cape Breton Island. The plane sloped down to eight thousand feet and I saw beside the Bras d'Or lake the tiny speck which was the house where my mother and sister at that very moment lay asleep. We did reach New York on schedule and that same day I ate my lunch in the Medical Arts restaurant on the corner of Sherbrooke Street and Guy. The man next to me at the counter asked where I had been and I told him I had been in the Scottish Highlands.

"It must have been nice," he said.

"It was. But it's also nice to be home."

Am I wrong, or is it true that it is only now, after so many years of not knowing who we were or wanted to be, that we Canadians of Scotch descent are truly at home in the northern half of North America?

1960

SINCLAIR ROSS (1908-   )

Born near Prince Albert, Saskatchewan, Sinclair Ross spent most of his life in Winnipeg and Montreal, but has lived in Spain for a number of years since retiring. He has published four novels—*As For Me and My House* (1941), *The Well* (1958), *A Whir of Gold* (1970), *Sawbones Memorial* (1974) and a collection of stories, *The Lamp at Noon and Other Stories* (1968).

In his writing, Ross studies both conflicts between man and nature and conflicts inherent in human relationships; his characters often suffer the effects of isolation and alienation. A meticulous craftsman, he writes in a spare and allusive prose style, with a sure use of the narrative voice.

The Lamp at Noon

A little before noon she lit the lamp. Demented wind fled keening[1] past the house: a wail through the eaves that died every minute or two. Three days now without respite it had held. The dust was thickening to an impenetrable fog.

She lit the lamp, then for a long time stood at the window motionless. In dim, fitful outline the stable and oat granary still were visible; beyond, obscuring fields and landmarks, the lower of dust clouds made the farmyard seem an isolated acre, poised aloft above a sombre void. At each blast of wind it shook, as if to topple and spin hurtling with the dust-reel into space.

From the window she went to the door, opening it a little, and peering towards the stable again. He was not coming yet. As she watched there was a sudden rift overhead, and for a moment through the tattered clouds the sun raced like a wizened orange. It shed a soft, diffused light, dim and yellow as if it were the light from the lamp reaching out through the open door.

She closed the door, and going to the stove tried the potatoes with a fork. Her eyes all the while were fixed and wide with a curious immobility. It was the window. Standing at it she had let her forehead press against the pane until the eyes were strained apart and rigid. Wide like that they had looked out to the deepening ruin of the storm. Now she could not close them.

The baby started to cry. He was lying in a home-made crib over which she had arranged a tent of muslin. Careful not to disturb the folds of it she knelt and tried to still him, whispering huskily in a sing-song voice that he must hush and go to sleep again. She would have liked to rock him, to feel the comfort of his little body in her arms, but a fear had obsessed her that in the dust-filled air he might contract pneumonia. There was dust sifting everywhere. Her own throat was parched with it. The table had been set less than ten minutes, and already a film was gathering on the dishes. The little cry continued, and with wincing, frightened lips she glanced around as if to find a corner where the air was less oppressive. But while the lips winced the eyes maintained their wide, immobile stare. "Sleep," she whispered again. "It's too soon for you to be hungry. Daddy's coming for his dinner."

He seemed a long time. Even the clock, still a few minutes off noon, could not dispel a foreboding sense that he was longer than he should be. She went to the door again—then

[1]A sound of lament or mourning.

recoiled slowly to stand white and breathless in the middle of the room. She mustn't. He would only despise her if she ran to the stable looking for him. There was too much grim endurance in his nature ever to let him understand the fear and weakness of a woman. She must stay quiet and wait. Nothing was wrong. At noon he would come—and perhaps after dinner stay with her a while.

Yesterday, and again at breakfast this morning, they had quarrelled bitterly. She wanted him now, the assurance of his strength and nearness, but he would stand aloof, wary, remembering the words she had flung at him in her anger, unable to understand it was only the dust and wind that had driven her.

Tense she fixed her eyes upon the clock, listening. There were two winds: the wind in flight, and the wind that pursued. The one sought refuge in the eaves, whimpering, in fear; the other assailed it there, and shook the eaves apart to make it flee again. Once as she listened this first wind sprang into the room, distraught like a bird that has felt the graze of talons on its wing; while furious the other wind shook the walls, and thudded tumbleweeds against the window till its quarry glanced away again in fright. But only to return—to return and quake among the feeble eaves, as if in all this dust-mad wilderness it knew no other sanctuary.

Then Paul came. At his step she hurried to the stove, intent upon the pots and frying-pan. "The worst wind yet," he ventured, hanging up his cap and smock. "I had to light the lantern in the tool shed too."

They looked at each other, then away. She wanted to go to him, to feel his arms supporting her, to cry a little just that he might soothe her, but because his presence made the menace of the wind seem less, she gripped herself and thought, "I'm in the right. I won't give in. For his sake too I won't."

He washed, hurriedly, so that a few dark welts of dust remained to indent upon his face a haggard strength. It was all she could see as she wiped the dishes and set the food before him: the strength, the grimness, the young Paul growing old and hard, buckled against a desert even grimmer than his will. "Hungry?" she asked, touched to a twinge of pity she had not intended. "There's dust in everything. It keeps coming faster than I can clean it up."

He nodded. "To-night though you'll see it go down. This is the third day." She looked at him in silence a moment, and then as if to herself muttered broodingly, "Until the next time. Until it starts again."

There was a dark timbre of resentment in her voice now that boded another quarrel. He waited, his eyes on her dubiously as she mashed a potato with her fork. The lamp between them threw strong lights and shadows on their faces. Dust and drouth, earth that betrayed alike his labor and his faith, to him the struggle had given sternness, an impassive courage. Beneath the whip of sand his youth had been effaced. Youth, zest, exuberance—there remained only a harsh and clenched virility that yet became him, that seemed at the cost of more engaging qualities to be fulfilment of his inmost and essential nature. Whereas to her the same debts and poverty had brought in a plaintive indignation, a nervous dread of what was still to come. The eyes were hollowed, the lips pinched dry and colorless. It was the face of a woman that had aged without maturing, that had loved the little vanities of life, and lost them wistfully.

"I'm afraid, Paul," she said suddenly. "I can't stand it any longer. He cries all the time.

You will go Paul—say you will. We aren't living here—not really living—"

The pleading in her voice now after its shrill bitterness yesterday made him think that this was only another way to persuade him. Evenly he answered, "I told you this morning, Ellen: we keep on right where we are. At least I do. It's yourself you're thinking about, not the baby."

This morning such an accusation would have stung her to rage; now, her voice swift and panting, she pressed on, "Listen, Paul—I'm thinking of all of us—you, too. Look at the sky—and your fields. Are you blind? Thistles and tumbleweeds—it's a desert, Paul. You won't have a straw this fall. You won't be able to feed a cow or a chicken. Please, Paul—say that we'll go away—"

"No Ellen—" His voice as he answered was still remote and even, inflexibly in unison with the narrowed eyes, and the great hunch of muscle-knotted shoulder. "Even as a desert it's better than sweeping out your father's store and running his errands. That's all I've got ahead of me if I do what you want."

"And here—" she flared. "What's ahead of you here? At least we'll get enough to eat and wear when you're sweeping out his store. Look at it—look at it, you fool. Desert—the lamp lit at noon—"

"You'll see it come back," he said quietly. "There's good wheat in it yet."

"But in the meantime—year after year—can't you understand, Paul? We'll never get them back—"

He put down his knife and fork and leaned towards her across the table. "I can't go, Ellen. Living off your people—charity—stop and think of it. This is where I belong. I've no trade or education. I can't do anything else."

"Charity!" she repeated him, letting her voice rise in derision. "And this—you call this independence! Borrowed money you can't even pay the interest on—seed from the government—grocery bills—doctor bills—"

"We'll have crops again," he persisted. "Good crops—the land will come back. It's worth waiting for."

"And while we're waiting, Paul!" It was not anger now, but a kind of sob. "Think of me—and him. It's not fair. We have our lives too to live."

"And you think that going home to your family—taking your husband with you—"

"I don't care—anything would be better than this. Look at the air he's breathing. He cries all the time. For his sake, Paul. What's ahead of him here, even if you do get crops?"

He clenched his lips a minute, then with his eyes hard and contemptuous struck back, "As much as in town, growing up a pauper. You're the one who wants to go, Ellen—it's not for his sake. You think that in town you'd have a better time—not so much work— more clothes—"

"Maybe—" She dropped her head defencelessly. "I'm young still. I like pretty things."

There was silence now—a deep fastness of it enclosed by rushing wind and creaking walls. It seemed the yellow lamplight cast a hush upon them. Through the haze of dusty air the walls receded, dimmed, and came again. Listlessly at last she said, "Go on—your dinner's getting cold. Don't sit and stare at me. I've said it all."

The spent quietness in her voice was harder even than her anger to endure. It reproached him, against his will insisted that he see and understand her lot. To justify himself he tried, "I was a poor man when you married me. You said you didn't mind. Farming's never been easy, and never will be."

"I wouldn't mind the work or the scrimping if there was something to look forward to. It's the hopelessness—going on—watching the land blow away."

"The land's all right," he repeated. "The dry years won't last forever."

"But it's not just dry years, Paul!" The little sob in her voice gave way suddenly to a ring of exasperation. "Will you never see? It's the land itself—the soil. You've plowed and harrowed it until there's not a root or fibre left to hold it down. That's why the soil drifts—that's why in a year or two there'll be nothing left but the bare clay. If in the first place you farmers had taken care of your land—if you hadn't been so greedy for wheat every year—"

She had taught school before she married him, and of late in her anger there had been a kind of disdain, an attitude almost of condescension, as if she no longer looked upon the farmers as her equals. He sat still, his eyes fixed on the yellow lampflame, and seeming to know how her words had hurt him she went on softly, "I want to help you Paul. That's why I won't sit quiet while you go on wasting your life. You're only thirty—you owe it to yourself as well as me."

Still he sat with his lips drawn white and his eyes on the lampflame. It seemed indifference now, as if he were ignoring her, and stung to anger again she cried, "Do you ever think what my life is? Two rooms to live in—once a month to town, and nothing to spend when I get there. I'm still young—I wasn't brought up this way."

Stolidly he answered, "You're a farmer's wife now. It doesn't matter what you used to be, or how you were brought up. You get enough to eat and wear. Just now that's all that I can do. I'm not to blame that we've been dried out five years."

"Enough to eat!" she laughed back shrilly, her eyes all the while fixed expressionless and wide. "Enough salt pork—enough potatoes and eggs. And look—" Springing to the middle of the room she thrust out a foot for him to see the scuffed old slipper. "When they're completely gone I suppose you'll tell me I can go barefoot—that I'm a farmer's wife—that it's not your fault we're dried out—"

"And look at these—" He pushed his chair away from the table now to let her see what he was wearing. "Cowhide—hard as boards—but my feet are so calloused I don't feel them anymore."

Then hurriedly he stood up, ashamed of having tried to match her hardships with his own. But frightened now as he reached for his smock she pressed close to him. "Don't go yet. I brood and worry when I'm left alone. Please, Paul—you can't work on the land anyway."

"And keep on like this?" Grimly he buttoned his smock right up to his throat. "You start before I'm through the door. Week in and week out—I've troubles enough of my own."

"Paul—please stay—" The eyes were glazed now, distended a little as if with the intensity of her dread and pleading. "We won't quarrel any more. Hear it! I can't work—just stand still and listen—"

The eyes frightened him, but responding to a kind of instinct that he must withstand her, that it was his self-respect and manhood against the fretful weakness of a woman, he answered unfeelingly, "In here safe and quiet—you don't know how well off you are. If you were out in it—fighting it—swallowing it—"

"Sometimes, Paul, I wish I were. I'm so caged—if I could only break away and run. See—I stand like this all day. I can't relax. My throat's so tight it aches—"

Firmly he loosened his smock from the clutch of her hands. "If I stay we'll only keep on like this all afternoon. To-morrow when the wind's down we can talk things over quietly."

Then without meeting her eyes again he swung outside, and doubled low against the buffets of the wind, fought his way slowly towards the stable. There was a deep hollow calm within, a vast darkness engulfed beneath the tides of moaning wind. He stood breathless a moment, hushed almost to a stupor by the sudden extinction of the storm and the incredible stillness that enfolded him. It was a long, far-reaching stillness. The first dim stalls and rafters led the way into cavernlike obscurity, into vaults and recesses that extended far beyond the stable walls. Nor in these first quiet moments did he forbid the illusion, the sense of release from a harsh, familiar world into one of immeasurable peace and darkness. The contentious mood that his stand against Ellen had roused him to, his tenacity and clenched despair before the ravages of wind, it was ebbing now, losing itself in the cover of darkness. Ellen and the wheat seemed remote, unimportant. At a whinney from the bay mare Bess he went forward and into her stall. She seemed grateful for his presence, and thrust her nose deep between his arm and body. They stood a long time thus, comforting.

For soon again the first deep sense of quiet and peace was shrunken to the battered shelter of the stable. Instead of release or escape from the assaulting wind, the walls were but a feeble stand against it. They creaked and sawed as if the fingers of a giant hand were tightening to collapse them; the empty loft sustained a pipelike cry that rose and fell but never ended. He saw the dust-black sky again, and his fields blown smooth with drifted soil.

But always, even while listening to the storm outside, he could feel the tense and apprehensive stillness of the stable. There was not a hoof that clumped or shifted, not a rub of halter against manger. And yet, though it had been a strange stable, into which he had never set foot before, he would have known, despite the darkness, that every stall was filled. They too were all listening.

From Bess he went to the big grey gelding Prince. Prince was twenty years old, with rib-grooved sides, and high, protruding hipbones. Paul ran his hand over the ribs, and felt a sudden shame, a sting of fear that Ellen might be right in what she said. For wasn't it true—nine years a farmer now on his own land, and still he couldn't even feed his horses? What then could he hope to do for his wife and son?

There was much he planned. And so vivid was the future of his planning, so real and constant, that often the actual present was but half-felt, but half-endured. Its difficulties were lessened by a confidence in what lay beyond them. A new house for Ellen, new furniture, new clothes. Land for the boy—land and still more land—or education, whatever he might want.

But all the time was he only a blind and stubborn fool? Was Ellen right? Was he trampling on her life, and throwing away his own? The five years since he married her, were they to go on repeating themselves, five, ten, twenty, until all the brave future he looked forward to was but a stark and futile past?

She looked forward to no future. She had no faith or dream with which to make the dust and poverty less real. He understood suddenly. He saw her face again as only a few minutes ago it had begged him not to leave her. The darkness round him now was as a slate on which her lonely terror limned itself. He went from Prince to the other horses, combing their manes and forelocks with his fingers, but always still it was her face he saw, its staring eyes and twisted suffering. "See Paul—I stand like this all day. I just stand still— My throat's so tight it aches—"

And always the wind, the creak of walls, the wild lipless wailing through the loft. Until at last as he stood there, staring into the livid face before him, it seemed that this scream of wind was a cry from her parched and frantic lips. He knew it couldn't be, he knew that she was safe within the house, but still the wind persisted as a woman's cry. The cry of a woman with eyes like those that watched him through the dark. Eyes that were mad now—lips that even as they cried still pleaded, "See, Paul—I stand like this all day. I just stand still—so caged! If I could only run!"

He saw her running, pulled and driven headlong by the wind, but when at last he returned to the house, compelled by his anxiety, she was walking quietly back and forwards with the baby in her arms. Careful, despite his concern, not to reveal a fear or weakness that she might think capitulation to her wishes, he watched a moment through the window, and then went off to the tool shed to mend old harness. All afternoon he stitched and rivetted. It was easier with the lantern lit and his hands occupied. There was wind whining high past the tool shed too, but it was only wind. He remembered the arguments with which Ellen had tried to persuade him away from the farm, and one by one he defeated them. There would be rain again—next year, or the next. Maybe she was right. Maybe in his ignorance he had farmed his land the wrong way, seeding wheat every year, working the soil till it was lifeless dust—but he would do better now. He would plant clover and alfalfa, breed cattle, acre by acre and year by year restore to his land its fibre and fertility. That was something to work for, a way to prove himself. It was ruthless wind, blackening the sky with his earth, screaming in derision of his labour, but it was not his master. Out of his land it had made a wilderness. He now, out of the wilderness, would make a farm and home again.

To-night he must talk with Ellen. Patiently, when the wind was down, and they were both quiet again. It was she who had told him to grow fibrous crops, who had called him an ignorant fool because he kept on with summer fallow and wheat. Now she might be gratified to find him acknowledging her wisdom. Perhaps she would begin to feel the power and steadfastness of the land, to take a pride in it, to understand that he was not a fool, but working for her future and their son's.

And already the wind was slackening. At four o'clock he could sense a lull. At five, straining his eyes from the tool shed doorway, he could make out a neighbour's buildings half a mile away. It was over—three days of blight and havoc like a scourge—three days so bitter and so long that for a moment he stood still, unseeing, his senses idle with a numbness of relief.

But only for a moment. Suddenly he emerged from the numbness; suddenly the fields before him struck his eyes to comprehension. They lay black, naked. Beaten and mounded smooth with dust as if a sea in gentle swell had turned to stone. And though he had tried to prepare himself for such a scene, though he had known since yesterday that not a blade would last the storm, still now, before the utter waste confronting him, he sickened and stood cold. Suddenly like the fields he was naked. Everything that had sheathed him a little from the realities of existence: vision and purpose, faith in the land, in the future, in himself—it was all rent now, all stripped away. "Desert," he heard her voice begin to sob. "Desert, you fool—the lamp lit at noon!"

In the stable again, measuring out their feed to the horses, he wondered what he would say to her to-night. For so deep were his instincts of loyalty to the land that still, even with the images of its betrayal stark upon his mind, his concern was how to withstand her, how to go on again and justify himself. It had not occurred to him yet that he might or should abandon the land. He had lived with it too long. Rather was his impulse to defend it still— as a man defends against the scorn of strangers even his most worthless kin.

He fed his horses, then waited. She too would be waiting, ready to cry at him, "Look now—that crop that was to feed and clothe us! And you'll still keep on! You'll still say 'Next year—there'll be rain next year'!"

But she was gone when he reached the house. The door was open, the lamp blown out, the crib empty. The dishes from their meal at noon were still on the table. She had perhaps begun to sweep, for the broom was lying in the middle of the floor. He tried to call, but a terror clamped upon his throat. In the wan, returning light it seemed that even the deserted kitchen was straining to whisper what it had seen. The tatters of the storm still whimpered through the eaves, and in their moaning told the desolation of the miles they had traversed. On tiptoe at last he crossed to the adjoining room; then at the threshold, without even a glance inside to satisfy himself that she was really gone, he wheeled again and plunged outside.

He ran a long time—distraught and headlong as a few hours ago he had seemed to watch her run—around the farmyard, a little distance into the pasture, back again blindly to the house to see whether she had returned—and then at a stumble down the road for help.

They joined him in the search, rode away for others, spread calling across the fields in the direction she might have been carried by the wind—but nearly two hours later it was himself who came upon her. Crouched down against a drift of sand as if for shelter, her hair in matted stands around her neck and face, the child clasped tightly in her arms.

The child was quite cold. It had been her arms, perhaps, too frantic to protect him, or the smother of dust upon his throat and lungs. "Hold him," she said as he knelt beside her. "So—with his face away from the wind. Hold him until I tidy my hair."

Her eyes were still wide in an immobile stare, but with her lips she smiled at him. For a long time he knelt transfixed, trying to speak to her, touching fearfully with his fingertip the dust-grimed cheeks and eyelids of the child. At last she said, "I'll take him again. Such clumsy hands—you don't know how to hold a baby yet. See how his head falls forward on your arms."

Yet it all seemed familiar—a confirmation of what he had known since noon. He gave her the child, then, gathering them both up in his arms, struggled to his feet and turned towards home.

It was evening now. Across the fields a few spent clouds of dust still shook and fled. Beyond, as if through smoke, the sunset smouldered like a distant fire.

He walked with a long dull stride, his eyes before him, heedless of her weight. Once he glanced down and with her eyes she still was smiling. "Such strong arms, Paul—and I was so tired with carrying just him . . ."

He tried to answer, but it seemed that now the dusk was drawn apart in breathless wait-ing, a finger on its lips until they passed. "You were right, Paul—" Her voice came whis-pering, as if she too could feel the hush. "You said to-night we'd see the storm go down. So still now, and the sky burning—it means to-morrow will be fine."
1938   1968

A. M. KLEIN (1909-1972)

Abraham Moses Klein was born in Montreal on February 14, 1909, the son of Jewish immigrants from Eastern Europe. He attended McGill Uni-versity from 1926 to 1930, and then studied law at the University of Montreal. He practised law in Montreal almost continuously since complet-ing his legal training in 1933.

Klein began to write and publish poetry while an undergraduate at McGill. He published four books of verse—*Hath Not a Jew* (1940), *Poems* (1944), *The Hitleriad* (1944), and *The Rocking Chair* (1948)—and one novel, *The Second Scroll* (1951). He also did a great deal of writing for Jewish periodicals, edited the *Canadian Jewish Chronicle*, and made an intensive study of James Joyce.

Klein's earlier poetry was concerned almost exclusively with the joys and sorrows of the Jew-ish people; in his later work he turned his atten-tion to his French-Canadian neighbours in the province of Quebec. He was a poet of strong feelings, who alternated between exaltation and lamentation something in the manner of the an-cient Psalmist of Israel. He was especially adept at seeing symbolic meanings in ordinary objects, and in re-creating experiences of physical exhil-aration such as swimming and snow-shoeing.

Illness forced a gradual retirement from writ-ing in the fifties; he died in 1972.

Autobiographical

Out of the ghetto streets where a Jewboy
Dreamed pavement into pleasant bible-land,
Out of the Yiddish slums where childhood met
The friendly beard, the loutish Sabbath-goy[1],
Or followed, proud, the Torah[2]-escorting band
Out of the jargoning city I regret
Rise memories, like sparrows rising from
The gutter-scattered oats,
Like sadness sweet of synagogal hum,
Like Hebrew violins   10
Sobbing delight upon their eastern notes.

[1]Goy: a Gentile, a non-Jew.   A Sabbath-goy turns on lights, lights stoves, etc. on the Sabbath
for an orthodox Jew; also a Jew who performs these functions.
[2]Name applied to the five books of Moses: Genesis, Exodus, Leviticus, Numbers, Deuteronomy.

Again they ring their little bells, those doors
Deemed by the tender-year'd, magnificent:
Old Ashkenazi's cellar, sharp with spice;
The widow's double-parloured candy-stores
And nuggets sweet bought for one sweaty cent;
The warm fresh-smelling bakery, its pies,
Its cakes, its navel'd bellies of black bread;
The lintels candy-poled
Of barber-shop, bright-bottled, green, blue, red;   20
And fruit-stall piled, exotic,
And the big synagogue door, with letters of gold.

Again my kindergarten home is full—
Saturday night—with kin and compatriot;
My brothers playing Russian card-games: my
Mirroring sisters looking beautiful
Humming the evening's imminent fox-trot;
My uncle Mayer, of blessed memory,
Still murmuring Maariv³, counting holy words;
And the two strangers, come   30
Fiery from Volhynia's⁴ murderous hordes—
The cards and humming stop.
And I too swear revenge for the pogrom.

Occasions dear: the four-legged aleph named
And angel pennies dropping on my book;
The rabbi patting a coming scholar-head;
My mother, blessing candles, Sabbath-flamed,
Queenly in her Warsovian perruque;
My father pickabacking me to bed
To tell tall tales about the Baal Shem Tov⁵,   40
Letting me curl his beard.
O memory of unsurpassing love,
Love leading a brave child
Through childhood's ogred corridors, unfear'd.

The week in the country at my brother's (May
He own fat cattle in the fields of heaven!)
Its picking of strawberries from grassy ditch,
Its odour of dogrose and of yellowing hay,—
Dusty, adventurous, sunny days, all seven!—

³The evening prayer.   ⁴An area in the Ukraine, site of a vicious attack upon the Jews in the late
  nineteenth century. These attacks were called "pogroms."
⁵Baal Shem Tov (1700-1760), a Hebrew teacher and healer of Eastern Europe, who founded
  the sect of Hasidim. He stressed an optimistic, joyful type of religion.

Still follow me, still warm me, still are rich
With the cow-tinkling peace of pastureland.
The meadow'd memory
Is sodded with its clover, and is spanned   50
By that same pillow'd sky
A boy on his back one day watched enviously.

And paved again the street; the shouting boys
Oblivious of mothers on the stoops
Playing the robust robbers and police,
The corn-cob battle,—all high-spirited noise
Competitive among the lot-drawn groups.   60
Another day, of shaken apple-trees
In the rich suburbs, and a furious dog
And guilty boys in flight;
Hazelnut games[6], and games in the synagogue,
The burrs[7], the Haman rattle[8],
The Torah-dance of Simchas-Torah night[9].

Immortal days of the picture-calendar
Dear to me always with the virgin joy
Of the first flowing of senses five

Discovering birds, or textures, or a star,   70
Or tastes sweet, sour, acid, those that cloy,
And perfumes. Never was I more alive.
All days thereafter are a dying-off,
A wandering away
From home and the familiar. The years doff
Their innocence.
No other day is ever like that day.

I am no old man fatuously intent
On memoirs, but in memory I seek
The strength and vividness of nonage days,   80
Not tranquil recollection of event.
It is a fabled city that I seek;

---

[6]Jewish children play with hazelnuts at the feast of the Passover.
[7]On the first day commemorating the destruction of the Temple in Jerusalem, Jewish
    people often throw burrs at one another to lighten an otherwise solemn and sad day.
[8]Haman rattle. The Book of Esther tells the story of Haman's attempts to destroy the
    Jewish people, and of Esther's success in defeating his attempts. On the Feast of
    Esther, the Book is read in the synagogue; each time Haman's name is mentioned, the
    children shake rattles.
[9]Portions of the Torah are read in the synagogue in order throughout the year. When the five
    books have all been read, and it is time to start again with Genesis, a dance or other
    celebration is frequently held.

It stands in space's vapours and Time's haze;
Thence comes my sadness in remembered joy
Constrictive of the throat;
Thence do I hear, as heard by a Jewboy
The Hebrew violins,
Delighting in the sobbed oriental note.

1943

The Rocking Chair

It seconds the crickets of the province. Heard
in the clean lamplit farmhouses of Quebec,—
wooden,—it is no less a national bird;
and rivals, in its cage, the mere stuttering clock.
To its time, the evenings are rolled away;
and in its peace the pensive mother knits
contentment to be worn by her family,
grown-up, but still cradled by the chair in which she sits.

It is also the old man's pet, pair to his pipe,
the two aids of his arithmetic and plans,   10
plans rocking and puffing into market-shape;
and it is the toddler's game and dangerous dance.
Moved to the verandah, on summer Sundays, it is,
among the hanging plants, the girls, the boy-friends,
sabbatical and clumsy, like the white haloes
dangling above the blue serge suits of the young men.

It has a personality of its own;
is a character (like that old drunk Lacoste,
exhaling amber, and toppling on his pins);
it is alive; individual; and no less   20
an identity than those about it. And
it is tradition. Centuries have been flicked
from its arcs, alternately flicked and pinned.
It rolls with the gait of St. Malo. It is act

and symbol, symbol of this static folk
which moves in segments, and returns to base,—
a sunken pendulum: *invoke, revoke;*
loosed yon, leashed hither, motion on no space.

O, like some Anjou ballad, all refrain,
which turns about its longing, and seems to move   30
to make a pleasure out of repeated pain,
its music moves, as if always back to a first love.

                                                              1948

For the Sisters of the Hôtel Dieu

In pairs,
as if to illustrate their sisterhood,
the sisters pace the hospital garden walks.
In their robes black and white immaculate hoods
they are like birds,
the safe domestic fowl of the House of God.

O biblic birds,
who fluttered to me in my childhood illnesses
—me little, afraid, ill, not of your race,—
the cool wing for my fever, the hovering solace,
the sense of angels—
be thanked, O plumage of paradise, be praised.

                                                              1948

Lookout: Mount Royal

Remembering boyhood, it is always here
the boy in blouse and kneepants on the road
trailing his stick over the hopscotched sun;
or here, upon the suddenly moving hill;
or at the turned tap its cold white mandarin[1] mustaches;
or at the lookout, finally,
breathing easy, standing still

to click the eye on motion forever stopped:
the photographer's tripod and his sudden faces
buoyed up by water on his magnet caught   10
still smiling as if under water still;
the exclamatory tourists descending the caleches[2];
the maids in starch; the ladies in white gloves;
other kids of other slums and races;

[1] A public official in the Chinese empire.
[2] A two-wheeled, horse-drawn vehicle used in Quebec.

and on the bridle-paths
the horsemen on their horses like the tops of f's:

or from the parapet make out
beneath the green marine
the discovered road, the hospital's romantic

gables and roofs, and all the civic Euclid[3]   20
running through sunken parallels and lolling
in diamond and square, then proud-pedantical[4]
with spire and dome
making its way to the sought point, his home.

home recognized: there: to be returned to—

lets the full birdseye circle to the river,
its singsong bridges, its mapmaker curves, its
island with the two shades of green, meadow and wood;
and circles round that water-tower'd coast;
then, to the remote rhapsodic mountains; then,   30
—and to be lost—
to clouds like white slow friendly animals
which all the afternoon across his eyes
will move their paced spaced footfalls.
1946-47   1948

[3]Father of geometry in ancient Greece.
[4]Boastful of one's learning.

IRVING LAYTON (1912-   )

During World War II, a second poetic movement began in Montreal. At first it centred in three little magazines, *Preview, First Statement*, and their joint successor, *Northern Review*. Associated with the movement were Patrick Anderson, P. K. Page, Irving Layton, Louis Dudek, Miriam Waddington, Raymond Souster of Toronto, and John Sutherland. These poets had in common a desire to make their poetry out of the lives and speech of the people around them, and to face squarely the political and social issues of their generation. They were left-wingers in politics, and were often angry at the injustice and complacency they saw about them.

Of this group, Irving Layton has gradually won recognition as the outstanding poet, although most of the others are still active. Layton was born in 1912 in Rumania, but was brought to Montreal as an infant by his parents. He went to Macdonald College during the depression on a government scholarship, and received his B.Sc. in Agriculture in 1939. During World War II he served in the Canadian Army, and on his discharge in 1943 he returned to Montreal and became active in the *First Statement* group. He also did postgraduate work in economics and political science at McGill, receiving his M.A. in 1946. He later taught at Montreal's Sir George Williams College (now Concordia University), the Herziliah High School, in various adult education centres and at York University in Toronto. His first volume of verse, *Here and Now*, was published in 1946, and it has been followed by over a dozen others. His collected poems, *Red Carpet for the Sun*, won the Governor General's Award as the best book of verse published in Canada in 1959, and another *Collected Poems* appeared in 1965. *The Unwavering Eye: Selected Poems 1969-75* appeared in 1975.

Layton is a complex and versatile poet. He can be tender and angry, humorous and bitter, sub-tle and coarse, joyful and sad in turn; he can write perceptive descriptions of the slum streets of a big city and equally observant pictures of natural scenery. But in all his work we can detect his fierce honesty and his intense vitality, his excitement at being himself.

Song for Naomi

Who is that in the tall grasses singing
By herself, near the water?
I can not see her
But can it be her
Than whom the grasses so tall
Are taller,
My daughter,
My lovely daughter?

Who is that in the tall grasses running
Beside her, near the water?   10
She can not see there
Time that pursued her
In the deep grasses so fast
And faster
And caught her,
My foolish daughter.

What is the wind in the fair grass saying
Like a verse, near the water?
Saviours that over
All things have power   20
Make Time himself grow kind
And kinder
That sought her,
My little daughter.

Who is that at the close of the summer
Near the deep lake? Who wrought her
Comely and slender?
Time but attends and befriends her
Than whom the grasses though tall
Are not taller,   30
My daughter,
My gentle daughter.

1955

Anglo-Canadian

A native of Kingston, Ont.
—two grandparents Canadian
and still living

His complexion florid
as a maple leaf in late autumn,

for three years he attended
Oxford

Now his accent
makes even Englishmen
wince, and feel
unspeakably colonial.

1956

The Bull Calf

The thing could barely stand. Yet taken
from his mother and the barn smells
he still impressed with his pride

with the promise of sovereignty in the way
his head moved to take us in.
The fierce sunlight tugging the maize from the ground
licked at his shapely flanks.
He was too young for all that pride.
I thought of the deposed Richard II.

"No money in bull calves," Freeman had said.   10
The visiting clergyman rubbed the nostrils
now snuffing pathetically at the windless day.
"A pity," he sighed.
My gaze slipped off his hat toward the empty sky
that circled over the black knot of men,
over us and the calf waiting for the first blow.
Struck,
the bull calf drew in his thin forelegs
as if gathering strength for a mad rush . . .
tottered . . . raised his darkening eyes to us,   20
and I saw we were at the far end
of his frightened look, growing smaller and smaller
till we were only the ponderous mallet
that flicked his bleeding ear
and pushed him over on his side, stiffly,
like a block of wood.

Below the hill's crest
the river snuffled on the improvised beach.
We dug a deep pit and threw the dead calf into it.
It made a wet sound, a sepulchral gurgle,   30
as the warm sides bulged and flattened.
Settled, the bull calf lay as if asleep,
one foreleg over the other,
bereft of pride and so beautiful now,
without movement, perfectly still in the cool pit.
I turned away and wept.

                                                       1956

Keine Lazarovitch 1870-1959 [1]

When I saw my mother's head on the cold pillow,
Her white waterfalling hair in the cheeks' hollows,
I thought, quietly circling my grief, of how
She had loved God but cursed extravagantly his creatures.

[1] The poet's mother.

For her final mouth was not water but a curse,
A small black hole, a black rent in the universe,
Which damned the green earth, stars and trees in its stillness
And the inescapable lousiness of growing old.

And I record she was comfortless, vituperative,
Ignorant, glad, and much else besides; I believe   10
She endlessly praised her black eyebrows, their thick weave,
Till plagiarizing Death leaned down and took them for his mould.

And spoiled a dignity I shall not again find,
And the fury of her stubborn limited mind;
Now none will shake her amber beads and call God blind,
Or wear them upon a breast so radiantly.

O fierce she was, mean and unaccommodating;
But I think now of the toss of her gold earrings,
Their proud carnal assertion, and her youngest sings
While all the rivers of her red veins move into the sea.   20
1945-68   1960

RAYMOND SOUSTER (1921-   )

Born in Toronto in 1921, Raymond Souster is thought of as a poet of that city. He has published more than a dozen collections, ranging from *When We are Young* (1946) to his collected poems, *The Colour of the Times* (which won the Governor-General's Award in 1964) to his most recent volume *Hanging In* (1979). He has also edited several anthologies of Canadian poetry.

Souster is a poet with a strong sociological impulse—that is, his poetry attempts to record the human condition at a particular point in history.

Like other young poets writing during the Second World War, he voiced working class concerns in a direct and colloquial manner. Throughout his career, Souster has sided with the victims of today's industrial society, celebrating the outcast's ability to survive and criticizing the instruments of mechanization and human waste. His best poems are based on direct observation of his immediate environment, sometimes with a quick flash of fantasy.

Flight of the Roller-Coaster

Once more around should do it, the man confided . . .

and sure enough, when the roller-coaster reached the peak
of the giant curve above me, screech of its wheels
almost drowned out by the shriller cries of the riders,

instead of the dip and plunge with its landslide of screams,
it rose in the air like a movieland magic carpet,
   some wonderful bird,

and without fuss or fanfare swooped slowly across
   the amusement-park,
over Spook's Castle, ice-cream booths, shooting-gallery.   10
   and losing no height

made the last yards above the beach, where the cucumber-cool
brakeman in the last seat saluted
a lady about to change from her bathing-suit.

Then, as many witnesses report, headed leisurely
   out over the water,
disappearing all too soon behind a low-flying flight of clouds.
1955   1955

Downtown Corner News Stand

It will need all of death to take you from this corner.
It has become your world, and you its unshaved
bleary-eyed, foot-stamping king. In winter
you curse the cold, huddled in your coat from the wind,
you fry in summer like an egg hopping on a griddle;
and always the whining voice, the nervous-flinging arms,
the red face, shifting eyes watching, waiting
under the grimy cap for God knows what
to happen. (But nothing ever does, downtown Toronto
goes to sleep and wakes the next morning   10
always the same, except a little dirtier.)
And you stand with your armful of *Stars* and *Telys*,[1]
the peak of your cap well down against the sun,
and all the city's restless seething river
surges beside you, but not once do you plunge
into its flood, are carried or tossed away:
but reappear always, beard longer than ever, nose running,
to catch the noon editions at King and Bay.

                                           1964

[1]Toronto's daily newspapers at this time were *The Toronto Star* and *The Toronto Telegram*.

MARGARET LAURENCE (1926-   )

Margaret Laurence has been the leading Canadian novelist of the past two decades; *The Stone Angel* (1964) is one of the most celebrated Canadian novels of the century. Her fiction explores the impact of small-town customs and conventions on individual lives—especially the lives of women—and the quest for the strength to overcome restrictions placed upon them.

Laurence was born in Neepawa, Manitoba. In 1947, after graduating from college in Winnipeg, she travelled with her husband, a civil engineer, to West Africa and then to England. Her first three books all dealt with life in Africa—the novel *This Side Jordan* (1960), *The Tomorrow-*

Tamer and Other Stories (1963), and the travelogue, *The Prophet's Camel-Bell* (1963). However, it is in the novels set closer to home that her skilful blending of psychological and social realism, along with a powerful use of symbolism, is most evident. The *Manawaka* books—four novels (*The Stone Angel, A Jest of God, The Fire-Dwellers* and *The Diviners*) and a collection of stories (*A Bird in the House*)—study individuals in the imaginary Canadian town of Manawaka. In the story which follows, taken from *A Bird in the House*, we are invited to enter the complex world of a young girl's emotions.

To Set Our House in Order

When the baby was almost ready to be born, something went wrong and my mother had to go into hospital two weeks before the expected time. I was wakened by her crying in the night, and then I heard my father's footsteps as he went downstairs to phone. I stood in the doorway of my room, shivering and listening, wanting to go to my mother but afraid to go lest there be some sight there more terrifying than I could bear.

"Hello—Paul?" my father said, and I knew he was talking to Dr. Cates. "It's Beth. The waters have broken, and the fetal position doesn't seem quite—well, I'm only thinking of what happened the last time, and another like that would be—I wish she were a little huskier, damn it—she's so—no, don't worry, I'm quite all right. Yes, I think that would be the best thing. Okay, make it as soon as you can, will you?"

He came back upstairs, looking bony and dishevelled in his pyjamas, and running his fingers through his sand-coloured hair. At the top of the stairs, he came face to face with Grandmother MacLeod, who was standing there in her quilted black satin dressing gown, her slight figure held straight and poised, as though she were unaware that her hair was bound grotesquely like white-feathered wings in the snare of her coarse night-time hairnet.

"What is it, Ewen?"

"It's all right, Mother. Beth's having—a little trouble. I'm going to take her into the hospital. You go back to bed."

"I told you," Grandmother MacLeod said in her clear voice, never loud, but distinct and ringing like the tap of a sterling teaspoon on a crystal goblet, "I did tell you, Ewen, did I not, that you should have got a girl in to help her with the housework? She would have rested more."

"I couldn't afford to get anyone in," my father said. "If you thought she should've rested more, why didn't you ever—Oh God, I'm out of my mind tonight—just go back to bed, Mother, please. I must get back to Beth."

When my father went down to the front door to let Dr. Cates in, my need overcame my fear and I slipped into my parents' room. My mother's black hair, so neatly pinned up during the day, was startlingly spread across the white pillowcase. I stared at her, not speaking, and then she smiled and I rushed from the doorway and buried my head upon her.

"It's all right, honey," she said. "Listen, Vanessa, the baby's just going to come a little early, that's all. You'll be all right. Grandmother MacLeod will be here."

"How can she get the meals?" I wailed, fixing on the first thing that came to mind. "She never cooks. She doesn't know how."

"Yes she does," my mother said. "She can cook as well as anyone when she has to. She's just never had to very much, that's all. Don't worry—she'll keep everything in order, and then some."

My father and Dr. Cates came in, and I had to go, without ever saying anything I had wanted to say. I went back to my own room and lay with the shadows all around me. I listened to the night murmurings that always went on in that house, sounds which never had a source, rafters and beams contracting in the dry air, perhaps, or mice in the walls, or a sparrow that had flown into the attic through the broken skylight there. After a while, although I would not have believed it possible, I slept.

The next morning I questioned my father. I believed him to be not only the best doctor in Manawaka, but also the best doctor in the whole of Manitoba, if not in the entire world, and the fact that he was not the one looking after my mother seemed to have something sinister about it.

"But it's always done that way, Vanessa," he explained. "Doctors never attend members of their own family. It's because they care so much about them, you see, and—"

"And what?" I insisted, alarmed at the way he had broken off. But my father did not reply. He stood there, and then he put on that difficult smile with which adults seek to conceal pain from children. I felt terrified, and ran to him, and he held me tightly.

"She's going to be fine," he said. "Honestly she is. Nessa, don't cry—"

Grandmother MacLeod appeared beside us, steel-spined despite her apparent fragility. She was wearing a purple silk dress and her ivory pendant. She looked as though she were all ready to go out for afternoon tea.

"Ewen, you're only encouraging the child to give way," she said. "Vanessa, big girls of ten don't make such a fuss about things. Come and get your breakfast. Now, Ewen, you're not to worry. I'll see to everything."

Summer holidays were not quite over, but I did not feel like going out to play with any of the kids. I was very superstitious, and I had the feeling that if I left the house, even for a few hours, some disaster would overtake my mother. I did not, of course, mention this feeling to Grandmother MacLeod, for she did not believe in the existence of fear, or if she did, she never let on. I spent the morning morbidly, in seeking hidden places in the house. There were many of these—odd-shaped nooks under the stairs, small and loosely nailed-up doors at the back of clothes closets, leading to dusty tunnels and forgotten recesses in the heart of the house where the only things actually to be seen were drab oil paintings stacked upon the rafters, and trunks full of outmoded clothing and old photograph albums. But the unseen presences in these secret places I knew to be those of every person, young or old, who had ever belonged to the house and had died, including Uncle Roderick who got killed on the Somme[1], and the baby who would have been my sister if

[1]World War I battle.

only she had managed to come to life. Grandfather MacLeod, who had died a year after I was born, was present in the house in more tangible form. At the top of the main stairs hung the mammoth picture of a darkly uniformed man riding upon a horse whose prancing stance and dilated nostrils suggested that the battle was not yet over, that it might indeed continue until Judgment Day. The stern man was actually the Duke of Wellington, but at the time I believed him to be my grandfather MacLeod, still keeping an eye on things.

We had moved in with Grandmother MacLeod when the Depression got bad and she could no longer afford a housekeeper, but the MacLeod house never seemed like home to me. Its dark red brick was grown over at the front with Virginia creeper that turned crimson in the fall, until you could hardly tell brick from leaves. It boasted a small tower in which Grandmother MacLeod kept a weedy collection of anaemic ferns. The verandah was embellished with a profusion of wrought-iron scrolls, and the circular rose-window upstairs contained glass of many colours which permitted an outlooking eye to see the world as a place of absolute sapphire or emerald, or if one wished to look with a jaundiced eye, a hateful yellow. In Grandmother MacLeod's opinion, their features gave the house style.

Inside, a multitude of doors led to rooms where my presence, if not actually forbidden, was not encouraged. One was Grandmother MacLeod's bedroom, with its stale and old-smelling air, the dim reek of medicines and lavender sachets. Here resided her monogrammed dresser silver, brush and mirror, nail-buffer and button hook and scissors, none of which must even be fingered by me now, for she meant to leave them to me in her will and intended to hand them over in the same flawless and unused condition in which they had always keen kept. Here, too, were the silver-framed photographs of Uncle Roderick—as a child, as a boy, as a man in his Army iniform. The massive walnut spool bed had obviously been designed for queens or giants, and my tiny grandmother used to lie within it all day when she had migraine, contriving somehow to look like a giant queen.

The living room was another alien territory where I had to tread warily, for many valuable objects sat just-so on tables and mantelpiece, and dirt must not be tracked in upon the blue Chinese carpet with its birds in eternal motionless flight and its water-lily buds caught forever just before the point of opening. My mother was always nervous when I was in this room.

"Vanessa, honey," she would say, half apologetically, "why don't you go and play in the den, or upstairs?"

"Can't you leave her, Beth?" my father would say. "She's not doing any harm."

"I'm only thinking of the rug," my mother would say, glancing at Grandmother MacLeod, "and yesterday she nearly knocked the Dresden shepherdess off the mantel. I mean, she can't help it, Ewen, she has to run around—"

"Goddamn it, I know she can't help it," my father would growl, glaring at the smirking face of the Dresden shepherdess.

"I see no need to blaspheme, Ewen," Grandmother MacLeod would say quietly, and then my father would say he was sorry, and I would leave.

The day my mother went to the hospital, Grandmother MacLeod called me at lunchtime, and when I appeared, smudged with dust from the attic, she looked at me distastefully as though I had been a cockroach that had just crawled impertinently out of the woodwork.

"For mercy's sake, Vanessa, what have you been doing with yourself? Run and get washed this minute. Here, not that way—you use the back stairs, young lady. Get along now. Oh—your father phoned."

I swung around. "What did he say? How is she? Is the baby born?"

"Curiosity killed a cat," Grandmother MacLeod said, frowning. "I cannot understand Beth and Ewen telling you all these things at your age. What sort of vulgar person you'll grow up to·be, I dare not think. No, it's not born yet. Your mother's just the same. No change."

I looked at my grandmother, not wanting to appeal to her, but unable to stop myself. "Will she—will she be all right?"

Grandmother MacLeod straightened her already-straight back. "If I said definitely yes, Vanessa, that would be a lie, and the MacLeods do not tell lies, as I have tried to impress on you before. What happens is God's will. The Lord giveth, and the Lord taketh away."

Appalled, I turned away so she would not see my face and my eyes. Surprisingly, I heard her sigh and felt her papery white and perfectly manicured hand upon my shoulder.

"When your Uncle Roderick got killed," she said, "I thought I would die. But I didn't die, Vanessa."

At lunch, she chatted animatedly, and I realised she was trying to cheer me in the only way she knew.

"When I married your Grandfather MacLeod," she related, "he said to me, 'Eleanor, don't think because we're going to the prairies that I expect you to live roughly. You're used to a proper house, and you shall have one.' He was as good as his word. Before we'd been in Manawaka three years, he'd had this place built. He earned a good deal of money in his time, your grandfather. He soon had more patients than either of the other doctors. We ordered our dinner service and all our silver from Birks' in Toronto. We had resident help in those days, of course, and never had less than twelve guests for dinner parties. When I had a tea, it would always be twenty or thirty. Never any less than half a dozen different kinds of cake were ever served in this house. Well, no one seems to bother much these days. Too lazy, I suppose."

"Too broke," I suggested. "That's what Dad says."

"I can't bear slang," Grandmother MacLeod said. "If you mean hard up, why don't you say so? It's mainly a question of management, anyway. My accounts were always in good order, and so was my house. No unexpected expenses that couldn't be met, no fruit cellar running out of preserves before the winter was over. Do you know what my father used to say to me when I was a girl?"

"No," I said. "What?"

"God loves Order," Grandmother MacLeod replied with emphasis. "You remember that, Vanessa. God loves Order—he wants each one of us to set our house in order. I've never forgotten those words of my father's. I was a MacInnes before I got married. The MacInnes is a very ancient clan, the lairds of Morven and the constables of the Castle of Kinlochaline. Did you finish that book I gave you?"

"Yes," I said. Then, feeling some additional comment to be called for, "It was a swell book, Grandmother."

This was somewhat short of the truth. I had been hoping for her cairngorm brooch on my tenth birthday, and had received instead the plaid-bound volume entitled *The Clans and Tartans of Scotland*. Most of it was too boring to read, but I had looked up the motto of my own family and those of some of my friends' families. *Be then a wall of brass. Learn to suffer. Consider the end. Go carefully*. I had not found any of these slogans reassuring. What with Mavis Duncan learning to suffer, and Laura Kennedy considering the end, and Patsy Drummond going carefully, and I spending my time in being a wall of brass, it did not seem to me that any of us were going to lead very interesting lives. I did not say this to Grandmother MacLeod.

"The MacInnes motto is *Pleasure Arises from Work*," I said.

"Yes," she agreed proudly. "And an excellent motto it is, too. One to bear in mind."

She rose from the table, rearranging on her bosom the looped ivory beads that held the pendant on which a full-blown ivory rose was stiffly carved.

"I hope Ewen will be pleased," she said.

"What at?"

"Didn't I tell you?" Grandmother MacLeod said. "I hired a girl this morning, for the housework. She's to start tomorrow."

When my father got home that evening, Grandmother MacLeod told him her good news. He ran one hand distractedly across his forehead.

"I'm sorry, Mother, but you'll just have to unhire her. I can't possibly pay anyone."

"It seems distinctly odd," Grandmother MacLeod snapped, "that you can afford to eat chicken four times a week."

"Those chickens," my father said in an exasperated voice, "are how people are paying their bills. The same with the eggs and the milk. That scrawny turkey that arrived yesterday was for Logan MacCardney's appendix, if you must know. We probably eat better than any family in Manawaka, except Niall Cameron's. People can't entirely dispense with doctors or undertakers. That doesn't mean to say I've got any cash. Look, Mother, I don't know what's happening with Beth. Paul thinks he may have to do a Caesarean. Can't we leave all this? Just leave the house alone. Don't touch it. What does it matter?"

"I have never lived in a messy house, Ewen," Grandmother MacLeod said, "and I don't intend to begin now."

"Oh Lord," my father said. "Well, I'll phone Edna, I guess, and see if she can give us a hand, although God knows she's got enough, with the Connor house and her parents to look after."

"I don't fancy having Edna Connor in to help," Grandmother MacLeod objected.

"Why not?" my father shouted. "She's Beth's sister, isn't she?"

"She speaks in such a slangy way," Grandmother MacLeod said. "I have never believed she was a good influence on Vanessa. And there is no need for you to raise your voice to me, Ewen, if you please."

I could barely control my rage. I thought my father would surely rise to Aunt Edna's defence. But he did not.

"It'll be all right," he soothed her. "She'd only be here for part of the day, Mother. You could stay in your room."

Aunt Edna strode in the next morning. The sight of her bobbed black hair and her grin made me feel better at once. She hauled out the carpet sweeper and the weighted polisher and got to work. I dusted while she polished and swept, and we got through the living room and front hall in next to no time.

"Where's her royal highness, kiddo?" she enquired.

"In her room," I said. "She's reading the catalogue from Robinson & Cleaver."

"Good Glory, not again?" Aunt Edna cried. "The last time she ordered three linen tea-clothes and two dozen serviettes. It came to fourteen dollars. Your mother was absolutely frantic. I guess I shouldn't be saying this."

"I knew anyway," I assured her. "She was at the lace handkerchiefs section when I took up her coffee."

"Let's hope she stays there. Heaven forbid she should get onto the banqueting cloths. Well, at least she believes the Irish are good for two things—manual labour and linen-making. She's never forgotten Father used to be a blacksmith, before he got the hardware store. Can you beat it? I wish it didn't bother Beth."

"Does it?" I asked, and immediately realised this was a wrong move, for Aunt Edna was suddenly scrutinising me.

"We're making you grow up before your time," she said. "Don't pay any attention to me, Nessa. I must've got up on the wrong side of the bed this morning."

But I was unwilling to leave the subject.

"All the same," I said thoughtfully, "Grandmother Macleod's family were the lairds of Morven and the constables of the Castle of Kinlochaline. I bet you didn't know that."

Aunt Edna snorted, "Castle, my foot. She was born in Ontario, just like your Grand-father Connor, and her father was a horse doctor. Come on, kiddo, we'd better shut up and get down to business here."

We worked in silence for a while.

"Aunt Edna—" I said at last, "what about Mother? Why won't they let me go and see her?"

"Kids aren't allowed to visit maternity patients. It's tough for you, I know that. Look, Nessa, don't worry. If it doesn't start tonight, they're going to do the operation. She's get-ting the best of care."

I stood there, holding the feather duster like a dead bird in my hands. I was not aware that I was going to speak until the words came out.

"I'm scared," I said.

Aunt Edna put her arms around me, and her face looked all at once stricken and empty of defences.

"Oh, honey, I'm scared, too," she said.

It was this way that Grandmother MacLeod found us when she came stepping lightly down into the front hall with the order in her hand for two dozen lace-bordered hand-kerchiefs of pure Irish linen.

I could not sleep that night, and when I went downstairs, I found my father in the den. I sat down on the hassock beside his chair, and he told me about the operation my mother was to have the next morning. He kept on saying it was not serious nowadays.

"But you're worried." I put in, as though seeking to explain why I was.

"I should at least have been able to keep from burdening you with it," he said in a dis-tant voice, as though to himself. "If only the baby hadn't got itself twisted around—"

"Will it be born dead, like the little girl?"

"I don't know," my father said. "I hope not."

"She'd be disappointed, wouldn't she, if it was?" I said bleakly, wondering why I was not enough for her.

"Yes, she would," my father replied. "She won't be able to have any more, after this. It's partly on your account that she wants this one, Nessa. She doesn't want you to grow up without a brother or sister."

"As far as I'm concerned, she didn't need to bother," I retorted angrily.

My father laughed. "Well, let's talk about something else, and then maybe you'll be able to sleep. How did you and Grandmother make out today?"

"Oh, fine, I guess. What was Grandfather MacLeod like, Dad?"

"What did she tell you about him?"

"She said he made a lot of money in his time."

"Well, he wasn't any millionaire," my father said, "but I suppose he did quite well. That's not what I associate with him, though."

He reached across to the bookshelf, took out a small leather-bound volume and opened it. On the pages were mysterious marks, like doodling, only much neater and more patterned.

"What is it?" I asked.

"Greek," my father explained. "This is a play called *Antigone*. See, here's the title in English. There's a whole stack of them on the shelves there. *Oedipus Rex*. *Electra*. *Medea*. They belonged to your Grandfather MacLeod. He used to read them often."

"Why?" I enquired, unable to understand why anyone would pore over those undecipherable signs.

"He was interested in them," my father said. "He must have been a lonely man, although it never struck me that way at the time. Sometimes a thing only hits you a long time afterwards."

"Why would he be lonely?" I wanted to know.

"He was the only person in Manawaka who could read these plays in the original Greek," my father said. "I don't suppose many people, if anyone, had even read them in English translations. Maybe he would have liked to be a classical scholar—I don't know. But his father was a doctor, so that's what he was. Maybe he would have liked to talk to somebody about these plays. They must have meant a lot to him."

It seemed to me that my father was talking oddly. There was a sadness in his voice that I had never heard before, and I longed to say something that would make him feel better, but I could not, because I did not know what was the matter.

"Can you read this kind of writing?" I asked hesitantly.

My father shook his head. "Nope. I was never very intellectual, I guess. Rod was always brighter than I, in school, but even he wasn't interested in learning Greek. Perhaps he would've been later, if he'd lived. As a kid, all I ever wanted to do was go into the merchant marine."

"Why didn't you, then?"

"Oh well," my father said off-handedly, "a kid who'd never seen the sea wouldn't have made much of a sailor. I might have turned out to be the seasick type."

I had lost interest now that he was speaking once more like himself.

"Grandmother MacLeod was pretty cross today about the girl," I remarked.

"I know," my father nodded. "Well, we must be as nice as we can to her, Nessa, and after a while she'll be all right."

Suddenly I did not care what I said.

"Why can't she be nice to us for a change?" I burst out. "We're always the ones who have to be nice to her."

My father put his hand down and slowly tilted my head until I was forced to look at him.

"Vanessa," he said, "she's had troubles in her life which you really don't know much about. That's why she gets migraine sometimes and has to go to bed. It's not easy for her these days, either—the house is still the same, so she thinks other things should be, too. It hurts her when she finds they aren't."

"I don't see—" I began.

"Listen," my father said, "you know we were talking about what people are interested in, like Grandfather MacLeod being interested in Greek plays? Well, your grandmother was interested in being a lady, Nessa, and for a long time it seemed to her that she was one."

I thought of the Castle of Kinlochaline, and of horse doctors in Ontario.

"I didn't know—" I stammered.

"That's usually the trouble with most of us," my father said. "You go on up to bed now. I'll phone tomorrow from the hospital as soon as the operation's over."

I did sleep at last, and in my dreams I could hear the caught sparrow fluttering in the attic, and the sound of my mother crying, and the voices of the dead children.

My father did not phone until afternoon. Grandmother MacLeod said I was being silly, for you could hear the phone ringing all over the house, but nevertheless I refused to move out of the den. I had never before examined my father's books, but now, at a loss for something to do, I took them out one by one and read snatches here and there. After I had been doing this for several hours, it dawned on me that most of the books were of the same kind. I looked again at the titles.

Seven-League Boots. Arabia Deserta. The Seven Pillars of Wisdom. Travels in Tibet. Count Lucknor the Sea Devil. And a hundred more. On a shelf by themselves were copies of the *National Geographic* magazine, which I looked at often enough, but never before with the puzzling compulsion which I felt now, as though I were on the verge of some discovery, something which I had to find out and yet did not want to know. I riffled through the picture-filled pages. Hibiscus and wild orchids grew in a soft-petalled confusion. The Himalayas stood lofty as gods, with the morning sun on their peaks of snow. Leopards snarled from the vined depths of a thousand jungles. Schooners buffetted their white sails like the wings of giant angels against the great sea winds.

"What on earth are you doing?" Grandmother MacLeod enquired waspishly from the doorway. "You've got everything scattered all over the place. Pick it all up this minute, Vanessa, do you hear?"

So I picked up the books and magazines, and put them all neatly away, as I had been told to do.

When the telephone finally rang, I was afraid to answer it. At last I picked it up. My father sounded faraway, and the relief in his voice made it unsteady.

"It's okay, honey. Everything's fine. The boy was born alive and kicking after all. Your mother's pretty weak, but she's going to be all right."

I could hardly believe it. I did not want to talk to anyone. I wanted to be by myself, to assimilate the presence of my brother, towards whom, without ever having seen him yet, I felt such tenderness and such resentment.

That evening, Grandmother MacLeod approached my father, who, still dazed with the unexpected gift of neither life now being threatened, at first did not take her seriously when she asked what they planned to call the child.

"Oh, I don't know. Hank, maybe, or Joe. Fauntleroy, perhaps."

She ignored his levity.

"Ewen," she said, "I wish you would call him Roderick."

My father's face changed. "I'd rather not."

"I think you should," Grandmother MacLeod insisted, very quietly, but in a voice as pointed and precise as her silver nail-scissors.

"Don't you think Beth ought to decide?" my father asked.

"Beth will agree if you do."

My father did not bother to deny something that even I knew to be true. He did not say anything. Then Grandmother MacLeod's voice, astonishingly, faltered a little.

"It would mean a great deal to me," she said.

I remembered what she had told me—*When your Uncle Roderick got killed, I thought I would die. But I didn't die.* All at once, her feeling for that unknown dead man became a reality for me. And yet I held it against her, as well, for I could see that it had enabled her to win now.

"All right," my father said tiredly. "We'll call him Roderick."

Then, alarmingly, he threw back his head and laughed.

"Roderick Dhu!" he cried. "That's what you'll call him, isn't it? Black Roderick. Like before. Don't you remember? As though he were a character out of Sir Walter Scott, instead of an ordinary kid who—"

He broke off, and looked at her with a kind of desolation in his face.

"God, I'm sorry, Mother," he said. "I had no right to say that."

Grandmother MacLeod did not flinch, or tremble, or indicate that she felt anything at all.

"I accept your apology, Ewen," she said.

My mother had to stay in bed for several weeks after she arrived home. The baby's cot was kept in my parents' room, and I could go in and look at the small creature who lay there with his tightly closed fists and his feathery black hair. Aunt Edna came in to help each morning, and when she had finished the housework, she would have coffee with my mother. They kept the door closed, but this did not prevent me from eavesdropping, for there was an air register in the floor of the spare room, which was linked somehow with the register in my parents' room. If you put your ear to the iron grille, it was almost like a radio.

"Did you mind very much, Beth?" Aunt Edna was saying.

"Oh, it's not the name I mind," my mother replied. "It's just the fact that Ewen felt he had to. You know that Rod had only had the sight of one eye, didn't you?"

"Sure, I knew. So what?"

"There was only a year and a half between Ewen and Rod," my mother said, "so they often went around together when they were youngsters. It was Ewen's air-rifle that did it."

"Oh Lord," Aunt Edna said heavily. "I suppose she always blamed him?"

"No, I don't think it was so much that, really. It was how he felt himself. I think he even used to wonder sometimes if—but people shouldn't let themselves think like that, or they'd go crazy. Accidents do happen, after all. When the war came, Ewen joined up first. Rod should never have been in the Army at all, but he couldn't wait to get in. He must have lied about his eyesight. It wasn't so very noticeable unless you looked at him closely, and I don't suppose the medicals were very thorough in those days. He got in as a gunner, and Ewen applied to have him in the same company. He thought he might be able to watch out for him, I guess, Rod being—at a disadvantage. They were both only kids. Ewen was nineteen and Rod was eighteen when they went to France. And then the Somme. I don't know, Edna, I think Ewen felt that if Rod had had proper sight, or if he hadn't been in the same outfit and had been sent somewhere else—you know how people always think these things afterwards, not that it's ever a bit of use. Ewen wasn't there when Rod got hit. They'd lost each other somehow, and Ewen was looking for him, not bothering about anything else, you know, just frantically looking. Then he stumbled across him quite by chance. Rod was still alive, but—"

"Stop it, Beth," Aunt Edna said. "You're only upsetting yourself."

"Ewen never spoke of it to me," my mother went on, "until once his mother showed me the letter he'd written to her at the time. It was a peculiar letter, almost formal, saying how gallantly Rod had died, and all that. I guess I shouldn't have, but I told him she'd shown it to me. He was very angry that she had. And then, as though for some reason he were terribly ashamed, he said—*I had to write something to her, but men don't really die like that, Beth. It wasn't that way at all.* It was only after the war that he decided to come back and study medicine and go into practice with his father."

"Had Rod meant to?" Aunt Edna asked.

"I don't know," my mother said slowly. "I never felt I should ask Ewen that."

Aunt Edna was gathering up the coffee things, for I could hear the clash of cups and saucers being stacked on the tray.

"You know what I heard her say to Vanessa once, Beth? *The MacLeods never tell lies.* Those were her exact words. Even then, I didn't know whether to laugh or cry."

"Please, Edna—" my mother sounded worn out now. "Don't."

"Oh Glory," Aunt Edna said remorsefully, "I've got all the delicacy of a two-ton truck. I didn't mean Ewen, for heaven's sake. That wasn't what I meant at all. Here, let me plump up your pillows for you."

Then the baby began to cry, so I could not hear anything more of interest. I took my bike and went out beyond Manawaka, riding aimlessly along the gravel highway. It was late summer, and the wheat had changed colour, but instead of being high and bronzed in the fields, it was stunted and dessicated, for there had been no rain again this year. But in the bluff where I stopped and crawled under the barbed wire fence and lay stretched out on the grass, the plentiful poplar leaves were turning to a luminous yellow and shone like church windows in the sun. I put my head down very close to the earth and looked at what was going on there. Grasshoppers with enormous eyes ticked and twitched around me, as though the dry air were perfect for their purposes. A ladybird laboured mightily to climb a blade of grass, fell off, and started all over again, seeming to be unaware that she possessed wings and could have flown up.

I thought of the accidents that might easily happen to a person—or, of course, might not happen, might happen to somebody else. I thought of the dead baby, my sister, who might as easily have been I. Would she, then, have been lying here in my place, the sharp grass making its small toothmarks on her brown arms, the sun warming her to the heart? I thought of the leather-bound volumes of Greek, and the six different kinds of iced cakes that used to be offered always in the MacLeod house, and the pictures of leopards and green seas. I thought of my brother, who had been born alive after all, and now had been given his life's name.

I could not really comprehend these things, but I sensed their strangeness, their disarray. I felt that whatever God might love in this world, it was certainly not order.

1970

ALICE MUNRO (1931-   )

Like Margaret Laurence, Alice Munro examines the struggle of girls and women coming to terms with themselves and with society's expectations. While she lacks Laurence's symbolism and deep probing of the psyche, she, too, writes with clarity and honesty of her subjects.

Munro was born in the small town of Wingham, Ontario, and began to publish short stories while still a student at the University of Western Ontario. In 1951 she married and moved to Victoria; she returned to Ontario a decade ago. Her first book, *Dance of the Happy Shades*, won the Governor-General's Award in 1968. This was followed by the novel, *Lives of Girls and Women* (1971), and another collection

of stories, *Something I've Been Meaning to Tell You* (1974). *Who Do You Think You Are?* (1978), her second novel, also won the Governor-General's Award.

For the most part, Munro's books vividly recreate life in a small Canadian town. She celebrates development into womanhood with awareness and acceptance of oneself; female readers especially appreciate her honest treatment of sexuality and the yearning for freedom expressed by her characters. Often, as in the following selection, she contrasts a lost and more sensitive world of yesterday with the values of today.

Dance of the Happy Shades

Miss Marsalles is having another party. (Out of musical integrity, or her heart's bold yearning for festivity, she never calls it a recital.) My mother is not an inventive or convincing liar, and the excuses which occur to her are obviously second-rate. The painters are coming. Friends from Ottawa. Poor Carrie is having her tonsils out. In the end all she can say is: Oh, but won't all that be too much trouble, *now*? *Now* being weighted with several troublesome meanings; you may take your choice. Now that Miss Marsalles has moved from the brick and frame bungalow on Bank Street, where the last three parties have been rather squashed, to an even smaller place—if she has described it correctly—on Bala Street. (Bala Street, where is that?) Or: now that Miss Marsalles' older sister is in bed, following a stroke; now that Miss Marsalles herself—as my mother says, we must face these things—is simply getting *too old*.

Now? asks Miss Marsalles, stung, pretending mystification, or perhaps for that matter really feeling it. And she asks how her June party could ever be too much trouble, at any time, in any place? It is the only entertainment she ever gives any more (so far as my mother knows it is the only entertainment she ever has given, but Miss Marsalles' light old voice, undismayed, indefatigably social, supplies the ghosts of tea parties, private dances, At Homes, mammoth Family Dinners). She would suffer, she says, as much disappointment as the children, if she were to give it up. Considerably more, says my mother to herself, but of course she cannot say it aloud; she turns her face from the telephone with that look of irritation—as if she had seen something messy which she was unable to clean up—which is her private expression of pity. And she promises to come; weak schemes for getting out of it will occur to her during the next two weeks, but she knows she will be there.

She phones up Marg French who like herself is an old pupil of Miss Marsalles and who has been having lessons for her twins, and they commiserate for a while and promise to go together and buck each other up. They remember the year before last when it rained and the little hall was full of raincoats piled on top of each other because there was no place to hang them up, and the umbrellas dripped puddles on the dark floor. The little girls' dresses were crushed because of the way they all had to squeeze together, and the living room windows would not open. Last year a child had a nosebleed.

"Of course that was not Miss Marsalles' fault."

They giggle despairingly. "No. But things like that did not use to happen."

And that is true; that is the whole thing. There is a feeling that can hardly be put into words about Miss Marsalles' parties; things are getting out of hand, anything may happen. There is even a moment, driving in to such a party, when the question occurs: will anybody else be there? For one of the most disconcerting things about the last two or three parties has been the widening gap in the ranks of the regulars, the old pupils whose children seem to be the only new pupils Miss Marsalles ever has. Every June reveals some new and surely significant dropping-out. Mary Lambert's girl no longer takes; neither does Joan Crimble's. What does this mean? think my mother and Marg French, women who have moved to the suburbs and are plagued sometimes by a feeling that they have fallen behind, that their instincts for doing the right thing have become confused. Piano lessons are not so important now as they once were; everybody knows that. Dancing is believed to be more favourable to the development of the whole child—and the children, at least the girls, don't seem to mind it as much. But how are you to explain that to Miss Marsalles, who says, "All children need music. All children love music in their hearts"? It is one of Miss Marsalles' indestructible beliefs that she can see into children's hearts, and she finds there a treasury of good intentions and a natural love of all good things. The deceits which her spinster's sentimentality has practised on her original good judgment are legendary and colossal; she has this way of speaking of children's hearts as if they were something holy; it is hard for a parent to know what to say.

In the old days, when my sister Winifred took lessons, the address was in Rosedale; that was where it had always been. A narrow house, built of soot-and-raspberry-coloured brick, grim little ornamental balconies curving out from the second-floor windows, no towers anywhere but somehow a turreted effect; dark, pretentious, poetically ugly—the family home. And in Rosedale the annual party did not go off too badly. There was always an awkward little space before the sandwiches, because the woman they had in the kitchen was not used to parties and rather slow, but the sandwiches when they did appear were always very good: chicken, asparagus rolls, wholesome, familiar things— dressed-up nursery food. The performances on the piano were, as usual, nervous and choppy or sullen and spiritless, with the occasional surprise and interest of a lively disaster. It will be understood that Miss Marsalles' idealistic view of children, her tender- or simple-mindedness in that regard, made her almost useless as a teacher; she was unable to criticize except in the most delicate and apologetic way and her praises were unforgivably dishonest; it took an unusually conscientious pupil to come through with anything like a creditable performance.

But on the whole the affair in those days had solidity, it had tradition, in its own serenely out-of-date way it had style. Everything was always as expected; Miss Marsalles herself, waiting in the entrance hall with the tiled floor and the dark, church-vestry smell, wearing rouge, an antique hairdo adopted only on this occasion, and a floor-length dress of plum and pinkish splotches that might have been made out of old upholstery material, startled no one but the youngest children. Even the shadow behind her of another Miss Marsalles, slightly, older, larger, grimmer, whose existence was always forgotten from one June to the next, was not discomfiting—though it was surely an arresting fact that there should be not one but two faces like that in the world, both long, gravel-coloured, kindly and grotesque, with enormous noses and tiny, red, sweet-tempered and shortsighted eyes. It must finally have come to seem like a piece of luck to them to be so ugly, a protection against life to be marked in so many ways, *impossible*, for they were gay as invulnerable and childish people are; they appeared sexless, wild and gentle creatures, bizarre yet domestic, living in their house in Rosedale outside the complications of time.

In the room where the mothers sat, some on hard sofas, some on folding chairs, to hear the children play "The Gypsy Song," "The Harmonious Blacksmith" and the "Turkish March," there was a picture of Mary, Queen of Scots, in velvet, with a silk veil, in front of Holyrood Castle. There were brown misty pictures of historical battles, also the Harvard Classics, iron firedogs and a bronze Pegasus. None of the mothers smoked, nor were ashtrays provided. It was the same room, exactly the same room, in which they had performed themselves; a room whose dim impersonal style (the flossy bunch of peonies and spirea dropping petals on the piano was Miss Marsalles' own touch and not entirely happy) was at the same time uncomfortable and reassuring. Here they found themselves year after year—a group of busy, youngish women who had eased their cars impatiently through the archaic streets of Rosedale, who had complained for a week previously about the time lost, the fuss over the children's dresses and, above all, the boredom, but who were drawn together by a rather implausible allegiance—not so much to Miss Marsalles as to the ceremonies of their childhood, to a more exacting pattern of life which had been breaking apart even then but which survived, and unaccountably still survived, in Miss Marsalles' living room. The little girls in dresses with skirts as stiff as bells moved with a natural awareness of ceremony against the dark walls of books, and their mothers' faces wore the dull, not unpleasant look of acquiescence, the touch of absurd and slightly artificial nostalgia which would carry them through any lengthy family ritual. They exchanged smiles which showed no lack of good manners, and yet expressed a familiar, humorous amazement at the sameness of things, even the selections played on the piano and the fillings of the sandwiches; so they acknowledged the incredible, the wholly unrealistic persistence of Miss Marsalles and her sister and their life.

After the piano-playing came a little ceremony which always caused some embarrassment. Before the children were allowed to escape to the garden—very narrow, a town garden, but still a garden, with hedges, shade, a border of yellow lilies—where a long table was covered with crepe paper in infants' colours of pink and blue, and the woman from the kitchen set out plates of sandwiches, ice cream, prettily tinted and tasteless sherbet, they were compelled to accept, one by one, a year's-end gift, all wrapped and tied with ribbon, from Miss Marsalles. Except among the most naive new pupils this gift caused no excitement of anticipation. It was apt to be a book, and the question was, where did she find such books? They were of the vintage found in old Sunday-school libraries, in attics and the basements of second-hand stores, but they were all stiff-backed, unread, brand new. *Northern Lakes and Rivers, Knowing the Birds, More Tales by Grey-Owl, Little Mission Friends*. She also gave pictures: "Cupid Awake and Cupid Asleep," "After the Bath," "The Little Vigilantes"; most of these seemed to feature that tender childish nudity which our sophisticated prudery found most ridiculous and disgusting. Even the boxed games she gave us proved to be insipid and unplayable—full of complicated rules which allowed everybody to win.

The embarrassment the mothers felt at this time was due not so much to the presents themselves as to a strong doubt whether Miss Marsalles could afford them; it did not help to remember that her fees had gone up only once in ten years (and even when that happened, two or three mothers had quit). They always ended up by saying that she must have other resources. It was obvious—otherwise she would not be living in this house. And then her sister taught—or did not teach any more, she was retired but she gave private lessons, it was believed, in French and German. They must have enough, between them. If you are a Miss Marsalles your wants are simple and it does not cost a great deal to live.

But after the house in Rosedale was gone, after it had given way to the bungalow on Bank Street, these conversations about Miss Marsalles' means did not take place; this aspect of Miss Marsalles' life had passed into that region of painful subjects which it is crude and unmannerly to discuss.

"I will die if it rains," my mother says. "I will die of depression at this affair if it rains." But the day of the party it does not rain and in fact the weather is very hot. It is a hot gritty summer day as we drive down into the city and get lost, looking for Bala Street.

When we find it, it gives the impression of being better than we expected, but that is mostly because it has a row of trees, and the other streets we have been driving through, along the railway embankment, have been unshaded and slatternly. The houses here are of the sort that are divided in half, with a sloping wooden partition in the middle of the front porch; they have two wooden steps and a dirt yard. Apparently it is in one of these half-houses that Miss Marsalles lives. They are red brick, with the front door and the window trim and the porches painted cream, grey, oily-green and yellow. They are neat, kept-up. The front part of the house next to the one where Miss Marsalles lives has been turned into a little store; it has a sign that says: GROCERIES AND CONFECTIONERY.

The door is standing open. Miss Marsalles is wedged between the door, the coatrack and the stairs; there is barely room to get past her into the living room, and it would be impossible, the way things are now, for anyone to get from the living room upstairs. Miss Marsalles is wearing her rouge, her hairdo and her brocaded dress, which it is difficult not to tramp on. In this full light she looks like a character in a masquerade, like the feverish, fancied-up courtesan of an unpleasant Puritan imagination. But the fever is only her rouge; her eyes, when we get close enough to see them, are the same as ever, red-rimmed and merry and without apprehension. My mother and I are kissed—I am greeted, as always, as if I were around five years old—and we get past. It seemed to me that Miss Marsalles was looking beyond us as she kissed us; she was looking up the street for someone who has not yet arrived.

The house has a living room and a dining room, with the oak doors pushed back between them. They are small rooms. Mary Queen of Scots hangs tremendous on the wall. There is no fireplace so the iron firedogs are not there, but the piano is, and even a bouquet of peonies and spirea from goodness knows what garden. Since it is so small the living room looks crowded, but there are not a dozen people in it, including children. My mother speaks to people and smiles and sits down. She says to me, Marg French is not here yet, could she have got lost too?

The woman sitting beside us is not familiar. She is middle-aged and wears a dress of shot taffeta with rhinestone clips; it smells of the cleaners. She introduces herself as Mrs. Clegg, Miss Marsalles' neighbour in the other half of the house. Miss Marsalles has asked her if she would like to hear the children play, and she thought it would be a treat; she is fond of music in any form.

My mother, very pleasant but looking a little uncomfortable, asks about Miss Marsalles' sister; is she upstairs?

"Oh, yes, she's upstairs. She's not herself though, poor thing."

That is too bad, my mother says.

"Yes it's a shame. I give her something to put her to sleep for the afternoon. She lost her powers of speech, you know. Her powers of control generally, she lost." My mother is warned by a certain luxurious lowering of the voice that more lengthy and intimate details may follow and she says quickly again that it is too bad.

"I come in and look after her when the other one goes out on her lessons."

"That's very kind of you. I'm sure she appreciates it."

"Oh well I feel kind of sorry for a couple of old ladies like them. They're a couple of babies, the pair."

My mother murmurs something in reply but she is not looking at Mrs. Clegg, at her brick-red healthy face or the—to me—amazing gaps in her teeth. She is staring past her into the dining room with fairly well-controlled dismay.

What she sees there is the table spread, all ready for the party feast; nothing is lacking. The plates of sandwiches are set out, as they must have been for several hours now; you can see how the ones on top are beginning to curl very slightly at the edges. Flies buzz over the table, settle on the sandwiches and crawl comfortably across the plates of little iced cakes brought from the bakery. The cut-glass bowl, sitting as usual in the centre of the table, is full of purple punch, without ice apparently and going flat.

"I tried to tell her not to put it all out ahead of time," Mrs. Clegg whispers, smiling delightedly, as if she were talking about the whims and errors of some headstrong child. "You know she was up at five o'clock this morning making sandwiches. I don't know what things are going to taste like. Afraid she wouldn't be ready I guess. Afraid she'd forget something. They hate to forget."

"Food shouldn't be left out in the hot weather," my mother says.

"Oh, well I guess it won't poison us for once. I was only thinking what a shame to have the sandwiches dry up. And when she put the ginger-ale in the punch at noon I had to laugh. But what a waste."

My mother shifts and rearranges her voile skirt, as if she has suddenly become aware of the impropriety, the hideousness even, of discussing a hostess's arrangements in this way in her own living room. "Marg French isn't here," she says to me in a hardening voice. "She did say she was coming."

"I am the oldest girl here," I say with disgust.

"Shh. That means you can play last. Well. It won't be a very long programme this year, will it?"

Mrs. Clegg leans across us, letting loose a cloud of warm unfresh odour from between her breasts. "I'm going to see if she's got the fridge turned up high enough for the ice cream. She'd feel awful if it was all to melt."

My mother goes across the room and speaks to a woman she knows and I can tell that she is saying, Marg French *said* she was *coming*. The women's faces in the room, made up some time before, have begun to show the effects of heat and a fairly general uneasiness. They ask each other when it will begin. Surely very soon now; nobody has arrived for at least a quarter of an hour. How mean of people not to come, they say. Yet in this heat, and the heat is particularly dreadful down here, it must be the worst place in the city—well you can almost see their point. I look around and calculate that there is no one in the room within a year of my age.

The little children begin to play. Miss Marsalles and Mrs. Clegg applaud with enthusiasm; the mothers clap two or three times each, with relief. My mother seems unable, although she makes a great effort, to take her eyes off the dining-room table and the complacent journeys of the marauding flies. Finally she achieves a dreamy, distant look, with her eyes focused somewhere above the punch-bowl, which makes it possible for her to keep her head turned in that direction and yet does not in any positive sense give her away. Miss Marsalles as well has trouble keeping her eyes on the performers; she keeps looking towards the door. Does she expect that even now some of the unexplained absentees may turn up? There are far more than half a dozen presents in the inevitable box beside the piano, wrapped in white paper and tied with silver ribbon—not real ribbon, but the cheap kind that splits and shreds.

It is while I am at the piano, playing the minuet from *Berenice*, that the final arrival, unlooked-for by anybody but Miss Marsalles, takes place. It must seem at first that there has been some mistake. Out of the corner of my eye I see a whole procession of children, eight or ten in all, with a red-haired woman in something like a uniform, mounting the front step. They look like a group of children from a private school on an excursion of some kind (there is that drabness and sameness about their clothes) but their progress is too scrambling and disorderly for that. Or this is the impression I have; I cannot really look. Is it the wrong house, are they really on their way to the doctor for shots, or to Vacation Bible Classes? No, Miss Marsalles has got up with a happy whisper of apology; she has gone to meet them. Behind my back there is a sound of people squeezing together, of folding chairs being opened, there is an inappropriate, curiously unplaceable giggle.

And above or behind all this cautious flurry of arrival there is a peculiarly concentrated silence. Something has happened, something unforeseen, perhaps something disastrous; you can feel such things behind your back. I go on playing. I fill the first harsh silence with my own particularly dogged and lumpy interpretation of Handel. When I get up off the piano bench I almost fall over some of the new children who are sitting on the floor.

One of them, a boy nine or ten years old, is going to follow me. Miss Marsalles takes his hand and smiles at him and there is no twitch of his hand, no embarrassed movement of her head to disown this smile. How peculiar; and a boy, too. He turns his head towards her as he sits down; she speaks to him encouragingly. But my attention has been caught by his profile as he looks up at her—the heavy, unfinished features, the abnormally small and slanting eyes. I look at the children seated on the floor and I see the same profile repeated two or three times; I see another boy with a very large head and fair shaved hair, fine as a baby's; there are other children whose features are regular and unexceptional, marked only by an infantile openness and calm. The boys are dressed in white shirts and short grey pants and the girls wear dresses of grey-green cotton with red buttons and sashes.

"Sometimes that kind is quite musical," says Mrs. Clegg.

"Who are they?" my mother whispers, surely not aware of how upset she sounds.

"They're from that class she has out at the Greenhill School. They're nice little things and some of them quite musical but of course they're not all there."

My mother nods distractedly; she looks around the room and meets the trapped, alerted eyes of the other women, but no decision is reached. There is nothing to be done. These children are going to play. Their playing is no worse—not much worse—than ours, but they seem to go so slowly, and then there is nowhere to look. For it is a matter of politeness surely not to look closely at such children, and yet where else can you look during a piano performance but at the performer? There is an atmosphere in the room of some freakish inescapable dream. My mother and the others are almost audible saying to themselves: *No, I know it is not right to be repelled by such children and I am not repelled, but nobody told me I was going to come here to listen to a procession of little—little idiots for that's what they are—* WHAT KIND OF A PARTY IS THIS? Their applause however has increased, becoming brisk, let-us-at-least-get-this-over-with. But the programme shows no signs of being over.

Miss Marsalles says each child's name as if it were a cause for celebration. Now she says, "Dolores Boyle!" A girl as big as I am, a long-legged, rather thin and plaintive-looking girl with blonde, almost white, hair uncoils herself and gets up off the floor. She sits down on the bench and after shifting around a bit and pushing her long hair back behind her ears she begins to play.

We are accustomed to notice performances, at Miss Marsalles' parties, but it cannot be said that anyone has ever expected music. Yet this time the music establishes itself so effortlessly, with so little demand for attention, that we are hardly even surprised. What she plays is not familiar. It is something fragile, courtly and gay, that carries with it the freedom of a great unemotional happiness. And all that this girl does—but this is something you would not think could ever be done—is to play it so that this can be felt, all this can be felt, even in Miss Marsalles' living-room on Bala Street on a preposterous afternoon. The children are all quiet, the ones from Greenhill School and the rest. The mothers sit, caught with a look of protest on their faces, a more profound anxiety than before, as if reminded of something that they had forgotten they had forgotten; the white-haired girl sits ungracefully at the piano with her head hanging down, and the music is carried through the open door and the windows to the cindery summer street.

Miss Marsalles sits beside the piano and smiles at everybody in her usual way. Her smile is not triumphant, or modest. She does not look like a magician who is watching people's faces to see the effect of a rather original revelation; nothing like that. You would think, now that at the very end of her life she has found someone whom she can teach—whom she must teach—to play the piano, she would light up with the importance of this discovery. But it seems that the girl's playing like this is something she always expected, and she finds it natural and satisfying; people who believe in miracles do not make much fuss when they actually encounter one. Nor does it seem that she regards this girl with any more wonder than the other children from Greenhill School, who love her, or the rest of us, who do not. To her no gift is unexpected, no celebration will come as a surprise.

The girl is finished. The music is in the room and then it is gone and naturally enough no one knows what to say. For the moment she is finished it is plain that she is just the same as before, a girl from Greenhill School. Yet the music was not imaginary. The facts are not to be reconciled. And so after a few minutes the performance begins to seem, in spite of its innocence, like a trick—a very successful and diverting one, of course, but perhaps—how can it be said?—perhaps not altogether *in good taste*. For the girl's ability, which is undeniable but after all useless, out-of-place, is not really something that anybody wants to talk about. To Miss Marsalles such a thing is acceptable, but to other people, people who live in the world, it is not. Never mind, they must say something and so they speak gratefully of the music itself, saying how lovely, what a beautiful piece, what is it called?

"The Dance of the Happy Shades," says Miss Marsalles. *Danse des ombres heureuses*, she says, which leaves nobody any the wiser.

But then driving home, driving out of the hot red-brick streets and out of the city and leaving Miss Marsalles and her no longer possible parties behind, quite certainly forever, why is it that we are unable to say—as we must have expected to say—*Poor Miss Marsalles*? It is the Dance of the Happy Shades that prevents us, it is that one communiqué from the other country where she lives.

1968

MORDECAI RICHLER (1931-   )

A native of Montreal and former student at Sir George Williams University, Mordecai Richler returned to Canada more than a decade ago, after spending many years living in Europe. He frequently travels across Canada giving readings; his opinions on the condition of Canada and its culture are often sought.

Although his first novels were written in Europe, only the first (*The Acrobats*, 1954, set in Spain) does not deal with the world of his childhood—the St. Urbain section of Montreal, a Jewish ghetto. He has become one of the best-known Canadian novelists of his generation, both here and abroad, particularly since *The Ap-*

prenticeship of Duddy Kravitz (1969), which has been an extremely popular novel. His more recent works—*St. Urbain's Horseman* (1971), and *Joshua, Then and Now* (1980)—have continued the exploration of his roots.

Richler is a satirist and a social realist; he writes, often bitterly and sarcastically, out of his "disgust with the way things are." He can also write with great sensitivity and humour, as is evident in the following selection.

Mortimer Griffin, Shalinsky, and How They Settled the Jewish Question

I was, at the time, beginning my first scholastic year as a lecturer in English literature at Wellington College in Montreal. You've probably never heard of Wellington. It's a modest institution with a small student body. There's the Day College, comprised, for the most part, of students who couldn't get into McGill, and the Evening College, made up of adults, most of them working at full-time jobs and trying to get a college education after hours. I was responsible for two Evening College courses, English 112 (Shakespeare) and English 129 (The Modern Novel). Shalinsky registered for both of them.

Until my fourth lecture I was only aware of Shalinsky as a ponderous presence in the third row. My fourth lecture dealt with Franz Kafka and naturally I made several allusions to the distinctively Jewish roots of his work. Afterwards, as I was gathering my notes together, Shalinsky approached me for the first time.

"I want to tell you, Professor Griffin, how much intellectual nourishment I got out of your lecture tonight."

"I'm glad you enjoyed it."

I'm afraid I was in a hurry to get away that night. I was going to pick up Joyce at the Rosens'. But Shalinsky still stood before my desk.

His wisps of grey curly hair uncut and uncombed, Shalinsky was a small, round-shouldered man with horn-rimmed spectacles, baleful black eyes, and a hanging lower lip. His shiny, pin-striped grey suit was salted with dandruff round the shoulders. A hand-rolled cigarette drooped from his mouth, his eyes half-shut against the smoke and the ashes spilling unregarded to his vest.

"Why did you change your name?" he asked.

"I beg your pardon. Did you ask me why I changed my name?"

Shalinsky nodded.

"But I haven't. My name is Griffin. It always has been."

"You're a Jew."

"You're mistaken."

Shalinsky smiled faintly.

"Really," I began, "what made you think—"

"All right. I'm mistaken. I made a mistake. No harm done."

"Look here, if I were a Jew I wouldn't try to conceal it for a moment."

Still smiling, blinking his eyes, Shalinsky said: "There's no need to lose your temper, Professor *Griffin*. I made a mistake, that's all. If that's the way you want it."

"And I'm not a professor, either. *Mr.* Griffin will do."

"A man of your talents will be famous one day. Like . . . like I. M. Sinclair. A scholar renowned wherever the intelligentsia meet. Thanks once more for tonight's intellectual feast. Good night, Mr. Griffin."

In retrospect, on the bus ride out to Hy and Eva Rosen's house, I found the incident so outlandishly amusing that I laughed aloud twice.

Joyce had eaten with the Rosens, and Eva, remembering how much I liked chopped liver, had saved me an enormous helping. I told them about Shalinsky, concluding with, ". . . and where he ever got the idea that I was Jewish I'll never know." I had anticipated plenty of laughter. A witty remark from Hy, perhaps. Instead, there was silence. Nervously, I added: "Look, I don't mean that I'd be ashamed . . . or that I was insulted that someone would think I was—Christ, you know what I mean, Hy."

"Yes," Hy said sharply. "Of course."

We left for home earlier than usual.

"Boy," Joyce said, "you certainly have a gift. I mean once you *have* put your foot in it you certainly know how to make matters worse."

"I thought they'd laugh. God, I've known Hy for years. He's one of my best friends. He—"

"*Was*," Joyce said.

"Look here," I said, "you don't seriously think that Hy thinks I'm an anti-semite?"

Joyce raised one eyebrow slightly—an annoying, college-girl habit that has lingered.

"Don't be ridiculous," I said. "Tomorrow, the day after, the whole thing will be forgotten, or Hy will make a joke of it."

"*They* have an excellent sense of humour," Joyce said, "haven't they? There's Jack Benny and Phil Silvers and—"

"Oh, for Christ's sake!"

Two days later a copy of a magazine called *Jewish Thought* came in the mail. Attached was a printed note, WITH THE COMPLIMENTS OF THE EDITOR, and underneath, penned with a lavish hand, *Respectfully, J. Shalinsky*. It took me a moment or two to connect Shalinsky, the editor, with Shalinsky, my student. I began to flip through the pages of the little magazine.

The editorial, by J. Shalinsky, dealt at length with the dilemma of Jewish artists in a philistine community. The lead article, by Lionel Gould, B. COMM. (McGill), was titled "On Being a Jew in Montreal West". Another article, by I. M. Sinclair, M.D., was titled "The Anti-Semite as an Intellectual: A Study of the Novels of Graham Greene". There were numerous book reviews, two sentimental poems translated from the Yiddish, a rather maudlin Israeli short story, and, surprisingly, "Stefan Zweig and J. Shalinsky: A Previously Unpublished Correspondence".

That night, as soon as my Eng. 112 lecture was finished, Shalinsky loomed smiling over my desk. "You got the magazine?" he asked.

"I haven't had time to read it yet."

"If you don't like it, all you have to do is tell me why. No evasions, please. Don't beat around the bush." Shalinsky broke off and smiled. "I have something for you," he said.

I watched while he unwrapped a large, awkward parcel. The string he rolled into a ball and dropped into his pocket. The brown wrapping paper, already worn and wrinkled, he folded into eight and put into another pocket. Revealed was an extremely expensive edition of colour plates by Marc Chagall.

"It occurred to me", he said, "that a man so interested in Kafka might also find beauty in the art of Marc Chagall."

"I don't understand."

"Would you be willing", Shalinsky said, "to write me a review, a little appreciation, of this book for the next issue of *Jewish Thought?*"

I hesitated.

"We pay our contributors, of course. Not much, but—"

"That's not the point."

"And the book, it goes without saying, would be yours."

"All right, Mr. Shalinsky. I'll do it."

"There's something else. You have no lectures next Wednesday night. You are free, so to speak. Am I right?"

"Yes, but—"

"Next Wednesday night, Mr. Griffin, the Jewish Thought Literary Society will be meeting at my house. It is a custom, at these meetings, that we are addressed by a distinguished guest. I was hoping—"

"What would you like me to talk about?" I asked wearily.

"Kafka," he said. "Kafka and Cabbalism. Refreshments will be served."

The address Shalinsky had given me was on St. Urbain Street. His house smelled of home-baked bread and spices. The livingroom, almost a hall once the double doors had been opened, was filled with folding chairs, all of them vindictively directed at the speaker's table. The walls were laden with enormous photographs of literary giants protected by glass and encased in varnished wooden frames. Tolstoi, a bearded scarecrow on horseback, glared at the refreshments table. Dostoyevsky and Turgenev, their quarrels forgotten, stood side by side. Opposite, Marcel Proust smiled enigmatically.

At dinner I was introduced to Shalinsky's wife and daughter. Mrs. Shalinsky was a round rosy-cheeked figure with a double chin. The daughter—plump, plum-cheeked Gitel Shalinsky—wore a peasant blouse laced tightly over a tray of milky bosom, and a billowy green skirt. Her thick black hair she wore in an upsweep; glittering glass ear-rings dripped from her cup-shaped ears. A wooden clasp, GRETA, rode one breast, and a rose the other. Throughout dinner Gitel never said a word.

I handed Shalinsky my twelve-hundred-word article on Chagall, titled—rather brightly, I thought—*The Myopic Mystic*. My editor pondered the piece in silence, waving his hand impatiently whenever his wife interrupted him, a frequent occurrence, with remarks like, "Chew your meat, Jake," and, in an aside to me, "If I gave him absorbent cotton to eat, you think he'd know the difference?", and again, baring her teeth in a parody of mastication, "Chew, Jake. *Digest.*"

Shalinsky read my article unsmilingly and folded it neatly in four.

"Is there anything the matter?" I asked.

"As an intellectual exercise your article is A-1, but—"

"You don't have to print it if you don't want to."

"Did I say I wouldn't print it? No. But, if you'll let me finish, I had hoped it would be a little more from the soul. Take the title, for instance. *The Myopic Mystic*," he said with distaste. "Clever. Clever, Mr. Griffin. But no heart. Still, this is a fine article. I wouldn't change a word. Not for the world."

The first of Shalinsky's guests arrived and he went into the livingroom with him. Mrs. Shalinsky excused herself, too, and so I was left alone with Gitel. "Your father", I said, "is quite an extraordinary man. I mean at his age to take university courses and edit a magazine—"

"*The Ladies' Home Journal*," Gitel said. "*There's* a magazine for you. But *Jewish Thought*. An eight-hundred-and-forty-two circulation, counting give-aways—that's no magazine."

"Your father tells me he's printed work by S. M. Geiger. He's a very promising poet, I think."

"Some poet. He comes up to here by me. Alan Ladd—there's another twerp. How long are you going to speak tonight?"

"I'm not sure."

"Make it short, Morty. The blabbers never get invited back."

Three-quarters of an hour after my lecture was supposed to have started, only twelve people, all middle-aged men, had turned up, though many more had been prepared for. "It's the rain," Shalinsky said. A half-hour later six more people had drifted into the livingroom: eight, if you counted the woman with the baby in her arms. Her name was Mrs. Korber. She lived upstairs and, in passing, I overheard her say to Mrs. Shalinsky, "Tell Mr. Shalinsky it's no trouble. Harry and the boy will be here the minute *Dragnet* is finished."

At that moment my jacket was given a fierce tug from behind. Whirling around, I was confronted by a small, wizened man with rimless glasses. "I am I. M. Sinclair," he said.

Retreating, I said: "You're a doctor, I believe."

"Like Chekhov."

"Oh. Oh, I see."

"I'm the only poet in Canada. Go ahead, laugh." Then, as though he were composing on the spot, I. M. Sinclair said: "I am an old man . . . an old man in a dry month . . . waiting for rain."

"You ought to write that down," I said.

"I have burned better lines. We have a lot to talk about, Griffin. The moment in the draughty synagogue at smokefall. . . ."

I broke away just in time to see Harry and the boy arrive. Shalinsky quickly called the meeting to order. There were three of us at the speaker's table—Shalinsky, myself, and a thin man with a fat ledger open before him. Shalinsky gave me a fulsome introduction, and Harry's boy—a fourteen-year-old with a running nose—poked two grimy fingers into his mouth and whistled. The others applauded politely. Then, as Mrs. Korber fed her baby with a bottle, I began.

"Louder," barked a voice from the back row.

So I spoke louder, elaborating on Kafka's difficulties with his father.

"What does he say?" somebody shouted. I waited while the man next to him translated what I had said into Yiddish. "Nonsense," his neighbour said. "A Jewish education never harmed anybody."

I rushed through the rest of my lecture, omitting half of it. A short question period was to follow. A Mr. Gordon was first.

"Mr. Griffin, my son is studying at McGill and he wishes to become a professor too. Now my question is as follows. How much can my Lionel expect to earn after five years?"

I had barely answered Mr. Gordon's question when a man in the back row began to wave his arm frantically.

"Yes," Shalinsky said. "What is it, Kaplan?"

Kaplan shot up from his seat. "I move a vote of thanks to Mr. Griffin for his excellent speech. I also move no more questions. It's nearly a quarter to eleven."

"Second both motions," cried a little man with thick glasses. "Segal. S,E,—no I—G,A,L. Get that in the minutes, Daniels."

A moment later Shalinsky and I were abandoned on one side of the room. Everyone else crowded round the refreshments table. I asked for my coat. At the door, Shalinsky thanked me profusely for coming.

"It's you I ought to thank," I said. "I enjoyed myself immensely."

"You see," Shalinsky said, "it's good to be with your own sometimes."

"Just what do you mean by that?"

Shalinsky smiled faintly.

"Look, will you please get it through your head that I'm not Jewish."

"All right, all right. I'm mistaken."

"Good night," I said, banging the door after me.

Joyce was waiting up for me in bed. "Well," she asked, "how did it go?"

"Skip it."

"What's wrong?"

"I don't want to talk about it, that's all."

"I don't see why you can't tell me about it."

I didn't answer.

"I mean you don't have to bite my head off just because I'm curious."

"There's nothing to tell."

"You've left a cigarette burning on the bureau."

"Oh, for Christ's sake. It would be so nice not to have all my filthy little habits pointed out to me for once. I know there's a cigarette burning on the bureau."

Retreating into the bathroom, I slammed the door after me. But even a bath failed to soothe my nerves. I lit a cigarette and lingered in the tub.

"What on earth are you doing in there?" Joyce shouted.

"Writing a book."

"Isn't he witty?"

"And next time you use my razor on your blessed armpits, kiddo, I'll thank you to wash it and replace the blade."

"Now who's pointing out whose filthy habits?"

I don't like mirrors. I make a point of never sitting opposite one in a restaurant. But tonight I had a special interest in studying my face.

"Mortimer!"

Mortimer, of course, could be a Jewish name.

"What are you doing in there?"

I'm a tall man with a long horse face. But my nose is certainly not prominent. Turning, I considered my face in profile. When I finally came out of the bathroom I asked Joyce: "Would you say I had a Jewish face?"

She laughed.

"I'm serious, Joyce."

"As far as I'm concerned," she said, "there's no such thing as a Jewish face."

I told her about the lecture.

"If you want my opinion," she said, "you wouldn't mind Shalinsky's notion in the least if you weren't a sublimated anti-semite."

"Thank you," I said, switching off the light.

An hour later, sensing that I was still awake, Joyce turned to me in bed. "I've been thinking, darling. Look, if—now please don't get angry. But *if* you were Jewish—"

"*What?*"

"I mean, if you have got Jewish blood I'd love you just as—"

"Of all the stupid nonsense. What do you mean, *if* I'm Jewish? You've met my parents, haven't you?"

"All I'm saying is that if—"

"All right. I confess. My father's real name is Granofsky. He's a goddam defrocked rabbi or something. Not only that, you know, but my mother's a coon. She—"

"Don't you dare use that word."

"Look, for the tenth time, if I had Jewish blood I would not try to conceal it. What ever made you think . . .?"

"Well," she said. "You know."

"Goddam it. I told you long ago that was done for hygienic reasons. My mother insisted on it. Since I was only about two weeks old at the time, I wasn't consulted."

"O.K." she said. "O.K. I just wanted you to know where I would stand if—"

"Look, let's go to sleep. I've had enough for one day. Tomorrow first thing I'm going to settle this matter once and for all."

"What are you going to do?"

"I'm going to start a pogrom."

"Some of your jokes", Joyce said, "are in the worst possible taste."

"Yes, I know. I happen to be cursed with what Hy calls a Goyishe[1] sense of humour."

The next morning I phoned Shalinsky.

"*Jewish Thought* here. Mr. Shalinsky is in Toronto. I'll have him get in touch with your office the minute he returns."

"Shalinsky, it's *you*".

"Ah, it's you, Griffin. I'm sorry. I thought it was Levite the printer. He usually phones at this hour on Thursday mornings."

"Look, Shalinsky, I'd like you to come over here at three this afternoon."

[1]From Goyim, the Yiddish word for Gentiles.

"Good."

Taken aback, I said: "What do you mean, *good?*"

"I was hoping you'd want to talk. Speaking frankly, I didn't expect it to happen so soon."

"Just be here at three," I said. "O.K.?" And I hung up.

By the time Shalinsky arrived I had amassed all manner of personal documents—my army discharge papers, passport, driving license, McGill graduation certificate, marriage license, a Rotary Club public speaking award, my unemployment insurance card, vaccination certificate, Bo-lo Champion (Jr. Division) Award of Merit, three literary cards, a parking ticket, and my bank book. On all these documents was the name Mortimer Lucas Griffin. Seething with suppressed anger, I watched as Shalinsky fingered each document pensively. He looked up at last, pinching his lower lip between thumb and index finger. "Facts," he said. "Documents. So what?"

"So what? Are you serious? All this goes to prove that I was born a white Protestant male named Mortimer Lucas Griffin."

"To think that you would go to so much trouble."

"Are you mad, Shalinsky?"

"I'm not mad." Shalinsky smiled, blinking his eyes against the smoke of his cigarette. "Neither do I want to make problems for you."

"What do I have to do to prove to you that I'm not Jewish?"

Shalinsky sifted through the papers again. "And what about your father?" he asked. "Couldn't he have changed his name without you knowing it? I mean, this is within the realm of possibilities, is it not?"

"Or my grandfather, eh? Or my great-grandfather?"

"You're so excited."

"I'd take you to see my parents, but they're both dead."

"I'm sorry to hear that. Please accept my condolences."

"They died years ago," I said. "A car accident."

"Is that so?"

"I suppose you think I'm lying?"

"Mr. Griffin, please."

"You're ruining my life, Shalinsky."

"I hardly know you."

"Do me a favour, Shalinsky. Cut my courses. I'll be grateful to you for the rest of my life."

"But your lectures are marvellous, Mr. Griffin. A delight."

"Some delight."

"Why, some of your epigrams I have marked down in my notebook to cherish. To memorize, Mr. Griffin."

"I've got news for you, buster. They're not mine. I stole them from my professor at Cambridge."

"So what? Didn't Shakespeare, may he rest in peace, steal from Thomas Kyd? The oral tradition, Mr. Griffin, is—"

"Shalinsky, I beg of you. If you won't quit my courses, then at least don't come to classes. If you'll do that for me I promise to pass you first in the class."

"Absolutely no."

Emptied, undone, I collapsed on the sofa.

"You don't feel so hot?" Shalinsky asked.

"I feel terrible. Now will you please go."

Shalinsky rose from his chair with dignity. "One thing," he said. "Among all those papers, no birth certificate. Why, I ask myself."

"Will you please get the hell out of here, Shalinsky!"

My parents were very much alive. But I hadn't lied to Shalinsky because I was afraid. There were my mother's feelings to be considered, that's all. You see, I was born an indecent seven months after my parents' marriage. They never told me this themselves. They always pre-dated the ceremony by a year, but once I accidentally came across their marriage license and discovered their deception. Not a very scandalous one, when you consider that they've been happily married for thirty-two years now. But the secret of my early birth belonged to my parents and, to their mind, had been carefully kept. There was something else. My father, a high-school teacher all these years, had been a poet of some promise as a young man, and I believe that he had been saving his money to go to Europe as soon as he graduated from McGill. He met my mother in his senior year, alas. I was conceived—suspiciously close to the Annual Arts Ball, I put it—and they were married. (A shock to their friends for, at the time, my mother was seeing an awful lot of Louis Cohen, a famous judge today.) Next year, instead of Europe, my father enrolled for a teacher's course. I have always been tormented by the idea that I may have ruined their lives. So I was certainly not going to open a belated inquiry into the matter for Shalinsky's sake. Let him think I was Jewish and that I was afraid to show him my birth certificate. I knew the truth, anyway.

But as far as Shalinsky was concerned, so did he.

Beginning with my next lecture he contrived to make life a misery for me.

"It seems to be your contention—correct me if I'm wrong—that Kafka's strict Jewish upbringing had a crippling effect on the man. Would you say, then, that this was also true of Hemingway, who had a strict Catholic upbringing?"

Another day.

"I may have misinterpreted you, of course, but it seems to me that you place Céline among the great writers of today. Do you think it possible, Mr. Griffin, that anti-semitism goes hand in hand with literary greatness? Answer me that."

Shalinsky filled all my dreams. He attacked me in alleys, he pursued me through mazes and, in a recurring nightmare he dragged me screaming into the synagogue to be punished for nameless iniquities. Many an afternoon I passed brooding about him. I saw myself being led up the thirteen steps to the hangman's noose, the despised strangler of Shalinsky, with—because of my ambiguous state—neither minister nor rabbi to comfort me. Because I was sleeping so badly, I began to lose weight, dark circles swelled under my eyes, and I was almost always in an unspeakable temper.

Fearful of Shalinsky, I cut *The Merchant of Venice* from Eng. 112.

"Ah, Mr. Griffin, a question please."

"Yes, Shalinsky,"

"It seems to me that in our study of Shakespeare, may he rest in peace, we have so far failed to discuss one of the Bard's major plays, *The Merchant of Venice*. I wonder if you could tell me why."

"Look here, Shalinsky, I do not intend to put up with your insolence for another minute. There are other problems besides the Jewish problem. This is not the Jewish Thought Literary Society, but my class in English 112. I'll run it however I choose, and damn your perverse Jewish soul."

With that, and the sharper exchanges that were to come, my reputation as an antisemite spread. Soon I found my self being openly slighted by other lecturers at Wellington. Several students asked to be released from my classes. It was rumoured that a petition demanding my expulsion was being circulated among the students with, I must say, huge success. Eventually, Joyce found out about it.

"Mortimer, this can't be true. I mean you didn't call Shalinsky a meddling Jew in class last week . . .?"

"Yes, I did."

"Is it also true, then, that you've stopped taking our newspapers from Mr. Goldberg because . . . you want to transfer our business to a Gentile store?"

"Absolutely."

"Mortimer, I think you ought to see an analyst."

"I'm crazy, eh?"

"No, but you've been overworking. I don't know what's come over you."

"Is this Hy's idea?"

She looked startled.

"Come off it. I know you've been seeing Hy and Eva secretly."

"Mortimer, how could you have written that article on Chagall for *Jewish Thought*?"

"What's wrong with it?"

"Did you have to call it 'A Jewish Answer to Picasso'? Hy's furious. He thinks that was so cheap of you. He—"

"I'll kill that Shalinsky. I'll murder him."

Joyce, holding her hands to her face, ran into the bedroom. Three days later, when I sat down to the tiresome job of correcting the Eng. 129 mid-term essays, I was still in a rage with Shalinsky. But I swear that's not why I failed him. His essay on Kafka was ponderous, windy, and pretentious, and deserved no better than it got: F-minus. Unfortunately for me, Dean McNoughton didn't agree.

"Not only do I consider this failure unwarranted, Griffin, but frankly I'm shocked at your behaviour. For the past two weeks charges of the most alarming nature have been flooding my office. I've been in touch with your wife who tells me you've been over-working, and so I prefer not to discuss these charges for the present. However, I think you'd best take the second term off and rest. Hodges will take your courses. But before you go, I want you to mark this paper B-plus. I think Shalinsky's essay is worth at least that."

"I'm afraid that's impossible, sir."

Dean McNoughton leaned back in his chair and considered his pipe pensively. "Tell me," he said at last, "is it true you offered to mark Shalinsky first in your class if he only stopped attending your lectures?"

"Yes, sir."

"I'm afraid I have no choice but to mark this paper B-plus myself."

"In that case I must ask you to accept my resignation."

"Go home, man. Rest up. Think things over calmly. If after three weeks you still want to resign. . . ."

I started impatiently for the door.

"I don't understand you, Griffin. We're not prejudiced here. If you're Jewish, why didn't you say so at first?"

Pushing Dean McNoughton aside roughly, I fled the office.

Joyce wasn't home when I got there. All her things were gone, too. But she had left me a note, the darling. It said, in effect, that she could no longer put up with me. Perhaps we had never been right for each other. Not that she wished me ill, etc. etc. But all her instincts rebelled against sharing her bed with a fascist—worse, a Jewish fascist.

I don't know how Shalinsky got into the house. I must have left the door open. But there he stood above me, smiling faintly, a hand-rolled cigarette in his mouth.

"My wife's left me," I said.

Shalinsky sat down, sighing.

"Joyce has left me. Do you understand what that means to me?"

Shalinsky nodded his head with ineffable sadness. "Mixed marriages", he said, "never work."

All this happened two years ago, and I have married again since then. I don't earn nearly as much money in my new job, and at times it's difficult to live with my father-in-law, but next spring, God willing, we hope to rent an apartment of our own (not that I don't appreciate all he's done for us).

I don't see any of my old friends any more, but my new life offers plenty of rewards. I. M. Sinclair, for instance, composed a special poem for our wedding and read it after the rabbi's speech.

> Lay your sleeping head, my love,
> human on my faithless arm . . .

When the last issue of *Jewish Thought* appeared, imagine my delight when I read on the title page: EDITED BY J. SHALINSKY AND M. GRIFFIN. Our circulation, I'm pleased to say, is rising steadily. Next year we hope to sell 1,500 copies of each issue. Meanwhile it's a struggle for Gitel and me. For me especially, as I am not yet completely adjusted to my new life. There are nights when I wake at three a.m. yearning for a plate of bacon and eggs. I miss Christmas. My father won't have anything to do with me. He thinks I'm crazy. Hy's another matter. He's phoned a couple of times, but I no longer have much use for him. He's an assimilationist. Last week my application for a teaching job with Western High School was turned down flatly—in spite of my excellent qualifications.

It's hard to be a Jew, you see.

1958

ALDEN NOWLAN (1933-   )

Born in Windsor, Nova Scotia, Alden Nowlan left school at an early age to work at a variety of occupations. After several years in journalism, mostly with the St. John *Telegraph-Journal*, he turned to writing full-time and has been writer-in-residence at the University of New Brunswick since 1963. He has published over a dozen collections of poetry (including *Bread, Wine and Salt*, which won the Governor-General's Award in 1967), a novel, a book of short stories, a collection of his newspaper columns, three plays, and several books of non-fiction.

Nowlan believes poetry is an intimate means of establishing communication with others; because of this desire for intimacy, his poetry is always aimed at one person, the individual reader. His early poetry deals realistically and compassionately with the lives of ordinary Maritimers; yet the poems are full of universal truths. An enemy of hypocrisy, he extols involvement and sincerity. As one might expect, Nowlan's own verse is marked by a disarming directness and naturalness of diction. Moreover, his poetry has become more personal and confessional over the course of his career.

Warren Pryor

When every pencil meant a sacrifice
his parents boarded him at school in town,
slaving to free him from the stony fields,
the meagre acreage that bore them down.

They blushed with pride when, at his graduation,
they watched him picking up the slender scroll,
his passport from the years of brutal toil
and lonely patience in a barren hole.

When he went in the Bank their cups ran over.
They marvelled how he wore a milk-white shirt   10
work days and jeans on Sundays. He was saved
from their thistle-strewn farm and its red dirt.

And he said nothing. Hard and serious
like a young bear inside his teller's cage,
his axe-hewn hands upon the paper bills
aching with empty strength and throttled rage.

1961

The Bull Moose

Down from the purple mist of trees on the mountain,
lurching through forests of white spruce and cedar,
stumbling through tamarack swamps,
came the bull moose
to be stopped at last by a pole-fenced pasture.

Too tired to turn or, perhaps, aware
there was no place left to go, he stood with the cattle.
They, scenting the musk of death, seeing his great head
like the ritual mask of a blood god, moved to the other end
of the field, and waited.   10

The neighbours heard of it, and by afternoon
cars lined the road. The children teased him
with alder switches and he gazed at them
like an old, tolerant collie. The women asked
if he could have escaped from a Fair.

The oldest man in the parish remembered seeing
a gelded moose yoked with an ox for plowing.
The young men snickered and tried to pour beer
down his throat, while their girl friends took their pictures.

And the bull moose let them stroke his tick-ravaged flanks,   20
let them pry open his jaws with bottles, let a giggling girl
plant a little purple cap
of thistles on his head.

When the wardens came, everyone agreed it was a shame
to shoot anything so shaggy and cuddlesome.
He looked liked the kind of pet
women put to bed with their sons.

So they held their fire. But just as the sun dropped in the river
the bull moose gathered his strength
like a scaffolded king, straightened and lifted his horns   30
so that even the wardens backed away as they raised their rifles.
When he roared, people ran to their cars. All the young men
leaned on their automobile horns as he toppled.

                                                                  1962

Ypres: 1915 [1]

The age of trumpets is passed, the banners hang
like dead crows, tattered and black,
rotting into nothingness on cathedral walls.
In the crypt of St Paul's [2] I had all the wrong thoughts,

[1] A World War I battle. The poet, like Canadian soldiers at the time, pronounces the name "Wipers."
[2] Cathedral in London where many great English heroes are buried.

wondered if there was anything left of Nelson
or Wellington, and even wished
I could pry open their tombs and look,
then was ashamed
of such morbid childishness, and almost afraid.

I know the picture is as much a forgery   10
as the Protocols of Zion,³ yet it outdistances
more plausible fictions: newsreels, regimental histories,
biographies of Earl Haig.⁴
                    It is always morning
and the sky somehow manages to be red
though the picture is in black and white.
There is a long road over flat country,
shell holes, the debris of houses,
a gun carriage overturned in a field,
the bodies of men and horses,   20
but only a few of them and those
always neat and distant.
                    The Moors⁵ are running
down the right side of the road.
The Moors are running
in their baggy pants and Santa Claus caps.
The Moors are running.
                    And their officers,
Frenchmen who remember
Alsace and Lorraine,⁶   30
are running backwards in front of them,
waving their swords, trying to drive them back,
weeping
          at the dishonour of it all.
The Moors are running.

And on the left side of the same road,
the Canadians are marching
in the opposite direction.

The Canadians are marching
in English uniforms behind   40
a piper playing 'Scotland the Brave'.

---

³The Jewish homeland, symbolic of Jewish national aspirations.
⁴British field marshal.
⁵British allies in World War I.
⁶Former French provinces which were part of Germany at this time; French resentment over this
    issue was a contributing factor to the outbreak of hostilities.

The Canadians are marching
in impeccable formation,
every man in step.

The Canadians are marching.

And I know this belongs
with Lord Kitchener's[7] mustache
and old movies in which the Kaiser and his general staff
seem to run like the Keystone Cops.[8]

That old man on television last night,   50
a farmer or fisherman by the sound of him,
revisiting Vimy Ridge, and they asked him
what it was like, and he said,
There was water up to our middles, yes
and there was rats, and yes
there was water up to our middles
and rats, all right enough,
and to tell you the truth
after the first three or four days
I started to get a little disgusted.   60
Oh, I know they were mercernaries[9]
in a war that hardly concerned us.
I know all that.

Sometimes I'm not even sure that I have a country.

But I know they stood there at Ypres
the first time the Germans used gas,
that they were almost the only troops
in that section of the front
who did not break and run,
who held the line.   70

Perhaps they were too scared to run.
Perhaps they didn't know any better
—that is possible, they were so innocent,
those farmboys and mechanics, you have only to look
at old pictures and see how they smiled.
Perhaps they were too shy

[7]British field marshal.
[8]Comic heroes of silent film.
[9]Soldiers hired for pay into foreign service.

to walk out on anybody, even Death.
Perhaps their only motivation
was a stubborn disinclination.

Private MacNally thinking: 80
You squareheaded sons of bitches,
you want this God damn trench
you're going to have to take it away
from Billy MacNally
of the South End of Saint John, New Brunswick.

And that's ridiculous, too, and nothing
on which to found a country.
                                Still
It makes me feel good, knowing
that in some obscure, conclusive way   90
they were connected with me
and me with them.

                                                        1969

LEONARD COHEN (1934-   )

Born into a wealthy Montreal family, Leonard
Cohen burst onto the Canadian poetry scene
with his first collection, *Let Us Compare Mytholo-
gies* (1966), while still a student at McGill. His
early promise was fulfilled in the sixties as he
published four more volumes of poetry and two
novels. Both his novels and his poetry, as well as
his career as a composer and singer of folk
songs, won him great popularity.

In the seventies, however, Cohen concentrated on his musical interests, publishing only
two volumes of poetry, both deliberately flat and
anti-romantic—*The Energy of Slaves* and *Death of
a Lady's Man*. He lived in Greece for some years,
but has since returned to Montreal.

Cohen's poetry ranges from the tender and
compassionate to the bitter and sarcastic, from
images of delicate beauty to the bizzare and sur-
real. His poems express a yearning for personal
salvation through the ecstasy of physical love, violence and art.

The Sparrows

Catching winter in their carved nostrils
the traitor birds have deserted us,
leaving only the dullest brown sparrows
for spring negotiations.

I told you we were fools
to have them in our games,
but you replied:

They are only wind-up birds
who strut on scarlet feet
so hopelessly far 10
from our curled fingers.

I had moved to warn you.
but you only adjusted your hair
and ventured:
    Their wings are made of glass and gold
and we are fortunate
not to hear them splintering
against the sun.

Now the hollow nests
sit like tumors or petrified blossoms 20
between the wire branches
and you, an innocent scientist,
question me on these brown sparrows:
whether we should plant our yards with breadcrumbs
or mark them with the black, persistent crows
whom we hate and stone.

But what shall I tell you of migrations
when in this empty sky
the precise ghosts of departed summer birds
still trace old signs; 30
or of desperate flights
when the dimmest flutter of a coloured wing
excites all our favourite streets
to delight in imaginary spring.

1954

For E.J.P.

I once believed a single line
    in a Chinese poem could change
        forever how blossoms fell
and that the moon itself climbed on
    the grief of concise weeping men
        to journey over cups of wine
I thought invasions were begun for crows
    to pick at a skeleton
        dynasties sown and spent
to serve the language of a fine lament 10
    I thought governors ended their lives

as sweetly drunken monks
telling time by rain and candles
    instructed by an insect's pilgrimage
        across the page—all this
    so one might send an exile's perfect letter
    to an ancient home town friend

I chose a lonely country
    broke from love
        scorned the fraternity of war   20
I polished my tongue against the pumice moon
    floated my soul in cherry wine
        a perfumed barge for Lords of Memory
to languish on to drink to whisper out
    their store of strength
        as if beyond the mist along the shore
their girls their power still obeyed
    like clocks wound for a thousand years
I waited until my tongue was sore

Brown petals wind like fire around my poems   30
    I aimed them at the stars but
        like rainbows they were bent
before they sawed the world in half
    Who can trace the canyoned paths
        cattle have carved out time
wandering from meadowlands to feasts
    Layer after layer of autumn leaves
        are swept away
Something forgets us perfectly

                                                    1964

Suzanne Takes You Down

Suzanne takes you down
to her place near the river,
you can hear the boats go by
you can stay the night beside her.
And you know that she's half crazy
but that's why you want to be there
and she feeds you tea and oranges
that come all the way from China.
Just when you mean to tell her
that you have no gifts to give her,   10

she gets you on her wave-length
and she lets the river answer
that you've always been her lover.
    And you want to travel with her,
    you want to travel blind
    and you know that she can trust you
    because you've touched her perfect body
    with your mind.

Jesus was a sailor
when he walked upon the water   20
and he spent a long time watching
from a lonely wooden tower
and when he knew for certain
only drowning men could see him
he said All men will be sailors then
until the sea shall free them,
but he himself was broken
long before the sky would open,
forsaken, almost human,
he sank beneath your wisdom like a stone.   30
    And you want to travel with him,
    you want to travel blind
    and you think maybe you'll trust him
    because he touched your perfect body
    with his mind.

Suzanne takes your hand
and she leads you to the river,
she is wearing rags and feathers
from Salvation Army counters.
The sun pours down like honey   40
on our lady of the harbour
as she shows you where to look
among the garbage and the flowers,
there are heroes in the seaweed
there are children in the morning,
they are leaning out for love
they will lean that way forever
while Suzanne she holds the mirror.
    And you want to travel with her
    and you want to travel blind   50
    and you're sure that she can find you
    because she's touched her perfect body
    with her mind.   1966

JOHN NEWLOVE (1938-   )

John Newlove was born in Regina in 1938. His mother was a school teacher and his childhood was spent in a number of Russian farming communities on the eastern edges of Saskatchewan. Newlove had lived in several parts of Canada before he accepted a senior editor's position at a Toronto publishing house.

A background of moving about the country is evident in Newlove's poetry as he contrasts the wild, vast stretches of the prairies with the barren wilderness of the city. His is a poetry of alienation, peopled with outsiders; intense love lyrics speak with unusual candidness and irony of failed relationships. Throughout his poems one senses the sanctity of the individual.

Newlove has published several poetry collections in the past two decades, notably *Black Night Window* (1968), *The Cave* (1970), and *Lies* (1972).

Good Company, Fine Houses

Good company, fine houses
and consequential people,
you will not turn me
into a tin factory.

I know where the lean and half
starved gods are hiding,
I have slept in their mountains.

I have slept among them,
in their mountains turning
nightmarishly between the rocks   10
and the reaching plants,

I have seen red eyes
on my throat from behind
every bush and waterfall,
greedy for blood.

Good company, fine people,
except for the shooting,
how much will your funerals cost

in your consequential houses?
I know where the god is   20
hiding, starved. I have slept
in the turning mountain.

1965

Lady, Lady

Lady, lady, I cannot lie,
I didn't cut down your cherry tree.

It was another man, in another season,
for the same reason.

I eat the stone and not the flesh,
it is the bare bones of desire I want,

something you would throw a dog,
or me, though I insult by saying so.

God knows it is not said
of your body, that it is like   10

a bone thrown to a dog,
or that I would throw it away, which

moment to moment I cannot remember
under those baggy clothes you wear—

which, if I love and tell,
I love well.

1968

MARGARET ATWOOD (1939-   )

Born in Ottawa in 1939, Margaret Atwood lived in a number of regions of Canada before starting her studies at the University of Toronto and Harvard University. She taught at several Canadian universities before settling on a farm in southern Ontario.

Atwood is an extremely prolific writer; just over forty, she has published eight volumes of poetry (her first, *The Circle Game*, won the Governor-General's Award in 1966) and five novels—*Edible Woman* (1969), *Surfacing* (1972), *Lady Oracle* (1976), *Life Before Man* (1979) and *Bodily Harm* (1981).

As a writer, Atwood is a determined anti-romantic. Her poetry strips away the comforting illusions of everyday life to reveal a world where the individual must struggle with his own perceptions just to maintain sanity. The mood is one of isolation and alienation; there are impenetrable barriers between the individual and the outer world and between individual human beings. Atwood uses the figure of the explorer or pioneer to represent modern man's search for identity. Startling images delivered in a matter-of-fact manner, as well as bizarre shifts in point of view and perception, give her work an immense original power.

This is a Photograph of Me

It was taken some time ago.
At first it seems to be
a smeared
print: blurred lines and grey flecks
blended with the paper;

then, as you scan
it, you see in the left-hand corner
a thing that is like a branch: part of a tree
(balsam or spruce) emerging
and, to the right, halfway up   10
what ought to be a gentle
slope, a small frame house.

In the background there is a lake,
and beyond that, some low hills.

(The photograph was taken
the day after I drowned.

I am in the lake, in the centre
of the picture, just under the surface.

It is difficult to say where
precisely, or to say   20
how large or small I am:
the effect of water
on light is a distortion

but if you look long enough,
eventually
you will be able to see me.)

1966

The animals in that country

In that country the animals
have the faces of people:

the ceremonial
cats possessing the streets

the fox run

politely to earth, the huntsmen
standing around him, fixed
in their tapestry of manners

the bull, embroidered
with blood and given   10
an elegant death, trumpets, his name
stamped on him, heraldic brand
because

(when he rolled
on the sand, sword in his heart, the teeth
in his blue mouth were human)

he is really a man

even the wolves, holding resonant
conversations in their
forests thickened with legend.   20

    In this country the animals
    have the faces of
    animals.

    Their eyes
    flash once in car headlights
    and are gone.

    Their deaths are not elegant.

    They have the faces of
    no-one.

1968

Dream 2: Brian the Still-Hunter

The man I saw in the forest
used to come to our house
every morning, never said anything;
I learned from the neighbours later
he once tried to cut his throat.

I found him at the end of the path
sitting on a fallen tree
cleaning his gun.

There was no wind;
around us the leaves rustled.   10

He said to me:
I kill because I have to

but every time I aim, I feel
my skin grow fur
my head heavy with antlers
and during the stretched instant
the bullet glides on its thread of speed
my soul runs innocent as hooves.

Is God just to his creatures?

I die more often than many.   20

He looked up and I saw
the white scar made by the hunting knife
around his neck.

When I woke
I remembered: he has been gone
twenty years and not heard from.

                                                                 1970

MICHAEL ONDAATJE (1943-   )

Michael Ondaatje was born in Sri Lanka, and educated in England. He came to Canada when he was almost twenty, studying at the University of Toronto and Queen's University. Besides writing and directing short films, he has also taught at York University for many years.

Ondaatje has an eye for the bizarre and abnormal, as one can infer from the titles of some of his collections—*The Dainty Monsters* (1967), *The Man with Seven Toes* (1969), *Rat Jelly* (1974)

and *Coming through Slaughter* (1976), his one novel. In 1979 he published *There's a Trick with a Knife I'm Learning to Do: Poems 1963-1978*. He is fascinated with the violence and energy of life, and sees the struggle for survival evident in even the domestic world. Intensely visual and dramatic, his poetry attempts to illuminate by coming at its subject from a sharp and unexpected angle.

A House Divided

This midnight breathing
heaves with no sensible rhythm,
is fashioned by no metronome.

Your body, eager
for the extra yard of bed,
reconnoitres and outflanks;
I bend in peculiar angles.

This nightly battle is fought with subtleties:
you get pregnant, I'm sure,
just for extra ground   10
—immune from kicks now.

Inside you now's another,
thrashing like a fish,
swinging, fighting
for its inch already.

                                                              1967

"The Gate in His Head"

for Victor Coleman[1]

Victor, the shy mind
revealing the faint scars
coloured strata of the brain,
not clarity but the sense of shift

a few lines, the tracks of thought

Landscape of busted trees
the melted tires in the sun
Stan's fishbowl
with a book inside
turning its pages   10
like some sea animal
camouflaging itself
the typeface clarity
going slow blonde in the sun full water

My mind is pouring chaos
in nets onto the page.
A blind lover, dont know
what I love till I write it out.

[1]Canadian poet, born 1944, who is concerned with linguistic precision and an almost improvisational
    (in the jazz sense) use of rhythm.

And then from Gibson's your letter
with a blurred photograph of a gull.   20
Caught vision. The stunning white bird
an unclear stir.

And that is all this writing should be then.
The beautiful formed things caught at the wrong moment
so they are shapeless, awkward
moving to the clear.

                                                                        1973

Bearhug

Griffin calls to come and kiss him goodnight
I yell ok. Finish something I'm doing,
then something else, walk slowly round
the corner to my son's room.
He is standing arms outstretched
waiting for a bearhug. Grinning.

Why do I give my emotion an animal's name,
give it that dark squeeze of death?
This is the hug which collects
all his small bones and his warm neck against me.   10
The thin tough body under the pyjamas
locks to me like a magnet of blood.

How long was he standing there
like that, before I came?

                                                                        1978

COMPLETE GLOSSARY

ABSTRACT DICTION. A word or phrase is abstract when it is not specific and definite in meaning.

Abstract words vary in their degree of indefiniteness. Such words as *nation, crime,* and *taxation* are not really specific, but they have more tangible meanings than *beauty, culture* and *honour*. Although modern writers favour *concrete* diction, eighteenth century poets were expected to speak of such philosphical abstractions as *Truth*, as in this excerpt from Alexander Pope's *An Essay on Man* (p. 198, l. 185-188):

> "That Reason, Passion, answer one great aim;
> That true Self-Love and Social are the same;
> That Virtue only makes our bliss below;
> And all our Knowledge is, *ourselves to know*."

ALLITERATION. A device commonly used in poetry and occasionally in prose: the repetition of an initial sound in two or more words of a phrase, line of poetry, or sentence ("The shallop flitteth silken-sail'd/Skimming down to Camelot:"—Tennyson's *The Lady of Shallott* p. 320).

ALLUSION. A reference, usually brief, often casual, occasionally indirect, to a person, event, or condition presumably familiar but sometimes obscure or unknown to the reader. Complex allusions abound in the work of such modern writers as T. S. Eliot—one cannot understand *The Love Song of J. Alfred Prufrock* (p. 462) without being aware of its classical and Shakespearean allusions.

ANALOGY. A partial similarity of features on which a comparison may be based: an analogy between the heart and a pump. In argument and persuasion, analogy is often employed as a form of reasoning in which one thing is compared to or contrasted with another. This simile from Pope's *An Essay on Criticism* is a type of analogy: "Tis with our judgments as our watches, none/Go just alike, yet each believes his own." (p. 193, l. 9-10).

ANTAGONIST. One who contends with, or opposes, another in a fight, conflict or battle of wills. In literature, such an adversary is the principal opponent, or *foil*, of the main character (Fortunato is the antagonist in Poe's *The Cask of Amontillado*, p. 357).

ARCHAISM. A word or phrase no longer in actual use, such as *enow* for enough and *gramercy* for thank you. Two archaic words appear in these lines from Coleridge's *The Rime of the Ancient Mariner* (p. 256, l. 11-12):

> "Hold off! unhand me, grey-beard loon!"
> Eftsoons his hand dropt he.

ASSONANCE. A resemblance of sound in words or syllables. Assonance applies especially to closely recurring vowel sounds in stressed syllables; it is a common device in poetry, particularly in the hands of a writer like Dylan Thomas "And as I was green and carefree, famous among the barns . . ." (*Fern Hill*, p. 447, l. 10).

ATMOSPHERE. This term, borrowed from meteorology, is used to describe the overall effect of a creative work of literature or other example of art. It involves the dominant mood of a selection as created by setting, description and dialogue. Note the powerful atmosphere Poe created through his description of the dark and deathly-still underground vaults in *The Cask of Amontillado*, p. 357.

BALLAD. A narrative poem composed in short stanzas and designed for singing or oral recitation. A ballad usually deals with an exciting or dramatic episode. See the selection of Middle English popular ballads, pp. 48 to 50.

BLANK VERSE. Unrhymed lines of ten syllables each, the even-numbered syllables bearing the accents, is called blank verse, or unrhymed iambic pentameter. This form of poetry is generally considered best adapted to dramatic verse in English; it was chosen by Milton for *Paradise Lost.*

CARPE DIEM. A Latin phrase meaning "seize the day." In literature, carpe diem refers to a theme or motif, chiefly in lyric poetry, that presents youth as short-lived and urges the pursuit of pleasure (see Robert Herrick's *To the Virgins . . .*, p. 134).

CLASSICISM. This term refers to a body of doctrine apparently derived from the qualities of early Greek and Roman culture as reflected in art and especially in literature. Classicism stands for certain ideas and attitudes such as formal elegance, correctness, simplicity, restraint, order, dignity, and proportion. In this text, refer to the writings of Jonson, Milton, Pope, Arnold, Eliot and Smith.

CONCEIT. A fanciful image or elaborate metaphor in which a writer describes a person or idea by use of an analogy which often seems farfetched and even startling. See Donne's famous comparision of himself and his wife to a pair of compasses (*A Valediction: Forbidding Mourning*, p. 125).

CONCRETENESS. Effective writers achieve concreteness in their work by giving it a quality of reality, specific elements that the reader can see, hear, feel, smell, or taste. Read Keats' *To Autumn*, p. 312.

CONFLICT. The opposition of persons or forces upon which the action depends in drama and fiction. One type of conflict is elemental or physical (as in Sinclair Ross's *The Lamp at Noon*, p. 531). Another type of conflict is social (as in Katherine Mansfield's *The Doll's House*, p. 434). A third kind of conflict is internal or psychological (as in Margaret Laurence's *To Set Our House in Order*, p. 548).

CONNOTATION. The suggestions and associations which have surrounded a word as contrasted with its bare, literal meaning, its denotation.

CRISIS. In drama and fiction, a crisis occurs when opposing forces creating conflict interlock in a decisive action on which the plot will turn. In Ethel Wilson's *The Window*, p. 495, the crisis occurs at the moment of the attempted robbery.

DENOUEMENT. This term refers to the outcome or result of any complex situation or sequence of events. Mr. Willy's new attitude toward his life is the denouement in Ethel Wilson's *The Window*, p. 495.

DIALECT. The language of a particular district, class, or group of persons; the sounds, grammar, and diction employed by people distinguished from other persons either geographically or socially. Note the references to dialect in Hugh MacLennan's *The Scotchman's Return*, p. 524.

DICTION. The style of speaking and writing as reflected in the choice and use of words. Diction refers to the selection and arrangement of words in statements and to the accuracy, emphasis and distinction with which they are written.

ELEGY. A mournful, melancholy poem, especially a funeral song or lament for the dead. Among well-known elegies are Gray's *Elegy Written in a Country Churchyard* (p. 215) and Milton's *Lycidas* (p. 144).

EPIC. A lengthy narrative poem in which action, characters and language are on a heroic level and style is exalted and even majestic. See *Beowulf*, p. 6.

EPIGRAM. A witty, ingenious, and pointed saying that is expressed tersely. Originally, an epigram meant an inscription or epitaph. Alexander Pope's remark in *An Essay on Criticism* (p. 193), "In poets as true genius is but rare,/True taste as seldom is the critic's share;" is an epigram.

ESSAY. A short literary composition on a particular theme or topic, usually in prose and generally thoughtful and interpretive. Because the term essay is applied loosely and widely, one basic division is helpful: *formal*—Dryden's *An Essay of Dramatic Poesy*, p. 171, and *informal*—MacLennan's *Scotchman's Return*, p. 524.

FIGURATIVE LANGUAGE. Deliberate and intentional departure from normal word meanings or word order to gain freshness and strength of expression. Figurative language is writing that makes use of one or more figures of speech.

FIGURES OF SPEECH. Expressive uses of language in which words are used in other than their literal senses so as to suggest and produce pictures or images in the reader's mind. Figures of speech may be divided into three classes: imagined similarities (such as allusions and similes); suggestive associations (hyperbole); appeals to the ear and eye (alliteration).

FORESHADOWING. Showing, indicating, or suggesting beforehand. In a literary work, foreshadowing provides a hint of what is to occur later. See Nathaniel Hawthorne's *The Ambitious Guest*, p. 348.

FORM. The manner and style of arranging and coordinating the parts of a composition, the structural pattern of a work of art. Form is more than an external scheme imposed upon subject matter; it should be considered the entire structural integration of expression and thought.

FREE VERSE. Verse that lacks regular meter and line length but relies upon natural rhythms. Free verse is free from fixed metrical patterns. See Irving Layton's *Anglo-Canadian*, p. 544.

GENRE. A category or class of artistic endeavour having a particular form, technique, or content; a synonym for type and kind. Genres in literature include the novel, the short story, the essay, the epic, etc.

HYPERBOLE. Obvious and deliberate exaggeration; an extravagant statement. Hyperbole is a figure of speech not intended to be taken literally; see Shakespeare's sonnet CXXX, p. 106, "If snow be white, why then her breasts are dun;"

IMAGE. The mental impression or visualized likeness summoned up by a word, phrase, or sentence. When Andrew Marvell wrote in *To His Coy Mistress* (p. 154): "But at my back I always hear/Time's winged chariot hurrying near;" he was describing the transience of life in the image of a hurrying vehicle.

IRONY. A figure of speech in which the literal meaning of a word or statement is opposite to that which was intended. Sometimes called the most ironic writing in all literature is Jonathan Swift's *A Modest Proposal* (p. 180), in which the author recommends the Irish sell their babies to English landlords for food.

LYRIC. A poem having the form and musical quality of a song; a short, subjective poem with a songlike outburst of the author's innermost thoughts and feelings. (See Christina Rossetti's *Song*, p. 340).

METAPHOR. An implied analogy which imaginatively identifies one thing with another. In Matthew Arnold's *To Marguerite—Continued* (p. 334), he compares isolation with the sea: "Yes in the sea of life enisled,/With echoing straits between us thrown."

METER. A poetic measure that refers to the pattern of stressed and unstressed syllables in a line of poetry. The number of stresses and syllables is fixed in the most frequent forms of meter in English verse; in some modern poets, regular meter is largely forsaken. Here is an example of verse in *iambic pentameter*:

> Thĕ cur / fĕw tōlls / thĕ knēll / ŏf pãrt / ĭng day,
> Thĕ lōw / ĭng hĕrd / wĭnd slōw / lȳ o'ĕr / thĕ lēa,
>
> Gray, *Elegy Written in a Country Churchyard,* p. 215, 1. 1-2.

MOTIVATION. Reasons and explanations for action through the presentation of convincing and impelling causes for that action. Revenge is the protagonist's motivation in Poe's *The Cask of Amontillado* (p. 357).

MYTH. A legendary or traditional story, usually concerning a superhuman being and dealing with events that have no natural explanation. Note Auden's use of the Greek myth of Icarus in *Musée des Beaux Arts*, p. 441.

ODE. Originally, a poem meant to be sung, but its meaning has been altered to apply to a lyric poem with a dignified theme that is to be phrased in a formal, elevated style. See Shelley's *To a Skylark*, p. 296.

OMNISCIENCE. Infinite knowledge; complete awareness or understanding; ability to see everything—a point of view in which the narrator is capable of seeing, knowing, and telling whatever he or she wishes (as in Frederick Philip Grove's *Snow*, p. 480).

PARABLE. A story designed to convey some religious principle, moral lesson, or general truth. Coleridge's *The Rime of the Ancient Mariner* (p. 256) has been called a parable of the human soul.

PASTORAL. A poem or other artistic composition dealing with the life of shepherds, or with serene and simple rural life (as in Milton's *Lycidas*, p. 144).

PATHOS. From a Greek word meaning "suffering," pathos refers to that ability or power in literature to call forth feelings of pity, compassion and sadness (as in Frederick Philip Grove's *Snow*, p. 480).

PERSONA. An invented person; a character in drama or fiction. In literary criticism, persona is sometimes used to refer to a person narrating or figuring in, for example, a poem—someone who may or may not represent the author himself. See Margaret Atwood's startling use of persona in *This is a Photograph of Me* (p. 586).

PERSONIFICATION. A figure of speech in which abstractions, animals, ideas and inanimate objects are endowed with human form, character, traits or sensibilities. In Keats' *Ode on a Grecian Urn*, (p. 310), a vase is referred to as a woodland recorder of events: "Sylvan historian, who canst thus express/A flowery tale . . ."

PLOT. In literature, plot refers to the arrangement of events to achieve an intended effect. A plot is a series of carefully devised actions that progresses to a climax.

POINT OF VIEW. In literature, point of view has several specific meanings: the position in time and space from which an author approaches and describes his material; the author's feeling and attitude toward his subject, and the relation through which a writer narrates or describes a subject—whether first, second, or third person.

PROTAGONIST. The leading character of a novel, drama, or other literary work. Mr. Willy is the protagonist in Ethel Wilson's *The Window*, p. 495.

REALISM. A theory of writing in which the familiar, ordinary aspects of life are depicted in a matter-of-fact, straightforward manner to reflect life as it actually is, often the lives of so-called middle or lower classes. See Morley Callaghan's *The Blue Kimono*, p. 510.

RHYTHM. Uniform recurrence (repetition) of beat or accent; the measured flow of words in verse or prose. Rhythm in verse is most often established by a combination of accent and number of syllables (see METER). In prose, rhythm is marked by variety of movement.

SATIRE. The ridiculing of folly, stupidity or vice; the use or irony, sarcasm or ridicule for exposing and denouncing the frailties and faults of mankind. See Dryden's *MacFlecknoe*, p. 168.

SETTING. In literature, the term is usually applied to the locale or period in which the action of a work takes place. For example, the setting of Hemingway's story, *In Another Country* (p. 473), is a hospital in Milan, Italy, during World War I.

SHORT STORY. A relatively short narrative designed to produce a single dominant effect, which contains the elements of drama. A short story concentrates on a single character in a single situation at a single moment, as in James Joyce's *Araby*, p. 416.

SIMILE. A figure of speech in which two things, essentially different but alike in one or more respects, are compared. In a simile the point of likeness is expressed by *like, as,* or *as if*. In A. M. Klein's *For the Sisters of the Hôtel Dieu* (p. 542), the poet compares the nuns in the following simile: "they are like birds,/the safe domestic fowl of the House of God."

SONNET. A poem of fourteen lines, usually in iambic pentameter, with rhymes arranged according to certain definite patterns. A sonnet usually expresses a single, complete thought, idea or sentiment. The sonnet was developed in Italy during the Renaissance and was introduced into England by Thomas Wyatt (p. 83) and the Earl of Surrey (p. 85).

STREAM OF CONCIOUSNESS. A manner of writing in which a character's perceptions and thoughts are presented as occurring in random form. In this technique, ideas and sensations are revealed without regard for logical sequences, distinctions between various levels of reality (sleep, waking, etc.) or syntax. This method of writing has been used by many authors, notably James Joyce, Virginia Woolf and William Faulkner.

STRUCTURE. The planned framework of a literary selection. For example, the structure of an essay depends upon a list of topics and the order of their presentation.

STYLE. The manner of putting thoughts into words; a characteristic mode of construction and expression in writing and speaking; the characteristics of a literary selection which concern form of expression rather than the thought conveyed.

SYMBOLISM. The practice of representing objects or ideas by symbols; expressing the invisible or intangible by means of visible or sensuous representations. Coleridge's *The Rime of the Ancient Mariner* (p. 256) is symbolism throughout: mankind's universal journey into despair and wickedness and then back to repentance, punishment and stability.

TONE. An author's attitude or point of view toward his subject; the devices used to create the mood and atmosphere of a literary work; the tone of voice assumed by the narrator or persona.

UNITY. Oneness; the state of being one. In literature, unity requires that a work should exhibit some principle of organization in which all parts are related to form an organic whole. Plot, characterization, mood or theme may each be a unifying force.

INDEX OF TITLES

INDEX OF AUTHORS

601